BOOK *Two*

# WORK

Division of labor,
co-operation, and
conflict in modern society

PERSONALITY

WORK

COMMUNITY

# An Introduction
# to Social Science

*Selected, written and edited by*   **Arthur Naftalin**

**Benjamin N. Nelson**

**Mulford Q. Sibley**

**Donald W. Calhoun**

**Andreas G. Papandreou**

**J. B. LIPPINCOTT COMPANY**        *Chicago, Philadelphia, New York*

*Printed in the United States of America*

In recent years an increasing number of American colleges and universities have launched programs of general education. These programs are designed to offer students a reasonably comprehensive and integrated framework of study within which they may develop an understanding of man in his complex relationships to the world of institutions, ideas, and values. This general education movement represents a reaction against the fragmentation in learning that has accompanied the emphasis on specialization in our culture. As our knowledge concerning man and the world has expanded, we have divided and subdivided the content of learning until today there is in all fields of higher education a large number of subfields and within each subfield a great proliferation of discrete courses. For the student who seeks a general education, the traditional liberal arts offerings are bewildering in their scope and diversity and frequently fail to provide that sense of integration and system which is requisite for meaningful study. The sense of integration and system which is prerequisite for the knowledge which *liberates,* the kind once distinctively sought by the *liberal* arts, has become at the moment almost impossible of attainment.

In their efforts at re-integration, different colleges have elected various approaches, and there is much lively debate among the respective planners as to which approaches are the more promising and which underlying assumptions have the greater validity. This is only to be expected, because what is involved in the general education movement is an effort to rethink the entire process of higher education and to fashion comprehensive programs and individual courses that manage to distil from the separate fields those principles, ideas, concepts, and data which, when appropriately joined, provide a meaningful framework.

Within the field of the social sciences, efforts at integration have taken various forms. One popular approach has been the survey course, which attempts to bring together and condense what are believed to be the essential elements of the several social science disciplines. Another widely used approach is the study of the history of Western civilization, which seeks to assist the student in identifying principles in historical change and to acquire a sense of the variety of forces that have shaped our heritage and which underlie contemporary institutions. Still another approach is one in which a group of selected contemporary issues having implications that cut across all the various disciplines is used as the core of the study. Some institutions have also been experimenting with courses designed to deal more directly with "training for citizenship in a democracy," or with the acquisition of values deemed appropriate for our age.

There is, therefore, little agreement and much uncertainty as to the most promising method of integrating social science materials for basic general education. As editors of this volume, we believe that the last word has yet to be spoken in this controversial field, and it is with a sense of severe limitation and an awareness of the extreme tentativeness of our effort that we present this volume of readings.

We regard the publication of this volume as part of a continuing experiment in the development of an integrated social science course. It grows out of our experience in developing the introductory social science course in the Department of General Studies at the University of Minnesota. It is designed to constitute the basis for an academic year's work at the undergraduate level, although many of the issues it develops will interest more advanced students as well.

Our effort at integration is based upon the study of three crucial aspects of man's many-sided life. We refer to these as *integrating themes* or as *problems,* and we distinguish them from current social *issues* such as housing, unemployment, race relations, or conservation. Our problems, by contrast with current social issues, are basic, enduring, and recurring. They affect every individual in every aspect of his life, and, as a result, we find they are useful points of focus for the gathering of selected basic data, crucial insights, and research methods from the various social sciences.

Our first integrating theme is the problem of achieving and maintaining an integrated and meaningful personality amid the complexities of modern life. Book One, therefore, deals with *Personality: The Human Individual and the Patterns of Culture.* Here we examine what not only social science but also natural science and the humanities have had to say—over the ages—on man's most basic problem, that of becoming a *person,* of being a *self,* of how an individual shapes, and is shaped by, his relations with other people and by the institutions that make up his contemporary world. We have deliberately attempted to avoid encouraging students that they are the hapless victims of a culture, itself without value.

Our second integrating theme explores the meaning of man's struggle to fashion a sustenance out of resources that are almost certain to be scarce in proportion to man's insistent needs and unstable wants. Again we attempt to discover how this struggle molds our culture and how the technology that man has evolved in waging the struggle shapes individuals and groups. Book Two is entitled *Work,* which, we feel, suggests the wide framework of problems of social or political economy, as is reflected in the subtitle, *Division of Labor, Co-operation and Conflict in Modern Society.*

The concluding problem can be viewed as the reverse of the emphasis on personality, which was the theme of Book One. In Book Three we return to our central questions and deal here with the processes of association, the affiliations within and interactions among groups, and the maintenance of the sense of *we-ness* and *belongingness* in society. Thus, Book Three, *Community: Group and Person in the Modern World,* considers the forces at work and the institutions that characterize our modern world and assays the various alternatives that man has pursued through the ages in his efforts to find social peace and harmony.

Our readings seek to develop these themes from all relevant points of view. We believe, too, that the social sciences are most fruitfully pursued when their close connection, not only with one another, but also with the humanities, is recognized. Both the social sciences and the humanities, after all, purport to treat of human nature in society and culture; and he who would comprehend the complexities of human personality and society cannot afford to ignore either the "scientist" or the "humanist." Social phenomena, we believe, call for ever more exacting, rigorous, and detailed analyses and, where possible, experimentations; but there are dimensions of those phenomena which can be grasped, if at all, only by the insights of the poet and the creative imagination of the novelist.

These considerations have led us to go beyond professional social scientists for our readings. We have summoned poets, philosophers, jurists, novelists, and theologians to contribute their quotas of knowledge and wisdom. We have also sought to combine readings presenting social science theory with case histories, descriptions of institutions, and "practical" illustrations. In short, it has been our wish to promote the humane study of human development, the humane study of human problems of our culture.

Many readers will note the absence in this volume of any formal, systematic treatment of the issues of social science methodology. This omission was deliberate. While we are aware of the great importance of methodology and of the many contributions made in this area by leading social scientists in recent years, we have found, on the basis of our teaching experience, that methodological problems are most effectively treated—at the undergraduate level of instruction—in connection with and incidentally to the substantive analysis. Methodological discussion in the abstract is often very sterile and dull, particularly for beginning students; but, developed in connection with a concrete problem of economics, it can be highly stimulating and enlightening. Then, too, methodological questions are raised at many points in the linking materials—general introductions, part introductions, and introductory notes to readings—written by the editors in an effort to bind the readings in a coherent way to the central theme.

Given this general framework and philosophy, it is not surprising that we should place great emphasis on the problem of values. The analysis of values and the attempt to dramatize or make vivid alternative value systems should be regarded as indispensable for, and inseparable from, any general education course in social science. That, at least, is the position we take in this volume. At almost every point in the readings questions of value are raised and students are challenged to relate the analysis of the readings to the moral choices which they have to make as men and citizens. The concluding Part of each Book is particularly devoted to problems of value as related to the analysis which has preceded it; but value patterns and issues are made explicit in connection with the other Parts as well.

The same scheme underlies each of our three books. In Part 1, we invite the students to consider the reputed shortcomings of one or another phase of our culture. In successive parts, we seek to acquaint students with research approaches and central hypotheses now accorded greatest respect by social scientists. The last Part of each Book inquires into the opportunities for improvements and seeks to weigh the relative values and costs of proposed changes.

Instructors in general social science courses may wish to use this volume with considerable flexibility. Those on the quarter system will perhaps find that the completion of one Book—and therefore one theme—per quarter is a fruitful scheme of organization. Those on the semester system will find a good breaking point at the end of Part 4 of Book Two. Or some might prefer to devote the entire first semester to Book One alone. It is expected, of course, that supplementary readings will be used in connection with each Book, and suggestions for such readings are given for each Part.

Some readings in the volume can be stressed more than others, and a few instructors will probably prefer to ignore certain readings altogether. It is recommended, however, that students read carefully the general introduction to each Book before proceeding to the readings. The general introduction, written by the editors, is designed to give the student an over-all picture of the problems which will be treated in the Book, to sketch out broadly the background and context of these problems, and, as has been noted before, to raise questions of methodology.

In the development of this volume we were aided in many ways by our colleagues in the Social Science Program at the University of Minnesota. For their suggestions and for their help in many phases of the work we wish to thank Edward Albertal, Chester L. Brooks, David Cooperman, Robert A. Endleman, Charles A. Gorder, Robert Jost, Virgil Kroeger, Robert H. Miller, Erma H. Olson, Martha Reed Petersen, Roger B. Page, T. Addison Potter, Fred A. Rainele, Miriam Richter, Alek A. Rozental, E. Victor Walter, J. Kingsley Widmer, Laurence Wyatt, and Muriel Wyatt.

We are especially grateful to Dean Russell M. Cooper, Chairman of the Department of General Studies, for his continued encouragement and assistance, and to Mrs. Nancy B. Miller for her assistance in the typing of manuscript and in many stages of the editorial work.

We should also like to thank the many publishers and copyright owners for the permissions they granted us to reprint the various selections. Each permission is individually acknowledged in the headnote appearing above that selection.

THE EDITORS

*University of Minnesota*
*Minneapolis*
*December, 1952*

‹‹‹‹‹‹‹‹‹‹‹‹‹‹‹‹‹‹‹‹‹‹‹‹‹‹‹‹‹‹‹‹‹‹‹‹‹‹‹‹‹‹‹‹

## Book Two

# WORK

*Division of Labor, Co-operation and Conflict in Modern Society*

## Part 4. The worker and the workless

## Part 5. Power and status in industrial society

## Part 6. The problem of economic instability

## Part 7. The state and economy

## Part 8. The future of work and community

BOOK *Two*

# WORK

~~~~~~~~~~~~~~~~~~~~~~~~~~~~~~~~~~~~~~~~~~~~~~~

*Division of labor,*

*co-operation, and*

*conflict in modern society*

# Work in the life of man

*❦ This Introduction by the editors explores the central themes involved in man's relationships in the economic order: his efforts to fashion a livelihood out of inevitably scarce resources, the effects upon personality and community of the division of labor, and the values fostered by the various forms of economic organization.*

In Book One we were concerned with the problem of personality and society. In a nutshell this problem involves the process by which the human being achieves a "character" or "personality." We considered such problems as the way the human biological organism functions, the way it tends to adopt the values of the society in which it lives, the way in which it tends to accept and "edit" the institutions in which it grows up, and the way in which it tends to adapt to the roles assigned to itself and to other people. We explored the methods by which human beings help to determine the course of history as well as the ways in which they seem to be determined by history. Personality formation is a process of interaction between the human organism and its natural and social environment. In Book One we focused on the first pole of the relationship—the individual. In Book Two we turn to the other pole—society.

This does not mean that in Book One we ignored social organization or that in Book Two we shall ignore the individual. It means rather that the perspectives of the two books differ. In Book One we were concerned with personality directly and with social organization indirectly. In Book Two we are directly concerned with social organization and indirectly concerned with personality.

## I. Problems and Perspective in Social Organization

### PERSPECTIVE AND CONCEPTUAL FRAMEWORK

Nobody can even begin to investigate the world without some sort of "conceptual framework." The point of view which one adopts inclines him to see certain facts and to ignore others. The perspective will give meaning to the facts. This is important, because some of us are deceived into thinking that the facts just "roll in" as soon as we expose ourselves to the world. Actually, this is not so, of course. Take yourself, for example, sitting in the classroom. You are all things to all men, depending on the point of view they adopt. To the physicist, you are a complicated combination of counterbalanced levers, or a system of energy. To the psychologist you are an individual with motivations, drives, inhibitions, responses, and complexes. To the sociologist you may be part of a complex institution called the university, or of a particular age group with particular problems, or a specimen of American culture. To the member of the opposite sex sitting next to you, you are a potential date. To the political organizer you are a potential supporter of his cause and possibly a cog in his political machine. To the theologian you are related somehow to God. The physicist, psychologist, sociologist, member of the opposite sex, political organizer, and theologian see "you" and study "you," but each from the viewpoint of his own particular interest will give a different account of "you." What is more, none of the six different stories about "you" may be "wrong."

Each of the observers looks at you from a particular angle of vision which leads him to stress certain things and not others. It is the standpoint or "conceptual framework" which gives "meaning" to the facts about you which he sees. The framework of the physicist is made up of such "concepts" as time, space, location, mass, and motion. The conceptual framework of the psychologist is made up of such "tools" as drive, motivation, inhibition. The conceptual framework of the sociologist uses such notions as institution, culture, age-group. The framework of the student beside you may embrace intelligence, sex appeal, imagined romance, and campus rating. The political organizer will think in terms of votes, majorities, and door-bell ringing. Concepts of the theologian may include such notions as revelation, soul, and immortality. It should be clear, then, that you or anything else in the world can be looked at from the standpoint of an indefinite number of different conceptual frameworks. Whether a "fact" will be used or ignored, stressed or treated lightly, will depend upon the conceptual framework of the person observing you.

The different frameworks which different observers may adopt in investigating human conduct are themselves not "natural" or inevitable. The framework a person develops will depend in great measure upon such things as the ways in which his culture has accustomed him to look at "the facts," the special slant which his own personality gives to his investigation, the particular things in which he is interested, and the "usefulness" of one framework as against another. Each of us, in other words, has to stand on a particular spot before he can look at a thing—it seems impossible to stand on all possible spots at once. This does not mean, of course, that anybody can find anything he wants to find. We assume that there is something "out there" to study, apart from and independent of the conceptual framework which we may use to study it. The framework is simply a means or tool for "getting at" the something outside the observer.

Now in social science it seems useful to look at "the facts" at different times principally from two different points of view. The first point of view we may call the *framework of individual action;* the second, we might designate the *organization framework.* In many ways, the first is a worm's-eye view, the second a bird's-eye view. If we look at what goes on in your classroom, for example, we may view it as the behavior of individuals with various motivations which bring and keep them there; or we may study it as the behavior of an organization called a "class," and ask, for example, how it is like and unlike other "classes," how a "class" of ten is different from a "class" of fifty, and so on. Either of the frameworks may be "translated" into the other. One observer may view your class as a complex system of personal actions; another observer may view you as a participant in the class. When we talk about the President of the United States or the treasurer of your fraternity we are concerned with the individual as part of an organization. When we talk about John Doe, we are, however, concerned with an individual as the focus of a vast and complex set of social relations and as the heir of a social tradition and culture.

What tools do we use when we approach John Doe through the framework of individual action? We may take as an example one set which has been outlined by the German social scientist Max Weber and his American interpreter and counterpart

Talcott Parsons.* What we study is the *act* of an individual. An act involves (1) an actor, (2) an end or goal, (3) the situation within which the agent or actor acts, and (4) some principle of selection of means for the achievement of the end. Suppose we take your behavior in college as the act we wish to explain. You are, of course, the actor. Your end or goal may be to become a medical student. Your situation is made up of certain conditions (such as the possession of a B.A. degree and the passing of certain courses) and certain means (such as taking your work at one accredited school or another). Some principle of selection leads you to go to school here rather than elsewhere, or to apportion your preparation between technical courses and general courses. There are other possible conceptual frameworks for investigating your actions, but this framework is an example of the kind of tools which may help reduce your thousand-and-one activities into "bundles" which help the observer understand you.

The "organization framework" deals with a system of actions of two or more people. When we speak of a college class as an "organization," we are speaking of the system of relationships between and among instructor and students. We can say, for example: "The organization of a class of ten is different from the organization of a class of 300." This may mean that the organization of the class of ten is made up (among other things) of "discussion" relationships between teacher and student, whereas the organization of a class of 300 is a set of "lecture" and "quiz section" relationships among instructor, students, assistants, and proctors. That a class of ten may, as an "organization," always be different from a class of 300 may be true no matter what individual persons or "actors" happen to be teachers and students. Certain

relationships seem to hold true; and classes of different sizes have different structures, regardless of personalities. Another way of illustrating the difference between the "action" and the "organization" framework is to point out that an organization may continue—sometimes for centuries—even though its membership constantly changes. Other examples of such complex sets of relationships—"organizations"—are the college or university as a whole, the Republican Party, the American Medical Association, the Roman Catholic Church, the United States Steel Corporation, and the "capitalist" or "socialist" social economic systems. We may investigate their structures also, and in this book shall investigate several of them.

To form an organization, people must work together (co-operate) so as to perform some common function. The people milling aimlessly around the town square on Saturday night are not an organization. Let them begin working together to fight a fire or a flood or to elect a certain candidate to office, however, and they become one. The fact that they perform a common function simply means that their actions all work together so as to carry through some activity, not that their motivations are necessarily all the same. Some people may co-operate to fight a fire because their families are in danger; others may co-operate because they will be thrown into jail if they do not; others may act because they fear loss of social prestige if they do not pitch in; while others may participate because they believe they would have a guilty conscience should they not help.

When relationships among people are consciously directed toward a goal of which they are all aware, when their activity continues over a considerable period of time, when certain people are assigned, or assume to themselves, the co-ordination of

ED. NOTE: * The outlines of Professor Parsons' position are developed in the following works: *The Structure of Social Action* (New York: McGraw-Hill, 1937, reprinted Glencoe, Ill.: The Free Press, 1949); *Toward A General Theory of Action*, edited with Edward A. Shils (Cambridge: Harvard Univ. Press, 1951); and *The Social System* (Glencoe, Ill.: The Free Press, 1951). A similar schema is suggested in Kenneth Burke, *A Grammar of Motives* (New York: Prentice-Hall, 1945).

their activities, and when these co-ordinated relationships have been given a name and formalized in an organization plan, we have a *formal* organization. Many important organized activities in any society are, however, *informal* rather than formal. People find themselves in a state of interdependence that has grown more or less spontaneously and did not come about as a result of anybody's conscious co-ordination toward a common goal. Society itself may be thought of as a vast informal organization with more or less uncertain boundaries. Institutions, common patterns of behavior, value systems, and languages are products of this vast informal organization we call society. Likewise, what has been called the "capitalist" system of economic organization is to a large extent informal rather than formal.

It should be remembered, of course, that any particular organization is never purely formal or purely informal. Even the most formal organization depends to a large extent upon informal relationships and activities; while in what seems to be a purely informal organization principles of formalization will always be present, if only in embryo.

## CO-OPERATION AND POWER IN SOCIAL ORGANIZATION

If we ask how, in an organization, the different activities of many people are pulled together so that the threads all join in a common function, we are investigating the problem of *co-operation* in organization. We shall study, on the one hand, the way in which the work of the organization is divided, and, on the other hand, the way in which it is co-ordinated. We shall thus discover *patterns of diversification* (another name for division of functions) and *patterns of integration* (co-ordination). When we have investigated these two aspects of any organization (factory, political party, women's club, army, economic system, football team) we may then be able to draw a chart which will help answer the basic question about co-operation in *any* organization: *How do so many people do so many different things and yet do the same thing?*

Even the simplest society needs integrative, co-ordinating forces if it is to survive as a society or an organization. A highly diversified society such as ours requires integrative forces that are subtler and more complex than those of simpler societies. For in our society there are more people to co-ordinate, and these people are much more unlike one another and are doing many more different things. There are two basic kinds of division of labor in our society. On the one hand, there is division of labor within formal organizations, such as the modern business enterprise. We need merely glance at an organization chart of a modern corporation to see how finely its work is subdivided. Executives, accountants, sales experts, mechanics, and skilled and unskilled laborers of all types are co-ordinated for the achievement of the corporation's goals.

On the other hand, division of labor takes place within society at large. One corporation manufactures steel, another automobiles, still another bread, and so on. Some of us become businessmen, others become clerks, mechanics, statesmen, professors, clergymen. Especially in our society, integration or co-ordination tends to take place in different ways in these two cases. Within a formal organization, the activities of the participants are consciously co-ordinated. Within the large informal organization, society, the vastly different activities of a tremendous number of people are made to pull in roughly the same direction through such forces as the market mechanism, the system of law, the value system, and the patterns of behavior that we call institutions.

If we ask what John Jones, James Doe, and Mary Smith do in an organization, if we ask who co-ordinates the work of John and James in one shop, and of Mary and her friend Jane in another, and if we ask who co-ordinates the work of the co-ordinators, we begin to see the patterns of co-operation (diversification and integration) in formal organization. If we ask how the activities of millions of people buying and selling in a "capitalist" economy somehow add up into a system, we begin to see the patterns of co-ordination in what is still in large part a vast informal organization.

There is, however, another aspect of all organization at which we must also look: *power*. Whenever there are relations between two or more people, one person may be in a better position to control the activities of others than are the others to control his. If three men are traveling in the remote wilderness and only one of them is an expert woodsman, it is very likely that he will in considerable degree control the actions of the other two: in this instance, certainly, knowledge is "power." The man with a gun is generally in a better bargaining position than the man without one. The man with money in the bank, or the man whose union has a strike fund in the bank, is in a more powerful position than the man without money. A scholar in a given field will develop influence in that field. The priest has influence and power over the believer. The man with the law on his side usually has power over the man who does not. The martyr helps to control the activities of some men and organizations even in the act of dying. The person who does not feel guilty about doing certain things may exercise power over the person who does.

An organization, whether formal or informal, may therefore be looked upon as a complex system of power relationships. When we look at an organization and ask *why* it is possible to co-ordinate people, and under what conditions they are co-ordinated, we are looking at power relationships. We may ask why Joe Doakes works in this factory, or works at all, why he accepts the orders of his foreman, why he works for a certain wage, neither more nor less, why he gets two weeks' vacation a year instead of three months' vacation or none, why he is or is not the beneficiary of a welfare fund or a clean rest room. If we ask these kinds of questions for all the workers in the factory, for all the people who co-ordinate them and for all the people who co-ordinate the co-ordinators, we will begin to get a picture of the *power*

*structure* of the factory. If we look at society as a whole, at the activities of employers' associations, labor unions, cartels, farm blocs, consumers' co-operatives—and ask "Who gets what, when, and how?"—we shall begin to get a picture of the power structure of the organization called our social economic system.

Within all types of organization we thus find patterns of co-operation and patterns of power. They are, of course, inseparable. No study of social organization can neglect either aspect.

### SOCIAL ORGANIZATION AND ECONOMIC ORGANIZATION

So far we have spoken of social organization in general. Book Two does not, however, endeavor to deal with all aspects of social organization. Rather, we have singled out for analysis one particular problem in the organization of human activities: we have called this "work" or *the organization of economic life*.

Work features all societies. It is the means through which we get the necessities and luxuries of life, and ultimately the way in which the vast majority of us stay alive at all. It has been a major theme of the world's great religions. According to one story, the First Man was cursed with work because of his disobedience to God. Some views even conceive of God primarily as the Great Workman. The organization of work being the means for keeping men and women alive, if the organization breaks down beyond a certain point, all social organization dissolves and people perish. Moreover, work, for most people, makes up more of life than any other single activity; and the conditions under which people work are to a large extent, therefore, the conditions under which they *live*. In tradition, story, and song, work and human happiness are closely linked, either in positive or negative terms. All the issues of co-operation and power, which constitute central themes, as we have seen, for the analysis of social organization in general, are particularly well reflected and illustrated in the social organization for work.

Economic life arises out of the fact that people have *wants* and that there are more human wants than there are available ways of satisfying them. Nobody can possibly have everything he might want; and with this fact begins "economizing," or the most efficient use or allocation of all available resources. There are some wants which inherently cannot be satisfied and others which can be satisfied only at the price of giving up other satisfactions. The desire to live forever on this earth will presumably never be satisfied and the limitations of the earth's resources make it certain that there is a point beyond which, even under the most ideal conditions, the material satisfactions of this world cannot be increased. Moreover, one satisfaction may exclude another: thus, one may visit Paris *or* Shanghai, but one cannot visit them both simultaneously. A man is able, perhaps, to marry one or more women, but he cannot marry all possible wives. He may be a beachcomber, but only by sacrificing the income and material goods which come from regular employment.

Certain wants, which are often referred to as basic needs, are relatively common to all human beings: the demand for food, shelter, clothing, companionship, security, and sex relations. But the experience of men has been that the satisfaction of "basic wants" does not put an end to the problem of wants in general. Wants seem to expand as they are satisfied. Many have thought that the wants of men may be insatiable.

Because all of a person's wants cannot be satisfied, everyone must erect, either consciously or unconsciously, a *want-scale,* or a *hierarchy of preferences.* At the bottom of this scale, let us say, are those satisfactions which he cannot do without. Farther up the scale are those satisfactions which he will seek if they can be achieved without sacrificing his most basic needs. Still farther up the scale are perhaps those satisfactions which he has renounced as unattainable.

One's want-scale (or "value system") is not necessarily conscious nor does it always remain the same. Among the greatest problems of some people is the fact that "they don't know what they want" and that what they desire today they may hold in low esteem tomorrow. The process of living is one of constructing a scale of wants and choosing from moment to moment which shall be satisfied.

So far we have spoken as though an individual lived, constructed, and sought to implement his want-scale in a vacuum. This is, of course, not true. Wants bring people immediately into interaction with other people. The wants of one person tend to conflict constantly with those of others. Just as an individual's wants cannot all be compatible with each other, neither can they be compatible with all those of other people. Moreover, most individual wants can be satisfied only through organized co-operation with others.

Thus, just as the individual's life organization is directed toward a "private" want-scale, so social organization is directed toward a social want-scale. The social want-scale, whereby society "decides" what wants shall be satisfied, in what order they shall be satisfied, and whose wants shall be satisfied, is often referred to as the social "value system."

We can now relate economic organization to human wants and social organization. It is characteristic of certain human wants that they can be satisfied through means which can be treated as commodities, that is, upon which a price can be put. Those wants which can be so satisfied are *economic* wants; those means of satisfaction which can be treated as commodities, or "priced," are economic goods and services. Apples, houses, and professional baseball games are, for example, usually commodities; sunshine, air, and love ordinarily are not. That aspect of social organization which satisfies economic wants is the economic organization of society. That part of the social want-scale in which the means of satisfaction carry a price-tag we may speak of as the economic sector of the want-scale.

Now the organization of economic life involves at least three great problems of "economizing," that is, of getting the most out of one's efforts. The first problem is that of deciding what "weight" or importance shall be given to purely economic values— the problem of how much of the time, energy, and attention of men shall be given to providing economic goods and services. "Man does not live by bread alone." Such highly prized human values as leisure, freedom, and happiness, in the most basic sense, carry no price-tag. Many religions have held, whether rightly or wrongly, that the "things of this world" are as nothing compared with the "things of the spirit." In more immediate terms, the problem is that economic production cannot take place without a sacrifice of something else. If the American economy could produce an average family income of $10,000 with a work-week of 40 hours, would this be more or less desirable than an average income of $6,000 with a work-week of 25 hours? If the material standard of living of the world could be doubled by a centralized regimentation of all work, would it be worth the sacrifice of freedom? In short, the first central problem of economic organization, in relation to the whole society, is to find ways of making economic values compatible with other values, and making choices between them when they cannot be made compatible.

The second central problem is that of setting up an *economic* preference scale— deciding what economic satisfactions shall be created, and for whom. Suppose it has been decided that economic activity shall be assigned a certain "weight" among all social activities. This might mean, for instance, that part of the total social life of America in 1955 should be the organization of enough time and energies to produce $300 billion worth of goods and services. Among all possible economic satisfactions, which shall be provided? Television sets or moving pictures? dresses or slacks? comic books or Bibles? guns or butter? Somehow, there must be provided a scale of economic preferences. And to whom shall satisfactions be provided? This issue is basically the problem of distributing scarce resources.

The third central problem of economic organization is that of securing the most efficient utilization of all resources available for the production of economic goods and services. In other words, how can we organize human and natural energies to do the jobs that have been decided upon? There are at least three aspects of this task. The first is the development of *material technology*. Economic progress—the vast increase in the store of such economic goods as food, shelter, and clothing—has resulted in large measure from finding ways of getting more out of the same amount of human energy, time, and effort by enlisting the services of machines. But economic progress has also arisen—and this is the second aspect of the problem of organizing human and natural energies—from *social technology*. This involves a discovery of the most "efficient" ways of subdividing and co-ordinating the activities of people in co-operative endeavor, whether within a physical plant or within a complex economy.

A third aspect of the task of organizing human and natural energies involves the problem of *human motivation*. Where "society" has "decided" upon a set of jobs to be done, and these requirements conflict with the wishes of any considerable number of individuals, the result is inefficiency or a complete breakdown of the socioeconomic organization. How can we make the social want-scale and the individual want-scales coincide? There are two basic ways in which this has been attempted. In the first, education, indoctrination, persuasion, force, or other means are used to shape or re-shape the individual's want-scale so that he is willing to perform the tasks demanded of him by society. In the second, efforts may be directed toward reshaping the social or economic want-scale so as to bring it more into line with an ever increasing number of individual desires. This may be done by changing the work process and its organization.

How different types of economic organization endeavor, consciously or by play of social "forces," to meet these problems of "economizing"—that is, of adapting human energies to the satisfaction of wants in a world of limited resources—is the central theme of this Book.

## II. *The Organization of Work and Division of Labor*

### WORK, DIVISION OF LABOR, AND ECONOMY

If each person were economically self-sufficient, there would be no problem of social organization arising out of work. Each individual would labor for his food, clothing, housing, and other necessities and luxuries; and there would be no buying, selling, or bargaining between and among persons. Problems of social organization, insofar as they arise out of man's work, come about only when division of labor begins to take place—when men come increasingly to depend upon one another for the performance of services. The Greeks had a word—*oikonomia*—which signified "rule" or "management" of a household— the manner in which the time, labor, and natural resources of the family were to be expended and ordered. In modern times this word *economy* has often been qualified by either "political" or "social," thus producing "political economy" or "social economy." Either of these expressions has come to signify the problems of "rule" or "management" or "ordering" of time, labor, and natural resources of that social organization, beyond the domestic household, which is based upon complex and minute division of labor. Our major problem of work is indissolubly linked with the degree to which division of labor has been developed and the way in which it is organized.

### BIOLOGICAL AND SOCIAL DIVISION OF LABOR

There is an interesting analogy between the development of biological organization and the growth of social organization, although the analogy should not be pressed too far (as it has been by some in the past). In high school biology classes you have doubtless studied the amoeba and the paramecium—one-celled organisms which perform all the functions of life through one unspecialized "cell." When the biological organization of life becomes more complicated, as you probably learned, specialization begins with the formation of colonies of cells which are still only loosely connected with one another. Finally, at some stage, the loosely-connected colonies of cells become more and more closely connected and the specialized functions of particular groups of cells within the whole colony become more pronounced. The result is a multicellular organism. As the multicelled animal organism specializes to a greater and greater degree within itself, co-ordinating centers for planning the work of the specialized groups of cells tend to develop. In the so-called "lower" orders of animal life, these co-ordinating centers (nervous systems and rudimentary brains) are relatively simple; but by the time we reach man, the function of co-ordinating and planning has attained enormous significance. As a matter of fact, as the "co-ordinating," "planning," and "imaginative" cells increase in importance, other groups tend to become less essential for survival. A leg, for example, is of enormous importance to a bear and its loss probably means death; for a man, however, the loss of a natural leg can in part be compensated for by a wooden leg and the man will be able, in most instances, to go about his work with only minor inconvenience.

Now something similar to this biological division of labor (and yet different, in many respects) seems to take place in society as men specialize more and more. With division of labor comes mutual interdependence and with interdependence the need for specialized organs of co-ordination and "clearing-houses" in order that the labors of specialized groups of men may be co-ordinated to common ends. Such "clearing-houses" and centers of co-ordination may be informal organizations like the market; or more formal organizations such as business corporations, the civil service, and the government. The more specialization develops, the greater is the need, on the whole, for clearing-houses and co-ordinating centers which are somewhat analogous to the brain of the biological organism.

## MARKET AND NONMARKET CO-ORDINATION

Allocation of resources and co-ordination of work may be accomplished either through the "market" or through various "nonmarket" co-ordinating devices. Under a pure "market" co-ordinating system, buying and selling of goods and services at prices determined solely by "supply" and "demand" would presumably mesh the activities of thousands of individuals in such a way that other devices would be unnecessary. Exchange values or prices of commodities and services would be fixed as a result of bargaining between relatively equal units (individuals). If there were too much cotton offered for sale at a given price, the price would immediately fall, warning cotton producers about possible "overproduction" and presumably diverting men's energies away from the production of cotton. One would decide one's occupation on the basis of probable market demand for one's services. If not enough resources were used in the production of a particular article and more than enough resources were going into another commodity, prices of the first would increase, thus stimulating individuals to produce more of the commodity desired; while prices of the second would correspondingly fall, thus discouraging use of resources in production of the second commodity. If one can imagine a very complicated pattern of "supply" and "demand" lines interweaving between and among sellers and buyers who have approximately equal bargaining powers, one will obtain some impression of what a "pure" market co-ordinating system would be.

It should be obvious, of course, that a "pure" market (or perfectly competitive) co-ordinating system has never existed in society as a whole. Essentially, such a system would require the uncoerced co-existence of approximately equal bargaining units having approximately equal access to the market. Such a scheme has existed only

in the imaginations of men. In actual fact, law, custom, and government regulation, as well as formal organization within the industrial and commercial realms, have always supplemented, and, in some instances, supplanted market co-ordination. Historically, market co-ordination has flourished within a rather detailed framework of nonmarket co-ordination; and the modern tendency all over the world has been to reduce market co-ordination and to exalt other techniques of integration. The growth of labor unions limits the individual in selling his services on the market and also restricts the employer in hiring and firing. Many prices are fixed by custom or by monopolistic combinations of various kinds. (In the sale of petroleum, for example, this is notoriously true.) Many governments have embarked upon programs of regulation—fixing minimum wages, maximum hours, and rates of interest, for example. The whole system of ownership of property is, in fact, part of the nonmarket framework within which the "market" operates. In totalitarian states the process of regulation reaches its optimum point; and the totalitarian ideal seems to look forward to a day in which market co-ordination will be completely eliminated.

There seem to be very deep reasons for the absence in human history of any pure market system. Men are not equal in physical or mental powers, nor do they have perfect and instantaneous knowledge of the values of all things. They cannot, moreover, be in different places at the same time. The conditions postulated for a pure market or perfectly competitive system have therefore never existed. Relationships of control and subordination, in addition, whether formal or informal, tend to modify the market system; and out of such relationships develop the rules and laws produced by nonmarket aspects of any political economy. In addition, the market itself would in many respects seem to be a cumbrous device of integration. No doubt it would produce a currency system; but the certainty and universal agreement seemingly necessary for such a system would always be subject to the hazards of an ever-changing market. It is for this reason that currency systems are established by the state and a definition of legal tender by the law, rather than by the market. Then, too, the slowness of market adjustments to the rapid changes in modern society has led many to press for still more extensive nonmarket controls in the hope that thereby adjustments to change can be made more rapidly.

The battle between market and nonmarket controls is central to the modern conflict of political ideologies. Essentially, those who favor market co-ordination are obliged to recognize that large sectors of every modern economy are actually controlled through nonmarket devices; hence they oppose the further invasion of nonmarket controls and plead for the elimination of many nonmarket controls which already exist. On the other hand, those who press for the extention of nonmarket controls of various kinds, including many socialists, are obliged to recognize that market co-ordination will have to be given a place in any economic system. The political issue thus actually becomes one of *degree* of market versus nonmarket controls.

### WORK AND PERSONALITY

The organization and co-ordination of work obviously cannot be separated from the development of personality, our theme in Book One. Division of labor, which is so important a key to the understanding of one pole of our analysis—social organization— is equally important in understanding the other pole—the individual. A specialist, for example, who learns more and more about a smaller and smaller area of knowledge, will have greater difficulty in seeing just where his work fits into the whole. A relatively self-sufficient farmer can see the immediate bearing of everything he does on the ultimate product: he has a hand in the whole process whereby a grain of wheat is turned into a wheat cake for the breakfast table. He is responsible for and can control, aside from the vagaries of nature, each stage of the process. But if the farmer is transformed into a specialized producer

of soy beans, his position is immediately changed. He can no longer control more than a minute fraction (planting and reaping soy beans) of the process whereby he lives. Where before he had only to suffer the frustrations and inconveniences of bad weather and bad personal health, he must now depend on the actions of remote corporations, banks, industrial workers, and government civil servants. To the frustrations of bad weather and bad health have been added the potential frustrations and worries of strikes, depressions, and other breakdowns over which he has no direct control. He is now at the mercy not only of the elements of nature but also of man's complex social organization. Or again, specialists in medicine may be experts on various parts of the body (dermatologists, oculists, gynecologists, etc.) or on the mind (psychiatrists); but, by virtue of their specialization (itself in part a product of social organization developed out of more minute division of labor), they may fail to understand the individual as a single organism in which the mind is not divorced from the body's physical structure.

Because modern division of labor tends to strip any one man of his power to create products from start to finish, it has been suggested by many writers that men have become mere cog-wheels in a machine over which they have little control. If one holds the value that persons should be considered as ends in themselves and not merely as means to the end of social organization, these writers go on, modern specialization of labor tends to deny this value and to be detrimental in its effects on human personality. Many industrial workers themselves seem to hold the same view, either implicitly or explicitly. Within political movements appealing to factory workers, for instance, there is often expressed the feeling that industrial workers are merely pawns manipulated for purposes not their own, "hands" controlled by some monster mechanical "brain" outside themselves. The men themselves take on machinelike characteristics: they tend to lose the capacity to criticize the process of which they are a part. One "radical" political versifier puts it this way:

*I work and I work and I work without reckon-*
  *ing,*
*Making, creating—endless the task!*
*For what? And for whom? I know not, I ask*
  *not;*
*Machine cannot answer, machine cannot ask.*

There is, however, another side to consider. Division of labor may make a man something of a cog, but it may also enable him to adapt his work to his talents. Reduce division of labor, and the specialist in psychiatry must know internal medicine, eye, ear, nose, and throat, and surgery as well; yet his particular talents might fit him best for psychiatry. Reduce division of labor still further, and the doctor must be his own janitor, general repairman, and stenographer. Reduce it yet more and the doctor-janitor-stenographer becomes lawyer and perhaps cook. Approached in this fashion, division of labor is found, in terms of human personality, to have creative potentialities because it enables the doctor to be a doctor and thus to realize the full use of talents that have both personal and social value. As a matter of fact, the term "civilization" has often been closely associated with the kind of social organization and culture produced by a high degree of specialization of work; and the term "barbarism," by contrast, has frequently been used to designate the cultures of those societies where work has not been highly specialized and where, therefore, potentially great musicians and scientists, for example, were "born to blush unseen and waste their sweetness on the desert air" because they could not specialize in those things for which they were best endowed. This suggests that a society can have too little as well as too much division of labor.

WORK, DIVISION OF LABOR, AND
MODERN TECHNOLOGY

The history of modern times is in considerable degree the story of the impact of machine production upon organization for work. The ideal of the medieval city—only partly achieved in practice, it is true—was one which held that each artisan should own the tools with which he labored and that there should be public regulation of wages, conditions of work, and the use of natural resources.

Special discussion of the phases in Europe's evolution from its predominantly rural-handicrafts foundations in the early Middle Ages to the triumph of the modern pattern of machine industry and intensive exchange through markets is reserved for the readings in Part 3. Here it suffices to recall that these developments were accompanied by an accentuated division of labor and by characteristically modern ideas about economic and social relations. The introduction of power-driven machinery in and on an expanding scale in the eighteenth century both necessitated greater subdivision of tasks and was itself partly an outgrowth of a more complex division of labor. The story of invention and the inventor is itself an interesting study in the history of work. In the initial stages of the modern period, invention of new machines was a kind of avocation—the inventor found in it a relief from his ordinary job. By the twentieth century, however, invention had become in some degree a profession to which one could devote a whole life, and the rapidity and scope of technological change were greatly enhanced.

Modern technology implies that one is dependent for the making of one's tools on a very large number of men. The hunter in the Stone Age shaped up the stone knife with which he hunted beasts and butchered his meat. But notice the complications of the process today: the simple stone tool has become a series of knives and other instruments, often organized into complicated machines for making sausage and for cutting, slicing, and canning meat. On any one machine hundreds and perhaps thousands of persons will have worked, long before the process of butchering and curing the meat takes place. A score of persons in Sheffield, England, may have worked on the knife which an employee in a Chicago packing plant uses; and a fellow-employee may be operating a sausage-stuffing machine into whose making went the labors of iron miners in northern Minnesota, steel workers in Pennsylvania, engineers from New York, petroleum workers in Oklahoma, and accountants in Chicago. And the inventor of the machine built upon the labors of pure and applied scientists back at least to the time of the ancient Egyptians. Thus the operator of the sausage machine, for example, finds himself dependent on thousands of other workers, dead and alive, for his tools and hence for his livelihood.

But he is dependent in another way as well. In a very simple division of labor and with primitive technological development, the tool which he uses will be so uncomplicated and individualized—a stone knife, for instance, or a hand loom—that the worker can and does "own" the tool himself. When, however, the tool becomes a complex machine, he is no longer able to purchase the tool himself, but must instead depend on those who have managed to accumulate vast savings or upon thousands of men who pool their savings for the purpose of buying the tool. These individuals and groups have been called "capitalists." Capitalists may be either individuals, private corporations that have gathered together in a common fund the financial means for the purchase of tools, co-operative societies pooling the resources of their members, or the whole community acting through the state (in the latter instance, we speak of "state capitalism," or "state socialism," depending upon the type of organization involved, the ends for which it is set up, and the theory upon which the collective enterprise is built). In most modern societies, capital may be supplied by any or all of these types of capitalists. But if the machine is not forthcoming from some kind of capitalist, the worker will in most cases have no work and hence no livelihood. Theoretically, he could return to the land and produce a living directly from the soil; but practically, this is in most instances difficult if not impossible.

The rise of a specialized group of capitalists is further illustration of division of func-

tion; for although the worker himself may have saved a little and thus furnished some capital himself, capital in modern industrial society is far from evenly distributed—the larger share of it tends always to be controlled by a relatively limited number of individuals and groups. This minority control of capital—and hence of thousands of livelihoods—gives rise to many of the most serious economic and political problems of modern industrial society.

From another point of view, the relationship of work and division of labor to technological development is illustrated by the history of warfare. In primitive warfare the soldier either makes his own simple weapons or calls upon an armorer and a few others to supply them. When he fights another soldier similarly equipped, the struggle tends to be an intensely personal face to face battle. But in modern warfare the man who drops an atomic bomb is only an infinitesimal part of the process whereby a city is destroyed. A thousand occupations and trades went into the making of the bomb and a hundred others (both in and out of the army) were necessary before the aviator was ready to drop it. An aviator's role in modern warfare is especially impersonal; he does not see the people whom his bomb kills, or, if he does, they are merely black dots without semblance of personality. The process is machinelike; the machine controls the man rather than the man the machine. And if one is a victim of the bomb, it is the same: a machine which was itself the product of a machinelike organization dropped the bomb; and no one person seems to be responsible.

The last two centuries have witnessed the migration of great numbers of men from field to factory. Metropolitan areas have grown enormously and with their growth has come further specialization in the division of labor. Because so many workers flocked to the cities, metropolitan areas grew enormously and with their growth came still further division of labor. And because machines had to be concentrated near the sources of power and raw materials and controlled centrally, a pattern of centralization in both economic and political life came to characterize the modern period. Technology had eliminated many of man's traditional loyalties—to village community, family, and local self-government—and had created instead the sovereignty of the machine and its twin requirements of population and industrial concentration and centralized controls. Never before in history, many suggest, have men been more subject to controls and directions by centralized power-holders—corporations, political parties, and states. Never before in history has the state had at its disposal such terrible weapons and such power.

But are concentration and centralization to continue indefinitely? Some observers believe they may not. There are those who argue that the very technology which contributed to industrial concentration is likely to destroy it. For example, cheap electricity, itself a product of modern science and technology, makes it possible to scatter industries over a wide area instead of concentrating them near sources of coal. The atomic bomb, which can destroy concentrated centers of industry, may put a premium on decentralization. Big cities may have to go —either through voluntary action by men or by destruction of frightful war. Perhaps we are living at the end of an era. The technology which gave birth to concentration and centralization may yet escort its children to the tomb. Whether complex technology will itself then join its children in the grave only the future can tell.

## OWNERSHIP AND CONTROL IN CORPORATE ORGANIZATION

The modern period began with a protest against medieval controls of economic life. The medieval system of thought had held that church and state should co-operate in regulating prices, wages, and commercial practices. These notions the early period of modern industrial society repudiated.

Instead, as machine production invaded larger and larger sectors of life and division of labor became yet more minute, men developed strong beliefs that as human beings became more and more interdependent, each man finding the place to which he was assigned by talent and individualistic competition, the necessity and desirablity of formal and public controls of the economic process would vanish. The belief that "market" co-ordination is sufficient to organize the world of work became a central canon of early nineteenth-century thought. Free competition in the market became the watchword; and it was believed that if each man sought only his own interest in his own way the general welfare would be maximized.

Unfortunately for this view, however, all men did not prove equal in economic bargaining power. Some were stronger than others. The strong combined to squeeze out weak competitors. Gigantic combinations of capital took the form of the legal device known as the limited liability company (where one's investment was the limit of one's liability in case of failure). As such companies grew and combined with one another (a process which was accentuated as technology became more complex and machines more costly), the competition envisaged and in part realized by the early modern period gradually faded away, until today the economic order has been described as in considerable degree one of monopoly and "monopolistic competition." And, with the growth of the number of stockholders in a corporation, their actual control of the corporation became increasingly a fiction. The American Telephone & Telegraph Company, for instance, to cite its latest circulars, has about a million shareholders scattered throughout the world. Under the law, they "own" the company. Obviously, however, they cannot, in any real sense, control its affairs: since they are scattered, real deliberation is impossible; and to imagine even half a million men being able to arrange their lives so that they can assemble for a long business meeting in a given place at a given time is certainly difficult.

Actually, while legal ownership remains in the shareholders, the making of decisions in the modern corporation has largely passed to technical managers and administrators. The managers have the knowledge necessary to operate a modern corporation —knowledge which, when combined with the ability to act quickly, confers upon them real power to control. Even the board of directors, nominally chosen by the shareholders to control the company, is often a mere pawn in the hands of the management which in legal theory is supposed to be subordinate to it. The law vests control in the legal owners (the shareholders) who theoretically act through the directors. Actually, however, this legal machinery tends to be bypassed and the principle of division of labor is found to operate here by separating the function of "ownership" from that of control, just as in an earlier period owership of capital was separated from labor power. In all areas of organized life, as a matter of fact, it should be remembered that, while legal ownership gives the *right* to control, the actual control may in practice reside elsewhere.

The growth of gigantic combinations of capital was accompanied by the development of enormous aggregates of labor. The "collectivism" of corporations—ownership of machines and factories collectively by large numbers of persons (whether organized as corporations, co-operatives, or government)—was met for bargaining purposes by the "collectivism" of labor unions —the pooling of the labor power of large numbers of workers. And here again the principle of division of labor can be illustrated, for just as the technical administrators of corporations became sharply differentiated in terms of control from those who remain the legal owners, so labor leaders often become "professionals" and become differentiated in psychology and outlook from ordinary union members who work in ordinary jobs. In form, members of the union control its affairs; but often actual control (including power to perpetuate themselves in office) is vested in business agents and other union officials. Thus major tendencies evident in business organization make their appearance in labor organization as well.

## WORK, DIVISION OF LABOR, AND CLASS

The rise of "industrial capitalism" was accompanied by a breakdown in many instances of traditional lines of social status and class. The celebration of industrial mobility upward and outward became a hallmark of the ideology which sought to justify the elimination of remaining medieval restrictions on individual self-assertion in the economic, social, and political spheres. And in considerable measure this ideology was reflected in practice: there was a great possibility that the manual worker might rise through his own efforts to become a proprietor, a factory owner. "From shirt-sleeves to millionaire before thirty" was often a reality. Of course, the principle could and did often work in reverse: a man could sink in the industrial and social scale as rapidly as he could rise. In theory, and not a little in practice, class lines were fluid and tentative.

In modern industrial society all this has become less true. The prospects that a manual worker will rise to become a proprietor have declined with the development of gigantic corporations. True, he may still rise into the "managerial" class, but even here, many observe, his prospects become increasingly slim. Both industrial and social "class" lines seem to be less tentative and fluid than in the early period of industrial society. In varying degrees, this fact tends to be reflected in changing attitudes on the part of manual workers. As workers become aware that their prospects of rising are few, they may, to use Marx's term, tend to become more "class-conscious."

Just what is meant by "class" as related to work and division of labor is often ambiguous. There are several ways in which the term has meaning. Marx defined "class" in terms of *relationship to the means of production*. In almost every industrial establishment there is a "class" system closely related to one's place in the industrial hierarchy. There are class differentiations associated with the division between white-collar and manual workers. To some extent, class is reflected in income figures, although this is not necessarily true (many manual workers, for instance, earn more money than many white-collar employees, yet the latter often look down on the former as "inferior" socially). More recently, sociologists have defined a "social class" as a group sharing *status and privileges*. Perhaps a rough idea of the social class to which you belong can be gained if you ask yourself whom you would and whom you would not invite to dinner with some degree of frequency. If you are a worker in a factory, would you invite your straw boss? The manager? A member of the Board of Directors? A large shareholder? A tramp? A lawyer? Class can be a very subtle and yet a very real factor in the lives of all kinds of workers: the nature of work organization and the psychology of workers are profoundly influenced by it. At the same time, class lines are in some measure determined by the nature of work organization and the particular system of division of labor involved.

### WORK AND UTILIZATION OF RESOURCES

A society which is so organized that each productive and distributive function is closely dependent upon every other for its continuance will, because of this very interdependence, be more subject to the possibility of periodic "breakdowns" of economic organization than a society in which interdependence is not highly developed. Thus, if the family lives on the land and produces almost all its own goods and services, what happens in China, while it may excite the philanthropic and intellectual interest of members of the family, will not affect its livelihood. If, however, the family is not self-sufficient but must depend on others for its farm machinery and on yet others for purchase of its products, it is likely to be directly affected by famines and wars in China. Moreover, the task of co-ordinating the activities of workers in a society based upon complex division of labor becomes such an enormous one that

any failure in prediction—a mistaken crop estimate, for instance, or overestimation of demand, or failure over a long period to introduce new machinery—is likely to mean that persons who were not directly responsible for the failures will nevertheless feel the economic impact of poor co-ordination. How to insure a "balance" between production and consumption of goods and services has become a serious problem for modern industrial society; and this problem is closely connected with the issue of adequate co-ordination.

Interdependence accompanied by defective co-ordination can thus lead to failure to utilize natural resources and failure also to provide the opportunity for men to labor. Just as complex division of labor gives rise to the possibility of greater production and a higher level of material well-being, so, on the other hand, it can lead to greater organizational waste (through unsatisfactory co-ordination and planning) than that existing in less complex societies. Unemployment of resources and unemployment of men have characterized industrial society. Typically, periods of relatively full employment have been followed by years of unemployment. These alternating periods of "prosperity" and "depression" have come to be called the "business cycle."

Students of economic problems have studied business cycles and have discovered several types of cycles. Obviously, many questions have been raised about them. What factors cause them? How are they affected by investment, production, and spending? What social losses are incurred as a result of their existence? How are they related to the problem of "co-ordination through the market"? Are there ways of co-ordination which would eliminate business cycles? Many of these questions will be explored in the following readings.

### WORK, COMMUNITY, AND STATE

In a situation where there were no division of labor the individual would, as part of his work, plan his own activities without concern for fitting his labor into the work of others. He would be self-sufficient and, so to speak, be his own "co-ordinator." Under division of labor, however, co-ordinating functions and organizations inevitably develop and with them emerge the vast problems having to do with the relationships of organization to the individual, of administrators to the administered, of the state (the most impersonal and all-embracing co-ordinating organization) to the citizen. Many of these problems will be considered at length in Book Three, which deals with the problem of Community. Here we touch upon certain selected aspects of these issues which are particularly connected with the problem of work and the organization for work.

(a) *Decline of Primary Groups.* The family is the primary group whose integrity and cohesiveness suffer most under a complex division of labor and modern technology. With the rise of mammoth cities, family size and solidarity diminish. The divorce rate rises. Social functions previously performed by the family are transferred to more formal and less personal organizations such as the state. Thus education and "social security" pass from the family and come to vest in the government. Such transfers in turn affect the problem of personality (the theme of Book One), on the one hand, and that of community (the subject of Book Three), on the other. The question arises as to whether there is not a limit to the functions which the state can perform well; and, in terms of power relations, whether the decline of primary groups does not put the individual more and more at the mercy of state power and minimize the effectiveness with which he can resist it. It seems likely that strong primary groups, such as the family and the well-knit neighborhood, are indispensable for personal liberty and the full flowering of the human personality.

(b) *Enhanced Roles of Politician and Lawyer.* To pull the parts created by division of labor into some kind of integration requires experts in conciliation and human relations. Politicians and lawyers are reflective of this need. The former attempt to secure the co-operation of apparently divergent interests and groups and to engineer some kind of acceptance of collective decisions. Lawyers become ever more essential due to the vast proliferation of laws which are, in turn, an accompaniment of enhanced division of labor. Even lawyers find the task of understanding the whole body of law increasingly difficult, for an eminent Justice of the United States Supreme Court was quoted recently to the effect that, even with all the help given him, he could not possibly keep up with major legal developments. Where organization is relatively simple and collective decisions few (under a regime where market co-ordination plays a predominant role, for example), politicians and lawyers operate within a narrow sphere. But where bargaining about wages becomes collective and corporations become great centers of political power, the labor union politician and lawyer and the politician and lawyer dealing with the organization of corporations become leading forces in the governance of society. Larger and larger spheres of life become "politicized" and "legalized" as co-ordination of work becomes increasingly of the "nonmarket" kind.

(c) *Rise of "Totalitarian" Theories and Practices.* It is not surprising that under such circumstances there should be modes of social organization and theories of government which would subject all of work and life to complete determination by the state. Such schemes and theories we call "totalitarian" because they would allow no area of life to be free from domination by collective decisions of the central government. They see man as wholly a creature of social organization with no dimensions of his existence transcending or escaping the "pole" of society. In the totalitarian view the very principle of individuality tends to be wiped out. Art, literature, sex life, domestic relations, and even thought itself exist at the mercy and by permission of the state. Since personality is not regarded as an end but only as a means for the enhancement of the political power of the state, the energies of all persons are harnessed for the ends of the state. Frequently, this means that men become mere instruments for the building of empire and the waging of war. Fascism, as one variety of totalitarian philosophy, glorifies war and argues that man achieves his "real" ends only by making war. In the Fascist view, then, the purpose of economic life and of work becomes war and destruction.

(d) *Managers, Administrators, and Bureaucrats.* Even in societies which can by no means be called "totalitarian" certain tendencies which exist in extreme form under totalitarianism are discernible. We have already observed that the task of administering business organization tends increasingly to be separated from ownership of business and that the legal owners of corporations usually do not in fact control the policies of the corporations. In government, too, this tendency is to be noted. Popular legislative bodies everywhere seem to be losing effective control of administration and technically trained administrators often make the policies which in theory should be made by legislative bodies. In labor organizations, leaders often control the unions even though in form they are merely employees of union members. In a highly complex division of labor, where the task of administering collective business becomes technical and involved, great power is conferred on the administrators, whether they be managers of corporations, civil servants, or professional trade union officials. Of course, this takes place only with the acquiescence, implicit or explicit, of those who are subject to the control of the managers, administrators, and bureaucrats; and one of the most important problems for the student of personality, work and community becomes that of *social control:* "Why do they acquiesce? What are the processes which lead them to believe they *should* subordinate themselves?"

(e) *Work and Problems of Democracy.* As specialists in co-ordination and administration grow in numbers and power, a most crucial issue is raised in those societies which theoretically exalt "democratic" values and are yet caught in the tendencies of modern social organization. In a society which wishes democracy—and hence presumably believes that co-ordination and planning should satisfy the needs and desires of the whole society and not the self-interest of the co-ordinating groups—how is it possible for the vast mass of men who are not experts in administration and co-ordination to control the experts? Or is it possible at all? Some would deny that it is possible. They argue that a bureaucracy always sets up goals of its own—self-preservation, enhancement of privileges, and expansion—which tend to run ahead of any controls which society may try to set up. How, the critics ask, can Congress really control the Atomic Energy Commission? How can the Board of Directors of the United States Steel Corporation control the vast bureaucracy technically trained to run that corporation? And while the power of administrators is growing, the tendency of men to subordinate themselves to administrative control seems also to grow. Extreme division of labor, the critics allege, makes it possible for rulers to "divide and rule." Each person is so much merely a cog in the machine of work organization that he finds it difficult to see himself as a whole personality opposing the wishes of his rulers. He becomes subject to a kind of fate; and his acquiescent subordination merely strengthens and makes possible the continuance and extension of irresponsible control by the administrators. How can the vicious circle be broken? Is it possible to reconcile a high degree of division of labor and specialization with the values of a democratic society—a society which emphasizes the values of equality, individual liberty, and effective control by the mass of men of their governors? Those who deny that such a reconciliation is possible contend that we must choose between a highly technological society with its accompanying specialization, on the one hand, and a democratic society, on the other: we cannot have both. This is one of the central problems of Community which will be explored in Book Three.

(f) *To What End?—Work and Values.* Men's work in human history has always been closely connected with their systems of value, their judgments of right and wrong, their conceptions of the moral order. Should work be regarded as something more than a means of getting a living? Is it a "curse of God" for sin, as some have held? Or, on the contrary, is it a necessary way of expressing one's personality and spirit? How should the products of human labor be distributed, particularly in a complicated society, where the connection between individual "worth" and the product of work is not always easy to trace? What about conflicts of value in problems of work organization? For example, if it can be shown by the social sciences that unemployment could be abolished, but only at the expense of those personal liberties (such as freedom of speech, press, and religion) which form part of the so-called democratic tradition, should we abolish it? As we have suggested elsewhere in this Introduction, questions of this kind depend upon one's whole system of values, and upon the relative weights one assigns to given values. What weights we assign to a series of values will depend upon our ultimate faith, or, otherwise stated, our orientation or world view. Historically, this faith or world view has often been closely associated with what we call religion; although it has also sometimes been stated in terms which do not use characteristically religious terminology. The kind of community we desire is thus expressed in our value system or scheme of ideals. The statement of ideals in the abstract is not enough in itself; but, coupled with social analysis and an attempt to relate such an analysis to our value scale, it is indispensable.

## III. The Plan of This Book

As you proceed in the following pages from Part 1 through Part 8, your knowledge of and insight into the world of work and economic organization should increase, each Part of the Book building upon the one which preceded it. The earlier parts are essential for a full understanding of the latter; the latter develop and complete the

earlier. The purpose is not merely, however, to discuss the social organization built up around the fact that men work, but also through discussion of this particular problem to illustrate the problems of social organization in general, and to lead thus into the broadest problems of Community posed in Book Three.

At the very outset, in Part 1, we take a preliminary look at some of the major economic problems which puzzle mankind in the twentieth century. In what respects have the ways of life of men and women everywhere been influenced by the spread of mass production and corporate ownership in the organization of large-scale enterprise? How do we explain the existence of want in the midst of an apparent plenty? How can we account for the persistence of stark poverty in so many parts of the world? In what measure have the turbulent political developments of our time—wars, revolutions, totalitarianism—been influenced by the instabilities of our economic arrangements?

Questions of this kind, obviously, cannot be answered without careful analysis of social economic organization. The remaining parts of the Book attempt to do just this. Thus Part 2 seeks to introduce you to central concepts in economic analysis. What are the important problems which any economy must attempt to solve? What are the major types of social economic organization? How do we go about analyzing the operation of an economy? Part 2, in short, provides the necessary frame of reference and a useful set of tools for the analysis which follows.

Part 3 then turns to an examination of "industrial society"—the kind of society which has increasingly characterized the world since the eighteenth century. What factors have led to the spread and predominance of the industrial pattern? How have men's ways of living been influenced by changes in technology? What was the impact of industrial society on non-industrial ways of life? What are the main characteristics of industrial society?

In Part 4, the readings seek to give you

some impression of the wide variety of occupations in an industrial society and some notion of how work and unemployment affect the personalities and outlooks of various kinds of workers. Division of labor *divides;* and in Part 4 we are told how it divides. We sample the various occupations of men and try to see the world from the several radically different perspectives involved.

Part 5 is concerned to show what factors shape power and status relationships in industrial society. As we have noted before, all social organization has two aspects—co-operation and power. Part 5 deals with the "power" aspect—or, as it has been put earlier—the problem of, who gets what, when, and how.

Elsewhere in this Introduction we have suggested that an important issue related to the problem of work is that of achieving "balance" between production and consumption of goods and co-ordination adequate to mesh the labors of men in such a fashion as to secure maximum utilization of resources. The readings in Part 6 concentrate upon this problem. What causes business cycles? What roles do investment, saving, and spending play in the imbalances so characteristic of industrial society? What policies, if any, can governments pursue which will "stabilize" an industrial economy—make sure that periods of "boom" and "bust" will not develop as they have in the past? What relationship do all these questions have to problems of so-called "underdeveloped" economies—those which have not yet been industrialized but whose fates are closely geared in the modern world to those more "advanced" economies which we call "industrial"?

In Part 7 we examine ways in which various systems have attempted to meet the problems of control and co-ordination which arise out of modern society and also consider proposed alternative systems. How do National Socialist aims and methods differ from British Socialist objectives and means? What is the case for socialism? The case against it? How does the social economic organization of the Soviet Union differ from that of the United States? How does it resemble the American system? What have been the actual effects of different ways of organizing economies on the production and distribution of such "noneconomic" values as personal freedom, civil liberties, and social equality?

Finally, in Part 8, we focus our attention upon the problem of "values" in economic life. What attitudes should we adopt as citizens to proposals for greater equalization of income and economic power? What potentialities for the future exist in industrial society? Are the men and civilization of the Atomic Age doomed to destruction, enslavement, and torment? Or, on the contrary, do the newly discovered forms of energy and automatic machinery afford us new ground for hope in the coming of a better world?

Thus in Book Two we move from (1) puzzling economic and social questions to (2) methods and major conceptions for analyzing social economic organization and major conceptions in analysis to (3) the development and nature of industrial society to (4) varieties of human work and the psychology of work in industrial society to (5) power and status relationships to (6) the problem of economic stability in industrial society to (7) alternative systems of co-ordination and planning to (8) discussions of work, social values, and the future of an extremely complex industrial society.

# PART 1

# Industrial society and its problems

❦ Our purpose in this Part is to "block out" some of the central problems which the organization of economic life creates for us as individuals and as citizens. These readings are designed to illustrate certain major dilemmas of economic life which we shall want to keep in our minds throughout the entire book.

The first reading, by PETER F. DRUCKER, tells us that we are living in a revolutionary period. The term revolution does not refer primarily to revolution in the political sense—as we speak of the French Revolution or the American Revolution—but rather to a profound and widespread change in our institutions and our way of life. It is in this sense of the term that we shall find our later authors speaking, for example, of the "Industrial Revolution." The great revolution of our time, in Drucker's view, has been the spread of the principles of mass production and corporate organization, which has led in every industrial country to the emergence of the modern large enterprise as the *"decisive,* the *representative,* and the *constitutive* institution." "Whether industrial society is organized under Capitalism, Socialism, Fascism, or Communism," Drucker declares, "the *enterprise* is its central institution, looks alike, behaves alike, and faces similar decisions and difficulties."

Drucker tells us that the revolution brought about by mass production is not primarily a revolution in material technology, not a mechanical revolution, but a revolution in the *human organization* of production. The model for the revolution through which we are now passing has been the industrial assembly line, which first came into existence in its present form in the automobile industry. What is significant about the assembly line, however, is not the mechanical arrangement of the factory, but the pattern of "rationalized" and highly co-ordinated organization of human activity which the factory involves. Nor is the "mass production" principle limited to the production of material commodities in the narrow sense: rather, the pattern has extended to all lines of production, so that the "assembly line" is found in commercial offices, the university, the hospital, the world of sports and entertainment, mass communications, and at many other strategic points in our society. Thus, for example, *Time, Life,* and *Fortune* are as much instances of this type of organization as a Ford factory. The spread of mass production means, above all, the *centralization* of control over the processes of production and the subordination of all individuals to the collective job of making a joint product. This subordination ordinarily involves the minute subdivision of the tasks assigned to each individual and, therefore, in the view of many, a separation of the worker, whatever his position in the hierarchy, from the direct control over the means of production, and a sense of alienation from other persons and from the task at hand.

The readings by HENRY GEORGE and RALPH BORSODI deal with special aspects of the dilemmas posed by our economic organization. George tells us that the past few centuries have been marked by a vast increase in the productive powers of the human race. This economic progress—by which we mean simply the increase in the production of goods and services—should have been expected to alleviate the poverty which had always previously faced or threatened men. But progress has by no means eliminated poverty; on the contrary, it seems to have made the problem of poverty more acute. The vast increase in the store of goods and services has tended to increase the material wealth of a large percentage of the population; but, in the process, George suggests, the individual has been torn loose from the "roots" which he once had in his home, garden, and community of friends ready to stand by in time of need. Industrial society has made him a rootless employee, compressed into barracks and cities when he has work and deprived of the soil on which he could formerly fall back when hard times set in.

George's analysis was written in the latter part of the nineteenth century. It is included here because it documents the fact that doubts about the workings of our economic organization are not something new which have arisen in the past few years, and because it has long been felt to constitute a classic statement of the paradox of poverty amid progress. We—as members of a relatively fortunate economic group in the world's wealthiest nation—may be inclined to believe that the problem posed by George is one of the past, now solved in the seventy-five years since he wrote. But what do we make of the evidence around us: the industrial slums of our own great cities, the rural slums of our Southern states and other agricultural sections, the conditions of the population of Europe or of those "underdeveloped" areas of the world where Western industrialism has gathered together the native populations for the production of rubber, tea, pineapples, and dozens of other mainstays of our "high standard of living"? Two-thirds of the world's population, it has been pointed out by Lord Boyd-Orr, a leading nutrition expert, go to bed hungry every night, and he suggests that this problem of hunger is one of the leading political issues confronting the world. Does it not appear that our own situation is not the rule in this world, but a fortunate exception? Perhaps we have *not* yet solved the problems posed by George: how to secure a production and distribution of economic satisfactions that will mitigate the contrast between "progress and poverty"; and how to stabilize economic life so as to bridge the gap between such "boom periods" as the present and such periods of widespread deprivation as the Great Depression of the 1930's.

The readings in this part thus contend that the performance of our economy is not satisfactory. Each writer has pointed up deficiencies, both from the standpoint of solving the problem of economic satisfaction and from the standpoint of contributing to human satisfaction in the broadest sense.

Shall we conclude, therefore, that our economy is unplanned, anarchic, and chaotic, and resolve our problems by adopting a program of centralized planning of production and distribution? Or is the "free-enterprise" economy really guided by an "invisible hand": the free play of supply and demand in the competitive market? Is it true, as Adam Smith and "classical" economists in general have tended to hold, that the free process of competition results in a more favorable and efficient allocation of resources and income to individuals than could any other system? Is it true, as many have also held, that the "free-enterprise" system is the only system compatible with personal and political liberty?

Will the ills and instabilities of industrial society be ended or minimized—as many have contended—by substituting public ownership and control of the means of production for the private enterprise system? Can our economic deficiences be remedied only by an increase of state power which, according to some writers, must deprive us of personal and political freedom? Can we remedy them *even if* we increase the planning powers of government? Is a certain amount of economic "planlessness" and a permanent gap between "promise" and "performance" in our economy the only way in which we can preserve these noneconomic values? Or is there some other scheme—a new program of "capitalism," or of socialism, or some "middle way"—whereby we can *both* organize our economic life so as to close the "gaps" which this section describes *and* maintain or increase our personal and political freedoms and other noneconomic satisfactions?

With these questions in mind, we may move forward into the parts which follow with a sense of why the materials in Book Two are crucial to our lives.

SECTION A

**The nature of industrial society**

# 1 Peter F. Drucker: *The Industrial World Revolution*

❦ *A new and terrifying society has emerged in the twentieth century—a society whose central institutions reflect the all-pervasive influence of mass production, specialization of labor, mechanized processes, and standardized products. Caught in the mesh of a highly complex organization over which he has little direct control, individual man tends to be reduced to a cog in a vast, impersonal machine. He is compelled to witness an endless succession of social upheavals—wars, depressions, dictatorships, concentration camps, and now the threat of annihilation.*

*Peter F. Drucker (1909–    ) is one of the leading analysts of the revolution which produced this new society. His writings define the rationale, structure, and impact of industrial organization, showing how the patterns of mass production and corporate management produce a form of organization that seems to operate with a momentum almost independent of the individuals who comprise it.*

*A native of Vienna, Drucker fled Europe during the Nazi regime. He was a member of the faculty of Bennington College (Vt.) for several years prior to 1949, and is now a consultant on problems of industrial management. The following selection is from his latest book,* The New Society: The Anatomy of the Industrial Order *(New York: Harper & Brothers, 1949, copyright by Peter F. Drucker, 1950), pp. 1–7, and is reprinted with the publisher's permission. Among Drucker's other works are* The End of Economic Man *(1939),* The Future of Industrial Man *(1942), and* The Concept of the Corporation *(1946).*

T̲he world revolution of our time is "made in U. S. A." It is not Communism, Fascism, the new nationalism of the non-Western peoples, or any of the other "isms" that appear in the headlines. They are reactions to the basic disturbance, secondary rather than primary. The true revolutionary principle is the idea of mass production. Nothing ever before recorded in the history of man equals, in speed, universality and impact, the transformation this principle has wrought in the foundations of society in the forty short years since Henry Ford turned out the first "Model T."

Though "made in Detroit," the impact of the new principle is not confined to the United States or to the old industrial territory of the West. Indeed, the impact is greatest on the raw-material-producing, pre-industrial civilizations. The sweep of mass-production technology is undermining and exploding societies and civilizations which have no resistance to the new forces, no background or habit-pattern of industrial life to cushion the shock. In China the mass-production principle, swept into the hinterland from the coastal cities by the forced migration of industries during the Japanese invasion, is destroying the world's oldest and hitherto its stablest institution: the Chinese family. In India, industrialization has begun to corrode the Hindu caste system: ritual restrictions on proximity and intercourse between castes simply cannot be maintained under factory conditions. Russia uses the new mass-production principle to try again where Byzantium failed: to mate Europa and the Bull, the technological fruits of Western thought with Oriental despotism, to produce a new world order which claims to be the legitimate heir to both East and West. In our own country the Old South, hitherto least touched by industry and still living in the ruins of its antebellum rural order, is speedily being "tractored off." Indeed, conversion of the Southern farm into a rural assembly line seems on the verge of "solving" the Southern race problem in a manner never dreamed of by either Southern Liberal or Southern Reactionary: by pushing the Negro off the land into the industrial cities.

At the time of World War I, only one generation ago, industry was, by and large, still confined to a narrow belt on either side of the North Atlantic. The only exception, the only successful transplantation of the machine to new soil, was in Japan. The representative unit of industry, even in the most heavily industrialized countries, was the family-owned or family-managed medium-size factory employing fewer than five hundred workers and differing from the workshop of pre-industrial days mainly in its use of mechanical power.

Today the situation is reversed. The areas not undergoing rapid industrialization are few and isolated; the representative, the decisive, industrial unit anywhere is the large, mass-production plant, managed by professionals without a stake in ownership, employing thousands of people, and altogether organized on entirely different technological, social, and economic principles. The change has been so great that, in retrospect, the typical factory of 1910 seems to have been closer to its great-grandfather, the artisan's workshop of pre-steam-engine days, than to its own son: the modern mass-production plant. The new industrial territories, only yesterday rural and largely innocent of machine and factory, are jumping directly into the mass-production age without going through the first "Industrial Revolution."

The geographic spread of the mass-production principle, its sweep in width, is accompanied by a sweep in depth: the penetration of the traditional pre-industrial and nonindustrial occupations. This aspect of the industrial world revolution is fully as important as the industrialization of the raw-material-producing countries.

The great bulk of productive work a generation ago was done in forms antedating industry by hundreds, if not thousands, of years. Even in the most highly industrialized country, it was completely nonindustrial in character. Only a minority of the people, though in some countries an important minority, lived and worked in an industrial world. Even in the most highly industrialized country, the mass-production principle was still regarded generally as a mere technique, such as the assembly line, and largely confined to the automobile industry.

Two World Wars showed that the principle which underlay Henry Ford's first plant forty years ago is completely independent of specific tools or techniques, and that it is a basic principle for the organization of all manufacturing activities. Today it has become abundantly clear that the mass-production principle is not even confined to manufacturing, but is a *general principle for organizing people to work together.*

The Russian collective farm was the first application of the principle to agriculture. Its labor organization which uses the individual as a highly specialized tool performing essentially one simple job repetitiously, its control through the state-owned tractor station, its system of compensation—all are applications of mass-production technology. Yet the Russian collective farm is already technologically as obsolete as an automobile plant of forty years ago. The fully mechanized cotton plantation in the Mississippi Delta, or the vegetable co-operative on the irrigated land of California's Central Valley, have gone much further in breaking with the pre-industrial traditions of agriculture. And in their grandiose scheme for raising peanuts in tropical Africa, the British proposed to reorganize a whole colonial empire on the mass-production basis. Yet agriculture has traditionally been regarded as opposite to, and incompatible with, industrialization, if not as the very symbol of the pre-industrial tradition.

Without assembly line or conveyor belt, clerical operations in large-scale business enterprises are today increasingly organized the same way in which Henry Ford organized the production of the Model T. The typists' pool of a large insurance company, check-sorting and check-clearing operations in a big bank, the sorting and filling of orders in a mail-order house, and thousands of other operations in business and government offices do not differ in substance from the automobile assembly line, however much they may differ in appearance.

Similarly, scientific research has been organized on mass-production lines. This has been true for many years in the engineering and chemical research carried on by American industry. The mass-production method is now being carried into medical and biological research. In the new Sloan-Kettering Institute for Cancer Research in New York—significantly founded by two pioneers of the automobile industry—concepts and methods of work are those of the assembly line. During the War the application of this mass-production principle to scientific research resulted in the atomic bomb, which could not have been produced by any other method. Even pure research, unconcerned with application, has been organized on the mass-production pattern in some of our most productive laboratories, such as those of the Bell Telephone System or of the General Electric Company.

The principle has even been applied successfully to work that has always been considered to be essentially personal in character. The efficiency and effectiveness of the Mayo Clinic, for instance, rests largely on its organizing diagnosis and examination into a production line. Henry Luce's "group journalism," by means of which *Time, Life* and *Fortune* are being produced, is largely assembly-line work.

Most startling, however, is the application of the principle to military organization. Of all pre-industrial types of organization, the army was the most highly formalized and apparently the most rigid. But the great Allied invasions of World War II were prepared and carried out as mass-production processes, with each officer doing only one highly specialized and largely mechanical task. He was seldom shifted from operation to operation, nor did he usually know where his piece fitted into the total. This application of the mass-production principle to the conduct of war was one of the most important contributions this country made to victory. It represented a greater change in the organization of warfare than anything that had been developed since Spain's *"Gran Capitan"* first created the concept of the modern army almost five hundred years ago.

"Industry" once meant any organization for human work. It was only during the eighteenth and the early nineteenth centuries, the era of the first "Industrial Revolution," that the term was narrowed to mean "manufacturing." With the second industrial revolution, the revolution of mass production, "industry" again reverts to its earlier meaning. The industrial principle of today, the mass-production principle, promises to put all major organizations for group work, no matter where or of what kind, on the same basis, and to organize them according to the same concept. It is not only the most revolutionary principle of production man has ever found but also the most general.

The mass-production principle is not a mechanical principle. If it were, it could never have been applied beyond manufacturing, and independently of assembly line, conveyor belt and interchangeable parts. It is a *social* principle—a principle of *human* organization. What was new in Ford's plant was not the organization of mechanical forces, but the organization of human beings performing a common task. And this explains the shattering impact of the new principle on traditional cultures, on the relationship between man and society, and on the family.

Of these impacts, *the divorce of the worker from the product and the means of production* is the most visible.

This separation has long been recognized. In the past it has always been blamed on the legal or economic "superstructure." It has been considered an accident, rather than an essential, of the industrial system. That was, for instance, Marx's premise and on it rest almost all his major conclusions. It was the premise of Marx's enemies, the Guild Socialists and the Syndicalists. It was shared by all other critical students of the effects of the first Industrial Revolution. It underlies the two famous Papal encyclicals on the industrial order, *"Rerum Novarum"* and *"Quadragesimo Anno."* There was a general belief that the worker would have control of production if only he were given legal control over the means of production.

In the mass-production system, this belief can no longer be maintained. The divorce of the worker from product and means of production is essential and absolute. It has nothing to do with legal control or political institutions. The worker by himself cannot produce. He must have access to that highly complex organization of men, machines and tools we call a plant. As we shall see, even the collective of the workers, such as a co-operative, a union or a syndicate cannot control this organization—except in a purely formal and entirely fictitious sense— let alone the individual worker.*

In fact, the worker no longer produces, even in the plant; he works. But the product is not being turned out by any one worker or any one group of workers. It is being turned out by the plant. It is a *collective* product. The individual worker usually is not even capable of defining his own contribution to the productive organization and to the product. Often he cannot even point to a part or a process and say: this is *my* work.

This applies wherever the mass-production principle has been applied. The most striking examples are indeed to be found outside of manufacturing. There are apparently no "means of production" in a clerical organization; but when a bookkeeper, a comptometer operator, a shipping clerk, is cut off from the organization he is completely helpless and unproductive. Similarly, an engineer or an industrial chemist is not productive unless integrated into the organization, no matter how highly trained he may be. Here it is clear that the productive unit, the "means of production," is the organization itself rather than any material tool.

There have always been trades and occupations where access to the organization was necessary if the individual was to be effective and productive. It has been a long time, for instance, since the individual soldier armed with his own equipment could go out and gain a kingdom all by himself as he does in the fairy tales. It is also true that, for his subsistence, the individual in all but a few societies is dependent on an exchange of products with his

ED. NOTE: * Many critics would regard this paragraph as too unqualified in its statements—particularly such statements as "It has nothing to do with legal control or political institutions."

neighbor—that is, on co-operation of some sort. But while not able to *subsist* independently, the overwhelming majority of the people living in any traditional society has always been able to *produce* independently, commanding not much more than the equipment they were born with or that they could make themselves. This applies not only to the hunter, the husbandman, and the farmer, but to the craftsman and to the professional in a traditional society. The tailor, the wheelwright or the baker, the priest, the medicine man and the scribe— they all could function productively as individuals.

In an industrial society the situation is reversed. It is only a very small minority of artists and professional men who can produce at all by themselves. All the others are dependent upon access to an organization to be productive. *It is the organization rather than the individual which is productive in an industrial system.*

This divorce of worker and means of production threatens the status and prestige system of any traditional society, whether of the West or of the East; it dissolves the traditional community and uproots the individual.

It also makes unemployment and the threat of unemployment unbearable—not because of their economic, but because of their social, consequences. This in turn imposes on government the new and unprecedented task of preventing and curing depressions, a job far beyond the ability of any government yet devised by man.

Finally, the divorce of worker and means of production makes the old problem of the concentration of power infinitely more urgent because it makes possible an altogether new total tyranny.

SECTION B

## The paradoxes of industrial revolution

# 2 Henry George: *Progress and Poverty*

❦ *The persistence of poverty in the modern world, despite the tremendous technological advances of the nineteenth and twentieth centuries, is a phenomenon of central importance in any analysis of contemporary political and economic life. One of the classic treatments of this paradox is that of Henry George (1839–1897) in his famous book,* Progress and Poverty *(1879), from which the following selection is reprinted.*

*At least in part because of the inspirational quality of their style, the writings of Henry George had a tremendous impact upon American thought before the end of the last century, and they have continued to be read by more recent generations. George was not formally trained in economics, being for the most part a publicist rather than a professional scholar. In 1886 he made an excursion into politics and was almost elected Mayor of New York City.*

*George's name is most popularly linked with the notion of the "single tax," a scheme under which all other forms of taxation would be replaced by a single tax on the value of land. This plan would confiscate economic "rent," which George saw as the root evil of the private enterprise economy.*

*The selection reproduced here is from the 1908 edition of* Progress and Poverty *(New York: Doubleday & Page & Company), pp. 3–11, and is reprinted with permission of his granddaughter, Agnes George de Mille. George's other works include* The Irish Land Question *(1881),* Social Problems *(1884),* Protection or Free Trade *(1886),* The Condition of Labor *(1891),* A Perplexed Philosopher *(1892), and* The Science of Political Economy *(1897).*

The present century has been marked by a prodigious increase in wealth-producing power. The utilization of steam and electricity, the introduction of improved processes and labor-saving machinery, the greater subdivision and grander scale of production, the wonderful facilitation of exchanges, have multiplied enormously the effectiveness of labor.

At the beginning of this marvelous era it was natural to expect, and it was expected, that labor-saving inventions would lighten the toil and improve the condition of the laborer; that the enormous increase in the power of producing wealth would make real poverty a thing of the past. Could a man of the last century—a Franklin or a Priestley—have seen, in a vision of the future, the steamship taking the place of the sailing vessel, the railroad train of the wagon, the reaping machine of the scythe, the threshing machine of the flail; could he have heard the throb of the engines that in obedience to human will, and for the satisfaction of human desire, exert a power greater than that of all the men and all the beasts of burden of the earth combined; could he have seen the forest tree transformed into finished lumber—into doors, sashes, blinds, boxes or barrels, with hardly the touch of a human hand; the great workshops where boots and shoes are turned out by the case with less labor than the old-fashioned cobbler could have put on a sole; the factories where, under the eye of a girl, cotton becomes cloth faster than hundreds of stalwart weavers could have turned it out with their handlooms; could

he have seen steam hammers shaping mammoth shafts and mighty anchors, and delicate machinery making tiny watches; the diamond drill cutting through the heart of the rocks, and coal oil sparing the whale; could he have realized the enormous saving of labor resulting from improved facilities of exchange and communication—sheep killed in Australia eaten fresh in England, and the order given by the London banker in the afternoon executed in San Francisco in the morning of the same day; could he have conceived of the hundred thousand improvements which these only suggest, what would he have inferred as to the social condition of mankind?

It would not have seemed like an inference; further than the vision went it would have seemed as though he saw; and his heart would have leaped and his nerves would have thrilled, as one who from a height beholds just ahead of the thirst-stricken caravan the living gleam of rustling woods and the glint of laughing waters. Plainly, in the sight of the imagination, he would have beheld these new forces elevating society from its very foundations, lifting the very poorest above the possibility of want, exempting the very lowest from anxiety for the material needs of life; he would have seen these slaves of the lamp of knowledge taking on themselves the traditional curse, these muscles of iron and sinews of steel making the poorest laborer's life a holiday, in which every high quality and noble impulse could have scope to grow.

And out of these bounteous material conditions he would have seen arising, as necessary sequences, moral conditions realizing the golden age of which mankind have always dreamed. Youth no longer stunted and starved; age no longer harried by avarice; the child at play with the tiger; the man with the muckrake drinking in the glory of the stars! Foul things fled, fierce things tame; discord turned to harmony! For how could there be greed where all had enough? How could the vice, the crime, the ignorance, the brutality, that spring from poverty and the fear of poverty, exist where poverty had vanished? Who should crouch where all were freemen; who oppress where all were peers?

More or less vague or clear, these have been the hopes, these the dreams born of the improvements which give this wonderful century its preëminence. They have sunk so deeply into the popular mind as radically to change the currents of thought, to recast creeds and displace the most fundamental conceptions. The haunting visions of higher possibilities have not merely gathered splendor and vividness, but their direction has changed—instead of seeing behind the faint tinges of an expiring sunset, all the glory of the daybreak has decked the skies before.

It is true that disappointment has followed disappointment, and that discovery upon discovery, and invention after invention, have neither lessened the toil of those who most need respite, nor brought plenty to the poor. But there have been so many things to which it seemed this failure could be laid, that up to our time the new faith has hardly weakened. We have better appreciated the difficulties to be overcome; but not the less trusted that the tendency of the times was to overcome them.

Now, however, we are coming into collision with facts which there can be no mistaking. From all parts of the civilized world come complaints of industrial depression; of labor condemned to involuntary idleness; of capital massed and wasting; of pecuniary distress among business men; of want and suffering and anxiety among the working classes. All the dull, deadening pain, all the keen, maddening anguish, that to great masses of men are involved in the words "hard times," afflict the world today. This state of things, common to communities differing so widely in situation, in political institutions, in fiscal and financial systems, in density of population and in social organization, can hardly be accounted for by local causes. There is distress where large standing armies are maintained, but there is also distress where the standing armies are nominal; there is distress where protective tariffs stupidly and wastefully hamper trade, but there is also distress where trade is nearly free; there is distress where autocratic government yet prevails, but there is also distress where political power is wholly in the hands of the people; in countries where paper is money, and in countries where gold and silver are the only currency. Evidently, beneath all such things as these, we must infer a common cause.

That there is a common cause, and that it is either what we call material progress or something closely connected with material progress, becomes more than an inference when it is noted that the phenomena we class together and speak of as industrial depression are but intensifications of phenomena which always accompany material progress, and which show themselves more clearly and strongly as material progress goes on. Where the conditions to which material progress everywhere tends are most fully realized—that is to say, where population is densest, wealth greatest, and the machinery of production and exchange most highly developed—we find the deepest poverty, the sharpest struggle for existence, and the most of enforced idleness.

It is to the newer countries—that is, to the countries where material progress is yet in its earlier stages—that laborers emigrate in search of higher wages, and capital flows in search of higher interest. It is in the older countries—that is to say, the countries where material progress has reached later stages—that widespread destitution is found in the midst of the greatest abundance. Go into one of the new communities where Anglo-Saxon vigor is just beginning the race of progress; where the machinery of production and exchange is yet rude and inefficient; where the increment of wealth is not yet great enough to enable any class to live in ease and luxury; where the best house is but a cabin of logs or a cloth and paper shanty, and the richest man is forced to daily work—and though you will find an absence of wealth and all its concomitants, you will find no beggars. There is no luxury, but there is no destitution. No one makes an easy living, nor a very good living; but everyone *can* make a living, and no one able and willing to work is oppressed by the fear of want.

But just as such a community realizes the conditions which all civilized communities are striving for, and advances in the scale of material progress—just as closer settlement and a more intimate connection with the rest of the world, and greater utilization of labor-saving machinery, make possible greater economies in production and exchange, and wealth in consequence increases, not merely in the aggregate, but in proportion to population—so does poverty take a darker aspect. Some get an infinitely better and easier living, but others find it hard to get a living at all. The "tramp" comes with the locomotive, and almshouses and prisons are as surely the marks of "material progress" as are costly dwellings, rich warehouses, and magnificent churches. Upon streets lighted with gas and patrolled by uniformed policemen, beggars wait for the passer-by, and in the shadow of college, and library, and museum, are gathering the more hideous Huns and fiercer Vandals of whom Macaulay * prophesied.

This fact—the great fact that poverty and all its concomitants show themselves in communities just as they develop into the conditions toward which material progress tends—proves that the social difficulties existing wherever a certain stage of progress has been reached, do not arise from local circumstances, but are, in some way or another, engendered by progress itself.

And, unpleasant as it may be to admit it, it is at last becoming evident that the enormous increase in productive power which has marked the present century and is still going on with accelerating ratio, has no tendency to extirpate poverty or to lighten the burdens of those compelled to toil. It simply widens the gulf between Dives and Lazarus, and makes the struggle for existence more intense. The march of invention has clothed mankind with powers of which a century ago the boldest imagination could not have dreamed. But in factories where labor-saving machinery has reached its most wonderful development, little children are at work; wherever the new forces are anything like fully utilized, large classes are maintained by charity or live on the verge of recourse to it; amid the greatest accumulations of wealth, men die of starvation, and puny infants suckle dry breasts; while everywhere the greed of gain, the worship of wealth, shows the force of the fear of want. The promised land flies before us like the mirage. The fruits of the tree of knowledge turn as we grasp them to apples of Sodom that crumble at the touch.

It is true that wealth has been greatly increased, and that the average of comfort, leisure, and refinement has been raised; but these gains are not general. In them the lowest class do not share.[1] I do not mean that the condition of the lowest class has nowhere nor in anything been improved; but that there is nowhere any improvement which can be credited to increased productive power. I mean that the tendency of what we call material progress is in nowise to improve the condition of the lowest class in the essentials of healthy, happy human life. Nay, more, that it is still further to depress the condition of the lowest class. The new forces, elevating in their nature though they be, do not act upon the social fabric

[1] It is true that the poorest may now in certain ways enjoy what the richest a century ago could not have commanded, but this does not show improvement of condition so long as the ability to obtain the necessaries of life is not increased. The beggar in a great city may enjoy many things from which the backwoods farmer is debarred, but that does not prove the condition of the city beggar better than that of the independent farmer.

ED. NOTE: * Thomas Babington Macaulay (1800–1859), the English historian.

from underneath, as was for a long time hoped and believed, but strike it at a point intermediate between top and bottom. It is as though an immense wedge were being forced, not underneath society, but through society. Those who are above the point of separation are elevated, but those who are below are crushed down.

This depressing effect is not generally realized, for it is not apparent where there has long existed a class just able to live. Where the lowest class barely lives, as has been the case for a long time in many parts of Europe, it is impossible for it to get any lower, for the next lowest step is out of existence, and no tendency to further depression can readily show itself. But in the progress of new settlements to the conditions of older communities it may clearly be seen that material progress does not merely fail to relieve poverty—it actually produces it. In the United States it is clear that squalor and misery, and the vices and crimes that spring from them, everywhere increase as the village grows to the city, and the march of development brings the advantages of the improved methods of production and exchange. It is in the older and richer sections of the Union that pauperism and distress among the working classes are becoming most painfully apparent. If there is less deep poverty in San Francisco than in New York, is it not because San Francisco is yet behind New York in all that both cities are striving for? When San Francisco reaches the point where New York now is, who can doubt that there will also be ragged and barefooted children on her streets?

This association of poverty with progress is the great enigma of our times. It is the central fact from which spring industrial, social, and political difficulties that perplex the world, and with which statesmanship and philanthropy and education grapple in vain. From it come the clouds that overhang the future of the most progressive and self-reliant nations. It is the riddle which the Sphinx of Fate puts to our civilization, and which not to answer is to be destroyed. So long as all the increased wealth which modern progress brings goes but to build up great fortunes, to increase luxury and make sharper the contrast between the House of Have and the House of Want, progress is not real and cannot be permanent. The reaction must come. The tower leans from its foundations, and every new story but hastens the final catastrophe. To educate men who must be condemned to poverty, is but to make them restive; to base on a state of most glaring social inequality political institutions under which men are theoretically equal, is to stand a pyramid on its apex.

All-important as this question is, pressing itself from every quarter painfully upon attention, it has not yet received a solution which accounts for all the facts and points to any clear and simple remedy. This is shown by the widely varying attempts to account for the prevailing depression.[*] They exhibit not merely a divergence between vulgar notions and scientific theories, but also show that the concurrence which should exist between those who avow the same general theories breaks up upon practical questions into an anarchy of opinion. Upon high economic authority we have been told that the prevailing depression is due to overconsumption; upon equally high authority, that it is due to overproduction; while the wastes of war, the extension of railroads, the attempts of workmen to keep up wages, the demonetization of silver, the issues of paper money, the increase of labor-saving machinery, the opening of shorter avenues to trade, etc., are separtely pointed out as the cause, by writers of reputation.

And while professors thus disagree, the ideas that there is a necessary conflict between capital and labor, that machinery is an evil, that competition must be restrained and interest abolished, that wealth may be created by the issue of money, that it is the duty of government to furnish capital or to furnish work, are rapidly making way among the great body of the people, who keenly feel a hurt and are sharply conscious of a wrong. Such ideas, which bring

ED. NOTE: * George is referring to the depression of 1873–81.

great masses of men, the repositories of ultimate political power, under the leadership of charlatans and demagogues, are fraught with danger; but they cannot be successfully combated until political economy shall give some answer to the great question which shall be consistent with all her teachings, and which shall commend itself to the perceptions of the great masses of men.

# 3 Ralph Borsodi: *The Conquering Factory System*

❦ *Man's growing knowledge of science and technology has given him a growing mastery over his natural environment. But the ultimate effect of the machine upon human personality and social life is less clear. Many leading social thinkers, among them Ralph Borsodi (1888– ), see modern man in the process of being dehumanized by his own inventions. They see man's cultural life—his art, his leisure, his philosophy—being invaded and warped by the influence of mechanization.*

*To counteract this imperialistic spread of technology Borsodi and others urge that people take up a closer relationship with the land, that they begin again to develop their powers of self-reliance, and that they join in a movement to decentralize the economic and social pattern of American life.*

*Borsodi, a leader in the decentralist movement, has written many books on the subject, among them* National Advertising vs. Prosperity *(1923),* Flight from the City *(1933),* Agriculture in Modern Life *(1939), and* Education and Living *(3 vols., 1943). The following selection is reprinted from* This Ugly Civilization *(New York: Simon and Schuster, 1929), pp. 183–99, with the author's permission.*

Factories, factory products, factory workers, factory customers—and a race dependent upon factories and factory goods—these are some of the fruits of the application of the factory system to the production of the things mankind needs and desires.

But they are not the factory's only fruits.

The factory has not been able to keep the factory system within the limits of its four ugly walls.

What is the factory system?

It is the group of methods used in manufacturing of which the most conspicuous are (a) systematic production; (b) standardization to insure uniformity of product; (c) division and subdivision of labor. These represent the application of the principle of efficiency to the work of producing the necessaries and luxuries of modern civilization.

Harrington Emerson, who has been called by an admirer [1] the "High Priest of the New Science of Efficiency," defines efficiency as "the elimination of all needless waste in

[1] Herbert N. Casson, "The Story of Emerson, High Priest of the New Science of Efficiency," *American Review of Reviews,* Vol. XIVIII, September 1913, pp. 305–15.

material, in labor, and in equipment, so as to reduce costs, increase profits, and raise wages." This definition should at once make clear the legitimate field of the factory system and also the limited sphere of activities in which its application is desirable. In a factory, which has its justification only in its capacity for producing the largest possible quantity of commodities at the lowest possible cost, the elimination of every waste is most desirable. But outside of a factory, in all the activities of man which have their justification primarily in the extent to which they enrich life, the quantitative criterion which efficiency enjoins becomes absurd. Life, if man is to dignify it by the way he lives, must be lived artistically. Not quantitative but qualitative criterions apply in home life, in education, in social activities, in literature, painting, sculpture. Yet the apostles of efficiency have not been content to limit its application to the factory. They have made efficiency a philosophy of life and are now busily engaged in applying the factory system to the regulation of every activity of civilized man.

In his introduction to his epoch making volume on "The Principles of Scientific Management," the late Frederick Winslow Taylor, the founder of the efficiency movement, said of the principles of which he was so ardent an advocate:

The same principles can be applied with equal force to all social activities: to the management of our homes; the management of our farms; the management of the business of our tradesmen, large and small; of our churches, our philanthropic institutions, our universities, and our government departments.[1]

What was merely the distant vision of Taylor in 1911 is today in process of becoming an accomplished fact. As we shall see, we are now in the process of fulfilling in every activity of life Taylor's prophetic words: *"In the past the man has been first; in the future the system must be first."*

In order to understand why the factory system has spread from the factory to every

aspect of American life a careful examination of the factory system in its original "habitat" is essential.

When the first manufacturers discovered that wealth could be accumulated much more rapidly by applying power to the making of one thing in one place instead of making many different things in one place, the first step in the development of the factory system had been taken. On the heels of this discovery came lower prices, made possible by economies in labor and ecomomies in material, and a ruthless war of extermination upon the guild, the custom, and the domestic systems of production.

The ubiquitous village smithy, where horses and oxen were shod and where practically everything which the neighborhood needed in the way of ironwork was made: agricultural implements—plowshares, boghoes, stone hooks, garden forks; carpenter's tools—broad-axes, pod-augers, beetles and frows; building hardware—hinges, latches, and locks; fire-place utensils—andirons, gridirons, cranes, tongs, and shovels; cooking utensils, cutlery and hundreds of other things, disappeared. The smithy's place was taken by mills and machine shops in each of which only one article or one commodity was made, or if a number of allied products were made, each was produced serially instead of on custom order.

The spinning wheels, the combs and cards, the reels and the looms and the loom rooms disappeared from the craftsman's shops and from the homes of rich and poor. These were replaced by mills in each of which only one process in the making of fabrics was carried on. One mill spun yarn. Another wove gray goods. A third dyed and finished them. Or mills confined themselves to only one fiber, to linen, to wool, to cotton, or to silk, and performed the various processes of manufacture in separate departments each of which made possible systematic factory production.

Much of the cooking and preserving disappeared from the home. Homes with kitchens, pantries, vegetable cellars, smokehouses and milk houses in which foods were cooked, smoked, pickled and pre-

[1] Frederick W. Taylor, *The Principles of Scientific Management* (New York: Harpers, 1911), pp. 7, 8.

served by the joint effort of the entire family were replaced by packing houses and canneries, in which foodstuffs were systematically packed and canned and bottled by the most approved factory techniques.

Serial production in the factory destroyed the very foundations of individual production. The factory owners, by concentrating systematically on one product, were able not only to outsell the craftsmen but to paralyze most of the productive activities in the home. The factory product, eventually, sold so cheaply that the workshop producers could not hope to meet its competition. It became so cheap that it did not even seem worth while for individuals to continue its production for their own consumption.

Yet in spite of the competitive advantage of very low costs of production, the early manufacturers found it difficult to put the craftsmen out of their misery. It took generations for the mills and factories to establish their present supremacy. It was only after the manufacturer discovered that concentration of production upon a single kind of goods made it possible to support systematic salesmanship that the old craft production really began to succumb. Systematic salesmanship made possible the profitable operation of the factory because it enabled the manufacturer to sell at a profit in territory where handicraft competition had been destroyed while selling at a loss in territory where it still survived. The factory was thus enabled to extend itself into new territory, selling if necessary at a loss until all neighborhood production ceased and then recouping its initial losses after the sale of its product had become firmly established.

Home and workshop products tended to vary not only in response to the moods and creative urge of the maker, but often in accordance with the needs, desires and idiosyncrasies of the consumer. Under such conditions eccentricity was no luxury. Personality could be catered to because individual taste was not penalized. Being made individually and serially, the products could be varied in size, in quality, and in design

to suit the maker or consumer without materially affecting the actual cost of production. But none of the economies of mass production, mass distribution, and mass consumption is possible if the finished product is permitted to vary in this manner. Serial production in the factory is dependent at all stages upon uniformities: uniformities of design, material, and workmanship. Each article exactly duplicates every other, not only because uniformity is essential for economical mass production, but because it is essential to the creation of mass consumption.

If the cooks in the canneries were permitted to vary each batch of soup as the spirit moved them, some of the cans of soup would contain more salt, others less; some would contain onions, others would have none; some would be thin, others would be thick. It would be obviously impossible to create a mass demand for the soup. Mass production is dependent upon mass consumption. The consumer must know beforehand just about what the soup is going to contain. The recipe, therefore, has to be a compromise which appeals to all kinds of demand. Taste has to be standardized, not only in soup, but in nearly everything that is consumed, or factory production becomes impossible.

The factory system involves an apotheosis of the mediocre. The least common denominator of taste is made the standard to which, on the score of efficiency, everything must conform.

. . . . .

The application of the three techniques which comprise the factory system to the production of the goods we consume has revolutionized life. It has enabled this civilization to realize the goal of increased profits, higher wages, lower prices. Material well-being has been increased; life in many obvious respects has been made less uncomfortable. Man has more shelter, more clothing, more creature comforts of all sorts than before.

It is only natural that those who have brought all this to pass should feel that the application of the factory system to all the activities of life, often under the *nom de plume* of "business methods," would result in equally startling improvements in every aspect of living. The factory system applied to the home should make the family happier; applied to the farm it should make the farmer more prosperous and farm products less expensive; applied to the business of our tradesmen it should add to their profits and make them serve their customers better; applied to the school it should produce a better educated citizen; applied to the church it should make our spiritual life richer; applied to philanthropy it should decrease the sum total of human suffering and make men more unselfish; applied to politics it should make government function more justly, more benignantly, more intelligently—above all more economically.

And this is precisely what we have in recent years begun to do. For better or worse, we have been systematizing all the activities of life; we have been transferring the "mechanizing" of life which began in the factory to the office, to the church, to the school, and to the home.

It is perhaps not correct to say that the application of the factory system to administrative and clerical work in offices of all kinds is an invasion of regions outside of the factory. The modern office should be considered a part of the factory, or at least of the industry with which it concerns itself even though it may be located in a city hundreds of miles from the place where manufacturing is actually carried on. And yet the invasion of administration by the factory system is worth mentioning because office workers generally, especially those occupying executive positions which correspond to the position of foreman and superintendents in factories, are fooled by their white collars and their more genteel clothes into total blindness to the fact that they are just as truly cogs in the industrial machine as are the men who work in overalls in the factory itself. Modern offices contain an increasing number of workers who are expected to perform their work well, just as are the machine operators in

the factory, but who, like the laborers, are not expected to rise higher.

*     *     *     *     *

But the invasion of fine arts by the factory system! Here indeed is an invasion of a sphere of activity which ought to be sacredly preserved for the creative expression of the individual.

Consider how modern literature—if we dare call much modern writing literature—is standardized by the demands of mass publishing. Author A has written an interesting short story about New York's East Side Jews. It has made a distinct hit. He must therefore fill book after book with stories devoted to the identical theme, or cease to be an author with a marketable commodity. Author B has written a dashing novel of the West and its cowboys. He must therefore endlessly repeat himself on the same locale and characters. The more uniform their stories, the more ideally they fit into the scheme of modern, factory methods of magazine and book publishing.

Of course, the factory system dominates the production of the American newspaper. The local news, unavoidably, must be written to fit local conditions, but aside from that, editorials, cartoons, "columns," comic strips, short stories, fashions, pictures, magazine sections, all are fabricated and syndicated by factory methods. You may move from New York to San Francisco—traverse the whole continent—and never for a day stop in a city in which some paper does not publish your favorite "column," your favorite comic strips, and your favorite poet's effusions.

*     *     *     *     *

The factory system has been applied in a most masterly fashion to the task of entertaining the masses. A populace bored to the point of inanity by the monotony of its work in office and factory, and supplied with ample leisure by the process of taking from the family most of the occupations which might make home-making interesting and important, has to be entertained. Entertainment is therefore provided which is quite as thoroughly standardized, as easy to assimilate, as little disturbing to the mind as is the work which they do while earning their daily bread. The movies, with standardized tragedies, comedies and news features, with standardized actors and actresses and standardized show houses, furnish a splendid means of escape into a world of adventure and apparent life. If the movies do not satisfy the masses every night in the week, there is the alternative of standardized vaudeville and standardized burlesque, and even without leaving the home to be entertained, there is the standardized entertainmnt of the radio, the phonograph, and the piano player. There is plenty of music, but it is mainly vicarious music, not music that is the product of personal effort. There is less of that kind of music and that kind of singing in the lives of the men and women of our factory-dominated civilization than in that of the African negroes in the forests. Family dancing and folk singing has gone the way of family and craft production: it has been systematized out of existence.

We buy our music today; we do not produce it ourselves. Perhaps the time will come when it can neither be produced or enjoyed by us.

Says Waldo Frank:

Art cannot become a language, hence an experience, unless it is practiced. To the man who plays, a mechanical reproduction of music may mean much, since he already has the experience to assimilate it. But where reproduction becomes the norm, the few music-makers will grow more isolate and sterile, and the ability to experience music will disappear. The same is true with cinema, dance and even sport. Only when the theatre for instance, is an ennobled symbolization of common social practice (as it was in Athens and in Medieval Europe) can it become an experience for the onlooker.[1]

·  ·  ·  ·  ·

The factory system dominates modern methods of education. The system begins in the nursery school. It ends in the university.

[1] Waldo Frank, "The Rediscovery of America," *The New Republic,* Vol. LIV, No. 693, March 14, 1928, p. 119 n. 1.

As more and more of the work of education is taken over by the school and less and less left to the home, schools become bigger and bigger institutions; the army of teachers becomes larger and larger; the educational system, more and more efficient. The modern school becomes more and more like a modern factory. It becomes an institution notable for its efficient equipment, efficient methods, and efficient personnel. The pupils go through the school in standardized classes; study a standardized curriculum; pass standardized examination; and emerge with standardized educations.

The work of teaching is divided and subdivided among specialists much as the work of making an automobile is divided and sub-divided among trained laborers in the automobile factory. Mathematics is taught by one teacher; history by another. There are plenty of teachers of mathematics who, though they probably did know enough history to graduate when they went to school, have forgotten all that they know of that subject and yet build splendid reputations in their specialty. True, the school can never hope to attain the degree of specialization which enables the automobile factory to train its workers for their tasks in a single day. But it can specialize to a point which will make it easy to use stupider and stupider types to perform each minute task in pedagogy; to shoot the teachers through normal schools more rapidly than before; to standardize systems and teaching techniques; in short, to apply the principles of efficiency to the whole task of running itself and of preparing the young for their factory-dominated futures.

Scholars may be as various in temperament and background as they can well be, but they must nevertheless be educated by a system in which they are treated as mere units in a carefully graded class of like units. They enter school as raw material in the kindergarten. The kindergarten prepares them for their primary work. They pass from one class to another; from the grammar school to the high school; from the high school to the college, and exit at various convenient stopping points along the route into the factory-world, much as raw cotton enters a mill at one point and finally emerges at another as finished cotton goods. Each individual yard is the same as every other yard. Each individual scholar tends to be the same as every other—educated for a place in the factory world, with the same identical range of reactions to factory, office, religion, politics, as the school and college boards consider it best for them to possess. They may, for instance, react either to Republicanism or to Democracy, but to Socialism, never!

. . . . .

Where has this factory system not gone? It has been applied to the most elementary aspects of life—to the feeding and sheltering of mankind. We eat in restaurants and lunchrooms dishes produced by factory methods out of foods which all came from factories, and we sleep in apartment houses and hotels in which every detail of living is as meticulously standardized as is every step in the making of a Ford car.

Strange as it may seem, some of the most acute students of civilization are completely blind to the deadening effect upon us of this systemization of all the ordinary activities of our lives. Havelock Ellis, who is not afraid to advocate the most revolutionary changes in our sexual customs, is yet willing to accept, with an amusing fatalism, the existing factory systemization of life as part of the solution of the problem of domestic happiness. He would make homes happy by destroying their every function except that of being dormitories for the couples who inhabit them. In an essay he urges mankind to replace the wasteful, extravagant, and often inefficient home cookery by meals cooked outside; "to facilitate the growing social habit of taking meals in spacious public restaurants, under more attractive, economical and wholesome conditions than can usually be secured within the narrow confines of the home," and "to contract with specially trained workers from outside for all those routines of domestic drudgery which are inefficiently and labor-

iously carried on by the household worker, whether mistress or servant." [1]

Is it really desirable to give up home cookery and to substitute for it mass cookery and mass service in restaurants? Wouldn't it be wiser to utilize our scientific knowledge for the purpose of making home cookery more attractive, more economical, more wholesome and to make homemaking a creative art rather than to abandon one of the few remaining economic functions of the home?

In our American cities we seem to be acting upon Mr. Ellis's prescription, according to Charles Laube, President of the National Restaurant Association.

Apartments have been largely responsible for the decline of the domestic kitchen. They are small and they aggravate modern wives who don't like to cook, anyway. The restaurateur has competed successfully against the home kitchen in the past because he has made money through labor-saving machines, electric dish washers and patented potato peelers. From now on success will lie in making his place more attractive, in dispensing atmosphere as well as good food. The restaurant will be decorated more artistically and a new type of waitress will appear—one who is prettier, more congenial and dressed becomingly.[2]

This is probably as it should be in a factory-dominated world. The "atmosphere," the artistic decorations, the prettily dressed homemakers are obsolete. All these must be transferred from the inefficient privacy of the home to a "spacious public restaurant" where they can be enjoyed en masse and in public.

In a civilization reflecting at every point the conquering factory system it is fitting to find that we have applied the factory system to the business of being born, of being sick, and in the end of dying and being buried. We now have maternity hospitals, nurseries, and nursery schools, sanitariums and even funeral churches, all of them efficient—and hard.

The modern mother is merely maternity

[1] Havelock Ellis, *Little Essays of Love and Virtue*, (New York: Doran, 1922, reprinted 1930), p. 96.
[2] Charles Laube, in *The New York Telegram*, May 25, 1928.

case number 8,434; her infant after being finger and foot printed, becomes infant number 8,003.

By virtue of the same mania for system, a modern corpse becomes number 2,432; while a modern funeral becomes one of a series scheduled for parlor 4B for a certain day at a certain hour, with preacher number fourteen, singer number 87, rendering music number 174, and flowers and decorations class B.

Thus the factory system begins and finishes the citizen of the factory-dominated world.

It introduces him to his world in a systematized hospital, furnishes him a standardized education, supports him in a scientifically managed factory, and finishes him off with a final factory flourish, by giving him a perfectly efficient funeral and a perfectly scientific entrance into the regions of eternal bliss.

## SELECTED REFERENCES FOR PART 1

ANGELL, NORMAN. *The Great Illusion.* New York: G. P. Putnam's, 1913.

Argues the wasteful character of war and political nationalism from an economic point of view.

ARNOLD, THURMAN W. *The Folklore of Capitalism.* New Haven: Yale Univ. Press, 1937. Contrasts the "realities" and the "myths" involved in the structure and working of our economic system.

BROOKINGS INSTITUTION. *America's Capacity to Consume.* Pittsburgh: The Eddy Press Corp., 1934.

———. *America's Capacity to Produce.* Pittsburgh: The Eddy Press Corp., 1938.

The central contention of these profoundly influential studies—issued during the Great Depression—is that the great mass of consumers received incomes too low to purchase the product of America's industry. The resulting misuse and disuse (idleness) of resources, they argued, could only be remedied if America's "capacity to consume" were geared to "America's capacity to produce."

BURCHARD, JOHN ELY (ed.). *Mid-Century: The Social Implications of Scientific Progress.* New York: Wiley, 1950.

A symposium, including contributions by Winston Churchill, Fairfield Osborn, Frank W. Notestein, P. W. Bridgman, and Senator Ralph W. Flanders.

DELAISI, FRANCIS. *Political Myths and Economic Realities.* London: N. Douglas, 1927.

Emphasizes the discrepancies between the international character of the division of labor and the nationalist character of political conceptions.

DEWHURST, J. FREDERIC, AND ASSOCIATES. *America's Needs and Resources.* New York: Twentieth-Century Fund, 1947.

A detailed study of today's accomplishments and tomorrow's prospects in the economic sphere. A handy illustrated presentation of this volume has been prepared by Thomas R. Carskadon and Rudolf Modley under the title *U.S.A.: Measure of a Nation* (New York: Macmillan, 1949).

HUNTER, MONICA. *Reaction to Conquest: Effects of Contact With Europeans on the Pondo of South Africa.* With introduction by Jan Christiaan Smuts. London: Oxford Univ. Press, 1936.

A case study in the impact of imperialism.

KAPP, K. WILLIAM. *The Social Costs of Private Enterprise.* Cambridge: Harvard Univ. Press, 1950.

Emphasizes the "wastes" inherent in the private enterprise system.

LIPSON, EPHRAIM. *A Planned Society or Free Enterprise,* 2nd ed. London: Adam and Charles Black, 1946.

"The lessons of history" applied to the problems of the modern economy.

McKINLEY, SILAS BENT. *Democracy and Military Power.* With an introduction by Charles A. Beard. New York: Vanguard, 1934.

Argues the intimate connection between the character of military technology and social structure.

MAYO, ELTON. *The Social Problems of an Industrial Civilization.* Cambridge: Harvard Univ. Graduate School of Business Administration, 1946.

Sums up the author's pioneering researches into personality and morale in the industrial community.

MEAD, MARGARET (ed.). *Co-operation and Competition Among Primitive Peoples.* New York: McGraw-Hill, 1937.

These studies query the inevitability or superiority of the system of competition by analyzing the contrasting ways of life among different peoples.

MEADOWS, PAUL. *The Culture of Industrial Man.* Lincoln, Neb.: Univ. of Nebraska Press, 1950.

A critical appraisal of modern industrial culture.

NEF, JOHN U. *War and Human Progress.* Cambridge: Harvard Univ. Press, 1950.

Traces the turmoil in recent politics to the collapse of traditional religious and cultural ideals.

OGBURN, WILLIAM FIELDING (ed.). *Technology and International Relations.* Chicago: Univ. of Chicago Press, 1949.

The editor again emphasizes the lag between "adaptive culture" and technology. Other papers demonstrate the effect of recent technological changes upon international relations.

POLANYI, KARL. *The Great Transformation.* With foreword by Robert M. MacIver. New York: Farrar & Rinehart, 1944.

Argues the thesis that the effort to achieve economic plenty and social welfare through the self-regulating market was doomed to failure. A critical evaluation of this argument is given by Allen Sievers, *Has Market Capitalism Collapsed?* (New York: Columbia Univ. Press, 1949).

ROEPKE, WILHELM. *International Economic Disintegration.* With appendix by Alexander Ruestow. London: William Hodge & Co., 1942.

Describes the breakdown in the world's economic organization.

———. *The Social Crisis of Our Time.* Chicago: Univ. of Chicago Press, 1950.

Argues the need for a third way, neither laissez-faire individualism nor Communist collectivism.

ROETHLISBERGER, FRITZ JULES, with W. J. DICKSON and H. A. WRIGHT. *Management and the Worker.* Cambridge: Harvard Univ. Press, 1946.

This detailed study of the Hawthorne Plant of the Western Electric Company is a major American contribution to social science in the present century.

SHIH, KUO-HENG. *China Enters the Machine Age.* Edited and translated by Hsiao-tung Fei and Francis L. K. Hsu. With foreword by Elton Mayo. Cambridge: Harvard Univ. Press, 1944.

Vivid description of the difficulties in transplanting industrial organization to the peasant society of China.

STALEY, EUGENE. *World Economy in Transition.* New York: Council on Foreign Relations, 1940.

Urges new conceptions of international political order to meet the needs of a world grown smaller as a result of modern technology.

TAWNEY, R. H. *The Acquisitive Society.* New York: Harcourt, Brace, 1920.

Contends that the "sickness" of modern society is exhibited by, and stems from, the unrestricted desire for, and pursuit of, economic gain.

VEBLEN, THORSTEIN. *The Engineers and the Price System.* New York: B. W. Huebsch, 1921; Viking, 1933.

———. *Essays in Our Changing Order.* Edited by Leon Ardzrooni. New York: Viking, 1934.

———. *The Instinct of Workmanship and the State of the Industrial Arts.* New York: Macmillan, 1914.

Veblen's writings charge that American economic institutions are dominated by absentee ownership and the cash-nexus. The "pecuniary calculus" of the price system, he thought, distorted the action of the "instinct for workmanship" and frustrated the hopes for full realization of America's productive potential.

WIENER, NORBERT. *The Human Use of Human Beings.* Boston: Houghton Mifflin, 1950.

Stresses the need for a more humane use of the newer resources of technology. Wiener's earlier work, *Cybernetics* (Cambridge: The Technology Press of Massachusetts Institute of Technology, 1948), is a pioneering treatise on "thinking machines."

WILLKIE, H. FREDERICK. *A Rebel Yells.* New York: Van Nostrand, 1946.

Offers an educational program which the author, a public-spirited industrialist, believes is suitable to a socially and economically progressive organization of production and society.

# PART 2

# Economy, society, and state

❦ Human beings have "economic problems" because their wants cannot be automatically satisfied. Far from being stationary either in kind or in intensity, wants vary from time to time and from place to place. Relative to these changing patterns of wants, the means of satisfaction—goods and resources—are inevitably scarce, available only in limited supply. For this reason, men are obliged to "economize," that is, to arrange ways of allocating their scarce resources so as to achieve a desired measure and variety of want-satisfactions. The basic elements in economic life are, therefore, *wants, scarcity,* and *organization.* In the words of the British economist, Lionel Robbins: "Economics is the science which studies human behavior as a relationship between ends and scarce means which have alternative uses."

Generally, men do not economize singly, in isolation from one another; rather, they join forces or are yoked together in the hope of multiplying their joint output. Men, in short, work together or "co-operate." What is commonly called "competition" need not, indeed, necessarily be thought of as opposed to co-operation. From a broader point of view, as has been suggested by William Graham Sumner, competition is a form of co-operation, namely "antagonistic co-operation."

In this Part, we shall attempt to establish some general principles of economic organization. The first reading, from *The Republic* by the ancient Greek philosopher PLATO, introduces us to the *division of labor.* The least complex form of human labor would occur in the hypothetical situation where everyone would be self-sufficient, that is, where every person would provide for himself, and only for himself, and everyone therefore would do much the same thing. Jobs arise, however, which one person cannot do alone; they require the co-operation of two or more people. Soon it appears that more will be produced if those who co-operate *specialize* in the tasks suited to their special capabilities and *exchange* the products of their labors. Plato presents the "logic" by which this division of labor among hunter, fisherman, and cobbler gives rise to a higher level of production; how this increased production demands new "specialties"; and how specialization, by giving rise to still greater satisfactions and still greater wants, creates a demand for still further subdivision of work. Ultimately, Plato concludes, complex division of labor tends to lead to the spread of expensive wants, luxurious habits, and imperialistic ventures.

Plato wrote about the division of labor in the "pre-industrial" society of ancient Greece. Two thousand years later, Adam Smith, living during the first flush of the industrial revolution of the eighteenth century, was to write about a second kind of division of labor—the division not *among* different occupations but *within* each occupation. This concept is essential for the understanding of the historical development of industrial society, which is given fuller treatment in Part 3.

At this point, however, we are interested primarily in noting how industry and manufacture have spread over the globe and how the world is not industrialized "all over" but is, rather, marked by "clustering" of industry and manufacture at some points while other areas continue to function in traditional pre-industrial patterns. The selection by HENRY M. KENDALL, ROBERT M. GLENDENNING, and CLIFFORD H. MACFADDEN discusses the general principles which determine the location of industry. This is particularly important because the satisfaction of even the most elementary wants of a large number of the earth's inhabitants depends upon either making the existing industrial "clusters" so productive that they can supply the underdeveloped regions of the globe, or upon finding ways of bringing industry to these nonindustrial areas.

In the reading from FRANK H. KNIGHT the principles and problems of economic organization are analyzed in greater detail. What are the functions, Knight asks, which *any* economy must perform? First, he says, it must decide what wants it is going to try to satisfy, since there is always scarcity and not all wants can be satisfied. Second, it must provide ways of organizing men and resources so as to provide the most "efficient" use of resources—land, technology, labor—in the satisfaction of the wants. Third, it must decide who is to get what: the economy must provide a method of distributing the social product. Fourth, the economy must choose between present and future satisfactions, between producing goods for immediate use (consumers' goods) and for use in further production (producers' goods). It must determine, in other words, the relationship between *consumption* and *investment* of the resources. Fifth and finally, the economy endeavors to co-ordinate production and consumption, so that all goods produced may be consumed, and depressions due to "overproduction" or "underconsumption" may thus be avoided.

Throughout history men have had varying notions as to how these functions of the economy are best performed. Knight believes that the systems which have been tried or seriously considered for the fulfillment of these objectives are essentially of five kinds.

In the society based on *status and tradition,* each person tends to have a fixed "place" and "worth," and the processes of production and distribution follow an unchanging pattern. In the society based on *autocracy* or *"military" organization,*

the processes are regulated and deliberately co-ordinated "from the top down."
In the *anarchist* society, by contrast, it is conceived that through good will and
intelligence people will work out their problems of economic and social organization more or less "spontaneously." The *democratic socialist* economy, Knight concludes, is a compromise between the authoritarian and the anarchistic. It is based
upon collective ownership of the major instruments of production; in socialist
theory, decisions are made by the democratic vote of the collective "owners."
Finally, in the society based on the *exchange system*—often referred to as *capitalism* or *free enterprise*—the major economic decisions are made through the "price
system."

The last of these forms—private enterprise—is the dominant organizational
pattern of modern industrialism, and the last part of Knight's essay deals with
the question of how the five functions of an economy are performed under this
system. He deals with it primarily in terms of the "circulation" of *goods* and *services* and of *money*. In all but the most primitive societies, exchange of goods and
services takes place not directly (through barter) but through the medium of
money. The function of money in exchange can be seen particularly at two points.
First, production gives rise to money *income;* second, this money income becomes
the instrument or medium through which goods are bought. Money, therefore,
appears first as the income received for participating in production; then it is
(or may be) spent to create *demand* for goods and services; thus it passes again
into the hands of producers, for whom it again becomes income. One can follow
this process if he will think of someone working, drawing a paycheck, spending
this paycheck, and then will ask himself what happens to these dollars after that.
Thus we get the "wheel of wealth": income—demand—production—income—demand—production, etc., etc.

There is another way of defining the roundaboutness or circularity in the
process of production and distribution in complex societies. The individual persons or households do not satisfy their wants directly by the immediate production of consumption goods. Rather, they contribute resources of one kind or
another, described as "factors of production," to business units known as "firms"
which specialize in the combination of these resources for the production of goods
and services. The individuals contribute land, labor, skill, capital, and other
valued resources and are paid for their contributions in the form of rent, wages,
profit, dividends, according to the supposed worth of these factors in market
prices. Many of the greatest problems which modern complex economies face
result from this circularity of the processes of production and exchange.

Opportunities for instability abound in any economy which is featured by
roundaboutness. It cannot be anticipated, where so many decisions are made in
so unco-ordinated a way, that households or firms can succeed in eliminating risk
and uncertainty in the conduct of their lives and enterprises. Sometimes it is supposed that social ownership of the means of production and programs of central

planning would eliminate all instabilities in the economy and end the risk of depressions and other violent fluctuations. The experience of recent years suggests that this is by no means certain. Unemployment, economic fluctuations, and depression may occur in socialist as well as capitalist economies. They owe their origin not to the forms of ownership or to the political structure of the state alone, but to the difficulties of co-ordinating decisions and of guaranteeing against uninsurable risks in an economic order marked by extreme circularity. Risk, uncertainty, and the possibility of loss may occur even where production is fully planned.

The adequacy of the free market system in performing the "five functions of an economy" has, on the other hand, also been vigorously challenged. In this system, anybody is legally free to spend his money "as he pleases," and the instruments of production are legally owned by private individuals who can use them "as they please" but are presumed to use them where they can get the greatest profit. Thus, all of the five basic problems of an economy are in theory solved by the "price mechanism," that is, by the actions of consumers spending their incomes "as they please," and by the actions of producers utilizing their resources where they will secure the greatest profit.

But the events of recent decades, in particular the Great Depression, have led many to question whether what Adam Smith called the "invisible hand" of the "free" price mechanism can do the job, at least unaided, and whether it may not be desirable to lay a "visible hand" upon the economy to regulate and stabilize its workings. The conviction that the problems of an economy do not necessarily solve themselves automatically has led to that approach to economic problems known as *national income analysis*. This approach views the national economy *as a whole* in much the same way in which an individual businessman views his *firm:* as an organization which has an annual output, an annual income, a balance sheet of output and income, an apportionment of income between production of new goods and services and maintenance and expansion of its "capital," and so on. As the individual entrepreneur, in theory, intelligently and deliberately decides how he shall make the best use of his resources, so national income analysis aims at understanding the "nation as a firm" so as to assist in the intelligent use of the nation's resources. National income analysis is not necessarily socialist or collectivist; it may, in fact, be employed to support and extend the system of "free enterprise."

In the reading by J. R. HICKS and ALBERT G. HART, we analyze the "nation as a firm," and consider some of the factors and processes necessary for an understanding of the economy-as-a-whole. They describe the roundabout process involved in the production of goods and services, showing how this roundaboutness becomes an important feature in the national economy of any modern state, because it means that the economy must divide its effort between making consumers' goods and producers' goods, and that the "stream of income" must divide between consumption and investment. The analysis of the "nation as a firm" requires the use of the concept of the "annual national income," and Hicks and Hart explain how this is calculated.

Underlying this kind of study are several important assumptions which may be summarized as follows: (1) It is possible to estimate how much a nation is capable of producing in a given year, to estimate its *level of full production.* (2) The "wheel of wealth" does not necessarily keep circulating so as to maintain "full production." (3) This is in large part because spending for consumers' goods, or investment in producers' goods, or both, may be insufficient to maintain demand for all that the economy could produce. (4) If this happens, resources—men and "capital goods"—will be left idle, and the goods and services which could have been produced will be lost. (5) It is possible, by understanding the "flow" of production and income in the "nation as a firm," to take steps to keep this from happening. (6) Other things being equal, it is desirable to keep the national income functioning at its most productive level.

A further word about the conception of annual national income should be added. Individuals and households, as we have noted, contribute factors of production to specialized units known as firms. These firms produce goods for exchange. Their product is the social product or the social output, and this is distributed to all who have made contributions: "rent" goes to those who have contributed land; "wages" to those who have contributed labor; "profit" to those who have assumed entrepreneurial risk; "dividends" and "interest" to those who have contributed capital. The income received by all firms and families constitutes the social or national income; thus, the social income is the equivalent of the social output. This income is spent, saved, and invested. The expenditure for consumption goods and for investment goods finances the purchase of the product and the making of new goods. Thus, the effective functioning of the economy depends upon a continuous flow of income, expenditure, and output. Much of the instability of the economy results from the lack of co-ordination among the various kinds of decisions and from "leaks" in the circuit flow of the income stream.

To summarize, this Part poses the problem of organizing the utilization of scarce resources for the satisfaction of human wants. It analyzes the development of division of labor and exchange as central processes in all advanced economies, and discusses the factors which give rise to the industrial division of labor and the distribution of industrial and nonindustrial areas over the globe. It attempts to present the basic functions which must be performed by any economy and some of the alternative systems through which they have been or might be performed. It analyzes in somewhat greater detail the way in which they are presumably performed in that economy known as the "exchange system," and it introduces us to the basic conceptions of the flow of production and income, or the "wheel of wealth," and of the "nation as a firm," whose processes can be studied and presumably influenced by intelligent action.

SECTION A

**Needs, wants, and society**

# 4 Plato: *Division of Labor and the State*

❦ *This discussion of the division of labor, from* The Republic, *by Plato (427–347 B.C.), while perhaps the oldest systematic treatment of the concept, is among the most illuminating ever written. It illustrates the effects produced upon their social and political life by changes in men's scale of values and by the evolution of their forms of economic organization. It attempts to account for the phenomenon of imperialism.*

*Plato, the leading disciple of the Greek philosopher Socrates, sought in* The Republic *to define and illumine the good society by recounting the dialogues of Socrates and his disciples. The following selection is from Book II of* The Republic, *and is reproduced from the translation by Benjamin Jowett.*

SOCRATES. A State arises, as I conceive, out of the needs of mankind; no one is self-sufficing, but all of us have many wants. Can any other origin of a State be imagined?

ADEIMANTUS. There can be no other.

Soc. Then, as we have many wants, and many persons are needed to supply them, one takes a helper for one purpose and another for another; and when these partners and helpers are gathered together in one habitation the body of inhabitants is termed a State.

ADEI. True.

Soc. And they exchange with one another, and one gives, and another receives, under the idea that the exchange will be for their good.

ADEI. Very true.

Soc. Then let us begin and create in idea a State; and yet the true creator is necessity, who is the mother of our invention.

ADEI. Of course.

Soc. Now the first and greatest of necessities is food, which is the condition of life and existence.

ADEI. Certainly.

Soc. The second is a dwelling, and the third clothing and the like.

ADEI. True.

Soc. And now let us see how our city will be able to supply this great demand: We may suppose that one man is a husbandman, another a builder, someone else a weaver—shall we add to them a shoemaker, or perhaps some other purveyor to our bodily wants?

ADEI. Quite right.

Soc. The barest notion of a State must include four or five men.

ADEI. Clearly.

Soc. And how will they proceed? Will each bring the result of his labors into a common stock?—the individual husbandman, for example, producing for four, and laboring four times as long and as much as he need in the provision of food with which he supplies others as well as himself; or will he have nothing to do with others and not be at the trouble of producing for them, but provide for himself alone a fourth of the food in a fourth of the time, and in the remaining three-fourths of his time be employed in making a house or a coat or a pair of shoes, having no partnership with others, but supplying himself all his own wants?

Adeimantus thought that he should aim at producing food only and not at producing everything.

Soc. Probably that would be the better way; and when I hear you say this, I am myself reminded that we are not all alike; there are diversities of natures among us which are adapted to different occupations.

ADEI. Very true.

Soc. And will you have a work better done when the workman has many occupations, or when he has only one?

ADEI. When he has only one.

Soc. Further, there can be no doubt that a work is spoilt when not done at the right time?

ADEI. No doubt.

Soc. For business is not disposed to wait until the doer of the business is at leisure; but the doer must follow up what he is doing, and make the business his first object.

ADEI. He must.

Soc. And if so, we must infer that all things are produced more plentifully and easily and of a better quality when one man does one thing which is natural to him and does it at the right time, and leaves other things.

ADEI. Undoubtedly.

Soc. Then more than four citizens will be required; for the husbandman will not make his own plough or mattock, or other implements of agriculture, if they are to be good for anything. Neither will the builder make his tools—and he too needs many; and in like manner the weaver and shoemaker.

ADEI. True.

Soc. Then carpenters, and smiths, and many other artisans will be sharers in our little State, which is already beginning to grow?

ADEI. True.

Soc. Yet even if we add neatherds, shepherds, and other herdsmen, in order that our husbandmen may have oxen to plough with, and builders as well as husbandmen may have draught cattle, and curriers and weavers fleeces and hides—still our State will not be very large.

ADEI. That is true; yet neither will it be a very small State which contains all these.

Soc. Then, again, there is the situation of the city—to find a place where nothing need be imported is well-nigh impossible.

ADEI. Impossible.

Soc. Then there must be another class of citizens wo will bring the required supply from another city?

ADEI. There must.

Soc. But if the trader goes empty-handed, having nothing which they require who would supply his need, he will come back empty-handed.

ADEI. That is certain.

Soc. And therefore what they produce at home must be not only enough for themselves, but such both in quantity and quality as to accommodate those from whom their wants are supplied.

ADEI. Very true.

Soc. Then more husbandmen and more artisans will be required?

ADEI. They will.

Soc. Not to mention the importers and exporters, who are called merchants?

ADEI. Yes.

Soc. Then we shall want merchants?

ADEI. We shall.

Soc. And if merchandise is to be carried over the sea, skilful sailors will also be needed, and in considerable numbers?

ADEI. Yes, in considerable numbers.

Soc. Then, again, within the city, how will they exchange their productions? To secure such an exchange was, as you will remember, one of our principal objects when we formed them into a society and constituted a State.

ADEI. Clearly they will buy and sell.

SOC. Then they will need a market-place, and a money-token for purposes of exchange.

ADEI. Certainly.

SOC. Suppose now that a husbandman or an artisan brings some production to market, and he comes at a time when there is no one to exchange with him—is he to leave his calling and sit idle in the market-place?

ADEI. Not at all; he will find people there who, seeing the want, undertake the office of salesmen. In well-ordered States they are commonly those who are the weakest in bodily strength, and therefore of little use for any other purpose; their duty is to be in the market, and to give money in exchange for goods to those who desire to sell, and to take money from those who desire to buy.

SOC. This want, then, creates a class of retail-traders in our State. Is not "retailer" the term which is applied to those who sit in the market-place engaged in buying and selling, while those who wander from one city to another are called merchants?

ADEI. Yes.

SOC. And there is another class of servants, who are intellectually hardly on the level of compaionship; still they have plenty of bodily strength for labor, which accordingly they sell, and are called, if I do not mistake, hirelings, "hire" being the name which is given to the price of their labor.

ADEI. True.

SOC. Then hirelings will help to make up our population?

ADEI. Yes.

SOC. And now, Adeimantus, is our State matured and perfected?

ADEI. I think so.

SOC. Where, then, is justice, and where is injustice, and in what part of the State did they spring up?

ADEI. Probably in the dealings of these citizens with one another. I cannot imagine that they are more likely to be found anywhere else.

SOC. I dare say that you are right in your suggestions. We had better think the matter out, and not shrink from the inquiry.

Let us then consider, first of all, what will be their way of life, now that we have thus established them. Will they not produce corn and wine and clothes and shoes, and build houses for themselves? And when they are housed, they will work, in summer, commonly, stripped and barefoot, but in winter substantially clothed and shod. They will feed on barley-meal and flour of wheat, baking and kneading them, making noble cakes and loaves; these they will serve up on a mat of reeds or on clean leaves, themselves reclining the while upon beds strewn with yew or myrtle. And they and their children will feast, drinking of the wine which they have made, wearing garlands on their heads, and hymning the praises of the gods, in happy converse with one another. And they will take care that their families do not exceed their means; having an eye to poverty or war.

GLAUCON. But you have not given them a relish to their meal.

SOC. True. I had forgotten; of course they must have a relish—salt and olives and cheese—and they will boil roots and herbs such as country people prepare; for a dessert we shall give them figs and peas and beans; and they will roast myrtle-berries and acorns at the fire, drinking in moderation. And with such a diet they may be expected to live in peace and health to a good old age, and bequeath a similar life to their children after them.

GLAU. Yes, Socrates, and if you were providing for a city of pigs, how else would you feed the beasts?

SOC. But what would you have, Glaucon?

GLAU. Why, you should give them the ordinary conveniences of life. People who are to be comfortable are accustomed to lie on sofas, and dine off tables, and they should have sauces and sweets in the modern style.

SOC. Yes, now I understand: the question which you would have me consider is, not only how a State, but how a luxurious State is created; and possibly there is no harm in this, for in such a State we shall be more likely to see how justice and injustice originate. In my opinion the true and healthy constitution of the State is the one which I have described. But if you wish also to see a State at fever-heat, I have no objection. For I suspect that many will not be satisfied with the simpler way of life. They will be for adding sofas and tables and other furniture; also dainties and perfumes and incense and courtesans and cakes, all these not of one sort only, but in every variety. We must go beyond the necessaries of which I was at first speaking, such as houses and clothes and shoes; the arts of the painter and the embroiderer will have to be set in motion, and gold and ivory and all sorts of materials must be procured.

GLAU. True.

SOC. Then we must enlarge our borders; for the original healthy State is no longer sufficient. Now will the city have to fill and swell with a multitude of callings which are not required by any natural want; such as the whole tribe of hunters and actors, of whom one large class have to do with forms and colors; another will be the votaries of music—poets and their attendant train of rhapsodists, players, dancers, contractors; also makers of divers kinds of articles, including women's dresses. And we shall want more servants. Will not tutors be also in request, and nurses wet and dry, tirewomen and barbers, as well as confectioners and cooks; and swineherds, too, who were not needed and therefore had no place in the former edition of our State, but are needed now? They must not be forgotten; and there will be animals of many other kinds, if people eat them.

GLAU. Certainly.

SOC. And living in this way we shall have much greater need of physicians than before?

GLAU. Much greater.

SOC. And the country which was enough to support the original inhabitants will be too small now, and not enough?

GLAU. Quite true.

SOC. Then a slice of our neighbors' land will be wanted by us for pasture and till-age, and they will want a slice of ours, if, like ourselves, they exceed the limit of necessity, and give themselves up to the unlimited accumulation of wealth?

GLAU. That, Socrates, will be inevitable.

SOC. And so we shall go to war, Glaucon. Shall we not?

GLAU. Most certainly.

SOC. Then, without determining as yet whether war does good or harm, thus much we may affirm, that now we have discovered war to be derived from causes which are also the causes of almost all the evils in States, private as well as public.

GLAU. Undoubtedly.

SOC. And our State must once more enlarge; and this time the enlargement will be nothing short of a whole army, which will have to go out and fight with the invaders for all that we have, as well as for the things and persons whom we were describing above.

GLAU. Why? Are they not capable of defending themselves?

SOC. No, not if we were right in the principle which was acknowledged by all of us when we were framing the State. The principle, as you will remember, was that one man cannot practise many arts with success.

GLAU. Very true.

SOC. But is not war an art?

GLAU. Certainly.

SOC. And an art requiring as much attention as shoemaking?

GLAU. Quite true.

SOC. And the shoemaker was not allowed by us to be a husbandman, or a weaver, or a builder—in order that we might have our shoes well made; but to him and to every other worker was assigned one work for which he was by nature fitted, and at that he was to continue working all his life long and at no other; he was not to let opportunities slip, and then he would become a good workman. Now nothing can be more important than that the work of a soldier should be well done. But is war an art so easily acquired that a man may be a warrior who is also a husbandman, or shoemaker, or other artisan; although no one in the world would be a good dice or draught player who merely took up the game as a recreation, and had not from his earliest years devoted himself to this and nothing else? No tools will make a man a skilled workman or master of defence, nor be of any use to him who has not learned how to handle them, and has never bestowed any attention upon them. How, then, will he who takes up a shield or other implement of war become a good fighter all in a day, whether with heavy-armed or any other kind of troops?

GLAU. Yes, the tools which would teach men their own use would be beyond price.

SOC. And the higher the duties of the guardian, the more time and skill and art and application will be needed by him?

GLAU. No doubt.

SOC. Will he not also require natural aptitude for his calling?

GLAU. Certainly.

SOC. Then it will be our duty to select, if we can, natures which are fitted for the task of guarding the city?

GLAU. It will.

# 5 Kendall, Glendenning, and MacFadden: *Resource Patterns and World Economy*

☙ *The particular kind of economic pattern a locality will have is dependent upon the interplay of many forces—the kind and amount of raw materials, the availability of power and labor supply, the level of communication and transportation, the state of technological development, and the prevailing cultural attitudes.*

*The following selection describes the process whereby these forces combine and interplay to produce industrial regions, showing how each region comes to occupy a certain place in the world division of labor. The reading is reprinted from* Introduction to Geography *by Henry M. Kendall, Robert M. Glendenning, and Clifford H. Mac-Fadden (New York: Harcourt, Brace and Company, copyright 1951), pp. 485–7, with the permission of the publisher.*

*Kendall (1901–    ) is Professor of Geography at Syracuse University; Glendenning (1905–    ) is Professor of Geography at the University of California at Los Angeles, and MacFadden (1908–    ) is also a member of the Department of Geography at U.C.L.A.*

Changes in the ways of life and ways of making a living for many of the world's inhabitants are indicated by the change in meaning of the word "manufacture" itself. Literally, the word means to make by hand. This is the old, original meaning. Today, it usually means to make, process, or fashion by the use of machines. Man has been manufacturing goods of one sort or another for several thousands of years, but only within the past two hundred has he learned to let machines do most of the work. The entire span of the Industrial Revolution, marking the significant change from human power and the home workshop to industrial power and the factory, is a matter of no more than the lifetimes of four or five persons. Such world-changing inventions as the steam engine, diesel engine, electric motor, ariplane, blast furnace, assembly line, and the use of mineral fuels and water power to make them function, occurred, in a sense, only yesterday.

For those parts of the earth which have become highly industrialized, the old ways of life have changed with surprising rapidity: vast population shifted from farms to urban centers; factories grew and encroached upon, or swallowed completely, many rural areas; persons by the millions were thrust closer to each other in teeming, smoky cities. Some nations, such as the United States, changed from the wilderness and the oxcart to huge cities and jet planes within less than one hundred and fifty years. The miracle is not that we face so many problems of adjustment and readjustment in the modern world, but that the problems are not more numerous and more serious than they are. Even many of the "far-away" places have been affected because some of the machines, literally "space-eaters," have so shrunk the world that today there are no two spots on earth which are more than fifty or sixty hours of flying time apart.

## LOCALIZATION OF MANUFACTURING REGIONS

Many factors and conditions underlie the world distribution of major manufacturing regions. Chief among them are type of culture, availability of raw materials, availability of power, amount and type of labor, nature and spacing of transportation facilities, capital, and nature and size of markets.

*Type of Culture.* Many peoples, even entire nations, have beliefs and follow ways of life that do not lead to industrialization. China is an example. Here the worship of the past, the long resistance to new ideas, and the emphasis on the family unit as opposed to national unity, are a few of the cultural factors which have prevented or hindered the growth of China as a truly important manufacturing nation. There are other peoples and nations in which the ideas and the manner of living are directly conducive to the origin and growth of manufacturing enterprises. In Great Britain, for example, opportunity for exercising initiative, the willingness to accept new ideas and new methods, and a rather pronounced national unity and political stability have fostered the growth of manufacturing.

*Raw Materials.* The creation of a *major* manufacturing region normally must be based on the occurrence of certain raw materials and the possibility of securing others. Again, the situation is different from one section of the earth to another. For example, Denmark is so poor in key industrial raw materials that she has not, and probably cannot, become a leading manufacturing nation. On the other hand, Germany, with an abundance of high-grade coal, to mention only one key ingredient, became one of the outstanding industrial nations.

*Power.* To make goods in the modern fashion demands more than the energy from human and animal muscles, for great amounts of readily controlled power are needed to make machines and to run them after they are built. So far, without attempting to guess what may eventually be done with atomic energy, solar power, or long-distance transmission of energy by radio, the world's industrial regions are mainly those with abundant coal. This is true despite the importance of power derived from water or from petroleum.

*Labor.* Modern industry, despite all the work done by machines, requires abundant labor of several sorts, from highly skilled to semiskilled to unskilled. Any manufacturing region needs all three types of labor, which are hired at salaries or wages usually ranging from very low to very high. In general, a region which has all three types readily available at *comparatively* low costs has a distinct advantage over regions which possess only one or two types. England has had all three; so have France and Germany.

So has the United States, although it has at times suffered in international competition because each of its labor types has been higher priced than those of other parts of the world. Contrariwise, certain other areas or countries have had either insufficient labor supply or an insufficiency of skilled and semiskilled labor; Australia exemplifies the former, India the latter.

*Transportation.* To manufacture goods requires the movement of raw materials of many kinds over long and short distances. Also, following manufacture, the goods must be distributed near and far to consuming areas. Without modern types of transportation and a sufficient fineness or detail of "transportation net," large-scale manufacturing is impossible. So close is the relationship that one may easily ascertain the *general world pattern* of major manufacturing regions by noting the portions of the earth in which transport lines, especially railroads, are numerous and are arranged in a network of fine mesh.

*Capital.* It goes almost without saying that manufacturing requires large financial resources. To buy raw materials, provide power for machines, pay wages and salaries, install and maintain transport systems, develop and retain markets, not to mention payment of taxes and other obligations, demands tremendous sums of money. Regions or nations with abundant capital or with abundant credit (which amounts to the same thing) are in position to become industrially important—others are not. The United States and Spain stand in strong contrast here, as do Switzerland and Paraguay.

*Markets.* The world's most important industrial regions are those which have large and fairly stable markets within their own limits. Although not commonly recognized, it is a fact that each such region is its own best customer. The West-European Manufacturing Region consumes most of its own products; the Northeastern Manufacturing Region of the United States does likewise. This in no way minimizes the importance of world trade in manufactured goods, because part of the flow, as in western Europe, crosses national boundaries. Also, the sale of manufactured goods in far-distant markets by nations which have dependable home markets plus major distant foreign markets is important. In general, the additional profit derived from distant foreign markets makes a great difference in the final "balance sheet." For example, the home market may "pay the bills," but no more, or very little more, while the distant markets, perhaps consuming only a small portion of the total production, may represent pure profit. To be sure, some countries within major manufacturing regions depend largely on distant foreign markets for the sale of the bulk of their manufactured products, but they are exceptional. Great Britain is the classic example, but even Britain sells much of its manufactures somewhere within the large manufacturing region of which it is a part.

*The Basic Factors.* The foregoing paragraphs suggest the complexities which have produced the modern world pattern of manufacturing regions. Reduced to simplicity, perhaps oversimplicity, one may say that manufacturing regions exist where there is the combination of sufficient technical knowledge, sufficient capital, and either large coal and iron ore deposits, or both. Certainly no *major* industrial regions exist where this combination is not present, and industrial regions which do exist without this combination are definitely not major. This in no way implies that the present pattern is necessarily permanent; in fact, the present pattern is itself the result of change. Cultures change, ideas spread, raw materials are exhausted in some areas and new sources are discovered in others, entirely new kinds of raw material come into use, populations grow or decline and with them go certain modifications of labor supply and of market—even capital "moves." The emergence of the industrial areas of the Soviet Union are good examples not only of change but of rapid change. Other examples are to be found in India and parts of South America.

## The tasks of social economy

# 6 Frank H. Knight: *Social Economic Organization*

❧ *Every economy may be viewed as a system of human actions and institutions intended to produce and distribute desired values and satisfy human wants. Societies may differ widely in their ideals and forms of organization, but all societies inevitably develop some scheme for allocating scarce resources, and these schemes profoundly influence the distribution of prestige, status, income, and power within a particular society. Moreover, it appears that the possible ways of organizing economies are not infinite in number; rather, the schemes adopted or proposed in human history seem to fall within a relatively small number of major types.*

*Perhaps the leading American analyst of the problems of social organization of economies is Frank H. Knight (1885–    ), retired Distinguished Service Professor of Economics and Philosophy at the University of Chicago and former president of the American Economic Association, from whose writings the following selection is taken.*

*This selection is excerpted from two essays originally prepared in 1934 for use in the social science program of the College of the University of Chicago. These essays have been reprinted in a volume,* The Economic Organization *(1951), published by Augustus M. Kelley. The selection is reprinted with the permission of Professor Knight and Mr. Kelley, from pp. 153–95 of Vol. II, the University of Chicago Syllabus for Social Sciences 3, 14th edition, 1948.*

### Social Economic Organization and Its Five Primary Functions

It is somewhat unusual to begin the treatment of a subject with a warning against attaching too much importance to it; but in the case of economics, such an injunction is quite as much needed as explanation and emphasis of the importance it really has. It is characteristic of the age in which we live to think too much in terms of economics, to see things too predominantly in their economic aspect; and this is especially true of the American people. There is no more important prerequisite to clear thinking in regard to economics itself than is recognition of its limited place among human interests at large.

*Common Definitions of Economics Much too Broad, though the Economic Conception of Life Is too Narrow.* In modern usage, the term economic has come to be used in a sense which is practically synonymous with intelligent or rational. This is the first and broadest conception of the term, within which we have to find, by narrowing it down progressively, a definition which will describe the actual subject matter of the science of political economy. It is in accord with good linguistic usage to think and speak of the whole problem of living as one of economy, the economical use of time, energy, etc.—*resource* of every sort. Many definitions of economics found in textbooks fall into this error of including virtually all intelligent behavior. One writer has actually given as his definition of economics the "science of rational activity." Others find its subject matter is "man's activity in making a living," or "the ordinary business of life." Such definitions come too near to saying that economics is the science of things generally, of everything that men are for practical reasons interested in. Such a definition is useless and misleading. It is necessary to devote a little time to making clear the restrictions which mark off the modestly limited domain of economic science within the inclusive sphere of knowledge as a whole.

In the first place, it should be understood that economizing, even in this broad sense of rational activity, or the intelligent use of given means in achieving given ends, does not include all human interests, and that the kind of knowledge on which such activity rests does not exhaust the field of human knowledge. It is, as we have said, one of the errors, not to say vices, of an age in which the progress of natural science and the triumphs of its application to life have engrossed men's attention, to look upon life too exclusively under this aspect of scientific rationality. It is requisite to a proper orientation to economic science itself as well as necessary to a sound philosophy of life, to see clearly that life must be more than economics, or rational conduct, or the intelligent accurate manipula-

tion of materials and use of power in achieving results. Such a view is too narrow. It implies that the results to be achieved are to be taken for granted, whereas in fact the results themselves are often quite as much in question as the means and procedures for achieving results. Living intelligently includes more than the intelligent use of means in realizing ends; it is fully as important to select the ends intelligently, for intelligent action directed toward wrong ends only makes evil greater and more certain. One must have intelligent tastes, and intelligent opinions on many things which do not directly relate to conduct at all. Not only are the objectives of action in fact a practical problem, as well as the means of achievement, but intelligent discussion of the means cannot be separated from the discussion of the ends.

Living is an art: and art is more than a matter of scientific technique, and the richness and value of life are largely bound up in the "more." In its reaction from the futility of medievalism and mystical speculation, the modern Western world has gone far to the other extreme. It loses much of the value of life through neglect of the imponderables and incommensurables, and gets into a false conception of the character of social and individual problems. Our thinking about life values runs too much in terms of material prerequisites and costs. It is an exaggeration which may be useful to say that economic goods as a class are predominantly "necessary" rather than truly valuable. The importance of economic provision is chiefly that of a prerequisite to the enjoyment of the free goods of the world, the beauty of the natural scene, the intercourse of friends in "aimless" camaraderie, the appreciation and creation of art, discovery of truth and communion with one's own inner being and the Nature of Things. Civilization should look forward to a day when the material product of industrial activity shall become rather its by-product, and its primary significance shall be that of a sphere for creative self-expression and the development of a higher type of individual and of human fellowship. It ought to be the first aim of economic policy to reduce the importance of economic policy in life as a whole. So it ought to be the highest objective in the study of economics to hasten the day when the study and the practice of economy will recede into the background of men's thoughts, when food and shelter, and all provision for physical needs, can be taken for granted without serious thought, when "production" and "consumption" and "distribution" shall cease from troubling and pass below the threshold of consciousness and the effort and planning of the mass of mankind may be mainly devoted to problems of beauty, truth, right human relations and cultural growth.

*The Actual Subject Matter of Economics.* What is discussed in the science of economics includes a relatively small fraction of the economic side of life taken in the broad sense. It has nothing to do with the concrete processes of producing or distributing goods, or using goods to satisfy wants. The study of these matters comes under the head of technology, including engineering, business management, and home economics. Economics deals with the *social organization* of economic activity. In practice its scope is much narrower still; there are many ways in which economic activity may be socially organized, but the predominant method in modern nations is the price system, or free enterprise. Consequently it is the structure and working of the system of free enterprise which constitutes the principal topic of discussion in a treatise on economics.

*The Meaning of Organization.* Everyone is familiar with the idea of division of labor —by which is really meant specialization of labor—and many economists have taken it as their point of departure in expounding the science of economics. This was the procedure of Adam Smith, for example, whose book, *The Wealth of Nations,* published in the year 1776, ranks as the first modern treatise on economics.

Modern economic society is often compared with a living body or "organism" and the comparison is certainly suggestive. The essential similarity and the fundamental idea for our purpose is precisely that of division of labor or specialization. But the expression "division" of labor, does not tell us enough. The idea is rather division into different *kinds* of labor. A number of men hoeing in a field or nailing shingles on a roof exemplify "division" of labor, but no organization. The problems of organization arise only when *different things are being done,* in the furtherance of a *common end,* and in definite relations to each other, i.e., in *co-ordination.* A single man in raising a crop or building a house shows division of labor in another sense, since he does many different things, but this is not yet organization in the sense with which we are concerned. The human body shows organization in the true sense, since the various "organs" not only perform different functions, but must all act in a substantially continuous manner and in proper adjustment to each other. Again, organization must be distinguished from co-operation; it involves co-operation, but more. If a group of men lift a stone which is too heavy for one to move alone, they co-operate, and increase their power by co-operation; their action is co-operative, but they are not organized, since they are all doing the same thing.

It is obvious enough that the economic or living-making activities of the modern world are very elaborately organized. . . . The problem of organization, which sets the problem of economic science, deals with the concrete means or mechanism for dividing the general function of making a living for the people into parts and bringing about the performance of these parts in due proportion and harmony.

More specifically, it is a problem of the social machinery for accomplishing *five fairly distinct functions.* Every system of organization must perform these tasks, and it is its success or failure in discharging these functions which determine its value as a system. Back of the study of economics is the practical need of making the organization better, and we can hope for success in this task only if we proceed to it intelligently, which is to say on the basis of an understanding of the nature of the work which a system of organization has to perform, and of the alternatives open in the way of possible types of organization machinery.

## THE FIVE MAIN FUNCTIONS OF AN ECONOMIC SYSTEM

The general task of organizing the economic activity of society may be divided into a number of fundamental functions. These are in fact very much interconnected and overlapping, but the distinction is useful as an aid to discussing the existing economic order both descriptively and critically, its structure as well as its workings. These functions fall into a more or less logical sequence. The first is to decide what is to be done, that is, what goods and services are to be produced, and in what proportions. It is the function of setting standards, of establishing a social scale of values, or the function of social choice; the second is the function of organizing production, in the narrow sense, of getting done the things settled upon as most worth doing; third is distribution, the apportioning the product among the members of society; the fourth is really a group of functions having to do with maintaining and improving the social structure, or promoting social progress.

1) *The Function of Fixing Standards; The Notion of Efficiency:* In a world where organizations were absent, where each individual carried on his life activities in isolation and independence of all others, the matter of standards would be simply a matter of individual choice. But when the production of wealth is socialized there has to be a *social* decision as to the relative importance of different uses of productive power, as to which wants are to be satisfied and which left unsatisfied or to what extent any one is to be satisfied at the expense of any other. In the case of an individual, choice need be made only among his own wants; but in a social system, the wants of different individuals also come

into conflict. As far as this is a quantitative question merely, of how far the wants of one are to be gratified at the expense of the wants of another, or left ungratified in favor of another, the problem is one of *distribution,* and will be noticed under another heading (the third function). But to a large and increasing extent, society finds it necessary or advisable further to regulate the individual's regulation of his own want satisfaction, to enforce a community standard of living. As a matter of fact, these two problems are closely interlaced, the question of *whose* wants and that of *which* wants are to be given preference, and in what measure. It is important to observe that they are largely the same question. The difference in the "amount" consumed by different persons is not mainly a difference in the amounts of the same commodities; different persons consume different things, which are quantitatively compared only through the agency of the value scale itself. Nevertheless there seems to be ample justification for a logical separation of the questions of what is to be produced from that of who is to get the product, and for discussing separately the relations between the two phases of organization.

A point of fundamental importance in connection with the question of standards is that of the origin or ultimate source of wants. The system of social organization does more than reduce individual values to a common denominator or scale of equivalence. In large part the individual wants themselves are *created* by social intercourse, and their character is also largely dependent upon the form of organization of the economic system upon which they are dependent for their gratification. . . .

The problem of standards or values occupies a key position in economics. The practical objective of economics, it must be kept in mind, is that of improving the social organization and increasing its efficiency. There is a common misconception that it is possible to measure or discuss efficiency in purely physical terms. The first principles of physics or engineering science teach that this is not true, that the term efficiency involves the idea of value, and some measure of value as well. It is perhaps the most important principle of physical science that neither matter nor energy can be created or destroyed, that whatever goes into any process must come out in some form, and hence as a mere matter of physical quantity, the efficiency of all operations would equal one hundred per cent. The correct definition of efficiency is the ratio, not between "output" and "input" but between *useful* output and total output or input. Hence efficiency, even in the simplest energy transformation, is meaningless without a measure of usefulness or value. In any attempt to understand economic efficiency, the notion of value is more obviously crucial since most economic problems are concerned with a number of kinds both of outlay and of return, and there is no conceivable way of making comparisons without first reducing all the factors to terms of a common measure. It will appear in due course that the science of economics is largely taken up with description and analysis of the process by which this common denominator of things consumed and produced by the economic system is arrived at, that is, with the *problem of measuring values.*

2) *The Function of Organizing Production.* The second step, logically speaking, after the ranking and grading of the uses to which productive power may be put, is that of actually putting them to use in accordance with the scale of values thus established. From a social point of view, this process may be viewed under two aspects, (a) the assignment or *allocation* of the available productive forces and materials among the various lines of industry, and (b) the effective *co-ordination* of the various means of production in each industry into such groupings as will produce the greatest result. The second of these tasks properly belongs to technological rather than to economic science, and is treated in economics only with reference to the inter-relations between the organization of society as a whole and the internal organization of the industries.

3) *The Function of Distribution.* This third function would not exist at all in an unorganized world. Each individual, acting independently of all others, would simply consume what he produced. But where production is socialized, the separate productive contribution of one participant in the process cannot be directly identified or separated. It is apparent that a modern factory operative, say one who spends all his time putting buttons on shoes or nailing the covers on packing cases, cannot live on his own product, physically interpreted. When we further consider that different individuals contribute to production in fundamentally different ways, many by furnishing land or other "natural resources" or material equipment or money or managerial or supervisory services, or by selling goods, and in other ways which make no identifiable physical change in any product, it is manifest that if everyone is to get a living out of the process some *social mechanism* of distribution is called for.

In this connection should be recalled the close relation between distribution and the control of production. The decision as to what to produce is closely bound up with the decision for whom to produce. There is also a close relation between the third function and the second. In our social system distribution is the chief agency relied upon to control production and stimulate efficiency. Ours is a system of "private property," "free competition" and "contract." This means that every productive resource or agent, including labor power, typically "belongs" to some person who is free within the legal conditions of marketing, to get what he can out of its use. It is assumed, and the course of the argument will show at length why it is true, that there is in some effective sense a real positive connection between the productive contribution made by any productive agent and the remuneration which its "owner" can secure for its use. Hence this remuneration (a distributive share) and the wish to make it as large as possible, constitute the chief reliance of society for an incentive to place the agency into use in the general productive system in such a way as to make it as productive as possible.

．　．　．　．　．

4) *Economic Maintenance and Progress.* There is no moral connotation in the term progress; it refers to any persistent cumulative change, whether regarded as good or bad. The principal forms of economic progress include, (1) growth of population and any cumulative change in its composition or education which affects either its productive powers or its wants; (2) the accumulation of material aids to production or "capital" of all kinds, including such permanent sources of satisfaction as newly discovered natural resources and also work of art; [1] (3) improvements in technical processes or changes in the form of business organization. It is to be noted especially that progress has two sorts of significance for the economic organization. First, it is one of the products or values created by the latter, at a cost; i.e., it involves using productive power for this purpose and sacrificing its use for other purposes; and second, it affects and changes the character of the economic system itself and the conditions under which the system works.

This fourth function of organization, especially the provision for progress, cuts across all the other three. It is a matter of standards or values to decide how much progress society can afford or cares to have at the cost of sacrificing present values, and what forms it shall take; it is a matter of productive organization to utilize the determined share of available productive power to bring about progress in the amount and of the kinds decided upon, and it is a problem of distribution to apportion the burdens and benefits of progress among the members of society. We may be reminded also that it is true of progress as of all other lines of human action that it comes within the field of economics just in so far as it is related to the organized system of producing and distributing the means of want satisfaction.

[1] Destruction and exhaustion of resources not replaced is also a progressive change.

The first three of these functions (or four, since No. 2 is really double, involving two aspects) are relatively "short-time" in character. They are all aspects of the general problem of an economic society working under "given conditions," in contrast with the fourth function which relates to the problem of improving the given conditions through the course of time. The first three therefore make up the problems of what may be called the "stationary economy." If society either could not or did not try to grow and progress and make improvements, its economic problem would be entirely within this field. But since economic societies do in fact face problems of growth and improvement, and make some effort to solve them intelligently, we have to add the fourth function, or group of functions. Such problems are frequently referred to under the head of "dynamic" economics; for reasons which cannot be given in detail here, this is a seriously misleading use of language, and they should be called simply problems of progress or historical problems.

The "given conditions" of the stationary economy are included under the three heads of *resources, wants,* and *technology,* which may be subdivided and classified in more elaborate ways.

．　．　．　．　．

*A Fifth Function: To Adjust Consumption to Production within Very Short Periods.* For completeness, this survey of functions should point out that within *very short* periods society faces still another set of "given conditions," hence still another type of problem, and in consequence its economic organization has still another task or function to perform, though this fifth function is rarely distinguished sharply from those of the "stationary economy" point of view. From this latter point of view, the problem is to adjust production to consumption under the given conditions. But in many cases, production cannot be adjusted quickly, while demand conditions do change rapidly; and in addition, production in many fields is subject to fluctuations from causes beyond control. In consequence, the supply of many commodities is fixed for considerable periods of time, on a level more or less divergent from the best possible adjustment to existing conditions of demand. The supply on hand is of course the result of productive operations in the past, and has to suffice until it can be changed. In agriculture this is conspicuously true. The crop of a given year has to last until the next year's crop is produced (except in so far as other parts of the world having different crop seasons can be drawn upon). In the case of manufactured goods, production is not definitely periodic, but it is still true that the rate of production frequently cannot be changed in a short time, to meet changes in demand, at least not without enormous cost.

It follows that over short periods consumption has to be controlled and distributed with reference to an existing supply or current rate of production, at the same time that adjustment of production to consumption requirements is being made as rapidly as practicable. . . .

ADVANTAGES AND DISADVANTAGES OF ORGANIZED ACTION

*The Reasons for Organizing Activity.* As previously remarked, a high degree of organization in human activity is a fairly recent development in the world's history, and is still restricted mainly to what we call the European peoples or cultures. The urge behind its development can be stated in the single word *efficiency*. The object of industrial activity is to utilize an available fund of productive agencies and resources in making the goods and services with which people satisfy their wants. Organized effort enables a social group to produce more of the means of want satisfaction than it could by working as individuals. During the course of history, the possibility of increased efficiency has led to an ever greater degree of specialization, which in turn has constantly called for a more elaborate and effective mechanism of co-ordination and control, just as the higher animals require an enormously more complex nervous and

circulatory system than the lower. It will be worth while to carry the analysis a little beyond the general notion of efficiency and see some of the reasons why specialized effort yields larger or better results. We must then turn to the other side of the picture and note some of the disadvantages of organization.

*The Gains from Specialization.*[1] The largest gain which the higher animals secure in comparison with lower, less organized forms, arises from the adaptation of structure to function. In the most primitive animals the same kind of tissue has to perform all the divergent functions of locomotion, seizing and ingestion of food, digestion, assimilation, excretion of waste and reproduction, while in the mammalian body the specialization of tissues and organs for the various functions and the increased efficiency with which all are consequently performed, are too evident to need extended comment. Some social insects produce physically divergent types of individuals adapted by structure to perform different functions. In the familiar case of the bees, the bulk of the community is made up of "workers" and the reproductive function is specialized in the queens and drones. Certain species of ants and termites present a very complex social structure containing a dozen or more structurally specialized types of individuals. One of the most interesting facts in regard to human society is the absence of definite structural specialization of individuals. Human organization is an artificial thing, a culture product. Natural differences undoubtedly exist among human beings, and are taken advantage of, more or less, in fitting individuals to specialized functions; but the differences seem to be accidental, and unpredictable. Certainly human beings do not become fused into a super-organism in the manner of the cells in an animal body. It is

[1] It will be recalled that we are using the word "specialization" instead of the familiar "division of labor," not only is labor divided, but it is differentiated and co-ordinated, and the other elements or factors in production are likewise "specialized" —often more extensively and vitally than the human factor.

in fact a matter of the greatest uncertainty and one of the most disputed questions in the whole field of knowledge, as to how far observed differences in kinds and degrees of capacity are innate and how far they are the result of "nurture" and the subtle influences of environment and social suggestion. The tendency of scientific study at the present time is to place more and more emphasis on the environment and less upon congenital structure. . . .

1) *Utilization of Natural Aptitudes; Especially Those of Leaders and Followers.* However, we are safe in asserting that there are some innate individual differences in human capacities and aptitudes, and the first in the list of gains from organization results from taking advantage of them. One social problem is to discover such differences and utilize them as far as possible. They can never be predicted with any certainty before the birth of the individual, in fact they cannot usually be discerned at any time in life from clear external marks; and in the course of the development of the individual they become so largely overlaid with acquired traits that they can never be separated from the latter. The most important natural differences of which we can be reasonably sure are those of physical stature and dexterity and (with much less certainty) of general mental activity. The most important differentiation in function, or division of labor, between individuals is the separation between direction and execution, or the specialization of *leadership.* . . .

2) *Development and Utilization of Acquired Skill and Acquired Knowledge.* The principal quality in man which gives him superiority over the animals is his ability to learn, including learning to know and learning to do. But even in man this capacity is exceedingly limited in scope in comparison with the whole range of acquired human knowledge and activity, and a large part of the gain from organizing activity comes from the increase in the efficiency of learning which is connected with reducing the field in which an individual must exercise his learning ability. Even the specialization

of leadership undoubtedly rests as much upon acquired as upon innate differences. In truth, the fundamental innate difference among men is in the capacity to learn itself. In other fields than leadership—fields of specialized knowledge and skill in the narrower sense—it is still more clearly impossible to separate the factor of innate capacity from that of acquired powers, and still more evident that the innate capacity itself is a capacity to learn rather than directly to perform. Even in the case of genius, what is inherited is an extraordinary capacity to learn, or learn to do, certain things, and the amount of actual specialization in the original bent is highly uncertain. In modern machine industry, where the operative is restricted to repetition of a few simple movements, an incredible increase of speed as compared with that of an untrained worker may be achieved in a short space of time. The operations generally involve movements very different from any which are natural to man as an animal, movements such as setting type, playing a musical instrument, or sorting mail matter into boxes; but they can be learned by any normal person, and when mastered they make possible the employment of a technology vastly more efficient than that of primitive industry. (See No. 5 below.)

3) *Changing Pieces of Work Cheaper, within Limits, than Changing Jobs.* The saving of time and effort in changing from one operation to another is the third gain from specialization. It is true that if a man performs the same operation repeatedly, he must change from one object, or piece of work, to another. But by the use of mechanical conveyors, scientific routing and the like, it is found that, *within limits,* the process of bringing to the workman a procession of shoes, automobile cylinders, or hog carcasses is far less costly than having him make the changes in position, changes in tools used, etc., involved in performing successively on any one of them the various operations necessary to complete the making of a product, as was done under old handicraft conditions. This gain is evidently rather closely connected with that

arising from specialized skill. It is to be especially emphasized, because so commonly overlooked, that in this connection there are offsetting costs, which only within limits are exceeded by the gains. Not only must the cost of changing jobs be compared with the cost of changing pieces of work as within a given factory. If each man completed a product, the workers would not have to be brought together into factories at all, a feature which also involves large costs, and neither would the materials have to be assembled from such a vast area or the product distributed back over a market perhaps nation-wide or even world-wide in extent. The costs of bringing together vast quantities of materials and of distributing the product tend in fact to offset very considerably the gains of large-scale production. These costs include not merely actual transportation, but marketing costs in the form of profits, risks and losses from inaccurate forecasting of demand, idleness due to over-production, storage, insurance and the like. The public has been educated by apologists for monopoly to over-estimate seriously the real gains from large-scale factory methods; these offsetting losses are rarely appreciated to the full.

4) *Natural Advantages in the Case of "Natural Resources."* However uncertain we may be as to the innate differences in men, there can be no question that the natural resources of different regions are suited to widely divergent employments. In such extreme cases as mineral deposits, for example, specialization to regions is absolute, since minerals can only be extracted where they exist, and this is quite commonly in places where any other industry is virtually out of the question. Also, "geographical" or "territorial" specialization is almost a physical necessity as between different climatic zones.

. . . . . .

5) *Artificial Specialization of Material Agents. Division of Operations Leads to Invention and Use of Machinery.* Even natural resources are never used in their nat-

ural state. The process of developing and adapting them to particular uses is generally more or less of a specializing process and may be compared to the "education" of a human being. When we turn to the forms of productive equipment usually classed as artificial—tools, machines, buildings and the like, it is evident that specialization goes very far indeed. A tool or machine is usually much more specialized than a human being can ever be, and its efficiency in a particular task is connected with the degree of its specialization. Many things can be done, after a fashion, with a hammer; only one with an automatic printing press or a watch-screw machine; but that one thing is done with wonderful precision and speed. Perhaps the very largest single source of gain from the specialization of labor is that it makes possible the development and use of machinery, the effectiveness of which is almost entirely a matter of its specialization to limited and relatively simple operations.

6) *Minor Technical Gains.* The gains from natural and artificial adaptation of men and things to tasks, plus that due to changing pieces of work instead of tasks (our number 3 above) do not exhaust the economies of specialization. There is an economy in co-ordination due to the fact that a specialized worker need have access only to the tools used for the operations he continuously performs, and not to all those used in making the article. This is practically rather an incidental matter, subordinate to the specialization of equipment. In primitive industry little is invested in tools, and a large investment carries with it specialization of both workers and equipment. We may note also as a final consideration in connection with this whole subject, that in many cases any sort of effective work involves the performance of different operations simultaneously, which of course necessitates specialization.

*Social Costs of Specialization.* All the gains from specialization are summed up in the one word, *efficiency;* it enables us to get more goods, or better; its advantages are *instrumental.* On the other hand, specialization in itself, is an evil, measured by generally accepted human ideals. It gives us more products, but in its effects on human beings as such it is certainly bad in some respects and in others questionable. In the nature of the case [1] it means a narrowing of the personality; we like to see people of all-around, well-developed powers and capacities. In extreme instances, such as the monotonous work of machine-tending, or repetitive movements at a machine-forced pace, it may be ruinous to health and maddening to the spirit. In this connection it is especially significant that the most important source of gain also involves the most important human cost. The specialization of leadership means that the masses of the people work under conditions which tend to suppress initiative and independence, to develop servility as well as narrowness and in general to dehumanize them.

*Technical Costs of Organization.* We have already mentioned the fact that there is another side to the technical advantages of specialization, namely the costs of assembly and distribution. This aspect of the situation is hinted at in the famous saying of Adam Smith that the division of labor is limited by the extent of the market, that is, really, by distribution costs. To these we must add the broader category of costs of organization in general. The existing social organization is called an "automatic" system, and in some respects it is such. But any system of bringing large numbers of people in intercommunication and co-ordinating their activities must involve enormous costs in actual human and physical energy. Organizations are like water-drops, or snowballs or stones, or any large mass; the larger they are the more easily they are broken in pieces, the larger *in proportion* is the amount of energy that must be consumed in merely holding them together. The larger the army the bigger the proportion

of officers, and the more unwieldy the aggregate, even then. The losses from this source in the modern world are stupendous. . . .

*Interdependence.* A final important disadvantage of organized production and distribution is the resulting interdependence of persons and groups. This interdependence is supposed to be mutual, in the long run; but for the time being, the persons who perform such functions as coal mining and transportation are very much more necessary to, say, school teachers or farmers than the latter are to them. Strikes or failures to function due to accidental causes produce a kind of suffering unknown in unorganized society, or even in small groups within which the pressure of public opinion is much more powerful. A phase of this interdependence manifests itself acutely in the ebb and flow of prosperity, particularly the recurrence of business crises bringing widespread distress.

## TYPES OF SOCIAL ORGANIZATION
### ECONOMICS AND POLITICS

*Social Organization and Biological Organism: Analogy and Contrast.* As an introduction to the survey and classification of forms of social organization it will be useful to revert briefly to the comparison between economic society and the human body—especially to emphasize the fundamental difference. In this comparison the human individual is said to correspond to the "cell," the ultimate unit of biological structure. Individuals, like the cells in an animal body, are aggregated into "tissues" and "organs," which carry on the elementary life functions, seizing nourishment, transforming it into a condition suitable for use or digestion, distribution, disposal of waste, etc. The analogy is indeed obvious, and no doubt useful within limits, if it is kept on the level of analogy and not pressed too far. However, reasoning from analogy is always dangerous, and the conception of the "social organism" has probably produced more confusion than enlightenment. The differences between society and an animal organism are practically

---

[1] Statements of this kind need a good deal of interpretation. In reality everything depends on the alternative system used as a basis of comparison. The idyllic system of universal craftsmanship certainly never existed historically; perhaps it could not exist; but we think we can imagine its existence.

more important than the similarities, for it is in connection with the differences that the social problems arise.

The division of labor between the organs of the body is based on an innate differentiation of physical structure, and the coordination of their activities is automatic and mechanical. The cells or tissues do not choose what positions they will take up or what functions they will perform, nor can they change from one position or function to another. They do not meet with any of the problems which make the study of human organization a practical concern; they have no separate interests which may conflict with each other or with those of the body as a whole, and there can be no competition among them in any but a figurative sense.

Human society is the opposite of all this. Definite machinery has to be deliberately designed to reconcile or compromise between the conflicting interests of its members. . . .

Planned provision must be made in human society for working out the division of labor, assigning the separate tasks to the various persons and apportioning productive equipment among them, for distributing the fruits of the activity, and even for determining the character of its own future life and growth.

*Types of Organization: (1) "Status" and Tradition, or the Caste System.* The nearest approach to a mechanical division and coordination of activity which is reached or can be conceived of in human society would be a universal system of *status* or "caste." It is possible to imagine a social order in which elaborate specialization of activities is achieved on a purely customary basis, and some approximation to such an ideal is found in the caste system of India. We can suppose that rigid social custom might fix all the details of the division of occupations and technique of production, the assignment of individuals to their tasks being determined by birth, while tradition would also set the details of the standard of living for everyone. Such a society would have to be nearly unprogressive, though

slow change in accordance with unconscious historical forces is compatible with the hypothesis.

.   .   .   .   .

2) *The Autocratic or Militaristic System.* The first step away from a caste system in the direction of increasing freedom is represented by a centralized, autocratic system most briefly described by comparing it with the organization of an army. In such a social order, worked out to logical completeness, the whole structure of society, the division of labor, determination of policies, and allocation of burdens and benefits, would be dictated by an absolute monarch. The individual need not be asked what he wants or thinks good for him in the way of either his consumption or his share in production. The idea of organization itself might be worked out to any degree of intricacy, and coordination might indeed be highly effective. In practice, such a system would have to contain a large element of caste, unless the family were abolished entirely, as in Plato's scheme for an ideal republic. The organizing principle is an autocratic system is personal authority resting upon "divine," or prescriptive, right.

It is to be observed that this principle, while theoretically reduced to a minimum in modern society, is actually, like that of tradition and caste, very much in evidence. The exercise of "authority," while limited in degree, is as real as either "free" exchange or persuasion, within the family, in the internal organization of business units and in the "democratic" system of government itself. . . .

.   .   .   .   .

3) *Anarchism as a Possible System.* In the third type of organization mechanism to be considered, we swing to the extreme opposite of the two preceding, from rigorous control by tradition or arbitrary authority to absolute freedom, or purely voluntary association. Whether such a system is possible, may well be doubted, as most of the world does doubt; but it is at least conceivable, and many cultivated and no-

ble minds have, as is well known, advocated attempting it as a practical program. The idea is simple enough; it is contended that if inequality and all hope or thought of exploiting or exercising authority over other men were abolished, people might agree voluntarily as to what were best to be done in the various contingencies of social life and the best method for doing it, and proceed accordingly, without any giving or taking of orders, or any threat of compulsion or restraint by force. It is not necessary to suppose that everyone would have to be all-knowing in regard to every sort of question. It is fully consistent with the theory of anarchy to have recourse to expert opinion; it must be assumed only that the experts would be able to agree, or that the mass of people would agree on which expert to recognize and follow. . . .

. . . . .

4) *Democracy or Democratic Socialism.* The two systems remaining to be considered represent combinations of or compromises between systems already named. The first, democratic socialism, is a compromise between the authoritarian and the anarchistic. The nearest approach to the freedom of anarchy which we even theoretically reach on any extended scale is the rule of the majority. In its main structural features a society organized entirely on this principle would resemble the autocratic, authoritarian system. The difference is that the controlling authority, instead of being an absolute autocrat, would itself be under the control of "public opinion," that is, the will of the majority of the citizens, expressed through some "political" apparatus. Again, the economic and political organizations would be fused and identified. This is the type of social structure advocated in the main by persons calling themselves "socialists" though by no means to the exclusion of other types of organization machinery, especially that of free bargaining. . . .

. . . . .

5) *The Exchange System.* The last type of organization machinery to be distin-guished is the one especially characteristic of modern western nations, in which the whole system is worked out and controlled through exchange in an impersonal competitive market. It is variously referred to as the competitive system, the capitalistic system, the system of private property and free exchange, individual exchange co-operation, and so on. Its most interesting feature is that it is automatic and unconscious; no one plans or ever planned it out, no one assigns the participants their rôles or directs their functions. Each person in such a system seeks his own satisfaction without thought of the structure of society or its interests; and the mere mechanical interaction of such self-seeking units organizes them into an elaborate system and controls and co-ordinates their activities so that each is continuously supplied with the fruits of the labor of one vast and unknown multitude in return for performing some service for another multitude also large and unknown to him. Although the actuality diverges in many respects from such a simple idealized description, the results which are in fact achieved by this method are truly wonderful. Like the other systems described, it does not exist and can hardly be thought of as existing in a pure form. But so large a part of the ordinary work of the modern world is organized in this way that such expressions as "the present social system" or the "existing economic order," are commonly understood to refer to the organization of provision for the means of life through buying and selling.

## The Price System and the Economic Process

### ECONOMIC ORGANIZATION AS A SYSTEM OF PRICE RELATIONS

Seen in the large, free enterprise is an organization of production and distribution in which the individual or family units get their real income, their "living," by selling productive power for money to "business units" or "enterprises," and buying with the money income thus obtained the direct goods and services which they consume. This view, it will be remembered, ignores for the sake of simplicity the fact that an appreciable fraction of the productive power in use at any time is not really employed in satisfying current wants but to make provision for increased want-satisfaction in the future; it treats society as it would be, or would tend to become, with progress absent, or in a "static" state. It also disregards the organization of activity in other ways than that of free enterprise; the latter is both the most typical and the most complex of the methods of organization in use in modern industrial nations, and the relation to free enterprise of other modes of organization—governmental industry, co-operation, the "handicraft" status (of agriculture, etc.) where the family unit produces and sells a product—is not an especially difficult problem when the working of a system of enterprise is understood. The general character of an enterprise system, reduced to its very simplest terms, can be illustrated by a diagram showing the exchange of productive power for consumption goods between individuals and business units, mediated by the "circulation" of money, and suggesting the familiar figure of the "wheel of wealth." At one

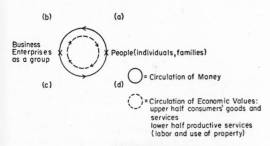

point on a circle we have the population as individuals (really families, always) and at the opposite point business enterprises as a group, including all the stages and branches of the productive organization in the broad sense of production which takes in merchandising, finance, etc. The circulation of money is a very literal fact. The upper and lower semi-circles respectively represent the two sets of exchange relations into which each person enters with business in the large, the "sale" of productive power and "purchase" of products. In the final result, it is a single exchange, of productive services for products, with money as an intermediary. It goes without saying that business enterprises consist in the large of the same individuals as "The People" (excluding dependent members of families and wards of the state). Yet it is a mere accident if any individual buys any products at all from the same enterprise to which he sells productive power or of which he is a member in any other capacity.

The nature of a business enterprise presents a problem of considerable subtlety. In its fully developed form it would be entirely separate from those who sell it productive power of any kind. In this theoretically pure form it rarely exists, but its character is approximated by a large modern corporation. The persons who make up or constitute the corporation may not furnish it with any considerable fraction of the personal services or of the material wealth with which it carries on its operations. The work, including that of management, may be performed by persons employed for wages or salaries, from common laborers up to the highest officials, and the property may also be hired from outsiders for a rental or an interest payment. If this were altogether the case, we should have the enterprise of abstract theory. In practice, of course, the men who make up the corporation as a legal entity generally do some of the work of the direction and still more commonly furnish some of the property value or "capital" with which it carries on its functions; but in many actual corporations both contributions approach the vanishing point if they do not disappear altogether. The nature of actual enterprises will be sketched somewhat more fully in a later chapter, but detailed discussion belongs to more specialized treatises.

It should be noticed that the "money" of the diagram represents the total social income, which takes on four different aspects or meanings at different points in its circular flow. Beginning with its expenditure by individuals for consumption goods and services—(a) on the diagram—it represents to the persons who pay it out the aggregate cost of living; to the enterprise to which it is paid (b) it is business receipts or income. As the enterprises pay it out for productive services it is (c) business expense or cost of producing goods, and to the individuals who receive it for the productive services it is (d) personal (or family) income, in the form of rent, interest and wages, or salaries, according to the kind of productive service and the terms on which the latter is sold.

The study of the price system narrows down to analysis of these two sets of prices and the interrelations between them, the prices of consumption goods and the prices of productive services. The two sets together control the process of production and distribution under free enterprise. Those individuals who do not sell productive power, but use their own labor, or property, or both, in making a product, with or without hiring the service of other persons or their property in addition, do not enter directly into the second of the two markets, but their position is not essentially changed by this fact. In effect they hire their own services from themselves, and their economic status is still determined by the total social situation. Those who render personal services, such as lawyers, doctors, etc., are especially likely to "work for themselves" yet increasingly such persons also are "employed" by an institution or corporation of some kind.

### PRICES AND THE TASKS OR FUNCTIONS OF ORGANIZATION

We shall now take up in slightly greater detail the manner in which the economic process is controlled by the two sets of prices. The four main tasks or aspects of organized activity are, as will be remembered, (1) to set standards for determining what things shall be produced and in what proportions, (2) to allocate resources to the various branches of production and combine or co-ordinate them effectively in each,

(3) to distribute the product, and (4) to provide for maintenance and progress.

1) *The Formulation of Standards for the Control of Production.* Under the system of free enterprise the first task is most obviously a matter of price, since it is precisely the prices of consumption goods and services which constitute the social measure of their importance. It is through its price that any good exerts the "pull" which assigns productive power to creating it. . . . The price measure is not a true index of social importance according to any recognized ethical standard, but it is the one in terms of which production is actually guided, insofar as the principles of free enterprise apply without "social interference" of any kind.

Prices also perform in the short run that special but highly important function as essentially the reverse of the above, namely that of adjusting consumption to production during the interval within which the supply cannot be changed.

2) *The Organization of Production.* Next after the problem of indicating the channels of greatest demand is the two-fold one of making production follow those channels, and of making it "efficient." This second task may be regarded as social business management. It covers (a) the allocation or assignment of productive resources, human and material, to the different lines of industry and (b) their effective *coordination* and direction. The latter, again, includes the location and lay-out of plants, selection of technical processes, determination of the scale of operations, marketing methods, internal personnel organization, and all matters affecting productive efficiency. In the control of production, the two sets of prices work together. Every enterprise is in competition . . . with other enterprises, both in the sale of products and in the purchase of productive services, labor, materials, etc. Each enterprise buys productive services and sells a product or products. The price it can secure for the latter is one factor in determining the price it can pay for the former, the other factor being the efficiency of the enterprise in

converting productive power into products. It is the prices offered for the productive services which actually determine their entry into the industries where demand is greatest and into the establishments within any industry which have the highest efficiency. But the prices of productive services reflect the prices of the products into which they ultimately flow. . . .

3) *Distribution.* The manner in which the product of industry is distributed among the members of society has already been indicated. Each responsible individual sells some productive service or services to some enterprise, or enterprises, and thereby obtains a money income, with which he buys products for consumption from various enterprises—(from "dealers" who buy them from the "producers" as the business world uses the term). It is evident that the share in the final produce which anyone is able to secure depends on (a) the amount of his *money income* and (b) its *purchasing power* over the goods which he desires to consume. But the first of these is determined by the prices of the productive services which he sells to industry, and the second is a matter of the prices of consumption goods, so that the shares in distribution are determined by the same two sets of prices already considered. The interconnection between the prices of final goods and those of productive services in a relation of mutual determination really ties all three of these major functions of organization intimately together; the interaction of the prices in the two markets sets standards, controls production and distributes the produce, and, as just observed, forms the main content of the study of economics.

4) *Economic Progress and the Price Regime.* . . . Progress involves many phases or aspects, which may be summed up under the three heads of changes in *resources* (as to amount and kind and distribution of ownership), changes in *technology*, including the technique of business organization, and changes in *wants*. Provision for and control over these progressive changes is one of the inescapable tasks of a system of organization. . . . Modern social organization is a mixture of most of the possible systems or methods. . . . The principal connection between the price system and social progress is mediated by the phenomenon of interest on capital. Most forms of progress call for the use of present resources in ways which are not immediately productive and hence are equivalent to the saving and investment of capital for a future return. Insofar, then, as progress is worked out through the price system at all, interest is the price through which control is chiefly exercised. According to the theory of enterprise, interest constitutes the incentive to save and invest, as well as the incentive to direct into the most productive channels the use of capital already saved. How far in fact interest is the effective stimulus to saving is an unsettled question, though there can hardly be doubt as to its significance in drawing accumulated wealth into productive use and into channels which promise larger rather than smaller returns. . . .

5) *Control of Consumption in the Period of Unalterable Supply.* There is for many commodities a short period within which the supply cannot be changed and the social problem is that of distributing the available supply over the period and among the consumers. . . . For some commodities, the price system has developed a complicated mechanism of speculative trading which works out the distribution of the supply. For others a less definite and formal procedure takes care of the problem more crudely.

SECTION C

**Production, consumption, and investment**

# 7 J. R. Hicks and Albert G. Hart: *Measuring Economic Growth*

❦ *The violent economic fluctuations and depressions of the twentieth century have led economists to give increasing attention to the entire framework within which a nation's economy operates. Traditionally, economic analysis had concentrated on the presumed behavior of imaginary firms in imaginary industries; the newer trend is to analyze dominant industries and the changing setting of institutions and laws. This latter method of analyzing the economy-as-a-whole has come to be called the national-income approach to economic analysis, which aims at defining the conditions that will assure the fullest possible employment of all productive resources, notably of labor.*

*The national-income approach is described in the following selection from* The Social Framework of the American Economy *by J. R. Hicks and Albert G. Hart. Copyright 1945 by Oxford University Press, pp. 28–46 and 141–59. This is an American edition adapted by Hart and based on Hicks'* The Social Framework: An Introduction to Economics *(1942). The selection is reproduced with the publisher's permission.*

*Hicks (1904–    ) is Stanley Jevons Professor of Political Economy at the University of Manchester and is the author of many volumes in the field of economic analysis, notably* Value and Capital *(1939). Hart (1909–    ) has also published many important studies on monetary and fiscal policies. He is Professor of Economics at Columbia University and has been engaged frequently as a consultant on economic matters by the United States Government.*

## Goods and Services

THE DEFINITION OF PRODUCTION

. . . We shall mean by Production any activity directed to the satisfaction of other people's wants through exchange; we shall use a Producer to mean a person engaging in production in this sense. A person whose wants are satisfied by such production we shall call a Consumer. . . .

Let us see what we are committed to by these definitions. The words producer and consumer are widely used in ordinary speech and in business. But in practical life they do not need to be used very precisely or uniformly, so that they are often used in senses which do not square with our definitions. Farmers, for instance, are fond of drawing a contrast between their own activities as "producers" of foodstuffs, and those of the traders or retailers, who merely sell or "distribute" them. On our definition the retailer is a producer just as much as the farmer. The work done by the retailer is a part of the process of satisfying consumers' wants, just as much as the work of the farmer. Milk on the farm and tobacco at the factory are of little use to anyone except the farmer and manufacturer themselves; milk on the doorstep and tobacco in the shop are provided, more or less, where and when the consumer wants them. . . .

The trader and retailer deal with material goods, but they do not make them. Their part is to take goods already made and to make them more useful by supplying them at the places and times at which they are wanted. But there are many sorts of workers who are not concerned with the production of material goods at all; doctors, teachers, civil servants and administrators, passenger transport workers, entertainers, domestic servants—all of these are producers in our sense, though they do not produce material products. They do useful work and are paid for it, consequently they count as producers. The things they produce are useful services, not material goods. It is convenient to say that the things produced by producers and consumed by consumers are of two kinds—material "goods" and immaterial "services."

The performance of such services as these is included in production. But if we are to be faithful to our definition, we may not say that all performance of services for other people counts as production. Production is activity directed to the satisfaction of other people's wants through exchange; thus it is only those services which are paid for that have to be included. The most important kind of services which, on this test, have to be left out are the services performed within the family—the work done by wives for their husbands, by parents in looking after their children, and so on. These services are not to be reckoned as productive, because they are not paid for. It is of course not very convenient that we have to exclude this essential work from our definition of production, but there does

not seem to be any help for it, if we are to have the advantage of using words in precise and well-defined ways.

. . . . .

## THE TIME TAKEN IN PRODUCTION. CONSUMERS' GOODS AND PRODUCERS' GOODS

On a certain day (say in the spring of 1939) the reader of this book will probably have eaten a piece of bread for lunch. Behind that piece of bread was a considerable history. A day or two earlier it was baked by a baker, who for his stage in the process of breadmaking used various ingredients, notably flour. Some weeks earlier the flour will have been milled out of wheat, various kinds of wheat being very probably mixed together. This wheat will have been harvested, probably during the year 1938, the precise date depending upon the part of the world from which it came. Some months before the time of harvesting the wheat must have been sown, and before the sowing the land on which it was grown must have been plowed. Taking this simple line of operations, from the plowing of the land to the bread on the table, not much less than a year can have elapsed between the start and the finish. Often it will be a good deal more than a year. But this is by no means the whole of the history behind that piece of bread.

At every stage in the process described— plowing, sowing, harvesting, threshing, milling, baking—power or fuel was needed. The power used for plowing may have been nothing more modern than the traditional horse. If so, that horse had to be fed, its feeding stuffs had to be grown, and the growth of the feeding stuffs extends the production process backwards for another series of months. Or the power may have been provided by a tractor; tractors use oil, so that the getting of the oil and its transport to the farm (another stage involving at least a month or two) have also to be reckoned into the process of production of the bread. The same will hold for the power (of whatever kind) used in harvesting, threshing, and milling, also for the coal or electricity used at the bakery. Of course many of these latter processes will be going on simultaneously, so that they do not lengthen the total time taken by the production. Nevertheless, when we have taken the power into account, the whole period looks more like two years than one.

Even this is not all. The tractor, the threshing-machine, the ships and railways used to transport the grain, the elevator used for storing it, the milling machinery used for making the flour, even the baker's oven—all these had to be made at some time or other, and the reason why they were made was because they would be useful in the manufacture of bread. Not of course this single piece of bread, which is far too humble an article to be able to claim for itself alone such mighty antecedents; but this piece of bread and millions like it are the reasons why the tractors and elevators and ovens and the rest of them were brought into being. All this elaborate equipment was in fact constructed as part of the process of manufacturing bread.

If at some date, three months or six months or a year before the bread appeared upon the table, we had examined how the process of producing it was getting on, we should have found that most of the equipment was already made and in use, while the raw material of the bread was still in the form of growing crops, or threshed wheat, or bags of flour. These things can all be looked upon as stages in the manufacture of the bread. Whatever stage has been reached, even if it is only the making of a tractor, or the building of a railroad tank car to transport the oil to feed the tractor, something has been done which will prove useful and help towards the final production of bread. The products which result from these early stages are useful products, but not products which are directly useful for satisfying the wants of consumers. Their use is to be found in their employment in the further stages, at the end of which a product which is directly wanted by consumers will emerge. It is convenient to use the term *goods* to cover the products of these earlier stages, as well as the final product which the consumer purchases. But the products of the earlier stages are called *producers' goods,* to distinguish them from the *consumers' goods,* which do satisfy the consumers' wants directly.

In our illustration, the bread is a consumers' good; the wheat, the flour, the tractor, the ship, the oven (and so on) are producers' goods.

．　．　．　．　．

## THE TIME TAKEN IN CONSUMPTION. DURABLE-USE AND SINGLE-USE CONSUMERS' GOODS

The production of any consumers' good one cared to select could be similarly shown to consist of a process, occupying in all quite a considerable time, and involving the production of a number of producers' goods on the way. It has next to be noticed that with some consumers' goods, but only with some, consumption is also a process taking an appreciable time. Consumers' goods can be divided, from this point of view, into two classes.

In the first class we have goods, like the bread of our example (and foodstuffs generally), which are used and used up in a single act. . . . Other consumers' goods which are of the same type are fuel, tobacco, matches, and writing-paper. I shall call these goods *single-use goods.* From the point of view of the consumer, services are similar in character to the single-use goods; but, as we have noticed, they are different on the production side.

The other goods I shall call *durable-use goods.* Houses, furniture, clothes, radios, bicycles, and automobiles are examples of this second class. Their common characteristic is that they can go on being used for considerable periods.

．　．　．　．　．

Most of the single-use goods which are purchased have to go on being purchased, week after week, day after day. To have had a good meal yesterday does not prevent one from wanting another good meal today; to have been warm last night does not prevent one from needing to be warmed again this afternoon. Durable-use goods, on the other hand, go on being useful for long periods after they have been bought. Thus they do not need to be bought continuously, but only when the want for them first appears, or when an old one has broken down or become impossibly shabby. It follows that while the purchase of most sorts of single-use goods will take place at fairly regular intervals, purchases of durable-use goods may be very irregular. This is a matter of considerable importance for the running of the productive process. If all the goods which consumers wanted were single-use goods, it would be comparatively easy to organize the economic system so as to keep it running continuously at the same level of activity. The production of durable-use goods is much harder to stabilize, just because the need to purchase such goods is so much less regular. Nevertheless, durable-use goods are of great importance to the consumer. Although food and warmth, the most urgent necessities, are single-use goods, some durable-use goods are essential at any standard of living, while at a higher standard they provide more solid satisfaction than single-use goods can do. Luxury single-use goods mainly take the form of entertainment; luxury durable-use goods range from good housing and good clothing to books and pictures and musical instruments and garden plants, the typical ingredients of a civilized life. People who buy these things can satisfy their wants for them without buying them so regularly as they would buy food. In consequence it is hard to arrange for their production in ways which may not involve economic disturbances. . . .

A SIMILAR DISTINCTION
AMONG PRODUCERS' GOODS

A similar distinction between single-use and durable-use varieties can be made for producers' goods. Some producers' goods are used up—though this may only mean that they have passed on to the next stage in their production—as soon as they are used at all. Others can go on being used in the same way for long periods. In the illustration we gave the wheat, the flour, and also the oil and the electricity were single-use goods in this sense; the tractor, the ship and the baker's oven were durable-use goods. Generally speaking, single-use producers' goods are the materials used in industry, though half-finished products ought also to be reckoned as single-use goods at another stage. Durable-use producers' goods are the instruments of production—tools, machinery, industrial plant of all kinds. The production of durable-use producers' goods is perhaps even harder to stabilize than the production of durable-use consumers' goods—for much the same reasons. But we are not yet in a position to deal with such questions.

## Consumption and Investment

### THE ANNUAL PERIOD

. . . The processes of production and exchange . . . go on more or less indefinitely; they have gone on since the dawn of history, and will go on as long as the human race exists. Although it is true in one sense that particular processes come to an end every day with the completion and sale of finished consumers' goods, these goods have usually been produced along with many others (the durable-use producers' goods used in making them are for the most part still in existence, and being used again). Thus it is very difficult to find a self-contained process which can ever be said to be really over, just as we have seen that it is very difficult to find a date when it can really be said to begin. The only way in which we can limit our investigations, so as not to have to deal with the whole of human history at once, is to select a particular period of time and to confine our attention to the working of the productive process during that period. Usually (though not always) the period which it is most convenient to take is a year.

. . . . . .

Let us therefore fix our minds on the working of the productive process during a particular year—say 1939. We must think of the whole stream of time as being spread out before us, like a film which has been unwound. We take our scissors and cut out a particular section of the film. Or we may say that we put a spotlight upon this particular year, leaving everything before it and after it in the dark. What is the effect of this limitation upon the classifications we have given?

## THE PRODUCTIVE PROCESS
## DURING THE ANNUAL PERIOD

During the year producers will be turning out services and goods of all kinds, single-use goods, durable-use goods, producers' goods, consumers' goods. Most of the single-use goods will be used up in the course of the year, the consumers' goods in the direct satisfaction of consumers' wants, the producers' goods in the making of consumers' goods. It is fairly evident that single-use producers' goods, produced and used up during the year, ought not to be reckoned as part of the total production or output of the year. If we were to include both the bread and the flour out of which it is made, we should be reckoning the same productive effort twice; if we did this, there would be no reason why we should not include the wheat as well, and even the wheat standing in the field as well as the threshed wheat after it has been harvested. Once we allowed ourselves to reckon in both the single-use consumers' goods and the single-use producers' goods out of which they are made, there would be nothing to stop us from dividing the process of production into a large number of stages and counting what is essentially the same product as many times as we like. This would make the result of our calculation completely arbitrary. "Double counting" of this sort has clearly got to be avoided.

Those single-use producers' goods which are produced and used up during the year must not be counted as part of the year's production. But does this mean that all producers' goods have got to be excluded? At first sight one might suppose so, but that is not the case. For the production we are concerned with is the production of the year 1939, and some of the durable producers' goods produced during 1939 will outlast 1939. We have to pay special attention to the carry-over from one year to another.

At the beginning of the year (the morning of January 1, 1939) there exists in the community a particular stock of goods, including some from all our four types, but among which the durable-use goods are no doubt predominant. These goods are inherited from the previous year; for the most part they are the result of production in that and in earlier years. The durable-use consumers' goods inherited from the previous year include the houses people are living in, the furniture they are using, the clothes they are wearing, and so on. The durable-use producers' goods will include the factories, the machinery standing in the factories, the railways, ships, trucks, tools, and so on which are available for use in production during the coming year. The single-use producers' goods which are inherited will include stocks of materials waiting to be sold. The single-use consumers' goods (not so many of these) will include such things as foodstuffs already in the larder; remembering that the retailer is also a producer, foodstuffs in the shops ought to be reckoned as producers' goods.

This is the position at the beginning of the year. Then the wheel of time rolls on, and the wheels of production begin to turn. The goods in the larder are used up, and replaced by new goods out of the shops— that is to say, producers' goods pass into consumers' goods. At the same time, the vacant places in the shops are filled by new producers' goods coming forward—that is to say, the materials existing on January 1st are worked on by labor, with the help of durable-use producers' goods, and turned by degrees into finished products. At the same time, other workers using other durable-use producers' goods are preparing new materials. And other workers are making new durable-use goods. So the process goes on, with a continual stream of new consumers' goods passing into consumption, and new single-use producers' goods poking their heads out of the productive process, only to be tucked in again.

Those producers' goods which are produced during the year, and used up in further production within the year, do not count as part of the year's output. They are taken to be included in the consumers' goods of which they are the materials. If we were allowed to extend our gaze into the indefinite future, we should presumably find all the producers' goods incorporating themselves in consumers' goods in this way; but we are not allowed to look forward indefinitely. The year has an end as well as a beginning; many of the consumers' goods in which the producers' goods of this year will be incorporated belong to future years, not to this year. There will be producers' goods left over at the end of this year, just as there were producers' goods left over to this year from the year before.

There is no reason why the quantity of producers' goods bequeathed to 1940 should be the same as that inherited from 1938. The single-use producers' goods inherited from 1938 will, for the most part, have been used up in the production of 1939; new goods will have been produced to replace them, but these new goods may be greater or less in amount than the goods which have been used up. Some of the durable-use producers' goods inherited from 1938 will also have been used up, or worn out, during 1939; and even those which are not worn out will be a year older in January 1940 than they were in January 1939; this will often mean that they have a year's less "life" left in them. Against this *wear-and-tear* or *depreciation* of the durable-use goods previously existing, has to be set the production of new durable-use goods; but the wear-and-tear may or may not be completely offset by the new production. If it is not completely offset, the quantity of such goods at the disposal of the community will be less at the end of

the year than it was at the beginning; if it is more than offset, the quantity at the end of the year will be greater.

The same process of using-up and replacing will occur with consumers' goods as well. The year 1939 will have inherited from its predecessors certain quantities of consumers' goods (mainly durable-use goods, houses and so on); it will hand on certain quantities to its successors. One of the tests of successful productive activity during the year is to be got by comparing the quantities at the end with those at the beginning.

## THE FACTORS OF PRODUCTION AND THE SOCIAL OUTPUT

The process of production during the year can therefore be described in summary fashion in the following way. At the beginning of the year, there exists a certain stock of goods (all our four kinds) which we may call the Initial Equipment. During the year the initial equipment is worked upon by labor, and there is produced from it a stream of goods. Some of these goods are producers' goods used up again within the year, so that they do not reckon into the year's output; the goods which are included consist partly of consumers' goods, consumed within the year, partly of new equipment, added to the initial equipment as a result of the year's production. The equipment which exists at the end of the year becomes the initial equipment of the next year; it equals the Initial Equipment of the first year *plus* the New Equipment which has been added *minus* the Wear-and-tear (and other using-up of equipment) which has taken place within the year. This is the scheme of the productive process which we need to have in our minds.

All the product or output of the year comes from Labor and the Initial Equipment; these are therefore called the Factors of Production. The output of goods consists either of consumers' goods consumed within the year (Consumption) or of New Equipment. We can therefore set out our scheme in the form of a table:

Factors of Production = Labor *plus* Initial Equipment

*They yield*

Product (or Output) = Consumption *plus* New Equipment

And for the effect on equipment of the year's production:

Initial Equipment 1940 = Initial Equipment 1939—Wear-and-tear during 1939 + New Equipment produced in 1939.

The classification set out in this table is of fundamental importance for the whole of that part of economics which we shall study in this book. Everything further we have to say is nothing but elaboration of it and application of it to practical problems. For when theory has reached this point, it does begin to be capable of being applied.

### COMPLICATIONS—LABOR SERVICES AND USE OF HOUSE-ROOM

Before we can proceed to these applications, it should first be noticed, however, that the table as it stands is not quite complete. In the first place, services have been left out of account, as Adam Smith left them out of account—and for what turns out to be substantially the same reason. Just as we have been learning to do, Adam Smith thought of the productive process as consisting of labor working on initial equipment, and making it grow into consumption goods and new equipment. And services did not fit into the picture properly; consequently he excluded them as "unproductive." We have decided not to take that way out, and so we must find some way of fitting services into our picture. We can really do so quite easily, if we include the services produced in the year as part of the consumption of the year, and allow for the possibility that these services may have been produced by labor alone, without making use of initial equipment to any important extent. (Of course—and this is even more true today than it was in Smith's time—services may require the assistance of durable-use goods from the initial equipment if they are to be produced. For in-

stance, passenger transport workers provide direct services, but they use a great deal of equipment in providing these services.) This, then, is one of the adjustments which have to be made.

The other adjustment concerns the durable-use consumers' goods, which are included in the initial equipment, and do in fact form an important part of it. Take, for example, houses. The houses which exist at the beginning of the year do for the most part go on being used during the year; they make themselves useful, very useful indeed. The use of a house is a thing for which people are prepared to pay; a man pays rent for the right to live in a particular house, just as he pays for the goods he (or his wife) purchases in the shops. We reckon the goods purchased in the shops as part of the consumption of the year, and since house-room is purchased by consumers in the same sort of way, it is convenient (even if it means some stretching of terms) to reckon the use of house-room as part of the consumption of the year, and consequently also to reckon it as part of the production or output of the year. Strictly speaking, we ought to do the same for all the durable-use consumers' goods contained in the initial equipment (automobiles, for example). But, largely because houses are very frequently rented by their occupiers, while automobiles are usually bought outright, it is usual (even if it is not very logical) to include in this way only the use of houses. Houses are in any case the most important type of durable-use consumers' goods.

Our revised table may therefore be written as follows:

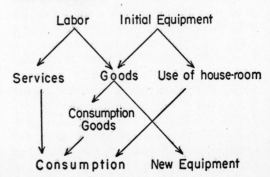

The new houses produced during the year are of course included in the new equipment.

## DEFINITIONS OF CAPITAL AND INVESTMENT

Our table is now complete, but before we can use it we must introduce two new terms. Instead of our phrase "initial equipment," economists usually employ the term "Capital" (or Wealth); instead of our phrase "new equipment" the term "Investment" (or Captial Formation) is now generally used. We had better familiarize ourselves with these important words.

I have so far avoided talking about capital and investment, because these are such outstanding instances of the way in which economists have taken words used by business men and given new meanings to them, meanings which are not (at least on the surface) the same as the business meanings. There is a relation between the meanings of capital and investment in economics and their meanings in business practice; we shall try to get that relation cleared up before we are done. But for the moment it is only the economic meanings which concern us.

In economics, the Capital (or Wealth) of a community consists in the stock of goods of all sorts possessed by the community (either by its individual members, or by associations of its members, such as governments) at a particular moment of time. Thus our "initial equipment" is the capital possessed by our community on January 1st. In economics, investment is the making of additions to capital. Thus the making of our "new equipment" is Investment (or Capital Formation).

In this terminology, the Factors of Production are Labor and Capital.[1] The goods and services produced by the factors of production are partly consumed within the year (consumption), partly used to make additions to capital (investment). In order to produce these goods and services, some part of the capital possessed at

the beginning of the year is used up (Wear-and-tear or Depreciation of Capital). The net addition to capital within the year is therefore the total production of additions to capital, with depreciation deducted. This net addition to Capital is called Net Investment. Consumption *plus* Net Investment *equals* Net Output. . . .

. . . . .

# The Social Output and the Social Income

## CONTRAST BETWEEN SOCIAL CAPITAL AND SOCIAL OUTPUT

The general picture of the productive process during any period . . . can be briefly described as labor working on capital to produce output. . . . The goods included in capital are those which exist at a particular moment of time; the goods included in output are those produced during a period of time. Some of the goods contained in output are durable goods, which will also count as parts of the community's capital at any time when they are simultaneously in existence. A house finished in April and a house finished in June are both in existence in July, and will count as parts of the community's capital in July. But a loaf of bread baked in April has been eaten before a loaf baked in June comes into existence; both loaves are part of the year's output, but there is no date at which they are both of them parts of capital.

Thus the social output consists of a different collection of commodities from that which makes up the social capital; but they are both of them collections of commodities including many different sorts. . . .

## IDENTITY BETWEEN SOCIAL OUTPUT AND SOCIAL INCOME ESTABLISHED IN A SIMPLIFIED CASE

The methods of computing the social output which are commonly employed depend on a very important economic principle, which is concerned with the close relationship between the value of the net social output and the total of the incomes of members of the community. . . .

[1] Land, which nineteenth-century economics used to reckon as a third factor of production, is here included in Capital.

It will be convenient to begin with a special case in which this principle is directly obvious. Let us suppose that the whole of the productive system of our community is organized in a single giant firm, which controls all the capital equipment, and employs the labor. This is very much the situation which would exist in a perfectly socialist community; the whole economic system of such a community would consist of a single firm, in which the State would own all the shares. We need not here suppose that the State owns the shares, as we do not want to bring the State into the picture just yet; we will suppose that the shares belong to a body of private shareholders, who may thus be regarded as the indirect owners of the capital equipment.

The net social output and the net output of our Firm are then one and the same thing. It consists, as we know, of the total amount of Consumption Goods and Services produced, *plus* net Investment, which is the increase in capital equipment brought about by the year's production. The wages of labor have to be paid out of the value of this output; but all the rest is profit, belonging to the shareholders.[1] The wages of labor are the incomes of the laborers; the profit left over is the income of the shareholders. The value of the social output is thus equal to Wages *plus* Profits; and Wages *plus* Profits equals the sum of incomes. The net social output equals the social income.

The same equality can be tested out along another route, by considering the way in which the incomes are spent. People will spend part of their incomes on buying consumption goods and services (buying them, of course, from the Firm, so that a part of its output is accounted for in this way); the rest they will save. Now when we say that a person saves a part of his income, we do not mean that this part of his income is not spent; saving is the opposite of consumption, not the opposite

[1] Since our firm controls the whole of production, there can be no purchasing of materials from other firms.

of spending. When a person saves, he uses a part of his income to make an addition to his assets; he is still saving, whatever form the additional assets take. Thus one possible way for a person to save would be by purchasing new equipment directly, and adding it to the assets in his possession at the end of the year. If we supposed that all the savings took this form, then it would be easy to see that the social income would purchase the social output. The part of the social output which consisted of consumption goods and services would be bought out of consumption expenditure; the part which consisted of the net investment would be purchased out of savings. Income as a whole would purchase output as a whole; we should have social income equaling social output along this route too.

Further, it is obvious that the equality would not be disturbed if we were to suppose that the savers, after acquiring the new equipment in this way, did not retain it in their possession, but lent it back to the Firm. The social income would still have purchased the social output; but the Firm would retain control of the new equipment, issuing shares in exchange for it. . . .

In order to arrive at this last situation, it would obviously be unnecessary for the actual goods which constitute the new equipment ever to pass directly into the hands of the savers. The savers might use their savings to acquire shares directly, and the Firm might issue the shares for them to acquire, without the new equipment ever changing hands. If the value of the shares issued was equal to the value of the savings, it would also be equal to the value of the net investment. . . .

So long as we assume that the whole of the capital equipment of the community is controlled by the single Firm, it is this last form which we ought to suppose the saving to take. People save by acquiring shares in the Firm; but the creation of the shares is only the reverse side of the accumulation of additional equipment by the Firm. When a person saves, he acquires the right to receive some part of the profit which will be earned by using the additional equipment which is being produced. He uses a part of his income to acquire a share in the indirect ownership of that new capital equipment.

Let us look . . . at the combined balance-sheet of firm and shareholders, . . . and see how it is affected by saving. Taking figures . . . appropriate for a giant Firm, we should have at the beginning of the year

| Assets (*billions*) | | Liabilities (*billions*) | |
|---|---|---|---|
| *Firm:* Real | | Capital stock, | |
| equipment | $100 | etc. | $100 |
| *Shareholders:* | | | |
| Shares of | | | |
| stock in firm | $100 | | |

At the end of the year we should have

| Assets (*billions*) | | Liabilities (*billions*) | |
|---|---|---|---|
| *Firm:* Real | | Capital stock, | |
| equipment | $105 | etc. | $105 |
| *Shareholders:* | | | |
| Shares of | | | |
| stock in firm | $105 | | |

The extra $5 billion of shares held by the shareholders are their savings; the extra $5 billion worth of real equipment is the net investment. Since the Firm's assets and liabilities must be equal *at both dates,* the savings must be equal in value to the net investment.

Thus the fact that people save by acquiring titles to the ownership of parts of the new equipment, instead of by acquiring new equipment directly, does not disturb the relationship between the social output and the social income. That relation can be summed up in the following very important equations:

*On the earning side*

Social = Wages = Social
Output + Income
Profits

*On the spending side*

Social = Consumption = Consumption = Social
Income + + Output
Saving Net Investment

.　.　.　.　.

. . . The part played by the giant Firm is exactly the same as that played in reality by all the firms which compose industry and commerce, when they are taken all together. Our Firm is simply the whole collection of actual firms rolled into one. . . .

The new points which emerge when we pull apart our giant Firm into the multitudinous separate firms, large and small, which correspond to it in reality, are only two in number. On the one hand, we have to take account of the materials and equipment [1] which are produced by one firm and sold to another, which uses them in its own production. These materials and equipment do not come into the picture, so long as industry and commerce are supposed to be amalgamated into one single Firm, because the passing on of materials from one stage of production to another is then a purely internal matter within the Firm. When the firms are pulled apart, the sale of materials looks just the same to the firm which sells them as any other sort of sale does. But since we have also to take into account the purchase of the materials by the firm which uses them, the sale and purchase of such materials will cancel out when all firms are taken together.

The other point which has to be taken into account when we have more firms than one is the possibility that a part of the shares (or other obligations) of one firm may be owned, not by private persons who are shareholders, but by another firm. If this happens, a part of the profits of the one firm will be paid out to the other firm; but here again, when all the firms are taken together, these transferences of profits will cancel out. The only profits left will be those which are actually paid out to private persons, or which remain as undistributed profits. A further consequence of this possibility is that savings lent to one firm may not be used as a means of increasing the capital goods in the possession of that firm, but may be lent again to some other firm. (An obvious example of this is the case of the banks.) These re-lendings,

[1] There are also certain services, such as transport and insurance, which are performed by one firm for another, so that their role is similar to that of materials.

too, will cancel out when all firms are taken together.

### THE PROFIT-AND-LOSS ACCOUNTS OF FIRMS AND THEIR PLACE IN THE SOCIAL INCOME

Thus the separation of firms makes absolutely no difference to our general argument. All transactions between firms cancel out, when all firms are taken together, as they have to be for calculation of the *social* income or output. But it will nevertheless be instructive to show in detail how the cancellation proceeds, by looking at the way in which firms do actually calculate their profits in practice. Firms calculate their profits by drawing up a profit-and-loss account; what we have now to show is the way in which the profit-and-loss account of a particular firm finds its place in those general accounts of the whole community, whose nature we have been investigating in this chapter.

The profits which are earned by a firm from the production of a particular year equal the value of its output *minus* the expenses to which it has been put in order to produce that output; but in the case of a firm which has obligations (shares or bonds) owing to it from other firms, the interest or dividends received from these other firms may also make a contribution to the firm's profits. The expenses of producing output include (1) wages and salaries; (2) cost of materials used up in order to produce the output; (3) cost of services, such as transport and insurance, provided by other firms; (4) depreciation of the fixed capital equipment. The profit left over after these expenses have been covered belongs to the owners of the firm's capital equipment, or to people who have lent money to it with which the equipment has been acquired; thus some parts of the profit may have to be paid out in rent of land or buildings (hired directly), or in interest on borrowed money; what remains is available for distribution to the firm's shareholders, though a prudent management will usually not distribute the whole of the

residue, but will keep back some part of it to add to reserves.

A typical profit-and-loss account could therefore be set out in the following form, which is substantially equivalent to that used in practice (the figures are only for purposes of illustration):

| | | | | |
|---|---|---|---|---|
| Value of output | $1,000,000 | Wages and salaries | $ 500,000 | ⎫ |
| | | Cost of materials | 200,000 | ⎬ Expenses |
| | | Transport, insurance, etc. | 25,000 | |
| | | Depreciation | 75,000 | ⎭ |
| Interest and dividends received from other firms | 50,000 | Rent of land or buildings | 50,000 | ⎫ |
| | | Interest to bondholders | 50,000 | ⎬ Profits |
| | | Dividends to shareholders | 100,000 | |
| | | Undistributed profits | 50,000 | ⎭ |
| | $1,050,000 | | $1,050,000 | |

Since the two sides add up to the same figure, we can re-arrange this account in another way, which is more convenient when we want to be able to consider all the firms in a community together. The account which follows has identically the same significance as that just given.

| | | | | | |
|---|---|---|---|---|---|
| Value of output | | $1,000,000 | Wages and salaries | | $500,000 |
| *less* | | | Profits | $250,000 | |
| Cost of materials | $200,000 | | *less* | | |
| Transport, insurance, etc. | 25,000 | | Interest and dividends received from other firms | 50,000 | |
| Depreciation | 75,000 | | | | |
| | | 300,000 | | | 200,000 |
| | | $ 700,000 | | | $700,000 |

This new way of writing the account has the advantage that the columns now add up to a total which is of great economic significance. The $1,050,000 to which the first account added up is not a figure which would have any significance except to the firm itself; the $700,000 which comes out as the total when the account is written in the second form is the net output of the firm [1] —its contribution to the net output of the community. If the accounts of all firms were written in the second form and the totals added together, we should get as a result

[1] This is frequently called the "value added" by the firm.

the net output of all firms together—the net output of industry and commerce, which corresponds to the net output of the giant Firm in our previous tables.

We can check up this correspondence on either side of the account. On the right-hand side, the net output of the firm is wages *plus* profits *minus* interest and dividends received from other firms. When all the net outputs are taken together and the totals added up, the parts of profits which are paid out to other firms will cancel out against the corresponding receipts by the other firms. The only profits which will be left are those which are paid out to private persons (shareholders, bondholders, or landlords), and those which remain as undistributed profits. The net output of all firms taken together is thus equal to

|  | Wages and salaries |
| *plus* | Profits paid out to private persons |
| *plus* | Undistributed profits |

But the total of these is just what the total of wages *plus* profits would be if industry were organized as a giant Firm; and we have seen that this is equal to the net output of industry and commerce.

Now look at the left-hand side. Here we have a similar cancelling-out to perform, because of the services performed by one firm for another, and because of the materials sold by one firm to another. The transport, insurance, etc., which figure among the expenses of production for most ordinary firms, are part of the output of such firms as railway companies and insurance companies, and cancel out against that output. Materials which are produced by one firm within the year, and used up by another firm within the year, are reckoned in the output of the first firm and in the cost of materials for the second; thus they also cancel out when the firms are taken together. But some of the materials which are produced during the year will not be used during the year, but will be added to stocks; some of the materials used during the year will not have been produced during the year, but will be taken from

stocks. Thus *all* materials will not necessarily cancel out.

When we have performed the cancellations, the sum totals of the left-hand sides for all firms taken together will come out as follows:

|  | Value of output of consumers' goods |
| *plus* | Value of new fixed capital produced |
| *less* | Depreciation of fixed capital |
| *plus* | Value of materials added to stocks |
| *less* | Value of materials taken from stocks |

which can also be written

|  | Value of output of consumers' goods |
| *plus* | Net investment in fixed capital |
| *plus* | Net investment in stocks of materials |

This is easily recognizable as the net output of consumption goods and investment goods produced by industry; that is, it is the net output of industry as before.

Thus the net output of industry and commerce is equal to the sum of the wages and profits derived from industry and commerce; . . .

## METHODS OF CALCULATING THE NATIONAL INCOME

The methods which are commonly used by statisticians for the calculation of the national output (or national income) now suggest themselves at once. Although there are certain corrections which have to be introduced when the simplifying assumptions are dropped . . . the connection between net national output and the sum of incomes remains close enough for it to be possible to approach the same problem from either side, from the side of output or from the side of income.

The most direct approach is the *income payments method*, which proceeds either by estimating the total amount of different types of income or by estimating the incomes received by persons of different types. In the United States, the total of income payments is built up by estimating total payrolls (including salaries), dividends and interest reaching individuals, net cash rents reaching individuals, and net profits of farmers and other self-employed, and a few minor items. From this total of 'income payments to individuals,' national income can be estimated by making adjustments for undistributed corporate profits, for non-cash rents, and for certain government transactions. In Great Britain, where the statistical source material is different in character, income is estimated for wage-earners, for persons liable for income tax, and for non-wage-earners not liable for tax; from the resulting total, national income is estimated by making adjustments for undistributed profits and for double-counting in the total. In principle a national total could be arrived at by making a field study to find the number of incomes in each range of income size, and adding the incomes so found; in practice such studies are so hard to carry out and the results are so imperfect that the total so derived is only a very rough check on the income payments total.

The second method is the census of production or *commodity flow* procedure, which begins from the output end instead of the input end. This consists in estimating net output either by industrial group or by type of final product. The standard American estimates on this basis have been compiled by using statistics on the flow of basic materials to gauge the flow of finished consumption goods and investment (or in the private language of American income

estimators, net capital formation). On the consumption side, commodity flow estimates yield in the first instance estimates of output at farms and factories, which have to be raised by an allowance for the final stages of production (i.e. transportation and marketing) and lowered by an allowance for business use of such commodities as gasoline which appear both as producers' and as consumers' goods. These figures have to be supplemented by figures for consumption services taken over from the expenditure estimates to be . . . ; and sometimes expenditure figures are substituted for commodity flow figures in the sphere of consumers' commodities. On the investment side, estimates are made of the total output of producers' durable-use goods and housing, and of the growth in inventories of other goods; this sum is called Gross Capital Formation. From this sum is subtracted an estimate of wear and tear on durable-use goods and housing (Capital Consumption), yielding Net Capital Formation (i.e. Investment) as a residual. Statistically this estimate is independent of that made by the income-payments method, and serves as control; for the United States the two methods give very similar results.

The third method is the *expenditure* procedure. This relies on retail trade data for consumption estimates; and instead of estimating net capital formation it involves estimating the amount of saving in different forms.

## SELECTED REFERENCES FOR PART 2

The number of volumes and articles bearing upon the issues of this Part is unusually large. This list is not meant to be complete. Treatises bearing on special aspects of economic development, such as business cycles and planning, are cited subsequently at appropriate points in the Selected References to the ensuing Parts.

For the sake of clarity, the items in the present Part are grouped under three headings: A. *Factors in Economic Development;* B. *History*

*of Economic Ideas;* and C. *Economic Analysis: Treatises and Texts.* Specialized studies on the economic evolution of the modern world are listed in Part 3.

No attempt is made under *Economic Analysis* to cite treatises prior to the reformulations of economic theory by the Austrian and British economists of the so-called "neo-classical" school of the third quarter of the nineteenth century. Full discussions of the publications and ideas of earlier writers will be found in the items listed under *History of Economic Ideas.*

## A. FACTORS IN ECONOMIC DEVELOPMENT

CARTER, WILLIAM HARRISON, JR., and RICHARD ELWOOD DODGE. *Economic Geography.* New York: Doubleday, 1939.

CHANG, PEI-KANG. *Agriculture and Industrialization.* Cambridge, Mass.: Harvard Univ. Press, 1949.

GRAS, N. S. B. *Business and Capitalism,* New York: Appleton-Century-Crofts, 1939.

LEITH, C. K., T. W. FURNESS and CLEONA LEWIS. *World Minerals and World Peace.* Washington, D. C.: The Brookings Institution, 1943.

MACLAURIN, W. R., with the technical assistance of R. JOYCE HARMAN. *Invention and Innovation in the Radio Industry.* Foreword by Karl T. Compton. New York: Macmillan, 1949.

MALINOWSKI, BRONISLAW. *Argonauts of the Western Pacific.* New York: Dutton, 1932.

MILLER, WILLIAM (ed.). *Men in Business: Essays in the History of Entrepreneurship.* Cambridge, Mass.: Harvard Univ. Press, 1952.

MOORE, WILBERT E. *Industrialization and Labor: Social Aspects of Economic Development.* Ithaca, N. Y.: Cornell Univ. Press, 1951.

SCHUMPETER, JOSEPH. *The Theory of Economic Development.* Translated by Redvers Opie. 4th printing. Cambridge: Harvard Univ. Press, 1951.

SWEEZY, PAUL M. *The Theory of Capitalist Development: Principles of Marxian Political Economy.* New York: Oxford Univ. Press, 1942.

VEBLEN, THORSTEIN. *The Theory of Business Enterprise.* New York: Scribner's, 1932.

WEBER, MAX. *The Theory of Social and Economic Organization,* being Part I of *Wirtschaft und Gesellschaft.* Translated from the German by A. M. Henderson and Talcott Parsons. Revised and edited, with introduction by Talcott Parsons. New York: Oxford Univ. Press, 1947.

ZIMMERMAN, ERICH W. *World Resources and Industries.* Revised edition. New York: Harper, 1951.

## B. HISTORY OF ECONOMIC IDEAS

FLUBACHER, JOSEPH F. *The Concept of Ethics in the History of Economics.* New York: Vantage Press, 1950.

GIDE, CHARLES, and CHARLES RIST. *History of Economic Doctrine,* 2nd English edition. Toronto: Clark, Irwin, 1948.

HALEVY, ELIE. *The Growth of Philosophic Radicalism.* Translated from the French by Mary Morris. New York: Augustus M. Kelley, 1950.

HEIMANN, EDWARD. *History of Economic Doctrines: An Introduction to Economic Theory.* London and New York: Oxford Univ. Press, 1945.

MITCHELL, WESLEY C. *Lecture Notes on Types of Economic Theory.* 2 vols. New York: Augustus M. Kelley, 1949.

ROLL, ERICH. *History of Economic Thought,* Revised Edition. New York: Prentice-Hall, 1942.

WHITTAKER, EDMUND. *A History of Economic Ideas.* New York: Longmans, Green, 1940.

## C. ECONOMIC ANALYSIS: TREATISES AND TEXTS

BOULDING, KENNETH. *Economic Analysis.* New York and London: Harper, 1941, revised 1948.

————. *A Reconstruction of Economics.* New York: Wiley, 1950.

BOWEN, HOWARD R. *Toward Social Economy.* New York: Rinehart, 1948.

BOWMAN, M. J. and G. L. BACH. *Economic Analysis and Public Policy,* 2nd Edition. New York: Prentice-Hall, 1949.

CLEMENCE, RICHARD V. (ed.). *Readings in Economic Analysis.* 2 vols. Cambridge: Addison-Wesley Press, 1951.

COMMONS, J. R. *The Economics of Collective Action.* With a biographical sketch by Selig Perlman. Edited, with introduction and supplemental essay, by Kenneth H. Parsons. New York: Macmillan, 1950.

DUESENBERRY, JAMES S. *Income, Saving, and the Theory of Consumer Behavior.* Cambridge: Harvard Univ. Press, 1951.

ELLIS, HOWARD S. (ed.). *A Survey of Contemporary Economics.* Philadelphia: Blakiston, 1948.

GAYER, ARTHUR D., C. LOWELL HARRISS and MILTON H. SPENCER (eds.). *Basic Economics: A Book of Readings.* New York: Prentice-Hall, 1951.

GRAHAM, FRANK D. *The Theory of International Values.* Princeton: Princeton Univ. Press, 1948.

HARROD, ROY F. *The Life of John Maynard Keynes.* New York: Harcourt, 1951.

———. *Towards a Dynamic Economics.* London: Macmillan, 1948.

HESS, ARLEIGH P., JR., ROBERT E. ALLMANN, JOHN P. RICE, and CARL STERN (eds.). *Outside Readings in Economics.* New York: Crowell, 1951.

HOBSON, JOHN A. *Confessions of an Economic Heretic.* London: G. Allen & Unwin, 1938.

HOOVER, GLENN (ed.). *Twentieth Century Economic Thought.* New York: Philosophical Library, 1950.

KATONA, GEORGE. *Psychological Analysis of Economic Behavior.* New York: McGraw-Hill, 1951.

KEYNES, J. M. *The General Theory of Employment, Interest, and Money.* New York: Macmillan, 1936.

———. *Laissez-Faire and Communism.* New York: New Republic, 1926.

KLEIN, LAWRENCE. *The Keynesian Revolution.* New York: Macmillan, 1947.

KNIGHT, FRANK H. *The Economic Organization.* New York: Augustus M. Kelley, 1951.

———. *Risk, Uncertainty, and Profit.* Originally published 1921. Revised edition, with new introduction and additional note by the author. London: London School of Economics and Political Science, 1949.

LERNER, A. P. *The Economics of Employment.* New York: McGraw-Hill, 1944.

MARSHALL, ALFRED. *Memorials of Alfred Marshall.* Edited by A. C. Pigou. London: Macmillan, 1925.

———. *Principles of Economics.* London: Macmillan, 1890, 1920, 1922.

MENGER, CARL. *Principles of Economics.* Translated by James Dingwall and Bert F. Hoselitz. Glencoe, Ill.: The Free Press, 1950.

MISES, LUDWIG VON. *Human Action: A Treatise on Economics.* New Haven: Yale Univ. Press, 1949.

MITCHELL, WESLEY. *The Backward Art of Spending Money, and Other Essays.* New York: McGraw-Hill, 1937.

MORGAN, THEODORE. *Introduction to Economics.* New York: Prentice-Hall, 1950.

PIGOU, A. C. *The Economics of Welfare,* 4th Ed. London: Macmillan, 1950.

ROBBINS, LIONEL. *The Economic Causes of War.* London: J. Cape, 1939.

———. *The Economic Problem in Peace and War.* London: Macmillan, 1947.

———. *An Essay on the Nature and Significance of Economic Science.* London: Macmillan, 1932.

SAMUELSON, PAUL A. *Economics—An Introductory Analysis.* New York: McGraw-Hill, 1948, revised 1951.

SCHUMPETER, JOSEPH. *Essays.* Cambridge: Addison-Wesley Press, 1951.

———. *Ten Great Economists: From Marx to Keynes.* New York: Oxford Univ. Press, 1951.

SPANN, O. *Types of Economic Theory.* Translated by E. and C. Paul. London: Blackwell, 1950.

WICKSELL, KNUT. *Lectures on Political Economy.* Translated by E. Classen and edited by L. Robbins. 2 vols. London: G. Routledge, 1934–35.

WICKSTEED, PHILIP H. *The Common Sense of Political Economy, and Selected Papers and Reviews on Economic Theory.* Edited with an introduction by Lionel Robbins. 2 vols. London: G. Routledge, 1944.

# PART 3

# The nature and impact of industrial society

❦ The nations of the world which today enjoy superiority in economic organization and production of economic goods are pre-eminently industrial in structure and outlook. By industrialism, it will be recalled, we have been referring primarily to a pattern of production centering around large-scale use of power-driven machinery.

The philosophies of work and wealth which appear to provide the most stimulating cultural setting for industrialism have been slow to mature. They were largely unknown to the societies of the ancient Orient, Greece and Rome, and the Middle Ages. Indeed, neither industrialism nor its characteristic philosophies became decisive for the conduct of most men of Western Europe until the third quarter of the eighteenth century, when the movement commonly known as the Industrial Revolution first emerged in classic form in Great Britain. From Britain this cultural scheme spread to the European continent and the United States, and in the twentieth century has been making its way at an accelerated pace into Russia, the Near and Far East, and Africa. One of the major functions of this Part will be to trace the origins, diffusion, and changing patterns of the culture known as industrialism.

The forms of social and political organization which are to accompany industrialism as it now spreads through previously undeveloped areas of the world are still in process of being determined. The political rivalries of the twentieth century revolve in no small degree about conflicts over the social and political framework by which production and distribution of economic and other values are to be guided.

Prior to the twentieth century, the leading centers of industrialism were characterized by a set of institutional and legal arrangements known as private-enterprise capitalism. Although the two—the new industrial order and the private enterprise system—have marched hand in hand in Western Europe and the United States, they need not necessarily go together. Industrialism is a *technological and productive organization;* private capitalism is a *social and political framework* marked principally by the private ownership of the means of production and the prominence of the "free market" as a mechanism for registering economic choices and for allocating resources. The link between the patterns has weakened since the last quarter of the nineteenth century, with the establishment of a trend toward more bureaucratic and centralized types of enterprise and state control. The Soviet Union has gone the farthest in the direction of centralized bureaucratic collectivism.

In this Part, we emphasize the central significance for Western culture of the relations between the technological setting and the social and political framework of economic systems. These raise a series of related problems. How has the division of labor, both in society generally and within any industrial or commercial enterprise, been affected by the changing patterns of technology and use of resources? What influence has the character of men's tools and machines had upon the way in which their joint labors are performed, and the way in which incomes, status, and power are distributed among them? What effect does relative access to raw materials have upon the relations of men and societies and upon their relative capacities to convert these raw materials into instruments of production?

Finally, in what measure can the "impersonalization" of relations and the "dehumanization" of man, which have, according to some, been aggravated since the rise of modern industry, be rightly charged against the capitalist system or the competitive ideal? Is it true, for example, as Karl Marx believed, that the adoption of social ownership of the means of production and centralized planning will eliminate inequalities of income and differences in social position and power? Is there evidence that the establishment of socialism or communism will put an end to the joylessness of work and the domination of the life of workingmen by management and the machine? In what measure are these developments likely to occur in any large-scale organization of enterprises, whatever the political setting, whether it be capitalist, socialist, communist, or anything else? How much reason is there to expect that a revolutionary change in economic and political forms will bring about a simultaneous liberation and integration of personality, work, and community?

Fuller discussion of these questions is reserved for later Parts of this Book, particularly Parts 5 and 7. This Part will provide a preliminary survey of the origin, spread, and impact of the new industrial culture.

Changing patterns of energy utilization and mechanical technique—what some have called changing "technological complexes"—are of great importance for every aspect of man's conduct and culture. Since the Middle Ages, the stages of technological evolution have been marked successively by the dominance of different kinds of power: water power, horse power, steam power, and electric power. In each epoch, as Lewis Mumford has contended in a series of notable volumes, the dominant kind of power and the techniques built upon it have tended to shape not only the organization of production but the whole pattern of social life and personality development.

But no technology or economic system develops except as an expression of human wants, values, motivations, ideas, and ideals. In understanding an economy it is, therefore, as important to understand its ideological background as it is to know its technological forms. Men do not always look upon work and wealth in the same way. The functioning of any economy depends upon the values—economic, aesthetic, ethical, and religious—which men place upon the work they must do and on the wealth they produce.

The selection from ADRIANO TILGHER helps us see how recent and unique is the structure of attitudes toward work which animates industrial society. Religious and ethical incentives for a life of strenuous manual exertion and systematic pursuit of profit are found rarely, if at all, in the teachings of the ancient Hebrews, classical Greek and Roman society, or among the early Christians. Men of the Middle Ages ascribed the highest value to the religious calling of the monks who, in the theory of the time, had fled secular society and its temptations to imitate Christ in His poverty, chastity, and humility within the walls of a secluded monastery.

Following Max Weber, Tilgher ascribes the adoption of a new attitude toward work and wealth to the influence of the religious teachings of the early Protestant reformers, especially Luther and Calvin. In the sixteenth and seventeenth centuries, methodical and conscientious labor in the calling assigned to or chosen by one within this workaday world (as distinguished from a monastery) came to be considered the most sanctified way of doing God's will. It is ultimately to the Protestant concept of impersonal service in a calling, Tilgher writes, that modern industry owes its underlying philosophy, namely, the sense of a mission to organize life for the reshaping of the face of the earth through and for greater and greater production of economic goods. This philosophy, Tilgher maintains, permeates industrial culture, whether religious or secular.

If Tilgher is to be believed, however, a decisive change in ideals concerning work and wealth is now occurring in Protestant lands, especially in the United States. A religion which encouraged men to work and save is giving way to a new religion, "the religion of large buying and amusements, a religion of comfort, . . . of cleanliness, a religion of the body." How, he asks, will this affect industrial culture?

Tilgher suggests another aspect of the modern changes in economic ideals which is critical for an understanding of subsequent readings in this Part—that is, the increasing "impersonalization" and "secularization" of life in our modern social order. Like the British historian, R. H. Tawney, in his *Religion and the Rise of Capitalism* (1926), Tilgher maintains that in modern "capitalist industrial society," economic life is usually held to be a sphere of activity separate from religion and ethics and governed by its distinct rules of conduct. In earlier days, by contrast, and notably in the Middle Ages, all aspects of life were subject to the authority of an all-embracing scheme of values, theological and moral. As business enterprise increased in scope and influence, religion and ethics were made purely "private" matters and ceased to have little connection with the life of workshop and market place.

The reading from HARRY ELMER BARNES presents a detailed, although highly condensed, chronological survey of the major developments in Europe's economic life and ideals from the Middle Ages to the advent of present-day mass production. Our survey begins in the more or less self-subsistent manorial economy, with its open fields, so-called common lands, and familialistic village organization. We turn then to the medieval city and note the growing conflict of interest between the artisans of the craft guilds, working for local consumers, and the great merchants and financiers, who reached out for foreign trade and investment. The power of these capitalist enterprisers, which received so great a stimulus from the Crusades, became decisive in the so-called "Commercial Revolution." One after another, blows were struck against the localism, the system of social and political regulation, and the premarket mentality of established trade and industry. The independent craftsman and his guild gradually disappeared. With the so-called "enclosure movement"—the consolidation of agricultural holdings, the enclosing of common fields—and the displacement of great numbers from villages to newly risen factory towns, the success of power-driven machines and the new patterns of industrial capitalism was assured.

Industrial capitalism has been undergoing rapid change for two centuries and the end is not yet in sight. Throughout the world, revolutionary innovations in the use of power, business organization, transport, and mass communication succeed one another at a pace which creates vast problems for all, whatever their social position and power. Morals, social and political thought, law, and religion are in continuous process of change.

During the nineteenth century, writers like Karl Marx called attention to the nature of the "factory system" which characterized industrial capitalism. They pointed out that in the factory the central unit of production became not the individual laborer, but the collective laborer—that is, the factory as a whole. Division of labor and specialization tended to limit the individual laborer to the "specialty of knowing nothing." Production through machinery was a decisive break with the past, for it withdrew from the worker the initiative and independence which the possession of tools had conferred upon him for so many centuries. Man was put in bondage to the machine and to its owner, the capitalist.

But this analysis is inadequate, according to our next author, HENRY FORD. As is well known, Ford helped initiate the revolution in mass production; and mass production and distribution has since set the pattern for industrial organization everywhere. For Ford, the central feature of mass production is the assembly line, with its intricate and highly efficient meshing of the innumerable parts into a finished product. In Ford's view, the teamwork of the assembly line immeasurably multiplied the production of low-price goods for mass markets and made possible a standard of living hitherto inconceivable. Ford specifically rejects the usual indictments against high-speed machine production. He insists that industry today produces goods of the highest quality, lightens labor, increases leisure, and provides opportunities for enjoyment unavailable to men in earlier days. In a truly competitive industrial society, Ford contends, rewards in the form of high profits go to those who render the most productive services to society.

The giant industrial establishment is also the theme of our last reading. Under the stimulus of the late Elton Mayo, research teams have investigated the effect of morale and group ideals upon productivity of factory workers. Other investigators have emphasized the significance of the status systems and supervisory structures of large-scale organizations.

A concise summary of the generalizations derived from work of this kind is found in the selection from BURLEIGH GARDNER. Gardner concentrates here on the pattern of hierarchy or formal organization which characterizes the modern industrial organization: a pyramid expanding downward from the "top brass" to the multitude of unskilled and semiskilled workers on the assembly line. Again we must remember that this description may apply not only to a plant producing automobiles, but that to a large extent it applies to any large-scale enterprise in our society. The importance of "informal organization"—relationships which do not appear on formal "blueprint" charts—should also be noted.

Gardner's essay points up sharply the spread of the "rationalization" of economic life, that is, the gearing of machines and persons into impersonal collective instruments whose aim is to produce with highest possible economic efficiency. With this issue we return to the problem posed in the first part of this Introduction: the relations between the technological complex known as industrialism and the social-political pattern of the enterprise system.

Many, including such thinkers as Karl Marx, believed that the "impersonalization" of social life and the "alienation" of the worker from his work were primarily due to the capitalist form of economic organization. Others, including the German thinker Max Weber, have asked whether the kind of large-scale impersonal organization depicted by Gardner is not the inevitable result of the vast expansion of the scale of the enterprise units themselves, regardless of whether they be organized capitalistically, socialistically, or in any other way. Our basic outlook on the future of society may depend on the answers we give to this question.

SECTION A

## Philosophies of work and wealth

# 8 Adriano Tilgher: *Work Through the Ages*

✸ *Most of us are aware that large-scale production of goods by machinery is a relatively new phenomenon in history. We know that before the age of industrialism men's tools were radically different from those of today. But when we pass from the instruments of work to ideas and attitudes about work, we are likely to make the error of believing that the ways in which we think and feel today are the ways men have always felt, and must always feel. It is therefore highly important that we see our own work ideals and values against the background of the philosophies of work which have been held in other cultures and other historical periods.*

*All kinds of ideas about work may be held within a given epoch of history, but in all probability a predominant motif will characterize each age. Adriano Tilgher (1887–1941), a noted Italian critic, historian, and philosopher, attempts in the following selection to compare ideals of work in various cultures and ages. His book,* Work: What It Has Meant to Men Through the Ages, *has been looked upon as a semiclassic. The reading here is from the English edition of this work, translated by Dorothy Canfield Fisher, copyright 1930 by Harcourt, Brace and Company. It is used with permission of the publisher.*

### WHAT THE GREEKS AND ROMANS THOUGHT OF WORK

To the Greeks work was a curse and nothing else. Their name for it—*ponos*—has the same root as the Latin *poena*, sorrow. For them *ponos* was colored with that sense of a heavy burdensome task which we feel in the words, *fatigue, travail, burden*. The turn of phrase which in English is restricted to downright drudgery, the Greeks applied to physical work of every sort.

Their poets and philosophers ring the changes on the same idea. According to Homer, the gods hate mankind and out of spite condemn men to toil. Xenophon called work the painful price the gods charge for the goods of life. Hesiod, to be sure, with his small farmer's ethical system, has no use for idleness and beggary, and preaches work. But he sees in it no inherent value or dignity, merely an escape from pinching hunger, from subjection to the rich and powerful, the only road to that degree of prosperity below which goodness and virtue are impossible. For Hesiod, too, life

without work would be the height of fe-
licity, a happiness the Golden Age knew,
which perhaps the future will know again;
but now, alas! the gods are displeased with
men, and have buried food under the earth
so that if man would eat he must first dig.

This point of view is typical. Most of
their thinkers grudgingly accept agriculture as not unworthy of a citizen, because
it brings a livelihood and independence—
that supreme ideal of the Greek spirit. Most
of them deplore the mechanical arts as
brutalizing the mind till it is unfit for thinking of truth, for practicing virtue. Free
artisans and craftsmen are scorned as hardly
better than slaves. Such intolerance was
natural in a society where the heavy labor
was done by slaves. . . .

. . . . .

Deep-rooted in Hellenic thought was the
conviction that the external world of material things is an endless recurrence of
phenomena which spring up and die down,
are born and pass away, are generated and
become corrupted, turning continually in
a circle on themselves, without beginning
or end, in an incessant change, ceaseless
and vain. To save oneself from the stormy
ocean of the exterior world, to retire into
the depths of one's own soul, secure from
change, concentrated in an unalterable
identity: this was for the Greeks the goal
of life. Hence any activity which brings the
spirit into close contact with the material
world seemed to them a painful humiliating necessity, to be reduced to the lowest
possible minimum, if possible to be eliminated altogether. Truth alone is the only
worthy concern for the spirit. Truth is an
ideal world, existing in itself before, outside of, and independently of the spirit,
secure from time and change, a world
which the spirit can know but cannot influence. Only by pure vision can the spirit
project itself into this eternal world, become one with it. Labor, therefore, which
contaminates the mind by contact with unstable matter, is clearly an enemy. It draws
the soul away from the roots of virtue in
the soul of whosoever submits to it, be he

slave or freeman. "The perfect constitution will turn no citizen into a working mechanic." Of all constitutions, those which
put power into the hands of the working
classes are judged by Aristotle to be the
worst.

Logically enough, although the Greeks
had the greatest respect for pure science
and were the first true creators of exact
science, they troubled themselves very little with its practical application. Archi-
medes, the greatest inventor of antiquity,
thought his devices poor things, adulterat-
ing the purity of ideas with matter, "for the
most part mere amusements and accessories
of Geometry." Logical again, the world's
greatest sculptors, they held even artistic
work in low esteem. Plutarch assures us
that no well-born youth would have chosen
to be a Phidias or a Polycletus.

As usual in abstract questions, Rome
copied Greece. At least Cicero speaks for
the majority of Romans when he lays it
down that there are but two occupations
worthy of a free man: first, agriculture;
next, big business, especially if it leads to
an honorable retirement into rural peace as
a country gentleman. All other pursuits are
vulgar and dishonoring, handcraft not less
than petty trade, the hiring out of one's
arms not less than usury. They chain the
soul to the desires of other men, to the thirst
for gain. Virgil alone seems to have had an
intuition that labor might be something
more than a prerequisite for personal well-
being and national greatness, that it might
be in itself a necessary element of a full
and worthy life, without which man would
not be man but a brute. "Under the reign of
Saturn," he sang, "the earth produced of
itself what was needful so that men in their
torpor were becoming as thick-witted as
dumb beasts. But Jove made life hard,
pierced the hearts of men with cares to stir
them from their idleness, and by the sting
of necessity, forced them to invent the
various arts." But this original conception
of work as a spur to man's development
rather than a drag upon it had to wait until the Renaissance before developing into
a complete and coherent philosophy of life.

Both Greeks and Romans saw clearly enough to link together their theory of work and their theory of wealth. So far as wealth might be useful in gaining the supreme ideal of life—man's independence of external things, self-sufficiency, satisfaction in himself—the ethics of antiquity accepted riches, but with the greatest distrust. Few of them, it is true, went as far as Antisthenes in holding wealth and virtue wholly incompatible. They tended rather to feel that poverty and riches were matters that did not affect virtue and happiness, but were good or bad according to the use made of them. . . .

. . . . .

THE HEBREW VIEW

Like the Greeks, the Hebrews thought of work as painful drudgery, but they did not stop with that thought. The Greeks could see no reason why man should be condemned to labor, nor "why from the blessed seats of its other-worldly home the soul fell here below upon earth," nor "Why does matter exist beside and outside of idea?" The Hebrew felt that he knew why our race is obliged to work. It was because it is its duty to expiate the original sin committed by its forefathers in the earthly Paradise. "If man," says the Talmud, "does not find his food like animals and birds but must earn it, that is due to sin."

For them, as for the Greeks, work is a hard necessity. But it is no longer a blind tragic necessity. It is accepted as a penalty, as an expiation, through which man may atone for the sin of his ancestors and reconquer his own lost spiritual dignity. Thus it takes on a certain worth and meaning. The Hebrews never saw laborers intent on their work in the fields without greeting and blessing them. But none the less work is a heavy yoke, hard to bear, and Ecclesiastes sighs, "The labor of man does not satisfy the soul."

Labor is the law of man's life; not of God's. The divine activity which created the world has nothing in common with human labor. The latter is toil; the first is almost play, a free expenditure of infinite energy which has no obstacles to overcome. "God, the Lord, fainteth not, neither is weary." Even so the work of man in the earthly Paradise before the fall was a playful and joyous overflowing of energy.

. . . . .

The Hebrew attitude toward work is just as logical as that of the Greeks, but it rests on different premises. For the Hebrew thinker, man's task is to lead the world, troubled and disturbed by man's abuse of his liberty, back to the cosmic unity and harmony which reigned when man was first brought into being by divine activity. The world is not merely something that exists but something that ought to exist, not a reality already complete, a field for passive contemplation. It is an ideal to be realized by man's efforts. It is the gradual and continuous process of restoration of the primal harmony destroyed by original sin. A process that will end in the reunion of justice and happiness, with the Kingdom of God upon earth.

. . . . .

. . . Rabbinical literature, without denying the coming of the Messiah, holds steadily to the view that the Kingdom of God will emerge slowly from present reality, thanks to the good will and work of man in brotherly relations with his fellow man. The Apocalypse puts the accent on the goal; Rabbinism, on the road which leads to it. In the thought of the Rabbis, work—not only intellectual but manual—re-acquires dignity and value. "Love work!" is the maxim of Samea. To work is to co-operate with God in the great purpose of the world's salvation. Man's labor tends to approach somewhat to that of God, for in the Cabalistic doctrines, the labor of man continues and prolongs the divine energy which overflowed in the act of creation. Even in Eden, Adam was obliged to earn his food, and driven out of Eden, was steadied by the necessity for increasing his toil. It is with work that God makes his bargain with man. It was God who taught Abraham the different kinds of work. The manna of the desert was not given the Israelites that they should eat in idleness, but that they might continue the labor of God's commanded migration. No labor, no matter how lowly, is so offensive as idleness, which creates lasciviousness and puts life itself in peril. The school of Rabbi Ismael prescribes that to the labor of the Law—contemplation—should be added the work of society—industry. The Pharisees maintain that the teaching of the Law is not enough. They exalt human manual labor, consider it preferable to idle contemplation and necessary to health, and they blame the father who does not teach his son an honest occupation. "Blessed the man who bows himself like an ox under the yoke, and like an ass to the burden." "He who lives by his labor is superior to the God-fearing man."

Nevertheless, although the Kingdom of God is indefinitely far away, that goal does not disappear from the Pharisee's horizon, and in that Kingdom there will be no place for work. The Pharisee too thought of the restored Kingdom as an era of blessed idleness, when the earth will bring forth of itself the best bread, and clothing already fashioned, and when one cluster of grapes will long refresh a whole family.

. . . . .

THE TEACHING OF JESUS

What value did Jesus set upon labor? The question is difficult and delicate because at first the answer appears self-evident. Text after text comes to mind, seeming to counsel an absolute trust in the Heavenly Father, a withering scorn of prudent work, and wealth.

We find Him saying in opposition to economic work, "Therefore I say unto you, take no thought for your life, what ye shall eat or what ye shall drink; nor yet for your body what ye shall put on. Is not the life more than meat, and the body than raiment?"

Behold the fowls of the air; for they sow not, neither do they reap nor gather into barns; yet your Heavenly Father feedeth them. Are ye not much better than they?

Which of you by taking thought can add one cubit unto his stature?

And why take ye thought for raiment? Consider the lilies of the field, how they grow: they toil not, neither do they spin:

And yet I say unto you, that even Solomon in all his glory was not arrayed like one of these.

Wherefore, if God so clothed the grass of the field, which today is, and tomorrow is cast into the oven, shall he not much more clothe you, O ye of little faith?

Therefore take no thought, saying, What shall we eat? or What shall we drink? Or, Wherewith shall we be clothed?

(For after all these things do the Gentiles seek) for your Heavenly Father knoweth that ye have need of all these things.

But seek ye first the Kingdom of God and his righteousness; and all these things shall be added unto you.

Take therefore no thought of the morrow: for the morrow shall take thought of the things of itself. Sufficient unto the day is the evil thereof.

Nor does he seem any more tolerant of wealth.

Lay not up for yourselves treasures upon earth, where moth and rust doth corrupt, and where thieves break through and steal:

But lay up for yourselves treasures in Heaven, where neither moth nor rust doth corrupt, and where thieves do not break through nor steal:

For where your treasure is, there will your heart be also.

Sell that ye have and give alms: provide yourselves bags which wax not old, a treasure in the Heavens that faileth not, where no thief approacheth, neither moth corrupteth. For where your treasure is, there will your heart be also.

No man can serve two masters: for either he will hate the one and love the other; or else he will hold to the one, and despise the other. Ye cannot serve God and Mammon.

But the cares of this world, and the deceitfulness of riches, and the lusts of other things entering in, choke the word, and it becometh unfruitful.

It is easier for a camel to go through the eye of a needle than for a rich man to enter into the Kingdom of God.

Jesus said unto him, If thou wilt be perfect go and sell that thou hast and give to the poor and thou shalt have treasure in Heaven: and come and follow me.

How did Jesus regard the pursuit of the world's goods? Clearly as a temptation, a peril to the soul. Not only the quest of riches, the mere having of riches makes doubtful the entrance to the Kingdom of Heaven. He who would be perfect must strip himself of everything—everything!—not only the superfluous but the necessary also, and give it to the poor. The teachings are meant literally. All attempts to soften them into metaphors or read into the gospels a justification of modern economics have been, and must be, vain.

And yet there is nothing of the ascetic in Jesus. Not from him comes the familiar doctrine that wealth in this world is the badge of the wicked, that he who hopes for salvation does well to renounce riches, secure in the hope that he shall be repaid tenfold when the unrighteous are despoiled at the day of judgment. Careful thought shows that when he preaches against wealth as an enemy, his point of attack is always that the getting and keeping of wealth fill the mind with care and anxiety, leave no time or strength for the real purpose of life, the service of God. Further than that he does not go. He does not hate riches or curse them or warn against them except as they turn the soul from God and his Kingdom. To work for them seems to him folly rather than wickedness. Such things come not from man's seeking: like all things they come from the bounty of God. For him the wise course and the good course are the same. Take no thought of the morrow: trust in God.

The true answer to the question: What value did Jesus set upon the world's goods and their pursuit? is that he set upon them no value at all. In and for themselves he ignored them. To be without material goods he thought no hardship, giving the righteous a future claim to the spoils of the wicked. That the unrighteous should prosper seemed to him no injustice, rather one more proof of the boundless goodness of God, who makes the sun to rise and the rain to fall alike on the just and the unjust.

It is idle to deny that Jesus denounced wealth and worldly care as barriers in the road which leads to God; that (even if they could be made harmless) he thought them vanities suited to the heathen rather than to the children of light. But we must remember that in their essence he did not condemn them; he passed over them as ethically neutral. This is not a quibble; the distinction is real. It is important, for, rightly understood, his teachings do away with the antithesis between material happiness and religious worth which lay at the bottom of the older visions of the Kingdom of God. They clear the ground for a future reconciliation of those two poles. But he did not himself attempt this reconciliation. He could not, wholly oblivious as he was of one of those two extremes of that antithesis —material goods.

.  .  .  .  .

## EARLY CHRISTIANITY

Primitive Christianity followed the Jewish tradition in regarding work as a punishment laid on man by God because of man's original sin. But to this strictly negative doctrine of expiation it added a positive function: to work is necessary not only to earn one's living, asking alms of no man, but above all so that the goods of fortune may be shared with one's needy brothers. Thus on work, as a means to charity, there falls a ray of the divine light that streams from charity. It is no longer possible to identify wealth with wickedness. Riches need no longer be shunned for the soul's health; shared with the poor, they bring God's blessing on the giver. Work thus gains a positive value. In addition it begins to be recognized as necessary to the health of body and soul, which without it would become bogged in idleness and fall a prey to evil thoughts and habits. It is the duty of the Christian brotherhood to give work to the unemployed so that no man need remain in idleness, but if he refuses to work, let him be cast out of the community.

Early Christian doctrine recognized no separation between mental and bodily work. The Jewish doctors of the Torah varied their study of the Law with the work of their hands.* In like manner Paul, missionary of the gospel:

Neither did we eat any man's bread for naught; but wrought with labor and travail night and day, that we might not be chargeable to any of you.

Not because we have not power, but to make ourselves an ensample unto you to follow us.

For even when we were with you, this we commanded you, that if any would not work, neither should he eat.

Nevertheless no intrinsic value is as yet recognized in labor. It gains a certain spiritual dignity, but only as a means to a worthy end. In itself it has no value, no importance. What more vain than labor to raise one's social position for the brief time the world shall endure? "Let every man abide in the same calling wherein he was called." Nor should the Christian lust after the things of the world lest he be turned away from the Christian life. He who is busy about many things and has a hand in many affairs must sin often and will hardly be saved. Therefore let him limit himself to one affair at most. With this advice, Hermas inculcates inertia and idle contemplation as a means of avoiding sin. He goes on to point out that riches detach the soul from God, that they are the bird-lime which holds the Christian in the life of heathendom.

.  .  .  .  .

Indeed all those early Christians were logical enough if we bear in mind that though they lived in the world, they kept themselves apart from it, waiting and longing for its end. Though bound by their bodies to the world of the relative, they fixed their spiritual eyes on the world of the absolute which does not pass away. Hence they felt no tie with the real and present world, no urge to better its conditions by work. They lived in the world only to renounce the world and bear witness to God. In the effort to make money and pile up ever more and more wealth, it was natural

that they should see the fountainhead of all moral and political iniquity.

The years rolled on and the yearned-for Kingdom always about to arrive, never actually did arrive and establish itself. Even the most faithful began to think of the next world as something far off in the future. They might believe in it as fervently as ever, but they no longer expected to find it just around the corner. Meanwhile the earthly world endured and promised to endure for many a year. Interest shifted to the problem of organizing the Christian brotherhood here on earth—to the Church Social questions (including that of work) could no longer be overlooked. Here as elsewhere it is St. Augustine who methodically thinks out the problem. He lays it down that work is obligatory only for monks; it supplies the needs of the monastery; it fosters brotherly love, purges body and soul of evil pleasures. In the lay world, rich people should prize and administer wealth as a trust from God. They may use it to pay for personal needs, to provide for their heirs, and for other charges fitting to their class; all else belongs to the poor, to charity.

Handcraft, tilling the soil, commerce on a small scale, these St. Augustine approves, though the seller must always be content with the "just price," and the taking of interest is abhorred as usury. But best of all is to give up owning property and live in a cloister. In the world, groups, classes, castes are to remain unchanged. Though they may spring from violence, they have their uses. Even slavery is permitted, although St. Augustine insists that slaves should have kind treatment. . . .

.  .  .  .  .

. . . Early Catholicism does something to dignify work, adds a new value, a spiritual dignity beyond that already granted by the conceptions of Israel. The aristocratic Greek scorn of the laboring classes dwindles. From the monasteries, above all from those of the Benedictines, where the

ED. NOTE: * Every Jewish boy, whatever his destined profession, was supposed to learn a manual trade. Thus St. Paul learned the trade of tent-maker and earned his livelihood by this means.

monks alternated work with prayer, where sons of nobles and princes bent their delicate bodies to humble labor, the cult of work spread into lay society. "Work, do not despair!"—the great words of St. Benedict ring down the centuries. Yet work is never exalted as anything of value in itself, but only as an instrument of purification, of charity, of expiation. . . .

. . . . .

. . . As the hope of the Kingdom of God on earth faded into the background, the church readjusted itself to the world, in the midst of which it organized itself as a self-contained society, perfect, divine, its eyes fixed on the one thing needful—the hereafter. The knife was laid at the root of every deep impulse which might have tied a churchman or devout layman to the earth, which might have led him to change its appearance by work. The interest in the hereafter overpowered any interest in the present, and the interest in the hereafter was satisfied by passive contemplation and meditation on God. The true Catholic can never feel a mission to change by his work the face of the earth and of society. For is he not already in this life a member of a society which cannot change because it is already perfect and divine?—which is in this world, it is true, but which fixes its gaze steadfastly on the world to come?

### SLOW GROWTH UNDER MEDIAEVAL AND MODERN CATHOLICISM

From the eleventh to the fourteenth century, Europe swarmed with heretical sects which almost threatened the existence of the Catholic Church itself. Since nearly all of them—Cathars, Waldenses, Poor Lombards, followers of Arnold of Brescia, Fraticelli and the like—insisted that every one, even the members of the clergy, should earn his living by the work of his own hands, it would be natural to suppose that they helped to raise the value of labor in men's minds. Not at all, quite the reverse. At bottom, they were thorough-going ascetics, misreading the message of Christ, scorning

wealth, exalting poverty to a positive religious sanctity, preaching work not because work is good but because they believed it painful, humiliating, a scourge for the pride of the flesh. Nor was the famous St. Francis of Assisi any less an ascetic. He lays on his Friars Minor the obligation of living by their own work, and this is to be only rough heavy manual work, with no other object than earning daily bread and a few coppers to be given as alms.

With the passing of the centuries, the Church, drawing closer and closer to the world, accepting worldly standards more and more, granted a fuller justice to labor and its fruits. In his encyclopaedic consideration of all things human and divine, St. Thomas Aquinas drew up a hierarchy of the professions and trades, according to their value to society. Agriculture he ranked first, then the handcrafts, commerce last of all. Money-lending he kept an outcast, since interest is not earned by work, and since the only rightful sources of property and profit are work and inheritance. Work he considered a necessity of nature. On work he founded his division of society into guilds and corporations according to the natural and divine plan. He held fast to the doctrine of the "just price," by which he meant just enough pay to assure the laborer and his family a bare livelihood.

Essentially, in his doctrine of labor, St. Thomas did little beyond dignifying into a philosophy the social practice of the bourgeois communes of his time. Yet, slight as the advance seems, judged by modern standards, it marks a great step forward in our history. From now on, in the Scholastic synthesis, work appears as a natural right and duty, the sole legitimate base of society, sole legitimate foundation for property and profit. . . .

. . . . .

But St. Thomas, too, puts ecclesiastical labor above work in the world, and places pure contemplation above all labor of all sorts. Like the mystic author of *The Imitation of Christ,* he finds the monk the truly religious man. Work is an obligation only insomuch as it is necessary to maintain the individual and the group of which he is a part. That end lacking, man does not need to work. He who can live without working is under no moral obligation to labor; much better for him to pray and contemplate God. High above merely material work, which limits the spirit to a small section of the world, stands contemplation, which takes the spirit into the divine order of things and enables the soul to perceive the purpose of God in its totality.

The status of mediaeval labor as described and regulated by St. Thomas is admirably reflected in those illustrated encyclopaedias, the great cathedrals built everywhere over Europe by the triumphant Catholic Church at the period of its greatest certainty and inner fullness. The cathedral welcomes among its other carvings those which show the humble gestures of daily work; the peasant is seen sowing, reaping, mowing, dancing in the wine vat. They are simple, serious representations, very close to suffering and toiling humanity, saturated with a manly religious feeling for work, austere and grave. But high, high above these representations of labor, throned and exalted, stand the images consecrated to learning and to contemplation.

Steadily the centuries piled themselves upon one another, and the Catholic Church, influenced by the economic practice of the industrial and commercial Italian republics, softened whatever was still too hard and mediaeval in the precepts of St. Thomas. Both St. Antoninus of Florence and Bernardino of Siena condemn idleness and extravagance, praise activity and industry, reprove avarice because a miser tends to do nothing but cling to his money-bags, fulminate against usury because it takes money which has cost no labor. They do, however, allow profits on investments, provided that the investor takes some part in the conduct of the enterprise. Thus capitalistic profit is encouraged as much as usury is repressed. Wealth and poverty, they hold, are in themselves neither good nor bad—may be either, depending on the use made of them. Nevertheless, of the two,

wealth is to be preferred, on condition that it is well employed.

.   .   .   .   .

With varieties and oscillations immaterial for our purpose, the Catholic theory of work continued along these lines during the following centuries. Nor was it able notably to overstep these limits even during its greatest effort to conciliate its ethical and religious principles with modern civilization. At the end of the nineteenth century and beginning of the twentieth, the orthodox movement known as Christian Democracy or Christian Socialism proclaimed labor as the foundation of all human progress, work a duty imposed by both divine and human laws. Every well-organized society should secure to its members the right to work as a natural consequence of the right to live, and further should grant to those unable to work the right to be cared for by those who do. So long as the interests of the community are respected, every man is free to choose his own work. Christian Socialism breaks the limits set by St. Thomas in recognizing that within the maximum and minimum set by society, man is absolute master of the rewards of his labor. But in affirming that the true source of prosperity is work, it harshly condemns modern capitalism—the economic system in which money of itself creates profits without personal work, and of itself automatically and endlessly increases. For the Christian Socialists, work is to be within the limits of natural law, which they consider to coincide with divine law. Confronted by this last law, work never rises to real independence, must remain simply a means subordinate to the end—which is life. And like life itself, it can never attain the dignity of being an end in itself, but must remain in the position accorded to life by the Catholic doctrine, as a mere means subordinate to the true end—which is the life hereafter. . . .

We have come a long way, it is clear, from the aristocratic Greek scorn of labor; but we have still far to go before we come to modern ideas. To reach them, we must pass through the Renaissance and the Reformation.

. . . . .

### THE PARADOX OF CALVINISM

With predestination as its keystone Calvin builds his logical, terrible philosophy of life. God is absolute power, illimitable energy, infinitely beyond the grasp of our reason, our ideas of justice. An abyss yawns between man and God, between the finite and the infinite. God is all, man is nothing. Man lives only to glorify God, and if he fails in this his fate is everlasting death. Now God has judged it fitting for his glory that only a small part of mankind (and this chosen regardless of good deeds or merit) shall know everlasting life. All other men must be eternally damned. No rational discrimination justifies to our eyes the frightfulness of this decree. It is precisely because of its frightfulness that the divine majesty shines from it. And since God changes not, nothing can win for man that divine grace which *ab aeterno* * he has not had; nothing can take it away from the man to whom it has been granted. This was an idea which did not fail to rouse infuriated resistance from other Reformed churches. Even Calvin himself did not state it in all its vigor until the third edition of the *Institutes*,† published after his death.

Thorough-going belief in predestination, one might suppose, would result in listless apathy—since man's fate is beyond his control. But when we forget the skeleton of abstract theology and think of the doctrine in terms of living human psychology, we will understand how it is that the dogma instead of condemning its believers to the stillness of death has roused them to the most prodigious fever of activity that the world has even known.

In the first place, while it is true that salvation cannot be won by taking thought, yet (putting the matter the other way around) the saved *do* take thought of their soul's health. The very fact of their election makes them turn to a deeper and fuller religious life. It follows therefore that the indifferent are evidently all damned—their light-hearted unconcern is a sure indication of lack of grace. Conversely those who agonize over the question of their salvation have at least a chance of finding themselves among the blessed . . . a thought which softens the horrifying and inhuman side of the doctrine.

Furthermore Calvin had a keen sense of the profound, irrational mystery of human individuality. A man's belief that he is of the elect comes from no other source than from his own individual, intimate, incommunicable experience. If he has not that belief, no church, no sacramental rites, not even Christ himself (who died for the elect alone), can take its place. Each man is face to face with the inscrutable majesty of divine omnipotence. In the terrible solitude round him, he has only the voice of his conscience telling him of his election, of his limitless responsibility, of his duty to serve God and to manifest his glory on earth.

But how shall a man be sure of his election? The firmest faith, the fiercest hope, may be nothing but a delusion! The only evidence lies in his daily life and deeds. For though he cannot win salvation by good works, nevertheless the zeal and power to do good works is a sign manual of God's favor. The elect do not live for themselves or for other men, but only for God, who is omnipotent and inscrutable Will. They are God's instruments—or rather they are no more than outlets through which the divine activity flows in its great task of bringing the glory of the Lord down upon earth. They do not act: God, acting through them, sets his own mark clearly on their lives and works. What more natural than for the man yearning to assure himself that his hope is not vain, to put himself to the test of trying to live as none but the elect

ED. NOTE: * "From eternity."

ED. NOTE: † The reference is to Calvin's great theological treatise, *Institutes of the Christian Religion*. The English translation is by John Allen; the Fourth American edition (2 vols., Philadelphia, 1843) has been often reprinted.

can live? What sort of life would that be? He must not stand idly contemplating, but must practice self-control, concentration, fight down the softness of his flesh, uproot whatever might bend his heart toward the idle, sinful world and its creatures. Yet he must not flee from the world. Meditation, striving toward inner purification, is of little value for him. His task is to act upon the world and its creatures and force them to become the visible mirror of God's glory. If he can do this, then his inner conviction of salvation may not be a vain hope. But he can never be sure. A true Calvinist can never rest in a peaceful proven certainty. His soul is always torn with burning doubt, torment, and subtle anguish from which there is no escape save in frantic activity, which will indicate to him and to other men the growing probability of his final salvation.

Self-control is no longer practical (as in Catholicism) as a means of cleansing and sanctifying man's natural instincts, but rather to preserve him in the God-given state of grace which he has always possessed. The distinction is fundamental. The Catholic believer tries to shape his natural instinct so that they will be drawn into a harmonious cosmos which will reflect divine life. For him, human nature is not wholly bad but only disorganized and perverted from its true end—that end to which it is his duty to lead it back. But Calvin looked on natural impulses only with horror and suspicion—vices to be rooted out relentlessly. He taught that natural man is wholly corrupt—the prey of death. Man redeemed by grace has nothing in common with natural man: he is the antithesis of natural man. He is a force from which all natural spontaneity has been eliminated: he is artificial and abstract Will.

Thus Calvin sets in motion a power that is hard, strong-willed, firm-fibered, deaf to sentiment, to fancy, to mystic ecstasies, to storms of passion. . . .

. . . . .

Calvinism is thus an appeal to will-power and action—a trumpet calling the faithful to battle against the prince of this world, against Satan. It makes no compromise with evil. It is a hard, harsh, violent, intolerant religion, but it signs no truce with injustice and wickedness. It enlists the believer as God's soldier, gives him a sword for one hand, a trowel for the other, and sets him to build the ramparts of the Holy City.

With Calvinism comes a new attitude toward labor. All men, even the rich, must work, because to work is the will of God. But they must not lust after the fruits of their labor—wealth, possessions, soft living. Their sweat and toil have value only as they help to establish the Kingdom of God on earth. And from this paradox—the command to ceaseless effort, to ceaseless renunciation of the fruits of effort—must needs follow a new economic practice. The miser's sterile hoarding, the money-lender's usury, are both swept away. A new use—the only worthy use—has been found for profit. As soon as earned it is used to finance fresh ventures, to breed new profit, again to be reinvested . . . and so on to the end of time.

All this sounds like the beginning of modern business. And so it is. Admitting all the other factors, when we search history for the first germ of capitalistic civilization, we find it quaintly but unquestionably in the worldly asceticism of Calvin, in his doctrine of unflagging ardor to make the earth the mirror of divine majesty.

With the new creed comes a new man, strong-willed, active, austere, hard-working from religious conviction. Idleness, luxury, prodigality, everything which softens the soul, is shunned as a deadly sin. Dislike of work is considered a sign that election is doubtful. Inactive contemplation is rejected, for God is too superior to his creatures to reveal himself to their comprehension, nor can they influence their salvation by mere taking thought.

Work alone suffices, and to please God, work must not be casual—now this, now that, now prolonged for the whole day, tomorrow laid down after an hour. Intermittent occasional work will not do. It must be methodical, disciplined, rational, uniform, and hence specialized work. To select a calling and follow it with all one's conscience is a religious duty. Calvinism thus lays the foundation of the tremendous discipline of the modern factory founded on the division of labor—very different from the easy-going ways of the independent artisan. Puritanism, developing out of Calvinism, goes still further and teaches that it is one's duty to extract the greatest possible gain from work; not for the love of money, nor to satisfy a thirst for pleasure, but so that more benediction may fall upon the head of the next needy person. Moreover, success (which is proved by profit) is the certain indication that the chosen profession is pleasing to God. The greater the profit, the greater the certainty of serving God with one's work. Puritanism thus opens to every calling whatsoever the prospect of unlimited profit. It not only permits, it consecrates, the effort to become wealthy. For the first time in history, wealth is reconciled with a good conscience. To wish to be poor is the greatest disservice to the glory of God.

Unlike Luther, Calvin considers it no virtue to remain satisfied with the class or the profession to which one is born. On the contrary it is every one's duty to seek out the profession which will bring to him and hence to society the greatest return. If that means abandoning an inherited trade or station in life, the change is not only permitted, it is ordered as a duty. Work is thus freed from hampering ideas of caste and is endowed with the greatest possible initiative. It becomes mobile, fluid, man-made rather than man-molding, rationalized.

Deny the world but live in the world, work in it, succeed in making yourself wealthy in order that the earth may reflect the majesty of God and of his saints! Such is the command of Calvin. And this command is the foundation of our modern age with its cult for work for the sake of work, of thrift, of wealth, with its abhorrence of rest and of pleasure.

. . . . .

## THE IDEA OF LABOR IN THE MODERN VISION OF LIFE

The modern idea of labor is the projection into theory of a new feeling in men's minds. That feeling has changed the face of the earth. Whole continents have been annexed to capitalistic civilization and despoiled of their natural resources, intact till now. Thousands of new cities have been founded and old ones changed from their foundation up. Agricultural and industrial production has been prodigiously increased, commerce intensified, the population of the world quintupled, and the human race amazingly brought together in time and space by the astoundingly sudden development of means of communication. Culture and hygiene are widespread as never before. Articles useful and necessary for life have to an extraordinary degree been placed at the disposal of all; articles which a few centuries ago were luxuries of the privileged classes are now in common use and regarded as common things. Ways of living and feeling have been highly standardized, and the barriers between town and country thrown down. Man has truly been made a citizen of an Earth miraculously unified. If Marx were alive today, not only would he have nothing to take away from the lyric praises of the achievements of the middle classes in the first pages of his Communist Manifesto but much to add to it.

This achievement and the immense benefits conferred on mankind by it are due, it is true, partly to the interweaving of a large number of historical circumstances which will never recur, and to incessant new discoveries in industrial technology. But, more than to any other cause, they are due to the prevalence of a new conception of the world and of life, to a new valuation of labor, thanks to which these historical events did not remain sterile, but were promptly utilized.

Consciously or unconsciously, man projects upon a cosmic plane and extends to the whole of the universe what he has learned in factories where industrial activity is constantly transforming the matter of the world. Industrial processes continually extend man's mastery over matter. He presses forward till he has again reached the limits of this new mastery and sees himself blocked by new obstacles. Strengthened by his preceding victory, he applies himself again to conquer these—and so on, world without end. Matter seems to him a moving frontier to the advance of industrial activity, a frontier which incessantly reappears, only to be pushed further on; it acts both as an obstacle which halts man's efforts, and as the solid fulcrum for the lever with which he moves the world.

．　．　．　．　．

In the fever of life and action man entirely loses sight of any possible life to come. Even if he does not formally deny its existence, the only world he cares about is the one in which he lives and works. The eternity of time, the infinity of space, which bowed down mediaeval and Renaissance man with their immeasurable weight, either disappear entirely from the modern consciousness or retire far into the background. His whole concern is with the point of intersection of the infinite lines of time and space. He lives entirely in the now and the here, where the spark of his activity gleams. Conscious of it or not, the modern man lives in a world without infinity and without eternity, in a world which he conceives as enduring in so far as the results of human activity pile themselves up like a snowball. The old sense of mystery gives way to our modern craving to find a practical solution to urgent problems.

To men who see life thus, work seems the summing up of all duties and virtues. It is in work that the man of capitalistic civilization finds his nobility and worth. His whole code of ethics is contained in the one precept, "Work!". . . In such a view of life "good" means active. Evil is synonymous with laziness, passivity, idleness. Moral progress consists of mounting from passivity into an activity continually purer and purer. The range of this activity has nothing fixed about it: it is a power which

by the law of its being continually grows greater the longer it persists, which by progressive stages gradually draws nearer to the infinite.

Activity is itself only in so far as it constantly advances beyond the position already attained, continually transcends the moment realized, never sleeps on its victories, but constantly draws nearer to the ideal (one that can never be realized) of an absolute and infinite activity. As a heavy layer of snow sliding down becomes an avalanche, so the very advance of activity makes it grow more active. The ideal goal is to make mankind the master of the world, the supreme power—God. Progress is the road which leads to this ideal. . . .

．　．　．　．　．

Modern man no longer seeks salvation by mastering his passions, by an ascetic absorption in the inner life of the spirit; but by work, with which he constantly transforms the external world; by work which contains, fused with itself, the infinitely numerous labors which preceded it and made it possible, work which will live again in the work of tomorrow made possible by it, work which survives the worker and confers on him a sort of earthly immortality. The holiness of work is reflected upon wealth and sanctifies it. Its usefulness is not at all that it may be spent and, in the Greek meaning of the word, enjoyed. That is of no consequence compared to its real purpose, which is to create new wealth, new work, new activity. For the modern man the pursuit of wealth is entirely different from the pursuit of pleasure. When he works hard to become rich it is to attain the condition which insures continually renewed activity. This explains, of course, why economics are at the center of the modern world.

In precapitalistic civilization, production was determined by demand, known and reckoned beforehand. Man manufactured no more than he knew was already wanted. Nowadays demand does not create supply. Supply, frantic to dispose of itself, rushes out to look up demand, engenders it, commands it, inflames it, sweeps it along toward the infinite and illimitable. We measure a nation's degree of progress by the amount of goods it consumes. When it constantly increases that amount, we say it is more progressive. The true heroes of the modern world are the great creators of wealth, the intensively working industrialists and entrepreneurs who produce wealth in constantly greater amounts, not with the egotistic purpose of enjoying it themselves, but so it may rain down on the world in life-giving floods, creating new wealth everywhere, new work, new activity. Such men are held something far better than the mere proprietors of the wealth they produce; they are its zealous, earnest, conscientious administrators. The wealth which makes other people hate and envy them gives them personally much less enjoyment than falls to the lot of their humble subalterns, unscorched by the divine fever of work.

Like all great civilizations, the capitalistic civilization of labor has its mythical hero: Faust. Faust sought happiness in all sorts of conditions and always failed to find it till in his old age he worked at the draining of a swamp, where some day a new nation was to live in fruitful toil. As he contemplates the future results of his work a beatific joy comes to him and he cries out to the moment as it passes, "Ah, stay! Thou art so fair!" He dies, and Mephistopheles is about to snatch his soul, but loses the wager, because in that moment Faust was enjoying a pleasure that lay not in the present but in the future.

True enough, by the law of its being, the civilization of labor bends its gaze on a future of which mankind is to be the artisan and creator. The dignity of labor is not based on its results, always vain and temporal, but on the fact that it permits the soul never to pause, always to ascend, and to find its peace in the very movement by which it flings itself forward, ever higher and further. If the *mot d'ordre* of Greek civilization was "Endure and abstain!" the slogan of our own, the civilization of labor, is "Work!"

## THE RELIGION OF WORK BEGINS TO FALTER

Now unless I mistake mere passing phenomena for true signs of the times, this great new religion shows symptoms of exhaustion, or at least of being in a dangerous crisis. It is certainly a serious matter that in the country which till yesterday was the veritable Holy Land of this new faith, in the United States of America, the religion of work should seem paradoxically but inevitably to be producing a religion its exact opposite, the religion of recreation, pleasure, and amusement.

In combination with other historical forces, the religion of work has created Greater Industry, which overwhelms the market by constantly huger avalanches of goods seeking purchasers. Hence Big Industry needs to create the demand which merchandise is to satisfy, to create conditions favorable for the consumption of the ever greater supply of goods which it is continually producing. This causes installment buying, high wages, short working days, all kinds of incitements to spend and especially to waste. These are all indispensable conditions if industry is to work full time at the highest rate of production. Thus in the very homeland of the religion of work a still later religion is growing up, the religion of large buying and of amusements, a religion of comfort, of well-being, of convenience, of cleanliness, a religion of the body. I mean those last three words to be taken literally—the Religion of the Body. This has a distinct tendency to relax the tautness of the will-to-work created by the religion of work and to break the psychological mainspring tempered and wound taut by that faith.

As far as that goes, the phenomenon is universal. Every country resounds to the lament that the work-fever does not burn in the younger generation, the post-war generation. If this is really true and if this condition lasts and becomes more marked, then the foundations of contemporary civilization have begun to crack. Nor may it be said that this slackening of the will-to-work does not affect the elite who direct affairs—the only persons of real significance in the matter, since the joy of creative work is their monopoly and does not touch the working classes. Observers of America unanimously report a new preference of American capitalists for safe investments, such as interest-bearing loans to foreign industries and foreign governments. Therefore in the very elite of America, the spirit of enterprise is giving way to the spirit of usury, which is in direct opposition to the capitalistic spirit and to the religion of work.

But let us pass over these, which may be only casual historical facts, evils for which history itself may be able to find a cure, and look for the root of this phenomenon. Like every great spiritual organism, the religion of work is based on a precarious balance between ideas and feelings, and changes its nature as it moves forward with the years. There is no doubt that the religion of work for the sake of work has given mankind peace, calm, and joy. The methodical discipline of professional work binds into a strong sheaf the scattered forces of the soul, frees men from doubts, anxieties, preoccupations, and sets the soul moving in a fine powerful rhythm which tends to perpetuate itself because of the very joy it gives. It is easy to make fun of the business man working from morning till night, wearing himself out to pile up wealth which he has neither the time nor the desire to enjoy. It is easy to accuse him of lack of spirituality. But that laborious existence engenders life in floods all around him; it gives him at times the divine joy of creation, and always (or almost always) the calm serenity of disciplined energies. . . .

In spite of this we must recognize that the state of mind of the modern successful worker rests upon a singularly unstable and precarious equilibrium of forces. On one hand, work must encounter something outside ourselves which at first resists and then yields to our labor. The joy of work is the joy of feeling our activity victorious over the resistance of the external world, the joy of feeling something becoming ours which at first was obstinately hostile to our will. But since we can only feel this joy if we care about this something-to-be-mastered, it is plain that work puts us in a state of dependence on the external world, condemns us never to be independent of it. This causes the pain of the worker who sees the fruit of his labor scattered, and the even keener suffering of the worker prevented by men or circumstances from doing the work for which he was born. Because work binds man to the world, the "I" to the "not-I," it multiplies the places through which the not-I can break in upon the I and wound it, and so of course multiplies the possibilities of suffering.

On the other hand work gives a man the joy of victorious force, bestows on him the harsh pleasure of feeling his personality triumphant. It tends to make a man feel that in himself alone is the source of all pleasure and joy. Since the joy which he seeks is to be found only in the possession of a powerful personality, the actual result of his work becomes a matter of indifference. The important thing is the joy of having been shrewd enough to accomplish that result. The more completely successful work makes a personality self-sufficing and self-governing, the more this personality tends to find its pride and joy in itself alone, in the consciousness of its own force and its own ability. It is no longer by accomplishing such or such a definite piece of work that the spirit finds peace; it is through work in general, any kind of work, the very act of entering into combat and conquering. Thus work tends little by little to change itself into a game in which the important thing is not the goal, but the skill of the player. But an activity which is separated only by a few degrees from games and sports sends down no deep taproots to the subsoil of human nature. It is a growth quickly laid low by the first high wind.

As soon as anyone realizes the tyrannical nature of this need to work he feels it to be a slavery, fetters to his personality which he must break. His mind opens out then to other needs, mounts to other needs, mounts to other ideals, wings its way toward other dreams. The divine madness of labor seems an unbearable chain, binding him to things outside his own nature, locking his soul into a narrow prison where its energies are impoverished and weakened. His soul longs to take pleasure in itself, in its own free play, in its inner harmonious rhythm. If it still feels the need of action, the activities toward which it yearns are those which do not enslave it to the world, but which are glorious with the light of art, or play, or luxury. Am I mistaken? It seems to me that our contemporary society is gravitating in this direction. If the very most modern era merits a name of its own, could it not be called the Age of Sport? New constellations keep rising on the horizon of the never-resting human soul. A revolution of incalculable importance in the history of contemporary civilization is perhaps upon us.

SECTION B

## The rise of industrial capitalism

# 9 Harry Elmer Barnes: *The Economic Development of Western Society*

❦ *The following selection by Harry Elmer Barnes (1889–    ), noted American historian and social scientist, traces the evolution of Western economic organization from the Middle Ages to the present day.*

*Barnes has taught at Columbia and Clark Universities, the New School for Social Research, Temple University, Smith College, and elsewhere. He has been a prolific writer, the range of his interests being indicated by a partial list of his publications: Sociology and Political Theory (1923), The Genesis of the World War (1926), The Twilight of Christianity (1929), History of Western Civilization (with Henry David), 2 vols. (1935), and Social Thought: From Lore to Science (with Howard Becker), 2 vols. (1938, revised 1952).*

*Our reading is excerpted from* An Economic History of the Western World *copyright, 1937, Harcourt, Brace and Company and reprinted with permission of the publishers.*

Aт the outset one must realize that during the Middle Ages agriculture was overwhelmingly predominant in the life and industry of man, and that the life of the great mass of the common people was, naturally, almost entirely agrarian. The manor implies a certain mode of landholding and cultivation; it was also the unit of medieval agricultural life. That it was more than that, however, the many—and usually inadequate—definitions of the manor indicate. The manor was the foundation stone of medieval rural organization and administration. It has been called "the simplest social organism above the family," which is, of course, a purely private group. The manor, in another sense, was the connecting link between two great medieval groups—the masses, who were concerned with providing the material necessities of life, and the classes, who provided protection, defense, and government both secular and spiritual. To the peasant the manor was practically the world itself, for he had few contacts outside of it.

．　．　．　．　．

In size, the manors varied widely. There seems to have been no customary area for the manor, or else we lack the necessary data to estimate an average size. It is unlikely that there were manors on which less than ten families lived. On the basis of a minimum 30-acre holding for each family, even such a small manor would contain at least 300 or more acres of arable land alone. There were no scattered farmhouses on the manor. The cultivators lived in small thatched houses or cottages, usually grouped together rather compactly in the center of the manor along the road running through the village. Almost invariably there was a stream near by, which supplied water for the animals and power for the mill. Around each house there was space enough for a tiny garden, a chicken run, and a shed for domesticated animals if they were not kept in or under the house. This closely massed collection of puny cottages constituted the medieval agricultural village.

With the village as a center, there extended out and around it the arable or cultivated fields, which could be reached from the village by lanes wide enough for the passage of carts. One could easily recognize that the arable land was divided into two or three major and distinct sections, each large field being subdivided into several smaller plots called shots, and these in turn divided into seemingly numberless strips of varying lengths. If the manor was

a large one, the village might nestle against the thick outer walls of the lord's castle. In a smaller one, the lord's manor house with the adjoining barn and stable would be situated on a choice site not far from, and perhaps facing, the village. Within the same section there stood a church, the dwelling of the priest, and a small cemetery. Near the manor house lay at least a part of the lord's demesne,[1] entirely his own land, and usually the best of the farm land on the manor. Finally, there was the common meadow, woodland, and waste land, shared by all the village peasantry.

In all, seven different agricultural divisions of land can be discovered on the typical manor: (1) The lord's demesne, cultivated both by special serfs of the demesne and by the villagers; (2) the lord's close, which was that part of the demesne rented to free or semiservile cultivators; (3) the tenures or shares of the villagers scattered in strips through the two or three large arable fields; (4) the meadow land; (5) the woodland; (6) the waste land; and (7) the land of the parish priest, either in a compact area or scattered in strips throughout the fields.

At the same time, another twofold division of the manorial land supplemented the above-mentioned agricultural divisions, and also indicated the dual nature and double mechanism of the manor. These two distinct sections were: (1) The land held in "villeinage"—that is, held of the lord by the tenants; (2) the demesne—the land cultivated for the direct and immediate benefit of the lord of the manor.

This latter division suggests the two viewpoints from which the manor may be regarded. On the one hand, the village community, with its somewhat extensive and peculiar form of self-government, was an association of peasants—that is, villagers—engaged in jointly working certain lands

[1] Not to be confused with the lord's domain—the sum total of the lord's manors. Part of the demesne often consisted of strips scattered throughout the arable fields worked by the peasants, though it was usually the lord's attempt, particularly in the late period, to concentrate the demesne, so far as possible, in a single plot.

for a livelihood. On the other hand, the manor was simply part of a fief, the estate or one of the estates of a lord, which supported and maintained him, his family, and his retinue. It had imposed upon it a particular type of economic administration that shaped the mode of life of the village community.

We have, then, in this double aim and organization a feature peculiar to the manor and sharply distinguishing it from both the modern large agricultural estate and the plantation of the ancient world. . . . The manorial system had a dual purpose—the providing of the villagers with their means of subsistence, and the lord with his profits. . . . These two aspects were more or less distinct, regardless of their intimate practical relationship. Sometimes they interacted harmoniously; sometimes they were unalterably opposed. From what has been said it will be clear that no matter how much the lord might desire and attempt to exploit the peasants and lands, it is not correct to assume that the manor existed and functioned for that purpose alone.

·  ·  ·  ·  ·

MEDIEVAL MARKETS AND FAIRS

Manorial economy permitted by its very nature only a minimum of commercial activity. Since most manorial units were nearly self-sufficient, their trade was necessarily limited to a few commodities, which were usually exchanged through barter for other products. Whatever trade went on was either in the hands of itinerant merchants or carried on at the markets situated outside a town or close by a monastery or castle. As the towns grew, the markets increased both in number and in importance.

Generally speaking, before the tenth century the local markets were the only important centers for the exchange of goods. These markets, continuing through the Middle Ages, are to be distinguished from the later fairs. The markets were local, or at most regional. Commodities from distant parts were not commonly found in them, and they were essentially designed for the exchange of local products. As an exchange and a distribution center for the locality the market played a most important role. The market days were specified and were held once or twice a week. Markets were established either by custom or by feudal or royal grant. They were generally encouraged by the feudal powers, for they meant an increase in tolls, taxes, and fees. The development of these markets indicates that medieval life was growing more settled. They implied a marked decline in petty peddling and a more extensive exchange of commodities.

With the appearance of more settled and civilized conditions a demand arose for a greater variety of commodities. At the same time, owing to a complexity of factors, especially the Crusades, commerce widened in geographic scope, and the so-called fairs appeared. Here were sold products not only of the particular region or country, but of foreign parts as well. The medieval fairs, while distinct from the markets, might be called "markets" for the sale of foreign goods and those coming from a distance. As compared to the market, the fair was not weekly, but seasonal. Dealing largely in imported commodities, it supplied a larger number of customers. Some of the great fairs, such as those of Champagne and Flanders, were really international in scope. There were smaller regional and even local fairs, serving as centers of still further local distribution of foreign goods.

·  ·  ·  ·  ·

The influence and significance of the fairs in medieval history is not easily exaggerated. Naturally enough, they acted as a stimulus not only to the internal and foreign trade of western Europe, but also to the industrial and agricultural activity of the localities in which they were held. They aided in transforming a barter economy into a money economy. Apart from purely economic considerations, the great fairs were in truth a civilizing force. They made possible important developments of commercial and international law. In bringing

together the products of different regions
and countries and promoting the mingling
of varied peoples, classes, and cultures,
they not only served to break down medieval isolation and localism, but they introduced new cultural and intellectual elements into the life of western Europe. No
other force is so destructive of bigotry and
provincialism as the contact of different
cultures and ideas. The medieval fair
probably did more to promote this process
than anything else before the overseas discoveries after 1492. Therefore it must be
accounted one of the most potent civilizing
forces in medieval European history.

FOREIGN COMMERCE DURING THE
MIDDLE AGES

Foreign trade . . . declined during the
Dark Ages. Yet there was greater commercial activity than earlier historians sus-
pected. . . . At one time it was generally
believed, and is still held by some excellent
scholars, that the Norse invasions of Britain
and the Continent in the ninth century almost extinguished whatever European commerce there had been. In the light of recent
research, this viewpoint has undergone re-
visions. True, the Vikings were pirates, sea
robbers. They were, however, traders at
the same time. Destructive as the Vikings
may have been in many respects, it appears
that their invasions actually stimulated
commercial activity. There is little question
that they stimulated commerce in France,
Russia, and the Mediterranean. On the
whole, both the variety and the volume of
commerce by the ninth century are being
recognized as greater than was previously
imagined.

· · · · ·

While the revival of foreign trade in
Europe became marked in the eleventh and
twelfth centuries, its origins are to be
traced to the preceding ones. The Crusades, important as they are in this respect,
cannot be accepted as the sole cause of the
commercial renaissance. For the European
cities along the Mediterranean already had
at least a small share in the Mediterranean

trade at the close of the tenth century and
in the early eleventh. Venice, for example,
was in steady contact with the Levant. By
the middle of the eleventh century, that is,
before the Crusades, the Italian cities were
playing considerable part in Mediterranean
trade, though Constantinople still controlled the Christian commerce with the
East.

It was cities such as Venice, Genoa, Pisa,
and Amalfi that profited most from the
trade revival and were the greatest immediate beneficiaries of the Crusades.
From the middle of the eleventh century,
then, trade between southern Europe and
the Orient kept constantly increasing.
France next felt the renaissance of mari-
time commerce in the twelfth century. By
the thirteenth, such an ancient port as
Marseilles was once more a thriving commercial center.

· · · · ·

Bringing the East and the West into
close contact, the Crusades introduced new
commodities into western Europe and
created new wants. The merchants, following the Crusaders and pilgrims, found new
markets and new sources of supply. The
richer and more cultured Near Orient was
opened up to European endeavor, and the
Mediterranean once more became the great
trade link between the prosperous East and
western Europe. . . . For the subsequent
history of Europe, the Crusades were far
more important as a commercial and cultural movement than as a religious foray.

· · · · ·

THE MERCHANT GUILD

Among the other effects of the revival of
trade upon western Europe were the
growth of a merchant class, the stimulation
of agricultural and industrial activity, and
the breakdown of the prevailing natural
economy. The last is perhaps one of the
most significant aspects of the revival of
trade. This breakdown ultimately resulted
in the general replacement of a natural
economy by a money economy—one of the
most far-reaching developments in the

Middle Ages. This implies that the trade revival brought with it the crucially important rise of capital and credit, which not only changed the nature of commerce, but also injected new energy and flexibility into all economic life.

The rise of capital not only widened the field of economic activity far beyond the limits possible under a natural feudal economy, but it made itself felt in other fields as well. The role that money played in the rise of the national state and the breakdown of the feudal order is very well established. It is sufficient here to note that in so far as the new money economy was a product of the commercial renaissance, the latter assisted in laying the foundations for the national state in late medieval times. Among the later results of the commercial revival, therefore, was the emergence of modern capitalism and politics. The trade revival of the period of the Crusades and thereafter, it must be recognized, produced only the first phases of a money economy. It created only the rudimentary emergence of capital and credit and the preliminaries of the national state. It remained for the expansion of Europe after the close of the fifteenth century to carry all these processes much further.

. . . . .

There was at first no clearly differentiated merchant class. In fact, the medieval tradition was anything but encouraging to its development. As we shall see later, a concern with economic matters "beyond what is necessary for subsistence" ran against the grain of medieval thought. The merchant had little place in the early medieval scheme of things. He was, as Professor Tawney observes, a late arrival "in a world dominated by conceptions hammered out in a pre-commercial age." As such, he never fully fitted into the ideal medieval structure, and later actually became a leading force helping on its disintegration.

The revival of commerce resulted in the creation of a distinct mercantile class in western Europe. The men who formed this class had no special niche in the medieval order as conceived by the medieval lawyers and unlike other classes they were not bound by customary or hereditary ties. Furthermore, the very nature of the feudal structure served as a check upon their economic progress. But they did possess one important bond in common—their commercial interests. On this basis they grouped together in associations in the mercatorial quarters for purposes of defense and the furthering of their common aims. These associations existed under various names, of which "guild" and "hanse" are most common. This appears to be the most plausible explanation of the origins of the merchant guild—the association for the protection and the promotion of the economic interests of the merchant group. It arose under the stimulus of the new economic conditions to achieve certain important practical ends in behalf of mercantile progress and the prosperity of merchants.

. . . . .

. . . The members of the guild were subjected to regulatory restrictions, and were under the protection of the entire guild. Members were permitted to sell their goods solely at stipulated times and specified places. Unfair business dealings and adulteration of goods on the part of the members were punished. Forestalling, regrating, engrossing,* short weights, and the sale of goods above the fixed price were all prohibited. On the other hand, if a guild member was unfortunate enough to fall into prison, the guild officials had to procure his release at the expense of the organization. A guildsman who met with misfortune was aided; sick members were visited; and the guild not only attended but also provided for the last rites of its members. From the viewpoint of business, far more important

ED. NOTE: * Forestalling consisted in buying up a commodity before it was put on the market for public sale; regrating was the buying up of large quantities of goods for sale at a profit; engrossing was "cornering" the market and thus creating a monopoly in a commodity.

than these fraternal aspects of guild activity [1] was the fact that each member shared in the monopoly of trade enjoyed by the guild as a whole.

The merchant guild was thus an association for the promotion of the economic interests of its members. This consideration determined its activities. In brief, its economic function was the control, to the point of monopoly, of the external trade of the town. . . .

．　．　．　．　．

In the functions of the merchant guild, the relationship between town and country is admirably illustrated. The urban community of northern Europe, Pirenne points out, was characterized by its agricultural nullity. Without the surrounding country its existence was impossible, for it produced no food supply. The countryside seemingly had the towns at its mercy. What the merchant guild did was to monopolize trade so that there remained no room for the independent middleman. Then the prices of foodstuffs could be depressed as far as possible, and the prices of commodities exchanged for them could be raised. The produce of the countryside was thus sold in the town market directly to the inhabitants. In the case of imported food produce, the importing merchant was compelled to allow the guild members to share in his purchases.

．　．　．　．　．

## MEDIEVAL INDUSTRIAL ORGANIZATION

The revival of trade notably increased the number of men engaged in industry and speeded up the development of urban industry. In competition with the free industry of the town, the unfree industry of the lord's domain was ultimately bound to decline. There grew up in the towns a special class distinct from the peasantry and free from the control of the lords. Possessing the knowledge of a skilled technique, these men provided for themselves by the

products of their "art" or craft. They were free artisans—free to choose their craft, since they were no longer attached to any special work, and free to dispose of their products as they wished. Instead of their producing for the domain or its lord, their market was now the town or the region.

The characteristic urban industrial establishment was the small workshop of the free artisan. In it he worked either alone, with the aid of his family, or more usually with the assistance of apprentices and journeymen. His tools were his own, and the raw materials that he worked up were frequently his as well. Sometimes his customers would furnish the raw material. He disposed of his produce in various ways. Aside from the sale of goods that had been ordered, he might sell articles in his workshop or market them himself. The artisan was, apart from the restrictions that encircled him, a small entrepreneur. He provided the tools, frequently the raw materials, always the labor—his own or that of his family or hired assistants—and finally disposed of the completed article. Since he was in part a merchant, it is understandable why the merchant guild at first included craftsmen.

The artisan rarely produced for a "blind" or unknown market. His production was usually determined by orders or by the usual amount of his sales. Working as he did on the orders of individual customers or producing for the town or regional market, he rarely ran the modern risk of overproduction. Though this circumscribed his gain, the return on his goods was wholly his own. He alone enjoyed the income from his labor. Of course, the element of profit entered where hired workers were involved. There the master craftsman received not only a return on his own labor, but also on that of others.

With the development of urban industry the number of those engaged in the crafts multiplied. With increasing demand, wider markets, and more elaborate industrial processes, the crafts became more specialized. . . .

[1] The merchant guild also had its festivities and ceremonies in which all the members participated.

The craft guild, viewed in its historical setting, unquestionably provided an excellent mode of supervising industrial processes. It is indeed to be doubted if any other type of economic organization has so well combined a concern for the welfare of the industrial classes with the dominating motive of excellence in workmanship. The craft guild also had at heart the reconciliation of the interests of both consumer and producer. Principles of professional honesty and craft unity gave a valuable social coloring to the more material and primary concern of the guild—the realization of common industrial interests.

### THE FUNCTIONS OF THE CRAFT GUILD

The economic functions of the craft guild were: (1) To regulate wages; (2) to fix prices and conditions of sale; (3) to determine the hours and the conditions of labor; and (4) to inspect workmanship and the quality of the materials. In all this was involved the local monopoly of each particular craft.

·  ·  ·  ·  ·

The regulation of wages was in accord with the idea of equalizing conditions among guild members and of destroying competition among them. The fixing of prices rested on the assumption that the work of all members of the guild was presumably of identical excellence, and upon the desire to maintain equality among the guild members. The success of price regulation depended upon the uniformity of the goods produced. When a great variety of goods began to be manufactured, and a diversity of grades began to prevail, control of prices was more difficult. To check both variety and diversity, all modifications and innovations were prohibited. A change in tools, material, or method would destroy the principle of guild equality as well as the uniformity of the type and grade of product. Technical improvements were frowned upon, and the guild acted as a brake on the development of industrial processes. Innovations did creep in, regard-

less of prohibitions, and complete equality and uniformity could never be maintained. When this effort failed, the rigid control of prices was bound to lapse.

·  ·  ·  ·  ·

In the craft guild there were masters, apprentices, and journeymen. The master may be distinguished as a fully fledged guild member in the sense that he played a direct part in the creation of guild rules and regulations and was controlled by them.

The apprentice was a boy or young man who was taught a particular trade by an accredited master workman to whom he was bound by his parents. Apart from the generally thorough technical preparation that the apprentice received, he was also given a moral education, apprenticeship being designed to make him socially useful as well as industrially skilled. The apprentice lived at the house of the master, who was to provide him with food, clothing, and the necessary chastisement, as well as to teach him the trade. On his part, the apprentice had to obey the master, conduct himself properly, and betray none of the master's secrets. During his period of service, the apprentice lived much as one of the master's family.

·  ·  ·  ·  ·

When his term of service was over, the apprentice became a journeyman,[1] and was employed by a master workman at specified wages. The journeyman was a candidate for mastership. At an earlier period in France the apprentice, having completed his training and proved his fitness, was eligible to mastership if he possessed the necessary capital. In time, several years' employment as a journeyman became customary before a craftsman could become a master. The years passed in working for wages served to endow him with experience and enabled him to accumulate the larger amount of capital called for by the

[1] From the French *journée*, that is, "day." The French terms for these wage-earners were *compagnons, varlets, locatifs*.

growth of industry. Before one could rise to mastership in England, he was generally compelled to work as a journeyman for two or three years. As a rule, the journeyman set himself up as a master when he was at least twenty-three years old, possessed sufficient capital, and had given the guild officials some proof of his skill as a workman. The common conception that a journeyman had to produce a *chef-d'oeuvre*, a masterpiece, before he could become a master, is in part erroneous. As an examination of the charters and rules of the craft guilds in Paris up to the fourteenth century shows, the candidate for the mastership was not usually required to submit a masterpiece. He frequently did have to submit to an examination, and he paid a fee to the guild when he became a master. It was only at the close of the Middle Ages that the candidate was sometimes compelled to produce a masterpiece in proof of his skill.[1] The purpose of this regulation, clearly, was to limit still further the number of masters.

. . . . .

With the increased wealth brought by flourishing industry, there grew up an industrial aristocracy based upon property. The journeyman was all too often doomed to remain a wage-earner. He could no longer look forward to certain promotion to the position of a master-employer. By virtue of his birth, which carried with it wealth and social position, the son of a master inherited his father's business—became a master without having to go through a period of training and without having to prove his technical and moral fitness. Industrial development, from this time on, held within itself one of the factors destructive of the craft-guild system. The appearance of a permanent class of wage-earners was at once a manifestation of, and a factor

[1] As a rule, however, the masterpiece was not a very difficult thing to turn out. It was usually a fair test of craft competence. An interesting survival of this requirement is the picture that every British artist is compelled to submit when he is received as a member of the Royal Academy.

contributing to, the decline of the craft guilds.

. . . . .

### THE PUTTING-OUT SYSTEM

We must now describe a new type of industrial organization, which at least partly replaced the guild system in those areas where it was introduced. The new so-called domestic or putting-out system developed as early as the thirteenth century in Italy, spreading gradually into the Rhine Valley, Flanders, and England. In Flanders it existed side by side with the independent guild system in the same towns, the two being applied to different industries. . . . The Commercial Revolution * greatly increased the number of merchant capitalists who supplied manufactured goods for consumption at distant places and times, and hence furthered the already discernible encroachment of the capitalistic organization upon the craft guild. The domestic or putting-out system was introduced into England in the fifteenth century, in the new and rapidly developing woolen and worsted industries.

Instead of having the workingmen collected in the household of a guild master, the workers under this system lived in their several dwellings, either in the towns or in the adjacent countryside. The person who really controlled all phases of this manufacturing process was known as a merchant capitalist, or more technically, in the woolen industry, as a clothier. He furnished the original capital with which to establish the business and sent out the raw materials to be worked up by the laborers living in their homes and performing the work at a rate agreed upon.[1] The representatives of the merchant capitalist could then go to the homes of the contract workers, leave more raw material, and collect the finished work. This merchant capitalist was not merely superimposed upon a single craft—his type was the organizing center of the whole

[1] Hence the term "putting-out" as descriptive of the system.

ED. NOTE:  * The Commercial Revolution was the great expansion of trade, usually dated from about the middle of the sixteenth century, which followed the break-up of the medieval economy.

group of crafts in the industry. For example, the clothier bought raw wool in the market or from the raisers, sent it in turn to spinners, weavers, fullers, and dyers, and finally marketed the finished product. Blackwell Hall in London became the great English cloth market.

At first the clothiers and the buyers of their goods met in a rather informal and haphazard fashion, but about the middle of the seventeenth century a special group of so-called factors appeared. They brought buyers and sellers together, collecting a fee or commission on sales. Later the drapers, who had been both retailers and wholesalers in the Middle Ages, gave up the retail trade and became wholesalers in the modern sense. They bought finished cloth from clothiers or factors and sold it to city retailers, provincial wholesalers, exporters, or foreign buyers. This transformation of the woolen industry and of the methods of selling cloth was completed by about 1750. England was then ready for the next step, the mechanical revolution in manufacturing technique. While the putting-out system was most completely developed in the textile industry, it was also applied in some measure to other industries, such as cutlery, leather, and iron.

There were many marked differences between the guild and the putting-out systems, but the most important were those which tended to develop a capitalistic tendency on the part of the merchant, the dominant figure in the process. Incidentally, in some ways the laboring groups in the scattered homes were rendered for a while more independent than under the old guild order, where the possibility of thoroughgoing personal supervision was much greater. At the same time, particularly in the later development of the putting-out system, the workers tended to lose their independence to the merchants, who often supplied them with both materials and tools. In this phase, some of the worst evils later associated with modern industrialism put in an appearance—woman and child labor, low wages, and "sweating" of the workers.

There were also defects in the putting-out system from the standpoint of the merchant capitalists. One of the greatest of these lay in the tendency of the unsupervised workingmen to loaf, particularly following the periodic pay days, after which one or all of the members of a family sometimes got drunk and remained intoxicated until the wages were used up. This had been more difficult in the old guild days and was even less possible when the factory came in later. There was also a great waste of time and money in sending out goods for the various processes of manufacturing, and in collecting them again. Nor was it easy for the capitalist to make certain of his ability to collect his manufactured product at the time he expected delivery, and a hitch early in the series of processes, say in spinning, delayed work all along the line. It was also difficult for him to supervise closely the quality and the style of his product, which was especially a drawback when new ideas and products began to be introduced. Finally, it was fairly easy for the workers to steal a portion of the raw material or to cheapen it by putting in substitutes. Material thus saved out could either be worked up by the employee himself or sold to a class of racketeering brokers who made a regular business of buying such stolen goods.

As a result of these manifold difficulties there was a tendency to grope after some method of securing better supervision of labor than any possible improvement of the putting-out system, however sweeping, seemed to offer. This led to the appearance of some large central shops—many writers call them factories—before the modern mechanical technique had been introduced. Workingmen could be assembled in a large building with spinning-wheels, hand looms, and the primitive appliances for dyeing and fulling. Here they could be kept at work by the representatives of the merchant capitalists. Viewed from the standpoint of personnel organization and discipline, this arrangement had all the advantages of the factory system, as we know it, except one—the cost of the tools was still so slight that the craftsman in most trades still had some chance to work for himself if he thought all the employers unjust. If it had become general, there is every reason to suppose that the central shop would have exhibited most of the defects and inconveniences of the factory system, such as crowded living-conditions and the centralizing of control in the hands of a few persons. Its slow growth and its restriction to a few industries suggest that the disadvantages of centralization before machines came in must have about balanced the advantages until the Industrial Revolution threw an overwhelming weight into the scales on the side of the factory.

. . . . .

### THE NATURE OF THE INDUSTRIAL REVOLUTION

The term "Industrial Revolution" should not be confined to any single type of economic development in modern times. Rather, a sufficiently broad conception must be adopted so that the term will embrace all of the diverse economic changes that have produced contemporary material culture, including the alterations in social institutions that have followed those economic transformations.

For the sake of clarity, the Industrial Revolution may be divided into three main phases: (1) The revolutionary changes in the technical methods of manufacturing, transportation, and the communication of information; (2) the rise of the factory system, viewed as a new method for the organization of industry and the discipline of labor; and (3) the general economic, social, political, and cultural effects of the new technology and the factory system upon Western civilization—in short, the technical process, the economic organization, and the sociological results.

### FROM TOOL TO MACHINE

The technological changes that formed the basis for the mechanical aspects of the Industrial Revolution rested, as we have just seen, to no small degree upon the progress that had been made earlier in natural and applied science. In the broadest sense, the revolution in technique consisted, in the first place, in the transition from a handicraft to a machine basis. There probably has never been a more revolutionary transition in human society than was embodied in the abandonment of the tool economy and the entry into the machine age. Man now became able to harness nature and to adapt it to his service through the medium of iron slaves. Not only was a new machine technique provided for the manufacturing of textiles; cheaper and more effective methods for the manufacturing of metal products were also developed. An improved type of motive power was found to drive the new machinery and the novel mechanisms of transportation. The steam engine, the internal-combustion engine, and the electric motor supplanted the ox, the ass, and the horse. Electricity, in the Second Industrial Revolution, was exploited in the interest of transportation facilities. It was also made the basis for a marvelous revolution in the communication of information, so that facts can be disseminated over any distance known to this planet, with the practical elimination of the time handicap. Finally, this easily gathered and rapidly transmitted information is now broadcast widely through the medium of the daily newspaper as well as the radio.

### THE RISE OF THE FACTORY SYSTEM

Equally novel was the appearance of the factory system as a new form of industrial organization and labor discipline. The old guild and putting-out systems had been based primarily upon personal relationships between the employer and employee in industry. Both of these older systems were compelled to give way to the factory system, once the machine technique had been introduced.

The term "factory system" is a little confusing, having been used in different senses by various writers. It is here employed to mean the labor (personnel) organization of the modern machine-equipped plant. It has been used by excellent authorities to designate any considerable aggregation of workmen, even with simple handicraft tools, under a single management. Such units might better be called "central shops," to avoid confusing voluntary centralization for convenience with the intricate and compulsory centralization of the labor force so characteristic of the machine age.

In the precise sense in which it is used here, the factory system was a necessary consequence of the modern machine technique. The bulky and complicated machinery that came in with the Industrial Revolution could not be installed in households. The factory system immediately produced a radically different type of industrial discipline. Far larger numbers of individuals were brought within one establishment, the personal relations between the employer and the employee tended to disappear, and the worker became regimented in all of his activities. With the growth of the factory system and of impersonal business enterprise, labor tended to become a commodity, bought and sold in the open labor market according to competitive business ideals rather than in accord with considerations of humanity. The factory worker was essentially at the mercy of the employer class, except in so far as labor organizations have gradually provided a means for collective bargaining and the effective defense of the workers.

### GENERAL MATERIAL AND CULTURAL RESULTS

The Industrial Revolution meant not merely a changed technique in manufacturing and transportation, and a new type of industrial organization. It also produced deep-seated and extensive economic, social, and cultural reactions. The mechanical technique, carried on under the factory system, led to an enormous increase in the volume of commodities produced; stimulated commerce; called for a much larger application of capital; reduced labor to a condition of general dependence upon the capitalist class; produced larger and improved banking and credit institutions; created corporations, trusts, holding companies, and other forms of large-scale industrial organization; and stimulated vast business combinations tending toward monopoly. Likewise, the new theory of business enterprise became triumphant. Immediate pecuniary profit became the chief motive of economic effort. The ledger circumscribed the economic perspective.

Social conditions were also profoundly altered. Civilization changed from a rural to an urban basis. The modern industrial city, with all its varied social problems, came into being. Population increased rapidly, so that the number of people living in Europe in 1900 was, roughly, double that in 1800. Great international shifts of population took place as a result of emigration from backward regions to more highly developed industrial areas.

The intellectual results of the Industrial Revolution were notable. The individual was enabled to receive information from all over the world, owing to the new methods of communication. He read books and journals to a far greater degree than ever before. Further, partly as a result of the gradual development of a class consciousness in the worker, came the achievement of free public education for the masses.

Along with these general intellectual and cultural gains of the Industrial Revolution a number of serious disadvantages have appeared. The nervous strains of the urban age have proved far greater than those of the earlier and simpler life of the country. Culture has tended to become standardized in terms of the machine technique. In enslaving the machine, man has himself been brought into bondage to the economic and social system that the machine technology created. The laborer has under capitalism become to a considerable degree merely a cog in a great industrial mechanism.

The political life of Europe and of the world was greatly modified by the Industrial Revolution. The middle class became all-powerful in the era of the industrialized state. This class provided political protection of its interests through constitutions and legislation based on the sanctity of property rights. But its ascendancy was soon challenged by the rising proletariat, whose growing participation in politics has created what we have today of modern democracy.

The development of the modern technique for transmitting information, perfected during the Second Industrial Revolution, made it possible for citizens of each of the great national states to feel and think alike through stimulation by uniform information. In this way the emotions of nationalism and patriotism, which had been stimulated by the revolutions of the seventeenth and eighteenth centuries, were made relatively facile and enduring. Telegraphs, telephones, radios, newspapers, and rapid transit have now made even great states psychologically smaller and more compact than a New England township was in the days of John Adams. Finally, the greatly increased productivity brought about by the new machine technology and factory system led to the search for new colonies, raw materials, and markets in oversea areas. This movement we speak of in history as modern national imperialism.

. . . . .

### THE TRANSIT OF
### THE INDUSTRIAL REVOLUTION

During the course of the nineteenth century, the industrial changes that had already affected England made their way not only to continental Europe and the United States, but all over the world. The industrialization moved in the form of a succession of expanding quasi-circular waves of which Western civilization has been the focus until very recently; first England, later Europe, and finally the United States.

The industrialization which, early in the nineteenth century, began its European expansion penetrated victoriously during the century into parts of the world outside of Western civilization. Country after country, continent after continent, joined the modern industrial world. Each decade of this movement fell heir to a richer technological heritage than the last. Speaking roughly, we can say that this process, which was typical of England in 1770–1820, penetrated continental Europe in the next forty years, the remainder of Europe and the

United States in the next thirty years, and moved to the other continents at the end of the nineteenth century. Stimulated by the World War, it became victorious over most of the world in the second quarter of the twentieth century, when it acquired and developed a revolutionary speed.

As a result of this development not only the physical distances, but the economic distances between the Western civilization and the former "backward countries" became shorter. In the first thirty years of the nineteenth century Western Europe was gradually becoming a common economic society. In the first thirty years of the twentieth century, the surface of our planet became the territorial basis of this society. The new century witnessed a trend towards the end of economic localism. But—and it is highly important—the quantitative growth of industrialization in general resulted in a qualitative evolution of special types of economy. In broad outlines, however, the industrial development of Europe and of the other regions followed the original pattern of growth laid down in England.

The general direction of the economic process in the century is clear. The nineteenth century transformed the local Western European economic civilization into a north-Atlantic one; the twentieth century strives to conquer the Pacific basin, and remaining regions of the world. The movement is from the West to the East, from the temperate zone to the tropics. This process, of course, was not simultaneous and equal in different regions of the world.

In the process of industrialization the world became one in the twentieth century —all countries, all nations, all continents, all corners of the world, move in the same general direction. Industrialization influences the powerful United States and small Liberia, the rationalized Germany and secluded Paraguay. Our entire planet is confronted with a grandiose movement of growing industrialization. The size of the movement is different, its coloring varies, its stages differ, depending on the local conditions of individual countries. But, in spite of the variety of incidentals, the startling uniformity of the development is obvious. The exceptions are few.

· · · · ·

### THE SECOND INDUSTRIAL REVOLUTION

There is considerable justification for describing as a "new" or "Second" Industrial Revolution the changes in applied science and industry since the middle of the nineteenth century, and particularly since 1900. Obviously, such an expression is an arbitrary one, and is no more valid than others that are conveniently employed to designate outstanding historical periods or tendencies. But its use is justifiable on the ground that the development of industry within the past eighty years or so does give evidence of certain characteristics which, in several respects, differentiate the more recent period rather clearly from the earlier phase of mechanical production that began around 1750 in England. The term "Second Industrial Revolution" should mainly impress the student with both the complexity and the increased speed of the industrial transformations since about the halfway mark of the nineteenth century.

The choice of the year 1850 as the date that demarcates the terminal years of the first Industrial Revolution, while to a certain extent arbitrary, is convenient and not lacking in historical logic. The essentials of the new mode of industrial production— the machine and the factory system—were solidly established in at least one country, England, and had already taken root or were beginning to be introduced in other countries by that time. Large-scale mechanical industry was an impressive fact, factories had been established, and industrial capitalism had already assumed a position of dominance. The earliest factory legislation had been placed upon the statute books. The middle of the last century is as logical a break as can be found between the first and second periods of modern industrial development. In some countries, as in Germany and Japan, the first and second Industrial Revolutions followed in rapid

sequence. Hardly had the machinery characteristic of the first been introduced when the early symptoms of the second began to appear. Our own generation is viewed as falling within the Second Industrial Revolution, but some students are now suggesting that certain postwar tendencies in Europe and the United States are so revolutionary in their significance that they give us grounds for speaking of still another or "Third" Industrial Revolution. Some writers place the first Industrial Revolution between 1750 and 1918 and hold that the Second Revolution begins with the latter date. To the author of this book, it seems better to regard a Third Industrial Revolution as getting under way after 1918.

· · · · ·

What are some of the changes that justify the term "Second Industrial Revolution"? 1. The earlier processes and tendencies have been enormously accelerated and striking new inventions have been made. 2. The stimulus to and the methodology of invention have been greatly modified and systematized. 3. Novel forms of power—especially electricity—have been discovered and utilized. 4. New machines, greater in size, more complex in construction and operation, and more delicate in adjustment, have been developed. 5. Machinery is becoming automatic and intelligence is transferred to the machine. 6. Precision instruments and machines have appeared. 7. Industry is becoming more completely dominated by science. 8. Synthetic products are replacing natural materials to an impressive degree. 9. The volume of industrial production has grown vastly. 10. Older methods of communication and transportation have been improved upon and new ones have been introduced. 11. Industrial capital has increased tremendously. 12. New forms of industrial organization have developed; a new relationship has sprung up between finance, banking, and industry, creating the era of finance capitalism. 13. More persuasive methods for promoting the sale of products have been worked out and employed in contemporary advertising. 14.

Through various devices of corporation finance control of business has been widely divorced from ownership. 15. Industry has become more thoroughly concentrated in areas best suited to combine advantages of labor supply, cheap raw materials, and market facilities. 16. New politico-economic policies have been formulated and pursued with far-reaching international consequences. 17. The workingman has been faced with new and difficult problems of life interests and class relationships.

. . . . .

### THE EVE OF THE "THIRD" INDUSTRIAL REVOLUTION

The advance of science and technology as applied to the steam and electric power industries has revolutionized the whole character of modern economic and social life. We seem to be entering a new age. If there is anything that would justify the concept of a "Third" Industrial Revolution it is this new era of power and the associated development of automatic machinery, both dependent upon applied electrophysics. Mr. Arkright has well summarized the character and significance of this revolutionary development in increased power:

The largest single modern turbine has a capacity of 300,000 horsepower or three million times the output of a human being on an eight-hour-day basis. But the turbine runs twenty-four hours a day, which man does not do, and hence its total output is 9,000,000 times that of one man. To say it in another way—four of these turbines have a greater energy capacity than the entire adult working population of the United States. At the present moment the United States has an installed capacity of one billion horsepower in engines to do work. What are these billion horses good for? Just one thing—to get work done. If these installed engines were operated continuously at capacity it would require fifty times the number of adult workers now living on the earth to equal this output by human labor alone. . . .

From these figures we may draw two conclusions:

1. The importance of man as a power unit in the United States is over.
2. The steady flow of this huge energy output has become so vital to our na-

tional existence that if we attempted to stop it and go back to hand labor we would die. Fire, disease, and starvation would do their work swiftly and ruthlessly.[1]

Another relatively novel and extremely portentous development in the realm of technology has been the recent growth of automatic machinery, namely, the removal of man two degrees from the actual burden of manual effort. Originally, man did the work himself or used tools. Then came the machines tended by men. Now we have machines watched and directed by other machines, thus vastly reducing the number of human beings needed to supervise mechanical processes and transferring intelligence from man to the machine. The basic nature of this change is well summarized by David Cushman Coyle:

In the power age there are two new mechanical factors. One is that electric power has made it possible to start and stop each machine in a factory independently by throwing a switch. The other is that the electric eye, the thermostat, and other instruments of the sort, have been developed to take the place of the human machine tender. From these inventions has grown a new conception, the automatic factory, where both the physical labor and the routine machine tending are done by non-human agencies. A few skilled mechanics and engineers are the only human beings about the shop.[2]

. . . . .

The coming of the automatic machine has given a new significance and seriousness to technological unemployment, that is, the tendency of machines to throw men out of work through displacing human effort by mechanical appliances.

Technological unemployment is no new thing. It is as old as the first stone culture of man—in other words, it goes back at least a quarter of a million years. The tool upset "prehistoric" industrial and social equilibrium as the machine has that of

[1] Frank Arkright, *The A B C of Technocracy* (New York: Harper, 1933), pp. 28–29.
[2] David Cushman Coyle, *The Irrepressible Conflict: Business vs. Finance* (privately printed 1932), p. 6.

modern times. When men first began to use stone implements and weapons the labor involved in protecting life and gaining a crude livelihood was greatly reduced. One man with an early paleolithic fist hatchet, fashioned from a large flint nodule, was worth as much as several who had nothing but their big jaws, bare hands, and chance clubs and stones to depend on. Specialization in the flint industry threw many of our "prehistoric" forefathers out of work. One skilled workman could turn out more fist hatchets, scrapers, and drills than a half-dozen novices. Systematic flintmining provided more good raw material than could be picked up sporadically by a multitude.

. . . . .

While technological unemployment has thus existed from the fist hatchet of the early Stone Age down to one of our modern match machines, that which faces us in the future is not only different in degree from anything in the past—it actually differs in kind. Therefore those who would allay our fears regarding technological unemployment by referring to facts and figures bearing on the period prior to, say, 1925 are ignoring the data that are really relevant to their problem. Talk about technological unemployment that overlooks the future implications of automatic machinery is blind and misleading.

No one has brought together the import of the impressive developments in the new technology better than Stuart Chase:

1. In the United States we have developed energy resources from coal, oil, natural gas, and water power until the total consumed has grown from 75 trillion British Thermal Units in 1830 to 27,000 trillion B.T.U. in 1930; while population has increased only twelve-fold.
2. We have developed prime movers (engines) to convert this energy into horsepower,

mechanical work, until the total now approaches one billion horsepower—capable of performing as much work as 10 billion men, some 250 times the working population.
3. We have developed a bewildering variety of clever machines to direct the brute power of the prime mover into thousands of useful operations, in manufacturing, agriculture, transportation, even in clerical work, merchandising, housework.
4. By virtue of these energy sources, prime movers and machines, the business of growing, manufacturing, and transporting economic goods is enormously accelerated. Due to the irresistible growth in the technical arts all three factors become constantly more efficient and more interlocked. The whole industrial system is approaching the status of one vast machine, the operation of every part of which depends upon the operation of every other part. If people in Texas do not consume automobiles, people in Detroit cannot consume as much food, whereupon farmers in Iowa cannot consume as many radios and harvesting machines, whereupon . . . The self-sufficient local community has gone forever. We are all tied together with chains of power and of steel.
5. The tendency in manufacturing and power production, and to a lesser degree in transportation, agriculture and clerical work, is in the direction of the full automatic process, where the machine does everything, the human muscle nothing. Such labor as is required increasingly takes the form of dial watching, control cabin work, switch throwing, inspection and set up. Even in this domain the photoelectric cell has been found to be a more dependable switch thrower than any human hand or eye.[1]

We have only scratched the surface of the remarkable developments that are taking place in the way of increasing energy for economic purposes and lessening the human factor in production. But even these sketchy summaries will demonstrate that if we are not already in the "Third" Industrial Revolution we are living on its eve. . . .

[1] Stuart Chase, *Technocracy; an Interpretation* (New York: John Day Co., 1933), pp. 23–24.

SECTION C

## Industrial production and the factory

# 10 Henry Ford: *Mass Production*

❦ *It is appropriate that the author of our reading on mass production should be the great wizard of automobile manufacture, Henry Ford (1863–1947). Perhaps more than any other person Ford was responsible for the development of industrial methods that were to revolutionize modern economy. Having fostered mass production in the automobile industry, he came to think of assembly-line methods as the key to greater production in all areas of economic life.*

*The rise of Henry Ford from machinist to ruler of a world industrial empire is a central part of the development of the modern world. Ford has recounted his views of the times he helped shape in several books, including* My Life and Work (1925), Today and Tomorrow (1926), *and* Moving Forward (1931).

*The selection which follows is reprinted from the* Encyclopedia Britannica (14th ed., 1929), pp. 38–41, *with the publisher's permission.*

The term mass production is used to describe the modern method by which great quantities of a single standardized commodity are manufactured. As commonly employed it is made to refer to the quantity produced, but its primary reference is to method. In several particulars the term is unsatisfactory. Mass production is not merely quantity production, for this may be had with none of the requisites of mass production. Nor is it merely machine production, which also may exist without any resemblance to mass production. Mass production is the focussing upon a manufacturing project of the principles of power, accuracy, economy, system, continuity and speed. The interpretation of these principles, through studies of operation and machine development and their co-ordination, is the conspicuous task of management.

And the normal result is a productive organisation that delivers in quantities a useful commodity of standard material, workmanship and design at minimum cost. The necessary, precedent condition of mass production is a capacity, latent or developed, of *mass consumption*, the ability to absorb large production. The two go together, and in the latter may be traced the reasons for the former.

THE ORIGINS OF MASS PRODUCTION

In origin mass production is American and recent; its earliest notable appearance falls within the first decade of the 20th century. The mere massing of men and materials is a procedure as old as the pyramids. Basic industries, like weaving, domestic baking, house construction and wooden ship building, are carried on, with only superficial changes, much as they were in ancient Egypt. Cottage manufactures and handicrafts moulded the practices of industry until the invention of the steam-engine. With the coming of power machines the seat of industry was removed from the homes of the people and a new work centre, the factory, was established. Much harsh criticism has been uttered against "the factory system," but it is perhaps fair to say that its first effect was to emancipate the home from being a mere adjunct to the loom or bench, and its later effect was to provide the home with means to develop the dignified status which it has now attained.

*The Factory System Giving Way.* The early factory system was uneconomical. Its beginning brought greater risk and loss of capital than had been known before, lower wages and more precarious outlook for the workers, and a decrease in quality of goods. More hours, more workers, more machines did not improve conditions; every increase did but enlarge the scale of fallacies built into business. Mere massing of men and tools was not enough; the profit motive, which dominated enterprise, was not enough. There remained the scientific motive which grew eventually into what is called mass production.

The new method came after the failure of the mercantile and financial emphasis in manufacture. The advent and progress of financial control of industry were marked by two developments, the corporation and the labour revolt. Artificial combination of industrial plants into vast corporations for financial purposes was the first movement toward *mass* in industry. It proceeded on the theory that complete financial control would automatically bring complete profit advantage. The theory ignored many vital principles of business and its fallacy became apparent, but not before serious social hostility had been incurred.

However, it was out of the social strife thus engendered that the idea began to emerge that possibly the difficulty lay in the neglect of scientific manufacturing principles. Industry was conceded to be necessary and useful; the service it rendered was regarded as of sufficient value to afford fair compensation for all engaged in it; it was therefore urged that the attention of management should be more directly focussed on the actual labour processes that were employed. This led to what was known early in the 20th century as the "efficiency movement" with its accompaniments of time-study and similar methods, although its roots were laid in the experiences of sound industrial observers as early as 1878. It cannot be said, however, that the efficiency experts did more than direct attention to the problem, by showing, in selected instances, how the then current methods were wasteful of men's earning power, and how their correction and improvement could lead to greater production, hence higher wages, and therefore a general betterment of labour relations. They emphasized a more intelligent management of methods than was then in use; they did not see that a wholly new method was possible which would simply abolish the problems of which the old method under the most intelligent management, was inevitably prolific. For example they dealt with methods which enabled labourers whose task was to load 12½ tons of pig-iron a day, to load 47½ long tons a day for an increase in the day's pay from $1.15 to $1.85. They did not see that another and better method might be devised which would make it unnecessary for a workingman to carry 106,400 lb. of pig-iron to earn $1.85. Mass production was not in their view, but only the alleviation of the worst errors of competitive factory practice.

*The Motor Industry Leads the Way.* To the motor industry is given the credit of bringing mass production to experimental success, and by general consent the Ford Motor Company is regarded as having pioneered in the largest development of the method under a single management and for a single purpose. It may, therefore, simplify the history of mass production and the description of its principles if the experience of this company is taken as a basis. It has been already suggested that mass production is possible only through the ability of the public to absorb large quantities of the commodity thus produced. These commodities are necessarily limited to necessities and conveniences. The greatest development of mass production methods has occurred in the production of conveniences. The motor vehicle represents a basic and continuous convenience-transportation.

Mass production begins, then, in the conception of a public need of which the public may not as yet be conscious and proceeds on the principle that use-convenience must be matched by price-convenience. Under this principle the element of service remains uppermost; profit and expansion are trusted to emerge as consequences. As to which precedes the other, consumption or production, experiences will differ. But granted that the vision of the public need is correct, and the commodity adapted to meet it, the impulse to increased production may come in anticipation of demand, or in response to demand, but the resulting consumption is always utilized to obtain such increase of quality, or such decrease of cost, or both, as shall secure still greater use-convenience and price-convenience. As these increase, consumption increases, making possible still greater production advantages, and so on to a fulfilment that is not yet in view.

The commodities that conduce to civilized living are thus far enjoyed by only a small fraction of the world's inhabitants. The experience of the Ford Motor Company has been that mass production precedes mass consumption and makes it possible, by reducing costs and thus permitting both greater use-convenience and price-convenience. If the production is increased, costs can be reduced. If production is increased 500% costs may be cut 50%, and this decrease in cost, with its accompanying decrease in selling price, will probably multiply by 10 the number of people who can conveniently buy the product.

## THE PRINCIPLES OF MASS PRODUCTION

As to shop detail, the keyword to mass production is simplicity. Three plain principles underlie it: (a) the planned orderly progression of the commodity through the shop; (b) the delivery of work instead of leaving it to the workman's initiative to find it; (c) an analysis of operations into their constituent parts. These are distinct but not separate steps; all are involved in the first one. To plan the progress of material from the initial manufacturing operation until its emergence as a finished product involves shop planning on a large scale and the manufacture and delivery of material, tools and parts at various points along the line. To do this successfully with a progressing piece of work means a careful breaking up of the work into its "operations" in sequence. All three fundamentals are involved in the original act of planning a moving line of production.

This system is practised, not only on the final assembly line, but throughout the various arts and trades involved in the completed product. The motor car assembly line offers an impressive spectacle of hundreds of parts being quickly put together into a going vehicle, but flowing into that are other assembly lines on which each of the hundreds of parts have been fashioned. It may be far down the final assembly line that the springs, for example, appear, and they may seem to be a negligible part of the whole operation. Formerly one artisan would cut, harden, bend and build a spring. In 1928 the making of one leaf of a spring is an operation of apparent complexity, yet is really the ultimate reduction to simplicity of operation.

*A Typical Operation Described.* For its illustrative value let us trace the course of a spring leaf after it has progressed from strips. (1) Beginning as a strip of steel prepared by the steelmill, it is placed in a punch press until it hits a stop, then trips the press. The cut-off and pierced piece falls on a belt conveyor which runs along the loading end of a series of heat-treating ovens. (2) A second workman takes the pieces from belt conveyor and places them on conveyor which passes through the furnace (in which temperature is automatically controlled); thence they are deposited at a certain temperature by this conveyor at the unloading end of the furnace. (3) The heated piece is lifted with tongs by a third operator and placed in a bending machine which gives the leaf its proper curve and plunges it in oil, the temperature of which is maintained at a definite degree by apparatus beyond the operator's control. (4) As the bending machine emerges from the oil bath, the same operator takes out the leaf and sets it aside to air-cool. (5) The leaf is then drawn by a fourth operator through molten nitrate kept at a regulated temperature. (6) A fifth workman inspects it.

As a set of springs on the Ford car requires on an average of 17 leaves, and 25,-000 springs are an average day's output, this operation must be visualised as employing a great battery of lines similar to the one briefly described. As all the leaves in a spring are of different length and curve, from the bottom or master leaf to the top leaf, this operation must be visualised as one of many carried on simultaneously by different batteries of machines, each battery working on its own special size. All of these lines, with their various machines and operations, are converging on the point where the leaves are assembled into springs. The leaf whose progress has been described is the simplest one.

The operation proceeds as follows: (7) A sixth workman removes the leaf from the conveyor which carries it from the molten nitrate, and inserts a bolt through this and the other leaves required in the spring. (8) A seventh workman puts the nut on the bolt and tightens it. (9) An eighth workman puts on the right and left hand clips and grinds off the burrs. (10) A ninth workman inspects it. (11) He hangs the spring on a conveyor. (12) The spring passes the tenth workman, who sprays it with paint, and the conveyor carries the

spring above the ovens where it was originally heated, and the radiated heat "force dries" the paint. (13) The conveyor continues to the loading dock, where the eleventh workman removes it.

One workman under the old system could attend the leaf through all these phases, or even make a complete spring, but his production would be limited. Where large quantities of the same article are to be made, the simplest operation may involve the whole time of one man. A one-minute operation will require one man a full day of eight hours to accomplish it on 480 pieces. Now this simple part, a spring leaf, must be identical in strength, finish and curve with millions of others designed to fulfil the same purpose, and this becomes a complicated and delicate procedure requiring automatic machinery, the most accurate of measuring devices, pyrometer controls, "go" and "no go" gauges—in fact, the best facilities that can be provided by modern management. The leaf described, which is a minor matter when compared with the whole great process, becomes a major matter when considered by itself; it must have its own supply of material delivered in sufficient quantities at indicated places—for example, steel at 1; heat at 2; power and oil at 3; molten nitrate at 5; bolts at 7; nuts at 8; clips at 9; paint at 12. In this process the secrets of many arts and trades are employed.

The story of this minor part illustrates what is meant by orderly progression of the article through the shop. It goes to meet other parts of the motor-car which have come from other parts of the plant by similar processes. The story illustrates also what is meant by delivering the work to the workman: every workman's task is prepared for him by some other workman, and delivered to his hand. The third principle also is illustrated—the analysis of a single job into its constituent operations. The simplicity of the part here described should not be permitted to exclude from view the multitude of other operations, ranging from the heaviest forgings to the lightest manipulations in bench assembly of delicate electrical instruments. Some gauge inspections involve measurements to the ten-millionth part of an inch.

The economies arising from this method are obvious. The machinery is constantly in use. It would be economically impossible to maintain all this equipment for the service of men occupied in the entire operation of making springs. Presses, furnaces, bending machines, oil baths would be idle while the workman progressed from operation to operation. Under mass production it is the work that progresses from operation to operation. Use-convenience in the commodity would be lessened, while price-convenience would be destroyed. Economy in machine hours is, however, only one element; there is also economy in time and material and labour. Mass production justifies itself only by an economy whose benefits may be transmitted to the purchaser.

## THE EFFECTS OF MASS PRODUCTION

But it is not the history and principle of mass production which provoke the widest discussions; the *effects* of it have been placed under scrutiny. What have been the effects of mass production on society?

(1) Beginning with management, where unquestionably mass production methods take their rise, there is a notable increase in industrial control, as distinguished from financial control. The engineer's point of view has gained the ascendancy and this trend will undoubtedly continue until finance becomes the handmaid instead of the mistress of productive industry. Industrial control has been marked by a continuous refinement of standardization, which means the instant adoption of the better method to the exclusion of the old, in the interests of production. Financial control was not, in its heyday, marked by a tendency to make costly changes in the interests of the product. The economy of scrapping the old equipment immediately upon the invention of the better equipment was not so well understood. It was engineering control, entrenched in mass-production methods, that brought in this new readiness to advance. In this way management

has been kept close to the shop and has reduced the office to a clearing house for the shop. Managers and men have been brought into closer contact and understanding. Manufacturing has been reduced to greater singleness of purpose.

(2) The effect of mass production on the product has been to give it the highest standard of quality ever attained in output of great quantities. Conditions of mass production require material of the best quality to pass successfully through the operations. The utmost accuracy must control all these operations. Every part must be produced to fit at once into the design for which it is made. In mass production there are no fitters. The presence of fitters indicates that the parts have been produced unfit for immediate placement in the design. In works of art and luxury this accuracy is achieved at the cost of careful handiwork. To introduce hand methods of obtaining accuracy into mass production would render mass production impossible with any reference to price-convenience. The standard quality of the product is guaranteed by the fact that machines are so constructed that a piece of work cannot go through them unless it exactly accords with specifications. If the work goes through the tools, it must be right. It will thus be seen that the burden of creation is on management in designing and selecting the material which is to be produced by the multiple processes utilised in mass production.

(3) The effect of mass production on mechanical science has been to create a wide variety of single-purpose machines which not only group similar operations and perform them in quantity, but also reproduce skill of hand to a marvellous degree. It is not so much the discovery of new principles as the new combination and application of old ones that mark this development. Under mass production the industry of machine making has increased out of all comparison with its previous history, and the constant designing of new machines is a part of the productive work of every great manufacturing institution.

(4) The effect of mass production on

employees has been variously appraised. Whether the modern corporation is the destruction or salvation of arts and crafts, whether it narrows or broadens opportunity, whether it assists or retards the personal development of the worker, must be determined by observable facts. A cardinal principle of mass production is that hard work, in the old physical sense of laborious burden-bearing, is wasteful. The physical load is lifted off men and placed on machines. The recurrent mental load is shifted from men in production to men in designing. As to the contention that machines thus become the masters of men, it may be said the machines have increased men's mastery of their environment, and that a generation which is ceaselessly scrapping its machines exhibits few indications of mechanical subjection.

The need for skilled artisans and creative genius is greater under mass production than without it. In entering the shops of the Ford Motor Company, for example, one passes through great departments of skilled mechanics who are not engaged in production, but in the construction and maintenance of the machinery of production. Details of from 5,000 to 10,000 highly skilled artisans at strategic points throughout the shops were not commonly witnessed in the days preceding mass production. It has been debated whether there is less or more skill as a consequence of mass production. The present writer's opinion is that there is more. The common work of the world has always been done by unskilled labour, but the common work of the world in modern times is not as common as it was formerly. In almost every field of labour more knowledge and responsibility are required than a generation or two ago.

*Some Criticisms Answered.* Mass production has also been studied with reference to what has been called the monotony of repetitive work. This monotony does not exist as much in the shops as in the minds of theorists and bookish reformers. There is no form of work without its hardness; but needless hardship has no place in the modern industrial scheme. Mass production lightens work, but increases its repetitive quality. In this it is the opposite of the mediaeval ideal of craftsmanship where the artisan performed every operation, from the preparation of the material to its final form. It is doubtful, however, if the mass of mediaeval toil was as devoid of monotony as has sometimes been pictured, but it is absolutely certain that it was less satisfactory in its results to the worker. In well-managed modern factories the tendency to monotony is combatted by frequent changes of task.

The criticism of mass production as a means of reducing employment has long since been out of court. The experience of the Ford Motor Company is that wherever the number of men has been reduced on manufacturing operations, more jobs have been created. A continuous programme of labour reduction has been paralleled by a continuous increase in employment. As to the effect of mass production on wages and the relations between managers and men, there is little need to speak. It is perhaps the most widely understood fact about mass production that it has resulted in higher wages than any other method of industry. The reason is at hand. The methods of mass production enable the worker to earn more and thus to have more. Moreover, the methods of mass production have thrown so much responsibility on the craftsmanship of management, that the old method of financial adjustment by reduction of wages has been abandoned by scientific manufacturers. A business that must finance by drafts out of the wage envelopes of its employees is not scientifically based. It is the problem of management so to organize production that it will pay the public, the workmen and the concern itself. Management that fails in any of these is poor management. Disturbed labour conditions, poor wages, uncertain profits indicate lapses in management. The craftsmanship of management absorbs the energies of many thousands of men who, without mass production methods, would have no creative opportunity. Here the modern method broadens instead of narrows individual opportunity.

(5) As to the effects of mass production on society, the increasing supply of human needs and the development of new standards of living are the elements to be estimated. The enlargement of leisure, the increase of human contacts, the extension of individual range, are all the result of mass production.

## 11　Burleigh Gardner: *Management and the Worker*

❧ *Many observers, including Henry Ford, tend to view the factory primarily in terms of its technological organization and of the relationship of man to machine. In recent years, social scientists have given increasing attention to the factory as a relationship of men to men, that is, as a social organization. In part, this emphasis developed out of a concern with causes of productive inefficiency and low factory morale. Investigators who began by assuming that "poor work attitudes" are largely the product of a worker's relation to the material conditions of work discovered that his relationship to the social environment in the factory may be more important in forming his work attitudes.*

*Burleigh Gardner (1902–　　) , the author of the analysis of the social system of the factory which follows, has taught at the University of Texas and Brown University. Since 1937 he has been associated with the Personnel Research Department of the Western Electric Company. Among his works are* Man in an Industrial Society *(1947) and* Human Relations in Industry *(revised edition, 1950). Our reading is taken from the last-named book, pp. 14–31, and is used with permission of the publisher, Richard D. Irwin, Inc., of Chicago.*

Examining the factory, we see it as a co-ordinated system of activities directed to the production of goods. It is like a machine of which the component parts are both objects and people, in which each part operates in a very definite and circumscribed way, but in which all parts combine to perform the functions for which the machine was built. . . . In such a system, each individual fits into a definite place within the total pattern. He has his job and his duties; he has his physical location; he is brought into contact with certain other people and objects; he has his circumscribed round of activities. In such a system, too, the individual is important only in terms of his activities and the way he fits into the activities of others. To put it another way, the whole forms a system of relationships in which each individual fills one position and must function according to the needs of that position.

The gross anatomy of the social structure of a factory forms a rough pyramid, with the workers forming a broad base level and the president or plant manager at the top. In between there are a number of layers which make up the supervisory hierarchy and which form a basic status system, with those at each particular level having the same rank in the structure. This structure is linked together from top to bottom by a series of superior-subordinate or boss-worker relations. These linkages running from top to bottom form the lines of authority by which the man at the top directs and controls the entire organization.

Besides the supervisory hierarchy and the lines of authority, there are vertical groupings or lines of cleavage which split the organization into units. These are best shown in the typical organization chart on which the various segments are represented with titles which indicate the differences in function of such units as engineering, manufacturing, and accounting. . . .

As in a physical organism, this whole social structure is linked together by processes of interaction and communication. There are definite channels along which information moves through the structure, the principal ones being the lines of authority and the various systems of reports by means of which certain information is collected and communicated upward through the structure. . . . In the factory, the bulk of information moves upward to the top of the structure, and the orders, questions, and other impulses move back downward. In addition there are a variety of mechanisms by means of which communication is maintained laterally through the system so that all kinds of information spread in all directions. Many of these processes are very irregular and informal, but they work very well. In fact, in most plants the "grapevine" plays an important role in keeping people informed and works faster than the formal channels.

A person's position in this structure determines to a large extent his behavior and his relationships with others and even the way he thinks about his job and the or-ganization. . . . In every case the individual must adjust his behavior to his place in the structure; he must adapt himself to the needs of the job rather than adapt the job to himself. Thus the individual is constantly subordinated to the structure, for otherwise it would be impossible to maintain the highly complex co-ordination of activities essential to the functioning of a modern factory. . . .

In addition to this formal organization, and existing with its framework, are elaborate patterns of relationships and activities which the people work out for themselves. For each worker there are patterns of individual friendships and dislikes, people he feels close to, whose feelings or values he respects, and those to whom he is opposed or indifferent. From these individual reactions arise the cliques, the informal leaders and their followers, the groups which oppose each other, and those who stand together on issues ranging from whether to open or close the windows to whether to strike or not. All these patterns of relationship and behavior are a spontaneous growth, influenced but not directed by the formal organization or by the intentions of management. They constitute the human element in the work situations and appear wherever groups of people are thrown into constant contact with one another.

. . . This structure [of formal organization] and its system of relationships is, for the most part, stable; it retains its pattern in spite of changes in personnel. People may come into the system, move from position to position in it, and move out again, yet the pattern remains intact. And while details may vary from time to time or from factory to factory, the basic elements are stable and appear in every large plant. This stability does not mean, however, that there is never any change, for there are constant changes in personnel, fluctuations in size, and various other modifications of the structure. In other words, the structure is not static or rigid, but it is stable within certain limits, in that the basic elements, the general patterns of interaction, remain the same.

This social system can be thought of as existing in such a state of equilibrium that it has a tendency to maintain itself intact against external forces. "By equilibrium" we mean a kind of balance of forces such that, when some change is imposed upon the system, forces are generated which resist the change and which may restore the original balance, once the outside pressure is removed. . . .

## THE SUPERVISORY HIERARCHY

. . . The heart of the social organization [of industry] is the relationship between the individual and his direct boss. This is the order-giving, as well as the status, relationship between superior and subordinate. Every person except one within the structure has a boss; and every boss, in turn, has his boss, until finally at the top of the heap we find that rare and practically sacred individual, the president, the owner, the big-shot-who-has-no-boss. . . .

The whole structure forms a neat pyramid, with the Big Boss at the top and each rank of lesser bosses increasing in numbers as they decrease in importance, until at the bottom of the supervisory structure there is the largest and perhaps the most misunderstood group, the foremen or first-line supervisors. The whole forms a status system with all foremen having a rank superior to the workers, all the next level outranking the foremen, and so on.

Although each department chief outranks every foreman, it does not follow that a foreman will take orders from any department chief or even from any superintendent. . . . Instead, each person has his own personal boss to whom he looks for orders and instructions, for praise and criticism, for rewards and punishments. This extends on up to the top, so that each person is linked up to the Big Boss through a series of these man-boss relationships. This forms what is known as the "line of authority," or "chain of command" in the army. Since each level has more persons in it than the level above, each boss, as a rule, has more than one person reporting to him.

This gives the fan-shaped pattern so well known on the formal organization charts, with a number of lines of authority merging at each level until finally they all merge into the supreme command of the Big Boss.

Just as the lines of authority converge toward the top of the structure, the lines of interest and attention converge too. In fact, everyone seems to be looking upward with his attention focused upon the people above him and especially upon his boss. His boss is the man who hands out the orders, assigns him to his work, gives him a pat on the back for a good job, and passes on a good word for him to the "higher-ups." And his boss is the man who can give him a dirty job to do, criticize him for doing it poorly, and give him a bad name up the line. His boss is his link with those above him in the structure. Thus the likes and dislikes of the boss, his moods and opinions, his comings and goings, his least comment and gesture, or the way he is distracted by that cute little redhead from the next department, all these are subjects of interest to his subordinates. . . .

While each boss is thus the center of attention from his subordinates, he in turn is busy watching his own boss and wondering about him. As a result he tends to look upon his subordinates in quite a different way. He rarely worries about their opinions of him. . . . He does not even remember that he is the center of their attention, and he is likely to be annoyed with them if they are upset by his indifference or demand a lot of his time.

Thus we have a series of man-boss relationships in which each person is intensely concerned with how his boss judges him and at the same time is busy judging his subordinates. Each is constantly looking at his subordinates, trying to determine how well they are doing their jobs, and how they might do better work, and each is constantly being irritated and disturbed when they fall short of what he thinks they should be doing. At the same time, his concept of the job is constantly being mixed up with what his boss will think and what *he* expects, until "doing a job" often becomes a matter of "doing what the boss thinks is good.". . .

The supervisory structure is, then, a status system in which it is accepted as a matter of course that each level has more status and prestige than the ones below it. . . . The problem of status or prestige does not end with this simple supervisory hierarchy, however, but intrudes itself into all sorts of situations and in innumerable guises. . . .

### SHOP-OFFICE DISTINCTIONS

In the first place we find important status distinction between shop and office or "white-collar" jobs. Despite the talk about the "dignity of labor" and the pleasures of working with your hands, there is an almost universal feeling that the office jobs are in some sense "superior" to the shop jobs and that the person who runs a typewriter or adding machine has a higher status than the person who runs a drill press. This feeling was well expressed by a girl working on a shop job, who said:

I'd really like to work in the office. Isn't it funny the way office people treat factory people? I don't see any difference between them myself, but the office people think they are so much better than the girls who work in the factory. Lots of them have the same education as the office girls, and we are just as refined as they are. They seem to think that factory girls are loud and rough, but there are just as many girls in the office who drink and smoke and are immoral as the girls in the shop. It just seems that having an office job makes them feel that they're better than we are. . . .

. . . The person who occupies the higher status position tends to identify himself with the status of his position until it becomes a part of him which he carries into all his contacts with those of lesser status. Thus the girl who had obtained an office job began to draw apart from her former factory friends, and the factory girl was looked down upon by the office girls whom she met in church. . . .

This interview . . . shows the general feeling of superiority which the higher status group has toward the lower. Not only

is their work felt to be of a higher order of importance or value, but they are superior beings. The office group tends to look down upon the shopworkers as inferiors in mind, manner, and morals. The shopworkers have grimy hands and poor taste, they say; they are loud-mouthed and use coarse language; they are less educated, or at least less intellectual. Although these attitudes of office workers may seem to be extreme expressions of feelings of superiority, similar feelings are expressed by every high-status group toward their "inferiors.". . .

### STATUS AND WAGES

The rate of pay or earnings is, of course, another important source of status differences. This is quite in keeping with a business or factory as an economic enterprise in which everything is supposedly evaluated in terms of money. Thus the higher the pay, the higher the status of the job or the individual. The ten-thousand-dollar-a-year man is far superior to the five-thousand-dollar man, or the dollar-forty-an-hour shopworker is superior to the eighty-five-cent man. . . . As a result, every work situation in which there is a gradation of wages has a status hierarchy revolving around these wages and one which is readily upset by any changes in the wage structure.

There is also a status system based upon the different kinds of jobs found in any work group. As a rule the jobs requiring the most skill are at the top and those requiring the least are at the bottom, although other factors may enter in to disturb such a simple arrangement. For example, a job which receives a great deal of attention and recognition from the boss may become the superior job even though other jobs in the group require more skill. Sometimes, too, jobs acquire status because they are always held by long-service people who receive recognition because of their service.

### SENIORITY AND STATUS

Seniority forms the basis for other status differences, with the old-timers feeling that they are somehow superior to the young people and newcomers. In most stable companies there is a feeling toward long-service people something like the attitude toward age which we find in our society generally. The youngsters are thought of as lacking in knowledge and understanding and are expected to give recognition and deference to their elders, while the very old have a place with certain rights and privileges because of their age. . . .

### ORGANIZATIONAL DIFFERENCES

There are also status differences among organizations, and in any plant there are usually certain organizations which are generally thought of as superior to others. The shop-office distinction accounts for some of this, as the strictly office organizations are usually superior to the shop organizations. As a result a typist or file clerk with the shop department is usually thought to have a "poorer," that is lower-status, job than the typist or file clerk in an accounting department. Also organizations such as engineering or sales, where much of the work requires technical skills or special training, are usually of status superior to shop or accounting organizations. In all such cases the feeling of superiority does not remain merely the prerogative of the salesman or engineers but carries over even to the most routine jobs in the organization. The office boy in the engineering department, for example, is apt to feel superior to the office boy in the accounting organization.

### COMPLICATING FACTORS

These status systems are not nicely co-ordinated, however, so that the older person always gets more money, has the better job, or is higher in the supervisory structure. We see old-timers in some of the poorest jobs at the lowest pay. We see bright young executives who, with only short service, have climbed high in the supervisory ranks. We see office jobs paying less than shop jobs, or skilled workers earning more than their foremen. We see innumerable complicating factors so that it seems impossible to present a simple picture of the status relationships between individuals within any plant or even in any one department.

We do find, however, that there is a feeling that these various status systems *should* be co-ordinated. This is most strongly expressed in the idea that superiors should earn more than their subordinates. Generally in the supervisory structure wages rise rapidly as you go up in the structure, and it is usually felt to be wrong for a foreman to get less pay than his subordinates. There is also some tendency for wages to increase with age, and a feeling that this should be so, especially when the rate of pay is not rigidly tied to the kind of job. Also the more highly skilled jobs are often held by the long-service people who have worked themselves up. Interestingly enough, the status difference between office and shop is usually not recognized in pay, especially at the lower levels. Apparently the office jobs are sufficiently attractive, especially to girls, that they are preferred even if the wages are lower, so that in many organizations we find these "better" jobs being paid considerably less than the others.

### "PLACING" PEOPLE

A matter of common interest and concern to everyone in the factory is the problem of "place" in the social organization. Everyone wants to know where other people "fit" in terms of the functional relations of the work and, what is to many even more important, in terms of the status systems. The newcomer is always faced by the questions, "Who are you?" and "Where do you fit?" In fact, one of the important aspects of getting acquainted on a new job is the process by which the newcomer finds out just where he belongs. He learns whom he will work with and what their relationship is to him and to each other; he learns who are his superiors in the line of authority, who can give him orders and who can not, to whom he should defer and whom he can ignore. All this is the real function of much of the introduction and conversation which often takes place when a new worker comes into a group. . . .

## SYMBOLS OF STATUS

Because of the importance of status, the individual himself is greatly concerned that he be placed properly, at least not in a position inferior to what he actually occupies. The private may be amused to be mistaken for a lieutenant, but the lieutenant who is mistaken for a private is really burned up. Undoubtedly that is one of the important functions of military insignia. In industry people feel much the same way, with the result that almost every large plant has developed its own insignia, its own set of symbols by means of which everyone can be placed properly in the status system. In general these symbols are not the simple and obvious types evolved by the armed forces but are much more subtle and indirect. The sort of clothes you wear, the desk you sit at, the position of your desk or work bench, the machine you operate, and many other things may indicate status. In fact, these things are often so indirect that the outsider is not aware that such a symbol system exists at all. . . .

Because of the importance of the distinction between shop and office, there is a strong tendency to differentiate between them in many ways, each of which becomes a symbol to indicate the position of the individual. While the nature of the work usually leads to a separation between office and shop groups, the separation itself becomes an important symbol of the difference in status. As a result, most office workers are upset and feel that they have lost status if they are moved from an office location to a shop location even though there is no change in the job. In most large plants where there is a separation of the office and shop organizations, there are usually separate washrooms for the office people, and any attempt to have the office people use the shop washrooms, or to bring shop people into the office washrooms, meets with the strong resistance from the office people. To be forced to share lockers or washrooms with these "uncouth and inferior" people is a bitter pill to the office people. . . .

In many companies there is a payroll distinction, too, between shop and office, the shopworkers being paid by the hour and the office by the week. Since both groups are actually paid every week, there is no obvious difference, yet the different payrolls assume the status differences of the two groups. And to move from the hourly to the weekly or salaried payroll is a step up in the world. In some cases this difference may be accentuated by having different time clocks or a different pay day for each group, so that there remains no doubt as to where a person fits. . . .

An almost universal characteristic of all types of status hierarchies is that certain prerogatives accompany high status; and as one ascends in the structure he acquires certain rights and privileges which are denied to those below him. Some of these rights have to do with the symbols of status themselves. As one is promoted, he acquires the right to display the insignia of his new place. Others are much more tangible rewards, such as increased freedom from restraints, special rights, additional pay, and so on. . . .

These symbolic distinctions are well shown, too, in the shop-office division, with the office usually having definite privileges denied to the shop. For example, office workers frequently have a longer lunch hour than shop; they may be free to leave their desks to go to the washroom whenever they please, while the shop is limited to fixed rest pauses. Through the device of the weekly pay, the office workers may take time off or come in late without penalty, while the hourly paid shop workers are usually paid only for the time they are actually on the job.

It is interesting that foremen are generally on the weekly payroll and so are grouped with the office people. It appears, then, that the ordinary factory is split into two groups, one of which is composed of the hourly-paid shop workers, the other of the weekly-paid office workers and the entire supervisory staff. The non-supervisory office workers, furthermore, tend to think of themselves as akin to the supervisory and executive group rather than to the shop workers.

Within the office group itself there is usually a high development of status symbols. Almost anything in the work situation seems to have potentialities for becoming such a symbol whether it be a desk, chair, telephone, location, arrangement of furniture, or whatnot. For example, a telephone directory usually becomes a sort of *Who's Who* which reflects status more than phone calls. Whether you have a telephone on your desk, or share one with the next desk, or have none at all may be a direct reflection of your status and is usually interpreted that way. In one large organization desks were an important symbol: the lowest clerical workers worked at tables, the next level had single-pedestal desks with one bank of drawers, the supervisors had larger, double-pedestal desks with two banks of drawers, and so on, up to the plant manager who had a great big desk of fancy woods. In such a system, to give a man a promotion without the proper desk would have given rise to elaborate speculations as to whether he really rated the title or just what was wrong. . . .

In the same way, offices for executives become important symbols of status. In most large organizations there are certain superior offices which, because of size or location, are preferred. Usually these better offices are occupied by the top-ranking men in the organization and reflect their status. Other offices may fit into the status pattern on the basis of their proximity to the "brass hats." Thus the office next to the president is superior to the one down the hall. Where offices occupy several floors of a tall building, the higher offices usually have the most status. The manager or president usually occupies the top floor, and the lesser officials are found somewhere below. In such cases moving to a higher floor is getting up in the world in more ways than one. The importance of location as a status symbol affects the people who work for executives, too, so that their secretaries, stenographers, and even their office boys, feel very strongly the status significance of working on the top floor or in the office next to the president's suite. . . .

Among shopworkers, on the other hand, there is not quite as much emphasis upon status symbols. In general, a person's position in the shop is pretty clearly shown by the work he is doing. The man operating an automatic screw machine is obviously different from the sweeper or material handler, the machinist is superior to his helper, and anyone familiar with shop work can place people easily in the general status system. This does not mean that shop workers are not concerned about status, but merely that the work itself provides fairly obvious status insignia.

With office people, however, as pointed out, the symbols of status are often a major concern and changes in them are sure to create disturbances. To account for such emphasis is difficult, but we may present two possible hypotheses. In the first place, the office and supervisory groups probably contain more people trying to get up in the world, who want to improve their status. And these people naturally want to display evidence of any gains; they want people to know where they belong. At the same time, the nature of office work is such that all jobs look alike from a distance; people sitting at desks writing and shuffling papers may be either important executives of the most unimportant clerks. For that reason it becomes important that the superior people acquire symbols to distinguish them from the rest. . . .

These status symbols are a constant source of conflict and anxiety. Each watches his equals lest they acquire symbols which he lacks; each longs to have the choice office or the large desk and schemes to get it; each judges the importance of his job by symbols which go with it.

As a result every change in arrangement, every movement of people or organizations, may upset the status systems and cause trouble.

## SELECTED REFERENCES FOR PART 3

ASHTON, T. S. *The Industrial Revolution*. London: Oxford Univ. Press, 1948.

A concise summary of the author's researches on the effects of the rise of modern industry on social life. Disputes many older views.

BOWDEN, WITT, MICHAEL KARPOVITCH, and ABBOTT PAYSON USHER. *An Economic History of Europe Since 1750*. New York: American Book Co., 1937.

Contains valuable maps, graphs, and bibliography.

BURLINGAME, ROGER. *Backgrounds of Power: The Human Story of Mass Production*. New York: Scribner's, 1949.

The latest installment in the author's panoramic survey of the relations between the developments of technology and society in the United States.

CLAPHAM, JOHN. *A Concise Economic History of Britain*. Cambridge, England: The University Press, 1949.

———. *The Economic Development of France and Germany*. Cambridge, England: The University Press, 1921.

Two of the most valuable of the distinguished historian's works.

CLARK, VICTOR. *History of Manufacture in the United States*. New York: McGraw-Hill, 1929.

An essential guide.

COCHRAN, THOMAS CHILDS, and WILLIAM MILLER. *The Age of Enterprise, a Social History of Industrial America*. New York: Macmillan, 1942.

A lively account of the growth of American big business.

COMMONS, JOHN R. *The Legal Foundations of Capitalism*. New York: Macmillan, 1924.

Stimulating discussions of the changes worked in and by the legal structure as a result of the development of capitalism.

———, ULRICH B. PHILLIPS, EUGENE A. GILMORE, HELEN L. SUMNER, and JOHN B. ANDREWS (eds.). *A Documentary History of American Industrial Society*. 11 vols. Cleveland: A. H. Clark Co., 1910–11.

A mine of materials.

DOBB, MAURICE H. *Studies in the Development of Capitalism*. London: G. Routledge, 1946.

Thoughtful papers by an avowed Marxist.

FAY, C. R. *Life and Labour in the Nineteenth Century*. Cambridge, England: The University Press, 1920.

A vigorously written survey by a specialist.

FORBES, R. J. *Man the Maker*. New York: Henry Schuman, Inc., 1950.

Subtitled: "A History of Technology and Engineering."

FURNESS, EDGAR S. *The Position of the Laborer in a System of Nationalism*. Boston: Houghton Mifflin, 1920.

Exposes the low view of the worker characteristic of the mercantilist economists of the seventeenth and eighteenth centuries.

HAMMOND, J. L. and BARBARA HAMMOND. *The Rise of Modern Industry*. New York: Harcourt, 1926.

Summarizes the authors' studies of the life of laboring men in the first phase of the Industrial Revolution.

HEATON, HERBERT. *The Economic History of Europe*. Rev. Ed. New York: Harper, 1948.

A standard text.

HERSKOVITS, M. J. *The Economic Life of Primitive Peoples*. New York: Knopf, 1940.

A summary of research.

HOBSON, J. A. *The Evolution of Modern Capitalism*. New York: Macmillan, 1949.

Illustrates the trend toward collectivism in the development of modern industry, enterprise, and society.

JOHNSON, E. A. J. *Some Origins of the Modern Economic World.* New York: Macmillan, 1937.

A popularly written account of the economic development of early modern Europe.

LIPSON, E. *The Growth of English Society.* New York: Holt, 1950.

A concise account of the author's extensive researches on England's economic development.

MANTOUX, PAUL. *The Industrial Revolution in the Eighteenth Century.* London: Basil Blackwell, 1928.

An outstanding treatise on the meaning and development of the Industrial Revolution.

PIRENNE, HENRI. *Economic and Social History of Medieval Europe.* Translated by I. E. Clegg. New York: Harcourt, 1937.

A masterly summary of medieval developments by the eminent Belgian historian. His account of economic and social unrest in the towns of Northern Italy and the towns of Flanders should help to dispel many popular illusions concerning the peacefulness and contentment of medieval men.

RICHARDS, AUDREY. *Hunger and Work in a Savage Tribe: A Functional Study of Nutrition Among the Southern Bantu.* Preface by Bronislaw Malinowski. Glencoe, Ill.: The Free Press, 1948.

Analyzes the division of labor and work ideals in primitive society.

SCHUMPETER, JOSEPH A. *Imperialism and Social Classes.* Translated by Heinz Norden. Edited with introduction by Paul M. Sweezy. New York: Augustus M. Kelley, 1951.

Contains two notable essays, "The Sociology of Imperialism" and "Social Classes in an Ethnically Homogeneous Environment."

SHANNON, FRED ALBERT. *America's Economic Growth,* 3rd Edition. New York: Macmillan, 1951.

A vigorously written text.

TAWNEY, R. H. *Land and Labour in China.* London: Allen & Unwin, 1932.

Economics and culture in a society now in the throes of the transition to industrialization.

————. *Religion and the Rise of Capitalism.* New York: Harcourt, 1926. Also, New York: Penguin Books, 1947.

A celebrated attempt to trace the connections between the Protestant Reformation and the rise of commercial capitalism. Tawney is particularly concerned with discovering how Western man came to consider economic life independent of ethics and religion. In his judgment the notion that "business is business" resulted from the breakdown of the medieval structure of moral and social thought from the sixteenth through the eighteenth centuries.

UNWIN, GEORGE. *Industrial Organization in the Sixteenth and Seventeenth Centuries.* Oxford: Clarendon Press, 1904.

Careful studies of industry and business organization in early modern England.

USHER, A. P. *A History of Mechanical Inventions.* New York: McGraw-Hill, 1929.

A basic guide.

VEBLEN, THORSTEIN. *Imperial Germany and the Industrial Revolution.* New York: Viking, 1939.

Emphasizes the significance for German development of its relative lateness in adopting the industrial pattern. Offers important clues for the understanding of economic and political rivalries among the Great Powers in the era of the First World War.

WEBER, MAX. *General Economic History.* Translated by Frank H. Knight. Glencoe, Ill.: The Free Press, 1950.

Posthumously published lectures on the evolution of capitalism by the author of *The Protestant Ethic and the Spirit of Capitalism.*

# PART 4

# The worker and
# the workless

❦ In this Part we continue our study of the impact of industrial society by looking closely at seven groups which are at least somewhat representative of the
variety of occupations in our economy. In the strict sense, the last of these groups
can hardly be called an "occupational" group, for it is made up not of people who
work, but of people who are unemployed. But if we think of the whole problem
in terms of the various occupational statuses which are allotted to different people, then we may think of "not working" as the particular lot which (at least for
a time) is assigned to certain members of our society, just as working as a waitress, a coal miner, or a banker, is the lot appointed to another person. If we look
at the problem in one way, indeed, we may observe that the industrial economy
has never succeeded in solving the problem of unemployment; and from this
standpoint, perhaps we may view unemployment as simply one of the many occupational "roles" produced by an industrialized and specialized economy.

One of the striking and important facts about the division of labor, as has
already been pointed out, is that each person tends to come to know more and
more about his own job, and less and less about everyone else's. Since one's job,
in terms of time spent at work, tends to occupy up to a half of every employed
person's waking day, and since the impact of his job does not begin when he
checks in in the morning or checks out at night, whole "ways of life" tend to form
around different occupations. One's occupation tends to determine the group with
whom one associates and one's "world-view."

This clustering of people into occupational groups more or less isolated from
one another has a host of important implications. One is the fact that although we,
as members of society at large, may be quite dependent upon another occupational group, we may know next to nothing about it. Thus, for example, GEORGE
ORWELL points out in our first selection that the work of the coal miner is indispensable to all the "higher" things of life and that the "higher" occupational
groups are at all times dependent upon the work of men in the mines. Yet this
life of the mines, and the total lives of those who work in them, may be as alien to
us as the life of some primitive tribe. At the same time—as, for example, when

the "public" is called upon to take a stand in a dispute in the coal industry—we must play a part, active or passive, in making decisions about a part of our economy of which we may be almost completely ignorant.

If we look at the problem from the standpoint of the miner—or the waitress, or the banker, or the white-collar worker, or the entrepreneur, or the hobo, or the unemployed person, who are the other occupational groups we shall study— then we may find that they are quite familiar with the narrow round of their own life, but are unable to get any sense of where it fits in, what it means, in the total picture of society. And since it seems that people find difficulty in doing work which is meaningless or whose meaning they do not understand, this fact raises a second and related problem which deserves our attention. How are people who are allotted to one economic role to understand the roles of others with whom they are interdependent; and how are they to relate the work they do to the on- going of the whole economy in such a way as to find meaning in it?

The first reading in this Part deals, as Orwell suggests, with an occupational group which may be considered typical of manual industrial labor. In Orwell's de- scription of the pits we can see clearly the phenomenon to which we have already alluded: the shaping of an *occupational type* through the work for which an oc- cupation calls. To be able to crawl through and work in openings which may be no more than waist or chest high, to be able to lift heavy loads in these surround- ings, requires a wiriness and a leanness, whether one be eighteen or sixty-five. The occupation of coal mining selects persons of a particular physical constitu- tion, and rejects those who do not meet specifications. Having selected them, it tends to mold them further into the occupational pattern. (In the case of the coal miner, his work requires that he keep thin). This selection and molding, which in the case of the coal miner takes a physically visible form, may in other occupa- tions take a less visible and more "psychological" or "social" form.

Thus, to those who are familiar with college professors or college presidents, it seems likely that they constitute an occupational "type" in much the same sense as do coal miners. It is likely that the occupation to which they are called selects people with certain temperaments and world-views; it is also likely that, once they have been "enrolled" in their occupation, their job tends further to shape their behavior, their mannerisms, and their interests.

Our second occupational type is the worker in the "service" trades, as repre- sented by the waitress. Perhaps the central characteristic of the waitress, as de- scribed by FRANCES DONOVAN, is the impermanence and uncertainty of her job. Again, on the one hand, this profession probably tends to select people who, for one reason or another, are unable or unwilling to accept a job which "ties them down"; on the other hand, the uncertainty and instability of the profession itself tends to develop and accentuate the tendency to be "mobile" and "footloose." One important effect, which the author points out, is the low morale among wait- resses as a group: each tends to look out for herself, co-operation among waitresses is low, and the occupation tends to be looked upon purely as a "job" which has to be done for a living.

The social position and ideology of the salaried or white-collar worker are described by CARL DREYFUSS. The author is particularly concerned with the "myths" which are built by people in this group in order to justify to themselves the job which they are doing: for the most part they think of themselves as belonging with "management" rather than with "labor," as doing jobs which require special independence, initiative, and responsibility, in spite of the fact that to a large extent they too are simply cogs in a "production line." Thus they may be willing to accept what are in fact quite menial and low-paid positions because of the prestige which they attribute to themselves by virtue of their occupational myths.

JOHN P. MARQUAND, in the next reading, takes us inside the life of an aspiring junior executive in a bank. One of the things particularly pointed out by Marquand is the intense insecurity of the professional person who is trying to "get ahead" in his hierarchy. On the one hand, he must present to the public the picture of a thoroughly solid, responsible person capable of handling the financial problems of those making ten times his own income, and must present to his associates the picture of a "good fellow" who is concerned with nothing except the "service" which his profession is presumed to perform. On the other hand, he may be lying awake nights wondering whether he or his rival is going to be promoted to the vacant desk of a vice-president, knowing that the minor employees probably already have a betting pool on which of the two is going to "make it."

The next selection, a thumbnail sketch by ROBERT FETRIDGE of the meteoric career of William Lear, a pioneer in many of the latest developments in the aviation industry, permits us to study the personality and role of another type of "worker" in our society, the enterpriser or entrepreneur. Judgments about the role of the entrepreneur in the modern economy have run the whole gamut from the indictment of the capitalist as the robber baron "expropriating" the fruits of the worker's toil, to the glorification of the enterprising businessman as the pathfinder of "progress," the indispensable agent of America's dynamic economy and high standard of living.

The story of the entrepreneur described in our selection sums up the major elements in the saga of the American businessman as hero. Like Andrew Carnegie, he started at the bottom. Like Henry Ford, he seems bent on always moving forward in the direction suggested by mechanical development. Like Walter P. Crysler, he promises to remain to the end "an American workman." Fetridge's sketch has been chosen because it does offer a most favorable view of the ideal of entrepreneurship, which continues to characterize American culture.

In the selection by NELS ANDERSON we meet three types who are generally considered as being on the fringes of the economy and of polite society: the hobo, the tramp, and the bum. The three groups are not to be confused: the hobo is a migratory worker who "works and wanders"; the tramp "thinks and wanders"; the bum "drinks and wanders." In the life-organization and the world-view of the hobo, especially important are his sense of the significance of his economic role (to him, the economy could not operate were he not on hand to perform seasonal and migratory labor); his sense of the superiority of the "mobile" way of life to that of the person "tied to his job"; and his strong sense of group morale and cohesion (we may contrast the hobo—who has a national organization, a newspaper, and a "college"—with the waitress, for example).

The final reading in this Part, from the PILGRIM TRUST study of the unemployed in Britain, is concerned both with the factors which "select" a person for "membership" in the group of the unemployed, and with the way in which the individual is shaped by his role. Here we are concerned with trying to understand what it means to be out of work. It should be remembered that although unemployment tends to select some people who are lazy, shiftless, and inefficient, this group does not by any means make up the major part of the role of unemployment during a great economic depression. Unemployment strikes at large groups of people who have been conscientious, hard-working, industrious, and possessed of all the virtues which are generally valued. What, the Pilgrim Trust selection asks, does it do to them, in terms of their political attitudes, their attitudes toward going back to work, their family and social life?

A mere listing of all the different occupations performed in the United States would fill many pages. Obviously, we have only begun to sample the varieties of occupational roles in our society. However, we have tried to select a representative sample, that is, one which will give us a feeling for the major types of occupational experience in our society.

We noted earlier that the differences of occupational experience in a complex society tend to isolate occupational groups from one another. Some writers have felt that the intensified division of labor in modern industry inherently creates a feeling of isolation and lack of coherence in life at large. Emile Durkheim (1858–1917) introduced the term *anomie* to designate the absence of common values or norms, and a lack of sense of rhyme or reason in life. Many more recent students have felt that economic matters such as wages and hours are far less significant as factors in explaining absenteeism, fatigue, low productivity, and labor unrest than are the aimlessness, the poor morale, and the lack of social cohesion or "team spirit" in the relations of individuals and groups in the industrial community and in society at large.

Other writers, however, point to increasing signs that new patterns of integration, revolving around the industrial unit, are under way. Today, as Peter Drucker has observed, the enterprise unit—whether it be an industrial plant, commercial firm, university, hospital, government bureau, or labor union—is tending to develop the character of an autonomous and independent *community,* with its own mores, rules, language patterns, ladders of mobility, and goals. The function men perform and the status they enjoy *within this unit* may come to be the decisive fact about their lives. Moreover, as this unit expands, it inclines to absorb into itself a complex of related functions, cultural as well as economic, and to take on the appearance of an *embracing society*. In time it might even become difficult to tell precisely which function, if any, is central to the life of the enterprise unit.

Thus, many large-scale corporations today perform all sorts of functions beyond the ones for which they were originally organized. Whether their business be that of automobile manufacturing, protection of the interests of labor, public administration, or the instruction of university students, these enterprise units are likely to own real estate, air fields, newspapers, radio stations, and to conduct commissaries, lunchrooms, hospitals, and educational and recreational programs. The sense of belonging which is denied to so many in the society at large is now achieved through identification with the goals, personnel, and way of life of the enterprise unit.

How profoundly these novel patterns are affecting political developments in the twentieth century will be discussed more fully in Part 5.

SECTION A

**The worker and his work**

# 12 George Orwell: *The Miner of Coal*

❦ *The life of the coal miner is largely shaped by the perils and tasks associated with employment in his particular industry. In a general sense, he may be regarded as a prototype of a whole range of manual workers in heavy industry and transport—the steel worker, the auto worker, the railroader, each of whom has a special outlook and style of life fashioned in large measure by the kind of work he is called upon to perform.*

*The following reading describes the coal miner's work, suggesting how it shapes his personality, his physique, and his social outlook. George Orwell, the author, was born in 1903 and died in 1950. He was an English novelist and essayist whose social criticisms gradually won for him a secure place in the world of letters. He was interested in the policeman, the dishwasher, the tramp, and the manual worker; and he was an acute analyst of such modern phenomena as imperialism and the totalitarian state. Among his writings are* The Road to Wigan Pier (1937); Animal Farm (1945), a *satire on dictatorship; and* Nineteen Eighty-Four (*1949*), *a novel which depicts the brutalization of life in a totalitarian world order.*

Our reading is taken from The Road to Wigan Pier, *pp. 21–35, and is used with permission of the publisher, Victor Gollancz.*

When you go down a coal-mine it is important to try and get to the coal face when the "fillers" are at work. This is not easy, because when the mine is working visitors are a nuisance and are not encouraged, but if you go at any other time, it is possible to come away with a totally wrong impression. On a Sunday, for instance, a mine seems almost peaceful. The time to go there is when the machines are roaring and the air is black with coal dust, and when you can actually see what the miners have to do. At those times the place is like hell, or at any rate like my own mental picture of hell. Most of the things one imagines in hell are there—heat, noise, confusion, darkness, foul air, and, above all, unbearably cramped space. Everything except the fire, for there is no fire down there except the feeble beams of Davy lamps and electric torches which scarcely penetrate the clouds of coal dust.

When you have finally got there—and getting there is a job in itself: I will explain that in a moment—you crawl through the last line of pit props and see opposite you a shiny black wall three or four feet high. This is the coal face. Overhead is the smooth ceiling made by the rock from which the coal has been cut; underneath is the rock again, so that the gallery you are in is only as high as the ledge of coal itself, probably not much more than a yard. The first impression of all, overmastering everything else for a while, is the frightful, deafening din from the conveyor belt which carries the coal away. You cannot see very far, because the fog of coal dust throws back the beam of your lamp, but you can see on either side of you the line of half-naked kneeling men, one to every four or five yards, driving their shovels under the

fallen coal and flinging it swiftly over their left shoulders. They are feeding it on to the conveyor belt, a moving rubber belt a couple of feet wide which runs a yard or two behind them. Down this belt a glittering river of coal races constantly. In a big mine it is carrying away several tons of coal every minute. It bears it off to some place in the main roads where it is shot into tubs holding half a ton, and thence dragged to the cages and hoisted to the outer air.

It is impossible to watch the "fillers" at work without feeling a pang of envy for their toughness. It is a dreadful job that they do, an almost superhuman job by the standards of an ordinary person. For they are not only shifting monstrous quantities of coal, they are also doing it in a position that doubles or trebles the work. They have got to remain kneeling all the while—they could hardly rise from their knees without hitting the ceiling—and you can easily see by trying it what a tremendous effort this means. Shovelling is comparatively easy when you are standing up, because you can use your knee and thigh to drive the shovel along; kneeling down, the whole of the strain is thrown upon your arm and belly muscles. And the other conditions do not exactly make things easier. There is the heat—it varies, but in some mines it is suffocating—and the coal dust that stuffs up your throat and nostrils and collects along your eyelids, and the unending rattle of the conveyor belt, which in that confined space is rather like the rattle of a machine gun. But the fillers look and work as though they were made of iron. They really do look like iron—hammered iron statues—under the smooth coat of coal dust which clings to them from head to foot. It is only when you see miners down the mine and naked that you realise what splendid men they are. Most of them are small (big men are at a disadvantage in that job) but nearly all of them have the most noble bodies; wide shoulders tapering to slender supple waists, and small pronounced buttocks and sinewy thighs, with not an ounce of waste flesh anywhere. In the hotter mines they wear only a pair of thin drawers, clogs and knee-pads; in the hottest mines of all, only the clogs and knee-pads. You can hardly tell by the look of them whether they are young or old. They may be any age up to sixty or even sixty-five, but when they are black and naked they all look alike. No one could do their work who had not a young man's body, and a figure fit for a guardsman at that; just a few pounds of extra flesh on the waist-line, and the constant bending would be impossible. You can never forget that spectacle once you have seen it—the line of bowed, kneeling figures, sooty black all over, driving their huge shovels under the coal with stupendous force and speed. They are on the job for seven and a half hours, theoretically without a break, for there is no time "off." Actually they snatch a quarter of an hour or so at some time during the shift to eat the food they have brought with them, usually a hunk of bread and dripping and a bottle of cold tea. The first time I was watching the "fillers" at work I put my hand upon some dreadful slimy thing among the coal dust. It was a chewed quid of tobacco. Nearly all the miners chew tobacco, which is said to be good against thirst.

Probably you have to go down several coal-mines before you can get much grasp of the processes that are going on round you. This is chiefly because the mere effort of getting from place to place makes it difficult to notice anything else. In some ways it is even disappointing, or at least is unlike what you have expected. You get into the cage, which is a steel box about as wide as a telephone box and two or three times as long. It holds ten men, but they pack it like pilchards in a tin, and a tall man cannot stand upright in it. The steel door shuts upon you, and somebody working the winding gear above drops you into the void. You have the usual momentary qualm in your belly and a bursting sensation in the ears, but not much sensation of movement till you get near the bottom, when the cage slows down so abruptly that you could swear it is going upwards again. In the middle of the run the cage probably touches sixty miles an hour; in some of the deeper mines it touches even more. When you crawl out at the bottom you are perhaps four hundred yards under ground. That is to say you have a tolerable-sized mountain on top of you; hundreds of yards of solid rock, bones of extinct beasts, subsoil, flints, roots of growing things, green grass and cows grazing on it—all this suspended over your head and held back only by wooden props as thick as the calf of your leg. But because of the speed at which the cage has brought you down, and the complete blackness through which you have travelled, you hardly feel yourself deeper down than you would at the bottom of the Piccadilly tube. . . .

It may seem that I am exaggerating, though no one who has been down an old-fashioned pit (most of the pits in England are old-fashioned) and actually gone as far as the coal face, is likely to say so. But what I want to emphasise is this. Here is this frightful business of crawling to and fro, which to any normal person is a hard day's work in itself; and it is not part of the miner's work at all, it is merely an extra, like the City man's daily ride in the Tube. The miner does that journey to and fro, and sandwiched in between there are seven and a half hours of savage work. I have never travelled much more than a mile to the coal face; but often it is three miles, in which case I and most people other than coal-miners would never get there at all. This is the kind of point that one is always liable to miss. When you think of a coal-mine you think of depth, heat, darkness, blackened figures hacking at walls of coal; you don't think, necessarily, of those miles of creeping to and fro. There is the question of time, also. A miner's working shift of seven and a half hours does not sound very long, but one has got to add on to it at least an hour a day for "travelling," more often two hours and sometimes three. Of course, the "travelling" is not technically work and the miner is not paid for it; but it is as like work as makes no difference. It is easy to say that miners don't mind all this. Certainly, it is not the same for them as it would be for you or me. They have done it since childhood, they have the right muscles hardened, and they can move to and fro underground with a startling and rather horrible agility. A miner puts his head down and *runs,* with a long swinging stride, through places where I can only stagger. At the workings you see them on all fours, skipping round the pit props almost like dogs. But it is quite a mistake to think that they enjoy it. I have talked about this to scores of miners and they all admit that the "travelling" is hard work; in any case when you hear them discussing a pit among themselves the "travelling" is always one of the things they discuss. It is said that a shift always returns from work faster than it goes; nevertheless the miners all say that it is the coming away, after a hard day's work, that is especially irksome. It is part of their work and they are equal to it, but certainly it is an effort. It is comparable, perhaps, to climbing a smallish mountain before and after your day's work. . . .

Watching coal-miners at work, you realise momentarily what different universes different people inhabit. Down there where coal is dug it is a sort of world apart which one can quite easily go through life without ever hearing about. Probably a majority of people would even prefer not to hear about it. Yet it is the absolutely necessary counterpart of our world above. Practically everything we do, from eating an ice to crossing the Atlantic, and from baking a loaf to writing a novel, involves the use of coal, directly or indirectly. For all the arts of peace coal is needed; if war breaks out it is needed all the more. In time of revolu-

tion the miner must go on working or the revolution must stop, for revolution as much as reaction needs coal. Whatever may be happening on the surface, the hacking and shovelling have got to continue without a pause, or at any rate without pausing for more than a few weeks at the most. . . .

It is not long since conditions in the mines were worse than they are now. There are still living a few very old women who in their youth have worked underground, with a harness round their waists and a chain that passed between their legs, crawling on all fours and dragging tubs of coal. They used to go on doing this even when they were pregnant. And even now, if coal could not be produced without pregnant women dragging it to and fro, I fancy we should let them do it rather than deprive ourselves of coal. But most of the time, of course, we should prefer to forget that they were doing it. It is so with all types of manual work; it keeps us alive, and we are oblivious of its existence. More than anyone else, perhaps, the miner can stand as the type of the manual worker, not only because his work is so exaggeratedly awful, but also because it is so vitally necessary and yet so remote from our experience, so invisible, as it were, that we are capable of forgetting it as we forget the blood in our veins. In a way it is even humiliating to watch coal-miners working. It raises in you a momentary doubt about your own status as an "intellectual" and a superior person generally. For it is brought home to you, at least while you are watching, that it is only because miners sweat their guts out that superior persons can remain superior. You and I and the editor of the *Times Lit. Supp.,** and the Nancy poets and the Archbishop of Canterbury and Comrade X, author of *Marxism for Infants*—all of us *really* owe the comparative decency of our lives to poor drudges underground, blackened to the eyes, with their throats full of coal dust, driving their shovels forward with arms and belly muscles of steel.

ED. NOTE: * *London Times Literary Supplement.*

# 13  Frances R. Donovan: *The Waitress*

❦ *Every occupational role has its place in the scale of social prestige, and this aspect of his job is of major importance in shaping the outlook and attitude of the individual worker. Service occupations generally have relatively low prestige, and the position of the waitress is marginal even within this group. Casual and transitory, her profession is still regarded as akin to domestic service. It does provide, however, a sense of personal contact and of status derived from the particular public served.*

*Mrs. Frances R. Donovan, the author of the following selection, has long been interested in the investigation of occupational roles and problems. She has written three studies, all based on her personal experiences:* The Woman Who Waits *(1920),* The Saleslady *(1929), and* The Schoolma'am *(1938). Before her retirement in 1945, Mrs. Donovan for many years taught school in Chicago. She now lives in Eureka Springs, Ark.*

*Our selection is excerpted from Chapter X of* The Woman Who Waits *(Boston: Gorham Press) and is reprinted with Mrs. Donovan's permission.*

The work of the waitress differs in the different types of restaurants and depends also upon whether she is a long or short-hour girl. The short-hour girl does little or no side work, but spends all of her time in waiting upon people while to the long-hour girls falls all the drudgery called in waitress language "side work."

In the hash-house, however, even the long-hour girl puts in the greater part of her time in waiting. This is because the hash-house serves meals continuously all day and all night. Short-hour girls come on only to handle the noon rush and the waiting at all other times is done by the long-hour girl. Most of the side work is done by Polish girls called porters who are hired for the purpose and the waitress in her leisure moments merely folds napkins, or wipes and fills sugar bowls, pepper and salt shakers, or catsup bottles.

In the tea room there is much more side work, tables to reset, silver to clean, glassware to wash and wipe, linen to count, and, in some places the dining-room to sweep.

In the Men's Grill at Usher Lane's there seemed to be little except side work. Each long-hour girl was given a section to clean; *i.e.*, a certain number of chairs, tables, booths, and buffets, two booths with a large table and two extra chairs in each besides the leather seats and woodwork, one large round table with six chairs, fifteen small tables with two chairs each, and a big party room containing an immense table and eighteen chairs. I also cleaned the woodwork and windows in this room. The tables and buffets had to be washed and the chairs and woodwork thoroughly dusted.

When this was done I put linen on all the tables: *i.e.*, centerpieces, plate doilies, and napkins, and then counted out silver and glasses for each table. This meant the counting and placing of sixty knives, sixty forks, sixty large service spoons, sixty teaspoons, sixty butter spreaders, sixty glasses, and sixty napkins and plate doilies.

After this task was finished I was expected to go to the kitchen to wipe sugar bowls or silver, and to pick chicken from bones or to shell peas, until eleven-thirty.

After dinner at three o'clock the girls all had certain jobs assigned to them as side work and these took from 3 until 5 P.M. My job was to clean and fill three hundred sugar bowls. Another girl cleaned ash trays, another salt and pepper shakers.

In fact almost the entire day at Lane's was spent in doing side work, only a couple of hours daily being devoted to actual waiting. I imagine that the men who go there have little idea of the amount of labor it takes to get ready for them before they come and to clean up after them when they leave. When a man pays fifty cents for a tiny chicken pie made up of a cover of puff paste, some gravy and a few bits of chicken, he is not paying for the ingredients in that pie; he is paying for the side work that has been done in the room where that pie is being served. The pie itself may be worth ten cents, the remaining forty cents pays for the service and the furnishings.

The hardest thing that the waitress has to contend with is the rush and this is to be met in every kind of restaurant at meal time, and I do not know whether it is worse at the hash-house where the men keep up a constant clamor but are content to have you throw the food down on the counter and let them eat it in the midst of the dirty dishes that you cannot get time to remove, or at Usher Lane's where if you fail to remember the square of peppermint that should accompany his finger-bowl, the wrathful gentleman will forget your tip.

But in any place the rush is nerve wracking. Your success in handling orders depends not only upon your own swiftness but upon that of the chef and pantry girl and also upon their mood at the time when you arrive. Chefs are usually good natured as well as efficient, but pantry maids are slow and stupid. The exceptions to this

rule were the Greek cook at Chiros' when I was there, who screamed angrily at us in Dago lingo and the pantry maid at the Hayden Square, a pretty rosey-cheeked girl who was both swift of hand and sweet of disposition.

The working conditions in the kitchen during the rush hour were worse at Lane's than at any other place that I worked. It was necessary to have so many dishes on which to serve the food and so many frills. Every little sprig of parsley, every tiny dish of relish, every little doilie of paper lace, meant a long delay, and when you had your tray all set up with the accessories, you had to stand in line an interminable time before the cooks filled your orders and another interminable time before the checker checked you out. The men get very impatient waiting, but the remark of one of the girls one day explains the situation. "It isn't because we are such bum hashers, it's the way this kitchen is run."

The reason this kitchen is so poorly managed is because all the kitchen help are women who can cook, but who have no ability to manage. They are paid from $4.00 to $7.00 or at most $10.00 or $12.00 (depending upon length of service with the company) per week, and naturally the most efficient women do not care for these jobs.

Another great occupational difficulty of the waitress is the lack of sufficient dishes, linen, and silver. I found this true in every place I worked except the Hayden Square Café, where there was always plenty. Of the hash houses, White and McCreary's was the best equipped. At the Café des Reflections the girls spent half their time running all over the dining-room in search of napkins, spoons, or glasses, or in washing dishes in the kitchen when about to serve an order.

The work of the waitress may be classified as casual labor. Occasionally a waitress stays a year or even several years in a place, but such instances are the exceptions. Fully 90 per cent of the waitresses whom I questioned told me they had spent at most only a few months at each job.

There is a variety of reasons for this. In

the first place it is easy for a waitress to be hired. She is required to give no references and she may not be asked where she has worked before. Sometimes she works weeks in a place without being asked to give her full name and her address. She is known simply as May or Susie. If the manager or the head waitress happens to be in need of help the waitress gets a job. She keeps it as long as she gives satisfaction or as long as she can get along with her fellow workers. In some places a girl cannot keep a job unless she meets with the approval of the cook. Quarrels are frequent between waitresses and those higher in authority, the "boss" or perhaps the cashier.

Sometimes the waitress is laid off because some more attractive girl has applied for her job. This was what happened to Millie who was working at the Taylor Café. A dashing blonde applied for a job in the afternoon and so pleased the eye of the young Greek who ran the place that Millie was laid off that night. To be laid off was for Millie a serious misfortune for she was a divorced woman with two children to support, and the loss of even one day's work meant a great deal to her.

The girls themselves, however, quit on the slightest pretext. A girl will work a few months at a good job, save some money, and then take a vacation and spend it all. She takes the gambler's chance on getting as good a job when she is ready to go back to work.

The work of the waitress is also seasonal in character as well as casual. In the summer there is always plenty of work. The summer hotels, amusement parks, golf clubs, and excursion steamers are all running then and require a great number of waitresses. The proprietor in the Loop has a hard time to secure enough help to handle his trade. But in the fall conditions are reversed, the proprietor has his innings. He has his choice of the most attractive and

efficient girls, and the others have a hard pull to get through the winter.

One day in the spring an old, broken waitress said to me, "There ain't no chance for an old hen to get a job now, but," she added gleefully, "summer is coming, and then we'll get even, they'll be glad to get us."

The wages of the waitress are about the same as those received by the ordinary office girl or typist, and a little better than those of the shop girl. For example, the steady girl in any type of restaurant receives not less than $8.00 per week for ten hours' work per day and more often she receives $10.00, and since the war, many places are paying as high as $11.00 and $12.00 per week.* The only exception that I know is Usher Lane's where the steady girl is paid only $6.00.

The dinner girl in the Loop is paid $4.00, $4.50 or $5.00 per week for three hours' work, the wages being a little less in the places where the tips are best. The two meal girl in the cafe is paid $6.00 or $7.00 per week and the supper girl in the neighborhood restaurant receives $4.50 or even $5.50 per week for three hours' work. The wages are a little better in the restaurants outside the Loop. This is because the waitress prefers to work in the Loop as she is then downtown where there is life and excitement and near the Alliance or the Union † which are her clubs, and where she meets her friends when her work is over.

The golf clubs and resorts pay the steady girls during the summer wages ranging from $30.00 to $45.00 per month with room and board. These places also need extra girls for week ends and holidays and pay $2.50 or $3.00 per day and carfare.

During the summer many of the girls work "extra" in the Loop as dinner girls; *i.e.*, they are sent out by the Alliance in answer to telephone calls to fill temporary

---

ED. NOTE: * It should be remembered, of course, that these are wages of the period immediately following the First World War. Prices and wages today differ from those of a generation ago, although the relative position of the waitress is probably about the same.

ED. NOTE: † The Alliance and Union were clublike employment agencies for waitresses.

vacancies. In this way the waitress is sure of 75 cents or $1.00 in wages for three hours' work and she can count on working every day that she goes to the Alliance for a job. This, with the $5.00 or $6.00 which she can earn in the week end insures her of an income of $9.00 or $10.00 every week.

But the waitress does not depend upon her wages alone for her income. The tips she receives are in some instances as great as and in some greater than her wages, and she receives tips in almost every place where she works although some places are better for tips than others, the cafe and the neighborhood restaurant being generally recognized as the best places in which to make tips.

The wages of the steady girl are not fair in proportion to the amount of labor which she performs. She does all the side work, puts in more than three times as many hours and receives only twice as much in wages as the short-hour girl. To be sure she is given three meals a day, but the short-hour girl is given two. The short-hour girl works only at the time when there is the best chance of making tips.

This injustice is particularly noticeable at Lane's, where the short-hour girl receives $4.00 for three and a half hours' work and has a better chance to make tips because she spends a half hour more in actual waiting than the long-hour girl does. The girls themselves spoke of this but I could not find out why the steady girl stood for it.

Often a girl works a dinner job in the Loop and also a supper job out south or north at a neighborhood restaurant. In this way she avoids the side work, has two or three hours off in the afternoon, and makes more money.

The waitress is markedly individualistic in her attitude toward life, and the status of her occupation as it exists today tends towards the individualistic. She does only what she has to do to earn her wages and her only real interest is in the tip. In her work she does not often consider the house, the manager, nor her fellow workers, but herself only, and she seldom hesitates to advance her own interests at the expense of others. For example, one evening at the Café des Reflections, I went out into the kitchen before the supper rush began and washed and wiped a number of spoons and brought them in to set up my tables. But before I could use them, a girl came along and grabbed up every one. I ran after her and said indignantly, "Those are my spoons, I had to wash them myself!"

"Well, they are mine now," she said with a laugh, and she would not give them back.

And often after your tables are all set up with glasses, silver, and napkins, a girl from another part of the room will come and steal your set-ups when your back is turned. Such a thing as team work among waitresses is unknown.

Another time I said to a girl, "It is a shame to use these nice linen napkins for side towels."

"We should worry!" she answered, with a careless shrug of her shoulders.

The work of the waitress, because it is so irregular in character, because it can be entered upon at any time without much previous training, and because the waitress can quit a job today and be very sure that she can get another just as good tomorrow, has but little disciplinary value. The attitude of the employer is an important factor also. He is too ready to discharge his help at the slightest provocation. Consequently they have no sense of security or permanence.

The work of the waitress, however, could be organized upon a distinctly social basis, and there might be great opportunities in this occupation if the waitress could be made to see the value of the individual to society, if her occupation could be made more creative.

I notice that the girls who worked in the Men's Grill at Usher Lane's had a more social and less individualistic attitude toward their work than at any other place, at least where I had worked, and the ones who had worked for any length of time were actually interested in working for the house. This was due to the attitude of their employer, who was a woman of character and refinement. She made them feel that they were part of a great organization and got them to look upon their work as a profession. She did not nag at them as most male employers do, but after clearly defining the work, placed the responsibility of its performance upon them.

The work of the waitress does not rank very high in the occupational scale. The waitress herself is ashamed of her job, and tries to conceal from her friends that she is a waitress. "What's the use of letting everybody know that you are a hasher?" she will say. And by working in the Loop or in some place far from her own neighborhood, she can easily conceal the fact that she is "hashing" for a living. This is particularly easy for the married woman, who usually works only as a short-hour girl.

I can, however, see possibilities in the occupation of waitress, although first there must be a change in the attitude of the employer and a recognition of length of service. Then a better class of girl might go into the work and the standards of the girl already in be improved. The "hiring and firing" of today is productive of great economic waste.

During my investigation, I have met one educated waitress, a graduate of an Eastern college. She belonged to the Alliance and worked in the Loop because she needed to earn her living. "I can earn just as much money and have a great deal more freedom than I could as an ordinary teacher and I meet more interesting people," she said, when I asked her why she was in the work, and she continued, "In the East you will find many college girls working as waitresses in the better class of places, but you do not find them here."

But while the income of the waitress, made up as it is of wages and tips, is much better than that of the office or shop girl and compares very favorably with that of the average teacher, stenographer, or well-paid saleswoman, she seldom saves any money, and is more often "broke" than women in other occupations. It is not that the wages of the waitress are too much. She can not live a decent life on less. She is dependent entirely upon her own resources, and does not, like the shop girl and the office girl "live at home." She needs all she makes. But what she needs more is education and a different attitude upon the part of the public towards her occupation.

# 14 Carl Dreyfuss: *The Psychology of Salaried Employees*

❦ *To understand what is involved in the relationship of the worker to his work in an industrial society, particular attention must be given to the position of the white-collar worker. His position—that of a manual worker on salary but with the psychological outlook of an executive or owner—reflects the strivings and searchings of the vast middle class whose ideologies and hopes make up much that is central in the industrial culture of today.*

*The selection which follows is excerpted from a study of German industry, Occupation and Ideology of the Salaried Employee, by Carl Dreyfuss. This work was translated by Ernst E. Warburg as a Works Projects Administration project under the supervision of a group of social scientists at Columbia University (1938). The translation is in two volumes and our reading is from Volume 2, pp. 133–5, 138–42, 143–6.*

Employees in various occupations and in different social positions, such as bank clerk, salesgirl, traveling salesman, stenographer, and manager, seem, at first glance, to have authority and responsibility in the artificial economic pyramid. All are swayed by a great many false conceptions as to their positions and functions in the process of distribution and by illusions as to the importance of their particular work, and their social status in general. . . . These employees differ [little] from laborers in their economic and social position and in their activities, but . . . their occupation offers [greater possibilities] for the formation of ideologies, and . . . this situation is taken advantage of by the employer in the exercise of ideological influences. Although the various grades of the business setup are sham and only a few occupations are unaffected by the extensive process of mechanization and standardization, nevertheless, in the consciousness of the majority of employees, their activity and position, in other words their occupation, appears to differentiate them fundamentally from the worker. An official publication of the *Deutschnationaler Handlungsgehilfenverband*, which, it is true, counts among its members more employees in higher positions than any other federation, emphasizes the fact that "commercial employees are different from all other gainfully occupied groups of the nation . . . that their duties are highly specialized, that there is almost no standardized work, and that, notwithstanding rationalization in large-scale enterprises, the skilled commercial employee cannot be dispensed with."[1]

Not all employees have this false conception. Recognition of actualities has progressed among the more enlightened, particularly when absolute dependence, monotonous work, and bad economic conditions no longer permit illusions as to individualized occupational activity to gain ground, and when sudden disappointment opens the eyes of the deluded employee. The majority, however, are convinced that they belong to a special estate which protects them from proletarization and regulates their social standing. The formation of estate consciousness—and this must always be emphasized—cannot be achieved except through psychic agencies, through satisfaction of instincts and impulses in work and position. Only these psychic processes can make ideological influences effective, only through their concurrence can social needs produce a consciousness which has not as yet adapted itself to the changed life of the employees.

.  .  .  .  .

After the complete change in economic conditions had swept away the old middle class in Germany and had converted it into proletarians, its members did not adapt their outlook to the economic revolution. This unchanged attitude has been an important factor in the formation of the concept "New Middle Class." Wide circles of employees eagerly embrace the illusion of an attachment to the bourgeoisie in order to escape from the lowest class into the shelter of this fictitious social stratum. As the goal of economic and social inclusion in the bourgeois class is unattainable, they have to content themselves with the idea of belonging to a stratum which, in its alleged position between the bourgeoisie and the proletariat, stands, after all, closer to the

[1] *Die Gehaltslage der Kaufmannsgehilfen*, Hamburg, 1931, p. 10.

former stratum. Thus they try to believe in the creation of a new social stratum—a desideratum and not a reality.

These illusions are based on occupational ideologies and fallacious notions of estate consciousness, which to no inconsiderable extent originate in influences exerted by employers. The employee with bourgeois inclinations clings tenaciously to the conception that his occupation lifts him from the mass of the exploited proletariat. He does everything in his power to hold on to this conception, even when his economic situation and social dependence have long ceased to serve as a proper basis for such notions.

Longing for promotion in his occupation and for social advancement give to the employee a strong integrating motive for the formation of estate consciousness; these two factors foster in him the illusion of belonging to the bourgeoisie or at least to the new middle class. Desire to identify himself with the employer (the emulation of whose standards is considered the highest aim) and the feeling of community of interests with the organization, produced by the influences already described, are stronger than the feeling of class solidarity with his coworkers. The extent to which employees regard themselves as one with the firm and the impelling effects of this ideology are shown by the words of one of them, in concluding the description of a large organization:

The 'House' is the world, our world, in which we feel happy or wretched, in which we complain and envy, reveal or disguise ourselves, attract and repel, where we work or loaf, love or betray, laugh or weep, where we flourish or fade—all of us, from the first to the last.[1]

An article entitled "Occupation as Life's Purpose," [2] published in the magazine of the *Verband weiblicher Angestellten,* (Female Employees' Union) elucidates the in-fluence of the unions on the formation of estate consciousness based on occupational ideologies. It enumerates several irrational factors which, in spite of present conditions, tend to awaken in the employee the illusion that his occupation is his life's purpose. Work, it is claimed, offers the healthy human being an opportunity to develop his strength, even in mechanized organizations. An occupation, the panegyric continues, becomes worthwhile because of the continuous struggle, "often against one's own will," for promotion and better working conditions. "The atmosphere of struggle in many occupations is a compelling incentive to the ambitious individual." Militaristic romanticism gives to the capitalistic form of the economy—so disastrous for the employees—a positive overvaluation. The desperate struggle for living conditions worthy of a human being and the futile efforts to escape from the herd of machine workers are bombastically glorified. When the employee goes about his mechanized tasks unwillingly and with resignation, performing work which corresponds so little to his conception of a commercial career and which has often brought him to a point of despair, he should say to himself that he profits by exerting all his strength to crush a "contrary personal will."

Inclusion of militaristic concepts in this web of occupational ideologies goes even further. Hard working conditions and strict service regulations are lifted from their true level as burdensome work factors into an illusory sphere of great importance. "Occupation signifies punctuality, reliability, and pleasure in neat and accurate accomplishment. All these factors are educational forces working towards the advancement of mankind." Even restrictions imposed upon the employee in the modern rationalized enterprise (and they tie him down as a laborer is held at the conveying belt) are pointed to as a source of benefit. "Work is tension and pressure. These, in the natural order of things, set free the pleasures of relaxation and leisure. Tension and relaxation give to human existence a happy and redeeming sense of rhythm." Every restric-

[1] Sling, "Und der Geist des Hauses," *50 Jahre Ullstein,* Berlin, 1927, p. 393.
[2] Emma Loewe, "Berufsarbeit als Lebenswert," *Die Handels-und Büroangestellte,* 36. Jahrgang, Heft 1.

tion, down to the most brutal oppression, may be glorified by a theory which praises hard and rigorous tasks because, in contrast, relief from them appears all the more beautiful.

.  .  .  .  .

In complete inversion of actual conditions, rationalization and the division of work resulting from it are used as arguments in proof of a "delegated employer function." The process of rationalization, which brought about increasing mechanization and standardization and deprived the employee of all independence and responsibility, is supposed to have made his occupation "skilled work." "The large-scale development of business, with its division of labor, has distributed the functions of the employer among groups of individuals. To this extent, the employee can be regarded as performing 'delegated employer functions.' " [1] Similar assertions, totally belying reality, are found in the annual report of the *Gewerkschaftsbund der Angestellten.* "Modernization, mechanization, and standardization have not destroyed the essentials of employee functions." [2] A leading article in the federation's newspaper reads:

If, on the one hand, the work of the employee is partly mechanized and standardized by structural changes, there is, on the other hand, an increase in that type of work which requires great intellectual ability and gives the employee, as intermediary between employer and laborer, a wide field of action and chances of promotion. [3]

The charitable veil of illusion is readily drawn over realities in order to conceal the insurmountable discrepancy between the independent employer possessing the means of production and the dependent, underpaid employee. However large the enterprise, however far advanced rationalization (which enslaves the employee masses and

condemns them to mechanized work), the illusion of "co-operation" of the commercial employee, "the right hand of the employer," will not disappear. "Though fewer and fewer commercial employees are able to establish themselves in business independently, strong personal ties and intimate relations with the firm—regarded by the employee as 'his own'—prevent the development of class consciousness in a Marxist sense." [4] Ideological influences spread by the employer come to light in the formation of such conceptions. The efforts to bind the employee to the organization, the pretense of producing true patriarchal relations by the creation of welfare services and institutions, such as company unions and house organs, are responsible for the talk of "personal ties and intimate relations," all this at a moment when, as a matter of fact, the trend toward large-scale enterprises has actually set up a well-nigh all embracing economic pyramid, the apex of which the average employee can never attain.

The work of the "estate conscious" commercial employee is supposedly ennobled by its intellectual value and by its resemblance to the duties of the employer. Such asseverations are made despite the fact that they are obviously at variance with reality. It is openly conceded that they contain more fiction than truth:

It cannot be denied that the work of the employee, however mechanized, rationalized, and specialized it may be, always differs from factory work. It has, notwithstanding necessary restrictions and limitations, many more intellectual elements. The employee feels that he has a distinctive personality, and therefore he clings to this conception of dissimilarity of work, not for the purpose of displaying misplaced arrogance but to save the remnants of a self-esteem necessary to everyone if life is to be bearable. He must in some way lift himself from obscurity, if he wishes to retain his respect for himself. He must be proud of something in the day's work if he is not to lose all feeling of human pride.

---

[1] Joseph Jahn, "Das Sozialbewusstsein der Angestellten," *Der Kaufmann in Wirtschaft und Recht,* 9. Jahrgang, Heft 6.

[2] Max Rössiger, *Der Angestellte von 1930,* Berlin, 1930, p. 58.

[3] George Borchardt, "Der Weg zur Persönlichkeit," *GDA–Zeitschrift,* 1932, Heft 5.

[4] From a report of the 1930 session of the *Deutschnationaler Handlungsgehilfenverband* in *Der Deutche,* 1930, No. 150.

This is the argument of a represenative of the *Deutschnationaler Handlungsgehilfenverband.*[1] When he fails of a suitable reply to rational considerations, he escapes into the darkness of irrationalism:

[1] Ernst Niekisch, "Ein Kracauer auf Entdeckungsreisen," *Deutsche Handelswacht,* 37 Jahrgang, Heft 2 and 3.

The employee who is still conscious of belonging to a special group is not merely a mass product. . . . His group consciousness makes him incalculable from a democratic standpoint; as a representative of an estate he is the embodiment of irrational masses, and everything that is irrational and incomprehensible is repugnant to democracy.

# 15 John P. Marquand: *The Aspiring Banker*

*At a point relatively high in the scale of social prestige we find the salaried professional group, of which the junior bank executive is an example. His work is characterized by a dramatic split between on-the-job manipulation of immense fortunes and a private life on a contrastingly modest income. He is continuously conscious of status and power relationships both within the banking firm and within the larger outside industrial society, and this preoccupation often results in his life being dominated by the thought and hope of upward promotion. This at least is what is suggested by the following reading, excerpted from the popular novel* Point of No Return *(1949), by John P. Marquand, and used with permission of the publishers, Little, Brown and Company.*

*Marquand (1893– ) is one of America's leading contemporary novelists. His recent works have constituted serious commentaries on the vagaries of modern society, with its emphasis on status and its worship of financial success. Marquand was awarded the Pulitzer Prize in 1938 for* The Late George Apley *(1937). Other recent novels include* H. M. Pulham Esquire *(1941),* So Little Time *(1943),* B. F.'s Daughter *(1946), and* Melville Goodwin: U. S. A. *(1951).*

Charles found a seat by a window and opened the *New York Times* to the financial page. There was nothing like competition. His mind had been working more alertly since he had met Roger Blakesley and everything assumed a new significance. They were both assistant vice-presidents in the trust department now, but they had both worked almost everywhere in the bank, except the vaults. Either could handle customers about as well as the other. They both were very bright boys, but he had never worried about Roger much until lately. There would have been no reason to do so now if Roger had gone to the war instead of using that period to make himself useful. The financial page was dull but Charles put his mind on it. . . .

Other banks, larger ones, were constantly advertising their friendly services and pointing out the almost insoluble personal complications faced by anyone who owned property in this period of economic change and regulation, but the Stuyvesant seldom advertised. It was a matter of deeds rather than words at the Stuyvesant, and it paid. The wills of deceased depositors were proof enough that the Stuyvesant had been an institutional friend through life. The Stuyvesant had been named an executor and trustee in hundreds of wills. The employees of the Stuyvesant understood rich clients and knew all the pains and drawbacks of being rich, although they were not rich men themselves. They had to deal familiarly, almost jovially, but always scrupulously with large sums of money, while living usually on modest salaries.

If you were successful at the Stuyvesant you ended by devolping a priestly, untouchable, ascetic attitude. You learned to think of your own financial life and your own problems as something apart from those other financial complications. If you did well enough to become an executive in the Stuyvesant, and this required a long time and an arduous apprenticeship, you found yourself solving the problems of individuals who had difficulty living within incomes approaching a hundred thousand dollars a year. You found yourself spending the working day discussing the investment of huge sums of money, only to get home yourself and to worry because the butcher's bill had risen some twenty dollars above the previous one. You had to debate the purchase or the sale of controls in business enterprises and then return home yourself to decide whether or not you could afford to buy a motor lawn mower, or a ready-made or a tailor-made suit. In time this gave you a split personality since you had to toss your own problems completely aside and never allow them to mingle in any way with those of clients and depositors when you reached your desk at the Stuyvesant. At your desk you had to be a friend and confidant, as professional as a doctor or a lawyer, ready and with an intelligent per-

spective for almost anything. Anthony Burton had once said that this attitude was one's responsibility toward society. . . .

Though you seldom talked of salaries at the Stuyvesant, your social status was obvious from the position of your desk. Charles occupied one of the two flat mahogany desks that stood in a sort of no man's land between the roll-top desks of the officers and the smaller flat-tops of lesser executives and secretaries crowding the floor of the bank outside the cages. A green rug extended from the officers' desks, forming a neat and restricted zone that just included Charles's desk and the one beside it which was occupied by Roger Blakesley. Charles could see both their names, Mr. Blakesley and Mr. Gray, in silver letters, and he was pleased to see that he had got there first from the eight-thirty, a minute or two ahead of Roger and Mr. Burton and ahead of everyone else near the windows.

Mr. Burton's desk, which had the best light, was opened already and so was that of Mr. Stephen Merry, the oldest vice-president, and so were all the others except one. This was the desk of Arthur Slade, the youngest vice-president of the Stuyvesant, who had died in a plane accident when returning from the West Coast six months before. The closed desk still gave Charles a curious feeling of incompleteness and a mixed sense of personal gain and loss because he had been more friendly with Arthur Slade than with anyone else in the Stuyvesant—but then you had to die sometime. Once Arthur Slade had sat at Charles's own place but that was before Mr. Walter Harry, who had been president when Charles had first come to the bank, had died of an embolism and everyone had moved like players on bases—Burton to Harry, Merry to Burton, Slade to the vacant roll-top—and so on down to Charles himself. The Stuyvesant was decorously accustomed to accident and death and now it was moving time again and it was so plain where one of two persons might be moving next that it was embarrassing. Any observing depositor and certainly everyone employed in the bank, right up to the third floor, must have known that either Mr. Blakesley or Mr. Gray would move to Arthur Slade's desk by the window. Undoubtedly they were making side bets out in back as Charles used to himself when he had first come there from Boston. Undoubtedly the clerks and the secretaries and the watchmen had started some sort of pool. . . .

Down there on the floor of the Stuyvesant you worked with the privacy of a goldfish. There might be certain sheltered corners in the neighborhood of the officers' desks, but there was no shelter at the edge of the green carpet where Charles and Roger Blakesley were stationed. They sat there in a kind of advanced bastion, barring the way to the higher executives, like a knight and a bishop on a chessboard, Charles sometimes thought, pieces expendable in a pinch, who had to pay for their own errors and for others' but who always must protect the rooks and the king and queen. Of course there was an outer ring of pawns in front. Individuals like Tom Joyce, his assistant, at his smaller desk well off the carpet, or Holland just behind him, or Miss Marble, were all protecting pawns. There was no physical railing to guard any of them from the customers.

Old Joe, who stood just inside the door, in a neat business suit instead of a uniform, was in the most exposed position, with duties roughly like those of a floorwalker in a department store. He was the one who helped with the counter checks and the deposit slips, who directed traffic and estimated the preliminary situation. It was he who decided that our Mr. Joyce or our Mr. Holland or, if it seemed justifiable, our Mr. Gray or Mr. Blakesley would be glad to help you.

Charles often wondered why this system of everyone's working in the open should exist. It might have been a part of the great tradition, stemming from the medieval days of the goldsmiths and the moneylenders, that all the workings of a bank should be as visible as the wheels and mainspring of a glass-enclosed French clock. It was perhaps a tradition that was deeply rooted in human suspicion regarding money and those who handled it. There must be positively no deception, everything open and aboveboard and nothing up the sleeve. If anyone had money in a bank, it seemed that he had an inalienable right to see the bankers sweating over it. Then, too, it established confidence to see a roomful of well-dressed, capable individuals sitting behind desks, reading, answering telephones, or moving in fixed orbits, according to their rank. You grew used to being an exhibit, of course, through time and training, and it was surprising how through sheer self-discipline you could avoid making mistakes of fact or even of judgment. You learned a lot about a certain kind of person there and certain facets of human nature. Granted that the clientele of the Stuyvesant was well above the average and that a high balance must be maintained for a checking account, you still met fools and rascals, and you encountered fear and hopelessness and avarice. Sometimes it seemed to Charles that all human behaviorism was mixed in some way with money.

# 16 Robert H. Fetridge: *The Entrepreneur*

☙ *The go-getting entrepreneur who is venturesome and imaginative and who has succeeded in building a personal fortune with his specialized know-how, is often identified as the "typical" product of American culture.*

*The history of America abounds in stories of entrepreneurial successes, of which the following selection is illustrative. This brief sketch describes the achievements of William Lear in the field of aviation. He meets the challenge to invent, reaches the pinnacle of success, and finds it impossible to retire. In this personality we find those qualities of imaginativeness, hard-headed business sense, inexhaustible energy, and skilled workmanship which sometimes enable their possessor, if he is lucky, to climb from penniless worker to aviation tycoon.*

*This article by Robert H. Fetridge, financial editor of the New York* Times, *is reprinted with permission of·the* Times *from the March 4, 1951, edition of that newspaper.*

He's a millionaire today and the inventor of the 36-pound automatic jet pilot that the "high brass" said couldn't be made, but back in the depression days he was broke. The stake he obtained then from an old Swedish friend in Chicago started him on the way to what is now termed a miracle of production.

William (Bill) P. Lear, chairman of Lear, Inc., who quit his formal education at the age of thirteen to become a $6 a week auto mechanic, probably has more "firsts" to his credit in the field of radio and mechanical aircraft controls than any other living individual.

He reached the pinnacle of his various achievements last year when he won the Collier Trophy for his automatic pilot which, in the words of the award, "makes possible the safe landing of jet aircraft regardless of extreme weather or visibility conditions."

The honor given Bill Lear brought into bold relief an entirely new personality in the aviation industry. But it also revealed a man with interests as wide as one could find in an individual. With only a primary school education he has advanced himself to one of the technical radio and aviation authorities in the world.

Probably half of the cost of modern military aircraft, as well as commercial or executive type plane is in the hundreds of accessories and equipment necessary to operate a flying machine in high efficiency and low accident standards. The layman has little knowledge of this increasing important phase of the aviation industry, but such advances contributed mightily to the amazing progress made by the United States in the field of aviation. Bill Lear has been in the front in supplying to military, commercial and private aircraft the means for "happy landings."

### ALL AUTOMATIC

Bill, the inventor of hundreds of devices ranging from one of the first automobile radios to the miniature motors that operate the engine cowl flaps on the B-29's in the last war is confident that eventually the human element will be eliminated completely from the operation of planes.

Now 48 years old, Bill flies about the country in his own plane and with the aid of his latest gadget—now being manufactured by his company for the jet fighters —finds time to read that latest book while aloft. He lets the automatic pilot do the work.

This chap who, back in the depression days, sat in his small office in New York and wondered where his next penny was coming from, now rules a company with thousands of employees and plants in three different parts of the country. But he's not an office boss. He's right out in the center of manufacturing activity, planning with his designers and engineers and often working around the clock to perfect a new development for air safety.

This enterprising Bill Lear has not confined his activities to aviation. His energy has spilled over into a variety of ventures, some of them very curious for a man intent on making flying as safe as humanly possible. He's the owner of Texas oil wells, the backer of Broadway musical productions, part owner of a silver mine in the mysterious Superstition Mountains in Arizona, and the manufacturer of soundproofing material and electric-eye devices.

He tried retiring to a life of ease a few years ago. But it just didn't work out. So, back into harness he went and with his return to the "shop" came the final perfection of the automatic pilot which now is standard equipment on the Army's jet fighters.

The wartime application of Lear's invention has been described by the high command of the Air Forces as the "basis of our capability to fend off enemy attack, no matter what the weather. It is the guts and core of the air defense of America."

Says Lear: "In my lifetime, I expect to be working on pilotless fighter planes, flown in satellite formation from a single mother ship. The human pilot in the mother ship will simply bring the satellites within range of the enemy—and take off. The satellites then will track down the enemy and fight him to destruction, all with completely automatic controls."

# 17 Nels Anderson: *The Hobo and the Tramp*

*❦ There is an underside to our industrial life peopled by a not inconsiderable number of men and women variously described as hobos, tramps, and bums. The hobo, in particular, helps to fill the demand for seasonal or irregular manual labor. Lacking social roots in any particular physical community, hobo, tramp, and bum are a somewhat romantic and footloose group, migrating from job to job or perhaps shunning work altogether.*

*They scoff at the strivings for social mobility and security characteristic of other occupational classes, preferring a life pattern that escapes many of the pressures of our industrialized order. In one sense the hobo is not unlike the go-getting, tradition-scorning entrepreneur: both cherish the freedom of the enterpriser. The businessman, however, never feels free unless he is busy, while the hobo feels free only if he is working where and when he pleases.*

*The lives of these people are described in this reading which is reprinted from a study,* The Hobo (1923), *by Nels Anderson, pp. 87–95, with the permission of the publisher,* The University of Chicago Press.

The term "homeless man" was used by Mrs. Alice W. Solenberger in her study of 1,000 cases in Chicago to include all types of unattached men, tramps, hobos, bums, and the other nameless varieties of the "go-abouts."

Almost all "tramps" are "homeless men" but by no means are all homeless men tramps. The homeless man may be an able-bodied work-man without a family; he may be a runaway boy, a consumptive temporarily stranded on his way to a health resort, an irresponsible, fee-ble-minded, or insane man, but unless he is also a professional wanderer he is not a "tramp." [1]

There is no better term at hand than "homeless men" by which the men who in-habit Hobohemia may be characterized. Dr. Ben L. Reitman, who has himself trav-eled as a tramp, in the sense in which he uses the word, has defined the three prin-cipal types of the hobo. He says:

There are three types of the genus vagrant: the hobo, the tramp, and the bum. The hobo works and wanders, the tramp dreams and wanders and the bum drinks and wanders.

St. John Tucker, formerly the president of the "Hobo College" in Chicago, gives the same classification with a slightly different definition:

A hobo is a migratory worker. A tramp is a migratory non-worker. A bum is a stationary non-worker. Upon the labor of the *migratory worker* all the basic industries depend. He goes forth from the crowded slavemarkets to hew the forests, build and repair the railroads, tunnel mountains and build ravines. His is the labor that harvests the wheat in the fall and cuts the ice in the winter. All of these are ho-bos.

M. Kuhn, of St. Louis (and elsewhere), a migrant, a writer, and, according to his own definition, a hobo, in a pamphlet en-titled "The Hobo Problem" gives a fairly representative statement of the homeless man's explanation of his lot.

The hobo is a seasonal, transient, migratory worker of either sex. Being a seasonal worker he is necessarily idle much of the time; being transient, he is necessarily homeless. He is de-tached from the soil and the fireside. By the nature of his work and not by his own will, he is precluded from establishing a home and rearing a family. Sex, poverty, habits and de-gree of skill have nothing whatever to do with

classifying individuals as hobos; the character of his work does that.

There are individuals not hobos who pose as such. They are enabled to do this for two rea-sons: first, hobos have no organization by which they can expose the impostor; second, the frauds are encouraged and made possible by organized and private charity. The hobo class, therefore, is unable to rid itself of this extremely undesirable element. With organiza-tion it can and will be done even if charity, which is strongly opposed by the hobo class, is not abolished.

Nicholas Klein, president of the "Hobo College" and attorney and adviser to James Eads How, the so-called hobo millionaire, who finances the "Hobo College," says:

A hobo is one who travels in search of work, the migratory worker who must go about to find employment. Workers of that sort pick our berries, fruit, hops, and help to harvest the crops on the western farms. They follow the seasons around giving their time to farms in spring, summer, and autumn, and ending up in the ice fields in winter. We could not get in our crops without them for the hobo is the boy who does the work. The name originated from the words "hoe-boy" plainly derived from work on the farm. A tramp is one who travels but does not work, and a bum is a man who stays in one place and does not work. Between these grades there is a great gulf of social dis-tinction. Don't get tramps and hobos mixed. They are quite different in many respects. The chief difference being that the hobo will work and the tramp will not, preferring to live on what he can pick up at back doors as he makes his way through the country.[2]

Roger Payne, A.B. and LL.B., who has taken upon himself the title "hobo phi-losopher," sees only one type of the wan-derer and that is the hobo. The hobo to him is a migratory worker. If he works but does not migrate, or if he migrates but does not work, he is not a hobo. All others are either tramps or bums. He makes no dis-tinction between them. The hobo, foot-loose and care-free, leads, Mr. Payne thinks, the ideal life.

Although we cannot draw lines closely, it seems clear that there are at least five types

[1] *One Thousand Homeless Men,* p. 209.

[2] *Dearborn Independent,* March 18, 1922.

of homeless men: (*a*) the seasonal worker,[1] (*b*) the transient or occasional worker or hobo, (*c*) the tramp who "dreams and wanders" and works only when it is convenient, (*d*) the bum who seldom wanders and seldom works, and (*e*) the home guard who lives in Hobohemia and does not leave town.[2]

### THE SEASONAL WORKER

Seasonal workers are men who have definite occupations in different seasons. The yearly circuit of their labors takes them about the country, often into several different states. These men may work in the clothing industries during cold weather but in summer are employed at odd jobs; or they may have steady work in summer and do odd jobs in winter. One man picks fruit in summer and works as a machinist in winter. He does not spend his summers in the same state nor his winters in the same city but follows those two occupations throughout the year.

Bill S. is a Scotchman and a seasonal worker. During the winter he is usually in Chicago. He works as a practical nurse. He is efficient and well liked by his patients and a steady worker during the winter. In summer he quits and goes to the harvest fields or works on a construction job. Since leaving his winter job (March to October, 1922) he has had several jobs out of Chicago none of which lasted more than a week or two. Between times he loafs on West Madison Street. He does not drink. He is well behaved. Seldom dresses up. When last heard of he was in Kansas City, Missouri, where he thought he would spend the winter.

Jack M. works on the lake boats during the sailing season. When the boats tie up for the winter he tries to get into the factories, or he goes to the woods. Sometimes during the tie-up he takes a notion to travel and goes West or South to while away the time. He has just returned from a trip East and South where he has been "seeking work" and "killing time" a week or so before the season opened. He has already signed up for the summer. He is loafing and lodging in the meanwhile on West Madison and South State streets.

[1] The seasonal worker may be regarded also as the upper-class hobo.
[2] The first three types of homeless men are described in this chapter. . . .

The seasonal worker has a particular kind of work that he follows somewhere at least part of the year. The hotels of Hobohemia are a winter resort for many of these seasonal workers whose schedule is relatively fixed and habitudinal. Some of these who return to the city regularly every winter come with money. In that case, they do not work until next season. Others return without money. They have some kind of work which they follow in the winter. The hobo, proper, is a transient worker without a program.

### THE HOBO

A hobo is a migratory worker in the strict sense of the word. He works at whatever is convenient in the mills, the shops, the mines, the harvests, or any of the numerous jobs that come his way without regard for the times or the seasons. The range of his activities is nation wide and with many hobos it is international. He may cross a continent between jobs. He may be able in one year to function in several industries. He may have a trade or even a profession. He may even be reduced to begging between jobs, but his living is primarily gained by work and that puts him in the hobo class.

E. J. is a carpenter. He was at one time a good workman but due to drink and dissipation he has lost his ability to do fine work and has been reduced to the status of a rough carpenter. At present he follows bridge work and concrete form work. Sometimes he tries his hand at plain house carpentry but due to the fact that he moves about so much, he has lost or disposed of many of his tools. A spree lasts about three weeks and he has about three or four a year. Sometimes he travels without his kit and does not work at his trade. He never drinks while working. It is only when he goes to town to spend his vacations that he gets drunk. He is restless and uncomfortable and does not know how to occupy his mind when he is in town and sober. He is fifty-six years old. He never married and never has had a home since he was a boy.

M. P. is interesting because he has a trade but does not follow it seasonally. He is a plasterer and he seems to be a good one. In his youth he learned the trade of stone mason. He

came to this country from England in his
twenties and he is past fifty now. He married
in Pennsylvania where his wife died and where
a daughter still lives. He became a wanderer
and for many years did not work at his trade.
He did various kinds of work as the notion
came to him. As he is getting older he is less
inclined to wander and he makes fewer ex-
cursions into other lines of work outside his
trade. During the past year he has not left Chicago and he has done little other than to work
as a plasterer. He lives in the Hobohemian
areas and is able to get along two or three
weeks on a few days' work. He seldom works
more than a week at a time. He takes a lively
interest in the hobo movement of the city and
has been actively engaged in the "Hobo College." Recently he won a lot in a raffle. It is located in the suburbs of the city. During the
summer (1922) he had a camp out there and
he and his friends from Madison Street spent
considerable time in his private "jungle."

The hobo group comprises the bulk of
the migratory workers, in fact, nearly all
migrants in transit are hobos of one sort or
other. Hobos have a romantic place in our
history. From the beginning they have been
numbered among the pioneers. They have
played an important role in reclaiming the
desert and in subduing the trackless forests.
They have contributed more to the open,
frank, and adventurous spirit of the Old
West than we are always willing to admit.
They are, as it were, belated frontiersmen.
Their presence in the migrant group has
been the chief factor in making the American vagabond class different from that of
any other country.

It is difficult to classify the numerous
types of hobos. The habits, type of work,
the routes of travel, etc., seem to differ with
each individual. Some live more parasitic
lives than others. Some never beg or get
drunk, while others never come to town
without getting intoxicated and being
robbed or arrested, and perhaps beaten.
One common characteristic of the hobo,
however, is that he works. He usually has
horny hands and a worker's mien. He aims
to live by his labor.

As there are different types of homeless
men, so different varieties of this particular brand, the hobo, may be differentiated.

A part of the hobo group known as "harvest
hands" follows the harvest and other agricultural occupations of seasonal nature.
Another segment of the group works in
the lumber woods and are known as "lumber jacks" or "timber beasts." A third group
is employed in construction and maintenance work. A "gandy dancer" is a man
who works on the railroad track tamping
ties. If he works on the section he may be
called a "snipe" or a "jerry."

A "skinner" is a man who drives horses or
mules.

A "mucker" or a "shovel stiff" is a man who
does manual labor on construction jobs.

A "rust eater" usually works on extra-gangs
or track-laying jobs; handles steel.

A "dino" is a man who works with and handles dynamite.

A "splinter-belly" is a man who does rough
carpenter work or bridge work.

A "cotton glaumer" picks cotton, an "apple
knocker" picks apples and other fruit.

A "beachcomber" is a plain sailor, of all
men the most transient.

For every vocation that is open to the
migratory worker there is some such characteristic name. In the West the hobo usually carries a bundle in which he has a bed,
some extra clothes, and a little food. The
man who carries such a bundle is usually
known as a "bundle stiff" or "bundle bum."
The modern hobo does not carry a bundle
because it hinders him when he wishes to
travel fast. It is the old man who went
West "to grow up with the country" who
still clings to his blanket roll.

### THE TRAMP

While the word "tramp" is often used as
a blanket term applied to all classes of
homeless and potentially vagrant or transient types, it is here used in a stricter sense
to designate a smaller group. He is usually
thought of, by those familiar with his natural history, as an able-bodied individual
who has the romantic passion to see the
country and to gain new experience without work. He is a specialist at "getting by."
He is the type that Josiah Flynt had in
mind when he wrote his book, *Tramping*

*with Tramps.* He is typically neither a drunkard nor a bum, but an easy-going individual who lives from hand to mouth for the mere joy of living.

X. began life as a half orphan. Later he was adopted and taken from Ohio to South Dakota. In his early teens he grew restive at home and left. But for brief seasons he has been away ever since and he is now past forty-five. He has traveled far and wide since but has worked little. He makes his living by selling joke books and song books. Sometimes he tries his hand at selling little articles from door to door. A few years ago he wrote a booklet on an economic subject and sold several thousand copies. During the winter of 1921–22 he sold the *Hobo News* each month. He is able to make a living this way. Any extra money he has he loses at the gambling tables. He spends his leisure time attempting to write songs or poetry. He knows a great deal about publishers but it is all information that has come in his efforts to sell his songs. He claims that he has been working for several years on a novel. He offered his work for inspection. He tries to lead the hero through all the places that he has visited and the hero comes in contact with many of the things he has seen or experienced in many cities but nowhere does his hero work. He enjoys life just as X. endeavors to do now. During the summer (1922) he has taken several "vacations" in the country for a week or more at the time.

C. is twenty-five years old. His home is in New York but he has not been home for more than ten years. He introduced himself to the "Hobo College" early in the spring of 1922 as "B-2." This name he assumed upon the conviction that he is the successor of "A-1," the famous tramp. He said that he had read "A-1's"

books and although he did not agree in every respect, yet he thought that "A-1" was the greatest of tramp writers. "B-2" claimed that he had ridden on every railroad in the United States. His evidence of travel was a book of post-office stamps. When he comes to a town he goes to the post-office and requests the postmaster to stamp his book much as letters are stamped. Another hobby he has is to go to the leading newspapers and endeavor to sell a writeup. He carries an accumulation of clippings. He has an assortment of flashy stories that take well with newspaper men. He claims that he has been pursued by bloodhounds in the South, that he has been arrested many times for vagrancy, that he is the only man who has beat his way on the Pikes Peak Railroad. He always carries a blanket and many other things that class him among wanderers as an individualist. He has been in the Army, saw action, and was in the Army of Occupation. He does not seek work. He says his leisure time can be better spent. He carries a vest pocket kodak. He says that the pictures and notes he takes will some day be published.

The distinctions between the seasonal worker, the hobo, and the tramp, while important, are not hard and fast. The seasonal worker may descend into the ranks of the hobos, and a hobo may sink to the level of the tramp. But the knowledge of this tendency to pass from one migratory group to another is significant for any program that attempts to deal with the homeless man. Significant, also, but not sufficiently recognized, is the difference between these migratory types and the stationary types of homeless men, the "home guard" and the "bum."

SECTION B

**The souls of the workless**

# 18 The Pilgrim Trust: *Men Without Work*

❧ *To understand the psychology and outlook of men and women who are involuntarily unemployed is not an easy task. Studies of their plight indicate that they live in a world radically different from that of the regularly employed. Ususally their lack of employment destroys their sense of independence and self-respect, of belonging, and of being wanted. For a few, the enforced "leisure" may mean an opportunity for personal release and greater community participation; but for most it means frustration and undermined morale.*

*In 1933, during the depths of the Great Depression, the Pilgrim Trust, a British philanthropic organization, financed an enquiry into the effects of unemployment and possible methods of overcoming it. The selection below is taken from the Pilgrim Trust report, Men Without Work (1938), Part II, pp. 143–76. The reading is reproduced with permission of the publisher, Cambridge University Press.*

One of the most frequently discussed of all the problems of unemployment is that of the willingness of the unemployed to work. The loss of the will to work may well be one of the disastrous effects of unemployment, and we were anxious to discover what the facts with regard to this might be. This involved an attempt to get behind the actual answers of those interviewed. We felt, and the opinion is confirmed by many who are in far closer permanent touch with the unemployed, that many of the answers given were "defensive" and do not represent a real attitude. If a man resents being asked about his anxiety to work, it is not necessarily an indication that he is trying to avoid it. It may show the sense of frustration that has come upon him from continuous refusals, or impatience at the inability of others to understand his difficulties. On the other hand, the evidence is incontestable that there are men who are "work-shy," and the experience of many Unemployment Assistance Board Officers, that an extensive investigation into certain sections of the register (especially among the young men under 25) may lead to a decline of numbers, cannot be ignored. If the threat of enquiries in itself proves enough to make men find work, it must mean that some men are avoiding it. We regarded it, therefore, as an important part of our work to try to throw some light on this question.

It is hazardous to attempt the simple classification of a complex thing such as a man's attitude to his work, and where figures are put forward in this section they must be treated with reserve. They may, however, serve as a general indication of the impression which we formed. There are, roughly speaking, three categories into which the sample can be divided in this respect, and throughout this section we shall be constantly referring to them. They are (i) those who think still only in terms of work; (ii) those who are beginning to accept unemployment as a normal state for themselves, though they still perhaps look for work, often as a matter of habit rather than with any conviction; (iii) those who have accepted unemployment as their normal state (sometimes because they have found satisfactory alternative activities) and for whom it would be hard to bring themselves to take work if it were available. We attempt to trace the process of "adjustment". . . by which the unemployed man gradually moves from one of these categories to another, and to give some estimate of their proportionate importance.

## LOSING WORK

One of the main differences between the "working" classes and the "middle" classes is the difference of security. This is probably a more important distinction than income level. If working men and women seem to be unduly anxious to make their sons and daughters into clerks, the anxiety behind it is not for more money but for greater security. Rightly or wrongly, they feel that the black-coated worker has a more assured position. The semi-skilled man is at the mercy of rationalisation. A week's notice may end half a lifetime's service, with no prospects, if he is elderly, but the dole, followed by a still further reduction in his means of livelihood when the old age pension comes. We take as an example a shoe laster from Leicester, who had worked thirty-seven years with one firm. "When I heard the new manager going through and saying: 'The whole of this side of this room, this room, and this room is to

be stopped,' I knew it would be uphill work to get something." He went on to describe to us how he had not been able to bring himself to tell his wife the bad news when he got home, how she had noticed that something was wrong, how confident she had been that he would get work elsewhere, but how he had known that the chances were heavily against him. For months and indeed often for years such men go on looking for work, and the same is true of many casual labourers. There were in the sample old men who have not a remote chance of working again but yet make it a practice to stand every morning at six o'clock at the works gates in the hope that perhaps they may catch the foreman's eye. There were young men who said that they could never settle to anything, but must be out all day, every day, looking for work. We had instances of men who had bicycled all over Lancashire and Yorkshire from Liverpool in the hopes of finding something. A young married man (aged 29) in Leicester, who was for some reason strongly criticized by the authorities for not looking for work, had tramped about for nearly a year in the hopes of getting some permanent, or at least temporary employment (his wife had gone back into service to make it possible for him to do so), but the only substantial work he had done during the whole period was pea picking. Another man, a shoehand, 38 years old, had come down on his own initiative from Lancashire, where the factory in which he worked had closed down, to Leicester. He was a neat, rather reserved type of man and had not perhaps the necessary push to squeeze himself into work, but he wanted it desperately. He tried to join the army and was refused for it, apparently on account of his age, and it was clear that as time went on he was getting a more and more defeatist attitude to work. He might go on trying, but his efforts were vitiated more and more by the knowledge that he was not going to succeed. The sample brought out scores of similar instances, but these two of comparatively young men in a city which by ordinary standards is exceedingly prosperous must stand for all of them. When a man is thrown out of employment the first thing that he wants is work, and very few of those who have a good employment history can settle down to accept the fact of unemployment till they have been out of work for months.

But when a man who has had perhaps ten years' steady employment is thrown on the streets, to look for work effectively is not always easy. A large number of the sample cases had lost good jobs at the time of the slump, when there was nothing else to be had. They had gone round from one works to another with hundreds of others all desperately anxious to secure employment, and failure after failure had gradually "got them down." The restlessness of which many wives spoke to us tells its own tale: "Now he's out of work he don't seem to be able to settle down to anything." When a man is out of work, anxiety is part of a vicious circle, and the more he worries, the more he unfits himself for work.

There were other symptoms of this nerviness. The high proportions of instances in which married men were living apart from their wives is certainly in some degree to be explained by it. Among many of the families visited, tension between man and wife was apparent. Thus we saw a man of 25 in Liverpool, who had had previously to 1935 a certain amount of work as a builder's labourer. At the time of the visit his wife was 19; they had been married when she was 16. The first child had died the day after it was born and the mother had suffered from anaemia and kidney trouble at the time. There was another baby a few months old, which was taken to hospital with pneumonia the night before the visit occurred. The man gave the impression of one who had been not unhappy for a time lounging, but was now getting to the end of his tether. Speaking of his wife, he said: "She's always crying. But crying don't make things no better": and the early marriage, poverty, illness, and finally the quarrel seemed to summarise in a single instance several of the worst features of the situation of the long unemployed. Friction may

come out in other ways, also. The children may get on a man's nerves if he is at home all day. "When he was out of work we were always having rows over the children. He will never let them do anything. It's much better now he is at work." In several cases where the wife was earning but the husband unemployed, there was evidently unhappiness as a result. A striking example occurred among the Liverpool visits, the case of a printer, 42 years old, who had lost his chance of re-employment at his old trade, through a dispute with the union. A few weeks before our visit occurred, he had left Liverpool in the hopes of finding work in the Midlands, and the wife showed one of us a touching letter in which he told her that he had got work at 25s. a week and enclosed 10s. for her. While he was out of work she had been working regularly, with the result that he only drew 5s. Unemployment Assistance. She described how she used to lie awake at nights and hear him "tramping up and down the garden path, or up and down in the parlour, and it made her nearly mad; and it made her nearly mad to feel that she was keeping him by her earnings and they gaining nothing by her work." There was a somewhat similar case in Leicester, where the woman had left her work because she could not bear to be the breadwinner while her husband, young and fit, did nothing; another in Blackburn where a young married woman, working, with an unemployed husband, said that "it made him wild" to be about with no money in his pocket. It is in the light of such cases that we should read the figures showing the numbers of men in the sample who were living apart from their wives.

Similar questions are raised by the case of the man whose allowance takes into account the fact that his children are earning sums which permit of their contributing to his support and the general upkeep of the household. There were in the sample instances of men over 55 years of age who were either not in receipt of any income from the Unemployment Assistance Board, or in receipt of small amounts, 5s. or 7s. 6d., from the Board, because it was held that the household resources were otherwise sufficient. This view would be justified if the household were taken as a unit. The fact remains however, that some men in this position feel the loss of an independent income, such as they enjoyed while on Unemployment Benefit, very acutely, and in many cases the home appears to represent two standards, the earning children being often smartly dressed and happy, while the fathers were shabby and suffering from a sense of their dependence. Such men gave the impression that they purposely avoided making any effort to keep up appearances in case the children might think that they were drawing an undue share of the family income. While among the sample as a whole, bitterness against the Unemployment Assistance Board is the exception rather than the rule, in cases of this kind it was the rule rather than the exception. The question has two sides, and we came across several instances in which children were behaving most unreasonably in refusing to contribute towards the household expenses the sum, not large, which the regulations expect of them. Nevertheless, there may be a case, even here, for making some larger payment from State funds.

The depression and apathy which finally settles down in many of the homes of these long-unemployed men lies at the root of most of the problems which are connected with unemployment. It is one of the reasons why they fail to get back to work. It is one of the reasons why the majority of them "have not the heart" for clubs or activities of other kinds, and it is one of the reasons why their homes seem so poverty-stricken. "I don't know how it is," said a young married woman in Blackburn, "but these last few years since I've out of the mills I don't seem able to take trouble, somehow; I've got no spirit for anything. But I didn't use to be like that." One of us who saw her had little doubt "how it was." The woman looked thin and ill, and it was clear that what food there was was going to the children. Such a simultaneous onset of physical

and psychological hardship can hardly help having serious results.

## WHAT WORK HAS MEANT

If we are to see how it gradually becomes possible for the worker to accept unemployment, it must be in the light of an understanding what work ordinarily means to him. The sample illustrated this, and showed how it differed as between individuals, as between places, or as between types of employment. Work provides for most people the pattern within which their lives are lived, and when this pattern is lost they have thrown on them a responsibility which, in the case of most unemployed men, their working lives have in no way qualified them to bear, the responsibility for organizing their own existence. They fall in ultimately with some new makeshift pattern.

"I was one of a gang," said a lad from Lancashire, "as we called it; there were twenty or more of us. We used to stay in bed late in the mornings so as not to need breakfast. I used to have a cup of tea, and then we would all go down to the library and read the papers. Then we went home for a bit of lunch, and then we met again at a billiard hall where you could watch the play for nothing. Then back for tea, and to watch the billiards again. In the evening we all used to go to the pictures. That was how we spent the dole money. In the end I thought I'd go mad if I went on like that. So I broke away from them and joined one of these P.T.* classes. But I found it made me so hungry that I couldn't go on with it. If I hadn't had the chance of coming to this place" (Wincham Hall, a college in Cheshire where educational courses for unemployed men are run) "I don't know what would have happened to me then. I felt like going under, I can tell you."

Sometimes life is less elaborately organized and gives a yet stronger impression of pointlessness: "You see that corner?" said a young man of 20 in the Rhondda, "Well, when I'm on my own, my time is spent be-

ED. NOTE: * Physical training.

tween here and that corner." One feature almost always stands out clearly, the days on which a man has to visit the Exchange and sign on to qualify for Unemployment Assistance: and the queue "at the Labour" plays a big part in the life of most unemployed men. But the first and most difficult feature of unemployment is the very obvious one that it leaves the unemployed man with nothing to do, and that, until he loses his job, he does not realise how much it means to him in this way. "Time," one man said, "is my worst enemy now."

A job has meant other things also. The skilled and semi-skilled man almost invariably has great pride in his work. He will tell you that his was the "finest pit in the world" or show you the tools he once used, or tell you of the different countries and continents to which in the old days the products of the factory where he worked used to go. "When you're working you feel like a cog in a machine. When you're out, you feel that no one has any use for you, and to see your wife busy makes you feel ashamed." "When you've a job you feel you're doing your bit for the Empire." This latter argument may not be very clear, but the feeling it expresses is clear enough—the feeling of uselessness with which many of the unemployed are obsessed. Their remarks often show, too, the interest they have had in the management of the firms with whom they worked. "Of course the old gaffer used to run the business properly, and then the new one came along and was always doing something else and spent most of his time on the booze and we didn't keep up to date; and at last the place was closed down and all of us were turned on to the streets. Most of us had been in the firm all our lives." The sample left no doubt that the majority of skilled and semi-skilled workers were normally deeply absorbed in their work. Often their manner suggested that their lives had been wholly centered in their employment, and that the friendships made in the course of it and the association which it brought with fellow-workers was the most valuable thing they had. Thus in Blackburn the sample included a woman who after many years' work as a weaver had lost her job because she rashly complained, on behalf of a large number of those who worked with her, of a new supply of material that they considered defective and as increasing considerably the labour of weaving. She had later been forced out of the union, because she worked "blackleg" outside Blackburn during a strike in the hope of thus recovering permanent employment. "I loved the mills," she said, "I loved the company and the people and everything about them. The mill was home to me. I'd do anything in the world if I could get back to them. I'd not mind working even if things were very much worse than they were before." Few men wear their hearts as openly as this on their sleeve: but the impression of isolation and loneliness which they give is, in its way, as vivid. What is sometimes the single link they have with their fellow-men has been severed.

But while the work done by the skilled or semi-skilled man is normally interesting enough to occupy his mind or at least continuous enough to give him the habit of working, the unskilled man is in a different position. Only if he is lucky does he get work with one firm which is continuous and carries him through the best part of his working life. More probably he never gets more than a few months' continuous work, after which he has to look for something else, and in many cases, it is only a matter of a few odd days' work occasionally here and there. Experiments have recently been made with regard to decasualizing dock work, and to a large extent they have been successful, but the problem nevertheless remains considerable even in docking, and much more considerable in unregistered casual labour. The spells of casual work which a "general labourer" finds for himself are often not enough to give men the habit of working. A young docker met in one of the Liverpool clubs described how as he was tramping down to the docks in the morning he would find himself turning into the club to spend the day there. He knew that the chances were against his getting work, even if he went to look for it. The club was comfortable and there was plenty to do, so that gradually it became more and more difficult for him to bring himself to take a job. He was an active and intelligent lad, and his case is illuminating. Work of the kind he does is clearly not going to provide that "pattern" of which we have spoken above. Though he may enjoy it while he is doing it, the chances are that it gives him no real interest and, as jobs get fewer and more far between, it does not worry him unduly, though his family feels the pinch soon enough. There are indeed casual labourers who are interested in their work; dockers with an extensive knowledge of the goods they handle, timber or whatever it may be—like one docker in the sample in Liverpool who had picked up a considerable knowledge of the fruit trade and was anxious to set up independently in it; and there are a few (like a splendid old workman whom one of us met in a common lodging-house in Leicester) whose interest in life has been to see the world and pick up jobs wherever they go to pay their way. But these are the exceptions. The ordinary unemployed "general labourer" in the sample evidently had very little interest in his work (though he often said he felt fitter while doing it) and this makes it much easier for him to acquiesce in unemployment.

Moreover, the general labourer on the dole has at least some form of security, and the frequency with which they find out that they are better off with regular money than many working, who get "rained off" for part of the week and draw only £1 or thereabouts in wages, shows clearly enough that they often appreciate this. Yet for these men, too, work means contacts with other men, and unemployment often turns them, especially the elderly, in upon themselves more and more. For many such men, shy, awkward and reserved, there is no other solution (if indeed they cannot be fitted back in work) than personal friendship, and even that will often fail to penetrate the isolation. It is not so difficult to help the elderly women, since their re-

sponse is readier, and they will let themselves go whole-heartedly in any social activities provided for them. Outside the Special Areas the problem of this isolation is particularly acute, since the proportion of elderly unemployed men who are living alone is particularly high. Thus in Deptford, in the age group 55–64, there were 25 "single men" (if one includes widowers and those living apart from their wives in this category) as against 29 married, that is to say, 46% were "single," while in Leicester there were 20 "single" and 26 married, the "single" men being 43% of the total. In Crook 10 were "single," 19 married (single 34%), and in the Rhondda 17 "single," 37 married (single 31%). Nothing is more urgent or more worth while than the attempt to do something for these older men, with whom may be reckoned for this purpose large numbers of old age pensioners above the age of 65. Things are being done, but not enough.

It remains to show in the figures this difference between skilled and unskilled. These are worked out, taking once more our three categories: those who refuse to accept unemployment, those who are on the way to accepting it, and those who have accepted it and would find it hard to bring themselves to take work, in the following table:

TABLE I. ATTITUDE TO NEW EMPLOYMENT, BY OCCUPATIONAL STATUS: MEN ONLY, EFFECTIVE RECORDS

| Attitude to New Employment | | Still thinking in terms of work | Beginning to accept state of unemployment | Adjusted to state of unemployment | TOTAL |
|---|---|---|---|---|---|
| *Status of worker* | | | | | |
| Minor commercial | | 13 | 11 | 8 | 32 |
| | % | 41 | 34 | 25 | 100 |
| Skilled | | 23 | 25 | 18 | 66 |
| | % | 35 | 38 | 27 | 100 |
| Semi-skilled | | 113 | 172 | 112 | 397 |
| | % | 28 | 44 | 28 | 100 |
| Unskilled | | 65 | 110 | 58 | 233 |
| | % | 28 | 47 | 25 | 100 |
| Submarginal | | 4 | 8 | 12 | 24 |
| | % | 17 | 33 | 50 | 100 |

The facts could hardly be clearer than they are there brought out. Here and there, it is true, other influences distort the result slightly; and if the rise in percentage for the lower status in column III is not regular, it is because the sample of semi-skilled men is weighted by the figures for the Special Areas, where "adjustment" to unemployment is for various reasons easier. As a whole, however, the table leaves no doubt whatever that the status of the worker plays a significant part in his attitude once he gets out of work. To the skilled worker work has meant something of real importance and interest, and he finds it hard to reconcile himself to the loss of it. For the unskilled worker this is less difficult, and for the "submarginal" case, the man who has done such casual work as requires neither intelligence nor physique, it is easier still. At the same time, though the change is quite clear, it is not violent. Table C 1 shows that to a high proportion of unskilled men work has meant enough to make them refuse adjustment to unemployment, and personal qualities are what obviously count most in causing the gradual drift into category III.

## THE EFFECT OF BAD WORKING CONDITIONS

So far those men have been considered for whom work was on the balance something which meant much to them and which it caused real distress to lose. But the effect of losing work may be different when unemployment, by breaking a connexion that has been accepted but never willed, gives men an idea of new possibilities, or at least a detestation of the work they used to do. This is common with those who have worked "underground," and occurs in some Lancashire towns among unemployed mill-workers, and it was noticeable too among the seamen of Liverpool. Conditions everywhere are changing, partly owing to the changing requirements of modern competition; and standards demanded by employees (e.g. by seamen, several of whom in the sample showed themselves well aware of the low wages

and discomfort of this occupation) are changing too. This is most clearly apparent in the mining industry. Thirty years ago the miners were an aristocracy of labour. Wages were good, the collier was a craftsman, and he generally served a kind of "apprenticeship" with his father. The demand for coal was increasing steadily, and the seams worked were generally thick. Now, however, mechanization has speeded up production underground and the pace of the men working at the coal face is forced for him; he is no longer his own master. The noise makes it difficult for him to hear the sound of cracks on which he used to depend to foretell falls of roof. "There's someone watching the conveyor all the time. If they see less coming along they're down on you in a moment. They use plenty of this (pointing to the mouth): all they need is whips." "I've always been used to look up, not to look down." "This is not work, it is murder."

Moreover, the unemployed miner believes (and it is difficult to disbelieve it, in face of the cases that are quoted) that many men are working regularly in the pits for a wage below the legal minimum, knowing that, if they complain, they will be "handed their cards"—"There is plenty waiting to take their place at a lower wage" —and putting up with their position because they hope that in the ballot for better seams they may soon be luckier. Mining is anyhow a dangerous occupation. In the course of the sample a young man of 28 was visited in the Rhondda. He was slightly lame, and he had done no regular work for thirteen years. He described how when he was 15 he was working underground and he was pinned up to the neck, by a fall of roof, and was not rescued for three hours. His case brings out the dangers of mining, but they can be easily illustrated in figures. The industry in South Wales leaves behind it a steady trail of human wreckage. The sample showed that almost exactly half of those miners over 45 who had been out of work for a considerable period in the Rhondda are in some way unfit.

It is, therefore, not surprising that many men should have had suggested to them by unemployment the possibility of giving up the industry entirely and adopting some different occupation, or should at least become more and more reluctant to return. It is no doubt possible to exaggerate this reluctance. As a collier of 52 told us, a man who by extraordinary persistence had succeeded at that age in fitting himself for a new trade, "If anyone were to ask for 4,000 men in Tonypandy, they would be forthcoming for the asking," and among them would be some who spoke of the dangers of mining as keeping them out of work, for the unemployed man is as human as anyone else and makes excuses on what might be called the "sour grapes" principle. But the sample leaves no doubt whatever that there is a substantial number who are reluctant to return to mining. As instances may be quoted a miner from the Rhondda who has made himself an expert gardener and talked lyrically of the discovery of the world above ground: "We people who work underground don't know anything about the things that make life worth living. Sometimes on the films I see one of those Californian giant Phloxes, and I think that is life": another, now working, who had made himself into a competent organist, and had evidently accepted only with great reluctance the offer of another mining job; a man of 33 in Crook who, thanks largely to his social activities, had succeeded in becoming thoroughly competent to undertake a clerical post, and described how as years went by his liking for the pit had been turned into fear of having to return to underground work. And the number of older people who said that they would on no account allow their sons to go underground, in view of conditions in the mines to-day, was considerable, which is only another side of the same reluctance. No doubt the realization that the job no longer gives the security that it used to give also plays a part.

The effects of this particular "adjustment" can be seen plainly in the figures. They show that, if we take the age group 28–42 in the Rhondda, 46 men come in the category II of those who are "beginning to accept unemployment as the normal state for themselves," as against 10 in category I, those who refuse to accept unemployment as a normal state, and 9 in category III, those who have accepted unemployment as the normal state and would find it difficult to work again if work was offered them. The corresponding figures for Liverpool are: 40 in group II, 31 in category I and 25 in category III. The majority of the unemployed Rhondda miners in this age group are finding it comparatively easy to acquiesce in unemployment because their old job has lost its attractiveness for them, though the majority of them also would take eagerly enough fair work of some other kind in the valleys if they had the opportunity of it.

. . . . .

### THE UNEMPLOYED COMMUNITY

If a man has been out of work for more than a year, and he sees hundreds of others similarly situated, it is natural that he should think less of the work he may never succeed in getting and more of "how to make do" in the circumstances. We have seen something above of the evolving of some pattern for existence that this necessitates, and the majority of men who have been unemployed for long have formed this pattern for themselves and follow it regularly day after day. Very often this "pattern" includes meetings with other unemployed men outside the Exchange or in the Public Library or the Unemployed Club. Here is one example in the life of a dock porter (age 35) in Liverpool: "I go round and meet a few of my friends and have a chat; then down to the Labour or the Unemployment Assistance Board and have a talk or a lounge about for a bit. Then I come back and have dinner. If anyone'll take me to the pictures in the afternoon I go there, once a week or more; or sometimes I go to a billiard hall and sit there. I don't do much reading except in the newspapers. I do no boot repairing, and don't do much carpentry, for if I do it people can tell it's not a proper job. What I miss is having a few shillings extra to go across the water at week ends, or to the football match. I often travelled to Manchester and beyond to watch the team playing."

This man, we were informed, was regarded by the officials as a "respectable type, eager to obtain work." In our view, he would have taken work if he had been offered it, but he had ceased to be "eager" for it. And as his day is like the day of tens of thousands who have been out of work long, so his attitude too is characteristic. He is coming to accept unemployment as something which is natural and inevitable. It means that he has to make some changes; that he cannot take a trip across the Mersey or to the Isle of Man as he used to do, but he gets accustomed to the economies. His life is switched down to a lower economic plane and no doubt at first he finds it hard, but especially where, as in the instance quoted, he has always been familiar with spells of unemployment, he ultimately settles down to a new routine of existence. And one thing above all makes this comparatively easy for him, if he finds himself a member of an unemployed community.

How much easier it is for an unemployed man who is associated with others like himself to become used to unemployment can be shown by a comparison between the Rhondda and Leicester. If we compare the oldest age group, 55–64, in these two places, the difference in "ease of adjustment" is at once apparent. The long-unemployed man in Leicester of that age is an isolated figure. In the Rhondda he is one of thousands. In the Rhondda it is easy for him to settle down, seeing how many others of his age are forced to do so, and something between a half and two-thirds of the men in this age group had so settled down. In Leicester that was true of about a quarter. In this town more than a fifth could not bring themselves to accept the fact that they would probably never work again, in the Rhondda less than a tenth.

In a prosperous area the unemployed community means not much more than the queue at the Labour Exchange, where the unemployed man signs on and draws his allowances. As each man is timed at the Exchange, the queues are largely voluntary, the men "hanging about" for a talk. Even in a prosperous area a man will see hundreds of others crowding in at the Exchange when he goes there, and often if he has not much enterprise and energy, he jumps to the conclusion that they are all in the same position as he is himself. "With so many young men out of a job, what's the use of a fellow like me going on looking?" The great majority of the young men are indeed only temporarily stopped, or, though out of work, will be fixed up with something in a week or two. The crowds round the Exchange are no indication of the extent of the real unemployment problem. But, if he can persuade himself that they are, this obviously makes it easier for him to accept his own position.

It is in the queue, at least in more prosperous places, that unemployed public opinion comes into being. Thus there are a number of standard complaints that one hears from one man after another, such as the complaint, made not only in Liverpool but in Leicester and London as well, that "everything is done here nowadays by this Irish labour." In most instances the complaint has little foundation, but it is passed on from one man to another because it is an excuse that each man can use readily for his own unemployment. When one of us was told in Liverpool by a coal-porter that "all the jobs nowadays are done by girls and machines," it was evident that this was an idea picked up in the queue, for even in these days there is not much displacement of coal-porters by female or mechanical labour. Another complaint for which there must be some foundation, but which is certainly exaggerated by unemployed public opinion, is that "work is only obtained through graft." Thus a Liverpool docker, to take one example of many, claimed that "most jobs go nowadays only to those who treat the bosses. The man upstairs is always at work like that. Any time in the pub you can see how it is done." Sometimes the complaint rang true enough, but in this instance, a rather disreputable young man who told us that "he'd been pretty lucky in his day" betting, it suggested an excuse rather than a reason for being out of work. It occurred frequently enough to show that it is a commonplace of unemployed gossip. In one case where it was mentioned by a more respectable man, he said that though he had often heard of it, an instance had never occurred within his own experience.

Evidently the unemployed clubs are in many places the subject of unemployed gossip in the queue, and the frequency with which the laconic criticism "dope" is made against them, suggested that it was also an idea originating in this way. It looks also as if many of the unjustified views of the Unemployment Assistance Board regulations are derived from the same source. Many unemployed men, for instance, conceal small occasional earnings for which no deductions would be made from their allowances. The printed leaflet which they all receive explaining the regulations stands little chance against this strong public opinion. Similarly, one reason why it has been difficult to get men to attend Government Training Centres in the past has been this unemployed public opinion, formed in the queue; for necessarily the unemployed man meets there the failures, and not the successes, since the latter, after their period of training, have passed into employment, generally in a new district. Some of the more respectable men described how they had at first dreaded the queue, and how gradually they had got used to it, and "if you talk about the right kind of things in the queue, racing and football, it isn't so bad as it might be."

An unemployed man's friendships are largely formed in this way, and when he speaks of "going about with a few other fellows" that is how he has generally found them. A striking instance of this is one of the small number of men in the sample

with prison records; a man who had served several short terms of imprisonment for house-breaking. He spoke after a time freely of the way in which this had happened. It was obvious that he was potentially a decent sort of man, and he had originally had good work which he left to emigrate. His passage to Canada had been guaranteed, but at the last moment, owing to the illness of his wife, he could not go, and it was impossible for him to get back to his old employment. "I'd never done anything of that sort when I was a child, but when I was out of work and we'd very little money I met one or two fellows down at the Labour who did that kind of thing and I thought I could do it too. It was exciting too, and once I got a bit of money that way it was very hard not to go on. But whenever I met a policeman it gave me the jumps, I never knew whether I'd come home again and I always knew they'd get me in the end. I never used to break into a house where there were people, but used to rob the coin meters in empty houses. Of course, I didn't want to take anything that belonged to anyone."

We have quoted him at length, for in so far as there is a connexion between unemployment and crimes against property, his case shows how that connexion may arise. But for our present purpose we note only the way in which he met his associates, since it shows how many unemployed men's associations are formed.

There are more specific organizations which help in the formation of this unemployed public opinion and help to keep the unemployed community together. In several of the towns visited, the National Unemployed Workers' Movement had representatives, who stood outside the Labour Exchanges, on pay day, collecting the penny a week from the "dole" money. The sample cases seen were not asked whether they belonged to it for obvious reasons (as they were not asked anything about their politics), but in a number of instances they volunteered information. One or two had dropped out because they did not think it any use, and there were some criticisms of the local personnel of the Movement, but the majority of those who spoke about it evidently valued it. There can be no doubt, however, that especially in more prosperous places, the tendency of organizations of this kind, as sometimes (though not by any means always) of the unemployed clubs, is with younger men at least to encourage them not to get work.

In places which are less prosperous the unemployed community is less militantly defensive owing to its very size. It is accepted, whereas in prosperous areas the attempt is made to ignore it. In Liverpool there are various reductions in price made for the unemployed and notices appear in the shop-window to that effect. They can get their hair cut cheaper, for instance, and in many places they can get cheaper cinema tickets. On Tyneside some of the unemployed club members get free passes into the cinema as often as three times a week. Such advantages may be set off partly, though not wholly, by those which an unemployed man in a prosperous place gets from the greater efficiency of the social services. We are not arguing for a moment that these things ought to be curtailed, for conditions are bad enough even when these few small advantages have been reckoned in. The point about them is simply that the unemployed man notices them, and that they help to reconcile him to his position. And if, as often happens in depressed places, two or three adult members of the family are out of work, the sense of belonging to an unemployed community is natural, and it is much easier to settle down. This was noticeable also in Liverpool, where we were sometimes told: "Why, there are only two families in this street where the man is working!"

. . . . .

### THE "WORK-SHY"

So much has been said of the unwillingness of the unemployed to work that it is important to get some idea of the proportion which the various types discussed bear to the whole problem, and we attempt such an estimate later. We still have to consider, however, other types, and in particular the type where there is no such explanation as a low potential wage for the adjustment which has taken place; where (to adopt the phrase which is generally used) the man is "work-shy."

From this type we should exclude all the older men. One factor common to prosperous as well as to depressed towns is the difficulty of older men obtaining work, once they lose it. Until measures are taken to create work for these older men, it is most desirable that they should be able to adjust themselves to the probability of not doing much work again for the rest of their lives, and it is cause for satisfaction rather than otherwise that some of them have found it possible to do so. Here the problem indeed is how to facilitate the adjustment where that has not occurred, for in a very large number of cases they refuse to make it. The older men were brought up with a different outlook and different standards from those which come to the younger generation, and many of them feel that they cannot be satisfied with the rest of their lives lived out "on the dole." Where, however, there is a large unemployed community such as in South Wales or Crook, the adjustment is more readily made, and a qualified observer who has known the Rhondda for fifty years said that in many ways the older men were probably now as happy as or happier than they had ever been. We are some way there towards the creation of a new "leisured" group of the old men who have been compulsorily retired from industry and yet are prepared to accept that as an opportunity to live as pleasant a life as their somewhat straitened resources will allow.

This adjustment has taken years to happen. The only question about it is how much harm is done by allowing such a group to exist among the nominally "unemployed." In the following table we compare the figures for the two places in the Special Areas with those for Leicester in order to show the extent to which such adjustment is taking place.

TABLE II. ATTITUDE: OLDER MEN 55–64

| Category | I | II | III |
|---|---|---|---|
| Rhondda | 3(7%) | 13(31%) | 26(62%) |
| Crook | 1(4%) | 7(31%) | 15(65%) |
| Leicester | 10(22%) | 22(49%) | 13(29%) |

The high percentages in category III in the two places within the Special Areas are most noticeable. The majority of the older men there know well enough that they will never work again, and they accept the fact. In Leicester, where there is great relative prosperity, adjustment is far more difficult.

That there is a certain number of "work-shy" men among the younger unemployed is of course not open to doubt, and the question is only what proportion they bear to the whole. In our view, the number is relatively speaking not large, and tends to be exaggerated by confusion with another group, which constitutes a much more troublesome problem, the men who have become diffident owing to continual unemployment, who find it more and more difficult to face repeated failures and who finally give up looking for work. Many such men have not in any way become used to unemployment; often there is no question of allowance approaching potential wages; nor is life made easy by associations, for many of them are living in isolation. It should be possible, if conditions of employment continue to be good, for the Exchanges to do much to help such men back to work. At present it is often assumed far too readily that because a man is young and has been out of work for some time, he is shy of work and therefore not the sort of man who can be sent for a job. Young men who are out of work in prosperous areas are not necessarily avoiding work, and if they sometimes answer shortly and "evasively," as we were told, to questions of the Board's Investigating Officers, it may be because looking for work has such humiliating associations for them that they hate the implied suggestion that they could get work if they tried.

The "work-shy" man is of a different type, though in a casual interview the two may not be easy to distinguish. The chances are that he is mixed up with some betting concern, or that he keeps greyhounds, or picks up something here and there in addition to his Unemployment Assistance by hawking or street singing. Often he does not even tell his wife whether he is working or not, and the share of the allowance which he keeps for himself is disproportionately large. He may be dressed rather flashily, and the chances are that he will complain of those men who won't work, contrasting them with the hard triers like himself. We may summarise the career of such a one, an extreme case, in a prosperous area: a married man aged 24. After leaving school in 1927 he was for a few months an errand boy. He subsequently worked for nearly a year in a factory, then was six months with a firm of builders in 1931. That same year he had two days of bill distributing, and two months in another factory. In the summer of 1934 he pushed a barrow hawking fruit. Interspersed with these jobs he had done some professional boxing in several different towns, and being at one time (before he was married) disallowed unemployment insurance on the grounds that he had voluntarily left good employment, he went off elsewhere with the friend with whom he lived, and by begging and singing in the streets for about two hours a day they used to earn 8s. or so, "enough to keep the wolf from the door." When a lad of 15, he was first fined for stealing, and subsequently bound over for two years for the same offence. Incidentally he told us that he used to have an allotment, but "got fed up when vegetables got pinched." In 1932 he was imprisoned for thirteen days for assault and at the end of 1934 he got six months hard labour for living on the immoral earnings of the girl he later married. His house was reasonably well furnished, and somehow he seemed to have acquired an excellent wireless set and apparently also a motor bicycle. One employer stated that it "appeared impossible for him to speak the truth, even when there was no reason for him to do otherwise." He had now evidently settled down on the allowance, eked out generously by less reputable sources of income, and expressed himself as quite contented. It would of course be easy to suggest many occupations in which such a man might do well. If, however, society can keep him quiet by paying him 33s. a week, it seems a not unreasonable bargain. But we have our doubts.

His is indeed an extreme case, though it must not be dismissed too readily for in each place visited there was, in category III, a sprinkling of men who had criminal records, or had been heavily fined for working with bookmakers. In Liverpool, for example, two or three of the men visited were of this type, like one with whom we had a useful interview in spite of a warning that he was a dangerous fellow who "throws culinary articles at his parents, habitually uses filthy language, frequents gambling clubs, and is a bookmaker's tout"; and that he "uses physical force where necessary." "A real clever boy," his mother (who saw the visitor first) described him. But the majority were less exciting, and much more depressing, as for instance a man of 25, living with his mother and sister. "When I called," our record notes, "at 12.15, he was still in bed. His mother opened the door. I heard her speak to him through the bedroom door. He said I should come again another time. When I asked him what time was suitable, he shouted it was no use, he would say nothing. His mother was very much afraid of him."

Almost always it is the same story: "Has not learned any trade." "Very little work since leaving school." "His mother says he would do better without the dole." "Gave the impression of not being over anxious to get another job." "Surly and reserved." "Said he wanted work, but I don't believe it." It would be mistaken, however, to assume that all these young men are necessarily inferior material. Anyone with experience of handling young men of 18 or 20 or so is aware of the odd aberrations for which allowances constantly have to be made, and obviously any aberration will be emphasized tenfold by the abnormality of prolonged unemployment. In one family

visited in Liverpool though the lad who was the sample case was still unemployed, his brother aged 25 was also seen, and he was back in good employment after being out for two years. He appeared a fine normal type, yet he described how difficult he had found it to force himself back to work, and his mother said that while he had been out of work "he was terribly surly. He used to go upstairs to his room and refuse to eat." If he had been visited by one of us at that time, he might perhaps have been classified in the third of our categories, but the classification would evidently have been wrong.

Yet this problem of the young unemployed man remains serious, perhaps the most serious of all the problems of the long unemployed. It is especially aggravated by the conditions of Liverpool, the depression, the casual character of much employment, and the low standard, material and nonmaterial, at which the Liverpool long unemployed are living. Here are the Liverpool figures for attitude to work split up into 15-year age groups.

TABLE III. ATTITUDE TOWARDS
EMPLOYMENT: LIVERPOOL

| Category | I | II | III | Total |
|---|---|---|---|---|
| Age 20–34 | 20(24%) | 39(46%) | 25(30%) | 84 |
| Age 35–49 | 26(33%) | 33(42%) | 20(25%) | 79 |
| Age 50–64 | 27(43%) | 24(38%) | 12(19%) | 63 |

It will be seen that eagerness for work declines steadily from the older men to the younger. We could wish that a larger proportion of the older men could accept the fact of unemployment, but they cannot, and we find that the proportion of them in category I is exceptionally high. Many of the middle-aged men with large families come into the group discussed above where the possible wages are so low that Unemployment Assistance is a satisfactory alternative, which explains the high proportion of middle-aged men in category II. What is most depressing, however, is to find from the figures of both category II and of category III that the young men are those who are most ready to accept long unemployment. It is hard to exaggerate the importance of this for the future. One other point must be mentioned here concerning the attitude of these young men. That association with an unemployed community which can be so powerful a factor in reconciling a man to unemployment is present probably more extensively here than in any other age group. Though they tend not to belong to specific organizations, the number who spend most of their time with other young men who are also out of work is large. In Liverpool these associations take chiefly the form of "cellar clubs." In Leicester it is the ordinary unemployed club which the young men patronize. But whatever the form, we find this feature regularly through the various areas into which the sample took us. It suggests at once one of the reasons for their continual unemployment, and also perhaps the possibility of a more effective institutional approach to them than has been made in the past.

## SELECTED REFERENCES FOR PART 4

BAKKE, E. W. *Citizens Without Work.* New York: Yale Univ. Press, 1940.

Subtitled: "A Study of the Effects of Unemployment Upon the Workers' Social Relations and Practices."

BARNARD, CHESTER I. *The Functions of the Executive.* Cambridge, Mass.: Harvard Univ. Press, 1938, rev. ed., 1948.

An effort, by a noted executive and social scientist, to develop a theory of the role played in social organization by executives and administrators.

BRIEFS, GOETZ A. *The Proletariat.* New York: McGraw-Hill, 1937.

The existence of an alienated proletariat, the author declares, constitutes a fundamental challenge to Western civilization.

CHASE, STUART. *Men at Work.* New York: Harcourt, 1941.

Popular essays on human relations in industry.

CHRYSLER, WALTER P. *Life of an American Workman.* In collaboration with Boyden Sparkes. New York: Dodd, Mead, 1937.

Self-portrait of a leader in the American automotive industry.

COTTRELL, W. FRED. *The Railroader.* Palo Alto, Calif.: Stanford Univ. Press, 1940.

A "participant observer's" report on the life of the railroader.

GINZBERG, ELI, SOL W. GINSBURG, SIDNEY AXELRAD, and JOHN L. HERMA. *Occupational Choice: An Approach to a General Theory.* New York: Columbia Univ. Press, 1951.

An attempt at describing "the sequence of occupational inclinations from late childhood to early maturity."

JOHNSON, GERALD W. *A Liberal's Progress.* New York: Coward-McCann, 1948.

The career of a "maverick" businessman, Edward A. Filene, noted for his innovations in merchandising and labor relations.

KOMAROVSKY, MIRRA. *The Unemployed Man and His Family.* New York: Dryden Press, 1940.

A careful study of the effects of unemployment upon the morale of the American workless and their families.

KRAUS, HENRY. *The Many and the Few: A Chronicle of the Dynamic Auto Workers.* Los Angeles: The Plantin Press, 1947.

An inside story of the Detroit sit-down strikes, sympathetic to the workers.

MAN, HENRI DE. *Joy in Work.* Translated from the German by Eden and Cedar Paul. London: G. Allen & Unwin, 1929.

——— *The Psychology of Socialism.* Translated from 2nd German edition by Eden and Cedar Paul. London: G. Allen & Unwin, 1928.

Critical examinations of Marxist theories concerning the joylessness of modern labor.

MILLER, DELBERT C. and WILLIAM H. FORM. *Industrial Sociology.* New York: Harper, 1951.

Subtitled: "An Introduction to the Sociology of Work Relations."

NEVINS, ALLAN. *John D. Rockefeller: The Heroic Age of American Enterprise.* 2 vols. New York: Scribner, 1940.

A sympathetic review of the career of the founder of the Standard Oil Company.

PARKER, CARLETON. *The Casual Laborer, and Other Essays.* New York: Harcourt, 1920.

Unusual insights into the psychological aspects of labor unrest by a neglected American economist who was one of the first to perceive the implications of Freudian psychology for the study of industrial relations.

REYNOLDS, L. G. and J. SHISTER. *Job Horizons: A Study of Job Satisfaction and Labor Mobility.* New York: Harper, 1949.

A critique of the presuppositions of classical economics concerning the worker's expectations and opportunities.

SATTERLEE, HERBERT L. *J. Pierpont Morgan.* New York: Macmillan, 1939.

An "intimate" and sympathetic portrait of the celebrated financier.

SLOAN, ALFRED P., JR. *Adventures of a White Collar Man.* In collaboration with Boyden Sparkes. New York: Doubleday, 1941.

The career and philosophy of a prominent industrial organizer and promoter.

SOMBART, WERNER. *The Quintessence of Capitalism: A Study of the History and Psychology of the Modern Business Man.* Translated by M. Epstein. London: T. F. Unwin, 1915.

One of the noted German economist's attempts to explain the evolution of the structure and spirit of capitalism.

STRIEDER, JAKOB. *Jakob Fugger, The Rich: Merchant and Banker of Augsburg, 1459–1525.* Translated by Mildred L. Hartsough.

Edited by N. S. B. Gras. New York: The Adelphi Co., 1931.

The life and times of the great German industrialist and financier of the sixteenth century.

SWARD, KEITH. *The Legend of Henry Ford.* New York: Rinehart, 1948.

A critical analysis of Ford's career and teachings.

TAUSSIG, F. W. and C. S. JOSLYN. *American Business Leaders.* New York: Macmillan, 1932.

A pioneering investigation on the social origins of the American business leaders. The materials on this theme are reviewed in William Miller's "American Historians and the Business Elite," *Journal of Economic History,* Vol. IX, 1949, 180 ff.

WALKER, CHARLES R. *Steeltown: An Industrial Case History of the Conflict between Progress and Security.* New York: Harper, 1950.

The story of the problems posed for management, labor force, and the community by the dismantling of a once-active plant.

WHYTE, WILLIAM FOOTE (ed.). *Industry and Society.* New York: McGraw-Hill, 1946.

Essays by Burleigh Gardner, W. Lloyd Warner and J. O. Low, Chester I. Barnard, Allison Davis, Everett Cherrington Highes, Mark Starr, Frederick H. Harbison, and the editor.

WILSON, LOGAN. *The Academic Man.* New York: Oxford Univ. Press, 1942.

The economic problems, social roles, and ways of life of college teachers.

ZWEIG, FERDINAND. *Life, Labour, and Poverty.* London: Gollancz, 1948.

———— *Men in the Pits.* London: Gollancz, 1948.

Closeups of the hopes and frustrations of the British working man.

❖        ❖        ❖

Some of the most striking accounts of occupational roles in American business and industrial life have been written by novelists and playwrights. Works by the following authors are particularly significant in this connection:

Saul Bellow (1916–    ); Erskine Caldwell (1903–    ); John Dos Passos (1896–    ); Theodore Dreiser (1871–1945); F. Scott Fitzgerald (1896–1940); William Dean Howells (1837–1920); Sinclair Lewis (1885–1951); Arthur Miller (1915–    ); Frank Norris (1870–1902); Budd Schulberg (1914–    ); Upton Sinclair (1878–    ); John Steinbeck (1902–    ); Frederick Wakeman (1909–    ); Jerome Wiedman (1913–    ).

# PART 5

# Power and status in industrial society

❦ Our main purpose in Part 5 is to examine the organization of power and status in industrial society. Who organizes and directs the affairs of our economy? Who has power to make decisions, and upon what is this power based? What means—from the threat of physical force, at one extreme, to the stimulation of spontaneous enthusiasm, at the other—are used to motivate participation in the economy, and who uses them on whom? What classes can be discerned, and what factors enter into their composition and structure?

In Section A we particularly wish to know what happens when an economy based in considerable degree on "market" controls (the free operation of "supply" and "demand" in the market) gives way to a "nonmarket" economy (one that is based on the limitation of competition and on decisions about production and distribution made by business combinations, labor unions, organizations of consumers, farmers' groups, and government). The first reading, from a NATIONAL RESOURCES COMMITTEE report, outlines the general nature of the problem. Here we are told that most modern industrial societies, and particularly the United States, combine market controls with an increasing number and variety of nonmarket controls. We must remember that this is primarily a difference of degree: an economy controlled by nothing but the forces of the market has never existed.

The very vigor of competition during the past century has itself been largely responsible for the decline of competition in our day. The strongest firms have tended to overcome their commercial rivals and to restrict the entry of aspiring competitors into business. Hence, various monopolistic practices have come more and more to be a characteristic of the "free-enterprise" economy. "Free enterprise" and not government has been largely responsible for the decline of "free enterprise." Mass production techniques themselves have called for greater aggregations of capital and a higher centralization of control. In many instances, economies resulting from size have appeared to make large combinations more efficient producers than a group of small competing firms would have been.

Within each large combination, moreover, ownership tends to be separated from control. Stockholders, the formal owners, being scattered and very numerous, cease to have any effective day-to-day influence in the government of the corporation. Actual control gravitates more and more into the hands of technicians and salaried administrators. Even boards of directors tend to be overshadowed by their employees, the administrators.

This reading further points out that organizations of businessmen and professional men—both the informal organization of the "corporate community" and the formal trade association—play a large part in the general structure of controls. A force counteracting the tendency for industrial control to become centered in large corporations and business combinations has developed with the growth of labor unions, which, in turn, however, have brought a further modification of the "free market" economy. To these control groups have been added organizations of farmers and, to a lesser degree, of consumers. Finally, government tends more and more to enter the picture with the professed objective of representing the "public" interest in a world of powerful conflicting pressure groups. In Part 7 we shall examine, in much greater detail, the role of government under various kinds of socio-economic organization.

But statistics about interest groups can hardly give us a complete picture of how nonmarket controls operate. The reading by DAVID LYNCH endeavors to make vivid for us the ways in which businessmen seek to eliminate competition, evade laws which have been passed to destroy monopoly, and harry potential competitors into conformity with respect to such crucial issues as prices and allocation of markets. Here we observe how "price leadership" is used to evade the antitrust laws, how "racketeering" is related to the problem of eliminating competition, and how advertising and patents are used to develop and sustain monopolies. There are, of course, many other techniques which are not examined in this particular reading.

The selection from the PRESIDENT'S ECONOMIC REPORT examines the problem of income distribution in an industrial society. Income distribution is closely related to all problems of power, prestige, and status. The larger one's income, the greater one's power and status is likely to be; conversely, the greater one's power and status, the larger, on the whole, will be one's share of the national income.

The reading by LEWIS COREY deals with class structure in the United States. Corey contends that there has been arising in the United States a "new" middle class, which promises, in the future, to assume an even greater importance in the economic and political life of the country. This selection, as Corey suggests, should be read against the background of two different visions of the future held during the nineteenth-century heyday of capitalism. Proponents of the private enterprise system tended to see the middle class of small shopkeepers and independent businessmen as the backbone of a free society, and to see the good society of the future as one based upon them. On the other hand, Karl Marx and others saw the middle class as the chief obstacle to be removed in reaching the good society and thought that the lower middle classes would gradually be "liquidated" by being forced down into the working classes as big business and industry expanded.

Corey argues that this proletarianization of the middle classes has not, in fact, taken place, although the "old middle class" has declined relative to other groups. The "new middle class" has rather arisen because, as business combinations and labor organizations grow in size and power, larger and larger numbers of people become salaried workers while not yet being psychologically or socially a part of the "working classes." It is this new middle class which Corey thinks gives us the key to many modern American phenomena in politics and social life generally. For salaried engineers, clerks, accountants, doctors, teachers, and administrators are neither the "old middle-class" shopkeepers and small businessmen nor are they manual workers. Yet their numbers have grown enormously.

The significance of labor unions in the structure of power and status is analyzed by C. WRIGHT MILLS. He discusses the organization and ramifications of American unions, providing a partial insight into the relationship between the leaders and ordinary union members. Labor unions are particularly important in an analysis of status and power because they represent a large group of producers whose interests do not necessarily coincide with those of consumers (as, of course, the interests of unions do not necessarily coincide with those of other producers, especially owners of capital). Like business combinations, they constantly seek to control the social machinery whereby incomes are distributed, prices fixed, and the consumer's dollar divided.

In the reading from the National Resources Committee it was suggested that stockholders no longer control the boards of directors and managers of large corporations but rather that managers and directors tend to control the stockholders. In labor unions, the Mills reading suggests, similar problems of internal control arise. While theoretically labor leaders are elected by and are responsible to union members, actually many union leaders tend to control the membership rather than to be controlled by it. As managers tend to become separated from directors and stockholders, so union leaders sometimes become largely independent of their members.

In the last reading in this Part, JAMES BURNHAM argues that modern industrial society is being increasingly ruled, not by capitalists, or by labor unions, or by politicians, but by what he calls the "managerial" class. Although the managerial *elite* is by no means identical with Corey's "new middle class," the growth in importance of the two groups stems from the same factor: the increasing role of technical and organizational skill in a society based upon large-scale production and wide division of labor.

Burnham extends the concept of "managerial control" to all aspects of society. The legal and formal control of industrial society may be, he says, in the hands of stockholders (who "own" the means of production), of the members of labor unions (who "own" their own labor power and have the right to strike), and of legislators (who are elected by the people and theoretically have the power to control through law). But the *actual* control, he contends, devolves more and more upon the managers of corporations, on business agents and other professional officers of unions, and on chiefs and directors of bureaus in government. This is true, Burnham argues, because these groups alone understand the technicalities and complexities of modern society. Their nominal "superiors"—stockholders, union members, and legislators—must therefore actually follow their lead and in effect be ruled by them.

Burnham's argument—that not only economic power but also power in the social structure at large, is passing into the hands of a "managerial class"—has been subjected to much criticism. One of the difficulties in evaluating his analysis, and in evaluating any effort to analyze power relationships, certainly grows out of the fact that although "power" is one of the most frequently used words in our language, it is also one of the most inadequately defined terms.

When we speak of and investigate economic power, we are speaking primarily of the different abilities of different persons and groups to determine how the functions of an economy shall be performed. In the broadest sense, when we speak of a person's "power" we mean his capacity to play an active part in shaping the whole world in which he lives. By political power we mean the capacity to play an active role in shaping the pattern of activities which we call government. Social power is the capacity to play an active role in the shaping of one's social organization. When we speak of status, we generally have in mind a picture of society, shared by its members, which usually takes the form of a ladder or pyramid, with some people "at the top" and sharing many social privileges, some "at the bottom" and sharing few.

Economic power is certainly closely related to all other forms of power and status. Since political activities require scarce resources or money, the distribution of economic power is closely related to the distribution of political power. For the same reason, it is also closely related to the distribution of social power and status.

Yet we must be on our guard against the assumption that there is a one-way road from economic power to the achievement of all other forms of status, prestige, and political power. The newly rich do not at once secure a rating in the Four Hundred. Under modern conditions, a man of great wealth may be severely limited in the amount of power he can exert, even over his own employees. Moreover, it should not be assumed that political power is necessarily any less primary or basic than economic power. Control of government is itself an important way of allocating scarce resources.

Burnham's argument serves to point up sharply the crucial question at stake in any analysis of the relationship between economic power and other forms of power and status: What is the significance for future social and political life—

particularly for those values which have been termed "democratic"—of the system of economic organization and power to which the modern industrial economy has given rise?

SECTION A

## The nature of controls

# 19 National Resources Committee: *The Structure of the American Economy*

❧ *The period between 1933 and the entry of the United States into the Second World War was marked by a revival of concern, on the part of individuals and government, about the extent and utilization of national resources. To investigate this problem, President Roosevelt appointed the National Resources Committee. The Committee published many reports, among them being* Our Cities (1937), Public Works Planning (1937), Regional Planning (1938), *and* Our Energy Resources (1939).

*One of the objectives of the Committee was to study the way in which the organization of the American economy affected the utilization of resources. This investigation led to the Committee's report entitled* The Structure of the American Economy (1939–40). *Our reading is excerpted from Part I, Chapter IX, pp. 153–70. After a brief theoretical analysis of the major types of economic control, the Committee endeavors in this selection to present a concrete picture of the way in which economic power—particularly of the "nonmarket" type—is distributed among different groups in the American economy.*

The major elements of control which are significant for the structure of the American economy are to be found in the great operating corporations, in the big financial institutions, in the trade and business associations, in the labor unions, in the farm organizations, in consumer organizations, and finally in the State and Federal Governments. If the economic controls associated with these organizations could be clearly delineated, the results would yield the main essentials in the structure of controls. . . .

THE CONCEPT "CONTROLS"

Because the term "controls" involves a relatively new economic concept, it is important to give it the greatest possible clarity. It is used here to refer to the ability of one individual or group to influence the policies in respect to the use of resources which are adopted by another individual or group. Thus, if a person can influence the production policy of a particular farmer by offering to buy his product at a price, by threatening to foreclose his mortgage, or by some other means so that the farmer raises one crop rather than another, to that extent the person is in a position to exercise some measure of control over the farmer's activity. Likewise, a factory superintendent is usually in a position to exercise a considerable measure of control over the activities of the workers in the factory during working hours. The management of a corporation similarly exercises a measure of control over the activities of subordinates, while the directors and the security-holders may, in turn, exercise varying degrees of control over the policies adopted by the management. Other groups, such as important buyers of a company's products, suppliers of raw material, financing agencies, labor unions, and government agencies, may exercise a considerable influence over the policies of an enterprise and to that extent share in its control. In each case, policies are developed with respect to the use of the resources available to the individual, or enterprise, or agency, and each of the persons or groups who influenced these policies may be said to have exercised some measure of control over them.

It is possible to conceive of a highly complex pattern of control running between all the individuals and groups in a society much as the physicist conceives of lines of attraction connecting all the stars and planets in the universe. In outlining the structure of controls, however, only certain major controls need to be considered.

## MARKET CONTROLS

Many of the threads of control exercised by individuals or groups are summarized in market phenomena. The influence which millions of bread consumers exercise over wheat farmers operates almost entirely through the influence of their demand on price and is thus summarized in the price of wheat. The controls exercised by millions of telephone users over the telephone systems are partly reflected in the demand for telephone service. To the extent that threads of control are summarized in market phenomena, they can be referred to as market controls and be analyzed as such. It is possible to imagine an economy in which all controls consisted of market controls. In such an economy, the policy of every enterprise would be so dominated by market controls reflected in market prices that no significant alternatives in price policy would be left to be influenced by nonmarket controls. In such a case, all controls would be covered by an analysis of markets.

## NONMARKET CONTROLS

However, in practice, market controls only partly determine the use of resources. In many producing units there is a wide latitude of choice in price policy, and economic controls not operating through the market are in effect. The extent of these nonmarket controls is suggested by the prevalence of insensitive administered prices * . . . and by the absence of free market prices in a large part of the American economy. Where policies with respect to the use of resources are only limited and not dominated by market controls, the nonmarket controls become a significant factor making for more or less effective use of resources. These nonmarket controls appear to build up into what has here been called a structure of controls, some of minor significance, some of major significance to the functioning of the national economy. The present outline of the structure of controls is concerned only with these major nonmarket controls.

Nonmarket controls may be said to be of major importance when policies affecting a very large number of persons can be significantly influenced. The major policies developed in large administrative organizations, such as an army or a large business corporation, usually are subject to a very considerable measure of nonmarket control and influence the actions of so many people in their use of resources as to be of sig-

---

ED. NOTE: * That is, prices which are fixed by business enterprises, or combinations of enterprises, so that they do not respond easily to the play of "supply and demand." Some methods of "administering" prices are dealt with in Reading 23.

nificance to the functioning of the whole economy. The nonmarket controls exercised by financial institutions through the handling of investment funds, and the nonmarket controls exercised by government through the regulation of business enterprises, through its fiscal policies, through the protection of property and enforcement of contracts, and through other major policies, likewise influence the activities of millions of people and are important to the structure of controls. Persons or groups in a position to influence policies at these points are, for this reason, in a position to influence to a corresponding extent the effectiveness with which the national resources are employed.

The nonmarket controls over policy are seldom sharply defined. Often the threads of nonmarket control build up in such a way as to result in many different foci of control, each focus having to do with some particular phase of activity. Thus, in a big corporation, while the main threads of control over operating policy may come to a focus in the hands of the corporation president, some threads of control are likely to rest with other groups; controls over financial policy may be partly focused in a special finance committee of the board of directors and partly focused in some bank or financial house to which the corporation is under obligation; the threads of control over labor policy may be divided between the corporation and a labor union, some threads focusing in the corporate management and some in the union officials; threads of control over some aspects of policy may rest with the government bodies, as in the case of minimum working standards or public utility regulation; still other threads may rest with some dominant buyer whose orders are so important that he can, within limits, dictate the internal policy of the corporation, say with respect to its policy toward labor organization; or a supplier of raw materials or of services may hold sufficient threads of control to influence or dominate corporate policy in particular respects. Thus, in any concrete situation, there is likely to be a complex network of controls, and a series of foci of varying degrees of importance, each concerned with some particular phase of activity.

The controls which come together at these different foci are sometimes direct and immediate, as in the case of a soldier and his immediate superior officer, or the worker and his shop foreman, but as often they are indirect and intangible. Sometimes they may operate simply through establishing a climate of opinion within which policies are developed. More often they impinge directly on the process of policy formation. The controls which a banker can exercise over a business enterprise may be only indirectly related to the process of borrowing. The controls exercised by Government through its monetary and fiscal policies often go largely unnoticed. The controls which a corporation exercises over public opinion through its institutional advertising are far from direct. . . .

The actual threads of control may be entirely informal or may be accompanied by a formal setting. For a business enterprise an organization chart may indicate the lines of control and responsibility with respect to its major policies. The corporate charter must set forth in some detail the formal division of controls between different groups of security holders and between the security holders and the management. Sometimes the formal lines of control and the actual lines may differ. In many corporations a majority of the stockholders are, as a matter of form, in a position to control the corporate enterprise, while, as a matter of fact, they are not in position to exercise actual control. Since the formal controls are often more easily ascertained than the actual controls, there is always danger of arriving at a false impression as to the locus of controls in any concrete situation. . . .

### THE BASIS OF CONTROLS

In the conduct of economic activity the controls exercised by individuals or groups arise from three main sources: possession of one or more of the factors of production, possession of liquid assets, and position in relation to a functioning organization.

Controls arising out of possession of the factors of production are relatively simple and direct. The farmer possessing land, tools, and seed is to this extent free of outside controls. The manufacturer possessing a factory can limit its use, usually determining when it shall be run and when it shall be closed. A strategically located worker may exercise some control over production through his freedom to quit work. Possession of one or another factor of production is thus one basis of control.

Possession of liquid assets, particularly the possession of salable securities and money, is a second source of economic controls. The possessor of liquid assets is in a position to buy action by others. Sometimes the mere possession of liquid assets without their actual expenditure can influence the action of others, though, for the most part, the controls derived from liquid assets depend on the expenditure of the liquid assets in the market.

The third and, for present purposes, the most important form of the economic controls exercised by individuals or groups arises from their position in relation to some functioning organization. The management of a large corporation may be able to exercise a significant degree of control over the use which is made of resources without itself owning any significant volume of assets. Because of its position in the corporate organization, the management shares in the controls arising from the assets of the corporation and the institutional relationships which develop out of its operations as a going organization. The leaders in a labor organization can exercise some control over production policy as a result of their position in an organization whose influence is based upon the labor factor of production. The leaders in a trade association similarly derive some measure of influence over the use of resources as a result of the organized relationship of its members. A government administrator is in a position to influence the use of resources as a result of his position in the governmental organization. . . .

The major importance of organizational controls is due, first, to the fact that the most significant nonmarket controls arise from organizations, and second, to the greater relative growth of such organizational controls. The great shift from a dominantly agricultural to a dominantly industrial economy during the last century has tended to expand organizational controls. The increased concentration of production into large corporate units, expansion of government functions, increased financial concentration, and growth of both labor organizations and trade associations all work in this direction. The expansion in the role of organization has reduced the relative importance of market controls and increased that of nonmarket controls to such an extent that market controls no longer dominate economic activity. Nonmarket controls have ceased to be isolated as incidental occurrences and have developed into an interrelated system of controls which is quite as important as the system of interrelated prices in determining the use to which resources are put. It is this system of nonmarket controls and its structure with which the remainder of this chapter is concerned.

### THE STRUCTURE OF CONTROLS

. . . In the following pages an attempt will be made to outline the main elements in the structure of controls, taking up, first, the controls exercised over the larger corporations, giving particular emphasis to the controls exercised by what might be called the corporate community; second, the controls exercised by the more important organizations of economic-interest groupings outside of the larger corporations; and finally, the controls exercised by government.

### CONTROLS OVER THE LARGER CORPORATIONS

A clear indication of the controls exercised over the larger corporations can be obtained by examining the 200 largest nonfinancial corporations and the larger financial corporations. . . . What persons or groups are in a position to influence the policies of these large corporations? What are the more important nonmarket controls?

*The Separation of Ownership and Control.* . . . It has long been customary to regard the stockholders of a corporation not only as the owners of the corporation but also as the main source of control over its activity. Yet, in practice, ownership of most of the larger corporations has become so dispersed that the stockholders have ceased to be able to exercise a very significant degree of control over corporate policy. Sometimes legal devices such as nonvoting stock and pyramided holding companies have been adopted to divest stockholders of effective control over corporate policy and personnel. On the whole, ownership and control have become separated in the larger corporations.

The inability of stockholders to exercise major control over corporate policies can be suggested by an examination of the stock ownership of the country's largest nonfinancial corporation, the American Telephone & Telegraph Co. At the end of 1935 there were 659,000 stockholders on the books of the corporation, a number almost equal to the number of potential voters living in the five smallest States. The holdings of different sized blocks of stock are indicated in Table I.

TABLE I. DISTRIBUTION OF STOCK OWNERSHIP, AMERICAN TELEPHONE & TELEGRAPH CO., 1935

| Number of shares held | Number of holders | Per cent of stockholders | Per cent of total number of shares |
|---|---|---|---|
| 1–5 | | 36.8 | 3.8 |
| 6–10 | | 20.7 | 6.1 |
| 11–25 | | 22.5 | 13.2 |
| 26–99 | | 15.9 | 26.4 |
| 100–999 | | 5.0 | 33.9 |
| 1,000–9,999 | | .1 | 11.4 |
| 10,000 and over | 43 | | 5.2 |

SOURCE: *Annual Report of the American Telegraph & Telephone Co.* for 1935.

The 43 largest stockholders, each owning 10,000 shares or more, together owned only 5.2 per cent of the total stock, while the 700 holding 1,000 or more shares together held only 16.6 per cent. In this largest of all corporations, stock ownership is so widely dispersed that no one person or small group is in a position to dominate the corporation as a result of stock ownership. Neither are stockholders as a group in a position to exercise significant control over corporate policy through majority vote. The policies of the corporation have seldom been presented to the stockholders for a vote before adoption, and even in the usual vote for corporate directors the proxy machinery * usually eliminates any significant control by stockholders. As a result, control over the policies of the American Telephone & Telegraph Co. lies only to a minor extent with its stockholders.

. . . . .

. . . A high degree of separation of ownership from control is disclosed in a . . . study based on information filed with the Securities and Exchange Commission. Many corporations are required to file with the Commission information on the total stockholdings of their officers and directors and stockholdings of other individuals and corporations holding 10 per cent or more of any of their voting issues. This information was available at the end of the year 1935 for 155 of the 200 large corporations listed by Berle and Means. A compilation based on these data is given in Table II.

For nearly half of these 155 big companies no one stockholder owned more than 10 per cent of the voting stock, and the officers and directors together owned less than 5 per cent of the outstanding stock. In only 15 companies did the officers, directors, and large stockholders appear to own 50 per cent or more of the voting stock, and in several of these cases the large stockholders were other corporations. For the 155 corporations as a whole the control

ED. NOTE: * The machinery whereby stockholders who do not attend the annual meeting may allow others to cast their votes. Thus, a few stockholders, often mainly officers and directors, may control (for voting purposes) thousands of shares not belonging to them.

## TABLE II. STOCKHOLDINGS OF CONTROLLING GROUPS

(Distribution of 155 large corporations according to proportion of voting stock owned by officers, management, and control group)

| Proportion of stock outstanding (per cent) | *Number of companies* | | |
|---|---|---|---|
| | All officers | Management (all officers and directors) | Control group (officers, directors and stockholders with 10 per cent of any voting stock issued) |
| 0–1 | 96 | 61 | |
| 1–3 | 25 | 30 | 73 |
| 3–5 | 10 | 21 | |
| 5–10 | 15 | 16 | 24 |
| 10–15 | 3 | 11 | |
| 15–50 | 4 | 14 | 43 |
| 50 and over | 2 | 2 | 15 |
| | 155 | 155 | 155 |
| Median holding as per cent of voting power | .40 | 1.74 | 5.40 |

SOURCE: Robert A. Gordon, "Ownership by Management and Control Groups in the Large Corporation," *Quarterly Journal of Economics*, May 1938.

groups owned approximately 12.4 per cent of the voting stock. Since this figure includes substantial stockholdings by other corporations, the stockholdings by individuals in a position to exercise dominant control over these corporations must have been appreciably less than 12.4 per cent of the total voting stock outstanding. No corresponding information is provided on the remaining 45 corporations. Twenty-one of them had dissolved, merged or gone into receivership, 16 did not have to file such information with the Commission because their stocks were not listed on any public exchange, and eight were not included in the compilation for miscellaneous reasons. Presumably, the stocks of the 16 corporations not listed on any exchange were closely held and largely subject to control by their owners, while in the case of the 15 companies in receivership, control over policy was almost completely taken away from the owners by court action.

It is clear, therefore, that for most of the largest corporations ownership and control

have become largely separated. . . . The lack of significant stockholder control over corporate policies may be regarded as the typical condition toward which the large corporate units have been tending. The main controls must be looked for elsewhere.

### MANAGEMENT THE CENTER OF POLICY FORMATION

Since the owners of the larger corporations do not in most cases exercise a significant degree of control over corporate policy, attention must be shifted to the management which is at the center of the forces influencing policy formation.

· · · · ·

The more important nonmarket controls impinging on corporate managements can roughly be grouped into three categories, (1) the corporate community, (2) other organized interest groups, and (3) government.

### THE CORPORATE COMMUNITY

If each corporate management were quite independent of every other corporate management and subject only to market controls in its development of policy, the structure of nonmarket controls might be of only secondary importance. In fact, however, there is a great deal of interrelationship between corporate managements. Partly through interlocking directorates, partly through the activities of the major financial institutions, partly through particular interest groupings, partly through firms rendering legal, accounting, and similar services to the larger corporations, and partly through intercorporate stockholdings, the managements of most of the larger corporations are loosely brought together in what might be called the corporate community.

*Interlocking Directorates.* The formal interrelationships between the larger corporations brought about through interlocking directorates can be seen by examining the directorates of the 200 largest nonfinancial corporations and the 50 largest financial corporations. . . . In 1935 only 25 of these corporations had no director in common with at least one other corporation on the list. One corporation, the Western Union Telegraph Co., interlocked with 35 other corporations on the list. . . .

TABLE III. NUMBER OF DIRECTORS AND THEIR HOLDINGS OF DIRECTORSHIPS IN 200 LARGEST NONFINANCIAL AND 50 LARGEST FINANCIAL CORPORATIONS, 1935

| Number of directorships held by a single individual | Total number of directors | Total number of directorships held | Cumulative number Directors | Cumulative number Directorships |
|---|---|---|---|---|
| 9 | 1 | 9 | 1 | 9 |
| 8 | 3 | 24 | 4 | 33 |
| 7 | 6 | 42 | 10 | 75 |
| 6 | 6 | 36 | 16 | 111 |
| 5 | 19 | 95 | 35 | 206 |
| 4 | 48 | 192 | 83 | 398 |
| 3 | 102 | 306 | 185 | 704 |
| 2 | 303 | 606 | 488 | 1,310 |
| 1 | 2,234 | 2,234 | 2,722 | 3,544 |
| TOTAL | 2,722 | 3,544 | | |

Altogether there were 3,544 directorships on the boards of these 250 corporations in 1935, and these positions were held by 2,725 individual directors. The distribution of the directorships, among individuals, is shown in Table III. Between them, 400 men held nearly a third of these directorships; 1,000 men held over half.

The extent of this interlocking and the magnitude of the assets involved are indicated in Table IV. Out of the 250 corporations, 151 companies, whose assets amounted to nearly three-quarters of the combined assets of the 250, were interlocked with at least three other companies in the group. There can thus be no question of the very extensive formal interlocking of the large corporations.

. . . . .

*Intercorporate Minority Stockholders.* A second influence tying together many of the large corporations results from extensive intercorporate stockholdings. In the case of at least 30 of the 250 large corporations, 10 per cent or more of the voting power derived from stock ownership was held directly or indirectly by another corporation in the group or by one of the 9 financial or holding companies not included in the list of 250 corporations but clearly part of the corporate community. In all but one of these cases, the corporate stockholders were the only stockholders with 10 per cent or more of the voting power. . . .

. . . . .

*Corporate Interest Groupings.* When the interrelationships between the larger corporations are carefully examined, company by company, groupings of more closely related companies emerge. . . .

TABLE IV. CORPORATIONS INTERLOCKING WITH ONE OR MORE OTHER CORPORATIONS AMONG 200 LARGEST NONFINANCIAL AND 50 LARGEST FINANCIAL CORPORATIONS, 1935

| Type of corporation | All corporations Number | All corporations Total assets | Corporations interlocking with one or more other companies Number | Corporations interlocking with one or more other companies Assets | Corporations interlocking with one or more other companies Per cent of total assets | Corporations interlocking with two or more other companies Number | Corporations interlocking with two or more other companies Assets | Corporations interlocking with two or more other companies Per cent of total assets | Corporations interlocking with three or more other companies Number | Corporations interlocking with three or more other companies Assets | Corporations interlocking with three or more other companies Per cent of total assets |
|---|---|---|---|---|---|---|---|---|---|---|---|
| Industrial | 107 | $ 25,140.6 | 91 | $ 23,022.3 | 91.6 | 71 | $16,261.9 | 64.7 | 60 | $14,645.5 | 58.3 |
| Utilities | 54 | 25,232.6 | 46 | 22,886.3 | 90.7 | 34 | 20,153.2 | 79.9 | 26 | 16,049.6 | 63.6 |
| Railroads | 39 | 23,874.0 | 38 | 23,705.9 | 99.3 | 36 | 22,796.2 | 95.5 | 31 | 20,146.1 | 84.4 |
| Banks | 30 | 20,707.6 | 30 | 20,707.6 | 100.0 | 28 | 20,223.5 | 97.7 | 22 | 16,921.3 | 81.7 |
| Other financial | 20 | 19,959.4 | 20 | 19,959.4 | 100.0 | 18 | 19,045.8 | 95.4 | 12 | 16,095.1 | 80.6 |
| All corporations | 250 | 114,914.2 | 225 | 110,281.5 | 96.0 | 187 | 98,480.6 | 85.7 | 151 | 83,857.6 | 73.0 |

A careful study of the interrelationships between the large corporations disclosed eight more or less clearly defined interest groups which so far overshadowed other groups as to justify the limitation of consideration to these eight groups. Together they include 106 of the 250 larger corporations and nearly two-thirds of their combined assets. The eight groups, each named according to some characteristic of the group, are listed in Table V, with an indication of the assets falling within each group. No attempt is made to include the assets of smaller corporations falling within the same sphere of influence though many such could be named.

The largest of the eight interest groups, that classified as the Morgan-First National group, includes 41 of the 250 larger corporations. It has been referred to as the Morgan-First National group, not because the separate companies are controlled by either J. P. Morgan & Co. or by the First National Bank of New York or by these two institutions in combination but rather because much of the interrelation between the separate corporations allocated to this group is brought about through these two institutions. Morgan & Co. and the First National have had a long history of close working relationships begun by the elder J. P. Morgan and the elder George F. Baker and subsequently developed on an institutional basis. Of the 39 corporations grouped with these 2 financial institutions, 10 had 2 or more directors in common with J. P. Morgan & Co. in 1935. However, information on interlocking directorates was in most cases incidental to the classification of a corporation to this particular group. In the case of 15 corporations classed with the Morgan-First National group, there was no interlocking of directorates with either of the 2 financial institutions while in 4 cases, corporations included in the 250 large corporations, were interlocked by directors with 1 or both of these institutions, but were not included in the 41 corporations constituting the interest group because other evidence pointed to the absence of a close relationship or was insuffi-

cient to substantiate such a relationship.

The corporations assigned to the Morgan-First National group include outstanding enterprises in most of the major lines of economic activity. The group is made up of 13 industrial corporations headed by the United States Steel Corporation and including corporations mining iron ore, copper, and coal, extracting oil, making steel and brass, fabricating electrical equipment, railway equipment, and plumbing and heating apparatus, and supplying bakery products, mail-order services, and Pullman services; 12 utility corporations, including the American Telephone & Telegraph Co., the International Telephone & Telegraph Co., and power companies controlling, in 1935, 37 per cent of the electric-generating capacity of the country, 11 major railroads or railroad systems controlling 26 per cent of the firstclass railroad mileage of the country; and 5 financial institutions including the 2 for which the group has been named. While it is certain that the extensive economic activity represented by these corporations is in no sense subject to a single centralized control, it is equally certain that the separate corporations are not completely independent of each other. The climate of opinion within which their separate policies are developed is much the same, many of the same people participate in the formulation and review of the policies of the separate corporations, financing is carried on for the most part through the same channels, and in many other ways this group of corporations constitutes an interrelated interest group.

The second interest group in importance has been named the Kuhn-Loeb group and consists primarily of railroads whose financing has for many years been handled by Kuhn-Loeb & Co. It includes 13 major railroads or railroad systems which together controlled approximately 22 per cent of the first-class railroad mileage in the country in 1935, The Western Union Telegraph Co., and one bank. Since it has never been the policy of Kuhn-Loeb & Co. to maintain more than a few of its contacts by means of directorships, these corporations are not linked to Kuhn-Loeb & Co. through directors except in three cases. There appears to be a much less close grouping of these corporations than in the case of most of those assigned to the Morgan-First National group.

While the two largest interest groups stem primarily from the activities of financial institutions, three interest groupings stem to a large extent from family interests not growing directly out of financial institutions. These are the groups named, respectively, as the Rockefeller, the Mellon, and the Du Pont groups. The largest of these, the Rockefeller group, includes six large oil companies and one bank. The oil companies are all successors to the old Standard Oil Co. which was dissolved by court decree in 1911, and together they control more than half the assets of the oil industry. In each of these companies, John D. Rockefeller and Rockefeller-endowed institutions together hold significant minority stock interests, usually the only large stock interests, representing from 7 to 24 per cent of the voting power in the different companies. Just how much control is exercised by Mr. Rockefeller over these companies is not clear. Very possibly it is mostly negative, but none the less real. Without going so far as to class these corporations as under common control, it is appropriate to treat them as belonging to a single interest group. The largest bank in the country, the Chase National Bank, is also assigned to this interest group.

The second of the family interest groups, the Mellon group, rests to a very much larger extent on ownership than is the case with the other groups covered. It includes

nine industrial corporations, one railroad, two utilities, and two banks. In the case of at least six of these corporations, a majority of the outstanding stock appears to be held by members of the Mellon family and their immediate associates. These closely held companies include the Aluminum Company of America, the Gulf Oil Corporation, the Pittsburgh Coal Co., and the Koppers Co., which indirectly controls many gas manufacturing plants. Most of the companies in this group center in Pittsburgh. Two Pittsburgh banks included in the group appear to be simply an integral part of the interest group rather than the center from which it derives its unity.

The third family group, the Du Pont group, includes only four companies, three industrials, and one bank, but all of these are of top rank in respect to size. Control over the separate companies arises primarily from substantial minority stock holdings. One Du Pont family holding company owned approximately 25 per cent of the voting stock of the E. I. du Pont de Nemours Co., which, in turn, owned approximately the same proportionate interest in the General Motors Corporation. Another family holding company owned approximately 20 per cent of the voting power in the United States Rubber Co. In each of these cases the minority stock holdings were sufficient to give the Du Pont interests working control in the corporations listed and the management of these companies reflects this fact. The bank included in this interest group appears to be incidental to the composition of the group.

The remaining three of the eight major interest groups appear to stem neither from

TABLE V. EIGHT INTEREST GROUPS AND THEIR ASSETS, 1935

(Millions of dollars)

| | Morgan First Nat'l | Rocke- feller | Kuhn- Loeb | Mellon | Du Pont | Chicago | Cleve- land | Boston | TOTAL ASSETS |
|---|---|---|---|---|---|---|---|---|---|
| Industrials | 3,920 | 4,262 | 0 | 1,648 | 2,232 | 858 | 1,066 | 425 | 14,411 |
| Rails | 9,678 | 0 | 9,963 | 153 | 0 | 0 | 0 | 0 | 19,794 |
| Banks | 4,421 | 2,351 | 548 | 672 | 396 | 2,595 | 338 | 740 | 12,061 |
| Utilities | 12,191 | 0 | 342 | 859 | 0 | 813 | 0 | 554 | 14,759 |
| TOTAL ASSETS | 30,210 | 6,613 | 10,853 | 3,332 | 2,628 | 4,266 | 1,404 | 1,719 | 61,025 |

particular financial institutions nor from particular families but rather to bring together corporations whose activity centers in particular localities. For this reason they have been named for the regions in which they center, the Chicago group, the Boston group, and the Cleveland group. In each case the group includes one or more banks located in the center for which the group is named, industrial activities carried on in the vicinity, such as meat packing in Chicago, shoe machinery in the vicinity of Boston, and steel in the Cleveland area, and in the case of two of the groups, local utilities. Just how closely knit these groups are it is not possible to say, but there can be little doubt that they exist as roughly interrelated groups.

### FORMAL ORGANIZATIONS REPRESENTING ECONOMIC INTERESTS

In addition to the informal but none-the-less significant groupings of controls which center in the corporate community, there are certain economic-interest groupings operating through formal organizations, which have a significant impact on the policies adopted by specific producing units. The most important of the economic interests formally organized are those of business, labor, farmer, and consumer. In each of these fields of economic interest, there are national organizations which aim to protect the special economic interests of their members. Associated with these national organizations or independent of them are smaller economic-interest groupings organized on a regional or functional basis which aim to further the particular economic interest with which they are concerned. These organizations function partly through the collection and dissemination of information to their members, partly through measures aimed to influence public thinking, partly through their impact on the process of government policy formation, and partly through the development of common policies which their separate members are encouraged to adopt. . . .

* * * * *

### ORGANIZATIONS BASED ON BUSINESS INTERESTS

The many organizations built on business interests do not fit into any simple pattern of activity. Some organizations, like the American Bankers Association, the Association of American Railroads, the Edison Electric Institute, the National Manufacturers Association, and the American Iron and Steel Institute, represent to a very considerable degree an extension of the corporate community, being made up of, or to a significant extent dominated by, the larger companies. Other organizations, like the National Retail Dry Goods Association and the Association of Retail Druggists, are made up for the most part of relatively small enterprises. Between these extremes lie many trade associations which are neither an integral part of the corporate community nor yet mainly outside it. Likewise, the functions performed by such associations vary in the widest degree.

In 1937 there were, in addition to the finance, railroad, and utility associations, over 2,400 national and interstate trade associations, each tying together, loosely or more closely, separate enterprises in particular industries. To these must be added the 4,100 State and local trade associations whose importance is primarily local, and the 5,400 local chambers of commerce.

Not all of these associations have the same significance for the structure of controls. Those which are primarily loose organizations, largely fraternal and promotional in their activity, presumably have little influence on policies adopted with respect to the use of resources. On the other hand, closely-knit associations which present a united front for an industry in dealing with labor, in disciplining recalcitrant members, in developing practices affecting prices and production, in influencing public thinking, and in affecting government policy may exercise a very considerable measure of influence over the policies developed in the use of resources. . . .

* * * * *

*Major Business Associations.* Probably the five most important business associations are the national associations in the fields of finance, railroads, utilities, manufacturing, and all business. The American Bankers Association has a membership which in 1938 accounted for over 90 per cent of the banking assets of the country. The Association of American Railroads represents within its membership practically the whole of the railway mileage of the country. The Edison Electric Institute covered through its membership approximately 90 per cent of the country's electrical generating capacity. The National Association of Manufacturers included manufacturing enterprises employing roughly a third of the workers in manufacturing industries. The Chamber of Commerce of the United States has not specialized but brings into a single organization 1,000 local chambers of commerce, 500 trade and other business associations, and 10,000 separate corporations and individuals carrying on all types of activities.

. . . . .

While the functions actually performed by these associations are varied and complex, there is a certain similarity in the character of their activities. Each of them acts as a center for the gathering of information and its dissemination to members. Each of them facilitates the development of common standards and policies within its particular sphere of productive activity. Each of them acts to develop agreement among its members with respect to governmental policies, and campaigns are carried on to prevent the adoption by government of policies believed to be harmful to their interests and to encourage the adoption of favorable policies. Finally, each of these business associations makes it a part of its program to try to influence public attitudes with respect to the activities and aims of its members and public policies likely to affect their interests. All of these association activities are aimed to influence, directly or indirectly, the policies adopted in the use of resources and constitute a

more or less significant part of the structure of controls.

. . . . .

## LABOR ORGANIZATIONS

Paralleling the large corporations and business associations are the organizations of labor, which occupy an increasingly important place in the structure of controls. Labor organizations exercise a measure of direct control over the use of resources both via the market, as they affect the relative bargaining strength of the parties and thereby the characteristics of the bargain in the labor market, and also administratively, to the extent that conditions of industrial operation are laid down by labor organizations or arrived at jointly by the representatives of labor and the representatives of business. In addition, labor organizations, like business organizations, affect the use of resources indirectly through their influence on government policy and on public thinking. . . .

. . . . .

## FARMER ORGANIZATIONS

Organizations of farmers constitute a third type of economic-interest grouping which is of importance to the structure of controls. Though less closely organized than either business or labor groupings, the many farm organizations, particularly the marketing and purchasing cooperatives, play a significant role in the field of agriculture and in reflecting the farm interest in the development of Government policy and in public discussion.

. . . . .

## CONSUMER ORGANIZATIONS

The fourth major economic-interest group, that of consumers, is relatively little organized. The leading national organization, the Cooperative League of the United States, is primarily a league of consumer-controlled producing enterprises affiliating 1,770 local cooperative enterprises in 1938 and with a total membership of 965,000. Other specific consumer interests, such as health and education, are reflected in national organizations, but there is no major national organization representing the consumer interest as a whole and apart from producing cooperatives.

.  .  .  .  .

### GOVERNMENT UNITS

Government units, Federal, State and local, provide the third set of nonmarket controls which, together with the market controls, constitute the essentials of the control structure. Because Government units are the primary organizations in the American economy through which the individuals and groups in the community are built into a social unity, they have powers and re-

sponsibilities which transcend those of any other type of organization, and the policies they adopt can vitally affect the use to which resources are put.

The controls which Government units can exercise arise primarily from organization, from the authority placed by society in the hands of government. To some extent they rest on the possession of the instruments of production, particularly public buildings and the public domain. Under certain circumstances they arise from the command over purchasing power. But in the main, the controls exercised by government rest on the complex social relationships which give government its special character.

## 20 David Lynch: *The Methods of Monopoly*

❦ *The previous reading attempted to describe the complex web of controls which makes up the fabric of power in the American industrial economy. A substantial part of that web is the control exerted by mammoth business units which tend to stifle competition. In recent years there have been several public investigations of the "imperfect competition" and monopolistic tendencies which characterize the American scene. From 1937 to 1939, the Temporary National Economic Committee (TNEC), a congressional body, inquired into the problem; and other studies were made by the House Judiciary Committee in 1945, the Smaller War Plants Corporation in 1946, and the Department of Commerce in 1950.*

*Our reading summarizes certain phases of the Temporary National Economic Committee inquiry. David Lynch, the author, was born in 1902 and has written the article on "Tariffs" in the* Encyclopædia Britannica Year Book of 1946; *Report on the Tariff Policy of Panama (1946); and* The Concentration of Economic Power (1946). *Our selection is excerpted from the latter work, pp. 173–229, and is reprinted with permission of the publisher, Columbia University Press.*

The ways of monopoly are protean; monopolists are less concerned with methods than with results. If one instrument is outlawed or for some practical purpose fails to produce the desired result, others are employed. For the purpose of effective discussion it will be necessary to assign names and to identify the principal techniques. More realistically, however, sharp boundary lines do not exist. Different methods may be employed at the same time to achieve the same ends, and their operations may so overlap and intertwine as to make them indistinguishable—merely differing aspects of the same method. There are no clear-cut categories, and hence the discussions which follow may appear to be repetitious at points. Nevertheless, an attempt will be made to assemble and synthesize the materials brought to the attention of the TNEC which show the nature and extent of monopolistic practices in the United States.

"Monopoly," of course, is not a precise word; it is subject to many interpretations and may thus provoke many misunderstandings and much needless quibbling. There are degrees of monopoly, varying from no control to complete domination. Moreover, domination may be achieved by one producer or by a combination of producers. Combination may be overt and tangible, or it may represent subtle and intangible alliances and understandings unrecognized by the consuming public and unreached by the monopoly laws. "Monopoly" is used here in its broadest sense and is intended to embrace all arrangements by which producers effect varying degrees of market control and by which they succeed in obtaining for themselves some of the benefits of monopoly price. Variations from pure monopoly have been discussed in recent years under more precise terms, which include "monopolistic competition," "duopoly," "oligopoly," and "imperfect competition." [1]

## PRICE LEADERSHIP

One of the most prominent types of monopolistic combination today is the loose, but effective, practice which has come to be known as "price leadership." Unlike the

trust, the pool, the holding company, the merger, and other methods of combination prevalent at the turn of the century, price leadership is inconspicuous and offers little tangible evidence of collusion or conspiracy, however obvious its results may be. The practice is similar to the price pool, but there is no overt evidence of its existence, and it often represents nothing more than a tacit understanding among producers to "follow the leader" in price policy.

Price leadership may become operative in a number of ways. Sometimes it results from an unwritten agreement among producers, arrived at after deliberation and consultation. At times it occurs when one producing unit is so large and possesses such industrial strength that it dominates the field, with the result that lesser firms, guided by prudence and experience, indicate their willingness to follow the policies of the leader. [2] It may develop in an industry where there are a few giant firms of approximately equal strength, each with a healthy respect for the power of the others and each reluctant to engage them in all-out competition. The result, therefore, may be a "live-and-let-live," "follow-a-leader" truce. Other instances have occurred in which militant and aggressive producers in a given field have employed duress to whip competitors into a price leadership program.

Price leadership commends itself to those seeking to control the market not only because it is effective but also because it is beyond the reach of the law. When no agreement exists and when there is no formal organization, it is quite impossible to show collusion or conspiracy. In fact, the defenders of price leadership have asserted that the very existence of the end product —uniform price—is in itself proof of effective competition, since in a regime of free competition all producers sell at one price —market price.

Prices determined under the price leadership regime probably constitute the most common form of controlled prices in the

[1] See Edward Chamberlain, *The Theory of Monopolistic Competition* (Cambridge: Harvard University Press, 1938), and Joan Robinson, *The Economics of Imperfect Competition* (London: Macmillan, 1933).

[2] *Hearings before the Temporary National Economic Committee,* Part 5, p. 1771.

American market. Though relatively unknown a few decades ago, price leadership was described to the TNEC as one of the most dominant of prevalent types of monopoly. In recent years this method of control has been common in the following industries: crackers, newsprint, steel, anthracite, gasoline, flour, corn syrup, stoves, tin plate, cigarettes, and milk bottles.

It should not be concluded from these remarks that the price leader policy is clandestine or that its existence is denied by industrialists with guilty consciences. On the contrary, the practice is openly referred to and discussed with frankness and candor. A few remarks by industrialists are illustrative. One corporation president said, "We generally make the prices"; [1] another told the TNEC, "I was very glad . . . of the opportunity to follow the Corporation's lead"; [2] others indicated that it was their practice never to initiate price changes but to meet them [3] and to follow a policy of "live-and-let-live." [4] One executive described the position of his firm thus: "We are too small to lead" [5] while another more supinely said, "We have to follow." [6] One industrialist testified that price leadership had been an established practice in his industry as far back as he could remember: "It is the custom of the industry. We have always done it." [7]

*Marketing Gasoline.* The instructions sent by its executive to the members of the National Association of Petroleum Retailers vividly describe the operation of price leadership.[8] After setting forth the intent of initiating a series of price increases for retail gasoline, the writer turned to the method by which uniform increased prices might be obtained. He proposed to emulate the example of the distributors.[9]

The answer has been before our eyes for many years. . . . In each territory there has been a supplier that was recognized as the market leader and other suppliers have merely met the competition set by the leader. . . . The dealers can do the same thing. . . . The leader must be a petroleum retailer and he must be followed by all other retailers in the territory.[10]

That such price control is a violation of the spirit and the purpose of the monopoly laws and constitutes a carefully implemented method of circumventing those statutes is emphasized by the care with which the trade association advised its members; concert, collusion, and "conspiracy against the public" was the aim and the purpose of the policy proposed, but all tangible evidence of such intrigue was to be avoided with meticulous care. The members of the trade association were told:

By this time you should be in a position to select your "market leader" who has the courage and those qualities of leadership that others recognize and will follow. After he is selected, give him your whole-hearted support. Remember to not agree upon a price, but each individual has the right to determine what he wants to do and to announce it, thus avoiding any conspiracy. Your "market leader" can set a price and the organization can send out a notice.[11]

Many independent retail gasoline dealers or their representatives testified that price leadership is a common practice at the filling stations. Usually the pace is set by one of the large integrated companies who, because of their oligopolistic positions, adopt the same policies and follow the same procedures. When one company posts a price cut, they all follow suit; when one posts a price raise, they fall in line.[12] Usually the market leader in a given area is the company which sells the largest gallonage in that area. Thus, the leader almost always is one of the great integrated companies and more often than not a member of the original Standard Oil group. Table

[1] *Ibid.*, Part 27, p. 14250.
[2] *Ibid.*, Part 19, p. 10592.
[3] *Ibid.*, p. 10659.
[4] *Ibid.*, p. 10679.
[5] *Ibid.*, Part 27, p. 14282.
[6] *Ibid.*, Part 5, p. 2087.
[7] *Ibid.*, p. 2099.
[8] *Ibid.*, Part 16, pp. 9040–9045.
[9] For examples of price leadership in the crude oil industry see *ibid.*, Part 14, pp. 7224, 7417.

[10] Hearings before the Temporary National Economic Committee, Part 16, p. 9045.
[11] *Ibid.*, p. 9040.
[12] *Ibid.*, Part 14, p. 7369.

18 lists the market leaders for various areas in 1939.

An interesting illustration of the *modus operandi* employed to implement price leadership came to light in the Ohio area. The Pennzoil Company regularly required its retailers to market its product at prices established by the Standard Oil Company.[1] Frequently retailers of Pennzoil products knew as far as a day in advance the nature of price changes announced by Standard. Mimeographed price notices published by Standard Oil were distributed by the Pennzoil Company to its dealers. A formal pool or a trust arrangement could scarcely have been more effective.

*The Steel Industry.* In 1936 the president of the United States Steel Corporation testified before a Senate committee that price leadership was characteristic of the steel industry. The following testimony is pertinent:

MR. IRVIN. I would say we generally make the prices.

THE CHAIRMAN. You generally make the prices?

[1] *Ibid.*, Part 16, pp. 8952–8974.

MR. IRVIN. Yes, sir; we generally make the prices, unless some of the other members of the industry think that that price may be too high and they make the price.

THE CHAIRMAN. You lead off, then, with a price charged, either up or down, at Gary, is that correct?

MR. IRVIN. Yes, sir. . . . We always notify the trade papers . . . and others interested as to what our prices are.

THE CHAIRMAN. Then the rest of them follow that?

MR. IRVIN. I think they do. That is, I say they generally do. They may quote the same price, but maybe they need some business and make a better price. We do not always know that until it is over.[2]

In the steel industry both the leader and those who were lead freely acknowledged that this practice was customary. Mr. Eugene C. Grace, representing the Bethlehem Steel Corporation, preferred to designate it as "meeting a competitive situation" when his company adopted pricing policies in concert with the United States Steel Corporation.[3] Whatever the lead of the latter,

[2] *Ibid.*, Part 5, p. 1867, and Part 27, pp. 14250–14251.

[3] *Ibid.*, Part 19, pp. 10586–10588, 10598–10603.

TABLE 18. MARKET LEADERSHIP IN THE PETROLEUM INDUSTRY, 1939

| Area | Price Leader |
| --- | --- |
| New York and New England | Socony-Vacuum Oil Corp. |
| Pennsylvania and Delaware | Atlantic Refining Co. |
| New Jersey, Maryland, District of Columbia, Virginia, North Carolina, and South Carolina | Standard Oil Co. of New Jersey |
| Ohio | Standard Oil Co. of Ohio |
| Kentucky, Mississippi, Alabama, Georgia, and Florida | Standard Oil Co. of Kentucky |
| Tennessee, Louisiana, and Arkansas | Standard Oil Co. of Louisiana |
| Michigan, Indiana, Wisconsin, Illinois, Iowa, Missouri, North Dakota, South Dakota, Nebraska, Kansas, and Minnesota | Standard Oil Co. of Indiana |
| Montana, Wyoming, Colorado, New Mexico, Idaho, and Utah | Continental Oil Co. |
| Washington, Oregon, California, Nevada, and Arizona | Standard Oil Co. of California |
| Oklahoma | Magnolia (subsidiary of Socony) |
| Texas | Magnolia or Texas Corp. |

SOURCE: Hearings before the Temporary National Economic Committee, Part 16, pp. 8880–8881.

whether the price change was up or down, the Bethlehem Steel Corporation followed. Mr. Grace appeared to be unable to cite any important instance in recent years when his company had taken the initiative or had been aggressive in quoting prices. He paid frequent tribute to the price leadership system and to the direction given it by the United States Steel Corporation. Some of his tributes were as follows: "It is a good guide for us"; [1] "We welcomed the opportunity"; "We needed it and we followed it"; [2] "I was very glad then of the opportunity to follow the Corporation's lead." [3]

Similarly, representatives of other steel companies indicated that they adhered to the policy fixed by the United States Steel Corporation. The president of the National Steel Corporation testified that his company never initiated a price and always met whatever price was established. He preferred to call this "meeting competition" rather than to recognize it for what it was —monopoly price through price leadership.[4] Obviously, when no one cuts the base price established by the leader and all meet that price simultaneously, that is not competition. This concept of competition was more realistically acknowledged by some to be a policy of "live-and-let-live." [5]

*Other Industries.* Despite the fact that the TNEC scrutinized the practices of only a few industries, it is significant that numerous instances of price leadership came to light. In addition to the steel and the gasoline industries, price leadership was found in the glass bottle, tag, group life insurance, and beryllium industries. . . .

### RACKETEERING

Sometimes it is the lure of monopoly profits which impels producers to restrain trade; sometimes it is the fear of cutthroat competition. Sometimes collusion is achieved through appeal to common interest or by the use of moral suasion mixed, perhaps, with intimidation and threats of economic sanctions. Then there is a type of "moral suasion" which employs less subtle and less civilized arts of persuasion. The racketeer takes recourse to violence, intimidation, and terrorism to obtain his ends. Racketeering may be, and has been, of course, employed for other purposes than to perpetrate a monopoly. Rackets have been used to extract tribute from members of a trade or to enable the members of the trade to exact tribute from the public. The latter, of course, are the subject of this discussion. The border line between the duress and the sanctions employed by a great many monopolistic groups, on the one hand, and the techniques of the racketeer, on the other, is indistinct, and it would be idle to give it definition even for the sake of precision. But clearly when resort is had to the destruction of physical property, to the infliction of bodily harm, or to intimidation by threats to commit such acts that border line has been crossed.

Monopolistic arrangements have been enforced in some industries by damaging goods, interfering with their movement, breaking windows, throwing bombs, setting fires, and assaulting tradesmen. Restraint of trade by such methods has been imposed upon various industries, including glaziers, laundrymen, bakers, building contractors, operators of garages and filling stations, as well as dealers in ice, milk, beverages, fish, poultry, and artichokes.[6]

Monopolistic racketeering is found principally among small-scale producers. It may exist with or without the trade association. Where oligopoly is not so apparent and the opportunity to "get together" not as convenient as it is in the mass production industries—which by their very nature have few producing units—the racket may substitute for reason and suasion. The Wickersham Commission made the following comment regarding this subject.

In this possibility of forcible suppression of competition is to be found one important rea-

[1] *Ibid.*, p. 10586.
[2] *Ibid.*, p. 10587.
[3] *Ibid.*, p. 10592.
[4] *Ibid.*, p. 10659.
[5] *Ibid.*, pp. 10678, 10679.
[6] Temporary National Economic Committee Monograph No. 21, pp. 293–298.

son why rackets tend to make especially rapid headway in lines of business having numerous small and actively competing units, where it is difficult to avoid so-called "cut-throat competition" which keeps all but the most efficient units at the starvation point. Open price-fixing agreements are forbidden by law, and probably would not be lived up to if made; but the racket may provide an effectively policed method of bringing about noncompetitive conditions.[1]

Four examples of racketeering sanctions, imposed to coerce reluctant competitors to participate in collusive practices, were brought to the attention of the TNEC: two in the retail petroleum trade, one in the milk industry, and another in the poultry industry.

*In the Oil Industry.* Retailers of petroleum products have organized from time to time to suppress price competition. Sometimes the organizers have resorted to "strong-arm" tactics to obtain results. A retail trade association with headquarters in Milwaukee, after advising its members how to regiment the trade, proceeded to suggest ways of bulldozing recalcitrant tradesmen into compliance. One course was called the "blockade method," involving the deliberate placing of obstructions between the retailer and his market. The blockade method was described by its advocate.

If you have to use the blockade method, be sure that it is friendly and peaceful, so as to prevent injunctions for disturbing the peace or disorderly conduct or assault, conducting yourselves as customers who are making small purchases and utilizing the free services which the station offers to the public, and block the driveways for a short time only—but during the busiest part of the day.

If the blockade is used as a means of bringing the price-cutters to reason, withhold the blockade during any negotiations that follow and remember to be firm and fair in your demands.[2]

[1] National Commission on Law Observance and Enforcement, *Reports*, Vol. V, No. 12, *Report on the Cost of Crime*, 1931, p. 410.
[2] *Hearings before the Temporary National Economic Committee*, Part 16, p. 9309; see also pp. 9040–9041.

The author of the above memorandum was apparently not averse to using other types of intimidation. This, however, did not represent an isolated instance of the use of the blockade. One dealer in Ohio who attempted to follow an independent pricing policy described how his hoses had been cut when he failed to adopt the prices suggested to him by the local gasoline retailers' association.[3] Moreover, members of the association drove into his station in large numbers, bought the minimum quantity of gasoline, demanded the maximum of service, remained inordinately long, and denied access to the station by the consuming public for a period of nearly two days. The following newspaper advertisement describes what happened to one retailer and represents an attempt to present his case to the court of public opinion.

One June 22nd and 23rd a large automobile caravan driven, fifty witnesses testify, by certain members of the Stark County Retail Gasoline Dealers Association and others, drove into the Red Head track-side gasoline station located at 522 Cherry Ave. NE., blocking the driveways with forty or fifty cars and trucks. Twenty-, fifty-, and hundred-dollar bills were flashed in payment of one-gallon purchases or less. Numerous services were requested, all with the obvious plan of tying up the station. When these "customers" ran out of service requests they still refused to move away from the pumps. Of course, this caused a general blockade of traffic, extending for several blocks, preventing the regular trade from getting gasoline. This un-American movement was the result of the Red Head being unwilling to enter into price collusion with its competitors to raise and peg gasoline prices in Stark County. A temporary injunction has been granted prohibiting this malicious mischief and other interference in the operation of the Red Head Station.[4]

*In the Milk and Poultry Industries.* A few large distributors controlled the retail sale of milk in Detroit. In 1936 a new enterpriser inaugurated a system of distribution over the counter from milk depots. His prices to consumers were substantially

[3] *Ibid.*, p. 8976.
[4] *Ibid.*, pp. 8979–8980.

lower than those charged from the wagon, and it appears that he paid more to the milk producer as well. The new distributor was not looked upon favorably by the milk combination, and he was soon subjected to various annoyances and interferences. Fighting brands were introduced, resulting in a substantial price war; state inspectors appeared on the scene to make an excessive number and an apparently capricious variety of inspections; the distributor's license was temporarily revoked, various legal interferences were instituted, bankruptcy proceedings were invoked, and threats of violence were made. In the same city another independent distributor had had his pasteurization plants bombed.

The New York live poultry market offers a notorious example of racketeering; for a number of years it was dominated by a small group of commissionmen, twenty-seven to thirty in number. To consolidate their position they allied themselves with four labor unions. Other commissionmen were excluded from the market by being denied access to the supply of labor. The rights to haul chickens and to supply coops and feed were dispensed as exclusive monopolies and were exercised to extract monopoly prices. Slaughterhouse owners were forced to purchase chickens from these commissionmen exclusively; those who attempted to do otherwise found their trucks overturned on the highways, discovered emery dust in their motors, or their chickens died from a diet of sand, gravel, and plaster of Paris, or were, perhaps, sprinkled with kerosene or poison.

. . . . .

### ADVERTISING

Advertising constitutes another barrier to free entry into the market and thereby lays the basis for monopoly. To the mind of the none-too-analytical layman advertising is a symbol of rigorous competition, but to the economically informed it is evidence of a restricted market. Obviously there are degrees of monopoly control, and there are degrees of product differentiation (intrinsic and imputed); this fact makes it difficult for the average citizen to comprehend the role of restraint which advertising performs. The owner of a product for which the price is competitively determined has nothing to gain from advertising. He can sell every unit he possesses at the market price, and were he to advertise "John Doe's field corn," he could sell no more and obtain no better price. The very purpose of advertising is either to carve out a monopolistic position for the product or to perpetuate or strengthen the position already obtained.

Before the epoch of modern advertising products could be established in the market by virtue of their reputation of quality and cost. Commodities formerly less complex and less a product of technology and chemistry could be analyzed more readily by the buyer. Consumers' goods and producers' goods, having become more complex, are sold less and less on the basis of tests which the consumer himself can apply and more and more in response to psychological appeal, ingenious presentation, colorful pretensions, and reputation built upon repetition. The eye, the ear, and the nose no longer can test the validity of claims and the efficacy of cures or discover the soundness of mechanical construction or the degree of freedom from harmful or worthless ingredients. That requires technical training and laboratory equipment beyond the reach of the consumer.

With the new pattern of technology, the new types of merchandising, the increased complexity of products, and the highly institutionalized and thoroughly organized advertising industry, the producer of a new product must run an expensive gauntlet before he can penetrate the market and reach the consumer. Ofttimes more important than the merits of his product and more expensive than his plant and equipment is the program of advertising which the producer must undertake to gain entry into the market. This barrier, though not insurmountable, is very substantial and frequently limits the field to the few who are able to finance such a program.[1]

[1] A striking illustration of this fact was the skill-

*The Tooth Paste Industry.*[1] A manufacturer of tooth paste described for the TNEC the all-importance of advertising to one attempting a start in that industry. In 1939 ten large manufacturers, producing ten branded products which through advertising had become household words, dominated the retail market. The new manufacturer proceeded to earn a place for his product—or attempted to do so—on its own merits without benefit of the heraldry and the psychological legerdemain of the advertising fraternity. The tooth paste he manufactured was based on a good formula and received the immediate approval of the American Dental Association (only one of the ten nationally advertised products had received this endorsement). He had also secured government contracts, thereby meeting the rigorous standards usually required in the case of such purchases. Moreover, the product sold to consumers at substantially one-half the retail price ordinarily charged for a similar package of the ten nationally advertised products. If cost and quality were sufficient to sell it in open competition, it should have sold. Another fact to its advantage was that retailers were able to profit more from the sale of each unit, being allowed a markup of 100 per cent as compared with only about 50 per cent in the case of the advertised products.

This manufacturer thus had for his product virtually every quality which should result in an active demand—every quality but one, access to consumers. Consumers had been pre-empted, as it were; they belonged almost exclusively to certain producers, quite as though territories had been allotted by a pool or a cartel. Whenever the manufacturer sought retail outlets, invariably he was greeted with the same response: "You have a very good product,

the price is right, your story is good, but bring customers to us. You bring customers into our stores to ask for your product and we will be very glad to carry it." [2] In other words, a good product is not enough. The producer must add another type of product differentiation; he must advertise to obtain a portion of the monopolized market. The producer literally found it necessary to buy his way into the market in order to have access to consumers. This approach he proceeded to investigate. After taking the matter up with several advertising firms, he discovered that it would cost $100,000 to make a preliminary survey to discover whether a national advertising program, if undertaken, would be successful. Such initial expense and the much greater costs which would follow to put the product across would be prohibitive, of course, to many producers, as it was to this one in particular. Monopolistic control of industry is, in part, a product of the inability of new enterprisers to enter the field; thus, heavy advertising costs have become an important barrier to free competition.

PATENTS

The monopoly problem today is more the product of a legal institution—the patent right—than it was in the days of pools, trusts, and combinations. From the patent laws there have evolved two classes of monopolies, one which was anticipated and planned for and the other, unintended and unplanned. Patents, by legislative intent, grant their owners the exclusive right, for a limited period, to make, use, and sell the patented article. This grant of monopoly is made to stimulate the inventive process and to foster technological progress. Many testified that such a result had been achieved.[3]

Another social product of the patent system has been the fostering of predatory business units and combinations. The border line between the lawful and social use of the patent monopoly, on the one hand, and the unlawful or predatory use, on the

---

fully managed advertising campaign of a powerful and well-established soap manufacturer to place the new product—"swan"—on the market during 1941–1942. This firm is reputed to have launched an advertising program costing more than $1,000,-000 to secure entry into the market for its product.
[1] *Hearings before the Temporary National Economic Committee*, Part 8, pp. 3396–3412.

[2] *Ibid.*, p. 3398.
[3] *Ibid.*, Parts 2 and 3.

other, is often indistinct, and to discover it requires careful examination and often the interpretation of the courts. The legal rights of the patent holder are not clear, and the distinction between the lawful and the unlawful must inevitably await the race between the prosecutor and the court, on the one hand, and the ingenuity of entrepreneurs on the other.

The patent right has made possible a variety of practices in restraint of trade. One involves the advantage afforded to existing patent holders in purchasing patents on new processes as they are developed. This advantage is most pronounced in the case of an owner of a basic patent who ofttimes is the only one to whom patents on improvements may be sold. Intrenched by his ownership of a basic process, he may, by acquiring the rights to all improvements, extend his monopoly almost indefinitely. Moreover, as the monopoly continues it may fan outward, as wider sectors of the economy are embraced. Not only may complementary processes be acquired through purchase, but competing processes as well. This may be done either to centralize control or to assure that the competing process never reaches the market. Patents also permit their owners to extend their monopoly over the patented article, ofttimes a machine, to its product. Hence, the holder of patents has been able to control prices at which others sell not only the patented article but also its product. Often this is achieved by licensing or leasing to manufacturers the use of patented machines. Still another practice involves the tying contract, whereby the patent owner requires users of the patented article to purchase nonpatented materials as well, thereby extending monopoly control into areas not intended by the law. The patent pool offers another obstruction to competition. Owners of competing and complementary processes may combine and, by their claims to almost all phases of the productive process, successfully obstruct others from operating or force them to accede to whatever terms are imposed.

The patent-protected monopolist frequently has recourse to numerous instruments of duress to secure compliance by unwilling producers. At their worst these devices resemble racketeering, since threats are made, weapons used, and the victim often finds it necessary to buy "protection." The method of "terrorism" in this case is harassment by litigation. Threats of litigation are often sufficient, since legal contests usually are expensive; the victim frequently finds it less expensive to become a licensee of the patent which he is presumed to infringe than to continue to pay large annual fees for litigation. The patent system permits powerful units or combinations to destroy small competitors by endless litigation or by threats of litigation, regardless of the merits of the small producer's case or of his product. Infringement suits may thus be employed to coerce independent producers to resign their patent rights to stronger combinations. By the use of interference proceedings smaller firms may be forced to barter away their patentable rights even before the patent is granted. . . .

SECTION B

**The distribution of income**

## 21 President's Economic Report: *Income and Saving in the United States*

❦ *One indicator of the way in which power is distributed in any society is to be found in the distribution of income, for income is clearly a form of power. Until recent years, data on income distribution in the United States were relatively incomplete and unreliable. Impetus was, however, given to the investigation of income distribution when Congress passed the Full Employment Act of 1946, which required President Truman, with the assistance of a Council of Economic Advisers, to report regularly to Congress on the economic state of the nation.*

*Our reading is taken from the* Economic Report of the President, *January 12, 1951, pp. 223–7. Among other things, these statistics suggest the enormous gulf between lowest and highest personal incomes and also the concentration of a substantial proportion of total income in the hands of a relatively few individuals.*

The people of the United States . . . can consider themselves fortunate that the period just ended was one of great progress in raising living standards. Not only has total personal income increased, but, as compared with the prewar period, a higher proportion of income now goes to the middle and lower income groups. Disparities between the quality and style of goods available to low and higher income groups have been narrowed. The outstanding example is perhaps automobiles, where low-priced cars are in elements of serviceability and many elements of style equal to those in high-priced ranges. The clothing of the average working girl is neat and modish, and to the casual observer little different from that of her wealthier sister; the variety of foods on sale in working-class

neighborhoods rivals that of high income localities.

Nevertheless, there are still large numbers of families in the United States with small or inadequate incomes. According to the *1950 Survey of Consumer Finances,*[1] in 1949, 33 per cent of the spending units in the economy had less than $2,000 money income before taxes, and an additional 21 per cent had between $2,000 and $3,000

[1] *The Survey of Consumer Finances* has been conducted annually in postwar years for the Board of Governors of the Federal Reserve System by the Survey Research Center of the University of Michigan. The detailed findings of the *Survey* may be found in the Federal Reserve Bulletin.

The Bureau of the Census data on family income in 1949 collected in connection with the Current Population Survey and the 1950 Census of Population will be published in the near future.

TABLE B-1. DISTRIBUTION OF
SPENDING UNITS AND TOTAL MONEY
INCOME BEFORE AND AFTER FEDERAL
INCOME TAX, BY INCOME GROUPS,
1949 [PER CENT]

| Income groups | Spending units [1] | | Total money income [2] | |
|---|---|---|---|---|
| | Before Federal income tax | After Federal income tax (disposable income) [3] | Before Federal income tax | After Federal income tax (disposable income) [3] |
| Under $1,000 | 14 | 15 | 2 | 2 |
| $1,000–$1,999 | 19 | 21 | 9 | 11 |
| $2,000–$2,999 | 21 | 23 | 16 | 19 |
| $3,000–$3,999 | 19 | 18 | 19 | 21 |
| $4,000–$4,999 | 11 | 11 | 15 | 16 |
| $5,000–$7,499 | 11 | 8 | 19 | 16 |
| $7,500–$9,999 | 2 | 2 | 20 | 15 |
| $10,000 and over | 3 | 2 | | |
| All cases | 100 | 100 | 100 | 100 |
| Median income [4] | $2,700 | $2,600 | ..... | ..... |
| Mean income [5] | $3,270 | $3,000 | ..... | ..... |

[1] The spending unit consists of all persons related by blood or marriage who live in the same dwelling unit and pool their income for major items of expense.
[2] Income data for each year are based on interviews during January, February, and March of the following year.
[3] Money income after deduction of estimated Federal personal income tax liability. See Appendix to Part III, *1950 Survey of Consumer Finances*, for method of estimating disposable income. Money income figures exclude capital gains or losses and tax estimates make no allowance for such gains or losses.
[4] The median amount of income is that of the middle spending unit when all units are ranked by size of income.
[5] The mean amount is the average obtained by dividing aggregate income by the number of spending units.

SOURCE: *1950 Survey of Consumer Finances*, sponsored by the Board of Governors of the Federal Reserve System, and conducted by the Survey Research Center of the University of Michigan.

income before taxes.[1] (See Table B-1.) Allowing for Federal income taxes, the proportion of spending units below $3,000 is raised to 59 per cent. State and local income taxes are not included in these computations, but in general they are not very important for lower income groups.

Table B-2 summarizes some of the data

[1] A spending unit consists of all persons related by blood, marriage, or adoption who live together and pool their income for major items of expense. A family may contain more than one spending unit: for example, an aged couple dwelling with children may have separate financial arrangements. Family income is on the average higher than spending unit income. According to the *Survey of Consumer Finances* for 1950, the mean family income in 1949 was $3,760 as compared with a mean spending income of $3,270.

TABLE B-2. DISTRIBUTION OF
CHARACTERISTICS OF LOW AND HIGH
INCOME GROUPS, 1949 [PER CENT]

| Characteristic of spending unit | Money income before taxes | | | |
|---|---|---|---|---|
| | Under $1,000 | $1,000–$1,999 | $2,000–$2,999 | $3,000 and over |
| Size: | | | | |
| One person | 44 | 37 | 24 | 9 |
| Two persons | 29 | 28 | 27 | 29 |
| Three or more persons | 27 | 25 | 49 | 62 |
| Race: [1] | | | | |
| White | 83 | 89 | 92 | 97 |
| Negro | 15 | 10 | 7 | 3 |
| Place of residence: | | | | |
| Metropolitan area | 14 | 23 | 28 | 39 |
| Other urban area | 35 | 41 | 39 | 38 |
| Rural area | 51 | 36 | 33 | 23 |
| Number of income receivers: | | | | |
| None | 3 | .. | .. | .. |
| One | 84 | 83 | 81 | 68 |
| Two or more | 13 | 17 | 19 | 32 |
| Age of head: | | | | |
| Under 25 years | 11 | 20 | 14 | 4 |
| 25–64 years | 54 | 65 | 77 | 90 |
| 65 years and over | 35 | 14 | 8 | 5 |
| Occupation of head: | | | | |
| Retired | 14 | 8 | 4 | 2 |
| Farm operators | 24 | 11 | 7 | 5 |
| Unskilled and service workers | 15 | 18 | 17 | 9 |
| All other occupations | 47 | 63 | 72 | 83 |
| Education of head: | | | | |
| No education | 9 | 4 | 2 | 1 |
| Grammar school | 61 | 47 | 45 | 29 |
| High school and colleges | 29 | 48 | 53 | 69 |
| All spending units [2] | 100 | 100 | 100 | 100 |

[1] Less than one-half of 1 per cent were "other" race.
[2] Detail for each characteristic will not necessarily add to 100 because of a small percentage of non-ascertainable cases.

SOURCE: Same as Table B-1.

with regard to characteristics of low income families which have been assembled by the *Survey of Consumer Finances*. These data indicate that there are some factors which tend to mitigate the degree of disparity between the status of the very low and middle income groups. For example, as compared with higher income groups, a greater percentage of the under-$2,000 group are one-person units, a larger fraction are retired persons, who in some cases have adequate savings, and a greater proportion live in rural areas, a considerable fraction are farm families, who may produce food and fuel for their own consumption.

After these qualifications are made, however, it is apparent that there still remains an economic and social problem of great magnitude. For example, 54 per cent of the under-$1,000 group and 65 per cent of the under-$2,000 spending units have heads between the ages of 25 and 64 years, a period of life in which earnings should be adequate. Over half live in metropolitan or other urban areas. A lack of adequate education is indicated in a large number of cases, since only 29 per cent of the under-$1,000 group progressed beyond grammar school. The position of families who must depend on the earnings of a woman head is particularly unfortunate, due to the pressure of family responsibilities and the discrimination against women in gainful employment. In the under-$2,000 family income group, according to statistics of the Bureau of the Census for 1948, 26 per cent of nonfarm families of two or more persons (whose heads were between 21 and 64 years old) were headed by women, as compared with only 6 per cent in higher income groups.[1]

Table B-3 shows that in 1949 a much

TABLE B-3. PERCENTAGE OF SPENDING UNITS WITHIN VARIOUS INCOME GROUPS HAVING INCOME FROM SELECTED SOURCES, 1949 [1] [PER CENT OF UNITS WITHIN EACH INCOME GROUP]

| Money income before taxes | Selected source of income | | | |
|---|---|---|---|---|
| | Wages and salaries | Pensions and allowances | Interest and dividends | Rent |
| Under $1,000 | 46 | 38 | 9 | 7 |
| $1,000–$1,999 | 75 | 36 | 7 | 6 |
| $2,000–$2,999 | 86 | 28 | 8 | 8 |
| $3,000–$3,999 | 91 | 23 | 11 | 9 |
| $4,000–$4,999 | 91 | 24 | 12 | 12 |
| $5,000–$7,499 | 87 | 18 | 20 | 13 |
| $7,500 and over | 60 | 9 | 43 | 23 |
| All spending units | 78 | 28 | 12 | 9 |

[1] In addition 9 per cent of spending units had income from farming and 9 per cent from unincorporated nonfarm business.

SOURCE: Same as Table B-1.

smaller proportion of the under-$2,000 income units received wages and salaries than in higher income groups, while a relatively high proportion received pensions and al-

[1] "Materials on the Problem of Low-Income Families" assembled by the staff of the Subcommittee on Low-Income Families of the Joint Committee on the Economic Report. 81st Cong., 2d sess., Table 6, p. 13.

lowances. The large number of units at all income levels receiving pensions and allowances as compared to interest, dividends, and rents is one of the more interesting findings of the consumer survey. In the $7,500-and-over group, a surprisingly small proportion, 60 per cent, received wages and salaries, while 43 per cent received interest and dividends. A relatively large number in the upper income groups also received entrepreneurial income.

The fact that expenditures of the lower income groups exceed the income of those groups by large amounts year after year indicates that some low income units have previously been in a more favorable position. Family income tends to rise with age of the head until about 45 or 50, after which it declines. Temporary business reverses, fluctuations in farm prices, sickness, and chance factors also contribute to shifting

TABLE B-4. PROPORTION OF SPENDING UNITS OWNING VARIOUS TYPES OF ASSETS, BY INCOME GROUPS, EARLY 1950 (PER CENT)

| Previous year's money income before taxes | Liquid assets[1] | Auto-mobile | Home or farm[2] | Other real estate[3] | Business Interest[4] | Corporate stock[5] |
|---|---|---|---|---|---|---|
| Under $1,000 | 44 | 24 | 50 | 9 | 3 | 2 |
| $1,000–$1,999 | 54 | 37 | 32 | 11 | 5 | 2 |
| $2,000–$2,999 | 68 | 54 | 40 | 12 | 5 | 5 |
| $3,000–$3,999 | 74 | 63 | 46 | 16 | 6 | 7 |
| $4,000–$4,999 | 86 | 74 | 55 | 18 | 10 | 10 |
| $5,000–$7,499 | 94 | 82 | 62 | 26 | 15 | 10 |
| $7,500 and over | 99 | 89 | 66 | 44 | 36 | 30 |
| All income groups | 69 | 55 | 46 | 16 | 8 | 7 |

[1] Includes all types of U. S. Government bonds, checking accounts, savings accounts in banks, postal savings, and shares in saving and loan associations and credit unions. Excludes currency.
[2] Owner-occupied home or farm.
[3] Real estate other than home or farm on which owner is living. Includes lots, one- or two-family houses, apartment houses, summer or week-end homes, commercial or rental property, farms owned by nonfarmers and additional farms and land owned by farmers, and other types.
[4] Full or part interest in a nonfarm unincorporated business or privately held corporation.
[5] Common and preferred stock of corporations open to investment by the general public. Excludes stock of privately held corporations, U. S. Government securities, and bonds of corporations and State, local, and foreign governments.

SOURCE: Same as Table B-1.

families from one income level to another. More data are needed on the degree of shifting up and down the income scale which families undergo over a period of years. The *Survey of Consumer Finances* shows that around 67 per cent of the under-$2,000 income group in 1949 were in the same or lower income group in the preceding year.[1]

About half the spending units in the under-$2,000 income group have assets worth at least $1,000, while one-fourth have

[1] Owing to a relatively large number of cases in which previous income was not ascertainable, these proportions are not exact.

assets worth $5,000 or more. As shown in Table B-4, 44 per cent of that under-$1,000 group have liquid assets, as compared with 69 per cent for all income groups, and 24 per cent own automobiles. The fact that a larger proportion of this income group own homes or farms than in the population at large indicates a disproportionate number of units with heads in older age classes.

SECTION C

## America's class structure

# 22 Lewis Corey: *The New Middle Classes*

*People not only vary in economic power and status as individuals—they also tend to cluster into power and status groups (or classes) according to the relationship which they bear to the process of production. These groupings tend to occur horizontally, separating those who engage in different types of occupations (for example, agricultural as against industrial working classes). They also form vertically within any given line of production (manual workers, white-collar class, and managerial class within any business).*

*Our reading analyzes class structure in modern American society. It is particularly interested in the changes which have taken place, and are taking place, in class alignments.*

*Lewis Corey was at one time an assistant editor of the* Encyclopædia of the Social Sciences *and was later Educational Director of the International Ladies Garment Workers Union. Since 1942 he has been a Professor of Political Economy at Antioch College. He is perhaps best known for his* The Crisis of the Middle Class *(1935). Our selection is reprinted from an article in* The Antioch Review, *Spring, 1945, pp. 68–83, with permission of the editors of* The Review.

## 1. CHANGES IN CLASS RELATIONS

Class relations have developed differently from the expectations of the early democratic and socialist philosophers. Democrats

foresaw the continuation and expansion of a middle-class democracy of small independent producers, in which a majority of the people draw their livelihood from property which they work and own. The early socialists, including Marx, prophesied that middle-class democracy was doomed by the concentration of industry and of property ownership, and the prophecy is largely fulfilled. But the Marxists were wrong, too, for there is no fulfillment of their prophecy of a rapid, inevitable polarization of classes into proletariat and bourgeoisie, with the virtual eclipse of the middle class.

Evidence is overwhelming that the early democrats were wrong. The middle class of small independent enterprisers grew in absolute numbers from 1870 to 1910 but underwent a relative decline; since 1910 the numerical size of the class has remained virtually stationary while it has considerably shrunk as a proportion of all gainfully occupied persons (Table 1). Its economic power has shrunk even more than its numerical strength because of increasing monopoly domination.

But while it has declined the old middle class has not disappeared, and it is still a class-political force to reckon with. Moreover, a *new* middle class of salaried employees has come into being that, since 1870, has grown faster than the proletariat.[1]

[1] Marx, with the foresight of genius, had glimpses of the new class development. "As modern society develops," said the *Communist Manifesto*, "the petty bourgeoisie sees the moment approaching when it will cease to exist as an independent section of modern society, *to be replaced*, in manufactures, agriculture and commerce, *by managers, superintendents and foremen.* In *Capital* Marx saw the increasing significance of management: "Not the industrial capitalist but the industrial managers are 'the soul of our industrial system' . . . management as a function [being] more and more separated from the ownership of capital." And in *Theorien über den Mehrwert* (v. III, pp. 59–60) Marx said: "That the middle class should grow and the proletariat, employed in production, become a relatively smaller part, even if it grows absolutely, of the whole population . . . is in fact the course of bourgeois society.". . .

TABLE 1. CLASS DIVISIONS IN THE UNITED STATES: 1870–1940

| (In thousands) | 1940 | 1930 | 1920 | 1910 | 1870 |
|---|---|---|---|---|---|
| I. FARMERS | 5,265 | 6,012 | 6,387 | 6,132 | 3,100 |
| 1. Owners | 3,227 | 3,463 | 3,954 | 3,864 | 2,325 |
| 2. Tenants | 2,038 | 2,549 | 2,433 | 2,268 | 775 |
| II. WORKING CLASS | 29,518 | 25,813 | 22,665 | 19,730 | 6,035 |
| 1. Industrial | 16,124 | 16,198 | 15,118 | 12,982 | 3,225 |
| a) Manufactures | 9,250 * | 9,150 | 9,450 | 7,425 | 1,812 |
| b) Mining | 824 | 887 | 982 | 862 | 179 |
| c) Transportation | 2,950 * | 2,961 | 2,386 | 2,204 | 465 |
| d) Construction | 3,100 * | 3,200 | 2,300 | 2,490 | 768 |
| 2. Farm Laborers | 2,312 | 2,606 | 2,217 | 2,658 | 1,500 * |
| 3. Other Workers | 11,082 | 7,456 | 5,329 | 4,089 | 1,310 |
| III. MIDDLE CLASS | 16,633 | 14,884 | 11,682 | 8,870 | 2,289 |
| 1. Old—Enterprisers | 3,863 | 3,751 | 3,350 | 3,261 | 1,532 * |
| a) Business | 3,382 | 3,304 | 2,943 | 2,895 | 1,304 |
| b) Professional | 481 | 446 | 406 | 366 | 128 |
| 2. New—Salaried | 12,769 | 11,580 | 8,332 | 5,609 | 756 |
| a) Technical-M'g'rial | 2,062 | 1,966 | 1,527 | 999 | 129 |
| b) Professional | 2,660 | 2,413 | 1,581 | 1,179 | 204 |
| c) Clerical | 3,889 | 3,345 | 2,719 | 1,403 | 68 |
| d) Salespeople | 3,347 | 3,003 | 1,877 | 1,595 | 282 |
| e) Public Service | 439 | 418 | 290 | 208 | 48 |
| IV. UPPER BOURGEOISIE | 240 | 300 | 200 | | |
| TOTAL | 51,656 | 47,457 | 40,935 | 34,733 | 11,424 |

* Partly estimated.

The final totals are all persons "gainfully occupied" or "the labor force" (new Census terminology) minus unpaid family farm workers. "Labor force" and "gainfully occupied" are not strictly comparable; the 1940 total is "labor force" and would be slightly higher if the older concept had been used.

Under "manufactures" are included some workers not working in factories. "Transportation" includes workers in communication industries. "Farm Laborers" includes only hired wage-workers. The "salaried" total includes "unspecified" salaried employees and telephone and telegraph operators (See Table 7). "Salespeople" includes "clerks" in stores. "Public Service" includes federal, state and local officials, police personnel and probation officers; it excludes doorkeepers, laborers and other wage-workers; and does not include the much larger total in government service.

SOURCE: Compiled, computed and arranged from material in *Population: Comparative Occupation Statistics for the United States, 1870 to 1940*, published by the U. S. Bureau of the Census. (Preliminary table.)

Let us look at Table 1 again. The working class increased slowly from around 53 per cent of all gainfully occupied persons in 1870 to a peak of 57 per cent in 1910; then it fell to 55 per cent in 1920, was stationary in the 1920's, and rose again to 57 per cent in 1940. But "working class" includes farm laborers and workers in domestic and personal service, while the "proletariat" in the Marxist sense is composed of industrial workers. The industrial proletariat reached its numerical peak in 1920 and has been almost stationary since, but its relative weight has fallen. From around 55 per cent of the working class in 1870 the industrial workers rose to a peak of 66 per cent in 1910 and 67 per cent in 1920, falling, however, to 62 per cent in 1930 and 55 per cent in 1940. This relative shrinkage in the proletariat appears clearly from another angle: as a proportion of all gainfully occupied persons the industrial workers rose from around 30 per cent in 1870 to 37 per cent in 1910 and 1920, falling to 34 per cent in 1930 and 31 per cent in 1940.

Two major factors underlie this shrinkage of the proletariat: the growing trend toward use of automatic machines and automatic plants, which displaces manual workers while it multiplies the number of technical-managerial and clerical employees; and the constant growth of professional and personal services, much of them to serve workers themselves as their living standards and leisure rise.

While the working class multiplied six times from 1870 to 1940, the middle class as a whole multiplied eight times and *the new middle class sixteen times*. The absolute numbers of the industrial proletariat has remained virtually stationary since 1920 while the new middle class scored an increase of 50 per cent. From an almost negligible proportion in 1870 the new middle class moved up to become 25 per cent of all gainfully occupied persons. Technical-managerial and professional employees alone have multiplied thirteen times since 1870, from 330,000 to 4,772,000.

This tremendous growth of the new mid-dle class is an integral part of basic economic changes in the structural set-up of capitalism:

1. The growing technical-scientific nature of industry, which calls for constantly greater numbers of technical employees.
2. The increasingly complex nature of production and distribution, and the separation of ownership from management in collective enterprise, which calls for constantly greater numbers of managerial employees.
3. The growing amount of planning, regulation, and control within industry, and the consequent need for more administration, which calls for constantly greater numbers of clerical employees.
4. The multiplication of goods and leisure, which calls for more employment in distribution and trade and for more personal and professional services, the performers of which are primarily members of the new middle class. The proportion of people employed in the production of physical goods fell from around 75 per cent in 1870 to 50 per cent in 1940. If incomes and leisure go up again, as they can, it will mean more employment in the performance of services.
5. The growth in the economic functions of government and of public services, which has brought the grand total of all public employees, federal, state and local, from around 175,000 in 1870 to 3,100,000 in 1930 and 3,200,000 in 1940, exclusive of relief workers. The small increase shown in 1940 over ten years earlier was due to contraction in state and local employment; federal employees rose from 580,-000 in 1930 to 1,000,000 in 1940. Around one-third of public employees are workers (including mail carriers); the balance of two-thirds are technical-managerial, professional, and clerical employees.

## 2. THE OLD MIDDLE CLASS

The economic basis of early middle-class democracy was the widespread ownership of small independent property in a society of small producers. But small ownership was disastrously limited by the onsweep of industrialism. In the America of the 1820's around 80 per cent of the people owned property from which they worked a livelihood; in the 1940's only 20 per cent do so, the great majority being now dependent on income from a wage-or-salary job.

Ownership of farms was the basis of earlier economic democracy. The absolute number of farmers kept on increasing until 1910, although they moved downward in a relative sense. But for twenty years thereafter the number of farmers remained stationary while population grew; and in 1940 there were fewer farmers than in 1910. Farmers today are not much more than 10 per cent of the gainfully occupied. The decrease in tenancy, from 42.4 per cent in 1930 to 38.7 per cent in 1940, did not represent an increase of free farmers but dispossession of tenants from the soil.

Small business enterprisers (Table 2) increased from 1870 to 1910, from 1,404,000 to 2,895,000; there was a small rise to 3,-304,000 in 1930 and hardly any change in 1940. The trend for the old middle class as a whole, including professionals, was pretty much the same, with a small increase from 1910 onward but a very large decrease as a percentage of all gainfully occupied persons. It is important to observe, however,

the relative and absolute decline in the number of independent *industrial* enterprisers (manufactures, construction, mining)—from around 425,000 in 1910 to 390,-000 in 1930 and 257,000 in 1940. The statistical decline may be a bit more than the actual decline, because the different years do not seem wholly comparable and because some of the 1940 decline may have been a temporary depression result, yet the downward trend is definite. Many independent industrial enterprisers have been wiped out by the war. Whether or not they stage a comeback depends upon postwar economic conditions and what kind of policy the middle class pursues.

Small independent enterprises have held their own in numbers only because of the very large increase in trade and personal services (some of which in 1940 was, however, a hangover of people opening small stores to escape unemployment during the depression of the 1930's).

Independent professionals, interestingly enough, have made little contribution to an increase of small enterprisers (Table 3). They made considerable gains from 1870 to 1910, multiplying nearly four times, but the later gains are small compared with the great gains of salaried professionals. Among professionals, too, employment becomes increasingly institutional. . . .

TABLE 2. ENTERPRISES: 1870–1940

| | 1940 | 1930 | 1910 | 1870 |
|---|---|---|---|---|
| Manufactures | 145,000 * | 207,901 | 235,618⎫ | |
| Building | 100,000 * | 167,512 | 174,422⎰ | 47,000 |
| Mining | 12,000 * | 15,511 | 14,287 | 500 |
| Trade | 1,926,000 | 1,800,000 | 1,278,000 | 440,000 |
| Laundry, etc. | 53,694 | 49,461 | 30,000 | 1,000 * |
| Entertainment | 70,844 | 67,744 | 34,347 | 1,185 |
| General Services | 535,000 | 467,000 | 390,000 | 110,900 |
| Garages | 100,000 | 95,000 | 18,000 | 2,000 * |
| Professional | 481,121 | 446,738 | 366,223 | 128,175 |
| Unclassified | 439,590 | 434,332 | 720,734 | 802,014 |
| TOTAL | 3,863,249 | 3,751,199 | 3,261,631 | 1,532,774 |

* Partly estimated.

Under "Laundry" are included laundry, cleaning, dyeing and pressing establishments. "Entertainment" includes theaters and motion picture houses, pleasure resorts, race tracks, etc. "General Services" includes hotels and boarding houses, eating and drinking places, barber and beauty shops, etc. "Garages" includes cab and truck owners, and, for earlier years, livery stables. "Professional" includes self-employed performers of professional services. "Unclassified" includes, especially for the earlier years, independent artesans and artisan shops.

SOURCE: Compiled, computed and arranged from material in *Population: Comparative Occupation Statistics for the United States, 1870 to 1940*, published by the U. S. Bureau of the Census. (Preliminary table.)

### 3. THE NEW MIDDLE CLASS

In some of its functions the new middle class of technical-managerial, professional, and clerical employees is not altogether new. There were office workers, public employees, a smattering of technicians and managers in early capitalism, some also in the commercial civilizations of antiquity. But their numbers were small and they were significant mainly in the repressive bureaucracy of the state. The new middle class is new in its numbers, in the variety and significance of its occupations, and in being a typical class product of large-scale collective economic activity.

The slowdown in expansion of the new middle class, as a result of the depression of the 1930's, was temporary unless there arises a new economic crisis. But a new crisis will engulf the working class, too. And the problems of policy created by the new middle class will become acute. Trends in the over-all class development since 1870 may be summed up:

The working class has grown proportionately more than twice as fast as the independent enterprisers.

The middle class as a whole has grown around 50 per cent more than the number of workers.

The new middle class has grown more than three times faster than the working class, eight times faster than the number of enterprisers, and two-and-one-half times faster than the middle class as a whole.

These are clear indications of the strength and significance of the new middle class.

#### TABLE 3. INDEPENDENT PROFESSIONALS: 1870–1940

|  | 1940 | 1930 | 1910 | 1870 |
|---|---|---|---|---|
| Physicians | 165,629 | 153,803 | 145,000 * | 60,000 * |
| Dentists | 70,601 | 70,344 | 39,597 | 7,988 |
| Other Medical | 48,458 | 48,187 | 19,755 | 5,585 |
| Lawyers | 180,483 | 160,605 | 114,704 | 39,791 * |
| Architects | 21,976 | 23,100 | 17,444 | 2,039 |
| Photographers | 37,641 | 32,805 | 31,775 | 7,652 |
| Artists | 62,485 | 57,253 | 34,094 | 4,120 |
| Authors | 14,126 | 12,325 | 4,324 | 1,000 * |
| TOTAL | 481,121 | 446,738 | 366,223 | 128,175 |

\* Partly estimated.

Under "Physicians" surgeons are included. "Lawyers" includes judges. "Other medical" includes veterinarians, osteopaths, chiropractors and healers. "Artists" includes sculptors and teachers of art. No attempt is made to classify other and newer professions.

The totals are functional, not arithmetical; they assume that an overall average of 10% of professional persons were salaried employees in 1910 and an average of 20% in 1930 and 1940.

SOURCE: Compiled, computed and arranged from material in *Population: Comparative Occupation Statistics for the United States, 1870 to 1940*, published by the U. S. Bureau of the Census. (Preliminary table.)

#### TABLE 4. TECHNICIANS: 1870–1940

|  | 1940 | 1930 | 1910 | 1870 |
|---|---|---|---|---|
| Chemists | 60,005 | 48,009 | 16,598 | 774 |
| Civil Engineers | 105,486 | 102,086 | 52,031 ⎫ | |
| Electrical Engineers | 55,667 | 57,259 | 15,125 ⎬ | 7,094 |
| Mechanical Engineers | 85,543 | 54,356 | 14,514 ⎭ | |
| Chemical Engineers | 11,600 ⎫ | 11,970 | 6,930 ⎭ | |
| Mining Engineers | 9,773 ⎭ | | | |
| Industrial Engineers | 9,803 | 3,261 | .... | 250 |
| Laboratory Technicians | 17,246 | 8,288 | 4,000 | .... |
| TOTAL | 355,123 | 285,229 | 109,198 | 8,118 |

Under "Chemists" are included assayers and metallurgists. "Civil Engineers" includes surveyors. "Laboratory" includes technicians and assistants; 1940 data is not comparable with earlier years.

SOURCE: Compiled, computed and arranged from material in *Population: Comparative Occupation Statistics for the United States, 1870 to 1940*, published by the U. S. Bureau of the Census. (Preliminary table.)

Its functions arise out of changes that have transformed capitalism and that carry into the future. They have brought a great increase in the number of technicians (Table 4). . . .

. . . The Census figures show an increase of forty times in the number of technicians, with 700,000 as the probable 1940 total. The greatest expansion has been since 1910 and there was no serious slowdown in 1940 because of the depression.

While the majority of technical engineers (electrical, mechanical, mining, civil) are in industry, 26.5 per cent of them were engaged in professional service in 1930, and 12.2 per cent in public service. . . .[1]

Any expansion of industry must neces-

[1] H. D. Anderson and P. E. Davidson, *Occupa-*

sarily increase the number of technicians and enlarge their strategic importance. Industry becomes more and more dependent on the possessors of technical knowledge and skills while the manual labor force dwindles, with increasingly more skilled workers being transformed into "junior technicians." The technician is master of the mysterious processes of a system of production which is infinitely more complex than production in the early stages of the industrial revolution. . . .

Technicians merge into the managerial group, which has grown fourteen times in number since 1870 (Table 5). Managerial

*tional Trends in the United States* (1940), p. 549. This is an excellent occupational study.

TABLE 5. MANAGERIAL EMPLOYEES: 1870–1940

|  | 1940 | 1930 | 1910 | 1870 |
|---|---|---|---|---|
| Agriculture | 62,778 | 70,583 | 52,811 | 2,000 * |
| Upper | 37,503 | ...... | ...... | ..... |
| Lower | 25,275 | ...... | ...... | ..... |
| Manufactures | 654,457 | 651,260 | 301,691 | 16,000 * |
| Upper | 312,000 * | 312,756 | 125,694 | ..... |
| Lower | 342,457 | 338,504 | 175,997 | ..... |
| Mining | 48,345 | 49,671 | 34,285 | 7,580 |
| Upper | 16,101 | 15,385 | 10,947 | 580 |
| Lower | 32,244 * | 34,286 | 23,338 | 7,000 * |
| Railroads | 111,311 | 153,996 | 113,003 | 25,000 * |
| Upper | 32,242 | 34,132 | 19,805 | ..... |
| Lower | 79,069 | 119,864 | 93,198 | ..... |
| Other Transport | 102,826 | 119,927 | 82,211 | 10,000 * |
| Upper | 50,882 | 63,352 | 34,490 | ..... |
| Lower | 51,944 | 56,575 | 47,721 | ..... |
| Communication | 40,024 | 34,182 | 16,551 | 300 * |
| Upper | 23,301 | 18,957 | 10,089 | ..... |
| Lower | 16,723 | 15,225 | 6,462 | ..... |
| Construction | 99,932 | 68,818 | 40,000 * | 12,000 * |
| Upper | 25,269 | 23,492 | 15,000 | ..... |
| Lower | 74,663 | 45,326 | 25,000 | ..... |
| Trade | 89,124 | 82,658 | 45,274 | 7,500 * |
| Upper | 50,000 * | 45,000 * | 25,000 * | ..... |
| Lower | 39,124 | 37,658 | 20,274 | ..... |
| Motion Picture | 2,100 | 1,923 | ...... | ..... |
| Garage | 21,250 | 19,247 | ...... | ..... |
| Banking | 95,000 | 93,356 | 56,059 | 15,000 * |
| Insurance | 39,735 | 33,997 | 9,501 | 1,000 * |
| Unclassified | 340,694 | 301,271 | 142,481 | 25,000 * |
| TOTAL | 1,707,576 | 1,680,889 | 893,867 | 121,380 |

* Partly estimated.

"Upper," managerial—managers, officials; "Lower"—foremen, overseers, inspectors.
"Other Transport" includes street railways, bus, taxicab, trucking, and shipping. "Communication" includes telephone and telegraph only. "Motion Picture, Garage, Banking, Insurance" include managers and officials only.

SOURCE: Compiled, computed and arranged from material in *Population: Comparative Occupation Statistics for the United States, 1870 to 1940*, published by the U. S. Bureau of the Census. (Preliminary table.)

employees are important in every field of activity, including government, although the largest proportion is engaged in manufactures. . . .

Around two-fifths of managerial employees are in the upper group, composed of officials and managers. The top layers of this upper group, the administrative officials, may be called "institutional capitalists" (for whom, however, power is a greater motive than profit, which largely explains why they merged so easily into fascism). They are identified with monopoly capitalism and imperialism and are, by and large, the heart of reaction. But this is not true of the whole managerial group, especially its lower layers which are frequently in conflict with the upper (evident today in the struggle of foremen to unionize against administrative opposition). . . .

In objective functional aptitudes and interests the technical-managerial personnel is not capitalist. It has an instinct for workmanship, which calls for doing a job of production, and its economic interests in terms of employment and income are promoted by full utilization of productive resources and their expansion. . . .

Salaried professionals scored an increase of thirty times from 1870 to 1940 (Table 6). They increased much more, and more rapidly, than independent professionals. They include not only groups specified in the table but also salaried physicians, surgeons, architects, lawyers, and others. . . . A wholly new group emerged, professional social workers. Many professionals are in the upper layers of management, while accountants are part of the administrative bureaucracy of corporate business. At least 125,000 salaried professionals (including technical-scientific personnel) are in the employ of the federal government, with many more, among them 1,100,000 teachers, employed by states, municipalities, and townships.

Among salaried professionals are the shapers of opinion and ideas: the teachers, editors, and reporters who, along with writers and artists, are the architects of ideology. They are the intellectuals—successors to the priests and medicine men of earlier religious civilizations. . . .

The economic status of salaried professionals is, in general, much inferior to that of the independents. Where the great ma-

TABLE 6. SALARIED PROFESSIONALS: 1870–1940

| | 1940 | 1930 | 1910 | 1870 |
|---|---|---|---|---|
| Teachers | 1,203,622 | 1,124,520 | 614,905 | 128,265 |
| Designers | 111,805 | 102,730 | 47,449 | 1,291 |
| Reporters | 63,493 | 51,844 | 34,382 | 5,375 |
| Musicians | 161,536 | 165,128 | 139,310 | 16,170 |
| Clergymen | 140,077 | 145,877 | 118,018 ⎫ | . . . . . . |
| Religious Workers | 35,172 | 31,290 | 12,970 * ⎬ | 44,934 |
| Social Workers | 75,197 | 32,241 | 3,000 * ⎭ | . . . . . . |
| Actors | 40,000 * | 37,993 | 28,297 | 2,066 |
| Librarians | 38,607 | 29,613 | 7,423 | . . . . . . |
| Trained Nurses | 371,066 | 294,189 | 82,327 | 1,204 |
| Accountants | 190,000 * | 191,571 | 39,239 | . . . . . . |
| Unclassified | 110,000 * | 95,239 | 12,061 | 5,000 * |
| TOTAL | 2,540,575 | 2,302,235 | 1,139,381 | 204,305 |
| Additional | 120,268 | 111,684 | 40,470 | . . . . . . |
| GRAND TOTAL | 2,660,843 | 2,413,919 | 1,179,851 | 204,305 |

* Partly estimated.

Under "Teachers" college professors and presidents are included. "Designers" includes draftsmen. "Reporters" includes editors. "Unclassified" includes professional apprentices and assistants and "other professional occupations." "Additional" is the sum of the assumptions made in Table 5 regarding the number of independent professionals who are salaried employees. Excluded are laborers and other wage-workers, keepers of billiard rooms and dance halls, and managers and officials which the Census lists under "Professional service."

SOURCE: Compiled, computed and arranged from material in *Population: Comparative Occupation Statistics for the United States, 1870 to 1940*, published by the U. S. Bureau of the Census. (Preliminary table.)

jority of independent professionals have yearly incomes above $2,500, most salaried professionals earn yearly incomes below $2,500 (comparable with most small independent enterprisers). . . .

Many technical-managerial and professional employees are, from the angle of their incomes, nearer to the workers than they are to members of their own class. In fact, millions of skilled union workers can earn more than millions of lower-salaried employees. Nevertheless, technical-managerial and professional employees are members of the new middle class. Most of them earn more than the workers; their occupations, their functions, and their potential (if not actual) incomes differentiate them from the workers. A worker who earns around $3,000–$3,500 a year knows that is the limit: he can earn more only by ceasing to be a worker. Technical-managerial and professional employees may earn only $2,000 a year, but they know they can earn more and they need not get out of their class to do so. . . .

This problem of class appears more sharply in the case of white collar workers, whose numbers jumped from around 375,000 in 1870 to 7,600,000 in 1940, an increase of twenty times (Table 7). Many white collar workers are difficult to classify. Salespeople and clerks in stores might be assigned to the working class, bookkeepers to the class of lower professional employees.

Yet objective and psychological considerations that are determining factors should be borne in mind.

One objective distinction can be made: the amount of education and training that is needed to qualify for a particular occupation. The professionals need more education and training than the white collars, and white collars (most of them at least) need more than the workers. An important class-psychological distinction is this: the white collar occupations (most, if not all, of them) were occupations that represented an upward move in the world, an escape from the working class. They were cleaner, with better hours and pay; they provided more security, social prestige, and chance to get ahead. In general the white collars developed within the middle class, as its lower layers, and with the psychological attitudes of that class. Hence their resistance to unionism, which is only slowly breaking down.

. . . Even if all white collar people are assigned to the working class there still remains a solid core of 9,000,000 members of the middle class, among them 5,000,000 technical-managerial, professional, and public employees. The total becomes larger as farmers (who are middle class, being proprietors) are added. . . .

· · · · ·

. . . It must be recognized that salespeople in stores are most akin to workers

TABLE 7. WHITE COLLAR WORKERS: 1870–1940

| | 1940 | 1930 | 1910 | 1870 |
|---|---|---|---|---|
| Bookkeepers, etc. | 741,308 * | 739,077 | 447,411 | 38,776 |
| Clerks | 1,973,604 | 1,795,000 | 639,000 | 29,801 |
| Stenographers-Typists | 1,174,886 | 811,190 | 316,693 | 154 |
| Clerks (store) | 525,591 | 401,991 | 387,183 | 80,000 * |
| Salespeople (store) | 2,200,000 * | 1,988,322 | 877,238 | 160,000 * |
| Commercial Travelers | 256,000 * | 223,732 | 163,620 | 7,296 |
| Sales Agents | 366,312 | 389,358 | 167,578 | 35,000 * |
| Operators | 250,821 | 316,638 | 137,684 | 8,406 |
| Unclassified | 118,000 * | 117,397 | 85,240 * | 15,000 * |
| TOTAL | 7,606,522 | 6,782,705 | 3,221,647 | 374,433 |

* Partly estimated.

Under "Bookkeepers" cashiers are included. "Clerks" excludes shipping clerks, who are listed with wage-workers. "Sales Agents" includes insurance and real estate agents. "Operators" includes telephone and telegraph operators. "Unclassified" includes railway mail clerks, etc.

SOURCE: Compiled, computed and arranged from material in *Population: Comparative Occupation Statistics for the United States, 1870 to 1940*, published by the U. S. Bureau of the Census. (Preliminary table.)

and that the relative position of white collars in general has seriously deteriorated since 1870. The working class has moved upward, the white collars downward. Division and subdivision of labor among clerical workers make their jobs more routine and uninteresting; a modern office more and more resembles a factory as machines in use multiply (office-machine operators almost doubled in 1930–40, rising from 36,-162 to 64,178); opportunities to get ahead are increasingly limited; differentials in pay shrink, and constantly larger numbers of wage-workers are better paid than most white collars. Finally, economic security is crumbling; in the depression of the 1930's, unlike the experience in previous depressions, nearly as many white collars, proportionately, were thrown into unemployment as wage-workers. The general situation is thus summed up in a Census analysis of the white collar worker:

The average salary is only enough to meet demands of a very moderate standard of living. Little is left for savings. He lives all too frequently—as do many workers—face to face with the hazard of unemployment and with the risk of dependency in his old age. . . . (White collars) are a class between the usually better-educated and better-paid professionals and the less well-educated but better-paid skilled workers. The skilled workers (and increasingly other workers too) often belong to unions, and many of the professional persons belong to the professional societies, but only a small proportion of the clerical workers are organized. As a class they are not yet fully group conscious. . . .

. . . . . .

The failure of socialism to grow among the American people, which always puzzled and irritated Marxists, becomes understandable in part as the changes in class relations are considered. Much of the socialist agitation was based on the argument that "opportunity has come to an end." But the emphasis always was on the opportunity to become independent businessmen. In this connection the socialist argument was largely true after 1910, although up until that year the opportunity, while diminishing, was still there. But a whole new field for "opportunity to rise in the world" was opened up by the astonishing expansion of technical-managerial and professional employment (in which may be included the upper layers of white collar workers). The form was new but it *was* opportunity and it offered "careers open to the talents." This, along with other factors—no American feudalism, the measurable completion in the 1820's–30's of the struggle for political democracy, the unparalleled economic expansion which brought to the American people the highest living standards in the world—distinguished this country from Europe and explains the failure of socialism. Its lessons must be learned to understand the present and project the future.

# 23 C. Wright Mills: *The New Men of Power*

❦ *Historically, the growth of business organization has been accompanied or followed by the development of labor organization. Business has usually opposed the initial organization of labor unions, often by such methods as espionage and armed violence. Nevertheless, and particularly since the New Deal, mammoth labor unions have taken their place alongside big business and big government as a major force in*

American society. With this growth in the size and importance of unions have arisen all those problems which had already manifested themselves in large-scale business and government: problems of leadership, bureaucracy, freedom and responsibility, and coercion.

In this reading, C. Wright Mills analyzes modern American labor organization from the standpoint of its internal structure and its relationship to organized business, to government, and to society at large. Mills is Professor of Sociology at Columbia University. His articles have appeared in the New Republic, American Journal of Sociology, Political Science Quarterly, and other journals. He edited, with H. H. Gerth, From Max Weber: Essays in Sociology (1946), and wrote, with the assistance of Helen Schneider, The New Men of Power (1948). He is also the author of White Collar: the American Middle Classes (1951). Our reading is excerpted from The New Men of Power, pp. 49–67, and is reprinted with the permission of the publisher, Harcourt, Brace and Company.

No matter what political publics may demand or the general public support, the labor leader can neither follow the first nor accept the second unless he is strong. No man is strong in the world of U. S. labor unless he has or is thought to have a strong union back of him. The power of the labor leader is bound up with the power of the union which he leads.

It is only because of his organization that the political publics make demands on the labor leader and the general public keeps him in focus. All his action, political and economic, is action with an eye on the state of his union.

### THE INTERNATIONALS

Workers come together to form local unions, which are the district units of nationwide unions. These national unions may be affiliated with the American Federation of Labor or the Congress of Industrial Organizations, or they may remain independent of both. The locals within a national union are under the control of the national headquarters, and the AFL and CIO are creatures of their respective national unions. Thus the key organization in the world of U. S. labor is the national union, which is often called the international because it may have members in Canada as well as in the United States. The 180-odd national unions, or internationals, are self-governing: they alone decide what they will do. The men operating these internationals are the men who run the union world of American labor.

Heading the international are the general officers, the president and the secretary of the union, who usually also serves as treasurer. In smaller unions the president, the secretary, and the treasurer may be the same man, but generally there are two top officers. In larger unions there are also one or more vice-presidents. Elected by a national constituency of union members, the national officers are often somewhat independent of pressure from particular local unions.

Attached to international headquarters are varying numbers of general organizers or "international representatives." Their job is to organize new locals and to serve as liaison agents between national headquarters and the lower segments of the organization. As links between the national officers and the scattered locals, they advise and service the locals, many continuously working assigned districts. These "international reps" are usually appointed as salaried employees, although in a few unions they are elected by the union's national convention. In many unions, they are attached primarily to given national officials and make up the cadre of the machine within the international.

The international's headquarters usually maintains an office staff. In the smaller unions, this staff may be altogether clerical and secretarial, but in the larger internationals, it is augmented by a sizable corps of professionals, appointed by the general officers. These professionals are lawyers, editors of the union's newspaper, and in an increasing number of unions, economists, statisticians, and research directors; they are the inside-the-union "intellectuals."

The international is composed of local labor unions, the bottom unit of labor organization. These locals contain the workers of a given plant or the craftsmen in a given labor market. The president and the secretary-treasurer of the locals are elected by the rank and file. In small locals, these officers continue to work at their trades, serving as part-time union leaders; in larger locals, the top officers are important members of the labor leader fraternity. Their job is to administer the affairs of their locals, and apart from collective bargaining, they are the labor leaders whom businessmen and personnel directors meet in the everyday round of work.

Most locals of any size usually have one or more business agents, who in older unions are generally elected by the members of the local or in newer unions (which have often grown fast and from the top down) are appointed by the national officers. In either case, the business agent is generally a full-time, paid organizer. He is a general manager and contact man. He provides the continuity and general supervision of the local's administration. His duties are as wide as the activities of the local. He sits with the executive board and the elected officers; he participates in every important meeting between the union and the companies; he is generally the depository of continuous union experience.

The locals have certain members working in the plants who hold the position of shop steward. They are usually chosen by the membership in the plant, although in some cases they are appointed by the local or international officers. These shop stewards are the backbone of the rank-and-file leaders, and as volunteers they help the union administer its domain. They do not receive union salaries, and although they have no formal voice in running the local, they do have a chance to acquire a following and gain influence.

There is a bewildering variety of organizational arrangements between the top national officers and the local labor leaders. Intricate mazes of delegate bodies crisscross one another in a pattern of elected and appointed authority. For example, there may be joint boards composed of all the locals in the international that have jurisdiction over a set of related crafts or occupations. These boards are composed of delegates from all the locals involved, and their purpose is to promote or secure united action among these locals. The boards may have firm control of their locals, may sometimes actually run them, or may be weak and dependent upon the constituent locals for their existence. In some unions, the boards are headed by men appointed by the international's president.

Some internationals may also have district councils, which have jurisdiction over the locals within a given territory. Coal, for instance, is divided into 30 district organizations, the heads of which nominally are elected by the locals but actually a majority are appointed by the president of the international. Steel has 40 district offices, and in each of them, a representative from the international holds forth.

One national union, for instance, has 251 locals, 19 joint boards, and 7 district councils, located in 238 cities, 32 states, and 4 Canadian provinces. This vast bureaucracy is a virtual job empire, securely integrated with a leading American industry and tying together an international labor union. In such internationals, there is much room for the "fixing" operations of a machinery of patronage built up and maintained by national officers.

All internationals began in one of three

ways: (1) A number of independently organized locals banded together to form a new national organization. (2) An organizing committee, attached to some existing labor body, created a new international by going out and organizing a number of locals and setting them up as more or less autonomous organizations. (3) Spontaneously organized locals appeared in an industry or occupation and were then gathered together by an organizing committee attached to some going labor body.

The international heads make decisions on broad questions—when to begin an organizing drive or when and how to handle a strike situation. The locals oversee initial as well as continuous grievance dealings, policies about participation in city politics, and dues collection. Such influence as the locals have over the national officers is mainly through the elected delegates they send to conventions; such power as the international officers have depends upon how much control they can exercise over a strategic combination of locals. The control of the international over its locals varies greatly from union to union. In general, however, power has shifted to the international officers and to their appointees in the union hierarchy. Thus the histories of the various internationals are case studies in the shaping of various types of bureaucracy.

### SIZES AND SHAPES

Fifty years ago, U. S. unionism was a small-scale affair. In 1900, there were 99 national unions, having a total of 833,600 members, 5.3 per cent of the wage and salary workers of the nation. In the five years after 1900, organizing surged, and from then until the first World War, the unions steadily made small gains. During and immediately after the first World War, membership boomed. Nineteen-twenty is the historical peak: 133 internationals had enrolled 4,961,000 members, 17.6 per cent of the wage and salary workers of the country.

The business boom of the Twenties was a bleak trade union slump: membership dropped from the 4,961,000 in 1920 to 3,-400,000 in 1925. The early years of the depression did not spur union growth. By 1935, the percentage organized was at its interwar low: 9.4 per cent of the wage and salary workers were in unions.

The big story for American labor unions begins just after 1935, the year of the great springboard, when the CIO drive got under way. All labor organizations were ramrodded to increased efforts: in the next decade total U. S. union membership rose from 3,400,000 to 13,600,000. The windfall years of the war did not altogether account for this jump—by 1938, the internationals had already climbed to 7,800,000. What happened during the war was merely a continuation of the trend that started during the later depression years. In 1944, some 34.4 per cent of all wage and salary workers in this country were members of labor unions.

Of the 182 internationals that were operating nationally in 1943, 55 per cent were founded before 1914, 14 per cent were founded between 1914 and 1934, and 30 per cent were organized after 1935. However, the growth in union membership has greatly exceeded the growth in the number of internationals. In 1900, 99 unions had an average membership of 8,400; in 1944, 182 unions had an average of 75,000 members. The average size of the 1944 international was almost nine times the average of 1900, but there were not even twice as many internationals in 1944 as in 1900.

These figures mean that a new institution is now part of the lives of many workers in America. Such numbers are the sure way to speak of the accumulated power of the unions. . . .

### THE RIVAL HOUSES

The all-powerful internationals of the union world are banded into two big agglomerates of American unionism—the American Federation of Labor and the Congress of Industrial Organizations, which derive their power from the internationals that compose them. Yet these blocs have power in and of themselves, and they exert it through wide-flung agencies.

. . . . .

The AFL was founded in the Eighties by Samuel Gompers, its president (except in 1894) until his death in 1924. For 36 years Gompers ran it, and in doing so, set many basic patterns of U. S. unionism. He is the spiritual grandfather of many of today's labor leaders. In 1924, William Green became the head of the AFL, and as of 1948, he has occupied the post for 24 years. From the turn of the century through 1935, about 80 per cent of the union members in this country belonged to AFL unions. Shortly after 1936 (the CIO was launched in 1935), the figure dropped to around 50 per cent and has since remained at approximately that level.

A leader's power in the labor union world rests primarily upon the number of workers organized under him. The powers within the AFL high councils obviously would have been disturbed if the millions of workers in the mass production industries had been taken into the AFL as big new industrial unions.

Yet governmental acts passed during the middle Thirties encouraged labor leaders to organize, and spontaneously formed locals were cropping up in whole brackets of industry. Quite clearly sections of the government as well as the workers were asking for unions.

The AFL was not able to meet a challenge of such magnitude. Its executive board, composed of international heads, the high powers in the trade union world, tried several times to loosen the jurisdictional tensions and to spread the unorganized workers among the existing job empires within the AFL, but it had no success.

Many AFL unions were of the craft type, but there was a secular requirement for industrial-type unions. A craft union is composed of workers who have identical types of skill and training, each worker carrying through to completion some whole process of work. An industrial union is composed of all the people who work in an industry, regardless of their skill, training, or function within the work-process. The diamond workers or the coopers are in craft unions; the automobile or the steel workers are in industrial unions. Between these polar types are many forms of union organization, composed of varying combinations of skill. For the sake of simplicity, we shall call the intermediary forms "amalgamated craft unions," for they are mainly composed of workers from related crafts. The men's clothing workers—the pressers, cutters, lapel makers, and so on—are in the Amalgamated Clothing Workers of America.

The type of union organization that prevails is more important for the jurisdictional problems it may lead to than for the pure sociological type it represents. John L. Lewis, head of the AFL organizing committee in the middle Thirties, though a conservative unionist, saw what was happening and what was demanded. He called for industrial unions, that is, for unions outside the existing domains, or unions which, if organized inside the existing domains, would certainly require new sets of machinery and would thus cause trouble within the upper circles.

Trouble or not, Lewis went on organizing, enrolling workers in steel, rubber, automobiles, regardless of their fields of employment within these industries. The executive board of the AFL told him to stop organizing in this wholesale and unjurisdictional manner. He refused. At the conventions of 1934 and 1935, he fought for industrial unionism. He lost the debates. In 1936, the ten unions involved were branded "dual unions," the worst phrase the other leaders could mouth, and expelled from the AFL. Three other unions left voluntarily. These 13 became the CIO, nucleus of the second house of labor and in time, almost as big as the first. At one stroke the AFL lost about 40 per cent of its total membership. . . .

Not all labor leaders and unions are inside one of these blocs. Some are independent or unaffiliated with any labor body. In the first quarter of 1947, 12 per cent of all union members were in independent unions, 39 per cent were in CIO unions, and 49 per cent were in the AFL.

Each international belonging to the AFL or the CIO is a sovereign body, and the federations do not often attempt to interfere in its internal business. The federations are dependent upon the internationals for monetary support. Why, then, are these autonomous and supreme internationals willing to pay from their treasuries to get a charter from the AFL or the CIO?

The American Federation of Labor and the Congress of Industrial Organizations try to assure an exclusive jurisdiction to the unions holding charters for given job empires. The Federation and the Congress will usually combat any union that tries to move in on the territory of another, even if vast portions of that territory are not being worked. But the leaders of an unaffiliated union may at any time find themselves facing a rival union backed by the money, organization, and unionizing talent of the AFL or CIO. If insurgents should form a majority within an international, the AFL is strongly inclined to continue recognizing the original leaders upon whom the charter was bestowed. Thus membership in the AFL or the CIO insures against rivalry from without and insurrection from within.

The AFL and the CIO represent labor before the legislative bodies of the states and of the nation. In so far as the member unions participate in decisions on legislative programs, they are part of what united political front labor has. Both affiliations help member unions in strike situations. They have no right to call upon the member unions to strike in sympathy, but they can, and do, back up the striking union with money and organizational talent. By its Union Label Department, the AFL helps its unions maintain the union label on goods that the members produce and boycott non-union-produced goods.

Both organizations lend their talents and money to their internationals for organizing purposes. In 1944, the AFL employed some 175 organizers; the CIO, 180. Usually, the organization of new fields is carried on by organizing committees; the people organized are then held in federal locals, directly attached to the bloc involved; and eventually they are assigned to existing unions or set up in new unions of their own. . . .

### THE STATES AND THE CITIES

All the locals belonging to affiliated internationals also belong to one of the AFL's 50 state federations [1] or to one of the CIO's 36 state industrial councils. Within each city, the locals belong to one of the AFL's 749 city centrals or the CIO's 232 city industrial councils.

Thus a local is part of an international, and through it, part of the AFL or the CIO. The same local may also belong to an AFL city central or a CIO city industrial council, which in turn belongs to a state federation or a state industrial council. Membership in these city and state organizations is optional, but the majority of the locals of internationals attached to the AFL or the CIO send delegates to the state and city bodies.

The primary task of the state bodies is political. They hold annual conventions at which legislative programs are formulated. The city organizations are more concerned with economic matters, but they, too, formulate policies concerning city politics; in both political and economic matters, the city units are the city-wide agencies of the locals composing them, and the clearing houses for political and negotiating purposes. Next to the local unions, the city units touch the members of the union more intimately than any other sections of the union hierarchy.

Both the city and the state organizations of the AFL and CIO are under cross-pressures. Their leaders borrow from and bestow power upon the internationals, the blocs with which they are affiliated, and the locals under their nominal jurisdiction. All these organizations, having members in the domain of a city body, may be represented in state federations or in one way or

[1] One for each of the 48 states, Alaska, and Puerto Rico.

another influence them. The composition of power in the AFL is such that it always tries to prevent city or state bodies from usurping power from any international. The city organizations are under the surveillance of the executive councils and can be expelled by them.

The internationals or the locals overshadow the city and state organizations in the handling of strikes and the framing of contracts. At most, the city and state agencies may attempt to integrate and help locals by providing techniques and information. If the head of a city central did more than that, the various internationals whose locals were involved would exert pressure on the head of the affiliate body of the offending city central, and then Green or Murray would act against the offending city central.

### WHAT IS ORGANIZED?

Labor leaders care nothing for the academic purity of definitions used to mark off the types of organizations which they lead. What they claim are job areas. They describe their jurisdictions, which is to say, the particular empires of jobs to which they have staked a claim. They do not do this to let the workers know where to go: they are talking to other labor leaders.

In the modern industrial world, and to a lesser extent in the world of labor unions, the craft has ceased to be the key unit of work and organization. Labor leaders, whether they want to or not, have to follow the contours of the industries that are open for organization. If they don't, and there is pressure for unionization, their unions will be by-passed by the mass of industrial workers. That is what happened in the middle and late Thirties. By 1940, only 9 per cent of the total union membership in the U. S. were in craft unions.

|  | Unions | Members |
|---|---|---|
| Craft ............ | 26% | 9% |
| Amalgamated craft . | 53 | 48 |
| Industrial ....... | 21 | 43 |
| Total ............ | 100% | 100% |

The average craft union in 1940 had about 16,200 members as compared with the average amalgamated's 43,000 and the average industrial's 98,500 members.

The craft unions are not only the smallest but also the oldest: 77 per cent of the craft unions, 60 per cent of the amalgamated craft, and 47 per cent of the industrial unions were organized before 1914. Only 7 per cent of the craft unions were organized after 1935, as compared with 20 per cent of the amalgamated craft and 28 per cent of the industrials.

Within each of the three types, the older union is generally the bigger, but there is a difference in the relation of the present size and age according to the type: the older craft unions are on the average ten times as large as the newer craft unions, whereas the older industrial unions average less than twice as large as the newer ones.

Most unions of the craft type are in the AFL; there is not one in the CIO, although it has many unions that are amalgamations of related crafts. Yet in 1936 it was not the principle of craft versus industrial unionism that caused the split; it was power among labor leaders, based on jurisdictional domains. Hutcheson's Carpenters Union, for instance, is a semi-industrial organization. It covers everything from the growing tree to the finished product: "Once wood, it is always the right of the carpenter to install it. . . ." These are the words of the same carpenter who is reputed to have said, "I'll see Lewis in hell before I see industrial unions." Power based on jurisdiction—that is the main issue which keeps the two organizations apart. It has remained the point of disagreement throughout the several formal attempts which, since 1936, have been made to get them together again.

In the early Forties, the members of the three major types of unions were divided between AFL, CIO, and independent unions in this way:

|  | Craft | Amalg. | Ind. |
|---|---|---|---|
| AFL .......... | 65% | 79% | 13% |
| CIO .......... | .. | 11 | 84 |
| Independent ... | 35 | 10 | 1 |
| Total membership ....... | 100% | 100% | 100% |

Clearly, amalgamations of crafts have occurred within and between a great many unions in order to minimize jurisdictional troubles, increase union strength, and make possible co-ordinated demands and actions. The median year of origin for craft unions is 1898, for amalgamated crafts, 1901, and for industrial unions, 1915.

Historically, labor unions have centered in construction, mining, and transportation, with manufacturing lagging. That pattern has now been reversed: between 1930 and 1940, the percentage of all union members who were in manufacturing rose from 24 to 43 per cent. Now for the first time, the manufacturing industries contain the bulk of the people who in one way or another are behind the power of the labor leaders.

Because craft-type unions predominate in the AFL, it is stronger in the building trades, mining, certain professional fields, personal service, and in transportation. The CIO is stronger in mass-production industries such as steel, textiles, automobiles, electrical equipment, and rubber. Here is the industrial composition within each union bloc:

|  | AFL | CIO | Ind. | Total |
|---|---|---|---|---|
| Raw materials . | 13% | 9% | .. | 13% |
| Manufacturing . | 29 | 75 | 7 | 43% |
| Building and construction . | 23 | .. | .. | 13 |
| Transportation and communication ...... | 17 | 8 | 64 | 17 |
| Trade ........ | 2 | 3 | .. | 2 |
| Service ....... | 17 | 5 | 29 | 14 |
| Total membership ....... | 100% | 100% | 100% | 100% |

Only 29 per cent of the AFL workers in 1940, against 75 per cent of the CIO workers, were in manufacturing industries. Furthermore, only one-third of the AFL manufacturing workers, compared with virtually all of the CIO manufacturing workers, were in industrial unions.

The question "What is organized?" may also be answered in terms of the white-collar and wage-worker components of the union membership. In 1900, 3.2 per cent of the white-collar employees and 5.8 per cent of the wage workers were in unions; today, 43 per cent of the wage workers, as compared with 15 per cent of the white-collar people, are unionized. There are many more lower-middle-class people in the unions than is generally realized: approximately 13 per cent of all union members are in white-collar unions.

There is some evidence that among wage workers, those having higher income and status are more likely to join unions, but among white-collar workers the reverse is true. The unionized ranks of both strata tend to come together, as it were, in a lower-middle-class grouping: this is the trade union bloc of the nation.

Before the CIO organizing drives, unions were, in the main, a monopoly of the skilled workers in certain industries: they were a trade aristocracy of labor. With the rise of the CIO, for the first time a large-scale arena for communication among many wage and salary workers was created. The progressive features of the CIO are due, in some part, to the fact that it has organized more than merely the skilled craft élite, just as its retrograde features are due, in some part, to the fact that it has not organized the lowest ranks of the wage workers but has become a new aristocracy of some of the industrial workers.

THE LEADERS AND THE LED

Some members of some unions are mere objects of manipulation; some participate actively in running the union. Some of the leaders are appointed and some are elected; some are paid and some work voluntarily. But always the relations between the leaders and the led are governed mainly by three facts: (1) the dues or the per capita tax which the local members pay to the national union and the money expended in locals by officers; (2) the elections and referenda, held in the locals, which formally determine the officers in the union hierarchy and their activities; (3) the machines the national officials may or may not control, which extend into the various locals.

The control of the first two, money and

elections, is set forth in the constitutions of the unions. The possibilities of building up and of maintaining the often crucial third factor—the machine—are also somewhat limited, if only formally, by the terms of the constitution.

At the convention, the business of running the union as a town meeting or as a leader's machine takes place. Therefore the frequency and the procedure of these conventions are crucial in relations between the leaders and the led. Some 32 per cent of the internationals hold a convention once each year, 36 per cent once every two years, 26 per cent every three to five years; the remaining 6 per cent set their next convention during a given convention or by referendum of the membership. There are cases where unions have not called conventions for long periods of time, but only a handful of internationals are guilty on that score.

The convention is the supreme authority and the only legislative body of the international. The delegates to the convention are usually local officers who, in the larger locals, are often accompanied by active rank-and-file leaders. Usually, "fixing" a union convention requires as much political maneuvering as does any Republican or Democratic Party convention.

Between the members in the local and the officers in the international headquarters, money is a continuing link: the locals are assessed by the internationals, and the latter pay for various local purposes out of the national treasury. One of the key powers of the national officers is this disbursement of national treasury funds. In unions as elsewhere, there is a finance of democracy and there is a democracy of finance.

All the money with which the internationals are run is collected by the locals. A per capita tax per member is paid by each local to its international each month. All this money comes from the fee that the worker pays when he joins or when he is reinstated, the regular dues (usually monthly), and special assessments that may be made for particular purposes.

Power has shifted from the locals to their internationals; centralization of money ha put power in the hands of the internationa officers, who in turn may use it t strengthen their position in locals wher their administration is weak.

Centralization of funds also tends t spread the risks of the union's life mor evenly among the locals. By putting strik funds in the hands of national officials, th locals weaken their own power but als increase, by a sort of insurance system, thei chances of weathering a period of strife This is especially important when union face big corporations whose executives en joy virtually absolute authority over far flung plants.

The democratic election of union officer is often accompanied by factional fights Democracy within the unions, as withi the nation as a whole, is usually a democ racy of machine politics imposed upon mass of apathetic members.

This process can be observed in the re election of union officers. Regardless of th merits of an incumbent, regardless of how successful he has been in running his office if he does not face the scrutiny of opposi tion in an open and free election, he is les likely to remain alert to what previous gen erations have called the "will of the ma jority."

The fact is that opposition in union elec tions is the great exception. The rule i lengthy tenure in office. The best study available shows that between 1910 an 1941, of 764 officers who won the election in 7 AFL unions, 634, or 83 per cent o them, ran for office unopposed. These wer all national officers. In the 63 presidencies 86 per cent were unopposed elections.

The elected leaders of the internationals thus show vigorous ability to perpetuate themselves in office. Daniel Tobin, the suc cessful candidate of the Teamsters in 1907 is still boss, and no one has opposed him since the election of 1910. Sidney Hillman late president of the Amalgamated Cloth ing Workers, was unopposed in office for over 25 years. William Mahon, head of the Street Railway Workers, has been head for over 40 years and unopposed for over 30.

William Hutcheson, chieftain of the Carpenters, has been their president since 1916;
D. B. Robertson, president of the Locomotive Firemen, was first elected to that position in 1922 and has served continuously
since; G. L. Berry of the Printing Press-
men's Union has held his office since 1906.*
For over a quarter of a century, John L.
Lewis has habitually expelled disruptive
elements that might upset his rule of the
Miners Union.

This lack of democratic opposition occurs
whether the election is by convention or by
referendum ballot of the membership. The
reasons for this have never been studied
systematically, but the scattered facts about
a miscellany of individual cases can be
pieced into a coherent story of why unions
tend to become autocratic and centrally
controlled.

As a union grows larger, there often tends
to be less interest among the membership
at large; effective desire for democratic
participation is lowered. The appeal to join
a union is seldom ideological. Bread-and-
butter reasons for joining as well as for
remaining a member go along with lack of
interest in union affairs as democratic
mechanisms.

As membership increases, there is also a
greater possibility for more patronage to be
controlled by union leaders. They can reward their friends and punish their enemies.
In fact, the machine power built up in this
manner may even make possible punishment severe enough to break men as union
leaders. Thus when John Brophy tried to
unify the opposition to John L. Lewis in
1926, Lewis declared the endeavor "a disruptive effort" and expelled Brophy and his
confreres from the union.

In passing, it must be mentioned that
intra-union discipline is often essential for
effective dealing with thoroughly autocratic
business institutions. The managers of corporations are not democratically elected by
the stockholders to represent their interests.
And in this respect, the unions are often
practically forced to borrow from their opponents an autocratic type of rule in order
to insure unity of action.

Over the last hundred years, the American unions have spread out with the national markets; on many of those markets,
no local organization can stand alone. The
distribution of power between the electorate in the locals and the labor leaders at
national headquarters is thus in large part
dependent upon the type of industry and
upon the size of the competitive labor market areas.

If power in most of the older internationals has gravitated from the local to the
national headquarters in the course of time,
in many of the newer unions power has
been concentrated at the top from the beginning. In many cases the men at the top
today are the men who formed the union.
In unions of either sort, a sudden flood of
new members tends to invite the leadership to tighten its grip.

Though many labor leaders retain office
only because of their grip on the union
machine or because of the indifference of
members, or both, some leaders also gain
additional security from the loyalty of a
hero-worshipping rank and file. In almost
all cases of long tenure, the men in power
have been sanctified by some battle through
which they successfully led the union. They
struggle with the birth of the union, they
lead a large strike, or they organize vast
numbers of new workers. The prestige John
Mitchell gained from leading the great
anthracite strikes at the turn of the century
was so great that he could not be successfully challenged as head of the Miners.

Democracy unambiguously means control of a responsible leader by the whole
rank and file. That requires a machinery
that forces the leader to remain alert to
the wants of the members, that keeps him
responsible. Another kind of mechanism
sometimes obtains equally popular results.
It is dangerous and may exist in the tight-
est dictatorships, but in American labor
unions it seems to occur more frequently
than the first-mentioned. This second type

ED. NOTE: * Mr. Berry passed away late in 1948.

evolves when an unchallenged leader consistently acts in the general interests of the
membership. It may result from a leader's
doing either what the members are interested in or what is to their interests. It may
come about by an identity of mental processes between the leaders and the led
("Hutcheson thinks just like an old carpenter") or by the members' absolute trust in
the leaders ("Ole John L. may be rough,
but he's always working for us") or by the
successful accomplishment of what all the
members agree is the most important matter ("He got us the dough, didn't he?").

When considering the undemocratic rule
and long tenure of many union chiefs, one
should remember that on occasion rank-
and-file leaders have upset the rule of the
big shots of the union world. Now, however, there is no general surge of rank-and-

ED. NOTE: * Communist Party.

file revolt against labor leaders. The old
left wing of the AFL, composed of social
ists and anarchist-syndicalists, is no more
Anyone who has watched a successful CP *
revolt knows that the CPers are not fo
rank-and-file democracy any more than the
vested interests they replace. And like the
old ruling class of Great Britain, the aristo
crats of American labor "buy up" the mili
tant, lower-rank upstarts who look poten
tially powerful.

But unions, like other American institu
tions, have to ride the cycle of slump and
war and boom. When times are bad and
there is demand that they be bettered, la
bor leaders must compete with each other
and with new leaders for rank-and-file al
legiance. Slump makes the rank and file
show its muscle, and the leaders of Ameri
can unions jump to more democratic action

# 24 James Burnham: *The Managerial Revolution*

❦ *Throughout this Part, our readings have suggested the tendency, in a large-scale
industrial society, for the significant economic groupings to become fewer in number
and larger in size. Wherever this has taken place, we seem to have seen the rise of
impersonal, centralized organization which has removed the average individual ever
farther from the apparent center of things. Whether as trade-unionist, stockholder, or
citizen, the individual finds himself increasingly subjected to rules and decisions made
by men whom he does not know and perhaps has never even seen. This rise of what
some have called "bureaucracy" has not, as is often believed, taken place only in government—it is equally the tendency in large-scale schools, industrial enterprises, banks,
unions, and churches.*

*What does this rise of "bureaucracy" mean for the future of our socio-political
order? It is to this question that James Burnham (1905–     ) addresses himself in this
reading.*

*Burnham has been a member of the Department of Philosophy at New York
University since 1929. For many years he was an active leader in "left-wing" political*

*movements, and is now identified as a militant anti-Communist. Among his writings are* Introduction to Philosophical Analysis *(1931),* The Machiavellians *(1943), and* The Struggle for the World *(1947). Our selection is from* The Managerial Revolution *(1941), pp. 71–88, and is used with permission of the publisher, John Day Company, Inc.*

The theory of the managerial revolution . . . holds, to begin with, that we are now in a period of social transition . . . , a period characterized, that is, by an unusually rapid rate of change of the most important economic, social, political, and cultural institutions of society. This transition is *from* the type of society which we have called capitalist or bourgeois *to* a type of society which we shall call *managerial.*

This transition period may be expected to be short compared with the transition from feudal to capitalist society. It may be dated, somewhat arbitrarily, from the first world war, and may be expected to close, with the consolidation of the new type of society, by approximately fifty years from then, perhaps sooner.

I shall now use the language of the "struggle for power" to outline the remaining key assertions of the theory:

What is occurring in this transition is a drive for social dominance, for power and privilege, for the position of ruling class, by the social group or class of the *managers* (as I shall call them, reserving for the moment an explanation of whom this class includes). This drive will be successful. At the conclusion of the transition period the managers will, in fact, have achieved social dominance, will be the ruling class in society. This drive, moreover, is world-wide in extent, already well advanced in all nations, though at different levels of development in different nations.

The economic framework in which this social dominance of the managers will be assured is based upon the state ownership of the major instruments of production. Within this framework there will be no direct property rights in the major instruments of production vested in individuals as individuals.

How, then, it will be at once asked (and this is the key to the whole problem), if that is the economic framework, will the existence of a ruling class be possible? A ruling class . . . means a group of persons who, by virtue of special social-economic relations, exercises a special degree of control over access to the instruments of production and receives preferential treatment in the distribution of the product of these instruments. Capitalists were such a group precisely because they, as individuals, held property rights in the instruments of production. If, in managerial society, no individuals are to hold comparable property rights, how can any group of individuals constitute a ruling class?

The answer is comparatively simple and . . . not without historical analogues. The managers will exercise their control over the instruments of production and gain preference in the distribution of the products, not directly, through property rights vested in them as individuals, but indirectly, through their control of the state which in turn will own and control the instruments of production. The state . . . will, if we wish to put it that way, be the "property" of the managers. And that will be quite enough to place them in the position of ruling class.

The control of the state by the managers will be suitably guaranteed by appropriate political institutions, analogous to the guarantee of bourgeois dominance under capitalism by the bourgeois political institutions.

The ideologies expressing the social role and interests and aspirations of the managers (like the great ideologies of the past an indispensable part of the struggle for power) have not yet been fully worked out, any more than were the bourgeois ideologies in the period of transition to capitalism. They are already approximated, however, from several different but similar directions, by, for example: Leninism-Stalinism; fascism-nazism; and, at a more primitive level, by New Dealism and such less influential American ideologies as "technocracy."

This, then, is the skeleton of the theory, expressed in the language of the struggle for power. . . .

But we must remember that the language of the struggle for power is metaphorical. No more than in the case of the capitalists, have the "managers" or their representatives ever got together to decide, deliberately and explicitly, that they were going to make a bid for world power. Nor will the bulk of those who have done, and will do, the fighting in the struggle be recruited from the ranks of the managers themselves; most of the fighters will be workers and youths who will doubtless, many of them, believe that they are fighting for ends of their own. Nor have the managers themselves been constructing and propagating their own ideologies; this has been, and is being, done for the most part by intellectuals, writers, philosophers. Most of these intellectuals are not in the least aware that the net social effect of the ideologies which they elaborate contributes to the power and privilege of the managers and to the building of a new structure of class rule in society. As in the past, the intellectuals believe that they are speaking in the name of truth and for the interests of all humanity.

In short, the question whether the managers are conscious and critical, whether they, or some of them, set before themselves the goal of social dominance and take deliberate steps to reach that goal, this question, in spite of what seems to be implied by the language of the "struggle for power," is not really at issue.

In simplest terms, the theory of the man-

agerial revolution asserts merely the following: Modern society has been organized through a certain set of major economic, social, and political institutions which we call capitalist, and has exhibited certain major social beliefs or ideologies. Within this social structure we find that a particular group or class of persons—the capitalists or *bourgeoisie*—is the dominant or ruling class in the sense which has been defined. At the present time, these institutions and beliefs are undergoing a process of rapid transformation. The conclusion of this period of transformation, to be expected in the comparatively near future, will find society organized through a quite different set of major economic, social, and political institutions and exhibiting quite different major social beliefs or ideologies. Within the new social structure a different social group or class—the managers—will be the dominant or ruling class.

.   .   .   .   .

### WHO ARE THE MANAGERS?

. . . Who are these managers, the class which is in the process of becoming the ruling class of society? The answer which interests us will not be given in terms of individuals: that is, we do not want to know that Mr. X, Miss Y, and other separate persons are managers. The answer that we need will be, first of all, in terms of *function:* by virtue of what function is it that we shall designate an individual as a manager? Whoever the individual may be, now or in the future, how are we to decide whether or not he is a manager? The functions that are of initial and prime importance to us are, of course, those functions in relation to the major instruments of production, since it is the relation to the instruments of production which decides the issue of class dominance, of power and privilege, in society.

The first part of the answer might seem to be only a verbal juggle and of no more value than any other verbal juggle: the managers are simply those who are, in fact, managing the instruments of production nowadays. Certainly, saying this does not appreciably advance our understanding. We must, therefore, investigate more carefully to see just who is doing the managing; and, in the investigation, we shall have to analyze out several ideas which are confusedly grouped together under the concept of "management."

It would seem obvious that in capitalist society it would be the capitalists who, in decisive respects at least, do the managing. If they do not manage the instruments of production, how could they maintain their position as ruling class, which depends upon control over the instruments of production? This is obvious, and the answer to this question is that they could not. It is the fact that during the past several decades the *de facto* management of the instruments of production has to a constantly increasing extent got out of the hands of the capitalists that so plainly proves society to be shifting away from capitalism and the capitalists losing their status as the ruling class. In ever-widening sectors of world economy, the actual managers are not the capitalists, the *bourgeoisie;* or, at the very least, the managerial prerogatives of the capitalists are being progressively whittled down. The completion of this process means the elimination of the capitalists from control over the economy; that is, their disappearance as a ruling class.

Let us make some distinctions: It is unnecessary to stress that the most important branches of modern industry are highly complex in technical organization. The tools, machines, and procedures involved are the results of highly developed scientific and technical operations. The division of labor is minute and myriad; and the turning out of the final product is possible only through the technical co-ordination of a vast number of separate tasks, not only within the individual factory, but in mines, farms, railroads, steamships, affiliated processors, and the like.

If we continue to look purely at the technical side of the process, we may observe the following: In comparison with the organization of industry in the period prior to modern mass production, the individual tasks, with the notable exception of a comparatively small percentage, require relatively less skill and training on the part of the individual worker. A century ago it took many years and considerable native aptitude to make a skilled general mechanic of the kind who then made engines or buildings or carriages or tools or machines. Today it takes a couple of weeks to make a worker ready to take his full place on a production or assembly line. Even so-called skilled work today usually needs no more than a few months' training. But, conversely, at the same time today a small percentage of tasks requires very great training and skill. Or let me put it in this way: within the process of production, the gap, estimated both in amount of skill and training and in difference of type of function, between the average worker and those who are in charge, on the technical side, of the process of production is far greater today than in the past.

From among those tasks which, today, require lengthy training and considerable skill, three may be separated out.

One type is found widely in those industries which, like the building industry, have not yet been organized in accordance with modern methods. There is, however, no technical reason why this has not been done in such industries. If it were done, the relative number of highly skilled workers in, for example, building would at once enormously decrease.

Another type consists of those tasks which need elaborate training in the physical sciences and in engineering. These have greatly increased in recent decades. A century ago, there were scarcely any highly trained chemists, physicists, biochemists, or even engineers functioning directly in industry, a fact which is plainly witnessed by the almost complete lack of educational facilities for training such industrial scientists and engineers. The comparatively primitive techniques of those days did not require such persons; today few branches of industry could operate without their constant services.

The third type consists of the tasks of

the technical direction and co-ordination of the process of production. All the necessary workers, skilled and unskilled, and all the industrial scientists will not turn out automobiles. The diverse tasks must be organized, co-ordinated, so that the different materials, tools, machines, plants, workers are all available at the proper place and moment and in the proper numbers. This task of direction and co-ordination is itself a highly specialized function. Often it, also, requires acquaintance with the physical sciences (or the psychological and social sciences, since human beings are not the least among the instruments of production) and with engineering. But it is a mistake (which was made by Veblen, among others) to confuse this directing and co-ordinating function with the scientific and engineering work which I have listed under the second type of task. After all, the engineers and scientists of the second type are merely highly skilled workers, no different in kind from the worker whose developed skill enables him to make a precision tool or operate an ingenious lathe. They have no functions of guiding, administering, managing, organizing the process of production, which tasks are the distinctive mark of the third type. For these tasks, engineering and scientific knowledge may be, though it is not always, or necessarily, a qualification, but the tasks themselves are not engineering or science in the usual sense.

It is this third type of function which, in the fullest and clearest meaning, I call "managing"; and those who carry out this type of function are they whom I call the "managers." Many different names are given them. We may often recognize them as "production managers," operating executives, superintendents, administrative engineers, supervisory technicians; or, in government (for they are to be found in governmental enterprise just as in private enterprise) as administrators, commissioners, bureau heads, and so on. I mean by managers, in short, those who already for the most part in contemporary society are actually managing, on its technical side, the

actual process of production, no matter what the legal and financial form—individual, corporate, governmental—of the process. There are, to be sure, gradations among the managers. Under the chief operating executives of a corporation like General Motors or U. S. Steel or a state enterprise like the TVA there are dozens and hundreds of lesser managers, a whole hierarchy of them. In its broader sense the class of managers includes them all; within the class there are the lesser and the greater.

But, it may well be commented, there is nothing new in the existence of managers. Industry has always had to have managers. Why do they suddenly assume this peculiar importance? Let us examine this comment.

In the first place, industry did not always require managers, at the very least not at all in the sense that we find them today. In feudal times the individual serf and his family tilled the small plot of soil to which he was attached; the individual artisan with his own tools turned out his finished product. No manager intervened to regulate and organize the process of production. Managers entered in only to the negligible sector of economy where larger-scale enterprise was employed.

Even in earlier capitalist times, the function of technical management was not crucial. The process of production was so simple, the division of labor so little developed compared to today, that hardly any special skill and training were necessary to carry out the functions of management. Nearly anyone who had any reasonable acquaintance with the industry in question could handle them.

Equally decisive for our purpose is the differentiation in *who* does the managing, what prerogatives attach to management, and how the functions of management are related to other economic and social functions.

In the earlier days of capitalism, the typical capitalist, the ideal of the ideologists before and after Adam Smith, was himself his own manager so far as there were managerial functions other than those assigned to some reliable skilled worker in the shop.

e was the individual entrepreneur, who wned the whole or the greater share of a actory or mine or shop or steamship comany or whatever it might be, and actively aanaged his own enterprise; perhaps to rere in old age in favor of management by is heirs. But, as is well known, the growth f large-scale public corporations along ith the technological development of aodern industry have virtually wiped such pes of enterprise out of the important ctions of the economy; with a few excepons, they remain only among the "small usinesses" which are trivial in their hisrical influence.

These changes have meant that to an ver-growing extent the managers are no nger, either as individuals or legally or istorically, the same as the capitalists. here is a combined shift: through changes the technique of production, the funcons of management become more distincve, more complex, more specialized, and ore crucial to the whole process of production, thus serving to set off those who erform these functions as a separate group class in society; and at the same time ose who formerly carried out what funcons there were of management, the *boureoisie*, themselves withdraw from manageent, so that the difference in function beomes also a difference in the individuals ho carry out the function.

. . . . .

Let us take a hypothetical and overimplified example in order to make more recise what is meant by "management" nd to separate this off from other ideas hich are often grouped with it. We will t our example be an imaginary automoile company. In connection with the ownrship, control, and management situation relation to this company, we may distinuish the following four groups:

1) Certain individuals—the operating xecutives, production managers, plant suerintendents, and their associates—have harge of the actual technical process of roducing. It is their job to organize the aaterials, tools, machines, plant facilities, equipment, and labor in such a way as to turn out the automobiles. These are the individuals whom I call "the managers."

It should be observed that the area of production which any group of them manages is most variable. It may be a single small factory or mine or a single department within a factory. Or it may be a large number of factories, mines, railroads, and so on, as in the case of the chief managers of the great United States corporations. In theory the area could be extended to cover an entire interrelated branch of industry (automobiles, mines, utilities, railroads, whatever it might be) or most, or even all, of the entire mechanism of production. In practice in the United States at present, however, there do not exist managers *in this sense* for whole branches of industry (with possibly one or two exceptions), much less for a major portion or all of industry as a whole. The organization and co-ordination of industry as a whole is carried on through the instrumentality of "the market," without deliberate and explicit management exercised by specific managers, or indeed, by anyone else.

2) Certain individuals (among whom, in the United States at present, would ordinarily be found the highest ranked and best paid of the company officials) have the functions of guiding the company toward a *profit;* of selling the automobiles at a price and in the most suitable numbers for yielding a profit; of bargaining over prices paid for raw materials and labor; of arranging the terms of the financing of the company; and so on. These functions are often also called those of "management" and those who fulfill them, "managers." However, there is clearly no necessary connection between them and the first type of function. From the point of view of the technical process of production, a car would be neither worse nor better because of what it sold for (it could be given away and still be the same car, technically speaking) or what the materials which went into it cost; nor, so far as technical problems go, does the difference between bank loans at 4 per cent or 5 per cent show up in

the power of the motor, or a change in dividend rate alter the strength of the frame.

In order to distinguish this group from the first, I shall call the individuals who make it up "finance-executives" or simply "executives," reserving the terms "management" and "managers" for the first group only.

3) Certain individuals (among whom in the United States at present would be many of the directors of the company and more particularly the bankers and big financiers who actually appoint the directors) have problems different from either of the first types. Their direct concern is not, or need not be, either the technical process of production or even the profit of the particular company. Through holding companies, interlocking directorates, banks, and other devices, they are interested in the financial aspects not merely of this automobile company but of many other companies and many market operations. They may wish to unite this company with others, in order perhaps to sell a stock or bond issue to the public, independently of the effect of the merger on the technical process of production or on the profits of our original company. They may want, for tax or speculative or other reasons, to lower the profit of this company, and could do so by, for example, raising prices charged by supply companies which they also were interested in. They may want to put some competitors out of business or influence politics or inflate prices; and any of such aims might be altogether independent of the requirements of production or profit in the particular automobile company. Any number of variants is possible. I shall call this third group the "finance-capitalists."

4) Finally there are certain individuals (a comparatively large number as a rule in the United States at present) who own in their names stock certificates in the automobile company and who are formally and legally the "owners" of our company. In fact, however, the great bulk of them, comprising in sum the legal "owners" of the substantial majority of the stock of the

company, have an entirely passive relatio to the company. The only right they posse with reference to the company is to re ceive, as against those who do not hav stock certificates registered in their name money in the form of dividends when o occasion dividends are declared by the d rectors.

This four-fold separation into "manag ers," "executives," "finance-capitalists," an "stockholders" is, in reality, a separation o *function*, of four of the types of relation i which it is possible to stand toward a ce tain section of the instruments of produ tion. It is theoretically possible, therefor that one and the same individual, or or and the same group of individuals, shoul perform all four of these functions, shoul stand in all four of these relations to tl instruments of production in question ( our hypothetical case, the tangible asse of the automobile company). That is, o and the same individual (Henry Ford, of some years ago, was a late and favori example) or group of individuals cou manage the production of the compan direct its policy so as to make a profit, i tegrate its activities in relation to banl and to other companies (if such were question), and be the sole stockholder of the company. Not only is such an identi possible: until comparatively recently, was normally the case.

Today, however, it is very seldom t case, especially in the more important se tions of industry. The four functions a much more sharply differentiated than the past; and they are, as a rule, performe by different sets of persons. It is not alwa so, of course; but it tends to become mo and more so. Even where there is ove lapping, where the same individual pe forms several of these functions, his activ ties in pursuit of each are easily separabl

Two further facts about these grou may be noted: In most large corporatior which together are decisive in the eco omy, the bulk of the stockholders, holdi in their names the majority of the shar of stock, have, as everyone knows, the pa sive relation to the company which b been referred to. With only the rarest exceptions, they exercise no real control over the company except for the minor element of control involved in their preferential sharing (as against nonstockholders) in the profits, or rather the declared dividends, of the company. But the third group in our list (the finance-capitalists) are also, some of them at any rate, stockholders. Together they usually do not own in the legal sense a majority of the shares, but they ordinarily own a substantial block of the shares, and have at their disposal liquid funds and other resources whereby they can, when need arises, obtain from the small stockholders enough "proxies" on stock shares to be able to vote a majority.

Thus this third group is in a legal position of ownership toward the company and the instruments of production included among the company's assets: if not with the unambiguous title of an earlier capitalist, who in his own name owned all, or a majority of, the shares of a company, at least to a sufficient degree to preserve the meaning of the legal relationship.

Sometimes the executives of Group 2 are also included in Group 4 and have substantial legal interests of ownership in the company (that is, have registered in their own or their families' names substantial blocks of the company's stock). But this is very seldom the case with the managers proper, with the members of Group 1; these ordinarily have no legal ownership interest in the company, or at most a very small interest: that is, they are not usually large stockholders in the company.

Second, there is a complete difference among these groups with respect to the *technical* role of their respective functions in relation to the process of production. The process of production is technically and literally impossible unless someone is carrying out the functions of management, of Group 1—not necessarily the same individuals who carry them out today, but, at any rate, someone.

Some of the finance-executive functions comprised in Group 2 are also technically necessary to the process of production,

though not necessarily in the same sense as today: that is, not necessarily (from a technical point of view) for the sake of profit as understood by capitalism. There must be some regulation of the quality, kinds, numbers, and distribution of products apart from the theoretic abilities of the instruments of production to turn products out. This regulation would not have to be achieved, however, as it is through the finance-executives, in terms of capitalist profits for the company. It could be done in subordination to some political or social or psychological aim—war or a higher standard of mass living or prestige and glory or the maintenance of some particular power relationship. In fact, with profit in the capitalist sense eliminated, the *technically necessary* functions of the finance-executives of Group 2 become part of the management functions of Group 1, if management is extended over all or most of industry. Management could, that is to say, absorb all of the technically necessary functions of the non-managing executives.

But, still from a strictly technical viewpoint, the remaining functions—the "profit-making" functions—of Group 2 and all the functions of Groups 3 and 4—finance-capitalist and stockholder—are altogether unnecessary (whether or not desirable from some other point of view) to the process of production. So far as the technical process of production goes, there need not be finance-capitalists or stockholders, and the executives of Group 2, stripped of many of their present functions, can be merged in the management Group 1.[1]

Not only is this development conceivable: it has already been almost entirely achieved in Russia, is approached more and more nearly in Germany, and has gone a considerable distance in all other nations. In the United States, as everywhere, it is

[1] I must warn that this fourfold division which I have made bears no relation to the usual division between "industrial capitalists" and "finance-capitalists." This latter distinction is of great importance in studying the historical development of capitalism, but seems to me of little value in the analysis of the structure of present-day capitalism. . . .

precisely the situation to be found throughout *state enterprise*.

This development is a decisive phase of the managerial revolution.

## SELECTED REFERENCES FOR PART 5

ADAMS, WALTER (ed.). *The Structure of American Industry.* New York: Macmillan, 1950.

Case studies of the mode of operation, and significance for the economy, of strategic industries.

AMERICAN ECONOMICS ASSOCIATION. *Readings in the Theory of Income Distribution.* Philadelphia: Blakiston, 1946.

Outstanding essays by leading American economists.

BERGE, WENDELL. *Cartels: Challenge to a Free World.* Washington, D. C.: Public Affairs Press, 1944.

A former official of the Department of Justice offers a sensational account of international cartels in peace and war.

BERLE, A. A., and G. C. MEANS. *The Modern Corporation and Private Property.* New York: Commerce Clearing House, 1932.

A noted account of the "silent revolution" wrought in American life by the "divorce of ownership from control" in corporate organizations.

BRADY, ROBERT A. *Business as a System of Power.* New York: Columbia Univ. Press, 1943.

Analyzes the role of business associations as power agencies.

BURNS, ARTHUR ROBERT. *The Decline of Competition.* New York: McGraw-Hill, 1936.

A detailed report on the scope of monopolistic combination and nonmarket co-ordination in the United States.

DIMOCK, MARSHALL. *Business and Government.* New York: Holt, 1949.
———. *Free Enterprise in the Administrative State.* University, Ala.: Univ. of Alabama Press, 1951.

Summarizes recent researches on the relations between business and government.

EDWARDS, CORWIN. *A Cartel Policy for the United Nations.* New York: Columbia Univ. Press, 1945.

A program to achieve workable competition in world trade.

FELLNER, WILLIAM. *Competition Among the Few: Oligopoly and Similar Market Structures.* New York: Knopf, 1949.

A careful technical study of the range and character of "imperfect competition" in our economy.

GORDON, ROBERT AARON. *Business Leadership in the Large Corporation.* Washington, D. C.: Brookings Institution, 1945.

The origins, status, and power of the American business leader.

HOBSON, J. A. *Imperialism, a Study.* London: Allen & Unwin, 1938.

Emphasizes the influence of economic factors on imperialist expansion and rivalry.

LANGER, WILLIAM. *The Diplomacy of Imperialism, 1890–1902.* New York: Knopf, 1935.

A historian reviews the theories and facts concerning national rivalries over spheres of influence.

LENIN, V. I. *Imperialism.* New York: Vanguard Press, 1933.

In this Communist statement, imperialism is claimed to be the symbol of the disintegration in the last phases of monopoly capitalism.

LINDBLOM, CHARLES E. *Unions and Capitalism.* New Haven: Yale Univ. Press, 1949.

Discusses the relationship between large unions and the structure of a society based on "free enterprise."

LOEVINGER, LEE. *The Law of Free Enterprise.* New York: Funk & Wagnalls, 1949.

Reviews judicial and administrative rulings concerning the conduct of business in the United States.

NUTTER, G. WARREN. *The Extent of Enterprise Monopoly in the United States, 1899–1939.* Chicago: Univ. of Chicago Press, 1951.

A statistical review of the evidence. Contends that the role of monopolistic combination in recent American development has been exaggerated.

ORTIZ, FERNANDO. *Cuban Counterpoint: Tobacco and Sugar.* New York: Knopf, 1947.

A study of a small nation whose economy is dependent upon an undiversified agriculture.

PERLMAN, SELIG. *A Theory of the Labor Movement.* New York: Macmillan, 1928. Reprinted, New York: Augustus M. Kelley, 1951.

Rejects the relevance of Marxist theories for the American labor movement, and explains and defends the "business unionism" associated with the American Federation of Labor.

ROSS, ARTHUR M. *Trade Union Wage Policy.* Berkeley: Institute of Industrial Relations, Univ. of California, 1948.

Wage determination, contends the author, cannot be understood without recognizing the role of unions as social and political groups.

SMALLER WAR PLANTS CORPORATION REPORT. *Economic Concentration and World War II.* Washington, D. C.: U. S. Government Printing Office, 1946.

Indicates the adverse effects of war mobilization upon the opportunities for growth of the smaller firms.

STALEY, EUGENE. *War and the Private Investor: A Study in the Relations of International Politics and International Private Investment.* Foreword by Quincy Wright: Introduction by Sir Arthur Salter. New York: Doubleday, 1935.

In the view of the author, "private investments seeking purely business advantages have rarely of themselves brought great powers into serious political clashes."

STEINDL, J. *Maturity and Stagnation in American Capitalism.* London: Blackwell, 1951.

An European observer assesses the evidence on a much-debated question.

STOCKING, G., and M. WATKINS. *Cartels in Action.* New York: Twentieth Century Fund, 1946.

———. *Cartels or Competition?* New York: Twentieth Century Fund, 1948.

An analysis of the extent of cartels, with a suggested program for control.

TEMPORARY NATIONAL ECONOMIC COMMITTEE. *Monographs,* 43 vols. Washington, D. C.: U. S. Government Printing Office, 1940–41.

The fruits of the two-year investigation of concentration of economic power by the Temporary National Economic Committee, these *Monographs* are among the most detailed pictures of American economic life in the twentieth century. The student of twentieth-century United States should know not only the *Monographs* but also the thirty-odd volumes of *Hearings* before the Temporary National Economic Committee.

# PART 6

# The problem of economic instability

❦ If we construct a chart and plot upon it the curve of "national income" for the United States throughout the last century and a quarter, we shall find that this curve does not take the form of a straight line—whether a *level* straight line, which would indicate a stable and stationery level of production, or an *ascending* straight line, which would indicate continuous and stable economic "progress." Rather, it takes the form of a series of "waves" with "crests" and "troughs." The idea of a curve of national income is simply a method—used in a number of charts throughout this Part—of indicating that *business in an industrial economy moves in "cycles" of relative prosperity and relative depression.* If we examine the cycles of economic development, we shall find that the history of the American economy shows a number of severe troughs—the Panic of 1837, the Panic of 1857, the Panic of 1893, the Panic of 1907, the postwar depression of 1920, and the Great Depression of 1929. Corresponding, roughly, are a series of periods of prosperity or "boom."

It is our purpose in this Part to examine *how* our economy behaves in terms of the level and stability of production, to ask *why* it behaves in this way, and to ask *what* (if anything) can or should be done about it. As we will remember from the reading by Hicks and Hart in Part 2, when we speak of crests and troughs of national income we are speaking of the rise and fall of production and the rise and fall in the consumption of needed or wanted satisfactions.

The final reading in Part 4 described some of the social effects of unemployment upon those who are out of work, as they grow out of the fact of being *workless* and as they grow out of the fact of being *without income.* These are some of the human experiences which are represented by the charts and curves which plot the "business cycle." The first reading in Part 6, a selection from the report of the NATIONAL RESOURCES PLANNING BOARD, describes the *economic* impact of the most recent and most severe of the troughs or "depressions" in the business cycle. From the standpoint of production, it tells us the extent of unemployment of resources—land, men, machines—which took place in the decade following 1929, a loss which can never be restored. From the standpoint of income and consumption, it tells us of what happened to diverse groups in the American economy as the Great Depression descended upon them.

Will this happen again? To begin to answer this question, we must analyze the process of production in the national economy of "capitalism." Why has our economic system followed so consistently, and sometimes so violently, the pattern of crest and trough, boom and bust? Is it because of factors peculiar to an economy based to a high degree on private ownership and market controls? Is it because of "rigidities" which are incidental or accidental, which enter in to disrupt the smooth flow of supply and demand, and without which the picture would be not a series of cycles but a smooth upward line of "progress"? Is it because of factors not peculiar to the private ownership system, but common to all *industrial* economies, "capitalist" and "noncapitalist" alike? These are some of the questions we must ask.

The second selection, from the *Treatise on Political Economy* written in 1803 by the French economist JEAN-BAPTISTE SAY, was for a century the "classic" statement of how the "wheel of wealth" is supposed to operate in a "free market" economy. When production takes place, Say asks, where does it find its market? The answer is that *it is bought by the income derived from other production*. All production which takes place is rewarded by income received by "entrepreneurs," "landlords," and "workers" who then spend it in buying the needed and desired goods of life. These may be either *consumers' goods*, for immediate enjoyment, or *production goods*. In the latter case, we may say that income has been *invested*. Thus production gives rise to income, income becomes demand, and demand creates further production: if we view the economy as a whole, production seems to create its own market, anything that is produced should find a buyer, and goods once produced could never go unbought. The "wheel of wealth," once set spinning, might ascend to *higher* levels of national income, but (barring destruction of resources or of population) it should never descend to *lower* levels. Say's argument seemed to provide the comforting assurance that, barring unforeseen external complications, the exchange economy would tend to operate at the point of *full-employment equilibrium*.

"Say's Law" seemed to be a theory which looked good on paper, but appeared to be contradicted by obvious facts. The first reading in this Part, for example, tells us that from 1929 to 1932, national production in the United States dropped by 40 per cent. This kind of thing had happened even a century earlier. So the problem became one of how to reconcile an apparently airtight theory with apparently contradictory facts.

Perhaps the most influential nineteenth-century effort to explain the facts was the theory of Karl Marx, later developed with some modifications by the British economist J.A. Hobson. It rested, basically, upon a denial of Say's Law. According to Say, income derived from production is necessarily spent in due time; and therefore, it must, soon after it becomes income, create a demand for further production, or for products which have already been created. But, said Marx and his followers, this is not necessarily the case as a matter of course. A poor man, drawing his paycheck, will probably spend it according to Say's Law. But a rich man, or a corporation drawing "earnings," may not, but may rather withdraw it from the "stream of wealth" in the form of *savings*. The greater the percentage of income going to the "upper-income brackets"—and we may remember that Marx predicted this amount would tend to increase—the greater the amount of income "drawn out" of the stream in the form not of buying, but of saving. When this takes place, production ceases necessarily to create its own demand; savings pile up in the hands of the rich; consumers do not have enough income to "buy back" the products of their economy; goods pile up on the shelves and the wheels of industry and business slow down or cease to move because there is no longer a market for their products. The economy has become the victim of a massive "over-production" or "underconsumption." Because of this tendency, and because of the increasing concentration of economic control, Marx saw the capitalist economy moving through a series of evermore severe depressions to a final catastrophic crisis.

The theory of "underconsumption" placed the blame upon the inequality of distribution of income inevitable in a capitalist economy. To it, the defenders of the "classical" theory made reply. The theory of "underconsumption," they said, assumes that a poor man's dollar may be spent, but that a rich man's dollar may be *not spent*. This, they were inclined to argue, is not possible. What happens to a rich man's dollar, or a corporation's dollar? First, it may be spent like the dollar of a poor man: in this case, it creates demand directly. Second, it may be invested in capital goods: in this case, it puts land, men, machinery to work. Third, it may be saved, by being put in a bank: but here the bank is a mere "stopping place" from which it is then lent out to consumers who wish to buy consumption goods, or producers who wish to invest in production. In any case, it returns to the "stream" in the same way as does the poor man's dollar. There can be no mass "underconsumption" attributable to the unequal distribution of income.

How, then, explain the fact that cycles do occur? Not through factors in the market system itself, but through flaws, accidents, and "rigidities." Goods may be available at a low price, but people may be unaware of their availability, and too much money may therefore go into an artificially inflated high price. Or workers may not know of the best job opportunities, or be unable or unwilling to move to the "best" jobs: since the "adjustment" of the market system assumes "free mobility of labor" to the place of "greatest opportunity," this immobility may throw a wrench in the wheels. Too much capital may be "sunk" or "fixed" in established lines of production, so that the allocation of resources cannot follow the lead of consumer demand. Monopoly or restriction of competition may enter in to artificially raise prices or curtail production. These are only a few of the possible flaws or rigidities, but the central point is that it was to these "accidents" that the ebb and flow of business was attributed, and not to anyhing *inherent* in the economy itself.

It was at this point that the author of our third selection, WILLIAM H. BEVERIDGE, began to study unemployment in the early years of the twentieth century. In this reading Beveridge tells us of the development of his thinking over a span of thirty years. At the beginning, he was inclined to accept the classical theory derived from Say's Law, and attribute unemployment to rigidities, to seasonal variations in production, to irregularity of employment in certain lines (such as dock work and shipping), or to the "frictional unemployment" due to the change from one job to another, under conditions where the worker did not know where to find employment. But as he followed the course of the business cycle in Britain, Beveridge began to question his earlier explanations, and to come more and more to the point of view that the cycle or trough and crest was not explainable in terms of merely incidental factors, but was rooted in the heart of the economy itself.

Probably the greatest single influence in changing Beveridge's thinking—as it was in changing the thinking of many other people—was the work of Sir John Maynard Keynes (1883–1946). Keynes agreed with the critics of the "underconsumption" theory that income might, *in the long run,* all be transformed into demand, no matter whose income it was. But, as Keynes said in a famous phrase, "in the long run we are all dead"; and it is the *short run* which is of practical importance. In the short run, at least, Keynes did not find that income must necessarily be transformed into demand for consumption goods (spending) and production goods (investment) in sufficient amount, and with sufficient rapidity, to maintain full utilization of the economy's resources. If the curve of production is to be "smoothed out," rather than being allowed to fluctuate violently in succeeding crest and trough, and if it is to be kept at the highest level of production of which the economy is capable, this will take place not through any "automatic steering wheel," but only through *deliberate public policy.*

The truth in the "underconsumption" theory Keynes reformulated in terms of the *consumption function:* the percentage of income an individual spends (his "propensity to spend") and the percentage he saves (his "propensity to save") are to a very great degree a "function" of the amount of income he draws. That is, the higher his income, the greater his ability to save, or, in Keynesian language, his "propensity to save"; and the higher the *general* level of income in an economy, the greater the general tendency to save and the greater the problem of making certain that saving becomes "translated" into spending or investment. Assuming that people have a "propensity," or tendency, to save, one must, Keynes pointed out, take into account the passage of time between the earning of income and its saving or investment: a dollar earned today and spent today does *not* have the same effect upon the economy as a dollar earned today and spent a year hence. For a dollar which is constantly in flow "multiplies" as it passes from hand to hand in a given time interval, into not one dollar of purchasing power, but several; the dollar which circulates less rapidly becomes, in effect, fewer dollars of actual purchasing power. This introduction of the "multiplier principle," and the recognition of the importance of *time*, brought in a "dynamic" analysis of production and consumption in place of a more "static" one.

There is no automatic mechanism, Keynes held, by which income "put in the bank" necessarily comes out again in the form of saving or investment. Whether it does so or not, or how long an interval elapses before it returns to the "stream," is determined above all else by the *expectations* of businessmen and other investors. This means that in good times, savings are likely to be reinvested rapidly; but in bad times, they are likely to "pile up" because everyone is "holding tight." Thus, just at the time when it is most important that the stream be kept flowing (in periods of depression and poor business "expectations") the stream tends to stagnate; and to this tendency is added people's *liquidity preference*, or their preference, especially in times of "trough," for having their money in a form where they can easily "get at it," rather than "tied up" in investment.

The selection from PAUL SAMUELSON reviews some of the important efforts to interpret the business cycle, with particular emphasis upon the tendency of investment to lag below the levels necessary for "full production." He points out that the most severe fluctuations are found in the *producers' goods* industries, that is, those which make the instruments of production; and he shows us that this is true because of the "acceleration principle," whereby relatively small changes in the demand for cotton shirts, for example, may give rise to very great fluctuations in the demand for the machinery with which these shirts are made, and in all the "heavy" industries which supply the raw material for machine-making. Samuelson's discussion is supplemented by the reading from the LEAGUE OF NATIONS report, which stresses the institutional factors which have rendered capitalist economies particularly unstable in recent years.

From here we move into the question of *policy;* that is, we assume that the economy is not automatically self-regulating, and ask what kinds of deliberate intervention might make for high production and economic stability. In the reading from the UNITED NATIONS report, we are presented with an official statement, by an international body, of the most general recommendations offered by a group of economists for maintaining economic stability. The authors tell us that these recommendations apply equally to "market" and to more "socialistic" economies, although public policy for full employment may be easier in societies which accept a greater degree of central control as part of their political and economic structure.

The problem of economic stability cannot, the United Nations report suggests, be solved on a purely isolated national basis, but must rather be solved in terms of the *world economy*. In the earlier readings in this Part we have already seen that the major curves of income and production for all large industrialized countries tend to coincide; that is, prosperity and depression, the fluctuations of the business cycle, tend to be worldwide. Our final selection, by HOWARD S. PIQUET, deals with the Point Four program and the international implications of full-employment policy.

In this Part, we are primarily concerned with the *economics of productive efficiency*. What this means, essentially, is that we are particularly concerned with trying to understand those factors, internal to the process of production, distribution, and consumption itself, which must be taken into account if we are to have steady and full utilization of the resources which are potentially available to us. This does not mean that "full production" is the only worth-while goal in life. In fact, there are conditions under which we should probably consider it a highly *undesirable* goal: we should probably question the desirability of attaining the highest economic "efficiency" if it were certain that it could be attained only by complete regimentation of everybody, or by making the process of work completely intolerable. The relationship between productive efficiency and the other values which are at stake in economic life is one with which we shall deal especially in Part 8.

SECTION A

## The impact of prosperity and depression

# 25 National Resources Planning Board: *Boom and Bust, 1920–1940*

❧ *Before the Depression of 1929 the average American was inclined to believe that a person's economic fate is always largely a matter of his own ability and initiative. The years 1929–39 saw a 40 per cent drop in total national income within the first three years, and a spread of unemployment and income loss over all geographical areas and all sectors of the population. This experience convinced a substantial number of Americans that a modern economic depression is a social catastrophe before which, once it is allowed to occur, even the most capable individual may be relatively helpless.*

*The following reading, from the National Resources Planning Board, discusses the effect of the Depression on national income, income distribution, and production. This Board was the successor to the National Resources Committee (see Reading 19), and had similar objectives. It was particularly concerned with the factors which produced the Depression of 1929, with the effect of the depression on the lives of workers, and with an analysis of policies endeavoring to control unemployment and establish a measure of social security. This selection is excerpted from the Board's report,* Security, Work, and Relief Policies *(1943), Chapter II, pp. 16–24.*

The 1920's constituted a period of rapid economic expansion which reached a peak in 1929. These years of rising national income, of expanding production and consumption, however, terminated in the severe economic decline of the early thirties, a decline of more serious proportions than in any previous depression. (See Figure 1.)

Among the many measures of the extent of the decline none is more significant than the reduction in the volume of goods and services produced. Total production in the United States amounted to 68.6 billion dollars in 1929, as measured in terms of 1939 prices. By 1932 national income produced had fallen by approximately 40 per cent to only 41.6 billion dollars in terms of 1939 purchasing power. The business situation slowly improved until 1937. However, as the total population had increased by over six million persons since 1930, per capita production was still considerably below the earlier high point. (See Figure 2.) Following a brief recession, total production again reached 69 billion dollars in 1939. The loss as a result of depression was so great that "if the economy had functioned at full capacity between 1929 and 1939, national income might have been from 20 to 30 billion dollars a year higher than it was."

Losses in production during the thirties had their concomitants in the financial realm. Bank failures, which had been recurrent in the twenties, rose to an unprecedented number in the early thirties. The resulting losses were enormous. It has been estimated that the total loss to unsecured depositors in suspended commercial banks during the years 1931–34 was more than 2.3 billion dollars, or almost three times the loss for the entire preceding decade. Industry drew upon accumulated reserves for operating expenses as well as for payment of dividends. Private savings were also drawn upon by all classes of the population to meet the emergency. Industrial life insurance in force declined over a billion dollars from 1930 to 1933. . . .

Huge amounts of productive capacity were unutilized, and new investment was sharply curtailed. Ordinary maintenance of plant and equipment was only partially provided for, and from 1931 through 1934 obsolescence and other deterioration of business plants and equipment actually exceeded replacements. As a result, the decline in production of durable goods was particularly sharp. Expenditures for new durable goods declined approximately 70 per cent from 1929 to 1933. The decline in consumption goods, though less severe, was likewise enormous. Consumer expenditures are estimated to have decreased 37 per cent from 1929 to 1933, while consumer credit, which had been employed increasingly during the twenties as a stimulant to greater consumption, declined by 41 per cent during the same period.

. . . . .

UNEMPLOYMENT

Individual security and welfare are dependent upon general economic conditions. For the entrepreneur, whether engaged in business or in agriculture, economic decline manifests itself in curtailed markets, falling prices, reduced profits, and actual losses. For the great majority of persons gainfully employed, however, economic decline means loss of wages and salaries as a result of unemployment and underemployment.

Unemployment is always present to some extent. Even during 1929 an average of 429,000 persons in the labor force were unemployed. At no time prior to the thirties,

**INDUSTRIAL PRODUCTION BY MONTH, JANUARY 1919—JUNE 1940 (adjusted for seasonal variations: 1935—1939 average = 100)**

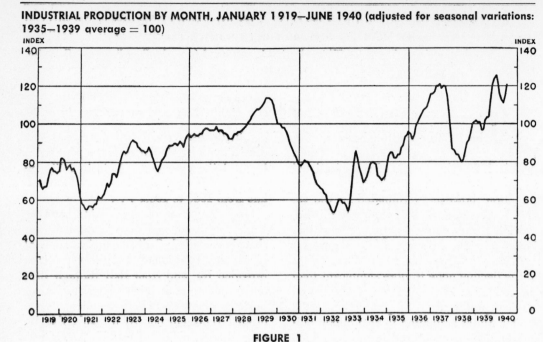

FIGURE 1

however, had unemployment been experienced by so large a proportion of the working population of the United States as at the trough of the depression of the thirties. In the depression year of 1921, unemploy-

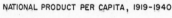

NATIONAL PRODUCT PER CAPITA, 1919-1940

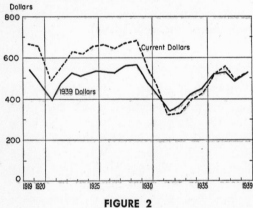

FIGURE 2

ment averaged 4,754,000 persons. The peak during the thirties was reached in March, 1933 when 14,762,000 persons, or 29 per cent of the total labor force, were estimated to be unemployed. The annual average of unemployment probably exceeded 10,000,-

000 persons in 1932, 1933, 1934, and again in 1938. In September 1937, the month of least unemployment since the bottom of the depression, there were still some 5,066,-000 persons out of work, despite the fact that there were at that time slightly more persons at work than in the average month of 1929. (See Figure 3.) The explanation for this seeming contradiction lies in the fact that between 1929 and September 1937 the labor force increased by about 4,795,-000 persons. This rapid expansion was a significant factor in the volume of unemployment and explains why increases in employment were not accompanied by commensurate declines in unemployment. At the opening of the new decade, January 1940, a total of 9,163,000 persons were estimated to be unemployed.

The figures just cited understate the total number of workers affected by unemployment because of the very considerable turnover among the unemployed population. The actual number of persons who experience a period of unemployment during any given year far exceeds the annual average. Moreover, in 1930–40, a large num-

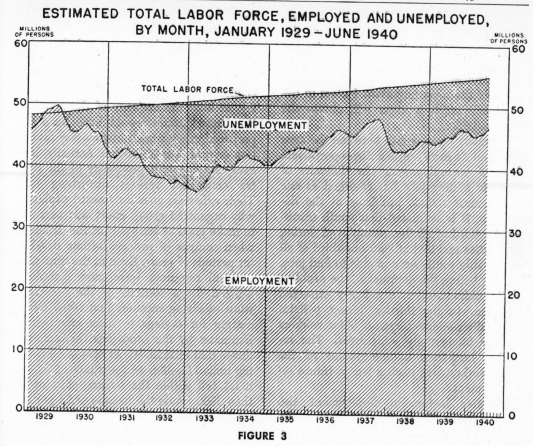

ESTIMATED TOTAL LABOR FORCE, EMPLOYED AND UNEMPLOYED, BY MONTH, JANUARY 1929 – JUNE 1940

**FIGURE 3**

ber of workers, while not wholly unemployed, suffered from underemployment in the form of partial unemployment. . . .

. . . . .

In addition to the workers actually unemployed or only partly employed, many others were forced down the occupational scale because of extensive unemployment and the resulting intensification of competition for available jobs. Semiskilled workers fell back into the ranks of the unskilled; skilled workers accepted semiskilled employment. This decline in occupational status naturally involved a reduction in income for the group affected.

The problems attributable to unemployment are aggravated, moreover, by the unevenness of its incidence. Some workers experience unemployment only intermittently, while others may be continuously

out of work for months or years at a time. As mass unemployment continues, the extent of long-term unemployment inevitably increases, and with it the chances for reemployment decrease for those who are idle for protracted periods.

Of 2,199,700 unemployed workers who registered for the first time with the United States Employment Service from July 1936 through March 1937, almost one out of three (32.3 per cent) had been out of work six months or longer. Nine per cent had been unemployed for at least four years. Among 4,736,000 persons who registered in the Unemployment Census of 1937 as totally unemployed during the week of November 7 to 13, 31.2 per cent had had no work at all for the preceding 12 months or more, and an additional 50.6 per cent had worked less than 27 weeks during the preceding year.

Since unemployment falls with unequal severity on the various categories of the working population, the problems of some groups are more acute than general data on unemployment indicate. Age, for example, is one of the most important factors in determining which workers will obtain the jobs available.

For many years, youth between the ages of 15 and 24 have borne a disproportionate share of unemployment. The difficulty of youth in finding jobs has emerged as one of the most serious problems of the depression. It is estimated that youth constituted a third of all the unemployed during the thirties and that at least one-third of all employable youth were unable to find jobs.

Long before the depression, the problem of the older worker in industry attracted attention. In the thirties, hiring policies which discriminated against older workers became increasingly widespread. The resulting long-term unemployment of the older workers was itself a bar to future reemployment. . . .

Selective factors in employment also worked to the disadvantage of Negroes. By virtually every census count in the thirties, Negro members of the labor force suffered a higher rate and a longer duration of unemployment than whites. . . .

. . . . .

INADEQUACY OF INCOMES

As a result of the economic conditions just described, the consumers of the Nation experienced a tremendous loss of income during the past decade with a resultant decrease, to the vanishing point in millions of cases, in the amounts of goods and services they were able to purchase. This was especially true of the low-income population.

From 1929 to 1933 total income payments to individuals declined from 82.5 billion dollars to 47.3 billion dollars, or 43 per cent. Per capita income payments declined from $679 in 1929 to $377 in 1933. For the farm population, the decline in income was even greater proportionately, with cash farm income decreasing from more than 11 billion dollars in 1929 to little more than 4.5 billion dollars in 1932.

It might have been expected that, since the depressed years of the thirties followed immediately upon the period of highest economic activity yet achieved by the country, at least the majority of the people of the United States would have been well prepared to withstand a temporary diminution or total loss of income. Actually, however, the apparent prosperity of the country concealed various disturbing facts. Their existence goes far toward explaining why organized group effort was necessary to make good at least part of the deficiency when sources of private income dried up for periods of years. Even at the time when national resources were most completely utilized, large sections of the population were receiving incomes that often left no margin for savings to meet emergencies. Estimates by the Brookings Institution indicate that in 1929, 10 per cent of all spending units (families and unattached individuals) fell within the income class of less than $500, while the income of 28 per cent was less than $1,000.

Consumers as a whole entered the depression period burdened with a volume of debt as a result of installment buying amounting to over 8 billion dollars. This fact, when viewed in conjunction with the losses in private savings resulting from bank failures in the years 1931–34, indicates that the ability of the population to meet serious losses of income from private resources was severely restricted.

In many sections of the country there were industries and occupational groups which failed to share in the economic upsurge of the twenties or were even at that time in a state of depression. Workers who had at best secured an uncertain livelihood were in no position to face any further inroads on their already limited economic resources.

Outstanding among the groups ill-prepared to face any further decline in private incomes were those who depended upon agricultural employment for their livelihood. The roots of the agricultural depression stretch back to the post-World War collapse of the early twenties from which farmers had been unable to recover fully when they were faced with the depression of the early thirties.

Among the nonagricultural population, there were sizable groups attached to industries whose difficulties considerably antedated the decline of the early thirties. Conspicuous among these was the New England cotton textile industry which, attracted by lower production costs, was moving to the South at a rapid rate during the 1920's. . . .

. . . . .

In 1935–36, when a considerable degree of recovery from the trough of the depression already had been achieved, 17 per cent of all spending units (over 6.7 million families and single individuals) in the United States received incomes of less than $500; a total of 47 per cent (more than 18.3 million) received less than $1,000; 82 per cent (almost 32.3 million) had incomes below $2,000. These incomes include estimates of the amount of public aid received by these families during the year and would have been lower, had these families not received socially provided income.

Families and individuals receiving incomes of less than $780 per year, representing one-third of all spending units, received only about one-tenth of the aggregate consumer income. On the other hand, consumer units receiving more than $1,450 annually, representing another third of all spending units, received nearly two-thirds of the total consumer income, while the middle third (families and individuals receiving between $780 and $1,450) accounted for about one-fourth of the aggregate consumer income. Spending units in the highest income brackets, over $3,400 annually, which represented about 5 per cent of all consumer units, received more

than one-fourth of the aggregate income. On a per capita basis, the income of consumer units consisting of one person only was three times as high as that of family units, but the income distribution of single individuals shows a larger proportion in the lower income brackets than does that of families. For example, no less than 61 per cent of all single-person consumer units received less than $1,000 per year, while among families the proportion was 42 per cent.

The lowest tenth of the families of two persons or more in the United States had incomes under $410 in 1935–36 and received less than 2 per cent of the aggregate income of all families. The highest tenth, comprising all families with incomes of $2,800 and more, received 36 per cent of the total consumer income.

In the South there was a particularly heavy concentration of families at the lowest income levels. In 1935–36 more than two-fifths of the families of two persons or more in that region had incomes below $750, while only about one-fifth of the families in the New England, North Central, and Pacific regions were similarly situated. In the Mountain and Plains area, with its large farm population, about one-third of the families received less than $750 in 1935–36. The relative number of families in each region having incomes of $3,000 and more, however, varied only from 6.5 per cent for the Mountain and Plains region and 7.1 per cent for the South to 9.0 per cent for North Central families.

Although total agricultural national income in 1940 was considerably higher than it was in the years 1935–36, it has been estimated that during this year one-half of all farm-operator families would have total net incomes of less than $940. The more fortunate half were expected to receive nearly four-fifths of the aggregate farm family income. . . .

SECTION B

**Economic realities and changing theories**

# 26 Jean-Baptiste Say: *The Inevitability of Equilibrium*

❦ *"Cyclical" fluctuations in business and production are at least as old as the Industrial Revolution. The rise of the industrial economy accentuated the dependence of the individual upon the general state of the whole economy in which he earned his livelihood, and motivated economists to try to explain and control the phenomenon of business fluctuation. The most influential early nineteenth-century theory was that of Jean-Baptiste Say (1767–1832), which held that production must always create its own market, and that general business failure must therefore be due to rigidities in the economy which create a deficiency in production.*

*Say is one of the leading figures in economic thought. He began his career as a merchant, but Adam Smith's* Wealth of Nations *stimulated him to study economics. Our reading is taken from Say's* A Treatise on Political Economy (*3rd American edition, translated from the 4th edition of the French by C. R. Prinsip, Philadelphia, John Grigg, 1827*), pp. 75–8, 83.

I t is common to hear adventurers in the different channels of industry assert, that their difficulty lies not in the production, but in the disposal of commodities; that produce would always be abundant if there were but a ready demand, or vent. When the vent for their commodities is slow, difficult, and productive of little advantage, they pronounce money to be scarce; the grand object of their desire is, a consumption brisk enough to quicken sales and keep up prices. But ask them what peculiar causes and circumstances facilitate the demand for their products and you will soon perceive that most of them have extremely vague notions of these matters; that

their observation of facts is imperfect, and their explanation still more so; that they treat doubtful points as matter of certainty, often pray for what is directly opposite to their interests, and importunately solicit from authority a protection of the most mischievous tendency.

To enable us to form clear and correct practical notions, in regard to the vents for the products of industry, we must carefully analyse the best established and most certain facts, and apply to them the inferences we have already deduced from a similar way of proceeding; and thus perhaps we may arrive at new and important truths, that may serve to enlighten the views of the agents of industry, and to give confidence to the measures of governments anxious to afford them encouragement.

A man, who applies his labour to the investing of objects with value by the creation of utility of some sort, cannot expect that the value is to be appreciated and paid for, unless where other men have the means of purchasing it. Now, of what do these means consist? Of other values, of other products, likewise the fruit of industry, capital, and land. Which leads us to a conclusion, that may at first sight appear paradoxical; *viz:* that it is production which opens a demand for products.

Should a tradesman say, "I do not want other products for my woollens, I want money," there could be little difficulty in convincing him, that his customers cannot pay him in money, without having first procured it by the sale of some other commodities of their own. "Yonder farmer," he may be told, "will buy your woollens, if his crops be good, and will buy more or less according to their abundance or scantiness; he can buy none at all, if his crops fail altogether. Neither can you buy his wool or his corn yourself, unless you contrive to get woollens or some other article to buy withal. You say, you only want money; I say, you want other commodities, and not money. For what, in point of fact, do you want the money? Is it not for the purchase of raw materials or stock for your trade, or victuals for your support? [1] Wherefore, it is products that you want, and not money. The silver coin you will have received on the sale of your own products, and given in the purchase of those of other people, will the next moment execute the same office between other contracting parties, and so from one to another to infinity; just as a public vehicle successively transports objects one after another. If you cannot find a ready sale for your commodity, will you say, it is merely for want of a vechile to transport it? For after all, money is but the agent of the transfer of values. Its whole utility has consisted in conveying to your hands, the value of the commodities, which your customer has sold, for the purpose of buying again from you; and the very next purchase you make, it will again convey to a third person the value of the products you may have sold to others. So that you will have bought, and everybody must buy, the objects of want or desire, each with the value of his respective products transformed into money for the moment only." . . .

Thus, to say that sales are dull, owing to the scarcity of money, is to mistake the means for the cause; an error that proceeds from the circumstances, that almost all produce is in the first instance exchanged for money, before it is ultimately converted into other produce: and the commodity, which recurs so repeatedly in use, appears to vulgar apprehensions the most important of commodities, and the end and object of all transactions, whereas it is only the medium. Sales cannot be said to be dull because money is scarce, but because other products are so. There is always money enough to conduct the circulation and mutual interchange of other values, when those values really exist. Should the increase of traffic require more money to facilitate it, the want is easily supplied, and is a strong indication of prosperity—a proof that a great abundance of values has been created, which it is wished to exchange for other values. In such cases, merchants know well enough how to find substitutes for the product serving as the medium of exchange or money: [2] and money itself soon pours in, for this reason, that all produce naturally gravitates to that place where it is most in demand. It is a good sign when the business is too great for the money; just in the same way as it is a good sign when the goods are too plentiful for the warehouses.

When a superabundant article can find no vent, the scarcity of money has so little

---

[1] Even when money is obtained with a view to hoard or bury it, the ultimate object is always to employ it in a purchase of some kind. The heir of the lucky finder uses it in that way, if the miser do not: for money, as money, has no other use than to buy with.

[2] By bills at sight or after date, bank-notes, running credits, write-offs, &c. as at London and Amsterdam.

to do with the obstruction of its sale, that the sellers would gladly receive its value in goods for their own consumption at the current price of the day: they would not ask for money, or have any occasion for that product, since the only use they could make of it would be to convert it forthwith into articles of their own consumption.[1]

This observation is applicable to all cases, where there is a supply of commodities or of services in the market. They will universally find the most extensive demand in those places, where the most values are produced; because in no other places are the sole means of purchase created, i.e. values. Money performs but a momentary function in this double exchange; and when the transaction is finally closed, it will al-

ways be found, that one kind of produce has been exchanged for another.

It is worth while to remark, that a product is no sooner created, than it, from that instant, affords a market for other products to the full extent of its own value. When the producer has put the finishing hand to his product, he is most anxious to sell it immediately, lest its value should vanish in his hands. Nor is he less anxious to dispose of the money he may get for it; for the value of money is also perishable. But the only way of getting rid of money is in the purchase of some product or other. Thus, the mere circumstance of the creation of one product immediately opens a vent for other products.

. . . . .

. . . The encouragement of mere consumption is no benefit to commerce; for the difficulty lies in supplying the means, not in stimulating the desire of consumption; and we have seen, that production alone, furnishes those means. Thus it is the aim of good government to stimulate production, of bad government to encourage consumption.

[1] I speak here of their aggregate consumption, whether unproductive and designed to satisfy the personal wants of themselves and their families, or expended in the sustenance of reproductive industry. The woollen or cotton manufacturer operates a two-fold consumption of wool and cotton, 1. For his personal wear. 2. For the supply of his manufacture; but, be the purpose of his consumption what it may, whether personal gratification or reproduction, he must needs buy what he consumes with what he produces.

# 27 William H. Beveridge: *Under-employment and the "New Economics"*

❧ *The first reading in this Part discussed the development of unemployment in the United States from 1929 through 1940, and the second reading presented a "classical" view of the causes of unemployment. In the selection below, one of the most prominent students of unemployment, the British economist Sir William H. Beveridge (1879–     ) tells us how his own views on unemployment evolved between 1909 and 1940. He shows why, in his judgment, the views of writers like Say were incomplete and why conceptions like those of Keynes are more nearly adequate.*

*Beveridge was for many years Director of the London School of Economics and Political Science, and Master of University College, Oxford. A prominent adviser to* the British Government, he was elected to the House of Commons in 1944 and was the author of the famous "Beveridge Plan" for comprehensive social welfare legislation.

His many writings include Insurance for All (1924), Causes and Cures of Unemployment (1931), Planning Under Socialism (1936), and The Price of Peace (1945). Our reading is reprinted from Full Employment in a Free Society by permission of W. W. Norton and Company, Inc., copyright 1945, pp. 42, 48, 90–7, 105–9.

Subtracting the unemployment rate for any group of employees from 100 gives a percentage which may be described as the employment rate, because it shows what proportion of every 100 men available for employment in that group were actually in employment at any time. The general employment rate derived in this way from the trade union returns is . . . represented graphically in Chart I. This Chart shows employment fluctuating continually up to

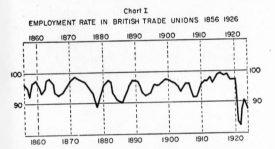

Chart I
EMPLOYMENT RATE IN BRITISH TRADE UNIONS 1856 1926

the first World War, in a succession of waves of unequal length. The crests of the waves, apart from the exceptional boom of 1872, are at about 98, representing 2 per cent of unemployment. The troughs, apart from the exceptionally severe depression of 1879 with more than 10 per cent of unemployment, are usually at about 92, representing 8 per cent of unemployment. . . . This trade union employment rate, in spite of its narrow basis, represents with a high degree of accuracy the course of industrial activity in Britain and is of fundamental importance for the study of the trade cycle. . . . The curve on Chart I shows in its latter portion the practical disappearance of unemployment during the first World War. . . , the high level of employment during

the immediate aftermath of war in 1919–20 . . . , and finally the catastrophic decline of employment and its lower general level from 1921 onwards . . .

The general unemployment rate, as given above, is a single figure for each month or for each year in Great Britain as a whole. This single figure covers a great variety of facts. "The persons recorded as unemployed month by month are not homogeneous. They are persons of different ages, sexes and capacities seeking employment in different industries and districts; they have been unemployed for widely differing periods of time . . ."

.  .  .  .  .

### THEORIES OF UNEMPLOYMENT

*Unemployment Diagnosis of 1909.* In my first study of unemployment, published in 1909, I was concerned to show how and why unemployment persisted, even though the demand for labour appeared to grow on the whole at least as fast as the supply of labour. I found the explanation on the one hand in the fluctuations of the demand, seasonal and cyclical, and on the other hand in the tendency of each industry to accumulate and retain reserves of labour greater than were needed to provide for local and individual changes in demand. The strength of this tendency to keep excessive reserves of labour varied from industry to industry, according to the numbers of separate employers, the frequency of engagements and the methods of engaging men, but the tendency was found, to some extent, in all industries. The same diagnosis of unemployment was made by the Royal Commission on the Poor Laws and the Relief of Distress which reported in February, 1909.

TABLE 1. GENERAL UNEMPLOYMENT RATE, 1921–1938

| Year | Percentage Unemployed | | Year | Percentage Unemployed | |
|------|---------------|---------------------------|------|---------------|---------------------------|
|      | Great Britain | Great Britain and Northern Ireland |      | Great Britain | Great Britain and Northern Ireland |
| 1921 | 16.6 | 17.0 | 1930 | 15.8 | 16.1 |
| 1922 | 14.1 | 14.3 | 1931 | 21.1 | 21.3 |
| 1923 | 11.6 | 11.7 | 1932 | 21.9 | 22.1 |
| 1924 | 10.2 | 10.3 | 1933 | 19.8 | 19.9 |
| 1925 | 11.0 | 11.3 | 1934 | 16.6 | 16.7 |
| 1926 | 12.3 | 12.5 | 1935 | 15.3 | 15.5 |
| 1927 | 9.6 | 9.7 | 1936 | 12.9 | 13.1 |
| 1928 | 10.7 | 10.8 | 1937 | 10.6 | 10.8 |
| 1929 | 10.3 | 10.4 | 1938 | 12.6 | 12.9 |

The policy of organizing the labour market, recommended by the Royal Commission and embodied in the Labour Exchanges Act of 1909, was described by me at the time as "a policy of making reality correspond with the assumptions of economic theory. Assuming the demand for labour to be single and the supply perfectly fluid, it is not hard to show that unemployment must always be in process of disappearing —that demand and supply are always tending to an equilibrium. The ideal for practical reform, therefore, must be to concentrate the demand and to give the right fluidity to the supply." [1]

It was not suggested, of course, either by the Royal Commission or by myself, that organization of the labour market was all that was required. The reality and the seriousness of cyclical fluctuation were fully recognized. The policies of 1909 included the regularization of employment by the use of public work; the Minority developed this idea into a proposal for a ten years' programme of work to be used deliberately to counteract cyclical fluctuation. The policies of 1909 included also unemployment insurance . . .

.    .    .    .    .

The idea that demand for labour as a whole might be failing to keep pace with the supply of labour was raised at that time only to be dismissed. It was ruled out by the Majority of the Royal Commission on theoretic grounds. It was ruled out in my study on grounds, not of theory, but of the facts as they presented themselves up to that time: "There is no general failure of adjustment between the growth of the demand for labour and the growth of the supply of labour. The forces which constantly tend to bring about this adjustment between the growth of the demand for labour and the growth of the supply of labour have not been brought to the limit of their power." But the limitations of this cheering conclusion were carefully noted:

The statement that the country is not overpopulated, and that its industrial system is still capable of absorbing the growing supply of labour, must always be something of the nature of a prophesy . . . Because up-to-date industry has expanded, the inference is made that it is still expanding, and capable of expansion. Because this expansion in the past has taken place through alternations of good years and bad years, the inference is made of any particular period of depression that it is only a temporary phase and will give way to renewed prosperity. All this, however, is far from inevitable. [2]

On the facts up to that time, the assumption of economic theory that demand in total could be left to look after itself appeared to be justified in practice. As the supply of labour had grown, so on the average had the demand for labour. With every pair of

[1] *Unemployment* (1909), p. 237.

[2] *Unemployment* (1909), pp. 14–15.

## Chart II

### GENERAL EMPLOYMENT RATE, 1921-1938 (Great Britain and Northern Ireland)

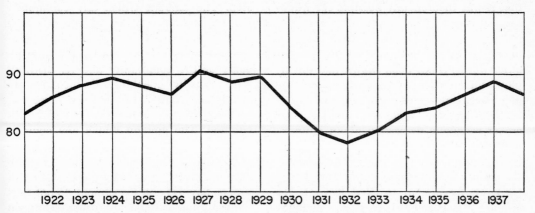

hands God sends a mouth. There had been a rising return to labour throughout the nineteenth century and this continued.

But even apart from the recurrent deficiency of demand through cyclical depression, the organization of industry was such as to involve serious unemployment in responding to demand: the main positive result of my first study was to show the scale and seriousness of frictional unemployment. My object in that first study was not to show that all was well with employment but to identify what was clearly wrong so as to exclude mistaken remedies:—

From the beginning to the end of fifty years of unprecedented industrial expansion unemployment has been recorded continuously, and has passed at intervals of seven to ten years from a normal to an acute phase. This in itself is enough to show that unemployment depends not so much on the volume of industry as upon the methods of industry, and while the methods remain unchanged, will continue or recur however the volume grows. A falling demand for labour may come as a symptom of national decay. A rising demand for labour will be no cure for unemployment.[1]

This was written when the unemployment rate recorded by the trade unions was running from 2 to 8. After the first World War a different scale of unemployment, with a rate running from 10 to 20 or more

[1] *Unemployment* (1909), p. 15.

had to be explained. The changed face of unemployment led naturally to new theorizing by economists about it. The first suggestion was that a general cause of the higher unemployment might be found in excessive wages. This was put forward prominently in Britain by Professor Pigou (*Economic Journal*, September, 1927) and from another angle by Professor Clay (*Economic Journal*, September, 1929).[2] The idea that high or rigid wages were an important cause of higher unemployment was substantially accepted by myself in the 1930 edition of *Unemployment*.

This potential effect of high wages policy in causing unemployment is not denied by any competent authority. . . . As a matter of theory, the continuance in any country of a substantial volume of unemployment which cannot be accounted for by specific maladjustments of place, quality, and time is in itself proof that the price being asked for labour as wages is too high for the conditions of the market; demand for and supply of labour are not finding the appropriate price for meeting.[3]

[2] J. M. Keynes, in lectures given at that time in London and Manchester, and reprinted as an article on "The Question of High Wages" in the *Political Quarterly* of January, 1930, emphasized the fact that in an international system high wages in a particular country, accompanied by mobility of foreign lending, might lead to unemployment. This is quite consistent with his subsequent criticism of Professor Pigou's general thesis as to the relation between wages and employment.
[3] *Unemployment* (1930), pp. 362 and 371.

It may be recalled that long before, in 1913, Professor Pigou had carried the argument about wages to the point of saying that it was theoretically possible for wage-rates at any moment to be so adjusted in every part of the industrial field "that no unemployment whatever can exist." "In other words, it has been shown that unemployment is *wholly* caused by maladjustment between wages and demand." [1]

*The Keynesian Analysis of 1936.* A new era of economic theorizing about employment and unemployment was inaugurated by the publication in 1936 of *The General Theory of Employment, Interest and Money* by J. M. Keynes,[2] now Lord Keynes. No account, however brief, of all the changes of economic thought and language induced by this epoch-making work can be attempted here. The gist of the new approach to the problem of employment that has resulted from it can be put shortly. Employment depends on spending, which is of two kinds—for consumption and for investment; what people spend on consumption gives employment. What they save, i.e. do not spend on consumption, gives employment only if it is invested, which means not the buying of bonds or shares but expenditure in adding to capital equipment, such as factories, machinery, or ships, or in increasing stocks of raw material. There is not in the unplanned market economy anything that automatically keeps the total of spending of both kinds at the point of full employment, that is to say, high enough to employ all the available labour. Adequate total demand for labour in an unplanned market economy cannot be taken for granted.

According to the Keynesian analysis, the possibility of prolonged mass unemployment lies in the fact that decisions to save

and decisions to invest are made by different sets of people at different times and for different reasons and may thus get out of step. The amount which any community will try to save is governed, not primarily by the outlets for saving, i.e. the opportunies for investment, but by the total income of the community and its distribution; broadly speaking, if incomes are evenly distributed, less will be saved out of the total than if they are unevenly distributed. The amount which any community will seek to invest is governed, not primarily by the amount of savings available for investment, but by expectation of profits. Savings and investment do not start with any initial tendency to march in step or bringing them together if they fall out. The rate of interest, which was supposed to serve this purpose, of regulating automatically the processes of saving and investment, fails to do so. If savings are tending to outrun investment, the rate of interest will fall only after a severe decline in the national income.

. . . . .

The argument . . . is not that the savings of a community in total can outrun the investment. In the sense in which these terms are used in the Keynesian analysis, the total savings that a community is, in fact, able to make, can never exceed the total invested: if a number of individuals in the community together try to save more than is being invested, the income of other members of the community will be correspondingly reduced; their losses in poverty and unemployment, their spending of former savings or running into debt will cancel out some of the savings of others and will thus reduce the total savings of the community to that which can be spent in investment. . . .

Saving in itself is merely negative; it means not spending. Saving may be desirable from the point of view of the individual who saves, in order to ensure to him the means of spending and of independence later. Apart from this merit of securing independence, saving in itself has no social

[1] *Unemployment*, p. 51 (Home University Library, 1913).
[2] . . . An excellent popular exposition of the Keynesian analysis is given by Mrs. Joan Robinson, in *The Problem of Full Employment*, published by the Workers' Educational Association as a Study Outline, and the analysis is explained and illustrated by the same author in *An Introduction to the Theory of Employment* (Macmillan, 1938).

irtue. The social virtue of saving by one person depends on there being someone else who wishes to spend the savings. This is obvious when the question is asked why, in war, saving is impressed upon all citizens as a duty, hardly second to that of giving their lives and their labour to the national cause. The answer is that in war the State has an infinite appetite for spending—is ready to spend all and more than all that the citizens can save. In spite of the war-savings posters, it is not the negative act of saving by the citizen that makes bombs and launches ships against the enemy, but the positive act of spending by the State. If neither the State nor anyone else is ready to spend savings, they are not a social but a self-regarding virtue. They may be no virtue at all.

· · · · ·

On the earlier teaching of the economists, moral and technical considerations in regard to the distribution of wealth had appeared to be in conflict. Moral considerations suggested the desirability of a more equal distribution of wealth, while technical considerations appeared to require great inequality as the condition of adequate saving. On the newer teaching of the economists . . . moral and technical considerations unite in favour of substantially greater equality of wealth than has obtained in Britain in the past.*

But, though actual saving in the Keynesian analysis is a mere residual, the amount which the individuals of a community will try to save, i.e. will not spend on consumption out of their incomes, is a factor of immense importance. The amount which the individuals of a community will try to save under conditions of full employment, with a given distribution of income, is the most important single economic fact about the community, for it commits the community to ensuring that that amount is spent by others, individually or communally, out of loans or from past savings, under penalty

of entering on a downward spiral of decreasing employment and growing poverty. By consequence it would be a matter of importance to have full and accurate information as to the sources from which the savings of a community come and as to the factors which influence saving. . . . The savings that tend to produce depression are the undistributed profits of companies and the large surpluses of a very limited class of owners of great wealth. The savings of most people are made for personal security; they merely postpone consumption; at any moment of time, while some are saving for future security, others are spending what they had saved in the past for this purpose and the two cancel out. . . .

The Keynesian analysis attacks directly and destroys one of the economic harmonies between savings and investment through the rate of interest, which according to older theory were assumed to keep the free capitalist system in prosperous equilibrium, with the demand for labour painlessly adjusted to the supply of labour. It destroys incidentally another of these harmonies also—the assumption made by Professor Pigou in 1913 that wage rates could be so adjusted as to abolish unemployment completely, and the inference that in any given situation employment could be increased directly by a general reduction of money wages. . . .

· · · · ·

The Keynesian analysis is of fundamental importance in making clear that the adequacy of the demand for labour as a whole to absorb the available supply should not be taken for granted. There may be unemployment through chronic deficiency of demand for labour, as well as unemployment through fluctuation of demand and through friction; demand for and supply of labour in total do not get adjusted automatically either by the rate of interest or by bargains about money wages. . . .

· · · · ·

ED. NOTE: * Keynesian economists, of course, were not the first to see this. Several socialist writers, including the American socialist Edward Bellamy (1850–1898) among others, had developed a similar analysis.

### THE NEW FACE OF UNEMPLOYMENT

Unemployment before the first World War appeared as an evil calling for remedy, but not as the most serious economic problem of its time. That it was this between two wars will be denied by few. The average rate of unemployment in Britain, that is to say the percentage of persons seeking work who could not find it, was between two and three times, most probably two and a half times, as high between the wars as it had been before the first World War. But doubling or trebling the rate of unemployment means much more than doubling or trebling the misery of unemployment, With unemployment at 5 per cent or less, the bulk of it consists of short interval unemployment of people who have not been idle long and can hope shortly to return to work. Unemployment at 15 per cent includes many who have been unemployed for long periods and have or are losing hope, as well as bodily vigour and the habit of work. Unemployment in Britain after the first World War had a new and grimmer face.

In this respect the experience of Britain accords with that of other industrial countries having similar economic systems. . . .

.  .  .  .  .

Nor is there room for reasonable doubt as to the direction in which the remedy [for mass unemployment] must be sought. The two approaches to the problem of unemployment in my first study of 1909 and in J. M. Keynes' General Theory of 1936, are not contradictory but complementary. The level of employment and unemployment at any time depends on the one hand, on the demand for the products of industry, and on the other hand, on the manner in which industry responds to the demand. In 1909, I assumed, in accord with all academic economists and most practical men, that, apart from the trade cycle, demand would look after itself. I was concerned mainly with the way in which industry responded to demand; the results of that study were summed up in its title—Unemployment:

A Problem of Industry. The revolution o economic thought effected by J. M. Keyne: aided by the experience of the thirties, lie in the fact that adequate demand for labou is no longer taken for granted. The Keynes ian analysis leads to the conclusion tha even apart from cyclical depression, ther may be chronic or nearly chronic deficienc in the total demand for labour, with fu employment a rare fleeting accident. J. M Keynes is not concerned with frictional un employment at all: it is excluded formall from his study. The Keynesian analysis doe not deny the importance of disorganizatio of the labour market as a cause of unem ployment. My first study did not deny th possibility of deficiency in total demand fo labour.

Both approaches are needed to-day. Th reality and the seriousness of the industria friction deduced by me from the limitec data available in 1909, are demonstrated b the analysis of unemployment between th two wars, based on the full data now avail able . . . ; this analysis shows, as a specia feature, the chronic hopeless unemploymen brought to particular regions by the shift ing of demand. The error of taking suffi ciency of total effective demand for granted on theoretical grounds, is made plain by th Keynesian analysis of 1936. Once that erro is shown, the burden of proof by facts tha an unplanned market economy can b trusted to maintain sufficient steady de mand for its products, rests on those who maintain this and the facts are agains them.

The new facts and the new theories o unemployment lead to the same conclusion that an unplanned market economy is les automatically self-adjusting at a high leve of employment than had been supposed in earlier times. . . .

.  .  .  .  .

The need for a new attack on the problem of unemployment cannot be denied to-day, except in a mood of unthinking optimism. The attack must be on three lines. There is unemployment due to chronic or recurrent deficiency of demand.

There is unemployment due to mis-direction of demand. There is unemployment due to the degree to which the labour market remains unorganized and to the manner in which particular industries respond to demand. The reduction of unemployment to a harmless minimum requires, therefore, measures of three kinds; measures to ensure sufficient steady demand for the products of industry; measures to direct demand with regard to the labour available; measures to organize the labour market and to assist the supply of labour to move in accord with demand.

SECTION C

## Explaining business cycles

# 28   Paul A. Samuelson: *Theories—Old and New*

🐦 *In this selection, Paul A. Samuelson (1915–   ), one of America's most prominent young economists, gives a concise and highly readable summary and analysis of the major theories of the business cycle which have been held up to the present. Following this analysis, Samuelson attempts to formulate a statement of the position at which business cycle theory now stands. Most, though not all, present-day economists would in general agree with his formulation.*

*Samuelson has been a member of the Economics staff of the Massachusetts Institute of Technology since 1940. He has been a consultant to the National Resources Planning Board, the War Production Board, and the United States Treasury. This selection is excerpted, with omissions, from Chapter 17 of his* Economics: An Introductory Analysis *(copyright 1948) with permission of the publishers, McGraw-Hill Book Company, Inc.*

Business conditions never stand still. Prosperity is followed by a panic or a crash. National income, employment, and production fall. Price and profits decline and men are thrown out of work. Eventually the bottom is reached, and revival begins. The recovery may be slow or fast. It may be incomplete, or it may be so strong as to lead to a new boom. The new prosperity may represent a long, sustained plateau of brisk demand, plentiful jobs, buoyant prices, and increased living standards. Or it may represent a quick, inflationary flaring up of prices and speculation, to be followed by another disastrous slump.

Such in brief is the so-called "business cycle" that has characterized the industrialized nations of the world for the last century and a half at least, ever since an elaborate, interdependent, *money economy* began to replace a relatively self-sufficient, precommercial society.

No two business cycles are quite the same; yet they all have much in common. They are not identical twins, but they are recognizable as belonging to the same family. No exact formula, such as might apply to the motions of the moon or of a simple pendulum, can be used to predict the timing of future (or past) business cycles. Rather do they resemble, in their rough appearance and irregularities, the fluctuations of disease epidemics, the vagaries of the weather, or the variations in a child's temperature.

To democratic nations, the business cycle presents a challenge—almost an ultimatum. Either we learn to control depressions and inflationary booms better than we did before World War II, or the political structure of our society will hang in jeopardy. For the ups and downs in business do not cancel out. At the top of the boom—if we are lucky!—there may be relatively favorable job opportunities for all who wish to work. Throughout the rest of the business cycle, men's lives are being wasted, and the progress of our economic society falls short of our true economic possibilities. If, as before the war, America marks time for another decade, the collectivized nations of the world, who need have no fear of the business cycle as we know it, will forge that much nearer or beyond us. Worse than that, peace-loving people who do not pretend to know very much advanced economics will begin to wonder why it is that during two World Wars individuals were freed for the first time from the insecurity of losing their jobs and livelihoods.

From these introductory remarks, it will be clear that the business cycle is simply one further aspect of the economic problem of achieving and maintaining high levels of jobs and production, and a healthy progressive economy.

. . . . .

Early writers on the business cycle, possessing little quantitative information, tended to attach disproportinate attention to *panics* and *crises* such as the collapse of the South Sea Bubble in 1720, the panic of 1837, the Jay Cooke panic of 1873, the Cleveland panic of 1893, the "rich man" panic" of 1907, and, of course, the super duper stock-market crash of "black Tuesday," Oct. 29, 1929. Later writers began soon to speak of two phases of business prosperity and depression, or boom and slump—with peaks and troughs marking the turning points in between.

Today, it is recognized that not every period of improving business need necessarily take us all the way to full employment. For example, throughout the decade of the 1930's there was a measure of recovery from the 1932–1933 trough levels but we could by no means speak of the period as being one of true prosperity. The prevailing fashion, therefore, is to follow the terminology of Wesley C. Mitchell long-time director of the nonprofit National Bureau of Economic Research and assiduous student of business cycles.[1]

The cycle is broken up by Mitchell and many other economists into four phases, the two most important ones being called the periods of "expansion" and "contraction." The expansion phase comes to an end and goes into the contraction phase at the so-called upper turning point (peak) called "recession." Similarly, the contraction phase gives way to that of expansion at the lower turning point (trough) or "revival.". . .

Each phase of the cycle passes into the next. Each phase is characterized by different economic conditions,[2] and each requires special explanatory principles. But let us continue a little while more with the facts before attempting analysis and theorizing.

How long are the usual economic cycles? This depends upon how many minor cycles you wish to count. Most observers have no trouble in agreeing on the major cycles, which run somewhere around 8 to 10 years

---

[1] W. C. Mitchell, *Business Cycles: The Problem and Its Setting* (New York: National Bureau of Economic Research, 1927).

[2] For example, during expansion, we find that employment, production, prices, money, wages, interest rates, and profits are usually rising, while the reverse is true during contraction.

in length. Everyone agrees that the late 1920's represent a period of prosperity and the early 1930's one of depression, and similarly with the past major business cycles. But not all economists attach much importance to the shorter minor cycles which are often to be seen in economic charts. In 1924 and 1927, there were small dips in business activity. Shall we call the 1920's, therefore, three different (minor) cycles or one major prosperity period? In an elementary introduction of this type, it is perhaps best to stick primarily to major business cycles. For our purposes we may accept Prof. Alvin H. Hansen's brief summary: [1]

The American experience indicates that the major business cycle has had an average duration of a little over eight years. Thus, from 1795 to 1937 there were seventeen cycles of an average duration of 8.35 years. . . .

Since one to two minor peaks regularly occur between the major peaks, it is clear that the minor cycle is something less than half the duration of the major cycle. In the one hundred and thirty-year period 1807 to 1937 there were thirty-seven minor cycles with an average duration of 3.51 years.

. . . it appears that the building cycle averages somewhere between seventeen and eighteen years in length, or almost precisely twice the length of the major business cycle. . . .

. . . American experience indicates that with a high degree of regularity every other major business boom coincides roughly with a boom in building construction, while the succeeding major cycle recovery is forced to buck up against a building slump. . . .

. . . the depressions which have fallen in the interval of the construction down-swing are typically deep and long. And the succeeding recovery is held back and retarded by the unfavorable depressional influence from the slump in the building industry.

### LONG WAVES?

Some economists, taking a broad historical view, like to speak of very "long waves,"

whose complete cycle length is about half a century. Thus from the end of the Napoleonic Wars in 1815 to the middle of the nineteenth century, prices tended to fall and times tended to be unusually hard, on the average. After the Californian and Australian gold discoveries following 1850, and as a partial result of the Civil and Crimean Wars, prices tended to rise. A new long cycle of falling prices followed the 1873 depression, tending to last until the 1890's when there was a great increase in gold production following the South African and Alaskan discoveries and improvements in gold refining. McKinley and the Republican party swam to prosperity and power on the crest of the new long wave.

Whether these long waves are simply historical accidents due to chance gold discoveries, political wars, and chance inventions, it is still too soon to say. [2]

### A FIRST CLUE TO THE BUSINESS CYCLE: CAPITAL FORMATION

Professor Hansen's emphasis on construction gives us our first clue as to the causation of the business cycle. Certain economic variables always show greater fluctuations than others in the business cycle. Thus, if it were to plot pig-iron production and anthracite-coal consumption side by side, we would hardly see the business cycle in the latter, whereas in the pig-iron series there would be little else to see but the business cycle. Why? Because anthracite is used largely for heating people's houses, and in both good and bad times most people are going to manage to keep reasonably warm. Pig iron, on the other hand, is one of the principal ingredients of capital and durable goods of all kinds: of plant equipment and durable machinery, of industrial and residential construction, of automobiles, washing machines, and other durable consumers' goods.

By their nature, such durable goods are

[1] Alvin H. Hansen, *Fiscal Policy and Business Cycles* (New York: W. W. Norton & Company, 1941), pp. 18–19, 20, 23–24.

[2] The interested reader may be referred to J. A. Schumpeter, *Business Cycles* (New York: McGraw-Hill Book Company, Inc., 1939), Chaps. 6, 7.

subject to violently erratic patterns of demand. In bad times their new purchase can be indefinitely postponed; in a good year, everyone may suddenly decide to stock up on a 10-year supply of the services of such durable goods. *Our first clue to the nature of the business cycle lies then in the fact that it is the durable or capital goods sectors of the economy which show by far the greatest cyclical fluctuations.*[1]

. . . . .

## A FEW THEORIES OF THE BUSINESS CYCLE

An industrious student could easily compile a list of separate theories of the business cycle which would run into the dozens.[2] Each theory seems to be quite different; but when we examine them closely and throw out those which obviously contradict the facts or the rules of logic, or which just appear to be conveying an explanation when really they are not saying anything at all—when we do all this, we are left with a relatively few different explanations. Most of them differ from each other only in emphasis. One man believes the cycle to be primarily the result of fluctuations in total net investment, while

[1] Lord Beveridge in his *Full Employment in a Free Society* (New York: W. W. Norton & Company, 1945) made a careful calculation of the degree of variability of the capital-goods industries in Great Britain ever since 1785 and found it to be twice as great as for other industries.

[2] We may just mention a few of the better known theories: (1) the *monetary* theory, which attributes the cycle to the expansion and contraction of bank credit (Hawtrey, *et al.*); (2) the *innovation* theory, which attributes the cycle to the clustering of important inventions such as the railroad (Schumpeter, Hansen, *et al.*); (3) the *psychological* theory, which treats the cycle as a case of people's infecting each other with pessimistic and optimistic expectations (Pigou, Bagehot, *et al.*); the *underconsumption* theory, which claims that too much income goes to wealthy or thrifty people compared with what can be invested (Hobson, Foster, and Catchings, *et al.*); (5) the *overinvestment* theory, which claims that too much rather than too little investment causes recessions (Hayek, Mises, *et al.*); (6) the *sunspot-weather-crop* theories (Jevons, Moore). The interested reader should consult G. Haberler, *Prosperity and Depression*, 3rd ed. (Geneva: League of Nations, 1944) or some other business-cycles text for further information on this subject.

another prefers to attribute the cycle to fluctuations in the rate of technological inventions and innovations, which act on business *through* net investment. A third man says that the root of the cycle is to be found in the fact that the creation of deposit money by our banking system causes investment spending to expand and contract so as to create boom and bust.

These sound like three different theories, and in most advanced textbooks they might be given the names of three different writers, but from our standpoint they are but three different aspects of the same process. (This does not mean that there is perfect agreement among all theories of the cycle or that there are not some important differences in emphasis between different writers.)

To classify the different theories, we may first divide them into the two categories of primarily external and primarily internal theories. The external theories find the root cause of the business cycle in fluctuations of something *outside* the economic system —in sunspot cycles, in wars, revolutions, and political events, in gold discoveries, in rates of growth of population and migrations, in discoveries of new lands and resources, and finally in scientific and technological discoveries and innovations.

The internal theories look for mechanisms *within* the economic system itself which will give rise to self-generating business cycles, so that every expansion will breed recession and contraction, and every contraction will in turn breed revival and expansion, in an irregular, repeating, neverending chain.

. . . . .

## SUNSPOTS AND RELATED PURELY EXTERNAL THEORIES

Not infrequently an amateur economist, often a scientist in some other field, will argue that sunspots, which have an average periodicity of some 11 to 13 years, have important effects upon the weather. This affects crops. Good crops cause low incomes and bad business. Or else it is the other way around, and good crops are supposed to mean prosperity. The sun-spot theorists cannot always make up their minds just which. In other versions, it is said that sunspots affect the intensity of solar radiation. Everyone knows that vitamin D depends on sunshine, and that people near the North Pole become despondent during the long winter nights. Hence, sunspots affect business by affecting pessimism, optimism, or health in general. One ingenious writer, dropping sunspots because they did not give an 8-year cycle, set forth the belief that whenever the planet Venus came between the sun and the earth, this caused magnetic absorptions and an 8-year business cycle. . . .

PURELY INTERNAL THEORIES

As against the crude external sunspot theory, we may describe a simple example of a possible crude internal theory. If machinery and other durable goods all had the same length of life, say 8 or 10 years, then we might try to explain a business cycle of the same length by this fact. If once a boom got started—never mind how —then there would be a bunching of new capital goods all of the same age. A few years later before these goods had worn out, there would be little need for replacement. This would cause a depression.

But after 8 or 10 years all the capital equipment would suddenly wear out and would all have to be replaced, giving rise to an inflationary boom. This in turn would give rise to another complete cycle, with a new cycle of depression and boom every decade. Thus, as a result of self-generating "replacement waves," we might have a purely internal business-cycle theory.

Actually, not all equipment has the same length of life; and not even all identical automobiles produced on the same day are in need of being replaced at the same time. Therefore, any bunching of equipment expenditures will tend over time to spread itself out, at most giving rise to weaker and weaker replacement peaks. Twenty-five years after the Civil War one might have observed a deficit of births because of that conflict. But another generation later and the dip would be hardly noticeable, while today it is just as if there had never been that particular violent disturbance of population. Replacement waves, therefore, are like a plucked violin string. They tend to dampen down and die away unless there is a new disturbance.

The laws of physics guarantee that friction will lessen any purely autonomous physical fluctuations. In social science, there is no law like that of the conservation of energy preventing the creation of purchasing power. Therefore, a much better example than replacement waves of a self-generating cycle would be the case where people became alternately optimistic and pessimistic, each stage leading as inevitably into the next just as the manic stage of an insane person leads eventually to the depressive stage. We cannot rule out such an internal theory. But neither can we be satisfied with it as it stands, for it does not explain a great deal.

COMBINING EXTERNAL AND INTERNAL ELEMENTS INTO A SYNTHESIS

Everyone has observed how a window or a tuning fork may be brought into pronounced vibration when a certain note is sounded. Is this vibration externally or internally caused? The answer is both. The sounded note is certainly an external cause. But the window or tuning fork responds according to its own internal nature, coming into strong resonance not with any sounded note but only with one of a certain definite pitch. It takes the right kind of trumpet to bring down the walls of Jericho.

Likewise we may look upon the business cycle as not unlike a toy rocking horse which is subjected to occasional outside pushes. The pushes need not be regular; great technical inventions never are. But just as the horse rocks with a frequency and amplitude that depends partly upon its internal nature (its size and weight), so too will the economic system according to its *internal* nature respond to fluctuations in external factors. Both external and internal factors are important, then, in explaining the business cycle.

Most economists today believe in a synthesis or combination of external and internal theories. In explaining the major cycles, they place crucial emphasis on fluctuations in *investment* or *capital* goods. Primary causes of these capricious and volatile investment fluctuations are to be found in such external factors as (1) technological innovation and (2) dynamic growth of population and of territory. With these external factors, we must combine the internal factors that cause any initial change in investment to be amplified in a cumulative, multiplied fashion—as people who are given work in the capital-goods industries re-spend part of their new income on consumption goods and as an air of optimism begins to pervade the business community, causing firms to go to the banks and the securities market for new credit accommodation.

Also, it is necessary to point out that the general business situation definitely reacts back on investment. If high consumption sales make businessmen optimistic, they are more likely to embark upon venturesome investment programs. Inventions or scientific discoveries may occur independently of the business cycle, but their economic introduction will most certainly depend on business conditions. If national income moves to a new postwar plateau which is some 50 per cent higher than prewar, we should expect that a considerable volume of capital formation (new machines, added inventories, construction) would be induced. Therefore, especially in the short run, investment may be in part an *effect* as well as a cause of the level of income.

In the longer run, no matter how high a plateau of income is maintained, the stock of capital goods will become adjusted at a higher level and new net investment will drop off to zero unless there is (1) a growth of income, (2) a continuing improvement of technology, or (3) a never-ending reduction in interest rates. The first of these processes, showing how investment demand may be induced by *growth* of sales

and income, has been given a rather high-sounding name—the "acceleration principle." Almost all writers bring it in as one strand in their final business-cycle theories. Let us examine how this internal cyclical mechanism works itself out and interacts with other factors.

## THE ACCELERATION PRINCIPLE

According to this law, society's needed stock of capital, whether inventory or equipment, depends primarily upon the level of income or production. Additions to the stock of capital, or what we customarily call *net* investment, will take place only when income is growing. As a result, a prosperity period may come to an end—not simply because consumption sales have gone down—but simply because sales have *leveled off* at a high level or have continued to grow but at a lower rate than previously.

A simplified arithmetical example will make this clear. Imagine a typical textile-manufacturing firm whose stock of capital equipment is always kept equal to about ten times the value of its yearly sales of cloth.[1] Thus, when its sales have remained at 6 million dollars per year for some time, its balance sheet will show 60 million dollars of capital equipment, consisting of perhaps 20 machines of different ages with one wearing out each year and being replaced. Because replacement just balances depreciation, there is no *net* investment or saving being done by the corporation. *Gross* investment is taking place at the rate of 3 million dollars per year, representing the yearly replacement of one machine. (The other 3 million dollars of sales may be assumed to go for wages and dividends.)

Now let us suppose that, in the fourth year, sales rise by 50 per cent—from 6 to 9 million dollars. Then the number of machines must also rise by 50 per cent, or from 20 to 30 machines. In the fourth year, 11 machines must be bought, 10 new ones

[1] We are ignoring any possible change in interest rates or degree of utilization of capacity in order to keep our discussion simple. This could be remedied. Also the reader may wish to include inventory change as well as equipment change in the analysis.

n addition to the replacement of the worn-out one.

Sales have gone up by 50 per cent. How much has machine production gone up? By ,000 per cent! It is this accelerated effect f a change in consumption on investment evels that gives the acceleration principle ts name.

If sales continue to rise in the fifth, sixth, nd seventh years by 3 million dollars, then ve shall continue to have 11 new machines rdered in every year. This is shown in able 1.

So far, the acceleration principle has iven us no trouble. On the contrary, it has iven us a tremendous increase in invest-nent spending as a result of a moderate ncrease in consumption sales. But now we re riding a tiger. Consumption has to keep ncreasing in order for investment to stand till! If consumption should stop growing t so rapid a rate—if it should level off in he seventh year even at the high level of 5 million dollars per year—then net in-estment will fall away to zero, and gross nvestment will fall back to 1 machine (see he table). In other words, a drop of zero er cent in sales has resulted in a 90 per

cent drop in gross investment and a 100 per cent drop in net investment!

The Lord giveth and the Lord taketh away. The acceleration principle is a two-edged sword. If sales should drop below 15 million dollars, gross investment would drop away to nothing; in fact, the firm would want to disinvest by selling off some of its machinery on the used-equipment market. It is now clear that a depression can set in just because consumption has stopped growing so rapidly, even if it has not dropped off absolutely, but only leveled off at a high level.

Needless to say, the curtailment of pro-duction in the machine-producing indus-tries will cause them to shut down, will curtail their income and spending on food and clothing, and lead to still further "mul-tiplier" changes in spending. This might ultimately cause textile sales to stop grow-ing altogether, or even to decline. This will cause a further accelerated drop in net in-vestment. Thus, we may be in a vicious circle whereby the acceleration principle and the multiplier interact so as to produce a cumu-lative deflationary (or inflationary) spiral.

It is easy to see that in the acceleration

ABLE 1. ILLUSTRATION OF THE ACCELERATION PRINCIPLE (IN MILLIONS OF OLLARS)

| Time | Yearly sales | Stock of capital | Net in-vestment | Gross investment, G. I. (N. I. + replacement) |
|---|---|---|---|---|
| First phase | | | | |
| irst year | $ 6 | $ 60 | $ 0 | 1 machine at $3 = $3 |
| econd year | 6 | 60 | 0 | 1 machine at $3 = $3 |
| hird year | 6 | 60 | 0 | 1 machine at $3 = $3 |
| Second phase | | | | |
| ourth year | $ 9 | $ 90 | $30 | (1 + 10) machines at $3 = $33 |
| ifth year | 12 | 120 | 30 | (1 + 10) machines at $3 = $33 |
| ixth year | 15 | 150 | 30 | (1 + 10) machines at $3 = $33 |
| Third phase | | | | |
| eventh year | $15 | $150 | $ 0 | 1 machine at $3 = $3 |
| Fourth phase (to be filled in by reader) | | | | |
| ighth year | $14.7 | . . . | . . | . . . |

principle we have a powerful factor making for economic instability. We have all heard of situations where people have to keep running in order to stand still. In the economic world, matters may be still worse: the system may have to keep running at an ever-faster pace just in order to stand still.

If business sales go up and down, the acceleration principle intensifies their fluctuation. It induces net investment on the upswing but causes about the same amount of net *dis*investment on the downswing. In the long run, if the system is growing because of population increase or higher real incomes, then the acceleration principle works primarily as a stimulating factor: growing national income causes extensive

growth of capital, which in turn means that investment demand will be brisk and unemployment relatively low.

The important lesson to be learned from this chapter is that the economic system is more or less without a steering wheel. There is no mechanism or automatic governor which keeps purchasing power right at the full-employment level, neither too low nor too high. On the contrary, even if businessmen and workers are doing their best and are acting intelligently and unselfishly, the system may still be in the throes of inflation or deflation, depending upon the chance circumstances of the complex interaction between investment and saving.

# 29 League of Nations: *Cyclical Patterns*

❦ *This reading supplements the preceding selection on the general nature of business cycles. It is an extremely concise statement of the "anatomy" of a depression, in terms of what happens to production, income, consumption, and investment as the business cycle swings from peak to trough and back to peak again. It is from Economic Stability in the Post-War World, which is Part II of the Report of the League of Nations Delegation on Economic Depressions (1945). Part I of the Report was entitled* The Transition from War to Peace Economy (1943). *The full report constitutes a valuable discussion of modern economic phenomena and theories.*

The ebb and flow of business, which we now characterize as the business cycle, take place in a given economic environment of institutions and habits. These tide-like movements appear to be an inherent characteristic of an individualistic economy and to be related to the process of capital accumulation and economic progress under that system. In more primitive societies they find their partial counterpart

in lean and fat years, in the alternation of abundance and famine.

## STRUCTURAL FACTORS

Progress in individualist economies has not taken the form of a steady uphill climb to new levels of output and well-being, but has been marked by successive spurts and halts, by alternations of periods of prosperity and depression. Each successive spurt differs in some ways from its predecessors; new paths are explored and fresh ground broken. Similarly the periods of arrested advance differ. But all periods of prosperity or of depression have certain characteristics in common. The former are marked by a rapid accumulation of real capital (investment by producers and consumers in durable goods) and of working stocks, associated with a general rise in incomes and demand; while periods of depression are marked by a sharp decline in the output of capital goods and in working stocks, associated with a general contraction of incomes and of demand.

As industrialization progresses and a greater proportion of the total productive forces of any country is devoted to the manufacture of capital goods, the instability of the economic system increases, depressions are liable to become more intense and the risk of unemployment becomes more serious.

Certain indirect effects of this industrialization accentuate the tendency to instability. Amongst those of particular importance are the effects of the slowing up of the rate of population growth which seems to accompany the process of urbanization, and the changes in demand to which increased wealth due to industrialization gives rise.

*1. Demographic Influences.* The first effect of the increased wealth and productivity in Western Europe, which was associated with the revolutionary technical developments and accumulation of capital in the last century, was an unprecedented increase in population. The improvement in health associated with the rising standard of living led to a spectacular decline in the death rate and consequent sharp increase in populations in the advanced industrial countries during the major part of the 19th Century. But this fall in death rates was accompanied or preceded by a fall in birth rates in industrial countries, the movement beginning in France as early as 1830, in Scandinavia and England after 1890, and in Germany, the Netherlands and Czechoslovakia after the turn of the century. Since 1910 the downward movement has been greatly accelerated and has been spreading since the last war to the industrial areas of North America, Oceania and elsewhere. In almost all highly urbanized countries the rate of population growth has in consequence flattened out, and declining population is to be foreseen if the anticipated excess of deaths over births is not made good by immigration. The following estimates for certain European countries, which do not include the effects of the present war, are characteristic. (See Table I.)

The rapid expansion of population during the nineteenth century probably helped to maintain active employment. Such an expansion gives rise to a relatively steady and persistent growth in the demand for such commodities of basic necessity as food and clothing, and the increase in the number of families provides a steady demand for new houses and all the durable goods (furniture, domestic appliances, etc.) con-

TABLE I. PAST AND FUTURE POPULATION TRENDS IN ADVANCED INDUSTRIAL COUNTRIES—TOTAL POPULATION (000,000's)

| | 1914 | 1940 | 1945 | 1950 | Projections [1] 1955 | 1960 | 1965 | 1970 |
|---|---|---|---|---|---|---|---|---|
| United Kingdom and Ireland | 46.1 | 50.2 | 50.6 | 50.6 | 50.2 | 49.4 | 48.2 | 46.8 |
| Sweden | 5.7 | 6.33 | 6.38 | 6.37 | 6.31 | 6.21 | 6.05 | 5.84 |
| Czechoslovakia | ... | 15.3 | 15.5 | 15.6 | 15.6 | 15.5 | 15.2 | 14.9 |
| Germany | 67.8 | 69.5 | 71.2 | 72.0 | 72.2 | 71.8 | 71.1 | 69.8 |
| Belgium | 7.7 | 8.31 | 8.35 | 8.34 | 8.27 | 8.16 | 7.98 | 7.76 |
| France | 39.8 | 41.2 | 40.8 | 40.3 | 39.7 | 39.0 | 38.1 | 36.9 |
| Total 6(5) countries | 167.1 | 190.8 | 192.8 | 193.2 | 192.3 | 190.1 | 186.6 | 182.0 |

[1] *The Future Population of Europe and the Soviet Union* (League of Nations, 1944, II, A. 2), pp. 56 and 75.

nected with the setting up of a home. Other types of investment, particularly schools, but roads, railways, and public utilities as well, are also related to the growth of population and increase steadily with population. At the same time an expanding population renders the economic system more adaptable to change. The labour force is younger and able more easily to learn new skills, and important shifts in demand and production can be met largely by a change in the flow of new recruits into industry instead of by the more difficult process of shifting those already employed.

A slowing up of population growth or a declining population affects employment and stability in precisely the opposite way. Certain types of investment opportunities—those particularly related to the number of households and to the size of the population—decline; the working population becomes older and less adaptable, while changing demands may involve shifting workers out of existing industries, with inevitable transfer frictions and unemployment. A retardation of population growth, moreover, renders consumers' demand more unstable. For with a smaller proportion of children in the population the demand for immediately consumable and indispensable goods such as food and clothing becomes relatively less important, and the demand for luxury or semi-luxury goods, more important. This latter demand can be and is postponed when times are bad, and is, moreover, peculiarly subject to changes in fashion and taste. A retardation of population growth thus has effects similar to those of an increase in national income in countries already relatively rich, and indeed is likely to be accompanied by or give rise to an increase in income per head.

2. *Increase in Income per Head.* Of the luxury and semi-luxury goods, some are durable—automobiles, refrigerators, wireless sets, etc.; others, though less durable, are subject to capricious changes of fashion; still others consist of services, such as entertainment or travel. The essential feature of the demand for all goods of this class is that it is less stable or dependable than the

demand for basic articles of food, dress, and housing; the automobile can be made to last another year; it is possible to get along with a smaller wardrobe; the holiday can be postponed until times improve.

The growing importance of this postponable and unstable personal consumption is an inevitable accompaniment to a rising standard of living. A wealthy community is more subject to the type of economic instability we have in mind than is a needy community, though it will be in a better position to weather bad times because it has reserves to fall back on.

3. *Increased Importance of Capital Goods.* The effect of the increasing instability of consumers' demand is reinforced by the growing proportion of the national income of richer countries which is saved and devoted to the production of capital goods. It is mainly this process of saving and investment which makes countries richer and renders labour more productive by providing it with more and better technical equipment. But the process of investment, in an individualist economy, is extremely unstable. It can cease altogether if the profit outlook seems dark, and in time of depression even gives way to capital consumption, the existing equipment not even being maintained.

Thus the increased relative importance of capital goods in total production tend (like the increased importance of durable and luxury goods in total consumption) to increase the instability of the economic system, while at the same time it also increases its dynamic power and render possible a higher level of satisfaction. When the business outlook darkens, or when there is some slackening in consumers' demand businessmen will tend to stop buying new machinery and plant and will satisfy demand with the existing plant. The more important the industries making plant, *i.e* the capital-goods industries, the greater the danger of a contraction in the demand for plant upsetting general economic activity.

In the immediate post-war years, however, there will be in certain countries very great demand for savings to rebuild the capital that has been destroyed during the war and to make up for the normal investment which had to be postponed during the war years. But when the reconstruction period is over, while savings may remain high or even grow with the restoration and increase of national wealth, opportunities for further investment at the intense reconstruction rate may well not prove to be available. Unless special steps are taken to increase consumption demand, or provide new investment opportunities either at home or abroad, serious unemployment may ensue in the investment industries, spreading to the consumption goods industries and involving the whole economy in a general depression.

4. *The Changing Distribution of Income.* In most advanced industrial states and in many others as well, the distribution of income during the present century has been rendered more even both by measures designed to relieve poverty, such as health and unemployment insurance, old age and widows' pensions, subsidies to consumers, etc., and by the application of progressive scales in direct taxation. In so far as these measures result either in maintaining demand in bad times, as does, for instance, unemployment insurance, or in increasing the proportion of the national income spent upon necessities, they have a stabilizing effect, which must be set against the tendency towards greater instability that we have mentioned in the last three sections.

On the other hand, unless met by suitable institutional adjustments, very steep gearing of taxes may tend to check progress by reducing the large personal incomes from which a considerable proportion of risk-bearing capital has been derived in the past and by narrowing the spread between the net return on funds put out at risk and funds maintained in relatively liquid form. We shall revert to this point in a later chapter, and would only observe here that different types of taxation may be required in highly advanced countries where the elements of instability are serious and in less developed countries where

rapid progress is likely to be a primary consideration.

5. *Growth of Rigidities.* While demand has been tending to become increasingly capricious, unpredictable and volatile, the productive process itself has become subject to increasing rigidities. The modern economic system imposes the need for great adjustments—and weakens the capacity to make them. Groups with great financial or political power—cartels, trusts, labour unions—have acquired monopolistic or semi-monopolistic control of important sectors of the economic system; and this control is sometimes exercised in ways detrimental to economic stability.

For it is a condition of stability that the economic system should be able to adapt itself smoothly and without any great friction to changes in demand and supply conditions, in technique and in invention. Changes in relative prices which alter the relative profitability of different lines of production constitute the process by which this adaptation is encouraged. Certain non-institutional factors, such as the increased importance of fixed capital, renders adaptation more difficult than previously; fixed capital cannot suddenly be re-invested in a different form to accommodate a change in demand. But more important have been the factors interfering, through organized control, with the formation of prices and preventing relative prices from accurately reflecting the demand for different classes of products and services. Concentration of control of a large portion of the output of important industries in the hands of a few producers, frequently behind high customs tariffs, has enabled them to pursue an independent price policy. To the extent to which they keep the prices of their products rigid when demand wanes they will tend to reduce demand still more, and throw more men out of work. In some countries agricultural interests have been strong enough to keep agricultural prices, through protection, quite out of line with the rest of the world, and have prevented adjustments where adjustments were required. At the same time, the trade unions

have rendered certain wage rates less elastic than in the nineteenth century and have
reduced the mobility of labours both from
occupation to occupation and from place
to place.

In consequence of these developments
there grew up in certain countries during
the inter-war period a price system which
was half free and half flexible—in some
parts of the economic system decreases in
demand resulted primarily in price reductions, while in other parts they resulted
primarily in a contraction of output and
the maintenance of prices. . . .

Rigidity in certain of the elements entering into costs tends to throw the burden
of price adjustments on others, and thus to
increase the price changes to which these
others are subjected. It would, however, be
dangerous to conclude dogmatically that
greater all-round flexibility of prices and
costs would necessarily make depressions
less severe. The essence of the question is
the effect of such flexibility on total purchasing power and demand, and there are
factors operating in both directions. On the
one hand, the restoration of profitable cost-
price relationships through a reduction of
costs which are out of line tends to stimulate investment and so to increase purchasing power. But if cost-reductions set up
anticipations of further cost and price reductions, producers may restrict their purchases and wait until prices are lower. If a
general reduction in wages leads to a decline in the purchasing power of the working classes, entrepreneurs' profit anticipations may be adversely affected and, in
spite of the fact that their liquid position
is improved through the reduction in wage
disbursements, they may be less willing
than they were before the wage reduction
to use their liquid balances and credit resources to replace plant and to produce. In
these circumstances there would be a net
contraction of purchasing power and a
deepening of the depression.

.   .   .   .   .

6. *Growth of State Intervention.* If we
examine the economic evolution of the last

century we shall find that it has led inevitably to the assumption by the state of
greater responsibilities in the direction of
economic life and to the general acceptance of the view today that the state has a
direct obligation to prevent serious depressions to the best of its ability, or, if they
occur, to take measures to overcome them.
The demands of a modern wealthy society
are more dispensable, more postponable,
than they were; they are less firmly supported by the needs for such simple things
as food and clothing of the coming generation; they no longer expand automatically
along foreseeable lines as population expands, but spread and ramify, start forward
violently and violently contract. Demand
was formerly met mainly by individuals or
small firms conducting a competitive struggle for existence, with high economic mor-
tality, and, through the process of evolutionary elimination, adapting themselves to
the changes in demand that resulted from
the slow swings of taste or from the gradual
growth of income per head as total national
production outran the expansion of population. As demand has become more varied,
the unit of production has grown and become less adaptable. The automatic elimination of surplus or inappropriate capital
equipment is no longer possible by the old
evolutionary means. Adaptation on the
scale required by the normal changes of
habit and wealth can only be effected by
the deliberate action on the large firm.
Much of the waste of the old ruthless system may be avoided. But if these large
undertakings fail to make the necessary adjustments, then progress may be seriously
impeded and depressions may develop into
violent crises. Intervention by the state may
be indispensable to assure that adjustments
are effected, and similarly intervention by
the state may be required to prevent the
collapse of some large enterprise which
would lead to widespread disaster.

In practice the role of the state in most
countries has become much wider than that
of an impartial director of traffic or umpire
in the conduct of business. The state has
itself acquired control of many of the larg-

est undertakings or natural monopolies, has substituted public for private monopoly, and has frequently entered the field of foreign commerce not simply to determine the rules of the game, but to participate in it itself. These centralized powers may be used in such a way as to maintain economic stability or in such a way as to increase rigidities and international instability. They afford an opportunity but also involve a risk.

SECTION D

## Full employment and public policies

# 30 United Nations: *Maintaining Effective Demand*

❦ *The previous readings were concerned primarily with diagnosis of the factors which enter into business cycles and depressions. The selection which follows is concerned primarily with prescription, that is, it deals with the problem of formulating adequate policies for maintaining full employment and avoiding depression. It is to be noted that the policies discussed do not go beyond those compatible with a capitalist or private enterprise economy, and that they do not discuss "war economy" as a policy for ensuring full employment.*

*The reading is taken from a report prepared by J. M. Clark, Arthur Smithies, Nicholas Kaldor, Pierre Uri, and E. Ronald Walker who were appointed by the Secretary General of the United Nations. The report is entitled* National and International Measures for Full Employment *(Lake Success, N. Y.: United Nations Department of Economic Affairs, December, 1949, UN Document E/1584), pp. 34–43 (with omissions).*

The problem of maintaining effective demand has two main aspects: how to secure stability, and how to secure an adequate level of spending. The problem of stability, in principle, could be tackled in two different ways: (1) by stabilizing the level of demand directly in those sectors of the economy which are primarily responsible for the fluctuations; (2) by neutralizing the effect of such fluctuations through compensating variations in the rate of expenditure on other goods and services. In both cases, the problem of ensuring stability of demand inevitably merges into the problem of ensuring an adequate level of demand. In the following section these two major methods of dealing with the problem will be treated in some detail.

## STABILIZING THE LEVEL OF INVESTMENT

Apart from cases in which the originating impulse of fluctuation is transmitted from abroad, the proximate cause of instability in the level of economic activity is the fluctuation in the level of capital expenditure, particularly of business investment in fixed capital or in inventories which . . . may be of a self-generating character. The problem of instability could therefore be largely solved if adequate measures could be devised to stabilize the rate of investment. Even investment stabilization may not, however, solve the problem entirely, since the expenditure of consumers on durable goods may exhibit features analogous to the expenditure on capital goods in the usual sense of the term. Nevertheless there can be little doubt that the fluctuations in business investment represent the major primary cause of economic instability.

Spontaneous tendencies to fluctuations in the level of productive investment may be regarded as inevitable so long as the decisions to invest are made by private business firms acting independently of each other. In a socialist state such fluctuations may be avoided by stabilizing investment through a government budget, though even in a socialist state irregularities in the investment process may arise as a result of the intricate problem of dovetailing a succession of specific investment projects, each of which is of limited duration. In economies in which production is carried on by private enterprise subject to direct government controls, stability in the level of investment may be secured by means of quantitative restrictions (such as building permits, allocation of basic materials, etc.) provided the current demand for capital goods of all kinds exceeds the effective supply. During the period of post-war reconstruction, this was generally the case in a number of industrial countries, so that the level of investment could be more or less effectively controlled by the government— the actual stability of investment depending on the practical effectiveness of the control measures. But while such measures of quantitative restriction may be effective enough in times when investment demand tends to be excessive, they are unavailing to maintain the level of investment once demand falls below the limit set by the supply of labour and basic materials.

In private enterprise economies, which operate with a free price mechanism, stability in the level of private investment could only be promoted by methods of indirect control. Such indirect control operates traditionally through the banking system, i.e., through the variation of interest rates and other conditions of credit. Past experience has shown that such monetary methods of control (like the methods of quantitative control discussed above) are more effective in placing an upper limit to investment than in preventing downward movement. But apart from monetary and credit measures, there may be at least two other ways in which the government can influence the rate of investment. One consists in influencing the timing of private investment projects through special tax incentives—the government offering special tax concessions or subsidies to firms which are willing to postpone or antedate their particular investment projects, so as to fit them into a more stable general pattern. This would require that the government obtain information on the investment plans of the individual firms for a sufficient time ahead to be able to exert an influence on the actual timing of their execution. It would also involve a highly complicated system of tax legislation and tax administration in order to devise and administer inducements that would exert a major influence on the timing of investment projects.

The second method of stabilizing the rate of investment consists in offsetting the fluctuations in private investment by countervailing fluctuations in public investment. The effectiveness of this method clearly depends on the size of the public sector of the economy which determines the scope for public investment. In economies where the only type of public investment consists of public works (such as the building of

highways, dams, bridges, navigation and ir-
rigation works, etc.), the possibilities of
stabilizing the rate of investment in this
manner will obviously be smaller than in
economies where housing, transport, public
utilities or other basic industries are also
under public control. It must be remembered, of course, that not all types of public
investment can be timed in such a way as
to fit in with the requirements of the general economic situation. In order to be effective, such a stabilizing policy would also
require (*a*) that the public authorities prepare in advance an adequate reserve of
suitable public investment projects which
could be put into operation as and when required; (*b*) that the government obtain advance information on the investment plans
of private firms, so as to be able to dovetail
public investment with private investment
effectively.

Economies that make widespread use of
central planning and control are obviously
in a better position to undertake the direct
stabilization of investment than private
enterprise economies relying on a free price
mechanism. There can be little doubt, however, that with properly thought out methods and sufficient preparation, private enterprise economies could also accomplish
far more in this direction than was thought
feasible in the past. . . . Some countries
are also accumulating a reserve of properly
elaborated public investment projects which
could be put into operation fairly quickly in
case of need. These methods are as yet in
their infancy and only experience will be
able to show to what extent they will succeed in imparting a greater degree of stability to the economic system.

If the level of investment were effectively
stabilized by any of the methods outlined
above (or some combination of them),
economies might still be faced with the
problem of ensuring that the total demand
for goods and services generated in the
economic system was adequate to ensure
full employment. If investment were stabilized at its long-term trend level (which
may be put somewhere mid-way between
the boom level and the depression level of

investment), no special problem need arise
in maintaining that level over longer periods, but the total demand for goods and
services generated at that level of investment would also be somewhere mid-way
between the boom level and the depression
level, so that it would not suffice to ensure
full employment. On the other hand, if an
attempt were made to stabilize investment
at levels approaching the peak periods of
activity, the continued high rate of investment would lead to a growing over-capac-
ity of plant and equipment, and would
thus require more and more compensatory
public investment to maintain it (or increasing subsidies to private investment),
which in turn would be likely to cause an
exhaustion of useful investment opportunities. In both cases, therefore, once the stability of investment is assured, there is the
additional problem of adapting the structure of the economy to a higher ratio of
consumption demand to investment demand which may be necessary in order to
secure adequate total demand at a level of
investment that is no higher than can be
sustained under conditions of stability.
This, of course, does not apply to underdeveloped or partially developed economies whose stock of capital equipment is
inadequate.

### STABILIZING AGGREGATE DEMAND

The alternative approach to the problem,
and one which may yield more effective results in highly industrialized countries, is
that of influencing the general level of consumer demand rather than attempting to
control investment demand directly. The
most promising methods of doing so are
through the revenue or expenditure programmes of the government, both central
and local. Certain kinds of government expenditures (e.g. consumers' subsidies, or
transfer payments such as family allowances and payments to the unemployed)
directly affect the purchasing power of consumers relatively to the level of incomes.
Similarly, changes in the level and structure of taxation directly affect the purchasing power of consumers. Hence, consumers'

expenditure can be raised or lowered by changes in taxes or in certain kinds of government expenditure. In this way, total effective demand could be stabilized even though fluctuations in investment demand itself were not eliminated. . . .

The activities of governments . . . will tend to exert a certain stabilizing effect on the economic system even in the absence of deliberate measures to raise consumers' demand in the face of a declining investment demand or vice versa. If the actual rates of taxation are not increased when the revenue of public authorities declines with a decline in income, the forces of contraction in the economic system will be weaker than they would be otherwise, and the downward spiral in production and incomes will come to a halt more quickly. If, furthermore, a decline in production and incomes itself leads to a rise in public expenditures (on account of unemployment compensation, for instance), the automatic stabilizing influence of governmental activities will be even greater. Looked at in another way, this means that if the fiscal policies of the state involve a growing budgetary deficit (or a declining budgetary surplus) in times of declining income, and vice versa, the actual fluctuations in income will be confined to narrower limits than if the public authorities attempted to achieve a balance between current revenue and current expenditure in each period. This stabilizing influence, moreover, will be all the greater, the larger the normal share of governmental expenditure in the total national expenditure. Such "built-in" stabilizing effects are, of course, far more effective in countries which have adopted a social security system and which, as a matter of policy, refrain from raising tax rates in times of declining national income. It would be desirable if governments reviewed their existing structure of social expenditure and their tax structure with a view to reinforcing the operation of such "built-in" stabilizers. It must be remembered, however, that such stabilizers, by the nature of the case, can only have the effect of dampening the range of economic fluctuations. They can mitigate the fall in consumers' demand that occurs in response to a fall in investment demand; they cannot conjure up an actual *rise* in consumers' demand that would be needed to offset the fall in investment demand.

A rise in consumers' demand could, however, be secured through budgetary measures if governments did not content themselves with the "built-in" stabilizers described above, but undertook positive counter-measures through counter-cyclical variations in the rates of taxation in force. If the rates of taxation were lowered in times of declining demand, and raised in times of rising demand, the purchasing power in the hands of consumers could be altered sufficiently to maintain total demand at a stable level. (A similar result could be achieved, of course, if instead of varying the rates of taxation, governments varied the rates of certain types of expenditure in a counter-cyclical manner—e.g. if the level of consumers' subsidies, or of family allowances, were raised in times of declining demand or lowered in times of rising demand.) Though this policy aims at stabilizing the total demand for goods and services and not the demand for each major component separately, it is not expected that any major fluctuations in employment would occur as a result. The recent experience of industrialized countries has shown that, provided total effective demand is maintained, the economic system is capable of dealing with considerable shifts in the distribution of demand without involving transitional unemployment.

Variations in the rates of taxation in force thus appear to offer for many countries a most effective and prompt method for maintaining the level of effective demand in the economy. The leading industrial nations of the world possess methods for estimating the effects of particular changes of tax rates on consumer demand with a sufficient degree of reliability to warrant the application of these methods; they also possess general taxes which could be altered at short notice and the effects of such changes would be transmitted fairly promptly. The most suitable taxes for such purposes are general sales taxes, social security contributions, or personal income taxes which in a number of countries are now collected on a "pay as you earn" basis. Though the income tax is normally an annual tax, we do not envisage any serious difficulties in introducing the adjustments required to make it possible for tax rates to be changed at more frequent intervals. In the leading industrial countries, the income tax is the most universal tax and is probably best adapted for this purpose. However, the use of social security contributions for this purpose would have the advantage of distributing the benefit of increased purchasing power over a wider range of the community than is possible through a reduction in personal income tax. . . .

If the future course of demand for goods and services could be forecast with sufficient accuracy, the necessary changes in taxation to maintain demand at a stable level could be planned ahead and, theoretically, put into effect simultaneously with any change in the level of national expenditure emerging from other causes, so that the actual level of expenditure could be kept stable. However, with the present knowledge of economic forecasting it would be utopian to expect that the necessary counter-measures to prevent fluctuations in national expenditure would generally be taken sufficiently early to prevent any actual variations from taking place. Though some governments do make regular forecasts of the trend of national expenditure and take these into account in determining the scale of taxation in con-

nexion with the annual budget, it may be inevitable that the major counter-measures intended to check a decline in production and employment should be taken in the light of actual events rather than on the basis of forecasts of future tendencies that have not yet materialized. Some decline in demand is therefore bound to occur before effective measures can be taken to check and to reverse the movement. In present circumstances this may be inevitable; what is essential is to ensure that such counter-measures are not taken too late, and that when they are taken they should be adequate for dealing with the situation. . . .

The basic principle underlying these recommendations is that compensatory measures aimed at producing an expansion of effective demand should be brought into operation automatically whenever the actual level of unemployment (as a percentage of wage-earners) exceeded a pre-announced level by a stated percentage, for three successive months. In our view, while the influence of chance factors would make it unreasonable to base policies on the actual record of any particular month, the record of three successive months should give sufficient indication of a trend to bring counter-measures into operation. The counter-measures could take the form of a stated reduction in taxation (whether of income tax or of a general sales tax) which, together with the secondary effects of the resulting increase in consumer expenditure, would generate an expansion of effective demand sufficient to bring unemployment within the full-employment target level.

# 31 Howard S. Piquet: *Point Four and World Production*

☛ *The preceding readings in this Part have discussed the problem of the business cycle and "full production" primarily from the standpoint of problems and policies within national economies. Our final reading considers the problem from the standpoint of the total world economy.*

*The United Nations has formulated a plan for technological assistance to underdeveloped areas and the leading world powers have all expressed their interest. American participation has taken the form of the so-called "Point Four" program for aiding underdeveloped areas with technical and financial assistance. With the Point Four program as a background, this reading classifies the nations of the world by income and standards of living. It dramatically exhibits the economic poverty of most of the world, and, by contrast, the relative luxury of a few sections. How, it implicitly asks, can the level of world production be raised, or the world product be redistributed, so as to mitigate these inequalities?*

*Howard S. Piquet (1903–   ) served with the United Nations Commission on Food and Agriculture from 1943 to 1945. Since 1934, he has been Adjunct Professor of Political Economy at the American University in Washington, D. C. He is the author of articles on tariffs and international organization. The following reading is excerpted from his article, "Point Four and World Production," The Annals of the American Academy of Political and Social Sciences, March, 1950, and is used with permission of the publishers.*

Practically speaking, countries may be grouped roughly according to their being developed, partially developed, or underdeveloped. It is not a question of there being only a small minority who have much or whether there are poverty-stricken areas within the country. It is, rather, a question as to whether the average inhabitant is reasonably well off in terms of worldly goods or whether he must get along on very little.

The best available yardstick for arranging the countries according to their stage of economic development [1] is the average annual per capita income of their inhabitants. According to estimates presented to the United States Senate by the National Advisory Council,[2] the 53 countries for which

[1] We are referring, of course, only to material development. There is no intention of implying anything with regard to cultural development. Some of the most economically backward areas of the world are among the oldest and most developed culturally. In some respects, an economically underdeveloped country, such as China, is more advanced than even the most industrialized countries.
[2] *Point Four*, Department of State, Washington, D. C., July 1949, pp. 92–93, 105.

per capita income figures for 1939 (the latest prewar year) are available can be arranged in three clearly distinguishable groups. Together these countries account for almost 85 per cent of the world's population.

The most advanced countries comprise Group I. There are 15 of them. They account for one-fifth of the world's population, and the weighted average per capita income of their inhabitants is $461.

The 10 countries in Group II account for approximately one-sixth of the world's population, and in 1939 their inhabitants had an average annual per capita income of $154. These might be called the partially developed countries.

Group III includes 28 countries, accounting for two-thirds of the world's population, with an average annual per capita income of only $41. These are the truly underdeveloped countries.[1]

Table 1 is taken from the report referred to above (pp. 104, 105).

## WORLD PRODUCTION

There is no adequate index to which we may turn in order to measure total world production, or to compare production of the underdeveloped countries with that of the more advanced countries. We can describe the situation in general terms and we can compare certain indices which, when taken together, provide overwhelming evidence of the wide disparity between living conditions among the two-thirds of the world's population who live in the underdeveloped areas and the remaining one-third.

Recent figures of the Statistical Office of the United Nations indicate that, in comparison with an annual average per capita income of $1,400 in the United States in

[1] The sensibility of the underdeveloped countries is illustrated by the evolution of the term "underdeveloped" as applied to them. At the Hot Springs Conference on Food and Agriculture, held in 1943, they were referred to in several draft resolutions as the "backward areas." The resentment aroused by this term resulted in its being changed to "undeveloped" countries. This, too, was unsatisfactory, and compromise resulted in the present designation.

TABLE 1. PER CAPITA INCOME, POPULATION, AND POPULATION GROUPS OF 53 COUNTRIES, 1939

| Country | Per Capita Income * (U. S. Dollars per Annum) | Rank | Population (in thousands)† | Population types‡ |
|---|---|---|---|---|
| *Upper Income Group* (Over $200) | | | | |
| United States | $554 | 1 | 131,416 | 1 |
| Germany | 520 | 2 | 69,317 | 1 |
| United Kingdom | 468 | 3 | 47,778 | 1 |
| Switzerland | 445 | 4 | 4,206 | 1 |
| Sweden | 436 | 5 | 6,341 | 1 |
| Australia | 403 | 6 | 6,997 | 1 |
| New Zealand | 396 | 7 | 1,642 | 1 |
| Canada | 389 | 8 | 11,368 | 1 |
| Netherlands | 338 | 9 | 8,834 | 1 |
| Denmark | 338 | 10 | 3,825 | 1 |
| France | 283 | 11 | 41,950 | 1 |
| Norway | 279 | 12 | 2,937 | 1 |
| Belgium | 261 | 13 | 8,396 | 1 |
| Eire | 248 | 14 | 2,946 | 1 |
| Argentina | 218 | 15 | 13,132 | 2 |
| *Middle Income Group* ($101–200) | | | | |
| Union of S. Africa | 188 | 16 | 10,251 | 1# |
| Finland | 184 | 17 | 3,684 | 1 |
| Chile | 174 | 18 | 4,940 | 2 |
| Austria | 166 | 19 | 6,650 | 1 |
| USSR | 158§ | 20 | 196,500‖ | 2 |
| Italy | 140 | 21 | 43,864 | 1 |
| Greece | 136 | 22 | 7,200 | 2 |
| Czechoslovakia | 134 | 23 | 15,239 | 1 |
| Hungary | 125 | 24 | 9,129 | 1 |
| Bulgaria | 109 | 25 | 6,308 | 2 |
| *Lower Income Group* ($100 and below) | | | | |
| Cuba | 98 | 26 | 4,253 | 3 |
| Yugoslavia | 96 | 27 | 15,703 | 2 |
| Poland | 95 | 28 | 35,090 | 2 |
| Japan | 93 | 29 | 72,520 | 2 |
| Venezuela | 92 | 30 | 3,650 | 3 |
| Egypt | 85 | 31 | 16,650 | 3 |
| Palestine | 81 | 32 | 1,502 | 3 |
| Costa Rica | 76 | 33 | 639 | 3 |
| Colombia | 76 | 34 | 8,986 | 3 |
| Peru | 72 | 35 | 7,000 | 3 |
| Panama | 71 | 36 | 620 | 3 |
| Ceylon | 63 | 37 | 5,922 | 3 |
| Mexico | 61 | 38 | 19,380 | 3 |
| Uruguay | 56 | 39 | 2,147 | 3 |
| Dominican Republic | 51 | 40 | 1,650 | 3 |
| Haiti | 50 | 41 | 2,600 | 3 |
| Nicaragua | 50 | 42 | 883 | 3 |
| Guatemala | 48 | 43 | 3,260 | 3 |
| Bolivia | 47 | 44 | 3,400 | 3 |
| Honduras | 45 | 45 | 1,090 | 3 |
| El Salvador | 45 | 46 | 1,745 | 3 |
| Brazil | 46 | 47 | 40,900 | 3 |
| Ecuador | 44 | 48 | 3,000 | 3 |
| Paraguay | 39 | 49 | 970 | 3 |
| India | 34 | 50 | 382,000 | 3 |
| Philippines | 32 | 51 | 16,300 | 3 |
| China | 29 | 52 | 450,000 | 3 |
| Indonesia | 22 | 53 | 69,435 | 3 |
| Total | | | 1,836,145 | |

\* SOURCE—Per Capita National Income, *Foreign Assets and Liabilities of the United States and Its Balance of International Transactions.* A Report to the Senate Committee on Finance by the National Advisory Council on International Monetary and Financial Problems, December 18, 1947.

† SOURCE—Statistical Yearbook, League of Nations 1941/42.

‡ Countries are grouped by population types as follows: Type 1: *Low growth potential.* Birth rates below 25 per thousand population. Low death rates. Small natural increase with prospect of relatively stationary populations in the future. Type 2: *Transitional growth.* Birth rates 25–35. Both birth and death rates generally falling. Rapid population growth. Type 3: *High growth potential.* Birth rates over 35. Death rates (but not birth rates) generally declining. Rapid growth in absence of civil disturbance, famine, and epidemic. The birth rates refer to average annual figures for the period 1931–1940. Official vital statistics were used where available, though for a number of countries these were corrected to take account of apparent underreporting of births. Birth rates were estimated from other demographic information for countries lacking official vital statistics.

§ SOURCE—P. A. Baran, "National Income and Product of the USSR, 1940," *Review of Economic Statistics*, November 1947. This applies to enlarged area after annexations in 1939–40.

‖ SOURCE—OIR, Department of State. Population after annexations in 1939 and 1940. Prior population 172,000,000.

# White population only.

1947, the annual average per capita income in twenty-five other nations, comprising together substantially more than one-half of the world's population, was less than $100 per year. The report [1] goes on to say that the economy of the underdeveloped areas is predominantly agricultural and that the "average output per person in agriculture in these areas is less than one-tenth of that achieved in more advanced countries."

More comprehensive figures are available for the prewar period. They are adequate for the present purpose, since there has been no substantial improvement in the past decade. In addition to per capita income estimates, there are data, by countries, for consumption of food and clothing, consumption of energy, freight carried, railroad mileage, motor vehicles registrations, and telephones in use. Data are also presented for a number of noneconomic factors, such as life expectancy, number of physicians and teachers per thousand of population, illiteracy, and tuberculosis death rates.

The accompanying chart is based on figures appearing in the recent report of the Department of State setting forth the administration's Point Four Program.[2] It shows vividly the wide differences among the three groups of countries with regard to each of these criteria. The percentage spread is particularly wide with respect to energy consumption, freight hauled, motor vehicles, telephones, illiteracy, and deaths from tuberculosis.

The unevenness of economic development in various parts of the world is not a mere accident. Those countries that are in the lead are there for numerous reasons, such as favorable climate, abundant natural resources, technological aptitude of the people, and political organization. To expect that all countries could, or should, be brought to the same degree of development would border on the unreasonable.

What President Truman's Point Four Program contemplates is that the gap between the economically most advanced and the economically most retarded countries should be narrowed by lifting the latter up closer to the former.

Nevertheless, it is interesting and informative to calculate, on the basis of such information as is available, what the potentialities are in the way of increased production. To do so is not to imply that such an increase will be the probable result of a vigorously administered Point Four Program, or that it would even be possible under *any* program. If the more backward countries can lift themselves even a fraction of the way toward such a goal, even over many years, the program will have been a success. For, as emphasized by the Department of State and by the United Nations, the success of a program for economic development depends upon a complex of factors—both economic and noneconomic—and will be measured, not in terms of years, but in terms of decades, if not generations.

If, in the three groups of countries described above, the countries of Groups II and III were to be lifted to the level of the Group I countries, so that the entire world would enjoy an average annual per capita income of $461, it would mean a global world income 2.3 times as large as that received in 1939. Obviously, such a figure is very rough; it is simply another way of saying that two-thirds of the world's population receives a per capita annual income only one-eighth as large as that received by the more favored one-third.

Even a modest improvement would mean a substantial percentage gain in the economic well-being of the submerged two-thirds. It would mean basic improvements in agricultural methods, more and better food, some industrialization, improvements in transportation and power production, more and better clothing, and in general a greater share in the things that constitute the difference between living and merely existing.

[1] *Technical Assistance for Economic Development,* United Nations, Lake Success, N. Y., May 1949 (E/1327/Add.1).

[2] *Point Four, op. cit.,* pp. 93–102. The chart gives the actual figures, but each one is drawn in percentage scale with either the Group I or the Group III countries shown as 100.

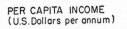

# INDICATORS OF DEVELOPMENT

## Economic Factors

100%

| Indicator | Values |
|---|---|
| PER CAPITA INCOME (U.S. Dollars per annum) | 461 / 154 / 41 |
| FOOD CONSUMPTION (Calories per day per capita) | 3040 / 2760 / 2150 |
| CONSUMPTION OF ANIMAL PROTEINS, (Ounces per day per capita) | 1.6 / .9 / .3 |
| CONSUMPTION OF FATS AND OILS (Ounces per day per capita) | 4.0 / 2.3 / 1.3 |
| CONSUMPTION OF COTTON, WOOL, AND RAYON (lbs. per annum per capita) | 18.63 / 7.52 / 4.80 |
| ENERGY CONSUMED (Hp. hours per capita per day) | 26.6 / 6.4 / 1.2 |
| ANNUAL FREIGHT CARRIED (Ton miles per capita) | 1517 / 927 / 58 |
| MILES OF RAILROAD (Per thousand sq. miles) | 40 / 29 / 13 |
| MOTOR VEHICLE REGISTRATIONS (Per thousand of population) | 111 / 7 / 1 |
| TELEPHONES IN USE (Per thousand of population) | 90 / 7 / 2 |

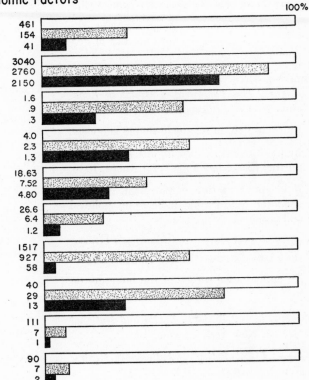

## Other Factors

100%

| Indicator | Values |
|---|---|
| PHYSICIANS (Per thousand of population) | 1.06 / .78 / .17 |
| ELEMENTARY SCHOOL TEACHERS (Per thousand of population) | 3.98 / 3.42 / 1.76 |
| LIFE EXPECTANCY (At birth) | 63 / 52 / 30 |
| TUBERCULOSIS DEATH RATE IN 1939 (Per 100,000 population) | 64 / 143 / 333 |
| PERCENTAGE OF ILLITERACY (Age 10 and over) | (under) 5 / 20 / 78 |

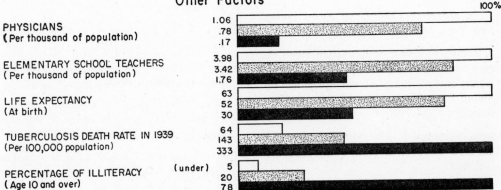

## SELECTED REFERENCES FOR PART 6

AMERICAN ECONOMIC ASSOCIATION. *Readings in the Theory of Income Distribution.* Philadelphia: Blakiston, 1946.

————. *Readings in Business Cycle Theory.* Philadelphia: Blakiston, 1944.

————. *Readings in the Theory of International Trade.* Philadelphia: Blakiston, 1949.

Papers by outstanding economists bearing on the causes, character, and remedies of economic fluctuations.

DILLARD, DUDLEY. *The Economics of J. M. Keynes: The Theory of a Monetary Economy.* New York: Prentice-Hall, 1948.

An exposition, in relatively simple language.

EZEKIEL, MORDECAI. *Jobs for All Through Industrial Expansion.* New York: Knopf, 1939.

A blueprint for full employment. Assumes need for considerable increase in political and economic centralization.

HABERLER, GOTTFRIED. *Prosperity and Depression.* Lake Success: United Nations, 1946.

An authoritative survey of the literature on business cycle theory.

HANSEN, ALVIN. *Business Cycles and National Income.* New York: Norton, 1951.

————. *Fiscal Policy and Business Cycles.* New York: Norton, 1941.

————. *Economic Policy and Full Employment.* New York: McGraw-Hill, 1947.

————. *Monetary Theory and Fiscal Policy.* New York, McGraw-Hill, 1949.

A leading supporter of Keynesian views argues for a vigorous public policy to counteract the tendencies toward unemployment resulting from the maturity of the American economy.

HARRIS, SEYMOUR E. *The National Debt and the New Economics.* New York: McGraw-Hill, 1947.

Argues, on the basis of Keynesian analysis, that expansion of the national debt does not imperil the stability of the American economy.

HAYES, H. GORDON. *Spending, Saving, and Employment.* New York: Knopf, 1947.

A readable popularization of the Keynesian theory of unemployment.

KLEIN, L. R. *Economic Fluctuations in the United States—1921–1941.* New York: Wiley, 1950.

A useful technical study.

KUZNETS, S. *National Product in Wartime.* New York: National Bureau of Economic Research, 1945.

A statistical compendium.

LERNER, A. P. *Economics of Employment.* New York: McGraw-Hill, 1951.

Analyzes public employment policy, with emphasis on the prevention of inflation under full employment.

METZLER, LLOYD, and others. *Income, Employment and Public Policy: Essays in Honor of Alvin H. Hansen.* New York: Norton, 1948.

A series of essays presenting newer views concerning the relation of employment to public policy.

MITCHELL, WESLEY C. *Business Cycles and Their Causes.* Berkeley: Univ. of California Press, 1941.

Papers by the leading American student of business cycles.

PIGOU, A. C. *Employment and Equilibrium.* London: Macmillan, 1941.

————. *Lapses from Full Employment.* London: Macmillan, 1945.

One of the best-known economic writers of modern times here indicates a departure from his earlier classical economic views.

ROBBINS, LIONEL. *The Great Depression.* London: Macmillan, 1934.

An analysis by the well-known British economist.

ROBINSON, JOAN. *Introduction to the Theory of Employment.* London: Macmillan, 1937.

A primer of the newer theories of fluctuation and fiscal policy.

SCHUMPETER, J. A. *Business Cycles.* 2 vols. New York: McGraw-Hill, 1939.

A monumental study of the course of economic development in the last two centuries, with particular stress upon the long trend factors in economic development.

TERBORGH, GEORGE W. *The Bogey of Economic Maturity.* Chicago: Machinery and Allied Products Institute, 1945.

Vigorously disputes the contentions of Alvin Hansen and others that the American economy faces maturity and impending stagnation.

WALLACE, HENRY A. *60 Million Jobs.* New York: Reynal & Hitchcock, 1945.

A full-employment program by the former Vice-President.

WECTER, DIXON. *The Age of the Great Depression, 1929–1941.* New York: Macmillan, 1948.

A chronicle of America during and after the Great Depression.

❋    ❋    ❋

Valuable materials on current problems will be found in the publications of the Department of Economic Affairs of the United Nations. See especially *International Capital Movements During the Inter-war Period* (1949); *Economic Development in Selected Countries,* 2 vols. (1947–1950); *Economic Survey of Asia and the Far East* (1949); and *Methods of Financing Economic Development in Under-Developed Countries* (1949).

# PART 7

# The state and the economy

In Part 6, we were concerned with the theory of the business cycle and of unemployment. In this Part, we turn to a more descriptive or empirical analysis of the ways in which different economies in our present industrial world have sought to solve the problems of large-scale economic life. By saying that in the previous Part we were primarily concerned with "theory," we mean simply that we were trying to find out what broad general *principles* have been distilled out of the many studies of national economies. By saying that in this Part we shall be more concerned with "empirical" material, we mean simply that we shall be primarily interested in *describing* how different economies have endeavored to work out basic principles in real life.

The major economies which we shall describe in this Part may be thought of as falling at different points on a continuum, according to the degree to which each is centrally planned. The idea of a continuum is simply that of a *continuous* line which we can imagine running from perfect competition at one end to perfect state monopoly at the other. Somewhere in between will be found all of the actual economies which now exist or ever have existed.

For, as we have seen, an economy based on "perfect competition," on *nothing* but pure market controls, has never existed in real life. Nor, may we imagine, will a "perfect state monopoly" ever exist in real life. Each is an "ideal type": that is, it is an abstraction which is constructed by extending or exaggerating the characteristics found in actual economies. Perfect competition, free enterprise, and laissez faire on the one hand and perfect monopoly, centralization, collectivism on the other, are simply the imagined end-points of the line on which all actual economies may be thought of as falling. Viewed this way, these ideal types are useful tools in thinking about these problems. They are "ideal" not in the sense that they are *desirable,* but in the sense that they are found in the realm of the imagination or of *ideas.* They are like a "perfect vacuum" in physics or a "perfect circle" in mathematics, neither of which has ever existed empirically.

The first two articles in this Part may be looked upon as marking out the two ends of this line or continuum: socialism and laissez faire. The articles by HENRY

D. DICKINSON and HENRY C. SIMONS are not, however, concerned so much with abstractions as with trying to show how these ideal systems could be approached in actual life. Dickinson begins with an analysis of the way in which capitalism is supposed to perform the functions of an economy, and leads from here into an analysis of the way in which it actually operates, especially with regard to the distribution of income. Capitalism, Dickinson believes, is unable—except, perhaps, for very brief periods of time—to perform the major functions of an economy with either justice or efficiency. Socialism aims to replace the evils of capitalism by a system which will stress collective planning rather than market controls. Dickinson deals at considerable length with some of the major objections which are leveled at socialism, especially the contention that it must necessarily curtail individual freedom. His general conclusion is that it may do so, but need not necessarily do so.

Simons believes that collectivism, planning, and socialism inevitably destroy individual liberties. He holds that democratic institutions arose with modern capitalism and that, if capitalism falls, they will fall too. He believes the most desirable economy approaches as closely as possible pure laissez faire and that the major economic evil is monopoly, whether it be on the part of overwhelmingly large corporations, labor unions, or the state. He argues for a "positive program for laissez faire" which would endeavor to maintain or restore free competition in all areas of economic life where it is possible: where it is not possible, the state should not endeavor to regulate and control, but to own and operate. One may well ask whether this leaves Simons' program as far from Dickinson's as it might seem to be at first glance.

The other selections in this Part analyze the operation of four major modern economies: the "mixed economy" of the United States; the "democratic socialist" economy of Great Britain; the "national socialist" economy of Nazi Germany; and the "soviet communism" of the U.S.S.R.

The selection by MERLE FAINSOD and LINCOLN GORDON summarizes a large number of the scattered materials on the American economy which have appeared throughout this book. The American economy appears here not necessarily as the *right* economy, but as one economic system among many. Fainsod and Gordon make explicit what is implied throughout the earlier readings: that the American economic system has for some time ceased to be one which could be described as a pure "free market" system. It has been a "mixed," or a "controlled capitalist" economy. This transition is not the product of one or another political regime, such as the New Deal; it is rather the product of the gradual extension of large-scale organization and "nonmarket" controls, both private and public. Fainsod and Gordon conclude by summarizing some of the main problems to be faced by a "mixed capitalist" economy, and by indicating basic principles of operation on which the majority of Americans seem to agree.

The readings by R. H. TAWNEY and SIR ARTHUR SALTER deal with the British economy as it developed, in the form of "democratic socialism," after the rise to power of the Labour Party in 1945. Tawney analyzes the main features of British socialism, which he sees to be (1) the redistribution of income through a variety of public services; (2) the undertaking of deliberate "contra-cyclical" policies intended to "smooth out" the business cycle and avoid depression; (3) the nationalization of several major areas of economic life; and (4) the extension of greater government control over many non-nationalized areas.

Salter sees as three of the major problems of British socialism: (1) the maintenance of incentives strong enough to motivate high production and economic "progress," as the motive of profit through private ownership becomes less effective; (2) the problem of establishing levels of income for different groups without becoming involved in inflation through "excessive" wage demands, on the one hand, or imposing an inflexible and arbitrary government control, on the other; and (3) the general problem of maintaining flexibility and decentralization of control in a "planned economy" which tends toward solving problems by greater and greater centralization.

The selection by WILLIAM EBENSTEIN analyzes and describes the "permanent war economy" of German "national socialism." Ebenstein points out that the term "socialism" does not, and cannot, convey the same meaning to a German that it does to a person in the Anglo-American world. To the Britisher or American, "socialism" is something new, a system that replaces an existing "free capitalist" economy. But Germany, Ebenstein tells us, has, in effect, never known the "free market" economy characteristic of British or American capitalism. As industrialism reached Germany, it tended to be organized in the form of large, semi-monopolistic concerns, without a transitional period of small "free enterprise"; when "socialism" began to come to Germany in the early part of the twentieth century, it was not a "socialism from the bottom," inspired by a mass movement against the "capitalists," but a "socialism from the top," a social welfare program initiated by the Kaiser's government.

Following the overthrow of the Kaiser, the Weimar Republic largely carried over the pattern of the centralized "social welfare" state. Thus when the Nazis came to power in 1933 and endeavored to put into operation a "totalitarian" economy geared for total and permanent war, its program of central planning was not opposed to the degree it might have been opposed in countries with a background of "free enterprise" and "liberal" political institutions. Ebenstein tells us that the Nazi economy was neither capitalist or socialist; its distinguishing feature was that it employed whatever means might be expedient—whether private or public—to maximize the war effort. In reading Ebenstein, we may have occasion to wonder whether the "permanent war economy," as he describes it, may be the model which many nations may be expected to approach in the near future.

This Part closes with a discussion of how Soviet Russia endeavors to perform the major functions of an economy. BARRINGTON MOORE, JR. believes that we cannot take at face value Russian claims that the masses play a large part in economic planning. He sees the structure of controls in the U.S.S.R. as a highly centralized system in which the most the masses can do is probably to suggest ways of more efficiently carrying through plans formulated by top bureaucrats. Discussing the ways in which Russia has endeavored to meet the problems of motivation and distribution, Moore says it has been forced to borrow many features of the profit motive, competition, and consumer sovereignty as they exist in capitalist economies. This does not mean, however, he contends, that it has in any sense become capitalist. What it does indicate, he believes, is that, on the one hand, the varieties of possible working economies are greater than is supposed by those who believe that nothing but a "free price system" can really perform an economy's "five functions," and, on the other hand, that the problems faced by *all* economies are more alike than has been supposed by those who have thought that all the problems of capitalist economy would be abolished with the abolition of private property.

In this Part, we try to survey the major national economies of our era. Though this survey is necessarily very sketchy, this Part endeavors to depict, in a concrete setting, some of the ultimate problems which must be faced in economic life and some of the difficulties which have been encountered by alternative systems in attempting to solve them.

SECTION A

**Liberty and security: the dilemmas of planning**

# 32 Henry D. Dickinson: *The Principles of Socialism*

❧ *"Socialism" is a term which has had many meanings, and attitudes toward socialist movements in modern times have varied from those of relatively uncritical acceptance to those which attack any idea associated with the word. On a scholarly level, socialist analyses and proposals in recent years have involved discussions of such problems as individual liberty in a socialist society, the possibilities of planning, and the compatibility or incompatibility of free consumers' choice with socialism.*

*Among the leading academic proponents of socialism has been the British economist Henry D. Dickinson. He was formerly a tutor at Oxford and is the author of*

Institutional Revenue (1932), *and* Studies in Capital and Investment (*with G. D. H. Cole and others, 1935*). *Our reading is reprinted from* The Economics of Socialism (*copyright 1939 by Oxford University Press, Inc.*), *with permission of the publisher. It examines what Dickinson sees as the defects of capitalism, defines socialism in terms of its basic proposals, and criticizes the charge that socialism is incompatible with individual liberty.*

Any society must have a method of determining what and how much is to be produced, of choosing between alternatives and of achieving its ends with the greatest economy of means. The method of a capitalist society is the system of production for profit and exchange upon the market,[1] modified by monopolistic combinations of capitalists, by trade-unions and by such occasional and irregular intrusions of deliberate social intervention as tariffs, marketing-boards, railway-rate regulation, factory acts, social insurance, etc. The productive energies of society are continually being diverted by the motive of private gain into the channels in which they will yield most profit to those who control them —that is to say, the greatest surplus of selling price over cost of production. Meanwhile competition, even if imperfect, is tending to equalize selling price and cost. Therefore, in theory, since sale price is determined by the consumer's effective demand, and cost depends upon the capacity of productive resources to satisfy demand in alternative uses, there should emerge the maximum satisfaction of needs with the minimum expenditure of resources. In reality this desirable result is attained only very imperfectly. Under capitalism, four causes contribute to falsify the readings of the price-index and hence to pervert the allocation of resources to production.

(*a*) The inequality of consumers' incomes systematically distorts the measure-

ment of social needs. A rich man wanting a country cottage for a few week-ends in summer can outbid two farm labourers who need shelter all the year round; two cottages are thrown together to make one weekend dwelling and two bread-winners have to seek work elsewhere at grave risk of unemployment or else add a six-mile tramp to their already fatiguing labours.

(*b*) Another all-pervasive cause of the falsification of the price-and-cost calculus is monopoly. The "invisible hand" which is presumed to maximize satisfaction operates only under conditions of perfect competition. But perfect competition is not a real entity; it is an abstraction born of the economist's urge to rationalize the working of the economic system. Even that degree of competition which, in John Stuart Mill's day, was enough to give the "invisible hand" good scope for its beneficent work only exists during a period of exceptionally rapid technical development: it is a fleeting transitional phase between one period of monopoly (mercantilism) and another period of monopoly (imperialism). Monopoly is the natural offspring of competition. Once it is established, the presumption no longer holds good that the distribution of resources produced by the self-interest of private entrepreneurs corresponds to the maximum satisfaction of consumers.

(*c*) The meretricious modern art of publicity makes it often more profitable for the manufacturer to spend money in making people want to buy the things that he produces, rather than on producing the things that people want to buy. This tendency is reinforced by the inevitable ignorance of the consumer, called upon to discriminate

[1] It is also the method of an economic system without large-scale production or large-scale marketing, but having private property and division of labour, in which goods are produced by small independent producers directly for a local market. This system is what Marx calls "simple commodity production."

between the properties of rival brands of tooth-paste, vacuum-cleaners, canned peaches, radio-sets, and artificial silk cami-knickers. It is often more profitable to advertise poor goods than to improve their quality.

(*d*) On the production side, money costs not infrequently fail to correspond to true social costs. Cheap goods can be made out of sweated labour; the costs of salvaging the human wreckage of industry being thrown on the relatives of the workers or on the general tax- or rate-payer. Costs can be cut by means involving the neglect of safety precautions, the pollution of the air by smoke, the contamination of rivers by noxious affluents, or the sacrifice of human life on the roads.

Nevertheless, the price-and-market system does give some sort of a solution, even though it be distorted and perverted by class privilege and exploitation, to the problem of the economic allocation of resources to the satisfaction of various and competing needs. . . .

### SOCIALISM

*General notion of socialism.* Ever since the early days of industrial capitalism, men have sought a remedy for its abuses and defects in some material reorganization of the economic system. In particular, the private ownership of the means of production has appeared to many reformers as the fundamental source of evil in the system. To some, such as James Mill and Henry George, it is the private ownership only of land and natural resources; to others, such as Major Douglas and Professor Soddy, it is the private ownership only of credit, that is the source of evil; but to the majority, the private ownership of *all* non-human means of production—factories, railways, machinery, and raw materials, as well as land and natural materials, and credit—has appeared as a barrier to the full utilization of

the resources of the world in the service c the needs of mankind. The author hold this last-expressed view. However impor tant historically may have been the specia role played by private property in land an minerals, or in credit facilities, as a facto in the evolution of class privilege, in th present stage of development of capitalism all forms of land and capital have becom merged in a single mass of privately owne means of production. The concrete goods o which this is composed have become inter changeable with one another; their specia nature—whether land, produced means o production, or intangible "productive re lations" such as credit—has become irrele vant. The ownership of a portion of thi mass confers the right to appropriate ; certain part of the income of society. I private ownership of productive resource. is to blame for the disharmonies of capital ism, it is private ownership of *all* means o production, and not of land, or credit, o some other part of the whole, that must b set in order.

.  .  .  .  .

Once private property in land and capita is established, there is a constant tendency for its ownership to become concentrated in fewer hands, until a definite class o owners of means of production ("capital-ists") emerges. The interests of this class are distinct from, and in many ways antagonistic to, those of the rest of the community. The class division between owners and workers begins.

The distribution of property tends to inequality and therefore the distribution of incomes derived from property tends to inequality. On the other hand, the distribution of incomes derived from work tends to be much less unequal. The reasons for this are legion. A few are:

1) Owing to the diminishing marginal utility of income,* the larger one's income

ED. NOTE:  * The reference to "marginal utility" of income and labor means, roughly, that the more income a person has, beyond a certain point, the less satisfaction he gets out of spending it, and the easier it is to invest it and thereby earn more income; whereas, after a certain point, each succeeding dollar earned by working is gained at a greater sacrifice ("takes more out of one.") Thus, says Dickinson, inherited or independent incomes tend to "snowball" at the expense of incomes earned by labor, and thus wealth tends to concentrate in the hands of the rich. "To them that hath, shall be given."

the easier it is to save out of it or otherwise use portions of it for the purpose of adding to one's property. The marginal disutility of labour, however, increases steeply after a certain point. Thus, while it is progressively easier to add to a property-income, it is progressively harder to add to a work-income.[1]

2) Owing to the working of the law of averages, the chances of total loss of capital diminish the greater the number of different portions into which it is divided for purposes of investment. The "small man" cannot easily or cheaply spread his risks in this way, and is thus more subject than the big investor to loss due to the vagaries of the market. (This is particularly noticeable in the general depressions that, under capitalism, periodically devastate the market economy.) If the "small man" seeks safety in gilt-edged securities or in conservatively managed investment trusts, he has to put up with a distinctly lower rate of return than the big operator can get on his capital with equal safety.

3) Exclusive market information and exclusive opportunities for investment on profitable terms are more likely to come to those who are already rich than to men of small means. Similarly, employment at a high remuneration is more readily obtained by those who are already well-to-do or who are connected by birth, education, or social ties with the rich than it is by poor men.

4) Once a society has begun to be stratified into classes on the basis of differences in income, the wealthier sections of the community in general contrive to monopolize the educational machine so that the necessary training and equipment for the better paid employments can only be acquired by those who already belong to the higher income classes.[2]

All these (and other) influences are cumulative in effect. There are, of course, counteracting influences, such as the tendency of the rich to relative sterility, extravagance and spendthrift behaviour (Veblen's "conspicuous waste"), the voluntary endowment of public institutions by the rich, and progressive taxation. But the general tendency, in a system of private free enterprise and private ownership of the means of production, is towards greater inequality and towards the stratification of society into antagonistic classes on the basis of wealth and of the origin of wealth. While minor divisions may be important, the division that dominates social life is that between the owners and the non-owners of the material means of production.

Socialism thus arises as the political objective of the nonowning class. In order to diminish inequality of wealth and to abolish the class stratification of society, socialists propose to abolish private ownership of the material means of production. Some method must be devised of administering the economic system after the expropriation of the existing private owners. This is the problem of the economics of a socialist community.

*Definition of socialism.* The definition of socialism that was generally accepted during the half-century between 1875 and 1925 is "social ownership of the means of production." Since that time the phrase "planned production" has been tending to take its place. There is a close connection between these two definitions. On the one hand, one of the chief advantages claimed for the socialization of the means of production is the elimination of the waste due to unplanned, chaotic, individualistic production. Individualistic production is coordinated, it is true, by the mechanism of price and the market; but it is subject to gross disturbances even in this sphere and it is fundamentally blind, purposeless, irrational, and incapable of satisfying many of the most urgent of human needs. On the other hand, so it is claimed by socialists, the planning of production is impossible on any basis less radical than the complete elimination of individual property rights in the means of production, at least in all the major branches of economic activity, and the transfer of these means of production to organs of collective economy. Only so

[1] See the present author's *Institutional Revenue,* ch. v, p. 26.
[2] See E. Ll. Lewis, *The Children of the Unskilled; Institutional Revenue,* pp. 58, 156; and *Political Arithmetic* (ed. L. Hogben), chs. viii, ix, x.

can the community sweep away the secrecy, arbitrary boundary lines, vested interests, overlapping of functions, waste, and monopoly that characterize private enterprise. One fundamental difference between socialism and capitalism will be the existence of an authority able to view the economic system as a whole and with power to make decisions involving the system as a whole. Another fundamental difference will be the fullest publicity of all relevant economic statistics throughout the whole system. All organs of a socialist economy will work, so to speak, within glass walls.

Socialism has also been defined *tout court* * as equality of income [1] and, although few socialists would adopt this definition without reserve, socialism of nearly all schools has been held to imply equality in one or other of the following senses:

(*a*) a greater approach to equality in the distribution of wealth;

(*b*) equality of economic opportunity, in a more genuine sense than that of bourgeois liberalism;

(*c*) distribution according to need rather than according to effort or product.

In effect, these three tend to the same result, since both equality of opportunity and distribution according to need would lead to greater equality of actual income than exists under capitalism, although not to an absolute arithmetical equality. Nor is the concept of greater equality unrelated to the definitions in terms of social ownership or of planned production. Since the most glaring inequalities of actual income and nearly all the inequalities of opportunity are based on the private ownership of land and capital, social ownership will almost certainly tend to greater equality. Also, since the object of genuine economic planning (as opposed to the sham "planning" which, like so-called "rationalization," is simply a euphemism for the restriction of production and the destruction

of machinery organized by monopoly-capitalism) is to substitute a conscious and direct relation of production to human needs for a relation arrived at by an indirect mechanism through the unconscious pushes and pulls of innumerable private interests in the market, a true planned economy would approach to some extent the ideal of distribution according to need.

The formal definition of socialism . . . is as follows:

Socialism is an economic organization of society in which the material means of production are owned by the whole community and operated by organs representative of and responsible to the community according to a general economic plan, all members of the community being entitled to benefit from the results of such socialized planned production on the basis of equal rights.

This definition includes the three elements of

(i) social ownership of the means of production,

(ii) economic planning,

(iii) equality.

It purposely, however, leaves vague two points:

(*a*) how society is to work the productive equipment that it owns, whether through government departments, public utility corporations, national guilds, co-operative societies, or what not;

(*b*) exactly how the social product is to be distributed, whether according to service or need, whether in separate shares to individuals, or in communal supplies and services.

But it does explicitly rule out irresponsible private enterprise, and the continuance of any form of privileged income or of class inequality in the division of the social product.

. . . . .

### PLANNING AND FREEDOM

The usual objection that is made to economic planning of any sort (and *a fortiori* †

---

[1] G. Bernard Shaw, *The Intelligent Woman's Guide to Socialism and Capitalism*, pp. 19, 49, 68, 94, 297, 343.

ED. NOTE: * Briefly, simply. † All the more.

to socialist planned economy) is that it necessarily destroys freedom. "Goods will be provided according to need, but according to the planning authority's idea of what people need and not according to their own idea of what they need." "People will be regimented and ordered to their various jobs without being allowed any say in the matter." The planner's motive, when it is not "the sadistic desire to destroy the rich," is "meddlesomeness," "the desire to assert themselves at the expense of others," or a plain "lust for power." "Scratch a would-be planner and you will find a would-be dictator."

Now there is no doubt that a planned economy affords great opportunities to any dictator who manages to capture the planning machinery; but dictatorship is not an inherent characteristic of planned economy. So much of the liberal indictment of planning must be admitted as refers to the *possibility* of the destruction of freedom under planned economy. In the hands of an irresponsible controller (or group of controllers) it *could* be made the greatest tyranny that the world has ever seen. But must we admit the *necessity* of such a destruction of freedom? Planning involves a conscious choice of ends. But may not freedom be the end chosen? Is it not possible to plan for freedom, for the abolition of the inequality which makes freedom a sham under capitalism, and yet retain enough of the price-system to ensure the satisfaction of a plurality of ends as expressed by individual consumers? Planning is a means, not an end, and it is as possible to plan for freedom as to plan for anything else. The end to which planning is directed depends on the wishes of that section of the community which can, in the ultimate analysis, control the actions of the planning body. The price of liberty is eternal vigilance, under planning as under any other system, and if people wish to be free they must deliberately choose freedom and pursue it.

It is claimed, however, that freedom is essentially incompatible with planning; that even if a socialist planner wished to realize freedom he could not do so and

remain a planner. The argument is that, since planning involves the deliberate choice of an end to be followed, it necessarily involves the rejection of all alternative ends and the abandonment of all possibilities of change. Now I believe this argument to involve a false antithesis. It is like the argument which asserts that import duties cannot be at the same time protective and remunerative. "Either the duty keeps out the foreign products or the foreign products enter in spite of the duty. In the first case the duty brings in no revenue; in the second case the domestic industry enjoys no protection." Of course, in actuality, *some* foreign wares may enter in spite of the duty, but less than would be imported if there were no duty. There may therefore be *some* measure of protection to home producers and *some* revenue for the treasury. So it is with the presumed antithesis of planning and flexibility. A plan can always be changed. When under the existing system a businessman plans the construction of a factory or a government commission plans the reform of an agricultural market, the decisions taken are not immutable, nor are they put beyond the pale of public discussion. What is true of the partial plans that can exist in the interstices of capitalism may be true of the more comprehensive plans of a socialist community.

But, it is agreed, decisions once taken cannot be modified without loss. As soon as the possibility of change is admitted the element of risk creeps into the economic problem. This must be admitted. Elasticity of organization and technique does introduce a penumbra of uncertainty into all economic calculations. If the community desires an economic machine that is responsive to changes in individual taste or productive technique it must pay for the advantages of flexibility by a certain margin of unavoidable loss. This is the cost of risk-bearing. It exists in planned as in unplanned economy. But is the only means of achieving flexibility the abandonment of the whole direction of resources to the company promoter and the advertising expert?

It is argued that the social cost of risk-bearing must be greater in a planned economy because wherever a wrong choice is made its effects are more widely spread, while individualism retains the saving grace of averages and random samples. But could the errors of a socialistic order well exceed those of capitalism as exemplified in the British stock exchange boom of 1928[1] or the orgy of foreign lending by America in 1927–8?[2]

It might be argued that, nevertheless, a planned society would generate a psychological atmosphere in which it would be difficult to admit mistakes or to change fundamentals of a plan. In particular, an unwillingness to sacrifice sunken capital would lead to the suppression of the desire to experiment and innovate. But this argument is refuted by those who object against planning that it tends to push technical improvements further than economic calculus would indicate. Surely the truth is that both tendencies will exist: the purely administrative type of mind will favour routine and a static order, while the technical mind will delight in novelty for novelty's sake. An effective system of social cost-accounting should be capable of holding the balance between these two opposing tendencies. We must have recourse to the devices of Measurement and Publicity.

But suppose that, in spite of our devices for securing a flexible equilibrium within planned economy, society does rush to one or another of these extremes—either a slowing down of material progress or a misplaced zeal for technical improvements unrelated to economic welfare—what then? Even the sternest critic of planning admits that the standard of living need not necessarily *fall*: economic progress will be slower than it might have been under an alternative system. But may it not be possible to balance the economic progress against other social ends—e.g. equality of oppor-

tunity and liberty for the common man? . . . There is not an all-or-nothing choice between a planned economy, rigidly unchangeable and unchanging, on the one hand, and a perfectly flexible market economy . . . on the other. It is a question of adjusting the proportions of conscious planning and of formal, market-economic freedom in order to maximize real social freedom. Some inequality, some rigidity, some irrationality, some lack of ideal symmetry and order, must perhaps be tolerated; but the resultant balance might conceivably produce a more satisfactory blend of order and freedom than that which we enjoy to-day.

. . . . .

Let us consider just what economic freedom means within the limitations of a socialist commonwealth. It certainly does not mean economic freedom in the sense in which the nineteenth-century economist understands these words. It does not mean freedom to own and to draw income from the ownership of land and other material means of production, although it is not incompatible with the personal *use* of such means of production (as under leases), nor with the personal ownership of tools and small machines such as an independent craftsman may use. But under modern conditions of technique the great mass of means of production exists in the form of machinery and equipment that can only be worked by labour associated on a large scale. And under socialism no individual or group of individuals may own the means whereby other men work and live. Nor does it mean freedom to organize production on individual lines for the sake of private profit, with all the secrecy, deception, speculation with other people's livelihood, and possibility of monopoly that this entails; although it is not incompatible with non-profit-making ventures on a co-operative basis for genuine experiment or for the provision by individually organized activity of highly specialized satisfactions of an aesthetic, literary, religious, or political nature. But it does mean freedom for the

---

[1] See "The Results of the 1928 New Issue Boom," *Economic Journal*, December 1931. Also *Macmillan Report* (Cd. 3897/1931), section 386.

[2] See League of Nations *World Economic Survey*, 1931–2, pp. 39, 42.

consumer, in the sense of a free choice of satisfactions within the limits of a system of prices reflecting the relative scarcity of different goods; and it does mean freedom for the producer, in the sense of a free choice of occupations within the limits of a system of wage-rates reflecting the relative social importance of different kinds of work. In other words, free price-formation is restored at the two ends of the chain of production, at the end of consumer's goods and at the end of personal productive services. It may be fairly claimed that, in these two respects, freedom will be more adequate than under capitalism.

For the consumer, liberty of choice will be implemented by the reduction of advertisement to its proper social function of stimulating interest and imparting information; whereas to-day the consumer is only too often "free" to choose between commodities whose real properties are obscured in a smoke cloud of misinformation and irrational appeal. Standardization of consumption goods is often decried as an infringement of the consumer's liberty of choice. In truth a considerable measure of standardization is a necessary condition of any rational liberty of choice. . . . An enormous variety of brands of chocolate, toothpaste, or petrol, a bewildering range of diverse kinds of clothes, furniture, and household gear, differing from each other by almost imperceptible shades of quality, far from offering the consumer increased opportunities of choice, really paralyse his powers of discrimination and decision. Only when the number of lines competing for his notice are reduced to a few varieties with well-marked characteristics does choice cease to be a mere gamble and become a rational decision. Moreover, the index of consumer demand will no longer be distorted by gross inequalities in consumers' incomes or by monopoly elements in the prices of goods.

For the producer, liberty of choice will be a reality when it is exercised with a full knowledge of the possibilities of the labour market and with full opportunities for training and equipment, unhindered by lack of means on the part of the candidate or the candidate's parents. Moreover, for those who dislike the prospect of salaried or wage-paid public employment, there will always be the emergency escape of the free-lance occupations and (possibly) of the private sector. . . .

Economic freedom in this sense is, however, only the beginning of freedom. . . . What socialists claim is that not merely economic freedom for consumers and producers but also liberty in the wider sense—political freedom as understood by the nineteenth-century liberals—is impossible under capitalism. Men cannot be free in a class-society: men cannot be free when the means whereby they live are owned by a few. The control over public opinion that is given by ownership of newspaper capital, like Beaverbrook's or Hearst's, the power of intimidation over votes that is possessed by a large local employer of labour, the power of wealth to impose its prestige upon wavering and indifferent voters—all these make a mockery of democracy under capitalism. Security of livelihood, a large measure of economic equality, the conscious control of social production by society— these are the guarantees of true liberty. Only by such restrictions as those mentioned at the beginning of this section can insecurity, inequality, and the arbitrary control of the private owner over men's destinies be kept at bay: only by these curtailments of liberty in small things can liberty in great things be purchased.

Liberals profess to fear the possibility of tyranny under socialism. As the sole employer and the sole purveyor of goods, the socialist commonwealth is expected to exercise its powers in the spirit of a monopolist under capitalism. But this expectation is no more reasonable than the expectation that a democratic state would reproduce all the vices of an absolutist or oligarchical state. Not the formal relations of economic or political organization, but the underlying social relations (and, above all, the relations of classes), are the decisive factor in the issue of freedom or tyranny. What is the source and origin of tyranny? Exploitation. Men tyrannize over other men, in political and economic relations, in order to obtain their services otherwise than by voluntary consent and co-operation. Abolish exploitation and substitute a society of freely co-operating agents, then the root cause of tyranny is taken away. If the basic cause of tyranny in the exploitation of one class by another is removed, there still remains the possibility of isolated and individual abuses of communally delegated power. This danger is a real one and the liberal's fear is to this extent justified. But the remedy is suggested by the historical parallel between the struggles for political and for economic rights. The task of the liberal in winning political liberty and equality was a twofold one. First, the control of the state-machine had to be wrested from the class that had previously monopolized it. The Sovereign People had to be placed on the throne of a Louis XIV. Secondly, the nature of the state-machine had to be transformed from an instrument of power into an instrument of service. The arbitrary elements in its action had to be abolished and it had to be made the means of serving the interests of all citizens on equal terms. In Dicey's words, the Rule of Law was set up. The same twofold task awaits the socialist, in establishing economic liberty and equality. First, the control of the economic machine must be wrested from the class that now monopolizes it. The community as a whole must step into the shoes of a J. P. Morgan or a Harry McGowan. Secondly, the nature of the economic machine must be transformed from an instrument of profit into an instrument of service. As part of this change a machinery of constitutional safeguards and guaranteed rights must be evolved. The Rule of Law must be extended from the political to the economic sphere. The part played in the bourgeois liberal order by property rights and enforcement of contract will be played in a socialist order by a Labour Code, which will enforce reasonable workshop customs and give remedies for victimization, and by a legally enforceable code of Consumers' Rights.

In a socialist society the distinction, always artificial, between economics and politics will break down; the economic and the political machinery of society will fuse into one. The problem of economic liberty will then become the same as the problem of political liberty. During the period of transition from a capitalist to a socialist society both forms of liberty may be abridged, just as during the early phases of the struggles which made possible the establishment of religious and political liberty those very liberties were temporarily eclipsed. Luther and Calvin persecuted, yet the ultimate influence of their teaching was tolerance; Cromwell and Robespierre ruled arbitrarily, yet the ultimate influence of their rule was to establish civil liberty. So Lenin and Stalin have shown scant respect for the preferences of the individual consumer, yet, if they shall have been the means of establishing a classless society, their ultimate influence will be for economic liberty. After a socialist order has been safely established, the *raison d'être* of restrictions on liberty will have ceased. There will no longer be a class with a privileged relation to the means of production. The planning authorities will become responsible to the whole body of the community.

This may be so, is the reply, but even a classless society may deny freedom of experience to minorities. Will those who manage the printing presses of the perfect socialist community be as ready to print Bibles or copies of *Science and Health* as to print Marx's *Capital,* in response to an equivalent effective demand of consumers? There is no reason why a socialist economy should not have room for voluntary associations formed for the publication of books, pamphlets, and periodicals. In this way, political, religious, and cultural minorities could express and propagate their views. But such associations would require, in addition, to obtain paper and the use of printing machinery from those organs of collective economy that owned and controlled them. Thus we arrive at the necessity of some machinery for vindicating consumers' rights, analogous to the legal machinery evolved by liberalism from 1776 onwards for vindicating the individual's political rights to life, liberty, and the pursuit of happiness.

Just as in the liberal political society of the nineteenth century the law was conceived of as a sort of automatic machine for defining and vindicating personal rights, that would operate indifferently whoever dropped the penny in the slot, whether he belonged to a majority or a minority; so a socialist community should conceive of the economic organization of society as a machine for satisfying individual needs, accessible on equal terms to all citizens. The socialist commonwealth ought to write into its constitution explicit guarantees of economic as well as of political liberty, and implement them by due process of law, especially in the matter of the printed and broadcast word.

We should not conceive of the administrative organs of a socialist economy as an extension of the powers of the *state*, but rather as the creation of the new form of activity of *society*. The state, as it exists under capitalism, is a product of class antagonism, and of national antagonism ultimately rooted in class antagonism. . . . With the achievement of a classless society, the state will undergo a complete transformation. Its functions as the bearer of authority will diminish largely in importance; its functions of impersonal administration in matters of common interest will probably gain in efficiency by being freed from association with its coercive functions. If it is desired to compare the organs of a socialist economy with existing institutions, an enlarged and universalized consumers' cooperative society would afford a better parallel than the political state.

But even under the most perfect constitution a democracy may act tyrannously to minorities: the ultimate guarantee resides not in written constitutions, but in the social structure of the community, thus ultimately in the material relations of production. The guarantee of liberty in a socialist community would be the absence of the causes which nowadays make human beings desire to deny one another liberty; in other words, the true pledge of freedom is the abolition of economic classes.

# 33 Henry C. Simons: *A Positive Program for Laissez Faire*

❧ *Is it possible, through deliberate public policy, to develop an economy based upon a consistent application of the principle of free competition? Is it desirable to do so? What would an economic system based upon a thoroughgoing policy of "laissez faire" look like? What institutions and practices current in our economic system would be changed by such a program, and what might be the results in terms of stability and productivity?*

*In the reading below, Henry C. Simons (1899–1946) directs himself to these questions. Simons was Professor of Economics at the University of Chicago and was throughout his career an opponent both of socialism and of what he regarded as the quasi-monopolistic economy of the twentieth century. He wrote A Positive Program* for Laissez-Faire (*1934*), Personal Income Taxation (*1938*), Economic Policy for a Free Society (*1948*), *and* Federal Tax Reform (*1950*). *Our selection is one of his best known essays and is reproduced from his* Economic Policy for a Free Society, *pp. 41–56, with permission of the publishers, the University of Chicago Press.*

We have witnessed abroad the culmination of movements from constitutional government to dictatorships, from freedom back to authority. This spectacle, for most of us, is revolting; and the experience, something to be avoided at all costs. Yet, faced with the same problems, we adopt measures and accept political slogans which call explicitly for an "American compromise," that is to say, for more authority and less freedom here and now. Thus do we justify and rationalize a policy and accelerating movement in a direction which we overwhelmingly disapprove.

The real enemies of liberty in this country are the naive advocates of managed economy or national planning; but with them we must agree on one vital point, namely, that there is now imperative need for a sound, positive program of economic legislation. Our economic organization is perilously near to disintegration and collapse. In earlier periods it could be expected to become increasingly strong if only protected from undue political interference. Now, however, it has reached a condition where it can be saved only through adoption of the wisest measures by the state. Modern democracy arose under conditions which made only negligible demands for intelligence in economic legislation; it remains soon to be seen whether democracy can survive when those demands are very great.

It is the main purpose of this tract to criticize current policies, simply by defining the main elements of a vitally different program. Part I undertakes to present the minimum of general analysis or diagnosis which seems essential for exposition of the program.

Much significance has been, and should be, attached to the simultaneous development of capitalism and democracy. Indeed, it seems clear that *none of the precious "freedoms" which our generation has inherited can be extended, or even maintained, apart from an essential freedom of enterprise—apart from a genuine "division of labor" between competitive and political controls.* The existence (and preservation) of a competitive situation in private industry makes possible a minimizing of the responsibilities of the sovereign state. It frees the state from the obligation of adjudicating endless, bitter disputes among persons as participants in different industries and among owners of different kinds of productive services. In a word, it makes possible a political policy of laissez faire.

.  .  .  .  .

The great errors of economic policy in the past century may be defined—and many of our present difficulties explained —in terms of excessive political interference with relative prices, and in terms of disastrous neglect of the positive responsibilities of government under a free-enterprise system. Our governments have tinkered interminably with relative prices (witness the tariff). On the other hand, they have never really tried to maintain effectively competitive conditions in industry (witness the "rule of reason" and the absurd grants of powers to corporations). They have evaded—when they have not abused—their responsibility of controlling the currency (witness the growth of private banks which provide, and potentially can destroy, all but a small percentage of our total effective circulating media). Moreover, they have scarcely recognized the obligation, or the opportunities, of mitigating inequality through appropriate fiscal practices—that is to say, through appropriate definition of the institution of property. Consequently, the so-called failure of capitalism (of the free-enterprise system, of competition) may reasonably be interpreted as primarily a failure of the political state in the discharge of its minimum responsibilities under capitalism. This view may suggest reasons for skepticism with reference to currently popular schemes for curing our ills.

It seems clear, at all events, that there is an intimate connection between freedom of enterprise and freedom of discussion and that political liberty can survive only within an effectively competitive economic system. Thus, *the great enemy of democracy is monopoly, in all its forms:* gigantic corporations, trade associations and other agencies for price control, trade-unions—or, in general, organization and concentration of power within functional classes. . . .

. . . . .

. . . For one who prizes political liberty, there can be no sanguine view as to where the proliferation of organization leads. If the state undertakes, under popular government (or perhaps under any other form), to substitute its control for competition in the determination of relative prices and relative wages, the situation must soon become chaotic. Congressional meddling with relative prices through tariff legislation has never hurt us severely, for we have had within our tariff walls an enormous free-trade area. The legislative history of the American tariff, however, does suggest most clearly the probable outcome of an experiment in the political manipulation of the whole structure of internal prices. That our political system could endure either the economic effects of such control or its consequences for political morality is at least highly improbable.

If popular government did for a time achieve that infinitely wise and effective control which would be necessary merely to prevent economic collapse, the system could not survive. Political determination of relative prices, of relative returns from investment in different industries, and of

relative wages in different occupations implies settlement by peaceful negotiation of conflicts too bitter and too irreconcilable for deliberate adjudication and compromise. The petty warfare of competition within groups can be kept on such a level that it protects and actually promotes the general welfare. The warfare among organized economic groups, on the other hand, is unlikely to be more controllable or less destructive than warfare among nations. . . .

Suppression of the competitive struggle within economic groups, and their organization into collective fighting units, will create conditions such that only ruthless dictatorship can maintain the degree of order necessary to survival of the population in an economy of intricate division of labor. . . .

. . . . .

It seems nowise fantastic, indeed, to suggest that present developments point toward a historic era which will bear close resemblance at many points to the early Middle Ages. With the disappearance of the vestiges of free trade among nations will come intensification of imperialism and increasingly bitter and irreconcilable conflicts of interest internationally. With the disappearance of free trade within national areas will come endless, destructive conflict among organized economic groups—which should suffice, without assistance from international wars, for the destruction of Western civilization and its institutional heritage.

Thus, the increasing organization of interest groups (monopoly) and the resurgence of mercantilism ("planning") promise an end of elaborate economic organization (of extensive division of labor, nationally and internationally), and an end of political freedom as well. . . .

. . . . .

Competition and laissez faire have not brought us to heaven. The severe depression, regarded as resulting from competition *instead of from the lack of it,* naturally produces an impairment of our affection for the system. But the widespread disposition to deprecate our institutional heritage seems explicable only in terms of general unwillingness and inability to consider seriously what the actual alternatives are—where new roads lead—or, whatever their destination, how much human suffering must be endured on the way. . . .

·  ·  ·  ·  ·

Let us consider now what circumstances are most inimical, within the old system, to production of a large social income (to economic efficiency). The effective functioning of our economic organization requires full utilization of existing resources, including labor, use of the best available technical methods, and, less obviously, economical allocation of resources among available, alternative uses. This latter aspect of the problem may well be emphasized here.

Any judgment of efficiency implies a standard or scale of values—merely physical efficiency is an absurd conception. For economic analysis, such a scale of values is available in the market values (prices) of commodities. These market values, being the result of competitive purchase by persons free to utilize purchasing power as they please, may be accepted as measuring roughly the relative importance (for the community) of physical units of different things. To be sure, these prices are the result of free disposition of purchasing power by individuals of widely different income circumstances. But the problems of efficiency and of inequality may usefully be separated for purposes of discussion—and properly, if one accepts the view that the appropriate measures for improving efficiency and for mitigating inequality are, within fairly wide limits, distinct and independent.

Efficient utilization of resources implies an allocation such that units of every kind of productive service make equally important (valuable) contributions to the social product in all the different uses among which they are transferable. Such allocation will be approximated if, by virtue of highly competitive conditions, resources move freely from less productive (remunerative) to more productive employments. It is an essential object of monopoly, on the other hand, to maintain an area of abnormally high yield (productivity) and to prevent such influx of resources as would bring the monopolized industry down to the common level. Any effectively organized group may be relied upon to use to this end the power which organization brings.

Monopoly thus means the exclusion of available resources for uses which, on the market-value standard, are more important, and, therefore, means diversion of resources to less important uses. Every organized group, whether of employers or of workers, possesses great power, both for exploiting consumers and for injuring other groups of producers to whose industries resources are diverted by virtue of the monopoly restrictions.

Such characterization fits best the case of the strongest and most nearly complete monopolies. For the more typical, partial monopolies (the organization basis for which the National Recovery Act has sought to establish everywhere), the situation is somewhat different and possibly worse from the viewpoint of the community at large. The looser forms of organization for price maintenance and output control (cartels, trade associations), while able to enforce output limitation upon existing firms, are seldom able to restrict the growth of investment (to control the number and size of firms); nor does their position permit them to withhold output quotas from newcomers in the industry. Such arrangements lead to gross wastage of investment as well as to exploitation of consumers. New firms, attracted by the high returns resulting from price maintenance, will construct plants; and they will be drawn into the organization and given their appropriate quotas (presumably on the basis of "capacity"). This means reduction in the quotas of other firms and increasingly meager utilization of plant capacity throughout the industry. Finally, producers within the organization may obtain, in spite of the price maintenance, no higher return on investment than prevails in competitive fields. But consumers will be paying heavily, in higher prices, for the policies of the organization; and the industry will end up with much smaller production, in spite of much larger total investment, than would have obtained under competitive conditions. . . .

The situation is strikingly similar with respect to trade-union monopoly, which usually involves a similarly partial monopoly power. The main device of trade union strategy is the maintenance of the standard rate of pay, through collective bargaining. The raising of rates of wages to a particular field above the competitive level, by whatever methods of coercion, serves to diminish the volume of employment available within that field—inducing economy of such labor by substitution (of machinery and of other labor) and relative contraction of the industries requiring such labor. If the organization admits newcomers freely and rations employment, the occupation may continue to grow in numbers, or fail to decline, in spite of decline in the total amount of employment available—the increased rate of pay more than offsetting, for a time, the reduction in employment available per man. As with the trade association, numbers may increase until the members are no better off than they would have been without any organization at all. Yet product prices in the industries concerned will be higher; and a large part of the community's labor resources will be wasted—a situation which roughly describes, except for the denouement, recent conditions in coal-mining in the Midwest. If the union can prevent entrance into the trade, if the older members are given full employment before newcomers are employed at all, or if the demand for this kind of labor is highly elastic, the effects of the wage control in this particular field will manifest themselves largely in diversion of labor into less important *and less remunerative* occupations. In any case, the diseconomies for the community are sufficiently evident.

The gains from monopoly organization in general are likely, of course, to accrue predominantly to the strong and to be derived at the expense of the weak. Among producers, organization is least expensive and most easily achieved, as well as most effective, within groups whose members are unusually large and prosperous at the outset. Among workers, the bias is not less striking. The most highly skilled and most highly remunerated trades are the trades where organization is least difficult and where the fighting strength of groups once organized is greatest. Little evidence, inductive or analytic, can be conjured up to support the popular conception of trade-unionism as a device for raising incomes at the bottom of the scale. Its possibilities lie mainly in the improvement of the position of labor's aristocracy—and largely at the expense of labor generally. Here as elsewhere the gains from monopoly are exploitative. The restriction of employment in the more remunerative occupations injures other laborers, both as consumers and as sellers of services rendered more abundant in other areas by the restriction.

Another major factor in the inefficient allocation of resources is to be found in government regulation and interference. Tariff legislation is again the main case in point, for the protective tariff is essentially a device for forcing resources from uses of higher to uses of lower productivity. Moreover, there are good reasons for believing that political controls will generally work out in this way. Government interference with relative prices is in the nature of arbitration of conflicts of interest between minority producer groups and consumers (the whole community); and such interference inevitably involves decisions which have regard primarily for the interests of the minorities. Producers are, from a political point of view, organized, articulate groups; and it is in the nature of the political process to conciliate such groups. Anyone may detect the notorious economic fallacies, and thus see the dictates of sound policy, if he will look at every issue from the viewpoint of consumers; but no politician can be expected to do this, or to act on his conclusions if he does, except in a world where legislators are motivated primarily by the desire to be retired at the next election. People as consumers are unorganized and inarticulate, and, representing merely the interests of the community as a whole, they always will be. This fact, perhaps, suggests the decisive argument for laissez faire and against "planning" of the now popular sort.

.   .   .   .   .

Public regulation of private monopoly would seem to be, at best, an anomalous arrangement, tolerable only as a temporary expedient. Halfhearted, sporadic, principleless regulation is a misfortune for all concerned; and systematic regulation, on the basis of any definite and adequate principle, would leave private ownership almost without a significant function or responsibility to discharge. Analysis of the problem, and examination of experience to date, would seem to indicate the wisdom of abandoning the existing scheme of things with respect to the railroads and utilities, rather than of extending the system to include other industries as well. Political control of utility charges is imperative, to be sure, for competition simply cannot function effectively as an agency of control. We may endure regulation for a time, on the dubious assumption that governments are more nearly competent to regulate than to operate. *In general, however, the state should face the necessity of actually taking over, owning, and managing directly, both the railroads and the utilities, and all other industries in which it is impossible to maintain effectively competitive conditions.* For industries other than the utilities, there still remains a real alternative to socialization, namely, the establishment and preservation of competition as the regulative agency.

Turning now to questions of justice, of equitable distribution, we may suggest that equitable distribution is at least as important with respect to power as with reference to economic goods or income; also, that the cause of justice, perhaps in both directions, would be better served if well-intentioned reformers would reflect seriously on what their schemes imply with respect to the distribution of power. Surely there is something unlovely, to modern as against medieval minds, about marked inequality of either kind. A substantial measure of inequality may be unavoidable or essential for motivation; but it should be recognized as evil and tolerated only so far as the dictates of expediency are clear.

If we dislike extreme inequality of power, it is appropriate to view with especial misgivings the extension of political (and monopoly) control over relative prices and incomes. Either socialization or the mongrel system of "national planning" implies and requires extreme concentration of political power, under essentially undemocratic institutions. A system of democratic socialism is admittedly an attractive ideal; but, for the significant future, such a system is merely a romantic dream. On the other hand, it seems unlikely that any planners or controllers, with the peculiar talents requisite for obtaining dictatorial power, would be able to make decisions wise enough to keep an elaborate economic organization from falling apart. Even if one regards that prospect as not unpromising, the implied division of power between controllers and controllees would seem an intolerable price for increased efficiency.

An important factor in existing inequality, both of income and of power, is the gigantic corporation. We may recognize, in the almost unlimited grants of powers to corporate bodies, one of the greatest sins of governments against the free-enterprise system. There is simply no excuse, except with respect to a narrow and specialized class of enterprises, for allowing corporations to hold stock in other corporations—and no reasonable excuse (the utilities apart) for hundred-million-dollar corporations, no matter what form their property may take. . . .

Another cardinal sin of government against the free-enterprise system is manifest in the kind of institution of property which the state has inflicted upon that system. It has lain within the powers of the political state, in defining rights of property and inheritance, to prevent the extreme inequality which now obtains; and the appropriate changes might still be effected without seriously impairing the efficiency of the system. In a practical sense, there is not much now wrong with the institution of property except our arrangements with respect to taxation. Instead of collecting their required revenues in such manner as to diminish the concentration of wealth and income, governments have relied on the whole upon systems of levies which actually aggravated inequality. Until recently (and the situation is not strikingly different now) governments have financed their activities largely by conglomerations of miscellaneous exactions which have drawn funds predominantly from the bottom of the income scale. Modern fiscal arrangements, like those of medieval barons, must be explained largely in terms of efforts to grab funds wherever they could be reached with least difficulty—to levy upon trade wherever tribute could most easily be exacted—and with almost no regard for consequences in terms of either economic efficiency or personal justice.

The problem of stabilization, of maintaining reasonably full employment of resources, calls for emphasis mainly upon two factors, one of which again is monopoly. If all prices moved up and down with substantial uniformity, changes in the general level of prices would have only unimportant effects upon the volume of production or employment. A major factor in the cycle phenomenon is the quite unequal flexibility of different sets of prices and, more explicitly, the stickiness of prices which, for the bulk of industry, determine out-of-pocket operating (marginal) costs. This stickiness of prices reflects, first, competition-restraining organization and, second, a widespread disposition to sacrifice volume to price— which is the characteristic exercise of monopoly power. Decisively important in the total situation is the exceeding inflexibility

of wages—the explanation of which would require attention to many factors, of which effective labor organization is but one. To some extent it reflects merely a subtle sort of defensive cooperation among workers to protect themselves in a market which is often only nominally competitive on the employers' side. To some extent it involves employer deference to an attitude of the public, which condemns wage-cutting and yet accepts wholesale discharge of employees as unavoidable and unreprehensible. More interesting than the stickiness of wages, if not more important, is the price policy in depression of those basic industries which have long since disciplined themselves along lines now widely approved, against "unfair" (!) competition. Equally significant, or more so, is the depression behavior of railroad rates and the charges in other public utilities subject to government regulation, especially freight rates. At all events, the existence of extreme inflexibility in large areas of the price structure is one of the primary factors in the phenomenon of severe depression. This inflexibility increases the economic loss and human misery accompanying a given deflation, and it causes deflation itself to proceed much farther than it otherwise would.

The major responsibility for the severity of industrial fluctuations, however, falls directly upon the state. Tolerable functioning of a free-enterprise system presupposes effective performance of a fundamental function of government, namely, regulation of the circulating medium (money). We should characterize as insane a governmental policy of alternately expanding rapidly and contracting precipitously the quantity of paper currency in circulation—as a malevolent dictator easily could do, first issuing currency to cover fiscal deficits, and then retiring currency from surplus revenues. Yet that is essentially the kind of monetary policy which actually obtains, by virtue of usurpation by private institutions (deposit banks) of the basic state function of providing the medium of circulation (and of private "cash" reserves). . . . Laissez faire, to repeat, implies a division of tasks between competitive and political controls; and the failure of the system, if it has failed, is properly to be regarded as a result of failure of the state, especially with respect to money, to do its part.

We have reached a situation where private-bank credit represents all but a small fraction of our total effective circulating medium. This gives us an economy in which significant disturbances of equilibrium set in motion forces which operate grossly to aggravate, rather than to correct, the initial maladjustments. When for any reason business earnings become abnormally favorable, bank credit expands, driving sensitive product prices farther out of line with sticky, insensitive costs; earnings become more favorable; credit expands farther and more rapidly; and so on and on, until costs finally do catch up, or until some speculative flurry happens to reverse the initial maladjustment. When earnings prospects are unpromising, credit contracts and earnings become still smaller and more unpromising. In an economy where costs (especially wages, freight rates, and monopoly prices in basic industries) are extremely inflexible downward,* the deflation might

continue indefinitely (until everyone was unemployed) if governments did not intervene (inflate) to save the banks or to mitigate human suffering.

Thus, the state has forced the free-enterprise system, almost from the beginning, to live with a monetary system as bad as could well be devised. If, as seems possible, both capitalism and democracy are soon to be swept away forever by a resurgence of mercantilism (by the efforts of persons who know not whither they lead), then to commercial banking will belong the uncertain glory of having precipitated the transition to a new era. Such is likely to be the case, even if our institutions survive this time the attentions of their misguided, if well-meaning, guardians. Capitalism seems to retain remarkable vitality; but it can hardly survive the political rigors of another depression; and banking, with the able assistance of monopoly, seems certain to give us both bigger and better depressions hereafter—unless the state does reassume and discharge with some wisdom its responsibility for controlling the circulating medium.

ED. NOTE:  * That is, these costs go down much less easily than they go up. They are "sticky" and likely to fail to fall in the downswing of the business cycle; this "stickiness" (unless, Simon says, counterbalanced by positive action) tends to prevent the readjustment called for by classical equilibrium theory.

SECTION B

## The great powers and their economic structures

# 34  Merle Fainsod and Lincoln Gordon: "Controlled Capitalism"—the United States

❦ *Throughout this volume, as is customary also in general discussion of the subject, the economy of the United States has been referred to as a "capitalist" or "free-enterprise" economy. As our earlier readings have shown us, however, this is an over-*

*simplification, useful only for certain purposes when we are making comparisons with other economies. Especially since 1900, the extent of governmental control of the economy, the forms of government regulation, and the degree to which government ought to guide economic affairs have been dominant themes of public discussion. It is important, therefore, in locating where we actually stand, to have a systematic summary of government's relation to the economy in the United States.*

*The following selection provides such a summary. It is excerpted from Chapters 1, 2, and 23 of* Government and the American Economy *(New York: W. W. Norton & Company, revised edition copyright 1948), by Merle Fainsod (1907–    ), who is Professor of Government and Administration at Harvard University, and Lincoln Gordon (1913–    ), who is Associate Professor of Business Administration at Harvard. It is reprinted with the publisher's permission.*

While it is impossible at the present time to anticipate either the volume or the duration of arms spending, or to appraise its future impact upon the economy, it may still be useful to summarize some of the basic characteristics of the economy upon which it is being superimposed. To do so is at least to indicate the context out of which present-day controls have emerged and with which they seek to cope.

In the first place, it is an economy characterized by considerable unevenness in distribution of income. According to the National Resources Committee study of the Distribution of Consumer Income in the United States in 1935–36,[1] more than 6,700,000 families and single individuals, or 17.01 per cent of the total, had annual incomes of $500 or less; more than 18,400,000, or 46.54 per cent of the total, had incomes of $1,000 or less; approximately 32,000,000, or 81.82 per cent of the total, had annual incomes of $2,000 or less. . . .

. . . . .

In the second place, it is an economy dominated on its industrial side by large-scale enterprise. Of the 1,730,000 employers covered by the Social Security Board records in 1937, 50 per cent of the employers, each one accounting for three or less employees, employed approximately 4 per cent of the workers. Seventy-six per cent of the employers, each one accounting for nine or less employees, employed only 11 per cent of the workers. At the other end of the scale, 1 per cent of the employers, each one accounting for 250 or more employees, employed 50 per cent of the workers. One hundred and ninety-five enterprises, approximately one one-hundredth of 1 per cent of the employer total, each enterprise employing 10,000 or more employees, accounted for 12.3 per cent of all workers.[2] The following table [3] indicates the importance of large-scale enterprise in four significant sectors of the economy:

| Activity | Percentage of total corporate assets accounted for by corporations with assets of $5,000,000 or more | Percentage of industry activity accounted for by corporations |
|---|---|---|
| Transportation and public utilities | 92.7% | 92% |
| Manufacturing | 65.8% | 92% |
| Mining and Quarrying | 64.8% | 96% |
| Finance | 77.7% | 84% |

As this table reveals, industry and finance are dominated by large-scale enterprise. On

[1] See *Statistical Abstract of the United States* (1939), p. 313.

[2] Temporary National Economic Committee, *Hearings*, Vol. I, pp. 99, 229 (1939).

[3] Table adapted from data in *ibid.*, pp. 108, 230.

the other hand, small business units are much more important in agriculture, retail trade, construction, and the service occupations.

In the third place, the economy is characterized by considerable concentration of control, with control particularly marked in certain areas. In 1929, according to the National Resources Committee, the two hundred largest nonfinancial corporations and their subsidiaries controlled 47.9 per cent of the assets of all nonfinancial corporations. By 1933, this proportion had increased to over 54 per cent.[1] The degree of control varies in different sectors and is not always a concomitant of size. The following table stresses concentration of control of output:[2]

| Product | Number of Companies | Per cent of output produced | Authority |
|---|---|---|---|
| Aluminum | 1 | 100 | Federal Trade Commission (1937) |
| Automobiles | 3 | 86 | Department of Commerce (1937) |
| Beef products | 2 | 47 | Federal Trade Commission (1935) |
| Cans | 3 | 90 | Federal Trade Commission |
| Cement | 5 | 40 | Federal Trade Commission (1931) |
| Cigarettes | 3 | 80 | Federal Trade Commission (1934) |
| Copper | 4 | 78 | Bureau of Mines (1935) |
| Corn binders | 4 | 100 | Federal Trade Commission (1936) |
| Corn planters | 6 | 91 | Federal Trade Commission (1936) |
| Iron ore | 4 | 64 | Bureau of Mines (1935) |
| Plate glass | 2 | 95 | Tariff Commission (1935) |
| Safety glass | 2 | 90 | Tariff Commission (1935) |
| Steel | 3 | 60.5 * | Tariff Commission (1935) |
| Whiskey | 4 | 58 | Federal Alcohol Authority (1937–38) |
| Zinc | 4 | 43 | Bureau of Mines (1935) |

* Steel percentage represents capacity, not output.

As this table indicates, in only one industry, the aluminum industry, does a single company completely dominate the industry. The characteristic pattern disclosed in the above table is that of a small group of enterprises, which together are able to control a large, and sometimes an overwhelming, proportion of the industrial output of a particular industry.

The consequences of this concentration are revealed in a fourth characteristic of the economy, the decline of competition in

[1] National Resources Committee, *The Structure of the American Economy* (1939), Part I, p. 107.
[2] This table is adapted from testimony before the T.N.E.C., Part I, *Economic Prologue*, p. 137.

many areas. In industries, such as those listed in the above table, prices are no longer determined altogether by the impersonal forces of supply and demand. Producers are in a position to influence price; prices become, in Gardiner Means's phrase, administered prices rather than market prices. Price control may assert itself in a variety of forms: by following the price leadership of a particular firm; by dividing or sharing the market; by price discrimination; by reducing output and employment rather than price in the face of declining demand; by the submission of identical bids; and by other forms of price behavior which indicate administrative co-ordination rather than co-ordination through the market place. The existence of a high degree of price control in some sectors of the economy and its absence in others tends to create serious problems of adjustment, as the example cited earlier of the relation of agriculture and industrial prices between 1929 and 1933 indicated. Disparities in the degree of price control exercised accentuate the effective bargaining power of the organized sector of the economy as against the unorganized; they also inspire counter-organization among the unorganized and efforts to utilize the instrumentalities of government to strengthen the bargaining power of weaker economic interests.

This emerging trend, which has run particularly strong in recent years, points to a fifth characteristic of the economy, the organization of hitherto little organized groups for effective economic action. The spread of trade associations, labor organizations, producers' co-operatives in the agricultural field, and consumers' co-operatives evidences the strength of this tendency in diverse fields. Particularly significant has been the recent invocation of governmental authority to buttress the bargaining power of some of these groups. Small independent firms, particularly in distribution, have sought to compensate for the mass power of large concerns through such legislation as the state chain-store tax and Fair Trade Acts, the Miller-Tydings Act, and the Robinson-Patman Act. Labor has attempted to strengthen its bargaining power by persuading government to set minimum labor standards and to guarantee and protect the right of collective bargaining. Farmers have organized to obtain large-scale government aid and to impose production, marketing, and price controls on the commodities which they produce. The result has undoubtedly been to increase the economic strength of hitherto weak interests; at the same time, additional rigidities are introduced into the economic system with possible lack of adaptive capacity in the face of changing economic conditions.

A sixth characteristic of the economy manifests itself in signs of increasing maturity. With the passing of the frontier and the exhaustion of free land, the period of land settlement has come to an end. Natural resources have largely been discovered and possessed. The rate of population growth is declining. The secular trend of industrial expansion appears to be no longer sharply upward. The community rate of savings continues high, but during the last decade the private sector of the economy has been unable to furnish adequate outlets for these savings in the form of new capital expansion. Businessmen have avoided large long-term capital commitments; new investment has been closely geared to the current rate of consumer demand.

As a result of these and other developments, still another characteristic of the economy crystallized—the increasingly important role played by government. The obligation of government to provide a measure of economic security was recognized. The limited, laissez-faire view of the state gave way to a new conception of the positive service state, with government assuming major responsibility for maintaining the stability of the national economy and conserving resources, natural and human. The budget became a vehicle to redistribute income, to provide social services, and to expand public enterprise.

Some of the salient aspects of this vast increase in the economic powers of government will be analyzed in the pages which follow. It is important to remember that this increase may be only partly accounted for by the depression ushered in by the stock market crash of 1929. In a larger sense, it represents a response to the new world created by modern technology and industry. The insecurities which they have generated have led to a growing dependence on government to redress the balance and guarantee well-being. The old economy of small trade, free competition, and equality of bargaining power lent itself to adjustments on the economic plane. There was relatively little pressure for government to intervene. The new economy of large-scale enterprise, concentration of economic power, administered prices, and maladjustment of income invites political adjustments. The pressure for government to intervene comes from disadvantaged business groups, as well as farmers, laborers, investors, and consumers. The new activities of government reflect these demands; they crystallize the adjustments of a democratic community to the facts of the new economy.

### THE ORGANIZATION OF ECONOMIC INTERESTS

Three basic interests—business, labor, and agriculture—seek to determine the content of public economic policy in the United States. Each has its own primary objectives, its own special resources, its own organizational forms, and its own tactics and strategy. Each, in turn, is a mosaic of many particular interests, not necessarily harmonious and frequently expressing their aspirations through independent political activity. The pattern of evolving public policy reflects the interplay of these interests, their strength and their weakness, their skill in accommodation, and their ability to capitalize such resources as they have at their disposal. A realistic analysis of the activities of government in the economic system must take these interests in account, must consider their claims and their demands and the intensity of the pressure which they are able to bring to bear on the process of determining public policy.

*The Politics of Business.* The business-man's concern with government is no new phenomenon; wherever business and government have coexisted, the problem of adjusting their relationships has always arisen. The nature of this adjustment has varied; for long centuries the businessman was consigned to an inferior social and political status. In the determination of public policy, he was subordinate to the warrior, the priest, and the landholder.

The rise of business influence in the Western World is a relatively recent development. With the industrial revolution, the modern businessman began to come into his own and assert a new-found independence. He exerted his power to cast off the burdensome restrictions of law and custom which had been evolved to fit the needs of a feudal-aristocratic landholding society. In Europe he met varying degrees of opposition. In England and France he was comparatively successful in overcoming the resistance of agrarian, military, and church groups; in Germany, Italy, and Russia he encountered much more effective resistance from these quarters.

America presented a different picture. There was no feudal heritage to surmount, though the rise of the Southern slaveholding aristocracy soon presented an American analogue. The Southern slaveholding aristocrats might look upon the businessman with contempt, but, while they could resist, they were ineffective in checking his expanding power. Such influence as they could exert to impede the triumph of business enterprise was destroyed by the outcome of the Civil War.

The Civil War ushered in a new era of business ascendancy. As the wealth and power of the business community increased, government became increasingly sensitive to its demands and wishes. The influence of the successful businessman permeated the whole life of society. Social values were primarily business values, and politics was geared to the aspirations of the dominant business interests. To be sure, the businessman rarely played a public role in the political process. For the most part, he depended upon professional politicians to effect the necessary adjustments between business activities and public policies. His influence, however, did not suffer in potency because it was indirectly exercised.

The post-Civil War consolidation of business influence did not go unchallenged. Beginning at least as far back as the seventies, a ground swell of anti-big business and antimonopoly sentiment became apparent. But, despite periodic upsurges of popular dissatisfaction, business leadership pursued its course and was able to dissipate dissent with the visible evidence of rising national prosperity. The golden age of Coolidge registered this trend at its apogee.

There are many signs to indicate that this social milieu is now in process of reorientation. The depression years bred renewed disenchantment with business leadership. Labor, agrarian, and consumer groups became bolder in demanding, and more successful in invoking, the aid of government. As confidence in business leadership was undermined, these groups turned to government to attempt to provide that co-ordination of economic activity which the business community in the depression years had failed to supply. An expanding network of regulatory statutes bore witness to the new trend. Businessmen found their calculations hedged about by the decisions of public officials, responding to group pressures which were not business pressures and seeking to protect interests which the businessman could not readily identify as his own. In the face of this apparent threat, business groups found themselves re-examining their political strength and resources, and readjusting their political methods in the hope of stabilizing their political relationships in a fashion more satisfactory to themselves. The American political front, which businessmen first conquered and then largely took for granted, has again become a vital arena and a scene of struggle in which many businessmen feel that the hegemony of business itself is at stake.

. . . . . .

*The Methods of Business Politics.* Practitioners of the politics of business have various methods at their disposal. One may be called the method of persuasion, a second the method of attrition, and a third the method of concession or compromise.[1] Each of these methods may be practiced by the same business groups at different times; sometimes, elements of each may be used at the same time.

The method of persuasion as used here embraces everything from direct economic pressure at one end of the scale to any form of presentation of business aims and objectives to the general public at the other end. Economic pressure may take the form of threats of economic injury for undesired conduct, or it may take the form of bribes or other kinds of rewards to induce desired conduct. The presentation of business aims and objectives may involve utilizing every medium of reaching the public or governmental agencies—radio, newspapers, motion-pictures, outdoor billboards, advertisements, booklets, speakers, and the like—and it may include every variety of effort to manipulate, mold, or affect public opinion.

* * * * *

*The Politics of Labor.* If organization be the *sine qua non* of power, labor has still to realize its potentialities. In spite of the tremendous stimulus to labor organization provided by the Wagner Act and other New Deal measures, in 1940 the number of organized workers, including those affiliated with the A.F. of L., the C.I.O., and the Railroad Brotherhoods, probably did not exceed eight million. This was less than 25 per cent of the approximately thirty-five

[1] Some would add a fourth method, the method of coercion. The use of "big-stick" methods has been particularly common in dealing with labor difficulties, although it has by no means been confined to that field. Business violence in the labor field has recently come in for elaborate scrutiny by the La Follette Committee on the Violation of Free Speech and Rights of Labor, and the findings of that investigation may be consulted to illustrate the strategy of coercion at work. See *Report* of the Committee on Education and Labor, *Violation of Free Speech and Rights of Labor* (76th Cong., 1st Sess., 1939). See especially *Report No. 6*, Part II.

million workers eligible for membership in unions. More than half of this eight million total of organized workers represented gains of recent origin.

Organization has proved most feasible among skilled urban workers, especially in mines, factories, building, and transportation, and has spread only slowly to the unskilled and to clerical and low-income professional groups. Even among the organized, internal cleavages have been widespread and recurrent. Sectional antipathies, opposition of skilled to unskilled workers, of rural to urban workers, craft rivalries, conflicts between craft and industrial lines of organization, nationalist cleavages among immigrants, opposition between "native" and "alien," violence and "racketeering," all have played their part in labor history. Employers and employees in a particular industry frequently act together to urge upon government their common interest in special protection against competitors. Thus, the "labor interest" is far from unified; the labor movement is far from unanimous in agreement on its objectives or its methods.

* * * * *

*The Politics of Agriculture.* Farmers, like businessmen and workers, seek to promote their interests through organization. The business community is bound together by a highly centralized system of banking, financial, and corporate interrelationships. The factory provides a natural nucleus around which labor can coalesce. But the task of bringing farmers together presents special difficulties—obstacles of isolation, distance, and inbred individualism which are not easily overcome. Diversities of interests among farmers themselves have accentuated these difficulties. Dairy farmers, grain growers, sheep and cattle raisers, cotton growers, and fruit farmers each have more or less distinct interests which induce commodity consciousness rather than a broader agrarian consciousness. Growers of export crops feel differently about tariffs than do producers of wool or sugar who enjoy protection. Farm owners do not necessarily share the outlook of farm tenants, farm laborers, or migratory workers.

Despite these differences and difficulties, and despite the dwindling importance of the rural element in the total population, the political strength of agriculture in recent years has been formidable. The explanation is many sided. The plight of agriculture has spurred co-operation and submergence of differences among farmers themselves. Government agencies, particularly under the New Deal, have provided a strong impetus to organization. With the emergence of sharp business-labor cleavages in the industrial sector of the economy, the political significance of the farmers as a balance-of-power group has increased. This factor becomes all the more important in national politics because the composition of the Senate ensures a majority of Senators from rural states and the apportionment of seats in the House of Representatives favors the rural population. This same tendency toward rural overrepresentation is also present in most state legislatures.

. . . . .

*The Problem of Pressure Politics.* The organization of economic interests to influence policy has increased in scope and intensity with the expansion of governmental authority in the economic realm. Pressure politics has become an inextricable part of the American system of representation; the result has been to create what Walter Lippmann has called "a policy of pressure groups."

Many have expressed concern lest the tendency of organized groups to put primary emphasis on their own economic interests lead to a dispersive type of group utilitarianism which completely loses sight of the general welfare and transforms the political arena into a "battle royal of interests." That this danger is real need not be denied. Its very existence emphasizes the need of synthesis and adjustment through the machinery of the democratic process. . . .

## PROBLEMS OF A "MIXED" ECONOMY

As the American economy adjusted itself to the changing demands of the postwar years the vast increase in the economic responsibilities of government, both national and international, was reflected in the various forms of government activity which developed to give expression to these responsibilities. While the extent of governmental intervention varied considerably in different sectors of the economy, the impact of public action was widely felt, and in some areas it was of crucial significance. The structure of controls had come to embrace such diverse methods as enforcement of competition through the antitrust laws; direct price fixing (all-encompassing in time of war and specifically directed in time of peace to utilities, transportation and such special commodities as milk); influencing supply as in agriculture and oil; providing information as under the Securities Act; a species of cartelization as under the now defunct NRA and the bituminous coal legislation; licensing as in radio broadcasting and the security markets; subsidies as in agriculture, ocean shipping and air transport; the utilization of governmental purchasing to set labor standards as under the Walsh-Healey Act; public enterprise as in the power, atomic energy, banking and credit, and housing fields; conservation of natural resources; the development of social security programs; large-scale foreign loans; fiscal policy as an instrument of cyclical control; and promotion and regulation of the activities of labor, business, and agriculture in a variety of miscellaneous ways. The result of these developments was to produce a "mixed" economy, an economy in which public enterprise, partially government-regulated private enterprise, and relatively uncontrolled private enterprise all existed side by side.

An economy so constituted presented many problems which grew out of its past experiences and developing responsibilities. The central one for the future was that of ordering the relationships between the various sectors of the economy so that it could make a maximum contribution to national and world well-being.

In a constitutional democracy such as ours in which organized interests found free expression, no single pattern of relations between government and the economy could be ordained as fixed and unalterable. The development of public policy reflected the changing aspirations of the dominant political groups as well as underlying technical, social, and economic developments. The vast expansion of the economic powers of government during the thirties represented an adjustment to the demands of political forces and disadvantaged groups which had been stirred to activity by a severe depression and a slow economic recovery. The altered framework of relations between government and business in that decade produced serious tensions which expressed themselves in the existence of widespread mutual distrust between government and business leaders.

Such tensions were perhaps the inevitable accompaniment of a period of rapid change. The increased responsibilities which had been assumed by government ran counter to previously accepted tenets of business leadership concerning the appropriate functions of government. The resultant frictions and cleavages had destructive potentialities in terms of community well-being. The full possibilities of synchronizing governmental and business efforts to overcome economic maladjustments were not adequately realized.

It became fashionable in some circles to insist that efforts to mingle public enterprise and public control with private enterprise were doomed to futility. Some proponents of the Either-Or method of analysis argued that the only ultimate choice was between complete government regimentation on the one hand, or wholly unrestricted and uncontrolled capitalism on the other. While this posing of alternatives had a certain polemic value in controversy over public policy, it became increasingly

clear, as America turned to more conservative leadership in the postwar period, that the new leadership was quite unprepared to conduct a great crusade to sweep away the whole structure of inherited government controls. Indeed, in the interim, the Social Security Act and much of the social legislation of the thirties had passed from an area of sharp controversy into one of relatively widespread public acceptance. Meanwhile, important new responsibilities such as those involved in the Employment Act and the Atomic Energy Act were being assumed by the government. While legislation such as the Taft-Hartley Act marked a considerable reversal of the labor policy of the thirties, it in no sense presaged an attempt to repeal all that the New Deal stood for. The bulk of the American electorate appeared committed to an intermediate position which sought to preserve civil and political liberties and the advantages of private enterprise and which at the same time looked to government to provide basic securities and to guide entrepreneurial dynamics in the direction of economic expansion and community welfare.

Stress on such values excluded both the possibility of totalitarian economic planning and reliance on an unlimited laissez-faire view of governmental functions. Despite profound differences at the polar extremes of American opinion, there remained a hard core of agreement which a substantial proportion of the electorate was apparently prepared to endorse. This area of agreement may be briefly summarized:

1) Public policy should be directed toward the maintenance of competition over as wide an area as possible, on a plane of minimum fairness and commercial decency; where competition is ineffective, it should be replaced by positive regulation of price policies, public enterprise, or other special treatment.

2) Government should fix reasonable minimum wages and maximum hours, eliminate child labor, and provide adequate care for the aged and the helpless.

3) Government should accept an obliga-

tion to sustain and improve the position of agriculture in the national economy.

4) Government should guarantee the provision of adequate basic services, preferably through private enterprise, but if necessary by providing them itself.

5) Government should be charged with the responsibility of conserving natural and human resources and of taking measures to prevent economic stagnation or retrogression. While agreement on the precise content of such measures might be difficult to obtain, recognition of a broad responsibility, such as is implied in the Employment Act of 1946, had become widespread.

6) Government should be viewed not as a substitute for private enterprise, but rather as a positive guiding force, helping to adjust the economy to the needs of the basic economic groups—consumers, agriculture, labor, and business—to whom it is directly responsible.

While these goals enlisted considerable agreement, the need of clarifying the objectives of public policy and of developing farsighted and co-ordinated policies capable of coping with America's postwar domestic problems and new international responsibilities remained acute. With the abandonment of war controls and with responsibility for important economic decisions divided and shared among business, labor, agriculture, and government, the basic problem of government remained that of facilitating accommodations, building community of purpose among conflicting groups, and shaping public policies which would both reflect common purpose and provide a creative response to the problems of the postwar world.

.   .   .   .   .

.  .  . The problem of using government creatively and effectively in a mixed economy to balance freedom and security and to reconcile economic progress and economic stability offered a continuing challenge to free societies and democratic governments from which there was no turning back.

# 35 R. H. Tawney / Arthur Salter: "Democratic Socialism"—Great Britain

❧ *The British "democratic socialist" experiment has aroused intense interest all over the world. Its nationalization measures, its health service, its vast extension of social security, and its economic planning have been widely studied. Some scholars regard the British program as a model for the rest of the world, while others regard it as a major threat to economic and political liberty.*

*Our present reading consists of two parts: (1) a selection from R. H. Tawney outlining what he believes are the major achievements of British socialism, and (2) an article by Sir Arthur Salter which poses certain unsolved problems involved in the nationalization (public ownership) of enterprise. Generally speaking, Tawney looks at British socialism with favor, while Salter tends to stress the difficulties involved.*

*R. H. Tawney (1880–    ) is Professor Emeritus of Economic History at the*

University of London. *Among his works are* The Agrarian Problem in the Sixteenth Century *(1912),* The Acquisitive Society *(1920),* Religion and the Rise of Capitalism *(1926), and* Land and Labour in China *(1932).*

Sir Arthur Salter *(1881–     ) was for ten years Gladstone Professor of Political Theory and Institutions at Oxford and for thirteen years a member of Parliament. Among his publications are* Recovery *(1932),* The Framework of an Ordered Society *(1933), and* Personality in Politics *(1947).*

## R. H. Tawney: *Britain under Socialism* *

A detailed analysis of the policies pursued since July, 1945, cannot here be attempted. Their international background . . . is, of course, of fundamental importance. If that crucial topic be omitted for lack of space, the principal new departures initiated by the Labour Government may conveniently be classified under three main heads. The first has been concerned with the extension and improvement of the various forms of communal provision—education, public health, insurance against sickness and unemployment, old age and widow's pensions, medical care and school-meals for children—which, though widely differing both in their purposes and their effects, are in England illogically grouped together under the un-illuminating name of the Social Services. Mainly under Conservative ministries, they had undergone, in the inter-war period, a development which, when allowance is made for the change in the price-level, had more than doubled the expenditure on them. The necessity both for their further enlargement and for their systematisation had become by 1939 common ground between parties.

The Coalition Government had taken some steps in that direction. It had been responsible in 1944 for a new Education Act, and, in the following year, for a Family Allowance Act. Of the latter something is said below; the former prepared the way

for the most far-reaching reconstruction carried out since a public system of education was first brought into existence. It affects every side of that system, from Nursery Schools or classes to the education of adults; but its most significant innovations were, perhaps, four. It substituted a universal system of secondary education for the selective arrangements which had hitherto existed. It fixed fifteen, instead of fourteen, as the minimum age for the cessation of compulsory education, with the addition that, as soon as circumstance allowed, attendance should be legally obligatory to sixteen. It abolished fees, and made secondary education free, in all but a small minority of secondary schools. It provided for the creation of a system of compulsory part-time continuation schools to follow full-time education up to the age of eighteen. Henceforward, therefore, all children, and not merely, as hitherto, a minority, will pass, between eleven and twelve, to one type or another of secondary school, and the disastrous gap between the school and industry will be partially bridged by continued education. Though piloted through Parliament by an enlightened Conservative minister, the measure owed not a little, it is fair to say, to the Labour Party, which has long given "secondary education for all" a prominent place in its programme. The duty both of enforcing the new mini-

ED. NOTE: * Reprinted from an article in William Scarlett (ed.), *The Christian Demand for Social Justice* (1950), a Signet Special book, pp. 106–115, with permission of Professor Tawney and Bishop Scarlett.

mum leaving age, in the teeth of short-sighted clamour that the shortage of workers made the reform inopportune, and also of bringing into operation other parts of the Act—in view of the shortage of materials for building schools no easy task—has devolved on the Labour Government. It had been decided before the conclusion of the war that the provision for university education required to be greatly expanded; and it was the first Labour Chancellor of the Exchequer who took the important step of enlarging and re-defining the powers and duties of the body—the University Grants Committee—on whose advice the State's financial aid to the Universities is given. The present Government's chief contributions to the Social Services have been made, however, in a different field. They consist of its Social Security and Health measures.

A system of pooling risks by unemployment and sickness insurance had been established in England before the first world war. Repeatedly extended in the next quarter of a century, it suffered, when the Labour Government came to power, from the gaps and inconsistencies to be expected after a long series of piecemeal modifications. The details of the new structure are necessarily complicated; but its larger outlines can be simply stated. In the first place, a comprehensive National Insurance Act has consolidated the former Health and Unemployment Insurance schemes; has placed them under a single Ministry of National Insurance; and has established a universal system, with standard contributions and benefits—both, but especially the latter, substantially increased—under which every citizen is insured against sickness and unemployment from the age at which compulsory education ceases to that at which he or she qualifies for a retiring pension, special provision being made for the needs of maternity, in the shape of a grant on confinement and allowances, up to thirteen weeks, in the case of mothers normally in employment, as well as for widows and orphans. In the second place, a further Act provides for the special case of injury or disease incurred by workers in the course of their employment. Henceforward, the injured worker, instead of being required to make good a claim, often stubbornly contested, to compensation under the Workmen's Compensation Acts, will receive as a matter of course, subject to periodical medical reports on his condition, industrial injuries benefit up to six months, and subsequently, if he suffers from permanent disablement, a disablement pension graded according to the degree of his incapacity.

The third piece of legislation, the National Health Act, is intended to make the best medical treatment available for the whole population, irrespective of the financial means of different families. It does not, as has been suggested, "nationalise medicine"; and the medical profession, which at first looked askance at the measure as threatening the independence of the private practitioner, decided, after some hesitation, to co-operate in making a success of it. It establishes a service free for all at the time of treatment, the cost of which will be met partly from insurance contributions, partly from local rates and partly from grants from the National Exchequer. Hospitals are transferred from the hands of Local Authorities and voluntary bodies —the latter often short of funds—to the Ministry of Health, under which they will be administered by Regional Boards, composed, to the extent of one-half, of medical practitioners, and, for the other half, of nominees of the Ministry and the Local Health Authorities. Doctors are at liberty to continue their private practices, or to enter the national service, or to combine the two, as they themselves decide. Provision is made for a wide development, as soon as circumstances allow, of Health Centres, equipped and maintained from public funds, where, when they so choose, they will engage in group practice. Finally, a principle not previously accepted in England has been embodied in an act already mentioned, the credit for which belongs to the Coalition Government. It is common knowledge that the period of maximum strain in a family occurs when several children have been born, and the eldest is not yet of an age to earn. The Family Allowance Act of 1945 is designed to meet that situation. It does so partly by establishing allowances in the shape of a small cash payment for each child after the first up either to the age when compulsory education ceases or to that of 16, whichever is the highest, partly by provision in kind, such as milk, vitamins, and cod-liver oil for expectant mothers and during the first year of a child's life, together with special supplies of the first for children of school age, and meals in public primary and secondary schools. Visitors to England periodically complain that milk is short. In reality, the average consumption per head is considerably higher than at any previous period. It is true, however, that, since a larger proportion of the supply than before 1939 goes to those, in particular children, who need it most, there is less for adults—other than invalids—who can contrive, without intolerable hardship, to moderate their appetite for it. It is a question whether that minute concession to Christian ethics can appropriately be regarded as an occasion for tears.

It is possible, by means of a wisely planned system of communal provision, to ensure that the whole population enjoys, as far as environmental influences are concerned, equal opportunities of health and education, and is equally protected against the contingencies of life. Such a system, therefore, is not an excrescence upon Socialist policy, but an essential part of it. It is an investment in the development of human energies, which will, in time, pay handsome dividends; and it was proper that a high place should be given by a Labour Government to the effort to create it. The second and third main departments of that Government's policy are on a different plane. They are concerned, not with sharing more equitably the wealth produced, but with organising more effectively the energies which produce it. They include anti-unemployment measures; the nationalisation of certain important services; and action to eliminate avoidable causes of inefficiency in the case of industries—which will for long remain the great majority—not yet promoted to the dignity of public ownership.

The steps taken under the first head may, at the moment, appear otiose. In order, however, to produce their effect, expedients to avert unemployment must be prepared in advance, at a time when, as to-day, the problem is the shortage, not of jobs, but of workers to fill them. The Labour Party does not share the belief expressed by eminent persons in the United States shortly before the catastrophe of 1929 that the level of productive activity can safely be left to take care of itself, nor does it take the view once fashionable both in that country and Great Britain that decisions based on the self-interest—enlightened or otherwise—of entrepreneurs and investors should be the chief factor determining it. On the contrary, it regards the economic waste and social misery caused by recurrent unemployment as a scandal to our civilisation, and holds that to take every possible step to prevent it is among the first duties of Governments. Thanks, largely, to the work of economic thinkers, such as Keynes and Beveridge, the partial, though doubtless not the complete, suppression of an evil till recently accepted, like typhus and cholera a century and a half ago, as though it were an Act of God, not the result of human folly and greed, no longer appears to be beyond the wit of man. . . .

In this matter the Labour Party makes no pretence to the possession of an infallible formula. It has merely sought the best advice available, and attempted to act on it. Given a planning organisation, to act as an economic general staff, the nucleus of which was created during the war, and which has now, with the necessary modifications, been placed under the Chancellor of the Exchequer, the first necessity was for the Government to be invested with adequate powers of control over the financial system. The principal means employed for that purpose have been three. The Bank of England has at last been added to the not inconsiderable number of Central

Banks in public ownership, and its power to issue directions to other banks has been increased. The war-time control of new capital issues by means of a licensing system has been continued, and the Treasury has been empowered to guarantee loans for the reconstruction or development of any industry up to a maximum of £50,000,-000, a figure which can, with parliamentary sanction, be increased. A National Investment Council has been established, to "advise and assist the Government in so organising, and, when necessary, stimulating, investment as to promote full employment." Henceforward, therefore, the main levers of short and long term credit will be in public hands, and it will be possible for both to be managed with a single eye to the public interest. Both a blunder, such as that of 1925, when, in deference to City sentiment, the export industries were sacrificed by the return to gold at too high a parity, and the recurrent imbecility of pouring capital into luxury flats, picture-houses and other investments which chance to hit the public fancy, at a time when coal and cotton were starved of the resources required to reconstruct them, are less likely to be repeated. Nor do measures of this order stand alone. Budgetary policy has an obvious bearing on the level of employment; and that favoured by Labour opinion has its contribution to make. Some twenty years have elapsed since it was remarked by a Royal Commission of unimpeachable propriety, presided over by a banker who was a pillar of respectability, that the social services, since they are not subject to sharp fluctuations, are a stabilising factor in the national economy; while it was the most eminent of modern British economists who wrote that "in contemporary conditions, the growth of wealth, so far from being dependent on the abstinence of the rich, is much more likely to be impeded by it." In combining an expansion of communal provision with a steeper graduation of taxation, the Government has complied with these prescriptions. A further, and more important, influence on the side of increased stability is likely to be exercised by a third element in its

policy. It is now generally agreed that fluctuations in investment have played a major part in producing alternations of boom and depression, and that those alternations are seen at their sharpest in the producer-goods industries. That public investment, which can be deliberately regulated from year to year, is likely, given a reasonable measure of prevision, to fluctuate less violently than that of private individuals and corporations is equally a truism. The larger, in short, the sector of the national economy in which investment can be made with some approximation to a settled plan, the greater the State's command of the means to neutralise the grave evils caused by the anarchic oscillations of private industry.

Since 1945, that sector has been in process of expansion. The Housing programme, under which, in the three years following the conclusion of the war, accommodation was provided for not far short of a million and a half persons; the town and country planning policy; the Distribution of Industries Act; and the development areas established under it, are cases in point. The transference, apart from the special case of the Bank of England, of half-a-dozen industries to public ownership, though primarily prompted by other considerations, is, in this connection also, not without its advantages. In considering the reasons for the adoption of a policy which, though not new in principle, is novel on the present scale, certain commonplaces, are, perhaps, in order. The line, in the first place, between the area of economic life resigned to the activities of profit-making entrepreneurs and that administered by public authorities has never possessed the fixity often ignorantly ascribed to it. In reality, as a glance at the history of Europe is sufficient to show, it has been repeatedly re-drawn; and an observer of that impressive Socialist undertaking, the TVA, may be pardoned for feeling some uncertainty whether even the most virtuous of peoples is an exception to that statement. *Prima facie*, there is nothing surprising in the view that, as circumstances change, a re-classification of the spheres of private and public undertakings is periodically required. Whether in any particular instance, it is desirable or not is a question to be decided in the light, not of resounding affirmations of the virtues either of free enterprise or of socialisation, but of the facts of the case. It is an illusion, to suppose, in the second place, that the advocacy of an extension of public ownership is either confined in England to members of one party or advanced by that party as a formula of universal application. Authorities whose political sympathies, if classifiable at all, are not to be grouped under any single heading, have recommended it, on grounds of practical expediency, in the case of monopolies—a large category—agricultural land, transport, coal and power. The Labour Party approaches the problem in an equally realistic spirit. It is true, of course, that great aggregations of economic power in private hands are open to objection on moral and political grounds, as a menace to democracy and freedom, and that Labour, which is rightly sensitive to their deleterious influence on the quality of civic life, looks to the extension of public ownership as one expedient, though only one, for averting that danger. Practical realities, however, determine that its policy in this field, as in others, shall not be wholesale and indiscriminate, but shall advance step by step, as a case for it is established. The result has been a process of selective nationalisation, undertaken when, on one or more of several different grounds, the balance of advantages favours that course.

In the case of the industries hitherto nationalised, such grounds have not been far to seek. Partly, it is to be presumed, for that reason, opposition to this aspect of the Government's policy has been less vocal than might have been expected. The transfer to public ownership of civil aviation and of long distance communications by cable and wireless passed almost unnoticed. The nationalisation of gas and electricity, if challenged in the House of Commons, stirred outside it only minor ripples. The more formidable task of converting into a unified service the railways, long distance

road haulage, and some sixty canal undertakings, together with subsidiaries such as the docks and harbours owned by bodies of several kinds, naturally aroused more anxiety; but, here again, objections had as their target less the principle of public ownership than specific questions relating to the structure and organisation of the new system. Just under thirty years ago, the recommendation that the mines should be nationalised, which was advanced by the majority of the Coal Commission presided over by the late Lord Sankey, aroused a storm of opposition. When, in 1946, that proposal became at last an Act of Parliament, not a dog barked. It is noticeable that a leading expert, whose strictures on the conduct of the industry by the Coal Board have aroused attention, accompanied them with a statement of his conviction that State ownership had been the correct policy.

The transfer of property in return for compensation, which nationalisation involves, is a means, not an end. Its purpose is to ensure that services, on which the general welfare depends, shall be conducted with a single eye to that objective, under authorities accountable for their proceedings to the public. Its success depends, therefore, not on the mere change of ownership, but on the degree to which advantage is taken of the opportunity offered by it to secure first-class management, to carry through measures of reorganisation which private enterprise was unable or unwilling to undertake, and to enlist the active co-operation of employees in increasing production. It is to be judged by its practical results on consumers, on workers and on the national prosperity; and, though the long decline in output, which went on in the Coal industry under private ownership, has been replaced since nationalisation by a slow upward movement, of results it is, as yet, too early to speak. Even, however, when this part of the programme of the present parliament has been carried to completion, some four-fifths of the industrial *personnel* of the country will continue to be employed in industries in private hands; and, while some of the latter are not open to serious criticism on the score of inefficiency, there are others whose condition leaves not a little to be desired. Policy here has followed several lines. The first step taken has been to throw on the industries in question the responsibility for preparing such plans for improvement as may be needed, by appointing "working parties" composed of employers and trade unionists, to submit reports on the subject to the Board of Trade. In the second place, the Government has taken powers, under the Industrial Organisation Act of 1947, to set up Development Councils to bring approved schemes of reorganisation into operation, and, in certain cases—for example that of the cotton industry, in which Parliament has empowered it to pay grants up to 25 per cent of the cost of re-equipment —has stimulated modernisation by financial assistance. Third, it has carried a Monopolies and Restrictive Practices Act, under which a Commission acting under the Board of Trade will inquire into such practices, and a competent Minister will have power, subject to affirmative resolutions in Parliament, to make orders prohibiting such of them as are found to be contrary to the public interest. Finally, and not least important, it has taken steps to ensure that the reproach of a neglect of the economic applications of science, which, though not generally true, had, in certain old-fashioned industries, too much validity, shall become a thing of the past. It has arranged for the supply of University-trained scientists to be largely increased; has made funds available to promote research, not only in technology, but in the economic and social sciences; has encouraged the establishment of an Institute of Industrial Management, partly financed from public funds, to conduct investigations into problems of management, and has expanded the activities of the public Production Efficiency Service, whose advice is available for all firms desiring it.

In the immense lottery of war, sacrifices neither are nor can be equally shared. The economic embarrassments inherited by Great Britain from a conflict in which she fought, like her principal antagonist, from the first day to the last, and was not careful, in contributing to the common cause, to consider her own future, have not been a trifle. Of the measures by which she is grappling with these inevitable difficulties, and will in due course overcome them, this is not the place to speak. Nor has the time yet come when the larger policies of her Government can be judged by results. Their tendency is, however, obvious. It will be interrupted by recurrent checks and throwbacks. Since, however, the force behind it is not merely a political party, but the set of British life, it will not be arrested. Like earlier movements in her history, which also wound their way amid shoals and sand-banks, it will produce, in due course, its distinctive social order.

If present indications may be trusted, that order will be found, as it develops, to differ not less from the capitalist plutocracies formerly predominant in Western Europe than from the Eastern dictatorships. Some of its characteristics, if only in embryo, can already be discerned. Parliamentary Government and personal liberty not only continue in England unimpaired, but derive a heightened significance both from the successful employment of the former to effect by consent changes elsewhere imposed by violence, and from the more positive content acquired by the latter as the result of the firmer guarantees for opportunity, economic security and social well-being now added to it. Private interests count for less as a determinant of economic strategy, and public interests for more. The preponderance which, in the fluctuating balance of power between property and creative work, formerly belonged to ownership is now passing to Labour. Social solidarity has been strengthened as the essentials of civilisation, once the privilege of a minority, have increasingly become a common possession. Judged by the distribution of income, a more equalitarian society than existed in pre-war England, and than exists to-day in the Soviet Union or in the United States, is in process of creation. "Choose equality and shun greed" is, doubtless, a far from all-sufficient formula. In a world, however, where Communist social theory and American economic practice agree in repudiating it, it is not, perhaps, a misfortune that one more people has been added to the small number of those disposed to take it seriously.

## Arthur Salter: *The Crux of Nationalization* *

A policy of nationalisation, of course, raises two kinds of problems. The first is to what sections of the economy it should be extended. Obviously, some industries are more appropriate than others. The public utilities, such as gas or electricity, which do not need to adapt their products to the changes of taste of foreign customers and have a comparatively uniform structure, are clearly the most suitable. There are intermediate cases where the balance of advantage is more doubtful. Such an industry as iron and steel is of quite a different character. There are many who, like myself, would be in favour of nationalisation, under appropriate conditions, for industries of the first class and strongly opposed to its extension to the second; and for these the exact delimitation of the frontier between the two classes presents an interesting subject of study and discussion.

The second type of problem is what, in the range selected for nationalisation, is the best form of administration. What administrative principles and methods will best secure the inherent advantages and mitigate or avert the inherent dangers? It is this second question only which is the subject of this article. I propose to describe what seem to me to be the three crucial administrative problems of nationalisation.

How can the incentives of competition, with prospective profit or bankruptcy,

which are found in private enterprise, be replaced? How can collective bargaining be adjusted to the different conditions of nationalised monopolies? And what safeguards can be found against the inherent tendency of bureaucracy to excessive centralisation? I shall, however, confine myself mainly to stating the problems, with only very tentative suggestions as to the lines upon which solutions may be found.

I ought perhaps first to say something of my personal attitude, so that the reader may better assess or discount what I have to say. . . . My discussion will . . . be inevitably influenced by my general political outlook, which is now nearer to the Right than the Left on current issues of controversy. . . . I have . . . been a Member of Parliament for thirteen years. And though I have been an Independent, and usually spoke and voted against the Conservative Government which was in office when I first entered Parliament, I have found myself increasingly in opposition to the Labour Government during the greater part of the last five years in which the new nationalisation has been introduced. . . . It is . . . my increasing conviction that at numerous crucial points the Government has introduced nationalisation on a large scale without having solved, or indeed seriously faced, the problems discussed in this article. It is not, certainly, due to an initial prejudice against nationalisation as such in appropriate cases. . . . I have always been deeply impressed with the dangers of the private ownership system in the case of services of great public interest in which monopoly could give great economies. . . . Moreover, like most others nowadays, I realise that, with modern economic development, the old laissez-faire private enterprise of competing units, if not corrected by public control (of which nationalisation of certain monopolies is a part), brings fewer benefits than in the past and very serious dangers and evils, novel at least in their scale.

But the fact is that both the private en-

ED. NOTE: * Reprinted from an article in *The Political Quarterly* for April-June, 1950, pp. 209–16, with the permission of the publisher.

terprise system, if left to itself, and not less a nationalised system, each present their distinctive inherent problems. In the case of the former, however, at least a great deal of intensive work has been done to find remedies for the inherent defects. In particular, the scientific research for correctives of the tendency of the private system to oscillate between periods of boom and depression, with large-scale unemployment in the latter, and the subsequent education of statesmen, bureaucrats and the public have had very important results. . . . We know now a great deal about the measures that can be taken to arrest the unemployment resulting from flagging home demand (though unhappily they could not help in the case of unemployment resulting from an inability to buy enough imported raw materials). Moreover, much is now known, and agreed by all persons of responsibility, as to certain useful forms of planned control at key points of the economic system, though there is also of course a wide area of controversy as to other forms and methods. . . .

The inherent problems and dangers of nationalisation are no less important and no less difficult. But no solutions have been found; though at least as problems they have long been familiar to all students of political institutions and frequently discussed.

The first of these, as I have said, is the adequate replacement of the pervasive, intimate and powerful compulsions of the profit and loss system. I am not among those who hold that other motives and other forces can never, under any conditions, be adequate. I was one among a small body of officials who had the task of bringing Lloyd George's National Health Insurance Act into operation in 1912. I do not believe that private enterprise could show a better example of either efficiency or ardour in tackling a new and difficult task. We worked as a team, with a pride and enthusiasm in our work, and were certainly as effectively stimulated to initiative and intense effort by our desire to see a great public service successful as if we had been engaged in a private enterprise dealing with a similar task. Indeed, when critics spoke of the civil servant's limitations, we reflected, with mingled pride and resentment, that private insurance had taken all the easier tasks—insurance against fire (where you can see the gutted house) or death (where you have the corpse) or sea accident (where the ship cannot hide itself), and left to the civil servant the kind of insurance which is most difficult of all. For there is nothing comparable to the ruins of a burnt house, or a dead body, or a wrecked ship when it is necessary to decide whether an ailing man (or, still more, a married woman, with domestic work at home) is or is not well enough to go to a factory. But in this case the advantages were exceptional. For a single task a large service could be formed from its most suitable officers. The creation of a novel enterprise is, moreover, in itself an inspiration. It is impossible to expect such team-work, or such ardour, when many schemes are launched and throughout the long years of normal administration. It is true that a high professional spirit in such a service as the Navy can give continued efficiency. But there the special character of the service, its relation to the security of the state, and the vivid memories of recent wars all give what is not available to a civilian service. It cannot be denied that in nationalised industries there is in practice nothing which encourages and compels efficiency, adaptability, initiative—and the rapid scrapping of the obsolete—which can compare with the ever-present consciousness of possible gain and possible ruin. In particular there is always a tendency to keep in existence, or to keep unduly large, an organisation created for a need of the moment which comes to an end or shrinks in scale. The immediate hardships to known colleagues of reduction of staff naturally bulk large in comparison with the fractional effect on the budget of a huge national concern, able with a monopoly to increase prices to the consumer, and beyond that to draw on the taxpayer. The danger, of course, is that, instead of painful but salutary bankruptcies of some small units of industry, the effects of sagging efficiency, higher costs and poor service may impose increasing burdens on the general economy of the state till it comes to disaster as a whole.

This is as much a central problem, and inherent danger, of nationalisation as the tendency to recurrent depressions with large unemployment is of the private enterprise system. It should, I suggest, be a main preoccupation of any government which is pursuing a policy of nationalisation to find or retain such safeguards against this danger as are consistent with its main purpose. There would, for example, have been something to be said, if it had been politically practicable, for nationalising electricity and gas, both intrinsically suitable for public ownership, in different Parliaments. In that case, the one first nationalised would have had, during its first formative period, the stimulus and standard of another industry providing lighting and heat, the consumers having some measure of choice between the two. That may be said to ignore the facts of political life. The necessities of a political programme, and the need to secure electoral support for it, prevent such prudent spacing. In any case, that is past history. I only mention it now to illustrate my point as to desirability of retaining some form of external standard when it is practicable. . . .

. . . . . .

I come now to the second crucial problem, that of collective bargaining as to wages and conditions of work in the nationalised monopolies. In relation to private industry, collective bargaining through the trade unions, with their accustomed traditions, has been of inestimable benefit. It has enabled labour to obtain its maximum share of the earnings of industry. Bargaining has, however, been kept within practicable limits through one salutary and indispensable safeguard which is inherent in the system of private and competitive enterprise. In every bargain, both sides always know that, beyond a certain point, though they may differ as to that point,

increased costs would bring bankruptcy, which would be disastrous to all in the industry. That safeguard no longer exists as an effective restraint in the nationalised monopolies. Since they are monopolies they can pass on increased wage costs to the consumer, who has no alternative, till he is himself broken. And if even then there is still a loss, the taxpayer, in spite of the illusory safeguards in some of the Acts, has to bear it. At least—and this is the decisive point—in the actual bargaining for higher wages or shorter hours there is no such compelling necessity of restraint recognised by both sides, as in the case of private industries which have to face competition and avoid bankruptcy. What, in these circumstances, is bound to be the result when a managing board is faced on the one hand with an insistent demand, and the immediate stoppage of a great public service if it is not granted, and on the other hand only with the fact that if the increased cost is incurred charges must be raised to the consumer and, if that is not enough, a net loss shown in the accounts? It is inevitable that costs and charges will rise, and rise out of relation to those in private industries, especially the exporting industries, which can neither sell to customers who have no alternative nor resort to the Treasury. A comparison of the movement of prices and of the profit and loss accounts of the nationalised concerns with those of private industries—iron and steel, for example—shows this tendency already in operation. Ultimately, the consequence must be that, instead of a few painful but salutary bankruptcies of particular competing units, the whole economy of the country is forced down together to lower levels. Nor is that all. Just as standards of efficiency cannot be maintained without the possibility of bankruptcy in the last resort of those who fall below them, so standards of work are bound to sag if there can be no dismissal in case of persistent slackness and absenteeism. But if there is a single employer for all of a particular kind of skill, dismissal, instead of merely compelling the skilled worker to seek work under another employer, may have the result of permanently degrading him to the status of a general labourer. In practice this will mean that dismissals will be too few to operate as a disciplinary influence, and when made will inflict an excessive penalty.

This problem must be solved if nationalisation is to be successful. . . .

.   .   .   .   .

Lastly, there is the excessive centralisation of management, to which bureaucracy always tends. Both the obvious conveni-

ences of a "functional" division of responsibility in great concerns, and the presumed necessity, in a public concern, of "uniformity" tend to favour centralised management. The inelasticity and inflexibility, which are fatal to efficiency, and the remote and impersonal control, which are fatal to human relations with workers in the industry, are always in the first instance less obvious to those who construct the new organisation. The evil consequences are left to develop gradually, to a point at which it may become almost impossible to find and apply a remedy.

# 36 William Ebenstein: *"National Socialism"—Nazi Germany*

❦ *Between 1933 and 1945, unemployment of men and resources was practically eliminated in Nazi Germany by the establishment of an economy whose major purpose was war. Men who before 1933 had been idle were now given work; members of the middle class, who had previously suffered from acute economic depression, now tended to find themselves re-established. The economic benefits of nazism to a large proportion of the German population were a powerful force drawing supporters to the regime which had accomplished this seemingly miraculous result. This does not mean that the Nazi economy "solved" all economic problems but simply that it gave the appearance, in the short run, of doing so. Also, the price of this apparent solution should be remembered—concentration camps, autocracy, brutality, and a war-dominated society.*

*The large measure of temporary economic success achieved by this "permanent war economy" should be kept constantly in mind in reading the following selection. The author points out the conditions peculiar to German historical development which made such an economy possible. It is important to compare the purposes and methods of the Nazi economy, as here described, with those of socialist Britain, the subject of our previous reading. It will also be profitable to compare the Nazi economy with that of the United States from 1940 to 1945, and with trends present in all the major world economies, geared as they are for another devastating world war.*

*The author, William Ebenstein (1910–     ), is Professor of Politics at Princeton*

*University. He has written* The Nazi State *(1943),* Great Political Thinkers *(1951) and other works. This reading is reprinted from* The Nazi State, *pp. 227–57. Copyright 1943 by William Ebenstein and reprinted by permission of Rinehart and Company, Inc., Publishers.*

## THE PLACE OF ECONOMICS IN GERMAN POLITICS

Germany was one of the great centers of European commerce from the late fourteenth to the early sixteenth century. A German family of trading genius, the Fuggers, was perhaps the richest single firm of that time. The decline of German economic power in the next two centuries was due to several factors. First, the great discoveries of the fifteenth and sixteenth centuries in Africa and America diminished the importance of the South German cities as outlets of Asiatic products in Central and Northern Europe. Spain, Portugal, Holland, France, and England assumed the position of commercial leadership formerly held by the prosperous cities of northern Italy and southern Germany. Second, these new competitors operated under the protection of unified national governments. They were thus able to found great trading empires overseas while Germany and Italy remained in a state of political anarchy for another three hundred years. The absence of national government in Germany before 1871 prevented the institution of uniform standards and policies without which modern business and industry cannot be carried on effectively. Third, the effects of the Thirty Years' War (1618–48) virtually destroyed the economic structure of the German people and retarded their general development for almost two centuries. The decline of the population from seventeen to four million gives an indication of the amount of human and physical destruction wrought by three decades of internecine warfare.

In more recent times, especially since the Industrial Revolution, economic institutions and ideas have never occupied in the German political pattern a position which was equal, or similar, to that in western nations. The great revolutions in England

(1688), America (1776), and France (1789) are not only symbols of the political ascendancy of the middle classes. In economic terms, these revolutions stood for the assertion of the productive superiority of the machine age over the agrarian feudalism of the traditional ruling classes. In this new economic philosophy of liberalism the state is held to be a necessary nuisance at best. In the free operation of the "laws of society," the "natural economic order" leads automatically to the greatest welfare of individual and society.

The German economic institutions and ideas since the Industrial Revolution have evolved along different lines. In the period before 1871, economic activities were spread over dozens of sovereign states and principalities ruled by absolute monarchs. Even within the individual states economic anarchy prevailed. In the Prussian provinces alone, 67 tariffs covering 3,800 commodities existed before 1816. . . .

The adoption of mild economic liberalism in the early nineteenth century was not the result of internal pressure as it had been in the great western nations. The temporary eclipse of Prussian military power in the period of the Napoleonic Wars forced a number of economic reforms on the Prussian government as well as on other German administrations. However, these reforms were introduced in Germany from above. . . .

Another factor made for state control of the economy in Germany: the late industrialization. This time factor, so important for an understanding of all phenomena relating to modern Germany, had a twofold effect. First, Germany was a country with ample but not abundant resources. She did not enjoy the advantages accruing from the possession of a great empire nor did she have the benefit of long-established commercial and financial relations with other nations. Since the state had never been ousted from its position as the authoritarian arbiter of all social issues, it was natural that it should assume the position of guidance and leadership in the process of Germany's "catching up" economically with the more advanced nations. Second, the classical period of early liberal economics in the western nations was coincident with the stage of economic evolution when owner, manager, and producer were still combined in one person or at least in one family. At that time, therefore, the individual business enterprise required relatively little fixed capital. The number of small and independent entrepreneurs was correspondingly high. The democratic systems in the west were based on the economic and political independence of these small business men and entrepreneurs.

When modern industrialism reached Germany in the second third of the nineteenth century, its technological structure and economic scale had changed considerably. The large-scale type of enterprise increasingly replaced the older and smaller units. The initial requirements in the outlay of capital goods and long-term overhead costs had risen enormously. In many cases the state alone could supply the necessary funds. In other cases it considered itself impelled to control the vast private funds needed for the establishment of the new large-scale type of enterprise. Technologically, this lateness of Germany was in many respects an advantage. She could avoid the piecemeal methods of trial and error and the resulting obsolescences of the industrial structures of those nations that had pioneered in the development of the machine economy. All this tended to increase the area of public control in Germany. At times this control assumed the form of outright ownership and management, as it did with the railways and most public utilities.

This factor of Germany's lateness raises serious questions concerning her political prospects. Germany was the first "late" country that supplanted a sort of state capitalism for the western economics of individual initiative. Later on, Russia, Japan, and other countries in Europe and overseas have demonstrated that the transition from the precapitalistic economy to the modern industrial system can no longer be accomplished without a strong dose of state control or outright state ownership. This raises the grave problem of whether political democracy on the western model can ever be established in those countries, for the historical origins of western democracy were so inextricably related to individual initiative and individual economic independence.

The domination of the state over economic institutions in Germany has had the effect of infusing them with the two most characteristic features of the German political system: army and bureaucracy. . . . Authoritarianism was typical not only of the relations between capital and labor. The internal organization of employers and employees was strictly disciplinarian and essentially based on the leadership principle long before the Leader was born.

The late penetration of modern industrialism and capitalism in Germany has had another interesting effect. Capitalism was, practically speaking, imposed by Prussia, first on her own citizenry after the Napoleonic Wars, and after 1871 on all Germany. As a consequence, Germany capitalism never commanded the fervent faith which the idea of free enterprise had instilled in those nations which had received its blessings through popular insistence rather than through bureaucratic imposition. . . .

* * * * *

### THE NAZI ECONOMY AS A PERMANENT WAR ECONOMY

As soon as Germany lost the World War of 1914–18 the first thought of her military writers and leading military men was to organize for the next war, which must be victorious for Germany. While the disillusioned German masses were bewildered by the course of events, the generals set to work preparing for the next war. . . .

Since 1933 the application of total politics and total war to economics has found expression in the new German science of *Wehrwirtschaft*, or economy of war. . . .

. . . . .

Many of these new *Wehrwirtschaftler* (war or military economists) have sought to define the exact nature of the Nazi economy as a permanent war economy. But all these definitions agree that a permanent war economy has to see to it that the total economy must be equal to the tasks of total warfare. The permanent war economy is the organization of the economy on military lines in time of peace for the preparation of total war. Practically, therefore, there can be no difference between the so-called peacetime economy and the wartime economy in a regime which is permanently in a state of war with its internal and external enemies. . . .

. . . . .

This characteristic feature of Nazism— that of obliterating the difference between the normal and the abnormal, and between peace and war—is also manifest in the field of economic theory and organization. And this character of the Nazi economy as a permanent war economy also explains why the endless discussion among foreign economists as to the socialist or capitalist nature of the German economy under the Nazi regime is largely artificial. The dispute between capitalist and socialist economists on this point tends to overlook the vital fact that capitalism and socialism are categories which relate to western welfare economics. Both capitalism and socialism aim at a welfare economy for the largest number of people in a national or world community. Their main point of division and disagreement lies in the distribution of goods. Whereas capitalism is willing to accept inequalities of income and property, socialism aims at a more equal distribution of both. The permanent war economy of Nazism cannot be defined in terms of socialism or capitalism because its basic social and political assumptions are different from those of either socialism or capitalism. Whereas the common objective of both is human welfare through economic means, the objective of the permanent war economy of Nazism is military strength and aggressive striking power regardless of the sacrifice of human happiness.

. . . The permanent war economy of Nazism is thus an economic system which cannot be subsumed under the western categories of either socialism or capitalism because the major inarticulate premises of both are fundamentally different from those of *Wehrwirtschaft*. This does not mean, of course, that the problems of rich and poor, of labor and capital, and other traditional economic issues, do not appear in the Nazi economic system. It merely means that these problems and their solutions in Nazi Germany must be related to the categories of the permanent war economy rather than to those of either socialism or capitalism, as these latter terms are understood in the west.

What confusion of thought can be produced by the introduction of these western concepts into the analysis of the German permanent war economy can best be seen, for purposes of illustration, from the Nazi use of the word "socialist." The Nazi party called itself the "National Socialist German Workers' Party." One could perhaps argue that it is neither national, nor socialist, nor German, nor a workers' party, nor a party at all. But taking just the socialist character of the party and of the Nazi economy into consideration, we find that Nazism has always prided itself in being socialist. However, the Nazi writers insist that their socialism is truly German and has nothing to do with western socialism. First, they point out that German (i.e., Nazi) socialism is national and not international as socialism elsewhere in the world. Second, Nazi socialism is not hedonistic like western socialism, because the aim of Nazi socialism is not the happiness of the largest number of individuals in society but the maximum strength of the state.

. . . . .

## THE ORGANIZATION OF
## THE ECONOMY

Before the Nazis came to power they had formulated an economic program of far-reaching significance. Points thirteen to seventeen of the party program contained the following objectives: nationalization of all trusts; profit-sharing in large concerns; extensive development of old-age pensions; nationalization of department stores and their lease to small merchants at cheap rents; land reform, including the abolition of interest on landed property.

In the first ten years of Nazi rule not a single one of these original economic objectives of the party has been translated into reality. Where business concerns or department stores have been confiscated, it was because they had been in Jewish hands. Even such property was not nationalized but merely transferred to "Aryan" competitors who had the right connections with the party leaders.

. . . . .

Immediately after the Nazis came to power they proceeded to co-ordinate all branches of the German economy along the authoritarian principle of Nazi leadership. After several preliminary and provisional measures the Minister of Economic Affairs was authorized by an act of February 27, 1934, to reorganize German trade and industry. Shortly afterward this reorganization was carried out. German trade and industry now form an "estate." It is a corporation of public law comprising all enterprises and constituting the sole legally recognized agency of formal representation. In addition to the estate of industry and trade there are the following estates: the Labor Front; the estate of artisans; the agricultural estate; the estate of transport.

The estate of industry and trade is subdivided both functionally and regionally. Functionally, it is made up of the following six major branches: industry, handicrafts, trade, banking, insurance, and public utilities. Each national branch is divided into regional and local subgroups. The regional organization of the whole estate has fourteen districts. The district organization comprises all territorial subgroups of the particular economic branches. The lowest territorial level is the local chamber of industry and commerce. This local body combines within itself all economic types on the local level.

In fact, every business, including public and governmental enterprises, is automatically a member of his particular national organization and of the local chamber of commerce. In essence, the organization of the estate of industry and commerce continues the German trade associations as they existed before 1933. What is new is, first, the compulsory membership of every businessman in Germany. Second, it is also new to bind together the previously existing national trade associations in industry, bank, and so on, into one "roof organization." Compulsory membership, unification of all trade associations, and the introduction of the leadership principle are the novel features of this reorganization.

The compulsory membership means that every businessman is obliged to pay dues and is subject to the jurisdiction, judicial and administrative, of his trade group. The unification of the previously existing separate national trade associations into one superagency has the purpose of unifying and facilitating the control of the government over all branches of trade and industry. The leadership principle, finally, is the symbol of the subservience of all, including the businessman, to the Nazi system of government.

The heads of the six national trade organizations within the estate are directly appointed by the Minister of Economic Affairs. Likewise, the heads of the fourteen subgroups of the branch "industry" are also directly appointed and dismissed by the minister in Berlin. Other major appointments are made by subordinate officials with the approval of the minister. The members of the local trade association have two legal functions: to declare whether the leader of the local trade association enjoys the confidence of the group, and to accept the annual report. However, the law explicitly states that even if the members express a lack of confidence in their local association leader, this refusal has no legal consequences. Similarly, the leader of the local chamber of industry and commerce, comprising all local trade associations of the different major groups and subgroups, is not dependent upon the consent or opinion of the members. The whole structure culminates in the National Economic Chamber (*Reichswirtschaftskammer*), which is the apex of all the functional and territorial organizations. Its leader and his deputies, two or more, are appointed and dismissed by the Minister of Economic Affairs.

The essential purpose of these trade associations, whether functional or territorial, is quite different from that of trade associations in a liberal political regime. Here again, names disguise realities. In a liberal society, trade associations are private organizations of citizens or corporate businesses designed to protect their group interests against the encroachments of other business groups and of the government.

In the Nazi economy, the trade associations are not organized for the purpose of protecting specific group interests against other group interests or the state. In the Nazi economy, the trade association has the name of its pre-Nazi predecessor, but actually it is a state agency to which all members of the particular trade group are compelled to belong as surely as they belong to the state. Membership dues are levied with the same compulsion as taxes are levied. There is no escape from either. Since the trade association in the Nazi economy is but a segment of the state bureaucracy, its purpose is the same as that of other branches of the state bureaucracy: to defend the interests of the state. Like other branches of the state bureaucracy, the trade association is merely a transmission belt for conveying to the regimented businessman the prescribed policies he is to carry out.

. . . . .

. . . German businessmen have learned since 1933 that they, like the rest of the German population, are completely subject to the political totalitarianism and arbitrariness of the regime. German courts have consistently followed the doctrine since 1933 that curtailments of property rights by public authorities are legal, even if the authorities have no specific legal authorization to effect such taking of property. Because the regime needs the technical and managerial skills of businessmen, it has retained them as a class. Individually, each member of the class knows that his life and property, let alone his pursuit of happiness, are not worth ten cents if he happens to fall into the party's disfavor. Major national decisions affecting the fate of business as a whole, such as the decision of war and peace, for instances, are taken with complete disregard of the views of the business class.

It is not easy to generalize on this issue because the permanent war economy of Nazism has affected the various groups of German business differently. The section of business which has benefited the most is big business. The reasons for that are not to be found in any innate preference of the Nazi leaders for big business or in their sense of gratitude for the support which they received from big business before 1933. The main reason is the transformation of the German economy into a permanent war economy. First, the technological demands of a war economy hit the existence of small firms more than that of large firms. . . .

Even before the commencement of war in 1939 the number of German handicraft firms had dropped by 12 per cent in the preceding three years. The small businessman and independent artisan has been forced out of business because he is technically less efficient than the large-scale enterprise in the armament economy. Even before the war the official organ of the artisans' trade associations exhorted its members not to be unhappy about their elimination from the German economy and their descent to the status of a wage earner, because "the ordinary working man lives a much happier life than the so-called independent businessman." The drafting of the owner of a small business for military service, compulsory in Germany since 1935, may often mean the permanent elimination of his business. . . .

Labor shortage is another reason for the elimination of the small businessman from the German economy. As soon as skilled labor became scarce as a result of the expansion of the armament industries, the government began to comb out the independent craftsmen. Several methods were employed: first, the government required in 1935 the Proof of Full Professional Qualification (*Grosser Befaehigungsnachweis*). This meant that these craftsmen who carried on their trade without having passed a master's examination would have to pass such an examination by 1939 or close shop. Those who were unable to pass the test had only one choice open: to sell their skill to a factory. Officially, the purpose of this decree was to cleanse the handicrafts from incompetent artisans and unhealthy competition. Actually, the objective was to force independent artisans into the ranks of industrial labor. As the expansion of the German war economy progressed, the pretenses of unhealthy competition and professional unfitness were dropped. A decree of February 22, 1939, to "Carry Out the Four Year Plan in Handicrafts," provided for the wholesale elimination of workshops. A similar decree of March 16, 1939, to "Eliminate Overcrowding in the Retail Trade" provided for the liquidation of shopkeepers. Another method of forcing out craftsmen and shopkeepers was the imposition of high taxes and dues on these groups. New high taxes and rigid collection of taxes in arrears often achieved this purpose. In addition, the government introduced in 1938 compulsory old-age insurance. Although one of the purposes of this legislation was to obtain additional financial resources for rearmament, the compulsory government insurance of craftsmen had also the aim of demonstrating to them that their social status was hardly different from that of factory workers who are also subject to compulsory government insurance.

The proletarianization of the German middle classes, their decline from a status of economic and psychological independence to that of factory workers, is one of the most dramatic events in recent German history. It is a change that has taken place as a consequence of many trends and tendencies in the Nazi system rather than as the result of one major decision. Therefore it has often escaped the attention of observers inside Germany and abroad. The long-term implications of this liquidation of the German middle classes may be the further lessening of the chances of liberal democracy in Germany. History has shown so far that liberal democracy was originally created and later sustained by the efforts and ideas of the middle classes. . . .

. . . . .

There is another reason why big business has a more favorable position than middle or small-scale business: Under the Nazi system the economy is riddled with red tape and bureaucracy. Practically every single step of the productive process must be approved by a government agency. The firm has to have permission to buy certain raw materials at home or abroad. This permission will, of course, be granted only if the final product serves in some way the cause of the war economy. If it has to buy the raw materials abroad, the firm will have to get permission from the Reichsbank for the necessary *Devisen,* or foreign exchange. The needed labor power will be assigned only if the government authority is satisfied that the work is for a nationally desirable purpose.

Likewise, the firm will obtain public orders only if it has the right connections. In all these innumerable steps, from the raw material to the final product, a German business firm must continually deal with government agencies. In a permanent war economy practically every available resource is made accessible to the individual businessman only on the basis of priorities obtained through contacts with government officials. This is where the big firm has a decided advantage, for it maintains regular contact men who act as the firm's "ambassadors" in its dealings with government agencies. . . .

*     *     *     *     *

The concentration of economic power under the Nazi regime can also be seen from the following facts: The average capital of German corporations was close to $800,000 in 1928–29. Eleven years later this average had risen to about $1,500,000, i.e., by 95 per cent. It is also interesting that the greatest increase occurred in the category of the industries manufacturing producers' goods which play an important part in a war economy. The rise in the averages for consumers' goods industries was only slight by comparison, as their position is relatively less significant in the structure of an expanding war economy.

*     *     *     *     *

The profit ratios in German industry according to types of industry show the same picture. Taking the movement of the profit ratios for two typical boom years, such as 1926 and 1938, we find that the average profit rate for all industries rose from 5.17 per cent to 5.66 per cent. Taking the heavy industries and the light industries for purposes of comparison, we find that the profit ratio in the case of the former rose from 2.10 per cent to 6.44 per cent, whereas in the case of the light industries this rise was only from 4.25 per cent to 6.02 per cent. Since heavy industries have a relatively higher capital concentration than the light industries, this means that big business was the greatest profiteer from the establishment of the war economy.

Another development which has greatly strengthened the hold of big business on the German economy to the disadvantage of small business is the compulsory cartelization since 1933. The Anglo-American common law has always been hostile to combinations of trade which limit competi-

tion within a particular trade or profession at the expense of the public. In the United States, "trust busting" has been for the last forty years one of the main issues of public policy. . . .

Historically, the attitude of the German people has been quite different. Since the rise of trusts and cartels in the early eighteen seventies Germans in general have accepted concentration of economic power and limitation of free competition. The late coming of industrialism in Germany meant that large-scale enterprise emerged at once in the transition from handicraft to machine production. The major industries of the German economy, such as steel, coal, and shipbuilding, were concentrated in the hands of a few big firms from the beginning. Likewise, the importance of the munition makers was officially stressed under Bismarck and the Kaiser, as it is today. But the German people also accepted trusts and cartels as a natural part of their industrial landscape because the whole structure of state and society was permeated with institutions in which the elements of bureaucracy and large-scale efficiency were stressed. The German army and bureaucracy were both big and powerful. Government was not decentralized through the distribution of power among different classes, parties, or regions. Centralization of political power as the accepted pattern of German politics made it appear natural for economic power to be concentrated similarly in relatively few enterprises.

Under the Weimar Republic several compulsory cartels were set up by parliamentary legislation. When the Nazis came to power they accelerated the rate of this traditional process in the German economy. . . . The cartels are not run on the leadership principle by government officials but by the firms which hold the majority. However, the term "majority" refers to the "quotas" assigned to each firm, and not to the absolute number of firms. In practice this means that a few leading firms holding the preponderance in the cartel control it. This makes for more efficiency, in the Nazi view, than democratic representation of individual firms.

The centralization of economic power has been increased by some political measures of the regime. First, Jews were robbed of their property in Germany. After 1939, the conquered populations were next. . . .

. . . . .

Since the conquest of country after country in the second World War Germany has pursued the deliberate policy of getting hold, by hook or crook (especially by the latter), of individual businesses in occupied countries. The technique first practiced against Jewish businessmen in Germany was faithfully copied with regard to all businessmen of the defeated nations. The important industrial and banking enterprises in Poland, Austria, Czechoslovakia, and France were taken over by a few big firms in Germany. . . .

. . . . .

The mobilization of all national resources for war was formally established by the Leader on October 18, 1936, when he instituted the Four Year Plan to make Germany independent of the importation of raw materials from abroad. In charge of the Four Year Plan is Marshal Goering, whose authority includes the power to legislate within the scope of his assigned task and to give orders to all government departments and party offices. The fact that he received more authority than anyone in Germany save the Leader points to the status of the war economy in the whole Nazi system.

While the foreign propaganda of the Nazis stressed the poverty of Germany, the home propaganda emphasized that Germany had more coal than any other nation except the United States, and that coal is the real source of modern industry and productive wealth. "Germany," Marshal Goering said in an address before German miners on January 11, 1941, "is not a poor country." [1] German engineers and chemists have been able to extract from coal an

[1] *Deutsche Allgemeine Zeitung*, January 14, 1941.

amazing number of products ranging from oil to synthetic rubber. Needless to say, the ersatz products gained through the Four Year Plan have been achieved at the expense of the German taxpayer. It is much cheaper to buy those materials abroad and ship them into Germany than produce them there as ersatz materials. But a permanent war economy calculates in terms of military strength and not of economic welfare.

On October 29, 1936, shortly after the establishment of the Four Year Plan, a Price Commissar was appointed by the Leader. The Price Commissar is directly under the general supervision of Goering in his capacity as Delegate in Charge of the Four Year Plan. He has control over all prices. Price regulations of all sorts had been in force since the summer of 1933, but the institution of the Four Year Plan and the transformation of the German economy into a total war economy in 1936 necessitated the regulation of all prices. The control of prices is achieved not only through the fixing of prices for the finished article but also through the control of the price factor for the various cost elements that make up the productive process. Regulations of such cost factors cover the interest rate, wages, rents, prices of raw materials, and the like. Full employment of all available man power and resources in a war economy makes such price regulation inevitable if inflationary tendencies are to be curbed as much as possible. They can never be fully avoided, as the experience of the first and second World Wars have shown in this country and in England, but such price fixing and controls can at least remedy the worst evils of inflationary tendencies.

The total war economy of the Nazi system was assigned in 1937 the task of collecting scrap and waste materials of all kinds that could be used by the rearmament program. A decree of August 11, 1937, ordered all municipalities of over thirty-five thousand inhabitants to organize the salvage of scrap and waste materials from the municipal garbage collections. The air-raid wardens are the official scrap collectors for their blocks. The Hitler Youth boys and girls are also engaged in the collection of waste and scrap materials. As this organization includes all German boys and girls from six to eighteen, there is an abundance of collectors. Since the spring of 1940 service of any type in the Hitler Youth can be ordered to all boys and girls over ten, and disobedience can be punished with arrest.

In 1940 the Four Year Plan was extended for another four years. It is not easy to say whether it has been a success. First, the price of the manufacture of ersatz materials has been the shortage of other materials caused by the excessive consumption of resources in the production of ersatz. The strains on the labor resources, electrical power, and transportation seem to have been especially serious. Finally, we should remember that since 1938 Germany has conquered country after country, and geared their resources to its own war economy. The Nazis have proceeded on the assumption that the best ersatz, and the cheapest at that, is to take the real thing from abroad by force instead of investing

so much labor and effort at home on ersatz articles. The mineral resources of Austria, Czechoslovakia, Poland, Belgium, and France have done more to alleviate the raw materials problem in Germany than any Four Year Plan.

Contrary to the commonly accepted doctrine that war does not pay, Germany has proved that it is much cheaper to seize the wealth and resources of other nations by conquest than to buy them from foreign countries or produce them at home in a roundabout fashion of ersatz procedures. The Four Year Plan was never designed to be a permanent solution for Germany's problem of raw materials because of the enormous economic waste that it involves if maintained over a long period of time. The sole purpose of the Four Year Plan was to make sure that Germany would win the Second World War for which she has been preparing since 1933; after victory all raw materials would be at the disposal of the German master race in an enslaved world. The purpose of the Four Year Plan was thus not economic but political and military.

# 37　Barrington Moore, Jr.: *"Soviet Communism"—U.S.S.R.*

*❦ The Soviet social and economic system has for a generation aroused the curiosity and excited the interest of the world. Yet it is difficult to secure the data necessary to describe with assurance and to assess its merits and defects objectively.*

*The following reading, based on Frank H. Knight's analysis (see Reading 6) discusses how the Soviet system makes four basic decisions—what to produce, how to combine necessary labor and resources efficiently, what proportion of labor and resources to devote to expansion and replacement of capital equipment, and how to distribute the products of the economy among the population. The author points out that the Soviet system, in establishing institutions to make these decisions, carries the principle of nonmarket co-ordination—of central planning and control—to extremes. In the Soviet system, by contrast with most other economies, market controls are mini-*

*mized. Hence, as Moore points out, problems which characteristically arise in non-market control systems—such issues as incentives, bureaucracy, and pricing—are particularly prominent in Soviet society.*

*The author of the selection, Barrington Moore, Jr. (1913–    ), is a Research Associate of the Russian Research Center at Harvard University. He is a student of comparative government and sociology. Our selection is reprinted by permission of the publisher from Moore's* Soviet Politics—The Dilemma of Power, *Cambridge, Mass.: Harvard University Press, 1950.*

It has been pointed out that any industrial economic system has to find ways and means for making four groups of decisions. First, it is necessary to decide what to produce. In the second place, decisions have to be made concerning the most efficient way of combining labor and resources in order to produce the guns, butter, and other myriad products of a modern industrial order. Thirdly, it is necessary to provide some means for deciding how much economic effort should go into the building of new plants and the replacement of equipment that has become worn out or obsolete. Finally, there have to be devices for ensuring the orderly distribution of the products of the economy among the population.[1]

The answer given to these problems by classical economic theory, and to a lesser extent by capitalist economic practice, is that the free play of the acquisitive impulses of the individual in an atomistic and competitive order of society will result in a maximum flow of goods and services. On the producer's side, the restless search for profit will supposedly lead him to find out what goods the consumer wants. The pressure from his competitors will supposedly compel him to manufacture these goods with a minimum output of labor and resources. Competition also forces the producer to sell his goods at a price that just covers the cost of production, including a return for his own managerial and entrepreneurial skills. On the consumer's side,

it is argued that the restless search for gain will send him into the employment that provides a maximum payment for his skills and efforts. Likewise, the acquisitive drives will compel the consumer to spend his earnings in the most efficient manner possible: that is, he will seek to purchase goods and services at the lowest possible price for comparable quality. In this way the consumer controls ultimately the activities of the producer, and the system of theorems is closed.

This system has been under attack ever since its formulation. At least in terms of institutional consequences, Marx and his followers have turned out to be the most important of the attackers. The essence of the Marxist attack lies in the denial of the assumption that the free play of acquisitive impulses among individuals will bring about a maximum of wealth and prosperity for all. Instead, Marx endeavored to show that under the operation of capitalist institutions the free play of such impulses would result in the rich becoming richer and the poor becoming poorer—in the famous "polarization of classes," culminating in the explosion of the class struggle in the proletarian revolution. This doctrine, too, has been subject to critical onslaught ever since it was first propounded.

In addition, Marx anticipated the viewpoint of some anthropologists in his denial that the "laws" of economics were laws in the same sense as the description of universal relationships observed and calculated by the natural scientists. Instead, according to Marx's argument, each type of

[1] We follow here with some variations the argument of Knight, *Economic Organization.*

social organization—slave economy, feudalism, and capitalism—displays economic and social relationships or laws of its own. With the advent of socialism, according to a famous phrase of Engels', man would make the leap from the realm of necessity into the realm of freedom. Marx coined no such phrase, and asserted more cautiously that in a socialist society man would still be subject to some restrictions and limitations, though these would not be the same as in capitalist society.

This denial of the axioms of classical economics was continued and elaborated by Lenin, Trotsky, Bukharin, and Stalin. At the same time, the Communists have taken over and modified some of the features of capitalist society, such as the utilization of status differentials and incentives, devices that received an oblique approval in Marx if not among his lesser followers. . . .

. . . . .

## WHO DECIDES WHAT TO PRODUCE?

The first question raised in the opening paragraph of this chapter may be used as a starting point: How does the Soviet system provide for reaching decisions on whether to produce guns or butter, machinery or knitting needles?

From the available evidence, it is reasonably certain that the major decisions on the general production goals of the Soviet economy, including the types of products and quantities of each, are now reached by the Politburo and embodied in the various Five Year Plans. This concentration of the decision-making power on matters of national import in the economic field parallels the political concentration of power. The present situation differs markedly from that before Stalin's accession to power. The First Five Year Plan was itself the product of discussions and small-scale trials that lasted from the November Revolution until 1929.

The highest planning body on economic affairs is the Gosplan (State Planning Commission). However, as the English economist Maurice H. Dobb, who is not one to emphasize the authoritarian aspects of the Soviet regime, points out, the Gosplan is an advisory body and "not an executive department of state." [1] It is a part of the Council of Ministers and, according to Soviet sources, receives its directives from them and from the Supreme Soviet.

During the war the power to reach economic decisions, as well as supreme political power, was concentrated in the hands of the Government Defense Committee headed by Stalin. In addition to Stalin, this Committee included Molotov, Voroshilov, Malenkov, Beriya, Kaganovich, Mikoyan, and Voznesensky, all, except the last, prominent members of the Politburo. In view of the overlap between the Politburo and the Council of Ministers, as well as between the Politburo and the Government Defense Committee, it is safe to assert that general decisions and directives originated in the Politburo during the war and originate there now.

The procedure by which the Five Year Plans are actually drawn up is quite complicated and need not be considered in detail here, especially since this aspect of the Soviet system has received considerable attention from Western writers. [2] It is sufficient to point out that in formulating the details of a Plan the Gosplan authorities must take careful account of existing capacities and resources, an operation which requires an accurate knowledge of such capacities and resources for the USSR as a whole. In the second place, the planners have to make sure that the plans for each industry and area match one another. . . .

The conclusion that the basic decisions concerning what to produce and in what quantities are made in their essentials by the Politburo goes directly counter to the official ideology, according to which the masses participate widely in the planning process and thereby help to control their economic destiny. A recent semipopular

[1] Dobb, *Soviet Economic Development,* p. 341.
[2] Among the most useful works are Bienstock, Schwarz, and Yugow, *Management,* chap. iv; Bettelheim, *La Planification Soviétique,* chap. iii; Baykov, *Development of the Soviet Economic System,* chap. xx; and Prokopovicz, *Russlands Volkswirtschaft,* pp. 255–83.

Soviet exposition of the planning machinery devotes a whole chapter to the participation of the masses in planning.[1]

An examination of this and other material bearing on this point throws very severe doubts upon the official contention. What happens, apparently, is that, under the stimulus of the Communist Party, the workers, factory directors, and collective farmers produce counterplans, in which they promise to carry out, or often to overfulfill, the official government plans. In 1947 and 1948 these counterplans have taken the form of long letters to Stalin, printed on the front page of the newspapers, in which groups of workers or farmers set themselves specific production goals that they are pledged to fulfill. Other forms of so-called mass participation in planning are the Stakhanovite movement and "socialist competition," in which various groups of workers or factories as well as collective farms vie with one another for prizes awarded to the group with the greatest output. All of these movements are carefully controlled and stimulated by the Party. . . .

### POSITION AND MOTIVATIONS OF THE SOVIET MANAGER

Once the decision has been reached concerning what goods are to be produced, there remains a host of decisions to be made concerning the most efficient combination of raw materials, factory equipment, and labor necessary to produce them. Under a capitalist system, the profit motive provides the major stimulus for the maximization of efficient production, and the bankruptcy court the chief negative sanction for inefficiency. The capitalist entrepreneur under textbook conditions is free to obtain his supplies of men and materials where he can find them. Actually, he does a great deal of shopping around for them. Likewise he makes the decision of whether or not to expand his plant by adding new buildings and machines. In practice, these decisions may be greatly influenced or limited by government authorities. The So-

viet manager enjoys only a very limited autonomy in the search for supplies, and on his own initiative can do next to nothing about the major aspects of the size and capacity of the plant entrusted to him by the state. This series of graded distinctions in the power to make important economic decisions, and in the motivations behind these decisions, is more important in practice at least than differences in property rights in distinguishing between the Soviet manager and his capitalist counterpart.

As a motivating force to interest the manager in the efficiency of his plant, the Soviets make use of the profit motive in a manner that has certain strong resemblances to familiar capitalist arrangements. The utilization of this device, often regarded as a distinctive feature of capitalism, is openly recognized and accepted in current Soviet doctrine. The Five Year Plan adopted in 1946 aims to "increase the importance of the profit motive and economic accounting as an additional stimulus to production." [2] Nevertheless, the operation of the profit motive is hedged in under the Soviet system by limitations on the opportunities to bargain for supplies, the centralization of decisions concerning plant expansion, and taxation policies that return most of the profit to the state. In this manner it is harnessed to the socialist chariot and prevented from becoming a force that might disrupt Soviet institutions.

To understand the operation of the profit motive and the limitations of the manager's power of decision, the Soviet production process at various points may be examined. Beginning at the point of sale, and working back from there, one may note that the products of a plant are sold at prices fixed by the government. Exceeding these prices is punishable by law. But the prices do not represent the money equivalent of the cost of production. The plant is expected to produce its goods at a cost that is less

[1] Sorokin, *Sotsialisticheskoye Planirovaniye*, chap. v.

[2] V. D'yachenko, "Khozraschet kak metod planovogo rukovodstva sotsialisticheskim khozyaistvom" (Business Accountability as a Method of Planned Management in a Socialist Economy), *Izvestiya*, April 4, 1946.

than the price set by the government. A so-called turn-over tax [1] and an amount included as the planned profit are added to the anticipated cost of production. Lowering the quality of the goods to increase the margin between cost of production and selling price is punishable by law. If the manager holds costs below the anticipated amount, the profits of the plant are increased. In 1945, the total profit for the Soviet Union as a whole amounted to 21,-051,000,000 rubles.[2]

At earlier stages in the production process, the limitations on the manager's power of decision and the operations of the profit incentive are connected with control over the physical equipment of the plant and over supplies of raw materials. The basic assumption of the Soviet system is, of course, that the manager is not free to buy or sell factories, which are regarded as government property entrusted to him to manage. In the process of spelling this principle out in actual legal and institutional forms, the Soviets have for some time drawn a distinction between what they call basic and circulating resources. Very different possibilities are open to the manager for the utilization of each.

The terms "basic resources" and "circulating resources" derive from the differences Marx believed he saw between the *means* of labor—factory buildings, machines, and so forth—and the *objects* of labor—raw materials, semifinished products, and the like. These differences would exist in any form of society, Marx declared. In general, the means of labor are regarded as the basic resources and the objects of labor as the circulating ones. The distinction between the two types of resources does not depend upon the nature of the object itself, but the purpose for which it is intended. Thus a linotype machine that is the product of a factory that makes them is part of the circulating resources of this factory. When the same machine is transferred to a printing establishment, it becomes part of the basic resources of this plant.

In practice, difficulties soon arose in the application of these distinctions. In 1923 it was decreed that basic resources were those that were not used up or destroyed in a single act of production—buildings, machines, and the like—and that circulating resources were those that could only be used once—fuel, raw materials, and others. In 1936 the definition of circulating resources was broadened to include objects whose useful life was less than a year, independent of their cost, and objects whose cost, independent of their useful life, was less than 200 rubles.

Basic resources cannot be bought or sold again by the individual manager.[3] In other words, the Soviet manager cannot increase or decrease the size and equipment of the plant entrusted to his care through buying and selling operations in the fashion of his capitalist counterpart. However, he does have a voice in the disposal of a small portion of the plant's profits which can be used for expansion. Thus the outlet for the operation of the profit motive is, in this part of the production process, a very small one.

Circulating resources provide the opportunity for the profit motive to serve as a stimulus to production and efficiency. The minimum of supplies necessary for the operation of the plant is determined according to the plan. The flow of supplies to the plant is controlled in different ways for different types of supplies, depending on the scarcity of the commodity concerned. Some of them may be purchased directly from other producers. The production plan for the individual plant includes a certain profit rate, called the planned profit. If the manager makes efficient utilization of his resources, he may exceed the planned rate of profit. Should this take place, the extra profit remains at the disposal of the plant. In 1940, 70 per cent of the cost of production for industry as a whole is reported to have been spent on raw materials, fuel, and

[1] A tax applied when goods enter consumption channels. . . .
[2] *Zasedaniya Verkhovnogo Soveta SSSR (Vtoraya Sessiya)*, October 15–18, 1946, p. 10.

[3] *Izvestiya*, April 4, 1946. . . .

other items that come under the definition of circulating resources.

In addition, the manager is permitted to add to his circulating resources through loans from the banks. These loans are supposed to be issued only for strictly defined purposes, though their utilization for purposes other than those defined is deprecated in strong enough terms to suggest that it may occur rather often. Such loans probably increase the leeway available to the manager in the making of production decisions, at the same time providing a further check upon managerial operations in a way that resembles banking control over production decisions in a capitalist society.

The disposition of the profit indicates further its limitations as an incentive. Part of it is taxed and part placed in the Industrial Bank (Prombank) for purposes of captial development within the industry. A third part goes into what is called the Director's Fund,[1] a slightly misleading name, since it does not appear that this fund is a direct reward for the manager.

The Director's Fund is primarily a way of rewarding the workers for energy and efficiency. Since the way the fund is expended is left partly to the discretion of the director, it is safe to assume that it represents a series of tempting prizes that the manager may distribute to those he chooses. In 1940 the amount distributed through the Director's Fund was 2,600,-000,000 rubles.[2] In some, presumably exceptional plants, individual workers received cash awards of 500 to 1,000 rubles.[3] Though payments into the Director's Fund were replaced by other rewards during the war years, they were revived again in 1946. Under the post-war legislation only 2 to 10 per cent of the planned profits may be credited to the Director's Fund, the percentage varying with different industries. A much larger proportion, between 25 and 50

per cent, of the profits in excess of the plan may be credited to this fund. This arrangement presumably acts as a stimulus toward greater profit on the part of both workers and management. The proceeds of the fund may be spent on improving the housing conditions of the workers and for other amenities, for individual bonuses, trips to rest homes, sanatoria, and the like. While the director has the right to allocate the fund, it does not appear that he may spend any of it upon himself.[4]

On the other hand, salary bonuses for the managers are closely related to profit, though not calculated as a percentage thereof. In coal mining, for each per cent of reduction of real cost of production below planned cost, the manager, assistant manager, chief and assistant engineers obtain a bonus of 15 per cent of their monthly salary. Similar rules prevail in other sectors of heavy industry. On occasion the total bonus granted to managers and engineers equals or exceeds their annual salary.

The Soviets have taken the profit motive of capitalist society and adapted it to the requirements of their own ideology and social system, hedging it in with numerous restrictions so that it may not act as a socially disruptive force. After 1929 they did much the same thing to the capitalist device of competition, which the Webbs described as being, under socialism, the use "of the sporting instinct to augment the wealth of the nation."[5] Socialist competition, as it is known in the USSR, usually takes the form of a race between two or more factories, or shops within factories, to see who can turn out the maximum output. It is thus closely allied to the Stakhanovite movement. The winners receive group publicity in the Soviet press, banners, and other symbols of achievement. During the war there developed, as part of the system of socialist competition, the "200 per cent movement," that is, groups of workers who fulfilled double the requirements of the

---

[1] Dobb, *Soviet Economic Development*, p. 354.
[2] Vladimirov, *"Za rentabel'nuyu rabotu predpriyatti,"* p. 30.
[3] Bogolepov, *Sovetskaya Finansovaya Sistema*, p. 13.

[4] *Sobraniye Postanovlenii*, no. 14 (December 27, 1946), section 272. The decree itself is dated December 5, 1946.
[5] S. and B. Webb, *Soviet Communism*, II, 740.

plan.[1] Whether this type of speed-up leads to an efficient utilization of men and machines is open to doubt, since it often leads to a rapid breakdown of both.[2] It should be noted that socialist competition, directed chiefly toward the quantitative maximization of output, differs sharply from competition in capitalist society, which takes the form of competitive bidding for labor and resources on the side of production, and in competition by price, quality, and services on the side of distribution.

In the light of the foregoing it is safe to conclude, as others have done, that non-economic incentives and checks play the more important role in producing the desired behavior on the part of the Soviet manager. Chief among these are the possibilities of advancement to positions of greater and greater responsibility and prestige for those who have learned to combine men, machines, and materials in the most efficient manner, and the probabilities of disgrace, or even active physical suffering, for those who fail to measure up to the assigned task. Economic failure is likely to be identified with sabotage, and hence becomes a "sin" in an even stronger sense than is the case in the United States, with severe penalties meted out in this life.

Though large allowances have to be made for the part played by earlier conditions and the relative smallness of the managerial group with which the Soviets began, it may also be concluded that the system has not inculcated through its rewards and penalties the habits of prompt decision-making and accurate attention to detail that are desired by the Soviet leaders. At a meeting of the Supreme Soviet in October 1946, the chairman of the budget commission repeated the typical complaint that many factory directors refuse to look at a balance sheet, to learn the cost of their products, or to eliminate unproductive expenditures.[3] Likewise, the Party press from time to time slashes away at managers who "look for a quiet life and sit with folded arms," paying no attention to cost and quality.[4] . . .

. . . . .

Throughout a considerable sector of the Soviet economy, that directly controlled by the secret police, the incentives provided by profit and competition appear to be almost totally absent. In this area political motivations, the need to eliminate political enemies, covered by euphemisms about the restoration of deviants to society (concentration camps are called "Corrective Labor Camps"), are combined with economic ones and may overshadow them. The extent of these operations remains a state secret that cannot be reliably penetrated from the available fragmentary information. They may be recalled, however, as a reminder that even in the Soviet Union more than one set of rewards and penalties operates within the economy.

### THE COLLECTIVIZATION OF THRIFT

According to classical economic theory, the resources needed for the construction of new plants and the replacement of worn-out machinery come from the sacrifice of present consumption. To a considerable extent they are derived in a capitalist economy from individual savings that are loaned to industry through the purchase of securities. Interest payments have been widely regarded as a form of reward for the sacrifice of present consumption, thus permitting the construction or replacement of capital equipment.

To some extent individual savings are a source of plant construction and replacement in the Soviet Union. The virtues of thrift are recognized there, too. As early as 1926 Stalin himself spoke out in favor of

---

[1] "Sorevnovaniye Sotsialisticheskoye" (Socialist Competition), *Kratkaya Sovetskaya Entsiklopediya*, pp. 1365–1366.

[2] For complaints about this in the Soviet press, see Gordon, *Workers Before and After Lenin*, pp. 406–408.

[3] *Zasedaniya Verkhovnogo Soveta SSSR (Vtoraya Sessiya)*, October 15–18, 1946, p. 32.

[4] "Peredovaya—rezhim ekonomii," *Bol'shevik*, nos. 23–24 (December 1946), p. 7. Since *Bol'shevik* is the organ of the Party Central Committee, its unsigned editorial introductions carry special significance.

interest payments as the normal way of "mobilizing" individual savings.[1] But they play a much smaller role in the Soviet Union than they do under capitalist conditions.

When the Soviets in the thirties started the drive for socialist industrialization, they could not, for a variety of reasons, afford to rely upon individual thrift alone, or upon voluntary abstention from consumption as a source of real capital investment. Perhaps the most important of these considerations was that the sacrifices required were too great for reliance on voluntary means. Nor could the regime permit people to save money with the idea that they would invest it wherever there was the greatest opportunity for profit. Both socialist doctrine and the requirements of the day demanded that decisions concerning real capital investment be centralized.[2]

For these reasons, capital investment has been, and is, financed very heavily out of the national budget. During the period of War Communism the economy operated for a time as if Soviet industry were one large factory. Assignments from the budget were the only resources of the individual plant, and all of its monetary income returned to the treasury.[3] This extreme centralization was subsequently abandoned and a number of other schemes tried out. During the thirties between three quarters and two thirds of the amounts devoted to capital construction were derived from the budget, the remaining portion being left to the individual enterprise to reinvest in its own operations, in ways apparently left to the manager's discretion.[4] During the war, and

subsequently, this amount has been much smaller.

. . . . .

DISTRIBUTION

In the Soviet system for the distribution of goods to the population at large, one may observe the same mixture of what are commonly considered socialist and capitalist principles as appear in the other aspects of their economic arrangements. The present arrangements for distribution are the product of a long period of trial and error. By the time of the outbreak of the Second World War, the system devised was to sell the products of socialist industry, as well as most of the products of agriculture, through government and cooperative stores at fixed prices. In addition, there is a free market for certain agricultural products. . . . In this system the turnover tax provides the means for matching prices to available supplies.[5] With certain relatively minor changes this is the principal arrangement in effect today. Under this system, incentives produced by inequalities in income have their full effect. Additional money income means an additional opportunity to purchase the necessities and good things of life. This situation is in accord with the socialist maxim, "From each according to his abilities, to each according to his work."

However, at various times and under emergency conditions, the Soviet regime, like its capitalist competitors, has found it expedient to resort to other distributive devices. One of these is, of course, rationing, which has existed from time to time, including the period of the Second World War. Wartime rationing was abolished on December 16, 1947, at the same time that consumer demand was checked by a devaluation of the currency. Special stores, where "members of the intelligentsia and highly skilled workers" could obtain various scarce goods, usually at higher prices

[1] Quoted by L. Valler, "Sberezheniya naseleniya v SSSR" (The Savings of the Population in the USSR), *Finansy SSSR*, p. 301.

[2] For a study of the consequences in terms of physical output and a comparison of rates of industrial growth in Tsarist times, see Gerschenkron, "Rate of Industrial Growth," *Journal of Economic History*, supplement VII (1947), pp. 144–174.

[3] K. Plotnikov, "Gosundarstvennyi biudzhet Sovetskogo Soiuza" (The Government Budget of the Soviet Union), *Finansy SSSR*, p. 140.

[4] Dobb, *Soviet Economic Development*, p. 381. According to a New York *Times* report of March 11, 1949, the proposed 1949 budget allotted 79 billion rubles for capital investment, in addition

to which 25 billion rubles would be derived from the enterprises' own funds.

[5] Dobb, *Soviet Economic Development*, p. 373. See also Voznesensky, *Voennaya Ekonomika SSSR*, p. 122.

than those in the regular distribution channels where the goods were often nonexistent, have been another distributive device."[1] Still another has been the organization of special canteens in the factories. During the war the role of farms that made special agreements with a particular factory, increased sharply. Before the war they accounted for only 4 per cent of the retail turnover in the USSR, while in 1942 they accounted for 28 per cent, and in special areas, such as the Urals, for as much as 45 per cent.[2] Despite these variations, the distribution of consumers' goods has by and large been based on the principle of "come and get it if you can afford it."

Even writers sympathetic to the Soviet Union assert that the system of retail distribution is one of the least successful products of the regime, and the Soviets themselves have denounced it perhaps more frequently than any other feature of their society. Service tends to be disinterested and slow. Little or inadequate attention is paid to local needs and tastes, or to seasonal requirements. "Stores are replenished with merchandise irregularly, and the most necessary goods are lacking." Store staffs are "neither accustomed to nor interested in laying in supplies on time or carefully storing perishable commodities."[3] The Webbs remark, "There have been not a few occasions when village and even city stores have been clamouring in vain for particular supplies, when these have been lying unopened, and even forgotten at some intermediate point."[4]

These difficulties may be attributed to both ideological and institutional sources. As Yugow argues, the nationalization and centralization of retail trade was undoubtedly premature in Russia, at least from a strictly limited economic point of view. It created an unwieldy and expensive bureaucratic apparatus that paid little or no attention to the habit, customs, and tastes

of the people.[5] Of perhaps even greater importance is the fact that while the reigning ideology romanticized the construction of industry, it did not provide motivations and rewards for the distributive side of the economic machine. Stalin recognized some of these difficulties. He endeavored to use his prestige to correct them and to develop a Bolshevik version of the American ideal of "service" in the course of his report to the Seventeenth Party Congress of 1934. His remarks are worth quoting in full as evidence of the difficulties derived from ideology:

> To begin with there is still among a section of Communists a supercilious, contemptuous attitude towards trade in general, and towards Soviet trade in particular. These Communists, save the mark, look upon Soviet trade as a thing of secondary importance, hardly worth bothering about, and regard those engaged in trade as doomed. Evidently these people do not realize that their supercilious attitude toward Soviet trade does not express the Bolshevik point of view, but rather the point of view of shabby noblemen who are full of ambition but lack ammunition. (*Applause*) These people do not realize that Soviet trade is our own, Bolshevik, work, and that the workers employed in trade, including those behind the counter—if only they work conscientiously—are doing revolutionary, Bolshevik work. (*Applause*) It goes without saying that the Party had to give these Communists, save the mark, a slight drubbing and throw their aristocratic prejudices on the refuse dump.[6]

In their various attempts to ameliorate this situation, the Soviet leaders have borrowed from the capitalist arsenal and endeavored to introduce the competitive incentive into the retail trade. These efforts parallel, though perhaps less successfully, the Soviet introduction of the profit motive into the production side of the economy. On the same occasion cited above, Stalin reported to the Party Congress that the various commissariats had been ordered by the Party to start trade in the goods manufactured by the industries under their con-

[1] Voznesensky, *Voennaya Ekonomika SSSR*, p. 129. These stores were also abolished on December 16, 1947.

[2] *Ibid.*, p. 124.

[3] Yugow, *Russia's Economic Front*, p. 89.

[4] S. and B. Webb, *Soviet Communism*, I, 324.

[5] Yugow, *Russia's Economic Front*, pp. 90–91.

[6] "Report on the Work of the Central Committee to the Seventeenth Congress of the CPSU," January 28, 1934, *Problems of Leninism*, p. 512.

trol. This led, he claimed, to an extensive improvement in the "competing" co-operative trade and to a drop in market prices.[1]

As happens in many cases of cultural borrowing, only the superficial aspects of an institution were taken over without the essential supporting arrangements, which in this case would have involved a general abandonment of socialist principles in favor of the free play of market forces. It is not surprising, therefore, that the difficulties have continued. Nor is it altogether surprising that the Soviets have continued to try to meet them in the same way. On November 9, 1946, the Council of Ministers again issued a decree that required the co-operatives to compete with the state monopoly of retail trade. Surplus agricultural products, formerly sold by the peasant on a local open-market basis, under the new arrangement are purchased by consumer cooperatives managed by Party officers. These foodstuffs are supposed to be distributed to the city population at prices not exceeding those charged in the special stores for the intelligentsia mentioned above. Producers' cooperatives likewise receive government assistance in the form of supplies and diminished tax burdens, while the prices of their products are set by government authorities.

Some of the ideas associated with the classical doctrine of consumer sovereignty have even been put forth by the Party press, which has warned the manufacturers of consumers' goods that the population will not take whatever goods the producer wants to turn out. . . .

.     .     .     .     .

SUMMARY AND CONCLUSIONS

In order to make their economic system work, the Soviets have arrived by a trial-and-error process at the stage where they have borrowed a number of the motivations of capitalism: inequality of rewards and incomes, the profit motive, and some of the superficial aspects of competition. These borrowings do not provide a warrant for the viewpoint that regards the Soviet sys-

tem as closely similar to capitalism. They do provide support for the assertion that a modern industrial society implies certain common problems and even certain common solutions. The extreme claim of universal validity for the principles of classical economics is not warranted according to the Soviet evidence. But neither is the extreme claim of cultural or institutional relativism established according to the same evidence.

The motivations generally lumped under the rubric of personal acquisitiveness, which Weber points out, are likely to crop up under widely disparate social situations, do not receive the scope and approbation that they do in the United States. The Soviet economic system is one that keeps them hemmed in at every turn and channeled into what are considered socially useful paths. To take their place other motivations and prestige rewards have been developed. Likewise, other justifications for the Soviet system have received wide dissemination: allegations concerning the greater security of the individual, and the system's claimed freedom from the corrosive effects of crises and unemployment. In this respect Soviet culture is still a materialist culture. The virtues claimed for the system are material virtues. There is none of the contempt for so-called debilitating material comforts displayed, if not practiced, by the leaders of Nazi Germany or Fascist Italy. The Soviet system of values is much closer to the American system in this respect than it is to Western totalitarian ideologies, or to the ascetic ideologies of the East.

In this system of values the conflict between authoritarian and populist elements finds a reflection in economic institutions. The belief that the masses must be led to their salvation played its role in the programs of forcible industrialization and collectivization. It may also be traced in the creation of a highly centralized system for the making of economic decisions. In its present form this highly centralized system is not yet capable of distributing to the people efficiently and courteously the ob-

[1] *Ibid.*, p. 513.

jects it produces. On the one hand, the system emphasizes the desirability of material goods; on the other hand, it is unable to satisfy this demand. The passage of time will reveal, unless an improbable catastrophe intervenes, whether or not this contradiction can be solved.

In general, however, the Soviets have come closer to achieving their original goals in the area of industrial institutions, regarded by their doctrine as crucial, than in any other. They have succeeded in imposing their ideology to a very great extent, yielding only at certain points and borrowing just enough from the capitalist competitors to make their own system function.

## SELECTED REFERENCES FOR PART 7

BARMINE, ALEXANDER. *One Who Survived.* New York: Putnam, 1945.

Autobiography of a former Soviet diplomat and industrial manager who fled to the U.S.A. Describes and evaluates the performance of Soviet industry.

BAYKOV, ALEXANDER. *The Development of the Soviet Economic System.* Cambridge, England: The University Press, 1946.

A careful survey of Russian economic development since the Bolshevik revolution.

BECKWITH, BURNHAM P. *The Economic Theory of a Socialist Economy.* Palo Alto, Calif.: Stanford Univ. Press, 1949.

An effort to provide a comprehensive economic theory for socialist societies.

BELLAMY, EDWARD. *Looking Backward.* New York: Houghton Mifflin, 1890.

This Utopian novel is one of the classics of socialist literature.

BIENSTOCK, GREGORY, HARRY SCHWARTZ, and AARON YUGOW. *Management in Russian Industry and Agriculture.* London: Oxford Univ. Press, 1944.

A documentary study on the social origin, economic role, and political power of managerial groups in the Soviet economy.

BRADY, ROBERT A. *Crisis in Britain.* Berkeley: Univ. of California Press, 1950.

An evaluation of the program of the British Labour Government.

BRUTZKUS, BORIS. *Economic Planning in Soviet Russia.* Trans. from the German by Gilbert Gardner, with a foreword by F. A. Hayek. London: Routledge, 1935.

A vigorous criticism of the shortcomings revealed in Marx's economic and social doctrines by the experience of early Soviet planning. The author, a Russian economist, was among the first to insist upon the Utopian character of much socialist and Bolshevik theory.

CHILDS, MARQUIS. *Sweden, the Middle Way.* New Haven: Yale Univ. Press, 1936. Also Penguin ed., 1948.

In the judgment of the author, Swedish society successfully combines "private" with "socialist" enterprise.

CILIGA, ANTON. *The Russian Enigma.* London: The Labour Book Service, 1940.

A Yugoslav communist traces the record of his disillusionment with the workings of the Soviet economy and state.

CLARK, JOHN MAURICE. *Social Control of Business,* 2nd ed. New York: McGraw-Hill, 1939.

An influential study of relationships between the economic and political orders.

DALLIN, DAVID, and BORIS NICOLAEVSKY. *Forced Labor in Russia.* New Haven: Yale Univ. Press, 1947.

This survey estimates the number of slave laborers in the Soviet Union at from seven to twelve million.

DURBIN, E. F. M. *Problems of Economic Planning.* London: B. H. Blackwell, 1949.

Elucidates present problems of British socialism.

EDWARDS, CORWIN D. *Maintaining Competition.* New York: McGraw-Hill, 1949.

Attempts to provide cues for a realistic program of workable competition.

FINER, HERMAN. *The Road to Reaction*. Boston: Little, Brown, 1946.

A point-for-point rebuttal of Friedrich A. Hayek's *The Road to Serfdom*.

HARRIS, SEYMOUR E. (ed.). *Economic Planning*. New York: Knopf, 1949.

A collection of useful papers.

HAYEK, FRIEDRICH A. (ed.). *Collectivist Economic Planning*. London: Routledge, 1935. Influential early discussions of the problems of achieving rational allocation of resources in a planned non-market socialist economy.

———. *The Road to Serfdom*. Chicago: Univ. of Chicago Press, 1944.

A well-known indictment of planning. Argues that planning and socialism are incompatible with individual political freedom.

HOFF, T. J. B. *Economic Calculation in the Socialist Society*. Translated from the Norwegian by M. A. Michael. London: W. Hodge, 1949.

A closely reasoned discussion of the much-debated issue.

JAY, DOUGLAS. *The Socialist Case*. London: Faber & Faber, 1948.

A British journalist, Financial Secretary to the Treasury in the Labour Government, here argues in a sophisticated way the case for a socialist society.

LIPPINCOTT, BENJAMIN (ed.). *On the Economic Theory of Socialism*. Minneapolis: Univ. of Minnesota Press, 1948.

Essays by the editor and Oskar Lange and F. M. Taylor attempt to disprove the contention of Ludwig von Mises that a rational socialist organization is impossible.

LITTLEPAGE, JOHN D., and BESS DEMAREE. *In Search of Soviet Gold*. New York: Harcourt, 1937.

A lively story of the Soviet mining industry in Siberia by an American engineer.

LOUCKS, WILLIAM NEGELE, and J. WELDON HOOT. *Comparative Economic Systems*. New York: Harper, 1938. Revised edition, 1951.

A useful compilation of materials on the economic systems of the world during the last three decades.

MISES, LUDWIG VON. *Socialism: An Economic and Sociological Analysis*. Translated by J. Kahane. London: J. Cape, 1936.

By the Austrian economist who has long been a leading critic of socialism.

NEUMANN, FRANZ. *Behemoth: The Structure and Practice of National Socialism*. New York: Oxford Univ. Press, 1942.

Emphasizes the Nazi opposition to labor unions.

SCHUMPETER, J. A. *Capitalism, Socialism, and Democracy*, 3rd ed. New York: Harper, 1950.

Distinctive discussions, critical of many current clichés, of the central problems of contemporary economic and political organization.

SCHWARTZ, HARRY. *Russia's Soviet Economy*. New York: Prentice-Hall, 1950.

A student of Soviet life here presents a general analysis of Russian economic organization.

WILLIAMS, FRANCIS. *Socialist Britain*. New York: Viking Press, 1949.

An account of Britain under the Labour Government.

WOOTTON, BARBARA. *Freedom Under Planning*. Chapel Hill: Univ. of North Carolina Press, 1945.

Discusses the principles under which, in the author's view, the scope of planning can be expanded without peril to precious freedoms.

# PART 8

# The future of work and community

✿ Our final Part presents an over-all view of the place which work occupies in human affairs. Our special concern here is to relate the problem of work to certain central ethical issues such as the distribution of resources, the development of personality, the role of education, the uses and value of technology, the problem of coercion, and the future of civilization in a technological age.

We have noted at many points that human societies are inevitably compelled to decide how to apportion goods and services which are relatively scarce. KENNETH BOULDING, in the first selection in this Part, warns us that too much stress can be placed upon the problem of distribution and not enough upon the problem of production. He reminds us that the problem of human want is still, first of all, not how to distribute an unlimited number of satisfactions, but how to produce enough to secure a reasonable supply of the world's goods for all people, regardless of the particular scheme used for apportioning them.

Those who look for an absolute and final standard of justice in distribution will, Boulding indicates, look in vain: how to apportion resources and satisfactions always has been a human *decision* and always must be. There is no magic formula. Proponents of "capitalism" have sometimes thought that the "free market" offered an absolute and infallible method for meting out each man's reward in terms of his *contribution* to the economy. But, he suggests, this standard supposes that a man's capacity to sell his services or his product to the "sovereign consumer" measures his total worth as a man and as a member of society; and this, many have been inclined to dispute. Proponents of other systems have advocated distribution according to *need*, or distribution on the basis of absolute *equality*. But both solutions, carried to their extreme, would be difficult or impossible to put into operation. How, he asks, are we to judge one man's need as against another's? Or, if we endeavor to reward all men equally, what will happen to the incentives upon which economic activity is based? Actually, Boulding holds, the absolute standards of distribution which some have advocated are important and useful not so much because it would be possible or desirable to put any single one of them into operation, but because they offer guideposts by which we may perhaps work out a composite standard which can be put into execution in real life.

A second crucial problem which has concerned us throughout this book is the impact of specialization and division of labor upon human beings, considered not only as economic producers, but as total persons. How, if at all, can the high degree of specialization upon which our economy rests be reconciled with the full development of human personality? Our guiding principle, it has been contended by some, must be a view which does not isolate economic activity from the rest of life, or reduce all of life to work and production, but one which sees man as producer as only one aspect of the whole man, and society as producer as only one aspect of the whole social organization of life. Those who take part in the process of production must, many contemporary educators claim, be given not a specialized training for a narrow trade, but a liberal general education. This means that the scientist, or the administrative person, or any other "brain" worker, should be so trained as to be intimately aware of, and experienced in, the "manual" aspects of production. Conversely, it means that the worker on the assembly line, particularly the manual worker, should be educated to an understanding of the meaning and the whole significance of the process of which he is a part, both as artisan and as citizen.

A narrow system of economic cost accounting may, it has been remarked, lead us to believe that the narrowing of man to the point where he is a fragmentary cog in the wheel is the most "efficient" basis for production. But this view may overlook the many hidden social effects of overspecialization, which cannot be added up on a business ledger, and overlooks the fact that production exists as a means to life as a whole, and not life as a whole as a means to production.

Our next section is devoted to two over-all views of the direction which the total organization of the "social economy" might take. The Utopian society envisaged by H. G. WELLS is one in which the evils which grow out of private ownership of the means of production and out of the haphazard "planlessness" of industrial capitalism, have been replaced by a "socialized" society guided by reason and intelligence. It took men, Wells tells us in describing his society of the future, many generations and severe catastrophes before they realized the "irrationality" of the economic order in which they had been living. But once they had "come to their senses," they then set about to organize a society in which even central government would be unnecessary, because all the functions of the economy and society would be performed by intelligent, capable, and "socialized" people, and thus would "mesh" themselves without central coercion.

WILHELM ROEPKE, in the next selection, voices extreme skepticism about all such large-scale, "rationalized" mass societies. The great enemy of all high human interests, he believes, is the "mass society," in which all people are "proletarianized," stripped of property, of "roots," and of "meaning" in either their work or their lives in general. "Planning," Roepke holds, is not a cure for this "proletarianization" of man. Rather, the desire for collectivism is a *symptom* of what "mass society" has already done to man, and a symptom whose further extension only worsens the disease. The "planned society," the centralized "welfare state," is to Roepke the last stage in the decay of all basic human values. It is for these reasons that he insists that we *must* find ways to decentralize; to abolish our vast over-grown cities and our vast, dehumanized and monopolistic industries; to restore enterprise to a scale small enough to allow the individual to feel himself a part of it; and to return man to a home of his own, a garden, and roots in property which he can call his own.

The possibility of a "rationalization" of economic life, through the increased use of automatic machines has been suggested in many recent books and articles. Norbert Wiener of the Massachusetts Institute of Technology, Dean Louis N. Ridenour of the University of Illinois, and others suggest that we may be on the verge of a new industrial revolution which will see the thinking and organization functions in society taken over to a large extent by "thinking machines," just as earlier a large part of the work of manual laborers was taken over by the semi-automatic production line. Where, they seem to wonder, will this kind of development, should it take place, lead us?

Many persons have felt that the "machine" has already become a monster which threatens to annihilate man, or at the least to destroy his civilization and his culture. This fear is symbolized in Mary Shelley's tale of Frankenstein's monster, the superhuman machine which destroyed its inventor. Is the Frankenstein's monster of super-technology going to destroy us in like manner, many have asked? Not necessarily so, says FRANZ BORKENAU. Or, he says, even given the chance that it may, there is no such thing as turning back. We must take our chances by going forward and endeavoring to harness technology in the service of human values. Those who say we have had enough of the machine and should give up our technology in order to recapture the values of the past overlook, Borkenau holds, the fact that technology is an integral part of human *knowledge*. One does not destroy the atom bomb, he would suggest, by destroying atomic *bombs*; it is the knowledge and not the artifact which persists as a part of our culture. To turn our backs upon technology and to endeavor to destroy it or limit its development would be to turn our backs upon human science and to prohibit the human quest for knowledge. Such an effort to recapture the values of a pretechnological age would mean not the realization of high human values, but the destruction of man's highest attributes: his capacity to think, to explore, and to create.

In these final readings, we endeavor to set the problems of economic life within the broad framework of social values. The formulation of an intelligent view of economic life rests—as does the formulation of an intelligent view of any aspect of life—upon an informed decision as to the *ends* which one desires and upon well-grounded knowledge as to the *means* by which they might be attained. Ends and means, values and techniques, interact with one another at every point in economic life as they do in all of life. Not all that is desirable is possible, not all that is possible is desirable; and in one's final judgment, one tries to ascertain how to secure the most of what is to be desired in the light of the opportunities and limitations at hand.

The readings in Part 8 are not, of course, presented as answers which we are to learn and accept. This would be impossible, even were it desirable, for the authors in Part 8 do not all agree with one another. What we have tried to do in this Part is to provide provocative statements on the broadest issues in economic life, with the hope that they may sharpen our thinking, bring to a focus the materials which we have studied in this Book, and perhaps inspire us to go on and help find better answers than these authors, or any other authors, have yet discovered.

SECTION A

**Distribution and justice**

## 38   Kenneth E. Boulding: *The Ethics and Economics of Equality*

❦ *Throughout history men have pondered the problem of how scarce goods shall be distributed. The problem is both an ethical and an economic one. Looked at from the standpoint of human justice, it becomes one of judging, according to some human standard, how much of the group product each person is morally entitled to receive. Viewed from the economic standpoint, it becomes one of judging what will be the effect upon economic productivity and stability, of different possible schemes of distribution.*

*Kenneth Boulding (1910–    ) is Professor of Economics at the University of Michigan. As an economist he has been very much concerned with the relationship between economics and ethics. In the field of economics he is the author of* Economic Analysis *(1941, revised 1948),* The Economics of Peace *(1945), and* A Reconstruction of Economics *(1950). He has also published a volume of poetry,* There Is a Spirit *(1945). Our reading is reprinted by permission of Prentice-Hall, Inc., from* The Economics of Peace, *pp. 102–3. Copyright 1945 by Prentice-Hall, Inc.*

Although from a realistic point of view economic progress is the most important economic problem to the majority of the world's population, yet the question of justice in distribution probably bulks much larger in the thought of the politically conscious elements. It is a commonplace of political oratory that "we have solved the problem of production, and it only remains to solve the problem of distribution." This sentiment is not confined to soapbox radicals; it might almost be described as the hallmark of liberal orthodoxy. . . .

. . . . .

## UNPRODUCTIVENESS IS THE MORE SERIOUS PROBLEM

It is of course true . . . that there is a very real problem of "distribution and purchasing power" to be solved. Americans in particular, who have bitter memories of a depression in which the paradox of "poverty in the midst of plenty" was all too apparent, and who observe great wealth and miserable poverty living almost side-by-side, may be excused for thinking that distribution and purchasing power are the fundamental problems. When we look at the world as a whole, however, it is all too clear that the problem of productivity—that is, of economic progress—is really the most important. The black mass of grinding poverty under which a half to three quarters of the world's people subsist is not due primarily to exploitation, or to bad distribution of income, or to lack of purchasing power. It is due to the sheer unproductiveness of the mass of human labor. In those regions where the standard of life has been most spectacularly raised during the past two or three centuries, this improvement has come about not primarily through a redistribution of wealth or income, but through the increase of per capita productivity. . . .

. . . . .

## PRODUCTION AND DISTRIBUTION ARE NOT SEPARATE PROBLEMS

There is another error involved in the orthodox liberal assumption which is likely to lead to trouble. It is the assumption that "production" and "distribution" are *separate* problems; that society, as it were, cooks up the total product first in her capacious ovens and then distributes it in a quite arbitrary and haphazard way to the re-

cipients who clamor around her table. In fact, production and distribution are not separate problems, but are merely different aspects of the whole economic process— not perhaps indissolubly wedded in all respects, but nevertheless connected by high degrees of kinship. The product and its distribution are mutually determined in the whole process of determining prices, outputs, and inputs. It is extremely important to know, therefore, what is the exact connection between production and distribution; how far can the state intervene in economic life in the direction of greater equality, for instance, without causing a decline in production? Is there indeed a clash between progress and security? Is there a conflict between the ideal of equal distribution and the ideal of economic progress, and if so, how far should we sacrifice the one in order to attain the other? These are questions of the utmost importance and are much neglected in contemporary liberal thought. This chapter does not propose to answer them completely, but to indicate some principles which are necessary to understand if an answer is to be found.

## ALL INCOME COMES FROM PROPERTY, EVEN WAGES

The first principle of distribution is that the distribution of income depends on the distribution of property, that is, of capital, for in the last analysis all income is derived from property. It might seem at first sight that income from labor (wages and salaries) is not income from property. In fact, however, we only receive wages and salaries because we have property in our own minds and bodies. Wages and salaries are incomes derived from the sale of the services of our minds and bodies. If we did not own these services, and particularly if we did not own the source of these services, we obviously could not sell them. Wages, therefore, are income derived from our property in our own minds and bodies. This is quite clear in a slave system, where a slave receives maintenance, not wages, like a domestic animal, and anything that he produces over and above his mainte-

nance belongs to his master. In a free society the fact is somewhat obscured because each man is his own slave, and consequently labor income is never capitalized;
we do not, in our accounting (as in strict
theory we should) place a capital value on
our own bodies and minds, and hence we
do not see our labor income as proceeding
from this capital embodied in our bodies.
A slave, however, does have a capital value
placed on him, because he can be bought
and sold. Hence, the labor income from a
slave is clearly the result of investment,
and the value of a slave depends on the anticipations of slave owners regarding the
future labor income to be derived from him,
just as the value of a house depends on the
anticipations of house owners as to the income to be derived from houses. The fact
that our property in our own bodies is not
transferable to others—that we have an
"inalienable right" to liberty—is responsible
for our failure to set a value on our bodies
in our accounts. . . .

. . . . .

### INCOME IS UNEQUALLY DISTRIBUTED
### BECAUSE CAPITAL IS

The problem of unequal distribution of
income therefore resolves itself into that
of the unequal distribution of capital in the
broad sense outlined above. The reasons
for an unequal distribution of income lie in
these historical forces which have led to an
unequal distribution of capital. The remedy
also for unequal distribution of income
must be found in setting up institutions that
will lead to a wider diffusion of capital and
will discourage its concentration into few
hands.

### INALIENABLE AND TRANSFERABLE
### CAPITAL

In this connection, we must distinguish
between *inalienable* capital, of which almost the sole example is our bodies and
minds, and *transferable* capital, ownership
of which can be transferred from one individual to another, including almost the
whole mass of *material* capital. There is a
certain amount of inequality in the distri-

bution of inalienable capital which is absolutely necessary and which cannot be
destroyed without destroying the productive process. Certain abilities, for instance,
are scarce, difficult to acquire, and perhaps
troublesome to exercise. The capital value
of the bodies of those individuals who possess these abilities must be high, or else
these abilities will not be forthcoming. In
the present state of human nature, at least,
unless a skilled engineer is paid somewhat
more than a common laborer, not enough
people will go to the trouble and inconvenience of becoming a skilled engineer.
It is true that the reward of skilled jobs and
scarce abilities lies partly in the pleasure
of skilled work and the prestige that is
attached to responsible positions. But these
things are not apparently enough to overcome the reluctance of mankind to acquire
skills and to take responsibilities in quantity adequate to meet the needs of society.
Nobody doubts that even if engineers and
managers were paid the same real wages
as common labor *some* people would be
willing, even on these terms, to spend years
of their life in training or to take on themselves the onerous load of managerial responsibility. But the fact that in a competitive society skill and responsibility nearly
always command a higher monetary reward
than common labor indicates that this
higher reward is necessary in order to induce a sufficient quantity of these scarce
abilities to be forthcoming. The experience
of Russian Communism is a good confirma-
tion of this principle. Starting with a pronounced equalitarian bias, the Russian system has been forced to introduce an increasing degree of inequality of personal incomes
in the interest of productive efficiency.

### ONLY TRANSFERABLE CAPITAL CAN
### BE EQUALLY DISTRIBUTED, AND
### THEN ONLY IN A SLAVE STATE

Somewhat different principles apply to
transferable capital, for in this case there
is no absolute reason why everyone should
not possess an equal amount. Nevertheless
such radical changes in our social institutions would have to be made if the equal

distribution of transferable capital were to be secured that we might well hesitate before setting up equal distribution as an end in itself. It is almost impossible to conceive of a situation in which individual ownership of capital is permitted and in which the historical process does not result in a certain inequality in distribution. This arises partly by chance, as fortune smiles on one individual and frowns on another, and partly through the differences in individual characters. Some individuals are of a frugal disposition and accumulate property; some are spendthrifts and dissipate what capital they have. Some individuals are able administrators of property, buying and selling wisely, so that the value of their possession continually rises. Others are careless administrators and their property declines in value. Inheritance also plays its part in creating inequalities; when wealthy families have few children, and intermarry, wealth becomes more concentrated. When the wealthy have many inheritors, and when the poor and the rich intermarry, wealth becomes less concentrated. As long as property is privately owned, therefore, and as long as the owner has a right to the income from his property, it is impossible to prevent the development of certain inequalities of ownership. Paradoxically enough, the most thoroughly equalitarian society would be a slave state, in which all individuals were slaves of the state and none owned property. It is the right of man to the produce of his own labor that results in the unequal distribution of property, for some will conserve that produce and some will squander it.

### THE STATE CAN AND SHOULD INTERVENE TO MAKE DISTRIBUTION MORE EQUAL

This is not to say, however, that the state should not or cannot intervene to secure a more equal distribution both of property and of income than would ensue if events were left free to take their course. The principal weapons at the disposal of the state in this connection are the inheritance laws on the one hand and the system of taxation on the other. If primogeniture is the rule, so that the estate of a father passes unbroken to the eldest son, inheritance works in the direction of a greater concentration of wealth. If, on the other hand, it is customary to divide estates among many heirs on the death of the owner, there will be a tendency for property to become more equally distributed. The most powerful weapon in the hands of the state for creating a more equalitarian society is, of course, taxation. Inheritance taxes have an important effect in breaking up concentrated wealth. A progressive income tax has an even more important effect in nullifying the effects of an unequal distribution of property. The distribution of income, up to a point, can be made much more equalitarian than the distribution of property by penalizing those with large incomes through progressive taxation. If a man with large property has to pay 80 per cent of his income in taxes, while a man with small property pays nothing, it is clear that the relative advantages of large properties are much diminished.

### LIMITATIONS ON THE DISTRIBUTIVE POWER OF THE STATE

Although the state by its tax system can modify considerably the distribution of incomes, its power in this respect is not absolute. There is some level of reward below which the owner of a factor of production will not feel it worth while to put his property to productive use. This level is usually called the "supply price" of the services in question. Thus, there is some wage below which a man will not work at a particular occupation; there is some rate of profit below which a capitalist would rather not hold his property in the form of productive goods, but would prefer to hold it idle in the form of money. This level of remuneration, however, is usually less than the income which the owner actually receives. Most men would be willing to continue at their present job even at a smaller wage and most capitalists would be willing to continue to hold goods at a lower rate of profit than they are now receiving. . . .

## THE CRITERIA OF DISTRIBUTIONAL JUSTICE

Before we can draw any conclusions as to distributional policy, it will be necessary to examine a little further what we mean by "distributional justice," or "social justice." What criteria can we set up to test the justice of any system or arrangement? Immediately we find ourselves in the presence of conflicting ideals. On the one hand, "justice" implies the rendering to each of his "deserts." The simplest and most practical expression of this criterion of justice would be "to each according to what he produces." On the other hand stands a rival criterion, the criterion of need. "To each according to his need" sounds as plausible, or even more plausible, than "To each according to his contribution."

### DISTRIBUTION ACCORDING TO CONTRIBUTION

Neither of these criteria is altogether satisfactory. The narrow ideal of justice that is based upon deserts leads us into hopeless contradictions. In the first place, how can we know what each deserves? "Use every man after his own desert and who should 'scape whipping?" It is a dangerous ethical assumption to identify "desert" with "contribution." Yet this identification seems to be the only solid ground in the midst of a bog of tentative opinion and groundless judgments. Who is to judge between "happy, undeserving A" on the one hand, and "wretched, meritorious B" on the other? The only concept of justice which permits of any objective solution on the criterion of desert is "reward according to contribution." The impersonal dictates of the market set prices for the services of the various factors of production, and the contribution to the total product made by any factor can be estimated by multiplying the price of these services by the quality rendered. This may be called the "pure capitalist" solution of the problem. If the market price of the services of my body is 40 cents an hour and I work 2,400 hours in the year, both the contribution that I make to the total value of the product, and the value of the reward that I receive for this contribution are equal to $960 a year.

### THE "PURE CAPITALIST" SOLUTION IS UNSATISFACTORY

For all its apparent logic, the pure capitalist" solution fails to satisfy us. In the first place, if we assume the rights of private property in transferable goods, it is likely to lead to a degree of inequality that we feel to be dangerous. We also have a strong feeling that income from material property, or from loans and bonds, is in some sense "unearned" in a way that income from personal exertion is not. Even our income tax law used to recognize the distinction, and "unearned" income was taxed at a higher rate than "earned income." The pure capitalist criterion, however, would treat all income alike, whether it was derived from property in our own bodies and minds or from property in stocks, bonds, and real estate. Finally, we are forced to recognize that society has certain obligations towards nonproducers, particularly towards children, old people, the sick, the insane, and the involuntarily unemployed. We must break down the criterion of "reward according to contribution" in some cases; hence, it loses its validity as a general formula. The reason for this seems to be that there is a certain sense of kinship that binds us all together and makes us feel in a measure responsible for the welfare of all. We must relieve the unproductive elements of society because in some sense they "belong" to us, just as a limb belongs to us. A craftsman does not deny his feet shoes because he earns his living with his hands. We cannot be pure individualists because we are not pure individuals; we are bound together in a social web that permits none of us to be either completely independent of others or completely nonresponsible for others. It is on this rock that the pure capitalist criterion splits.

### THE "PURE COMMUNIST" CRITERION IS ALSO UNSATISFACTORY

Should we, then, go to the other extreme and adopt what may be called the "pure communist" criterion—"from each according to his abilities, to each according to his needs." There is much that is superficially attractive about the idea of distribution according to need. Nevertheless, on examination it turns out to be full of difficulties, both theoretical and practical. Just as it is impossible to judge the deserts of another, so it is impossible to judge his need. The criterion of need, therefore, breaks down on two grounds: theoretically, because it is essentially mechanistic; practically, because it presents an administrative problem of impossible complexity.

### DIFFICULTIES OF DISTRIBUTION ACCORDING TO NEED ILLUSTRATED BY RATIONING

Nothing illustrates these difficulties better than the problem of rationing scarce supplies. The simplest method of apportionment is, of course, to give everyone an equal share. This has been done—in wartime, for instance—in the case of sugar and coffee. Equal distribution, however, is clearly inequitable, for needs are not equal. Some like sugar, some do not; some bake cakes, some do not; some are diabetic, some are not. Hence, rationing means no hardship for some, and considerable hardship for others. The equal rationing of coffee is even more inequitable—a household where only one member drinks coffee feels no pinch, whereas a household of heavy coffee drinkers is sharply restricted. Gasoline rationing is even more difficult. With the same ration, A is happy, B is not; for A the car is a luxury, for B it is a necessity. Even for the simplest needs, therefore, equal rationing is hopelessly unjust. Hence, there must be graduated rationing; special food rations for heavy workers, special gasoline rations for heavy drivers, and so on. The attempt to ration for individual needs, however, results in a piling of board on board and application on application until red tape engulfs everybody. Even in the case of such basic "need" as food, rationing cannot be applied as a universal principle. If all food were rationed, no matter how carefully the ration is graduated according to age, sex, and occupation, some would starve and some would be relatively comfortable,

for nutritional requirements differ markedly from person to person. It is a basic principle of food rationing in wartime, therefore, that some important source of calories must be left unrationed—such as bread in England or potatoes in Germany.

### THE "POINT PRICE" SYSTEM

It is significant that as the technique of rationing develops it tends to approximate more and more to a price system, using the criterion of effective demand rather than of need. Point rationing is a partial return to a price system; what is, in effect, a supplementary money is issued (the ration tickets), and demand is equated to supply by adjusting "point prices" rather than the regular money prices. But whereas money prices can adjust to every local situation, rising to accommodate a temporary scarcity and falling to relieve a temporary glut, "point prices" have to be fixed by the rationing authority at regular intervals. Errors in the setting of point prices therefore lead to large wastages of perishable products before they are adjusted. Any "administered" price system is bound to run into these difficulties, and as the control of distribution necessarily involves control of prices, controlled distribution likewise runs into a similar administrative impasse.

### DIFFICULTY OF ESTIMATING "NEEDS"

If the criterion of need is so difficult to apply even in the case of basic necessities, how much more difficult would it be to apply it to the luxuries and conveniences of life! The thought of distributing phonograph records, books, travel, and the like according to individual need by some rationing authority is one before which the stoutest communist might quail. It may be objected that we can still permit goods to be allocated through the price system, so that there is a certain amount of consumers' choice, and yet ration *incomes* according to need. But what standards could we follow in such a case? Should we give all university graduates double the income of high school graduates, because presumably a college education breeds expensive tastes?

There is simply no administrative solution to the problem of allocation according to need, once we get away from the barest necessities, and even there the administrative problem is almost insuperably difficult and can only be solved by rule-of-thumb methods.

### "NEEDS" AND "ABILITIES" DO NOT CORRESPOND

There is, however, an even more fundamental objection to the pure communist criterion. It is that abilities and needs are not likely to correspond. The things we most want to do (the activities miscalled "leisure") do not in general produce a sufficient quantity of the commodities that we need. This is the fact which makes necessary the whole system of economic values and institutions. . . .

. . . . .

### THE ABOLITION OF EXPLOITATION AND DISCRIMINATION

There is another ideal which is continually present in the discussions of distributional justice—connected perhaps with those mentioned above and yet important enough to deserve independent consideration. This is the ideal of the abolition of exploitation and discrimination. . . .

. . . . .

It remains to consider the conclusions for economic policy which follow from this discussion. They may be summarized as follows:

1) Although the problem of distribution is in reality less important than that of economic progress, the state has an obligation to intervene in this matter in order to prevent exploitation and discrimination and in order to prevent anyone in the society falling below a basic minimum standard of life.

2) There are several methods available for the elimination of exploitation and discrimination. As this is always due primarily to a monopolistic situation, it is important that all such conditions, where they cannot be broken up by law, should be regulated by law. Labor unions have an important function in preventing the exploitation of individuals. Minimum wage laws may also accomplish this end. It is more difficult to prevent the exploitation of groups. Particularly is this true where the exploiters are not the employers, but the organized workers. A tight craft union with restricted membership is as much a monopoly as the old Standard Oil Company and needs regulating just as much. A degree of regulation aimed simply at preventing unreasonable obstacles to membership, and eliminating obstructions to economic progress would probably be adequate. Direct legislation aimed against discrimination is also possible, and is a little-tried field. The Fair Employment Practices Committee is an example of something that could be made much more general and permanent. Many political and sectional interests stand in the way of a federal anti-discrimination law; nevertheless, it is a completely logical development of the American ideal and should not prove impossible to put through.

3) The state has an obligation to see that nobody falls below a certain basic minimum standard of life. The level of the basic minimum which a society can afford depends on the economic productivity of society, and in particular on its "economic surplus." If the problem of distribution is to be solved, then, it is extremely desirable to develop a large economic surplus. There are two ways of achieving this end. The most important is the direct encouragement of economic progress. Not to be neglected, however, is the development of a social pressure against riches and the display of wealth, and in favor of simple and frugal standards of life. This is of particular importance in countries where productivity and the economic surplus are low, for under these circumstances it is impossible to achieve a reasonable rate of economic progress unless consumption can be forced below the meager level of production, so as to permit of accumulation. Even in rich countries, however, provided that monetary and fiscal policies are devised that will ensure full employment, it is highly desirable

to educate the people in favor of simple standards of life. In the richest of contemporary societies, and still more if we take into account the world as a whole, the abolition of poverty will require a considerable restriction of consumption on the part not only of the well-to-do but of the middle classes. . . . Our slogan . . . in the field of distribution should be "it's ridiculous to be rich!"—the natural corollary being, in the field of full employment, "it's ridiculous to be poor."

4) The principal instrument in the redistribution of income is, of course, the system of public finance. By taxing the rich and giving benefits to the poor, a society can materially change its distribution of income, provided that its taxes do not dig below the economic surplus. One of the more difficult problems in this connection is how far the benefits should be in cash and how far in kind. Some of the benefits, of course, must be in the form of free services—for example, education, public health, and so on. Some of them should probably be in the intermediate form of insurance benefits. There is, however, a large debatable ground between, say, the advocates of relief in cash and the advocates of relief in

kind. There is also a difficult problem concerning the recipients of benefits. Every member of a society, rich and poor alike, might be regarded as sharing a potential property right in the economic surplus, and therefore entitled to a money income from the state—an income which would, of course, be taxed away again in the case of the rich. There is a certain attractive simplicity about this idea of a "social dividend." If it were much above a bare subsistence, however, it might have a detrimental effect on productivity, for many would not wish to supplement this income by working. The alternative solution of a complex system of social security benefits is probably more desirable, though less elegant. In this connection, the special position of children deserves notice. A large proportion of "primary poverty" is due to the existence of large families. A wage that supports two in comfort brings starvation to a dozen. If we admit the logic of public education, we must also admit the logic of public responsibility for the nutrition, health, and clothing of the child, for it is absurd to give a child education which he cannot absorb because of his poverty and malnutrition. . . .

SECTION B

**The quest for a humane society**

# 39 H. G. Wells: *Work and State in Utopia*

❦ *The more complex and minute the division of labor, the more complicated and centralized the social organization tends to become. But complicated organization tends to produce bureaucracy, a high degree of coercive power in the hands of a few people, and irresponsibility in those occupying positions of control. Thus, in addition to the immediate psychological and sociological problems posed in the previous reading, division of labor poses the political problem of power in social organization. Is*

*there a way out—one which will preserve the benefits of technology and high speciali-*
*zation, and yet avoid the increasing coercion of the individual by social, economic, and*
*political organizations, particularly by the state?*

*H. G. Wells (1866–1946) believed there is a way out. His basic argument, as pre-*
*sented in the following reading, was that if men will study social organization seriously,*
*using the methods of science, they will be able to find ways of eliminating the coercive*
*factor in society altogether. Wells was a leading literary figure for half a century. Al-*
*most all his novels and stories have social themes, and several of them develop his*
*utopian notions. Among his many works are* A Modern Utopia *(1905),* The New
Machiavelli *(1911),* God the Invisible King *(1917), and* Men Like Gods *(1923). Our*
*reading is taken from the last-named book with permission of The Macmillan Com-*
*pany and the estate of H. G. Wells.*

T hen do you mean to say," he continued, addressing the Utopians with an expression of great intelligence, "that your affairs are all managed by special bodies or organizations—one scarcely knows what to call them—without any co-ordination of their activities?"

"The activities of our world," said Urthred, "are all co-ordinated to secure the general freedom. We have a number of intelligences directed to the general psychology of the race and to the interaction of one collective function upon another."

"Well, isn't that group of intelligences a governing class?" said Mr. Burleigh.

"Not in the sense that they exercise any arbitrary will," said Urthred. "They deal with general relations, that is all. But they rank no higher, they have no more precedence on that account than a philosopher has over a scientific specialist."

"This is a republic indeed!" said Mr. Burleigh. "But how it works and how it came about I cannot imagine. Your state is probably a highly socialistic one?"

"You still live in a world in which nearly everything except the air, the high roads, the high seas and the wilderness is privately owned?"

"We do," said Mr. Catskill. "Owned— and competed for."

"We have been through that stage. We found at last that private property in all

but very personal things was an intolerable nuisance to mankind. We got rid of it. An artist or a scientific man has complete control of all the material he needs, we all own our tools and appliances and have rooms and places of our own, but there is no property for trade or speculation. All this militant property, this property of manoeuvre, has been quite got rid of. But how we got rid of it is a long story. It was not done in a few years. The exaggeration of private property was an entirely natural and necessary stage in the development of human nature. It led at last to monstrous results, but it was only through these monstrous and catastrophic results that men learnt the need and nature of the limitations of private property."

Mr. Burleigh had assumed an attitude which was obviously habitual to him. He sat very low in his chair with his long legs crossed in front of him and the thumb and fingers of one hand placed with meticulous exactness against those of the other.

"I must confess," he said, "that I am most interested in the peculiar form of Anarchism which seems to prevail here. Unless I misunderstand you completely, every man attends to his own business as the servant of the state. I take it you have—you must correct me if I am wrong—a great number of people concerned in the production and distribution and preparation of food; they inquire, I assume, into the needs of the world, they satisfy them and they are a law unto themselves in their way of doing it. They conduct researches, they make experiments. Nobody compels, obliges, restrains or prevents them. ('People talk to them about it,' said Urthred with a faint smile.) And again others produce and manufacture and study metals for all mankind and are also a law unto themselves. Others again see to the habitability of your world, plan and arrange these delightful habitations, say who shall use them and how they shall be used. Others pursue pure science. Others experiment with sensory and imaginative possibilities and are artists. Others again teach."

"They are very important," said Lychnis.

"And they all do it in harmony—and due proportion. Without either a central legislature or executive. I will admit that all this seems admirable—but impossible. Nothing of the sort has ever been even suggested yet in the world from which we come."

. . . . .

The conversation continued desultory in form and yet the exchange of ideas was rapid and effective. Quite soon, as it seemed to Mr. Barnstaple, an outline of the history of Utopia from the Last Age of Confusion onward shaped itself in his mind.

The more he learnt of that Last Age of Confusion the more it seemed to resemble the present time on earth. In those days the Utopians had worn abundant clothing and lived in towns quite after the earthly fashion. A fortunate conspiracy of accidents rather than any set design had opened for them some centuries of opportunity and expansion. Climatic phases and political chances had smiled upon the race after a long period of recurrent shortage, pestilence and destructive warfare. For the first time the Utopians had been able to explore the whole planet on which they lived, and these explorations had brought great virgin areas under the axe, the spade and the plough. There had been an enormous increase in real wealth and in leisure and liberty. Many thousands of people were lifted out of the normal squalor of human life to positions in which they could, if they chose, think and act with unprecedented freedom. A few, a sufficient few, did. A vigorous development of scientific inquiry began and, trailing after it a multitude of ingenious inventions, produced a great enlargement of practical human power.

There had been previous outbreaks of the scientific intelligence in Utopia, but none before had ever occurred in such favourable circumstances or lasted long enough to come to abundant practical fruition. Now in a couple of brief centuries the Utopians, who had hitherto crawled about their planet like sluggish ants or travelled parasitically on larger and swifter animals, found themselves able to fly rapidly or speak instantaneously to any other point on the planet. They found themselves, too, in possession of mechanical power on a scale beyond all previous experience, and not simply of mechanical power; physiological and then psychological science followed in the wake of physics and chemistry, and extraordinary possibilities of control over his own body and over his social life dawned upon the Utopian. But these things came, when at last they did come, so rapidly and confusingly that it was only a small minority of people who realized the possibilities, as distinguished from the concrete achievements, of this tremendous expansion of knowledge. The rest took the novel inventions as they came, haphazard, with as little adjustment as possible of their thoughts and ways of living to the new necessities these novelties implied.

The first response of the general population of Utopia to the prospect of power, leisure and freedom thus opened out to it was proliferation. It behaved just as senselessly and mechanically as an other animal or vegetable species would have done. It bred until it had completely swamped the ampler opportunity that had opened before it. It spent the great gifts of science as rapidly as it got them in a mere insensate multiplication of the common life. At one time in the Last Age of Confusion the population of Utopia had mounted to over two thousand million.

"But what is it now?" asked Mr. Burleigh.

About two hundred and fifty million, the Utopians told him. That had been the maximum population that could live a fully developed life upon the surface of Utopia. But now with increasing resources the population was being increased.

. . . . .

The overcrowding of the planet in the Last Age of Confusion was, these Utopians insisted, the fundamental evil out of which all the others that afflicted the race arose. An overwhelming flood of newcomers poured into the world and swamped every effort the intelligent minority could make to educate a sufficient proportion of them to meet the demands of the new and still rapidly changing conditions of life. And the intelligent minority was not itself in any position to control the racial destiny. These great masses of population that had been blundered into existence, swayed by damaged and decaying traditions and amenable to the crudest suggestions, were the natural prey and support of every adventurer with a mind blatant enough and a conception of success coarse enough to appeal to them. The economic system, clumsily and convulsively reconstructed to meet the new conditions of mechanical production and distribution, became more and more a cruel and impudent exploitation of the multitudinous congestion of the common man by the predatory and acquisitive few. That all too common man was hustled through misery and subjection from his cradle to his grave; he was cajoled and lied to, he was bought, sold and dominated by an impudent minority, bolder and no doubt more energetic, but in all other respects no more intelligent than himself. It was difficult, Urthred said, for a Utopian nowadays to convey the monstrous stupidity, wastefulness and vulgarity to which these rich and powerful men of the Last Age of Confusion attained.

("We will not trouble you," said Mr. Burleigh. "Unhappily—we know. . . . We know. Only too well do we know.")

Upon this festering, excessive mass of population disasters descended at last like wasps upon a heap of rotting fruit. It was its natural, inevitable destiny. A war that affected nearly the whole planet dislocated its flimsy financial system and most of its economic machinery beyond any possibility of repair. Civil wars and clumsily conceived attempts at social revolution continued the disorganization. A series of years of bad weather accentuated the general shortage. The exploiting adventurers, too stupid to realize what had happened, continued to cheat and hoodwink the commonalty and burke any rally of honest men, as wasps will continue to eat even after their bodies have been cut away. The effort to make passed out of Utopian life, triumphantly superseded by the effort to get. Production dwindled down towards the vanishing point. Accumulated wealth vanished. An overwhelming system of debt, a swarm of creditors, morally incapable of helpful renunciation, crushed out all fresh initiative.

The long diastole in Utopian affairs that had begun with the great discoveries, passed into a phase of rapid systole. What plenty and pleasure was still possible in the world was filched all the more greedily by the adventurers of finance and speculative business. Organized science had long since been commercialized, and was "applied" now chiefly to a hunt for profitable patents and the forestalling of necessary supplies. The neglected lamp of pure science waned, flickered and seemed to go out again altogether, leaving Utopia in the beginning of a new series of Dark Ages like those before the age of discovery began. . . .

. . . . .

What happened, Mr. Barnstaple gathered, was a deliberate change in Utopian thought. A growing number of people were coming to understand that amidst the powerful and easily released forces that science and organization had brought within reach of man, the old conception of social life in the state, as a limited and legalized struggle of men and women to get the better of one another, was becoming too dangerous to endure, just as the increased dreadfulness of modern weapons was making the separate sovereignty of nations too dangerous to endure. There had to be new ideas and new conventions of human association if history was not to end in disaster and collapse.

All societies were based on the limitation by laws and taboos and treaties of the primordial fierce combativeness of the ancestral man-ape; that ancient spirit of self-assertion had now to undergo new restrictions commensurate with the new powers and dangers of the race. The idea of competition to possess, as the ruling idea of intercourse, was, like some ill-controlled furnace, threatening to consume the machine it had formely driven. The idea of creative service had to replace it. To that idea the human mind and will had to be turned if social life was to be saved. Propositions that had seemed, in former ages, to be inspired and exalted idealism began now to be recognized not simply as sober psychological truth but as practical and urgently necessary truth. In explaining this Urthred expressed himself in a manner that recalled to Mr. Barnstaple's mind certain very familiar phrases; he seemed to be saying that whosoever would save his life should lose it, and that whosoever would give his life should thereby gain the whole world.

. . . . .

The impression given Mr. Barnstaple was not of one of those violent changes which our world has learnt to call revolutions, but of an increase of light, a dawn of new ideas, in which the things of the old order went on for a time with diminishing vigour until people began as a matter of common sense to do the new things in the place of the old.

The beginnings of the new order were in discussions, books and psychological laboratories; the soil in which it grew was found in schools and colleges. The old order gave small rewards to the school-master, but its dominant types were too busy with the struggle for wealth and power to take much heed of teaching: it was left to any man or woman who would give thought and labour without much hope of tangible rewards, to shape the world anew in the minds of the young. And they did so shape it. In a world ruled ostensibly by adventurer politicians, in a world where men came to power through floundering business enterprises and financial cunning, it was presently being taught and understood that extensive private property was a social nuisance, and that the state could not do its work properly nor education produce its proper results, side by side with a class of irresponsible rich people. For, by their very nature, they assailed, they corrupted, they undermined every state undertaking; their flaunting existences distorted and disguised all the values of life. They had to go, for the good of the race.

"Didn't they fight?" asked Mr. Catskill pugnaciously.

They had fought irregularly but fiercely. The fight to delay or arrest the coming of the universal scientific state, the educational state, in Utopia, had gone on as a conscious struggle for nearly five centuries. . . .

But the service of the new idea that had been launched into the world never failed; it seized upon the men and women it needed with compelling power. Before the scientific state was established in Utopia more than a million martyrs had been killed for it . . . point after point was won in education, in social laws, in economic method. . . .

. . . . .

Every Utopian child is taught to the full measure of its possibilities and directed to the work that is indicated by its desires and capacity. It is born well. It is born of perfectly healthy parents; its mother has chosen to bear it after due thought and

preparation. . . . Kindness and civility becomes ingrained habits, for all about it are
kind and civil. And in particular the growth
of its imagination is watched and encouraged. . . .

If the individual is indolent there is no
great loss, there is plenty for all in Utopia,
but then it will find no lovers, nor will it
ever bear children, because no one in
Utopia loves those who have neither energy
nor distinction. There is much pride of the
mate in Utopian love. And there is no idle
rich "society" in Utopia, nor games and
shows for the mere looker-on. . . . It is a
pleasant world indeed for holidays, but
not for those who would continuously do
nothing. . . .

. . . . .

Utopia has no parliament, no politics, no
private wealth, no business competition, no
police nor prisons, no lunatics, no defectives
nor cripples, and it has none of these things
because it has schools and teachers who are
all that schools and teachers can be. Politics,
trade and competition are the methods of
adjustment of a crude society. Such methods of adjustment have been laid aside in
Utopia for more than a thousand years.
There is no rule nor government needed by
adult Utopians because all the rule and government they need they have had in childhood and youth.

Said Lion: "Our education is our government."

# 40 Wilhelm Roepke: *Mass Society, Person, and Community*

❦ *Some will argue that the idea of a noncoercive "mass" Utopia, such as that outlined by Wells in the preceding selection, is only a dangerous illusion. Among them is
Wilhelm Roepke (1899–      ).*

*Among the greatest evils in modern society, Roepke maintains, are the "proletariani-
zation" of men and the impersonalism characteristic of an economy where property is
held in massive units, whether the ownership be private or public. Proletarianization,
as Roepke uses the term, means the uprooting of men from their attachment to the
land and their separation from direct and personal ownership of property. Insofar as
the development of modern technology is responsible for this, Roepke suggests, it
must be controlled and limited, not extended. He would like to see a large degree of
decentralization, the establishment of peasant proprietorship as a pattern of agrarian
organization, and the revival of handicrafts to take the place, in part, of the machine.*

*Roepke, a native of Germany, has taught at the Universities of Jena, Marburg,
and Istanbul. Among his works are* Crises and Cycles *(1936),* The Nature and Solution of the German Problem *(1947),* Civitas Humana *(1944), and* The Social Crisis
of Our Time *(1950). Our reading is reprinted from the English translation (1948) of*
Civitas Humana *by Cyril S. Fox, with permission of the publisher, William Hodge
and Company, Ltd.*

Closely connected but in no wise identical with all this congestion and regimentation [of modern man] is that pathological process which we designate proletarianisation, and indeed in its widest material as well as immaterial sense of uprooting, nomadisation and finally that anonymous and impersonal collectivist social services mechanism. That this is one of the very worst sins of our western society, and that it is a prime duty to rescue the proletariat from a type of existence wholly unsuited to human beings and to assimilate this body with the rest of the nation and thus make citizens of them is an unassailable truth. Probably there are even now people who are unconscious of the full weight of this crime against society, its true nature and the far-reaching consequences it involves. Many still believe that the wretchedness of the proletariat is due to insufficient wages and too long hours of work. From this they draw the conclusion that it is merely a simple matter of material standards of life which can be settled only by means of higher wages and shorter working hours. The majority of measures of traditional social policy are directed solely toward this end, that is, the English "Beveridge Plan" which has led to a certain superficial jubilation not only does not depart from this line but even pursues it to its utmost limit. This point of view does but illustrate the blindness with which some people view the material things in life as the most important and neglect the deeper lying problems of human nature.

And there are others who seem so accustomed to the proletarianisation of society that the thought scarcely enters their heads that this state of affairs should or can be changed. These people only prove how short our memory is when we maintain that so it must be and that there is no alternative. . . . It may be remembered that it was Jefferson's nightmare that the peasants and workers who comprised the population of the United States of America at the end of the eighteenth century would become changed one day into a propertyless and nomadic proletariat on the one hand and a capitalistic plutocracy on the other. . . .

It is appalling to think of the tearing speed with which this process of proletarianisation has been taking place everywhere and going hand in hand with technical progress in big business, with the uncanny growth of big cities and industrial areas, with the depopulation of the open countryside owing to measures inimical to the peasants, and with that increase in population with the unfortunate results of which we are already only too familiar. This proletarian existence which is rapidly becoming the destiny of human beings and which must be regarded as a type of life, of work and of habitat wholly unsuited to human beings, represents a pathological state of affairs which has never been witnessed in our history before to the same extent. Although this is not yet the predominant situation even in the large industrial countries, at least, apart from the collectivist nations, it has given its stamp more and more to our whole civilisation. However, this deterioration has affected individual countries to a very varying extent. Some countries, like England and the United States, are threatened in a high degree, whereas others, like Switzerland, can be looked upon as "slight" cases. We should consider those countries as rabidly proletarianised in which the disappearance of the country folk and craftsmanship, the spread of giant works and the concentration of property have all led to a large part of the population becoming dependent, propertyless, urbanised wage-earners and made to fit into the hierarchy of the commercial and industrial mammoth concern. . . .

We know well how deeply we err if we maintain that proletarianisation is a natural process, that things could not have been otherwise and that there is no alternative. Who and whatever must be held responsible, let it suffice that in recent generations, and in a manner as yet unrealised by many, whole masses have been torn away from the anchor of property, with the result that these people are living from hand to mouth, that they—and fundamentally this applies to all of us, including us economists—have become accustomed to think almost exclusively in terms of money income, and indeed together with their property they have lost their conception of it as a category of importance and desirability for human beings; that with comprehensible energy substitutes for security and for existence are being sought which previously long-term working conditions, property, savings, self-help, professional and family solidarity would have guaranteed; and lastly that this substitute has now apparently been found in the modern government with its social services and in its impersonal and mechanical solidarity of mass.

The proletariat is lacking in precisely that which characterises the peasants and the craftsmen, wholly apart from the purely material aspects of life; the independence and autonomy of their whole existence, their roots in home, property, environment, family and occupation; the personal character and the traditions of their work. Thus it is becoming clear to us that what the proletariat lacks is at bottom that form of existence which is appropriate for human beings and which affords us the kind of satisfaction that we experience when we live in harmony with those deeper forces of our nature and of which we are barely conscious. Proletarianisation means nothing less than that human beings have got into a highly dangerous sociological and anthropological state which is characterised by lack of property, lack of reserves of every kind (including the ties of family and neighbourhood), by economic servitude, uprooting, massed living quarters, militarisation of work, by estrangement from nature and by the mechanisation of productive activity; in short, by a general devitalisation and loss of personality.

．　．　．　．　．

. . . Work instead of being a satisfaction and fulfilment of life becomes a mere means and the hours spent at work a mere

liability, whereas normally these ought to represent an asset in the balance-sheet of life. Compensation for this state of affairs is sought all the more eagerly in consumption, but more often than not this means compensation in pleasures and distractions which are no less mechanical and void than the work. This floating humanity, the modern nomads as may well be understood—feel an intense longing for something which must be lacking to a great extent in such an existence, i.e., security and stability.

Congestion, regimentation, proletarianisation, collectivisation and the disappearance of the little properties of the masses, who incidentally are being continually recruited afresh from the crumbling middle classes, all these are discharged like a river into a mass delta, ordered, led and always further financed by the state, and in conjunction with the state together with its apparatus for taxation and "social services," produce a society which is drying up individuality in favor of collectivism and which is finally reducing human beings to the level of state slaves. . . .

．　．　．　．　．

. . . The sickness of our society is so severe, so all-embracing and so deep-rooted that no programme for a cure exists which we can produce out of a hat and hand over to Parliament to put into effect tomorrow, no Beveridge Plan in which everything is beautifully calculated, and no projects of vast organisation provided with a well thought-out clockwork mechanism. In fact thinking in terms of such plans and programmes belongs, as we have seen, rather to just that atmosphere which itself has been created by congestion and masses. The task of finding a remedy is exceptionally difficult and complex, so much so, that the working out of the details far surpasses the capacity of a single individual and must be dependent upon the co-operation of all who have recognised the urgency of the matter, and who, instead of directing their impatient questions at us, would do better to begin by asking themselves what is to be done. Which means that, armed with full knowledge of the fundamental disease and of the essence of congestion and proletarianisation, one must approach all the detailed questions of economic and social reform; one must fearlessly take account of the hideous development of our circumstances—the big city, the gigantic works, the rootlessness, the propertylessness, the loss of personality, the devitalisation, the estrangement from nature—and no less fearlessly draw the consequences.

It is only right that all these thoughts should occupy every single individual wherever he or she may happen to be, by day and by night, and torment him or her as much as it does the author of this book and his friends. They are thoughts which are characterised by moving in only one direction; *away* from centralisation in every connection, from all agglomerations, from the city pen and the factory coop, from accumulations of property and power which corrupt the one and proletarianise the other, from the soullessness and lack of dignity of labour through mechanised production and *towards* decentralisation in the widest and most comprehensive sense of the word; to the restoration of property; to a shifting of the social centre of gravity from above downwards; to the organic building-up of society from natural and neighbourly communities in a closed gradation starting with the family through parish and county to the nation; to a corrective for exaggerations in organisation, in specialisation, and in division of labour (with at least a minimum of self-maintenance from one's own soil); to the bringing back of all dimensions and proportions from the colossal to the humanly reasonable; to the development of fresh non-proletarian types of industry, that is to say to forms of industry adapted to peasants and craftsmen; to the natural furtherance of smaller units of factories and undertakings as well as to sociologically healthy forms of life and occupation, approaching as closely as possible that ideal border-line of peasant and craftsman; to the breaking-up of monopolies of every kind and to the struggle against concentrations of businesses and undertakings

where and whenever possible; to the breaking-up of the big cities and industrial districts, and to a properly directed country-planning having as its aim a decentralisation of residence and production; to the re-awakening of professional sentiment and to the restoration of the dignity of all honest labour; to the creation of conditions which render possible a healthy family life and a non-artificial manner of bringing up children; to the resurrection of a cultural hierarchy which will put an end to the tumults of ambition and give each rung of the ladder its appropriate place. . . .

. . . . .

We can now see our way to a programme of economic and social reform; one that . . . looks . . . to changes in outlook and to well-considered assaults on strategic points of economic and social life. Quite the most important of these strategic points is the question of the restoration of property for the masses, something which should do away with that leading characteristic of the proletariat, namely the lack of property.

The "restoration of property." That would seem to be a pretty radical demand. . . .

In the *first* instance, a policy of this nature demands as its most important prerequisite that people really want to possess property. As distinct from income which everybody wants as a matter of course, property requires a certain exertion on the part of the will and a particular attitude of mind, things which are anything but matters of course. And the difficulties with which we meet when we recommend decongestion and deproletarianisation reveal how a century of proletarianisation has weakened the desire for property. All would like "to possess," and no revolutionary policy is so popular as that which would snatch from one to give to another. But "to hold"? This presupposes more: frugality, the capacity to weigh up the present and the future, a sense of continuity and preservation, the will to independence, an outstanding family feeling. Hence a successful policy having as its object the restoration of property—and this differentiates it fundamentally from the customary demagogic tub-thumping rubbish—does not begin with a promise but with a demand, a moral appeal, and with a work of education. If we are successful in really re-awakening the desire for property an important step towards the restoration of property will then have been taken.

Now we come to the *second* point, namely, the difficulties and limitations which will have to be encountered in connection with the inevitable encroachments upon the existing division of property. A policy of this nature certainly has two aspects to it just as property itself, to which the homely and heartfelt words of Bacon are most appropriate: "Wealth is like muck. It is not good but if it be spread." Property concentrated in the hands of few is liable to abuse and represents the reverse side of the picture of the lack of property on the part of the masses, but when reflecting labour and social functions, and being of reasonable extent, it is a blessing. The former should be discouraged and the latter promoted. The restoration of property implies the simultaneous combatting of feudal and plutocratic property in which case property has not only lost its social significance, but is at the same time antagonistic to the conception of small-holdings for the broad masses. Indeed it presupposes their lack of property just as in feudal times. Concentration of property which usually implies concentration of the means of production, is in effect the negation of property in its anthropological and social sense. It is the preliminary step to that utmost concentration of property—and hence its disappearance—demanded by the socialists. If its restoration requires its decentralisation this means that an energetic "No" must be combined with an equally energetic "Yes." A "No" to concentration of property, a "Yes" to its decentralisation.

.  .  .  .  .

. . . It is of some consequence to state concretely what is precisely meant by the term property, which entity we are desirous of creating for those who have none for the purpose of redeeming them from their proletarian existence. Clearly not shares in the Royal Dutch Company or a motorcar, but something which fulfils the function of property, which gives to existence stability, solidity and roots. And it must preferably be property possessing some vital significance. This means on the one hand property which can be productive, on the other, which can provide a home. The concentration of property signifies to a large extent concentration of the means of production and thus the question arises how is decentralisation possible here? So long as the technical and organisational advantages of the big concerns render impossible a decentralisation of the concrete property of production one would have to be satisfied with the democratisation of titles to the property, the shares in other words. This would lead to many disadvantages. It would be infinitely more satisfactory, if possible, to bring about a decentralisation of such property by means of an increase of small and medium-sized concerns. . . .

Fortunately there is a form of property which in a wonderful way combines two characteristics. That it can be completely decentralised, and that it represents the most vital of all forms of property. We are referring to the land. This form of property possesses the still further important characteristic that it can embrace also the Home. It is that form of property which in this double capacity can make an end of proletarianisation even where, as in many industrial centres, as regards the individual's job, decentralisation is in practice out of the question. The industrial worker whom we cannot metamorphose into a craftsman, can and ought to become at least the proprietor of his own residence and garden—or allotment—which would provide him with produce from the land, i.e., his own land, during his voluntary (or involuntary) leisure and an occupation besides his regular job. This would also render him finally independent of the tricks of the market with its wage and price complexities and its business fluctuations. On the one hand we ought to maintain in being and increase to the utmost of our power the number of peasants, craftsmen and small business people, in short, all who are independent and provided already with their own house property and means of production. On the other hand where this is not possible it should be our aim to procure the worker or employee at least the equivalent of such an existence by providing him with a minimum of property, and by letting him have a house and garden of his own. If there be such a thing as a social "right" this is a "right to property," and nothing is more illustrative of the muddle of our time than the circumstance that hitherto no government and no party have inscribed these words on their banner. . . .

Decentralisation of habitat by means of ownership of house and garden implies that new conditions must be created in which a genuine and natural family life can thrive. To this belongs not only Pestalozzi's "Magnetism of the Hearth" but also what we might call the "Magnetism of the Garden." The garden is not only "the purest of human pleasures" (Bacon) but also offers the indispensable natural foundation for family life and the upbringing of children, and furthermore, a decentralised existence gives the family with many children those conditions which transform a heavy burden to be endured with resignation and avoided if possible into something natural, stimulating and immediately worth-while, something for which one can strive without too great moral exertion.

SECTION C

**The march of technology**

# 41   Franz Borkenau: *Will Technology Destroy Civilization?*

❦ *It has been seriously argued that technology might destroy civilization. Some thinkers, viewing technology's destructive potentialities—as represented, for example, by the atomic bomb—have suggested that it is time to call a halt to technological change. This view holds that, since man is apparently unable to control his technology for nondestructive ends, we must either destroy technology or technology will destroy us.*

*The author of this reading questions whether technology will destroy civilization. True, he argues, a new barbarism or primitivism is quite possible, given the tensions in modern culture and organization. But, he says, barbarism is usually the prelude— perhaps, it is true, after years of suffering and chaos—to a new civilization. Creative forces are released in a period of chaos and those forces eventually develop a new order (or cosmos). To attack technology, moreover, in the author's view, is to attack science and learning in general; so that unless one is willing to repudiate man's highest spiritual attributes, it is difficult with consistency to attack technology as such. The essay concludes with the author's belief in the possibility of human progress, which, he argues, implies belief in God.*

*Franz Borkenau (1900–    ) is the author of* Austria and After *(1938),* World Communism *(1938),* The New German Empire *(1939), and* The Totalitarian Enemy *(1940). Our reading is reprinted from the January, 1951, issue of* Commentary *with permission of the publisher.*

A common and increasing disillusionment with technology today marks contemporary thinkers of the most divergent tendencies. A classic expression of this feeling was Aldous Huxley's *Brave New World,* a utopian novel portraying a world whose every problem and every difficulty has been solved by technology, but which for this very reason has become emptied of all meaning. Arnold J. Toynbee, though not envisaging any utopian ultimate in technology, also seems to lean to the view that modern technology is at bottom worthless —for "mankind's serious business is religion"; all that we need in the way of secular culture was already produced by the Greeks—in our technological efforts we are only the bad imitators of a past civilization.

The same tendency of thought has had such important representatives in Latin countries as Ortega y Gasset and Paul Valéry. But it has met with its strongest response in Germany. I mention here in particularly only the Jünger brothers. Ernst Jünger, in his book *The Worker,* unlike Huxley, does not "reject" technics on aesthetic grounds or any other; but his positive conception of a perfect *"Arbeitertum"* (workers' civilization) came very close to Huxley's utopia and yielded nothing to it in point of horror. Friedrich Georg Jünger for his part has launched an all-out campaign against technology—to what effect, we can see in Otto Veit's *Die Flucht vor der Freiheit* ("Flight from Freedom," Frankfort 1948), which by a startling simplification would hold technology responsible for all that endangers our culture today.

Let me say at once that I do not deny the dangers of technology, which are tremendous. But what strikes one constantly about these lamentations over the evils of technology is their minimization of its unique achievements in modern times, achievements by no means limited to the sphere of the "practical." On the contrary, spiritual values of the highest order are inseparable from technology. Nor can you draw a line between technology and science—if only because without modern instruments there would be no modern science, as without science there would be no technology.

No one will deny that our science, in the course of its development from Galileo to Einstein and from Boyle to Planck and Rutherford, has penetrated the "interior of nature" as never before. Even supposing that technology is in fact as destructive in its consequences as many now claim it to be—is that all there is to it? For my part, I believe that as surely as the human spirit exists to illumine the cosmos with its knowledge, so surely does the modern conquest of nature represent this spirit's sublimest, most heroic achievement. . . .

In dismissing as an incidental matter the knowledge we have finally won of the basic structure of the material world, the critics of technology for the most part overlook the fact that these very insights have given us a glimpse into the basic structure of all existence, spiritual as well as material. Are these insights tragic in their refutation of cherished illusions?—well, all culture is tragic, all culture is paid for by the surrender of primitive consolations of the human soul. And may one not ask whether the real threat to culture does not perhaps come from those who have not the fortitude to face up to the consequences of this greatest of human triumphs, and must therefore take flight from reason?

But is the flight from reason and technology at all possible? We ought to put this question to ourselves, not in any aesthetic and utopian fashion, but in complete and deadly earnest. Let us say, conditionally, "yes," a flight is possible. The condition is: the reduction of the "white" population to a fraction of its present size; for the present European and American population levels, unlike the Asiatic, are dependent entirely upon technology. A sharp fall in our population is, of course, not out of the question. It is unfortunately more than merely conceivable that an atomic war should utterly destroy tens of millions of lives as well as our technological resources and abilities. In the absence of such an event, technology will certainly endure, so that we can only discuss the possibility of its disappearance by assuming an atomic catastrophe.

Bertrand Russell recently suggested that such a disappearance might be effected by a destructive outbreak of mass hatred against technology following an atomic holocaust. This vision of an outraged humanity turning upon science is an ever recurring one. Spengler, it might be remembered, held that technology was something specifically "Western": peoples of alien cultures mastered technology only in order to use it in their struggle against the West; with the downfall of the West, they would cast it aside as "a monkey would a walking stick." Toynbee, too, would seem to expect much the same thing.

But is not Spengler's dark estimate of the future of technology intimately connected with his gross underestimation of what was really taking place in science? It was around 1914 that Spengler, himself originally a mathematician, disputed the possibility of any further significant advance in scientific theory, conceding a future only to purely practical technology. Obviously he mistook the actual depth of the current of science—mistook it grossly. Recent scientific developments, flatly contradicting him, have completely revolutionized our conception of the world. Hence a discussion of

ED. NOTE: * Before the Common (or Christian) era.

the problem cannot start out from any notion of a decline or "end" of science, but must begin by answering the question: *Is it conceivable that, as a result of enormous material and spiritual catastrophes, all the knowledge and skills we have acquired in the last three hundred years should be lost?*

Pointing to earlier cases of cultural decline does not in itself mean very much. To draw a parallel between our own situation and the decline into barbarism and the "dark ages" that marked the end of antiquity is certainly misleading. As Spengler pointed out, there is always more than one parallelism to choose from. You have to have what Spengler calls a "physiognomic pulse" to understand which parallels are valid and which are not. The parallel with the decline of antiquity is not. Although it is true that there was a sharp falling-off of urban life at that time, no real deterioration took place in technology. One of the most important arguments against a too simple notion of progress is contained in the fact that from the end of the Old Kingdom in Egypt (3rd millennium BCE *) until the 11th century of our era, actually no real change occurred in technology—a state of affairs that speaks stronger than anything else for the Spenglerian thesis of the distinctively Western character of technology.

But there are two sides to this coin of "Western science." Not only modern machine technology, but also something so seemingly insignificant as the European method of harnessing draught-cattle, profoundly affects population growth, the rise of cities, etc. Will other, "colored" civilizations cast this achievement aside as a monkey would a walking stick? If not, where is the point beyond which they will refuse to borrow from Western culture? Or, as in Samuel Butler's *Erewhon*, will some one year finally be fixed, and all technological innovations made prior to it accepted, and all those made afterwards rejected?

. . . . .

. . . Toynbee, with his particularly strong antipathy to modern technology, goes so far as to consider the possibility of our technological development leading to the complete destruction of all civilized peoples and the elevation of the Central African pygmies to the position of the chief bearers of human culture. Against such a view of things there is little one can say in the way of conclusive argument. But an examination of historical precedents will disclose another perspective.

When one surveys all of human history, it can be seen that the periods in which cultures decline are indispensable intervals of cultural renewal. In the "dark ages" the modern Western spirit was gestative. The historical process just referred to, whereby a new culture results from the assimilation of elements from different older cultures, takes place without exception amid the catastrophic collapse of all the older cultures figuring in the process—takes place, that is, amid the upsurge of barbarism.

Vigorous and independent cultures resist to the death the challenge of a different culture. In their late stages they do not undergo a process of change, but tend rather to harden and grow rigid. Only when this period of rigidity is followed by collapse, does the creative process of fusion begin. This mechanism of cultural renewal, the decisive connecting link in the chain of human history, can be unhesitatingly called history's most universal law, admitting of not one exception. *A chaos precedes every cultural cosmos.* Chaos is not downfall, not ruin. It is the necessary connecting link between the end of one creative process and the beginning of another.

We hear it said that, regardless of the outcome of the present struggle between East and West, the world is "entering an era of barbarism." What in actual fact is "barbarism"? It is not the same thing as cultural primitivism, a turning-back of the clock. It is rather a phenomenon that manifests itself within the temporal and spatial boundaries of high cultures. It is a condition in which many of the values of high culture are present, but without that social and moral coherence which is the pre-condition for a culture's rational functioning.

But for this very reason "barbarism" is also a creative process: once the over-all coherence of a culture is shattered, the way lies open to a renewal of creativity. To be sure, however, this way may be through a collapse of political and economic life, and centuries of spiritual and material impoverishment and terrible suffering. Our own particular brand of civilization and culture may not survive unimpaired, but the fruits of civilization and culture, we may be sure, will in some form survive. There is no historical warrant for believing that the slate will be wiped clean.

Let us try for a more balanced perspective of this whole popular question of "the threatened disappearance of civilization." It is hardly to be doubted that we are now living at the beginning of a period of "barbarism." It cannot logically be proven that, like every earlier crisis of its kind, it will be a creative transition and not the end, although an inner consciousness should tell us that the highest stage reached in the development of the human spirit could hardly be the immediate prologue to its final downfall. The legend of the Tower of Babel has indeed a point for us, insofar as it is true that, build we ever so high, an end is reached to all our building. Yet the truth of the legend is temporally circumscribed: for the end was no end at all, but a new beginning—over and over again we build our Tower, and right now higher than ever. And here, if I may, I should like to take leave of history.

I have already expressed my repugnance to an attitude that, in dealing with the problem of technology, would ignore the *truth* of modern science. Spengler vainly sought to demonstrate that Euclidean geomtry was true only for antiquity. The fact is of course that it is true for all ages, only we have come to understand that it is a partial truth, that it is true when certain postulates are given. The same thing holds for modern technology and science. Once discovered, these truths are a universal possession of humanity, because they are not only human truths, but in accord with cosmic reality. Very possibly such truths can be lost sight of in chaotic transitional periods, but is it conceivable that they should vanish as if they had never existed? Or isn't it far more likely that, after having been purged in the fires of a great cultural change, they should first really begin to shine forth?

And now the cat is indeed out of the bag, I have gone and blabbed my faith in progress, that unpardonable sin. Yet I do not mean that automatically, steadily accelerating progress in which Condorcet, Hegel, and Buckle believed, not a progress that can dispense with cycles and relapses, not a progress on an ever rising historical escalator that one can commit oneself to with smugness and equanimity. Still, much has happened in the course of our evolution from primordial atom to amoeba, from amoeba to man, and from Peking Man to Planck and Rutherford; and it seems absurd to me to imagine that in all this there is little more that is worthy of philosophical and religious notice than is involved in lamenting the sins and sufferings of existence.

We all know that the chief concern of the opponents of this qualified belief in progress is with the "timeless," and it is to the "timeless" that I too am led. The kernel of the faith in progress, it turns out, is a faith in the effective significance of objective truth in human life. Is it an accident that all those who deny progress, from Spengler to Barth, are the very ones who deny the efficacy of all the truths that man perceives by his unaided intellect? And is not truth one of the chief aspects of the divine? And in this respect, on the same level with morality? To deny the truths perceived by man, is it not to deny the stamp of divinity upon creation? Is not faith in progress perhaps in the end only a faith in God's positive working in history—and not outside of history?

## SELECTED REFERENCES FOR PART 8

ČAPEK, KAREL. *R. U. R. (Rossum's Universal Robots).* Translated by Paul Selver. New York: Doubleday, 1923.

A "fantastic melodrama" depicting a revolt by "mechanical men" embittered at the treatment accorded them by their human creators.

CARNEGIE, ANDREW. *The Gospel of Wealth.* New York: Century, 1900.

The social philosophy of the famous steel man; he holds economic inequality to be both inevitable and desirable but insists that the rich have an obligation to use their wealth for the promotion of the public welfare.

CARVER, T. N. *The Religion Worth Having.* Boston and New York: Houghton Mifflin, 1912.

Illustrates what Max Weber called the "Protestant ethic." The author believes the "religion worth having" is the one that does the most to stimulate productivity.

CHASE, STUART, in collaboration with MARIAN T. CHASE. *Roads to Agreement.* New York: Harper, 1951.

Stresses the implications of recent studies in group dynamics for the improvement of the quality of collective decisions and the peaceful settlement of conflicts.

CLEETON, G. U. *Making Work Human.* Yellow Springs, Ohio: Antioch Press, 1949.

Emphasizes the noneconomic aspects of work and tries to show how one's vocation can take on moral significance.

DREHER, CARL. *The Coming Showdown.* Boston: Little, Brown, 1944.

A socially minded engineer turned publicist offers a blueprint of an American economic organization intended to combine the merits of social planning and individual liberty. The argument and the evidence reveal the influence of Thorstein Veblen and the so-called "technocrats."

DUBREUIL, HYACINTHE. *Robots or Men?* Translated by Frances and Mason Merrill. New York: Harper, 1930.

A French workman and union official offers his first-hand observations on the effect of advanced American industrial methods on personality and culture.

FORD, HENRY and SAM CROWTHER. *My Life and Work.* Garden City, N. Y.: Doubleday, 1922.

The late industrialist assesses the significance of his own career and describes the ideals which he believes guided him.

GANDHI, M. K. *Autobiography: The Story of My Experiments with Truth.* Translated by Mahadev Desai. Washington, D. C.: Public Affairs Press, 1948.

The late leader of the Indian independence movement explains the sources and significance of his resistance to large-scale mechanization of industry.

GIEDION, SIEGFRIED. *Mechanization Takes Command.* New York: Oxford Univ. Press, 1948.

A strikingly illustrated documentary survey on what modern mass production has meant in respect to the conduct and enjoyment of life in its most intimate aspects. Includes chapters on the significance of mechanization of the processing of food and the furnishing of the home.

GRAHAM, FRANK D. *Social Goals and Economic Institutions.* Princeton: Princeton Univ. Press, 1942.

A "liberal" economist offers a program of progressive economic policy for a democratic society.

HOBSON, J. A. *Work and Wealth, A Human Valuation.* London: Allen & Unwin, 1941.

The somewhat unorthodox British economist analyzes economic phenomena in terms of their ethical and social implications.

KNIGHT, FRANK H. and THORNTON W. MERRIAM. *The Economic Order and Religion.* New York: Harper, 1945.

A distinguished economist and religious leader debate the implication of Christian teachings for the achievement of economic plenty and political freedom.

KROPOTKIN, PETER. *Mutual Aid: A Factor in Evolution.* New York: McClure, Phillips & Co., 1902.

In this famous book the author argues that co-operation has been at least as important as conflict in animal and human evolution to "higher" levels of life.

MAY, HENRY F. *Protestant Churches and Industrial America.* New York: Harper, 1949.

An investigation of the ways in which the values of secular industrial society affected the course of Protestant thought on economic and social issues in the nineteenth century.

MENGER, ANTON. *The Right to the Whole Produce of Labour.* Translated from the German by M. E. Tanner. Introduction by H. S. Foxwell. London and New York: Macmillan, 1899.

A critical examination of Socialist theories of distribution.

MORRIS, WILLIAM. *News From Nowhere.* London: T. Nelson & Sons, 1911.

Morris paints his picture of the ideal society, one in which large cities have been destroyed, coercion abolished, and men's creative possibilities released from the repressions which the author sees as inevitable in a capitalist industrialist society.

MOORE, WILBERT. *Industrial Relations and the Social Order,* Revised Edition. New York: Macmillan, 1951.

Reviews the literature and problems of industrial organization in different cultures.

MUMFORD, LEWIS. *Story of Utopias.* Introduction by Hendrik Willem Van Loon. New York: Boni and Liveright, 1922.

A challenging account of the great contributions to progress made by men's great plans for social regeneration.

PIUS XI. *"Quadragesimo Anno"* in *Five Great Encyclicals.* New York: Paulist Press, 1941.

The late pope here presents the Roman Catholic view on labor and the problems of industrial society.

RAUSCHENBUSCH, WALTER. *Christianizing the Social Order*. New York: Macmillan, 1912.

A classical "liberal Protestant" view of the problem of work in relation to the social order.

ROETHLISBERGER, FRITZ. *Management and Morale*. Cambridge: Harvard Univ. Press, 1941.

Valuable summary of the findings of the group of researchers affiliated with the Harvard School of Business Administration.

SHAW, GEORGE BERNARD. *The Intelligent Woman's Guide to Socialism and Capitalism*. New York: Brentano's, 1928.

The late dramatist's defense of equality in distribution.

SHELLEY, MARY GODWIN. *Frankenstein: or The Modern Prometheus*. New York: Dutton, 1927.

An early nineteenth-century portrayal of what might happen if man-made mechanical monsters should suddenly free themselves from the control of their creators.

SINCLAIR, UPTON. *The Jungle*. New York: Viking, 1910.

A novel vividly describing the meat-packing industry in the early years of the twentieth century. Sinclair portrays the industry as having utter disregard for human values and maintains that only in a socialist society will men be accorded the dignity due them.

SLICHTER, SUMNER H. *The American Economy: Its Problems and Prospects*. New York: Knopf, 1948.

A "conservative" defense of the values which the author finds in the American economy.

SUMNER, WILLIAM GRAHAM. *What Social Classes Owe Each Other*. New York: Harper, 1883.

The eminent American social scientist warns against the evils he believes to be attendant upon attempts to guarantee equality for all.

SWEEZY, PAUL M. *Socialism*. New York: McGraw-Hill, 1949.

An analysis by an economist sympathetic to Marxian socialism.

TANNENBAUM, FRANK. *A Philosophy of Labor*. New York: Knopf, 1950.

A defense of the ideals of the American labor movement.

ULAM, ADAM B. *Philosophical Foundations of English Socialism*. Cambridge: Harvard University Press, 1951.

Traces the growth of socialist thought in Great Britain.

WELLS, H. G. *The Time Machine*. New York: Random House, 1931.

————. *A Modern Utopia*. New York: Scribner, 1905.

These two volumes present Wells' views of the effects of capitalist and socialist organization on man's values.

WIENER, NORBERT. *Cybernetics; or Control and Communication in the Animal and the Machine*. Cambridge, Mass.: The Technology Press of the Massachusetts Institute of Technology, 1948.

Wiener maintains that "thinking machines" may be expected to play a greatly expanded role in many areas of the world's work in the near future. He is acutely conscious of the revolutionary social possibilities of "mechanical" brains.

WRIGHT, AUSTIN T. *Islandia*. New York: Farrar and Rinehart, 1942.

A novel idealizing a decentralist scheme of society and arguing the importance for personal development of direct access to the land.

WRIGHT, DAVID McCORD. *Capitalism*. New York: McGraw-Hill, 1951. (Economics Handbook Series.)

————. *Democracy and Progress*. New York: Macmillan, 1948.

The author stresses the vital connections between free enterprise, economic growth, and democratic process.

❦ *This is a composite index of names appearing in Books One, Two, and Three* (Personality, Work, Community). *Roman numerals preceding each page number refer to Book Numbers.*

~~~~~~~~~~~~~~~~~~~~~~~~~~~~~~~~~~~~~~~~~~~~~~~~~~

❦ *This is a composite index of subjects appearing in Books One, Two, and Three (Personality, Work, Community). Roman numerals preceding each page number refer to Book Numbers.*

Absentee ownership (in farming), effects of, III:168–190

Absolutism, theories of, III:244

Acceleration principle, related to capital, production, and income, II:260–2

Acquaintanceship, in the small town, III:198–200

Adaptive culture, and cultural lag, I:115

Adjustment, and listening to radio serials, I:335–7

Administration, in social groups, III:33–4

Administrators, enhanced power in modern society, II:19

Advertising, as a monopolistic device, II:200; as promoting monopoly in tooth paste industry, II:201

Age of Reason, and natural harmony, III:360

Aggregate demand, and economic stability, II:269–71

Aggression, channeling of, I:227, 373–81; and human nature, I:362–4; and kinship, I:374–8; and leadership, I:267; as a natural attribute of man, I:354; and occupational system, I:378–9; sources of, I:355

Agriculture, Greek attitude toward, II:93; in the Middle Ages, II:106–8

Aikens v. Wisconsin, cited, III:332

Alcoholic psychoses, in cities, III:215

American Bankers Association, as an organization based on business interests, II:192

American Federation of Labor, II:217, 218, 219, 220

American Iron and Steel Institute, II:192

American Telephone and Telegraph Company, II:15

Americanization, I:324–7

Anabaptists, and the Hutterite creed, III:310

Anarchism, as a "natural society," III:308–9; political theories of, III:238, 303; and social organization, II:67–8

Andamanese, relative isolation of, III:84

Anomie, meaning of, II:140, III:26

Anonymity, as characteristic of psychological crowds, III:128

Anti-Christ, as opposing kingly office of Christ, I:322

Anus, as source of pleasure in the young, I:359

Apprenticeship system, decline of, III:37; in the Middle Ages, II:112–3

Army, leadership and libido in, III:131, 132, 133

Art, fulfillment through, I:50; and human life, II:36

Artisan, in medieval Europe, II:111

Arvin (California), characteristics of, III:170–190

Asceticism, and the Hutterites, III:316–7; and the monastic ideal, I:110; and the Protestant ethic, I:111

Assimilation, and immigration in American culture, I:311–4

Association of American Railroads, II:192, 193

Atlantic City, crime and "politics," III:226–9

Austria-Hungary, and the problem of cohesion, III:13

Authoritarianism, and American culture, I:249; and the home, I:248; and the personality of a "Fascist," I:235–45

Authority, and hatred of parents, I:250; and the "moral order," III:15–6

Autocracy, in labor unions, stimulated by business autocracy, II:223

Auto-eroticism, role in child's life, I:157

Autonomy, and the moral judgment of the child, I:217–9

Babies, influence of, I:133

Banker, as an occupational type, II:153–5

Barbarism, and division of labor, II:13; and the revival of civilization, II:357

Bias, as tainting all human knowledge, III:329

Biological organization, and social organization, II:66–7

Biology, and constitutional determinants, I:67

Biotic community, composition of, III:61; man's place in it, III:62–3

Birth, and the factory system, II:40–1

Bookmaking, as part of gangster monopoly, III:225

Boss, his role in factory organization, II:129–30

Bradfield v. Roberts, cited, III:343

Bridges v. State of California, cited, III:338

Business, as closely related to crime, III:147

Business cycles, and capital formation, II:257–8; and changing distribution of income, II:265; and demographic influences, II:263–4; and effective